once owned by K. J. Maidment, ed of Minor Attic Orators (Loeb), fellow of Merton

BIBLIOTHECA CLASSICA.

EDITED BY

GEORGE LONG, M.A.
FORMERLY FELLOW OF TRINITY COLLEGE, CAMBRIDGE,

AND THE

REV. A. J. MACLEANE, M.A.
TRINITY COLLEGE, CAMBRIDGE

THE PHAEDRUS OF PLATO.

WITH

ENGLISH NOTES AND DISSERTATIONS

BY W. H. THOMPSON, D.D.

LONDON.
WHITTAKER & CO., AVE MARIA LANE,
GEORGE BELL, YORK STREET, COVENT GARDEN
1868.

LONDON
GILBERT AND RIVINGTON, PRINTERS,
ST JOHN'S SQUARE

THE

PHAEDRUS OF PLATO.

WITH

ENGLISH NOTES AND DISSERTATIONS

BY

W. H. THOMPSON, D.D.

MASTER OF TRINITY COLLEGE, CAMBRIDGE, AND

LATE REGIUS PROFESSOR OF GREEK.

Φιλόμυθος ὁ φιλόσοφός πώς ἐστιν —ARISTOTLE

LONDON.

WHITTAKER & CO, AVE MARIA LANE,

GEORGE BELL, YORK STREET, COVENT GARDEN

1868.

CONTENTS.

ERRATA.

Page 11, note, line 21, *for* Plut. Men *read* Plut. Mor.
— 37, note, line 12, *for* παρ' θεοῖς *read* πὰρ θεοῖς
— 55, note, line 31, a comma is needed after 'the form so called'
— 61, note, line 15, *for* ἐπωνουμίᾳ, *read* ἐπωνυμία,
— 64, note, line 4, *for* Ruhnk. and Tim. *read* Ruhnk. ad Tim.
— 107, note, line 32, *for* diacritic *read* diaeretic
— 122, note, line 37 *for* ὔλην *read* ὕλην
— 143, note, line 7 from the bottom, *dele* comma after γράψει
— 162, line 23, *for* which that desire *read* which desire
— 167, line 22, *for* the existing *read* the then existing
— 168, bottom of the page, *for* notions *read* notices

PREFACE.

Of this edition of the Phaedrus it may be said, and with better reason than Porson says of his Hecuba, "tironum usibus destinata est." The Introduction and the first Appendix were read, together with much that is now left out, by way of prolegomena to lectures delivered to University students in the year 1859; and the notes, though not reduced to their present form until the year following, had in substance been written for the same hearers. The second Appendix, on Isocrates, was composed in 1861, also for oral delivery, though to a somewhat different audience Very little has been added either to the notes or the dissertations, but pains have been taken in the correction of errors, and the omission or abridgment of controversial matter. The edition would probably have seen the light some years earlier, but I had laid it aside, together with one of the Gorgias framed on the same plan, in the hope of recasting both and adapting them to a more comprehensive scheme, which for various reasons is now abandoned. If this present 'opella' should be found useful to those for whom it is principally designed, the Gorgias will probably follow it at no long interval

In editing this dialogue, I have made no new collation of manuscripts, but the text has of course been carefully compared with the Various Readings, especially those of the 'Clarkian' or 'Bodleian,' as given by Gaisford,—readings which are often suggestive, even when false Of original emendations but few have been introduced, and those not, I trust, very violent. For instance, in page 92 (260 c), for the received *προσενεγκεῖν*, I have suggested *πρός γ' ἐνεγκεῖν*. Ibid. for the readings, evidently corrupt, of the codices, I have restored from Hermeias *οὐ κρεῖττον γελοῖον καὶ φίλον ἢ δεινὸν καὶ ἐχθρὸν* [*εἶναι*]. The ejection of *εἶναι*, which is not found in these scholia, I have contented myself with recommending. Its absence might be defended by 238 E, *κρεῖττον δὲ καὶ ἴσον ἐχθρόν*.

In p. 100 (263 A), *τῶν ὄντων* has been taken into the text from one MS., in place of the too long received *τῶν τοιούτων*.

In p. 55, I have ventured to adopt a happy suggestion of my friend Dr. Charles Badham, whose name will frequently occur in these notes. Instead of the received *ἐκ πολλῶν ἰὸν αἰσθήσεων* I read *ἰόντ'*; a daring change, for which I can give no reason except the reason of the case.

One nearly certain emendation has been overlooked. The invocation to the Muses, in p. 237 A, is thus quoted in the Homeric Allegories of Heraclitus: *ἄγετε δή, ὦ Μοῦσαι, εἴτε δι' ᾠδῆς εἶδος λιγείας εἴτε διὰ γένος τι μουσικὸν ταύτην ἔσχετε τὴν ἐπωνυμίαν κ.τ.λ.* (P. 119, ed. Mehler.) Here *λιγείας* is of course wrong, but Cobet has rightly inferred that *τὸ Λιγύων*, which stands very awkwardly after *μουσικὸν* in the received text, ought to be ejected as a gloss upon *γένος τι μουσικόν*, which is the true reading of the passage. This, I think, is rather confirmed than refuted by the order of the words given by Dionysius of Halicarnassus, *εἴτε διὰ γένος τὸ Λιγύων μουσικόν* (de Demosth. § 7, p. 969, Reiske), which is apparently a transitional reading.

In the matter of orthography, I have followed to a considerable extent the practice of the so-called Atticists. For instance, *ἐλεινός*, *ἑόρακα*, *κλῄω* are invariably read in place of the common forms, *ἐλεεινός*, *ἑώρακα*, *κλείω*. In elision, I have stopped very far short of Hirschig's and Cobet's practice, having yet to be convinced that all Attic writers are equally averse to the so-called 'concourse of vowels.' This dogma was certainly not held by the ancient critics. Dionysius of Halicarnassus, one of the earliest and best witnesses to Attic practice, assures us that while writers in the *γλαφυρὰ καὶ θεατρικὴ λέξις*, of which Isocrates was a master, shunned as much as possible the *σύγκρουσις φωνηέντων*, those of an austerer type rather courted it, and he quotes instances of this collision from Demosthenes himself, which, as he thinks, increase the *σεμνότης* of the passages in which they occur. Dion Hal. de Isocr Jud § 2, vol v. p 538, Reiske Ibid. vi., pp. 964, 1069, 1076, 1090 (de adm. vi dicendi in Demosth. §§ 4. 38. 40. 43).

Of Plato's practice in this respect Dionysius gives us no direct information, but from § 3 of the Judicium de Isocrate, we may fairly, I think, infer that it was a mean between that of the smooth, or polished, and that of the 'austere' school To his testimony add the following, from one of the more judicious of the rhetoricians of the Empire *περὶ δὲ συγκρούσεως φωνηέντων ὑπέλαβον ἄλλοι ἄλλως. Ἰσοκράτης μὲν γὰρ ἐφυλάττετο συμπλήσσειν αὐτά, καὶ οἱ ἀπ' αὐτοῦ. ἄλλοι δέ τινες ὡς ἔτυχε συνέκρουσαν καὶ παντάπασι· δεῖ δὲ οὔτε ἠχώδη ποιεῖν τὴν σύνθεσιν, ἀτέχνως αὐτὰ συμπλήσσοντα καὶ ὡς ἔτυχε· διασπασμῷ γὰρ τοῦ λόγου τὸ τοιοῦτον καὶ διαρρίψει ἔοικεν· οὔτε μὴν παντελῶς φυλάσσεσθαι τὴν συνέχειαν τῶν γραμμάτων· λειοτέρα μὲν γὰρ οὕτως ἔσται ἴσως ἡ σύνθεσις, ἀμουσοτέρα δὲ καὶ κωφὴ ἀτεχνῶς, πολλὴν εὐφωνίαν ἀφαιρεθεῖσα, τὴν γινομένην ἐκ τῆς συγκρούσεως, κ.τ.λ.* (Demetrius *περὶ ἑρμηνείας*, c. 68, in vol ix. p 34 of Walz's Rhetores Graeci) Any one who will compare Hirschig's text with that of Bekker will perceive my motive for introducing these quotations.

In interpreting this dialogue it has been my duty to refer to my predecessors, in particular to Heindorf, Ast, and Stallbaum From the first, when I have differed, it has been with reluctance, for no editor has so fine a sense of Platonic usage Ast's larger Commentary is full of learned illustrative matter, excerpts from which appear in these notes He also earned the thanks of editors of the Phaedrus by publishing the Scholia Hermiae entire in his edition of 1810 Many extracts from these will be found in this edition, for amidst a heap of Neoplatonic rubbish, they contain occasional learned and even sensible remarks They are also not without their use in fixing the text of disputed passages, for the 'lemmata' which they contain differ, sometimes for the better, though sometimes also for the worse, from the received readings. The text of Hermeias[1], as given by Ast, sorely needs revision, and I have had to make some obvious corrections in the passages quoted.

In illustrating the subject-matter of the dialogue, frequent reference has been made to the valuable and interesting essays of Leonhard Spengel; nor must I omit to mention a very painstaking and learned, though not well-written, monography on the Phaedrus, by the late Professor Krische of Gottingen. There is also a clever analysis of the dialogue by Sallier, in the French Academy of Inscriptions for 1736, of which the poet Gray's Argument is an abridgment. The notes written by Gray himself are so much to the purpose, that one regrets that they are not more numerous. Some of them the reader will find quoted in this edition and also a few adversaria of Godfrey Hermann,—possibly published elsewhere, but taken by me from the margin of his copy of Heindorf's Phaedrus, which was bought, at the sale of his books, for the Public Library of this University.

The dates given above will show that in preparing this edition I have made no use of some valuable additions to Platonic and the kindred branches of literature which have recently appeared. This, I am aware, is no recommendation; but I have not of late had the time necessary for a careful comparison of my own views either with those of Mr Grote, in his great work on Plato and the Socratics, or of my friend Mr Cope in his learned Prolegomena to the Rhetoric of Aristotle, or, lastly, with those of Professor Lewis Campbell, who, in his edition of the Sophistes and Politicus, has treated of the "dialectical method" with much judgment and ability.

I cannot end these observations better than in the words of a

[1] He was contemporary with Simplicius, Damascius, and the other survivors of the Platonic succession, who were silenced by the edict of Justinian, A.D. 529. [illegible]

veteran interpreter, whose writings gave a great stimulus to the study of Plato in Germany in the early part of the century "In scriptore tali qualis Plato est, permulta inveniri quae sua quisque ratione intelligat atque judicet, per se patet, quocirca haud mirabor, si varia, partim etiam iniqua, de meis annotationibus judicia in medium prolata videro"

TRINITY COLLEGE, CAMBRIDGE,
February, 1868.

INTRODUCTION.

PART I.

ON THE SUBJECT AND INTENTION OF THE PHAEDRUS.

Few of the Platonic dialogues have provoked so much controversy as the Phaedrus. This distinction it owes, partly to the complexity of its structure and the variety of its contents, and partly to the interest attached to it in consequence of a generally believed tradition that it was the earliest offspring of its author's philosophical genius. Hence have arisen two questions, neither of which, perhaps, can be said to have received a final answer. (1) What is the main scope and purpose of the dialogue, and what the relation its several parts bear to each other? (2) What is its relation to other dialogues? Is it to be regarded as a preface to the whole series, or to any assignable part of the whole series, or is its office that of a supplementary and subordinate, rather than of a vital and integral part of the system implied or developed in the Platonic writings?

That the first of these questions, that which relates to the leading idea of the dialogue, has been answered very variously, is evident from the bare enumeration of the different headings which the Greek commentators have prefixed to it. Φαῖδρος ἢ περὶ καλοῦ—Φ. ἢ περὶ ἔρωτος—Φ. ἢ περὶ ῥητορικῆς—περὶ τἀγαθοῦ—περὶ ψυχῆς—περὶ τοῦ πρώτου καλοῦ—περὶ τοῦ παντοδαποῦ καλοῦ—such are the titles by which scholars or philosophers have recorded their several impressions.[1] None of these second titles possess the slightest authority; for we may be quite sure that the only one prefixed by the author

[1] Krische, über Platons Phaedrus, pp. 3, 4, where the references are given. "Hujusmodi additamenta a recentioribus esse profecta, jam Proclus significavit ad Plat. Polit. p. 350. 24—καθάπερ ἄλλαι τῶν ἐπιγραφῶν, προσθέσεις οὖσαι τῶν νεωτέρων." Ast ad Pl[illegible]

was that by which the dialogue was known to his disciple Aristotle, who quotes it by the sole name Phaedrus[2] The discrepancy of view implied in these contradictory headings is no proof that the problem defies solution, but may be regarded as an intimation that we must look for such solution rather to Plato himself than to his commentators. That the Phaedrus is a mere congeries of poetical descriptions, of brilliant metaphysical speculations, acute logical discussion, and satirical literary criticism, is a supposition which no one who has read one of the more considerable Platonic dialogues with attention will easily entertain. That it was not so regarded by its author, is pretty evident from his own testimony, for he tells us that "every written composition should resemble a living creature in its structure: it should have an organized body of its own, lacking neither head nor foot, but possessing a centre and extremities, adapted each to the other and in perfect keeping with the whole[3]" This precept we cannot suppose to have been consciously violated by its author in the very dialogue in which it occurs, a dialogue in which his literary ability shines with greater lustre than perhaps in any other of his compositions

The Phaedrus may fairly be described as a dramatized treatise on Rhetoric. The popular treatises on this art and their authors are held up to ridicule both in this dialogue and in the Gorgias: but in the Phaedrus Plato furnishes us with a scheme of a new and philosophical rhetoric, founded partly on 'dialectic,' and partly also on psychology,—the science which distinguishes the principles of human action, and the several varieties of human character upon which the orator has to work, in producing that "Persuasion" which is acknowledged to be the final cause of his art. 'Ρητορικὴ πειθοῦς δημιουργὸς[4] is a definition which Plato virtually accepts in common with his opponents; but, unlike them, he follows out the principle to its logical results, which, as he shows, had escaped the notice of all teachers of Rhetoric from Tisias down to his own time

For this exposition he prepares the way by an elaborate dramatic introduction A speech of Lysias is read by Phaedrus, and severely criticized by Socrates[5] The speech is an address of a lover to a youth whose favour he tries to win, and its merit is supposed to consist in the originality of the thesis it enforces, ὡς μὴ ἐρῶντι μᾶλλον ἢ ἐρῶντι δεῖ χαρίζεσθαι Socrates finds the discourse full

[1] [illegible] 7 11, ed Oxon [3] Phaedr p 264 c
[4] [illegible] to the same effect: λόγου δύναμις τυγχάνει ψυχαγωγία 271 c
[5] [illegible] 236 b

of tautology and deficient in invention. His young friend, unable to deny the justice of the criticism, insists that Socrates shall make a better speech on the same theme. This, after coquetting awhile, Socrates consents to do, and so far fulfils his engagement as to prove satisfactorily that it is better for the ἐρώμενος to reject the proposals of his ἐραστής[6]. This done, he suddenly breaks off, horror-struck at the impiety of which he had been guilty in putting a vile meaning upon the sacred name of Love[7]. He would gladly depart, but an inward voice[8] commands him first to make his peace with the offended son of Aphrodite—a "god and goddess-born." He will follow the precedent given by Stesichorus, who, struck with blindness for reviling the fair Helen, composed a palinode, in which he proved her good as fair, and thereupon straightway regained his sight. He, Socrates, will recite a palinode in which due atonement shall be made to the injured majesty of Eros. Then follows that famous rhapsody on Love, which Socrates describes as "a kind of mythic hymn," but which is quite as remarkable for its philosophic as for its literary and poetical merits[9]. It has accordingly made a deep impression upon successive generations of Platonic students, some of whom[1] have erroneously regarded it as the really important portion of the Phaedrus, to which the elaborate discussion on rhetoric which follows it is to be interpreted as merely accessory. In the course of the subsequent conversation[2], the second λόγος ἐρωτικὸς is more than once referred to by Plato, but without any reference to the passion of which it professes to treat, or to the matter, speculative or mythical, which it contains. It is used by its author for one purpose, and one only—to exemplify the dialectico-rhetorical theory evolved in the sequel of the dialogue.

Readers of the Gorgias naturally ask, How is it that Plato devotes a work so elaborate as the Phaedrus to the illustration of that art of rhetoric which in the former dialogue he pointedly condemns; which he pronounces to be no art, but a mere trick acquired by practice (ἄλογον πρᾶγμα, τριβή, ἐμπειρία), destitute of all scientific principle, and capable of subserving none but the most unworthy ends? Those who adhere to the tradition that the Phaedrus is a juvenile composition, are compelled to suppose that Plato, when he wrote the Gorgias, had survived the illusions of his youth—had, in fact, changed his mind, and ceased to regard Rhetoric as worthy the

[6] P. 237 B—241 D. [7] P. 243 D. [8] P. 242 B.

[9] A less favourable view is taken by Col. Mure, who calls it "an eloquent mystification." A more indulgent phrase-maker might call it a "romance of the soul."

[1] As Ficinus. See his "Argument," prefixed to the English reprint of Bekker.

[2] Which begins p. 257 B, and continues to the end of the dialogue.

attention of a philosopher. This opinion appears to me quite untenable. In the first place, the supposed second thoughts of the Gorgias are by no means the better thoughts. The view adopted in the Phaedrus is both more moderate and more deep and true than the narrow and passionate special-pleading of the Gorgias, a dialogue (as I may attempt to show hereafter) not improbably composed while the wound inflicted on Plato's feelings by the unrighteous doom of his master was still but half healed. In the second place, there are two passages in the Phaedrus, in which an unprejudiced eye cannot fail, in my opinion, to detect an allusion to the deprecatory language employed in the Gorgias. In Phaedr. 260 E, Socrates exclaims: "I seem to hear the approaching steps of a band of antagonist arguments (λόγοι) loudly protesting that Rhetoric is no art, as she lyingly pretends, but an ἄτεχνος τριβή." These personified λόγοι can be none other than those with which we are familiar in the Gorgias. No one before Plato ever used the phrase ἄτεχνος τριβή, nor is there any dialogue except the Gorgias in which the import of the terms τριβή and ἐμπειρία, as distinguished from τέχνη, is explained. In that dialogue the utmost pains are taken by Socrates to render them intelligible to the untutored apprehension of Polus, whereas here their meaning is assumed as self-evident. The distinction is repeated in p. 270 B, and there, as here, allowed to pass without comment or objection.

Lastly, if we refer to dialogues which we know for certain to contain the deliberate opinions of Plato's riper years, we find him assigning to Rhetoric much the same rank as that which it holds in the Phaedrus. In the Politicus (p. 304 A), for instance, he speaks of Rhetoric as an art of co-ordinate dignity and importance with the arts of the General and the administrator of justice: and he describes the functions devolving upon the rhetor in a well-ordered commonwealth, in terms which are but the application of a passage in p. 270 B of the Phaedrus. This passage of the Politicus is interesting in itself, and throws much light not only upon the Phaedrus, [illegible] for that very curious feature in Plato's writings, the frequent use of the philosophical mythus. "To what art," it is asked, "are we to [illegible] the office of persuading the vulgar, by a method mythological [illegible] than didactic[1]?" "This function also," says the younger [illegible], "we must appropriate to Rhetoric." To the same effect [illegible] Phaedrus in this dialogue, where he describes the office of [illegible] τὸ δικαιοσύνης τε καὶ ἄλλων ὧν λέγεις πέρι μυθολογεῖν[4].

[illegible]

[illegible] Phaedrus, τῇ δὲ (ψυχῇ) λόγους τε καὶ ἐπιτηδεύσεις νομίμους [illegible] πειθὼ ἣν ἂν βούλῃ καὶ ἀρετὴν παραδώσειν (p. 270 B). There is an

These passages, taken in connexion, explain what might otherwise seem obscure, viz Plato's motive for selecting Love as the theme both of Lysias' speech which he condemns, and of the two counter speeches of Socrates. They at the same time account for the discrepancy, in one point of view real, in another only apparent, between the mode in which Rhetoric is handled in the Gorgias and in the Phaedrus In the Gorgias the ῥήτωρ and the demagogue are identified, and the Rhetoric which Socrates assails is that of the Agora and the Law Courts But in the ideal Monarchy which is sketched in the Politicus, as well as in the ideal Aristocracy of the Republic, there is no room for either Pleader or Demagogue. Eloquence is thenceforth to exert her powers in what Plato conceived to be the nobler task of swaying and moulding the affections of the citizens into conformity with the principles of a State founded in righteousness She was to be the handmaid at once of Philosophy and of Political, or, what in the ancient view was the same thing, of Ethical Science Πείθουσα τὸ δίκαιον ξυνδιακυβερνᾷ τὰς ἐν τῇ πόλει πράξεις . . κεχώρισται πολιτικῆς τὸ ῥητορικὸν ὡς ἕτερον εἶδος ὄν, ὑπηρετεῖ μὴν ταύτῃ (Pol 1 1), or, as Aristotle, entirely in the spirit of his master, remarks: "Rhetoric is properly an offshoot of Dialectic, and of the science of morals, which is Politic properly so called[5]"

Now, setting aside political uses, which are not contemplated in the Phaedrus, the Rhetoric of which the Erotic Discourse is an example is precisely that which Plato describes. As its author explains[6], the discourse commences with a definition framed on dialectical principles. Having determined Love to be a Madness, it proceeds to investigate the varieties of Madness, and singles out that special variety to which Love belongs It is, therefore, an example of a Rhetoric which is an "offshoot" of Logic or Dialectic[7]; for Dialectic it is which teaches us how to define "per genus et differentiam" It is also a μυθολογία περὶ δικαιοσύνης καὶ ἄλλων ὧν ἔλεγε πέρι—"a mythical discourse touching Justice and other topics of Socratic discourse" It relates to Justice, for that virtue, according to the Platonic Socrates, consists in the due subordination of the lower appetites to the Reason, aided, not thwarted, by the im-

ambiguity in the word μυθολογεῖν, which may bear the general meaning 'fabulari,' 'sermocinari' Heindorf denies that it has any more special meaning in this passage, but I think the context, coupled with the parallel passage in the Politicus, would justify the restricted and more usual meaning Compare Rep 377 C

[5] συμβαίνει τὴν ῥητορικὴν οἷον παραφυές τι τῆς διαλεκτικῆς εἶναι καὶ τῆς περὶ τὰ ἤθη πραγματείας, ἣν δίκαιόν ἐστι προσαγορεύειν πολιτικήν Rhet. i 2, § 7.

[6] Pp 263 D 265 E

[7] Rhetor sine dialectica nihil firmi docere potest Et e contra Dialecticus sine rhetorica non afficit auditores. Utramque vero conjungens docet et persuadet Luther in Epist ad Gal c 5

pulsive or irascible principle; and this subordination is figured by the charioteer holding well in hand the restive steed, while he gives the rein to his nobler and upward-striving yoke-fellow[3]. It may also be justly said to embrace the other customary topics of Socratic discourse, for we recognize, under but thin disguises, all the peculiarities of the Platonic psychology the immortality, antecedent and prospective, of the soul, its self-moving or self-determining properties ("freedom of the Will"), its heavenly extraction, its incarceration in the flesh, and the conditions of its subsequent emancipation finally, that singular tenet of *ἀνάμνησις* which, in the Phaedo and elsewhere is insisted on as one of the main props of the doctrine of immortality: and that not less characteristic doctrine of ideas or archetypal forms with which the theory of *ἀνάμνησις* is bound up The speech is, moreover, manifestly psychagogic, to borrow Plato's term designed, that is, to sway the Will of the hearer *πλάττει τὴν ψυχὴν τοῖς μύθοις, μᾶλλον ἢ τὰ σώματα ταῖς χερσίν*, as the licensed mythologer is said to do in the Republic (b. ii 377 c) It is an instance of that species of rhetoric which alone seemed to Plato desirable or salutary: a rhetoric which, *mutatis mutandis*, answers sufficiently well to our eloquence of the pulpit as distinguished from the eloquence of the bar the senate, or the hustings[4] It is intended to prove, by a living example, that the art which, as ordinarily practised, was a tool in the hands of the designing and ambitious, is capable of being turned by the philosopher to the better purpose of clothing in an attractive dress the results of his more abstruse speculations; and also of stimulating the minds of his disciples, if only by working in them that wonder which, as Plato elsewhere says, and as Aristotle said after him, is the fountain of all philosophy In one word, the Erotic Discourse may be regarded as a master-piece of its author's myth-making genius the exemplary specimen of an art of which he has left us many other instances, but none so brilliant and elaborate[1]

In one respect, indeed, this discourse may be said to differ from other philosophical myths which are scattered in the Platonic

[3] Appendix I p 161

[4] [illegible] the decided preference of Isocrates over Lysias (in this dialog) [illegible] for the dicastery, Isocrates for the closet, and had is the *φιλοσοφία* [illegible] in his speeches undoubtedly "philosophia quaedam," [illegible] ng in the business-like speeches of Lysias It evidently [illegible] speak as civilly of Isocrates as he could, if only by way [illegible] *λογογράφος* Political sympathies may also have had [illegible] was an aristocrat and "laudator temporis acti"

[1] [illegible] 77 [illegible] passage which is a description of the *ἐρωτικὸς λόγος* and [illegible] which it was framed Note esp the clause, *ποικίλῃ μὲν ποικίλους* [illegible] *ἁρμονίους διδοὺς λόγους ἁπλοῦς δὲ ἁπλῇ*

writings, it is, in most of its parts, a deliberate allegory, in which the thing signified is designed to be intelligible to the instructed hearer or reader. This is not always nor usually the case with the Platonic myths, in most of which the sign and the thing signified are blended and sometimes confused, as in myths properly so-called; so that it is hard to say how much is (supposed) truth and how much fable[2]. This distinct allegorical character has led some modern writers to regard the Erotic Discourse in the light of a mythical proem to a course of philosophy hereafter to be developed in a graver and more didactic manner by means of dialogues as yet unwritten, while other writers, for similar reasons, have treated the entire dialogue as a composition answering to an inaugural lecture, published by Plato on the occasion of opening his school in the Academy after his return from Sicily. The first of these hypotheses is adopted by Schleiermacher, the second by C. F. Hermann, the former of whom regards the Phaedrus as a preface to the entire series of Dialogues, the latter as a preface only to those composed after the date before mentioned. I am unable to adopt either view. First, because, as it seems to me, the mythical representations in the Phaedrus presuppose, on the part of its readers, a certain familiarity with the cardinal points of the Platonic morals and psychology, which it was impossible that any circle of Athenian readers could have possessed at the beginning of Plato's professorial life. Secondly, because both theories will be found incompatible with that unity of design which should characterize a work of high literary art, and which, if we are content to look upon it as a treatise on Philosophical Rhetoric, does really characterize the Phaedrus. Thirdly, because, as we have seen, such hints as Plato himself has vouchsafed to give us, point in the direction indicated[3], and Plato's intimations of his own meaning, even when slight and cursory, and

[2] As instances of this fusion, take the mythic account of a state of retribution after death at the end of the Gorgias, and that of the migration of souls, &c., in the tenth book of the Republic, also the splendid description of the process of Creation in the Timaeus.

[3] That the Phaedrus of the dialogue is supposed to be something of a Platonist, is evident not only from his want of curiosity as to the meaning of the many fine things said in the Erotic Discourse, but from his familiarity with other Platonic distinctions, such as that between pure and mixed pleasures (258 E). "It is pleasures like these," says Phaedrus, "which alone make life desirable (the pleasures of hearing and reading discourses), not those which are necessarily preceded by pain and uneasiness, which is the characteristic of nearly all the pleasures of the body, on which account the latter are deservedly styled slavish." The distinction, expressed in this offhand manner by Phaedrus, is in the Philebus given as the result of a careful metaphysical analysis (Phileb. 31 seqq.). The same theory of mixed pleasures is also implied in the description of the throbbing and pain attendant on the growth of the wings pictured in the Erotic Discourse, p. 251.

still more when, as in this dialogue, quite explicit, are of more value than the theories of his most ingenious expositors.

We may add to these reasons the not unimportant one, that Aristotle seems to have taken a view of this dialogue similar to that which we have adopted. His three books of Rhetoric are, in effect, an expanded Phaedrus. He accepts Plato's views of the subordinate relation of Rhetoric to Dialectic, and of the necessity of a thorough dialectical training to the future orator. He accepts also the view that he who would work effectually on mankind must first acquaint himself with human nature, with the springs of action and the varieties of character, so as to know by what arguments such and such classes of men are most easily swayed; and he agrees with Plato in condemning as unscientific the *τέχναι* or Arts of Rhetoric which existed in great numbers in his time. Like Plato too, he regards rhetorical figures and the arts of style (*εὐέπεια λόγων*) which composed the body of the popular treatises, as mere accessories to a philosophical theory of Rhetoric, not as essential or integral parts of the science. His second book is, in great part, but a working out of the three precepts laid down in the Phaedrus[4]. "Any one," says Plato, "who really means to give us an Art of Rhetoric worthy of the name, must first accurately describe the human soul: telling us whether it is one and uniform, or whether it admits of as many varieties as the body. Secondly, he must tell us how the different parts of the soul act, also how they are affected, and by what agencies. Thirdly, he must be able to classify (*διατάξασθαι*) the different kinds of arguments, as well as the different modifications of soul, and the affections of which these are susceptible, and then fit the several arguments to the several mental constitutions, and show why such and such souls are necessarily wrought upon by such and such discourses." With these three conditions of a *τέχνη ῥητορική* Aristotle faithfully complies. His first book contains a classification (*διάταξις*) of the different *πίστεις* or modes of producing persuasion; his second embraces (1) a careful analysis of the *παθήματα*—the affections of which human nature is susceptible, and also of the causes by which such affections are called forth; (2) a descriptive catalogue of the various modifications of human character, and the sort of arguments adapted to each[5].

The third part of Rhetoric, the Praecepta bene scribendi, to which

[4] p. 271.

[5] Thus the 2nd chapter treats of anger, its causes and the modes of allaying it. The 4th of *φιλία* and *μῖσος*, the 5th of Fear, the 6th of Shame, &c. Again, in the 12th chapter he describes the *ἤθη* of young men, in the 13th of old ones, in the 14th of persons of middle age: after which he describes the effects upon the character of nobility, wealth, power, &c.

Socrates allows a certain subordinate value, but which, when severed from dialectic and psychology, he pronounces rank quackery[6], is altogether evaded in the Phaedrus. Socrates approaches the subject[7] only to dismiss it with a few characteristic remarks on the greater value of oral, i. e. conversational, as compared with written instruction. These remarks are introduced by a singular mythus, the scene of which is laid in Egypt, the supposed mother-land of written discourse. The moral of the tale is, that the art of writing operates on the memory and intellect rather as a sedative than as a stimulant; that it fosters the conceit of wisdom, δοξοσοφία, rather than wisdom itself. This, it may be observed, is a view of his own art not likely to be taken up by a young writer; and the passage, so far as it goes, may be used as an argument against the early date of the Phaedrus. It is evidently Plato's object to exalt the art of Dialectic at the expense of Rhetoric; and we find in this portion of the dialogue a justification of the oral exercises which, as we learn from other sources, formed part of the teaching of the Academy, and which were ridiculed and disparaged both by the teachers of Rhetoric and the comic poets[8]. Aristotle, however, though, as we have said, he also treats the εὐέπεια as an accessory rather than an essential part of a systematic Rhetoric, devotes to it a considerable portion of his third book; in which he handles the subject with his usual good sense, and in a manner more entertaining than might have been expected. His estimate of the Sicilian school of rhetors agrees with Plato's, and the third chapter of his third book περὶ ψυχρᾶς λέξεως is filled with instances of their bad taste.

This view of the Phaedrus may offend those who are in the habit of looking upon its theory of Love as one of the most sublime and characteristic mysteries of Platonism. But the question now before us is not the importance of the subject-matter, but the place which the Discourse on Love was designed by its author to fill in the general scheme of the Dialogue, and what is the point of view from which we can contemplate the Phaedrus with satisfaction, as a living and harmonious whole (ζῷον συνεστός). Now that Plato himself professed to hold an humbler view of the use of mythical compositions than that which has found favour with later Platonists, we may satisfy ourselves by reference to his own words[9]. "Shall we say," exclaims Socrates, "that the philosopher who possesses clear conceptions of Justice, Beauty, and Goodness, will exhibit less discretion

[6] 268 A. [7] 271 B.
[8] As particularly by Epicrates ap. Athen. ii. 59 C. Meineke iii. p. 370.
[9] p. 276 C.

than the husbandman in disposing of these his precious seeds of truth?" "Surely not," says Phaedrus. S.—"He will not then set himself, by way of a serious occupation, to write his thoughts in water, or be content with sowing them in ink with his pen, in the form of discourses, which are incapable of defending themselves against assailants, or even of conveying a complete idea of the truth." Ph.—"That is most unlikely." S.—"It is so; and it will therefore be by way of pastime that he will sow his seed in such soil, writing, when he writes at all, for the purpose of laying up precious memorials against oblivious age, for himself in case he live to be old, and for all that pursue the same philosophic career. He will look fondly on these tender growths of his genius, and will find in them a choice substitute for the coarser recreations of the vulgar." Ph.—"Such pastime, Socrates, is as noble as those of the multitude are poor and contemptible: happy he who is able thus to amuse himself, who can weave stories (μυθολογοῦντα) about Justice and the other matters upon which you discourse![1]" In this passage we may read Plato's explanation of his own purpose in writing, and of his practice of interweaving subtle dialectical controversy with discourses half playful, half serious, in which philosophical truth is blended with poetic fiction in varying proportions. Literary skill was not the attainment on which Plato most prided himself, or which he most admired in others. He wore it "lightly, like a flower," esteeming poetry and eloquence as dust in the balance when weighed against philosophic insight and dialectical subtlety. The man he was prepared to run after (κατόπισθε μετ' ἴχνιον ὥστε θεοῖο[2]) was one who knew how to collect and divide, to elevate common notions into scientific conceptions, to separate genera into their species by strict rules of art, to find the One in the Many and the Many in the One,—in a word, the consummate dialectician.

The original passage of which this is a part is well worthy of consideration. It professes to give us the key to Plato's philosophical method, and more than one of his dialogues may be viewed as a commentary upon it. In the Sophistes and Politicus he has given us elaborate specimens of his art of Division, διαίρεσις, or, as we should call it, Classification, with which in the former dialogue he has interwoven a refutation of the Eleatic or Eristic Logic, which was based on a principle antithetic to his own.

[1] Compare Timaeus 59 D, where he speaks of the unrepented pleasure (ἀμεταμέλητος ἡδονή) afforded by speculating on physics, in accordance with τὴν τῶν εἰκότων μύθων ἰδέαν. This will be a philosopher's recreation (παιδιὰ μέτριος καὶ φρόνιμος), in the intervals of his dialectical exercises.

[2] p. 266 B.

PART II

ON THE PROBABLE DATE OF THE PHAEDRUS[3]

THE notion that the Phaedrus was the earliest of Plato's philosophical productions rests mainly, if not entirely, so far as external evidence is concerned, upon a passage of Diogenes Laertius, who lived in the third, and one of Olympiodorus, who lectured on Plato and his philosophy in the sixth century after Christ. The passage of Diogenes occurs in the twenty-fifth chapter of his life of Plato (b. iii. § 38), a chapter containing six or seven unconnected notices of more or less interest, but of which two at least are demonstrably erroneous[4]. After speaking of the tradition that the books of the Laws were left by Plato at his death ἐν κηρῷ, i. e. written on wax tablets, and that his scholar Philippus of Opus, the reputed author of the Epinomis, first wrote them out fair, Diogenes proceeds as follows: Εὐφορίων δὲ καὶ Παναίτιος εἰρήκασι, πολλάκις ἐστραμμένην εὑρῆσθαι τὴν ἀρχὴν τῆς πολιτείας, ἣν πολιτείαν Ἀριστόξενός φησι πᾶσαν σχεδὸν ἐν τοῖς Πρωταγόρου γεγράφθαι ἀντιλογικοῖς. λόγος[5] δὲ πρῶτον γράψαι αὐτὸν τὸν Φαῖδρον· καὶ γὰρ ἔχει μειρακιῶδές τι τὸ πρόβλημα. Δικαίαρχος δὲ καὶ τὸν τρόπον τῆς γραφῆς ὅλον ἐπιμέμφεται ὡς φορτικόν[6]. "Euphorion and Panaetius have stated that the opening sentence of the Republic was found with

[3] The following chronological table will assist the reader:—

Plato was born B.C. 427 or 429				
—	became acquainted with Socrates	407 or 409	an. aet.	20.
—	left Athens *mortuo Socrate*	399	—	28 or 30.
—	said to have returned thither	395	—	32 or 34.
—	began to teach in the Academy	386 perh.	—	40 or 42.

[4] Aristotle is made to say that "the diction of Plato is intermediate between that of prose and poetry," evidently a misrepresentation of Rhet. iii. 7. 11, where the philosopher speaks only of the *Phaedrus*, in which he says that this style was adopted ironically (μετ' εἰρωνείας). He is also represented as having been the only one of Plato's audience who had patience to hear to the end the dialogue περὶ ψυχῆς, i. e. the Phaedo. The genuine tradition on which this preposterous story is founded is well known and sufficiently probable. It was an oral discourse περὶ τἀγαθοῦ, not the reading of the Phaedo, which thinned the philosophic circle.

[5] Vulg. λόγον, corrected by Cobet in his ed. of D. L.

[6] Of the authorities here quoted

Aristoxenus was a disciple of Aristotle,	flor. circ.	320 B.C.
Dicaearchus do. do.	— —	326—287
Euphorion a poet and historiographer	— —	240
	born 274, d.	221
Panaetius	flor. circ.	113

The last is called "gravissimus Stoicorum" Cic. de Off. ii. 14. 51. He was a Platonizing Stoic however—"Semper in ore habuit Platonem," de Fin. iv. 28. 79, "dissentit in nonnullis a Platone suo," Tusc. i. 32. 69, e. g. with reference to the Immortality of the Soul.

the words written several times over, and each time in a different order, which Republic, Aristoxenus says, was almost entirely contained in the Antilogica of Protagoras; there is also a report that the first dialogue he (Plato) wrote was the Phaedrus: for indeed the subject of that dialogue is one which a very young man would naturally choose. But Dicaearchus censures the style of the entire dialogue, which he thinks in bad taste[7]." In this passage Diogenes agrees perfectly with the statement of Olympiodorus, who says in his life of Plato, τοῦ Πλάτωνος τοῦτον πρῶτον γράψαντος διάλογον, ὡς λέγεται. In other words, the belief that Plato wrote the Phaedrus first was a common rumour, founded on the juvenile character of its πρόβλημα—its theme, or subject proposed for discussion,—which those who accept the tradition suppose to be Love[8]. Others think that the story was borrowed from Dicaearchus, in which case it is conceivable that the "report" was an inference founded on his impression of the dialogue, which he deemed unworthy of an adult Plato. And this seems to be Schleiermacher's view, which is not on the whole improbable[9]. However this may be, the rumour was unknown to Cicero, who was familiar with the writings both of Aristoxenus and Dicaearchus, especially with the latter, whom he repeatedly quotes. In the Orator, c. xiii 41, occurs the following passage: "Isocrates videtur testimonio Platonis aliorum judicia debere contemnere. Est enim (ut scis) quasi in extrema pagina Phaedri[1] his ipsis verbis loquens Socrates: 'Adolescens etiam nunc, o Phaedre, Isocrates est: sed quid de illo augurer libet dicere. Quid tandem? inquit ille. Majore mihi ingenio videtur esse quam ut cum orationibus Lysiae comparetur. * * * * * Inest enim natura philosophia in hujus viri mente quaedam.' Haec de adolescente Socrates auguratur. At ea *de seniore* scribit Plato, et scribit aequalis, et quidem, exagitator omnium rhetorum, hunc miratur unum."

We are compelled to infer from this passage that Cicero conceived the Phaedrus to have been written when Isocrates had reached at least his full maturity (*senior*), in other words, long after the time at which the conversation between Socrates and Phaedrus is feigned to have taken place. Plato himself was but six years the junior of Isocrates, and, therefore, could not have been a young man at a time

[7] φορτικὸν seems to mean 'inflated,' 'turgid,' 'overdone,' 'pompous.' φορτικὸς καὶ ὑπέρογκος occur together in Dion. Hal.

[8] Perhaps because Aristotle says, ὅτι οἱ νέοι ἐρωτικοί. Krische über Platons Phädrus, p. 5. But the καλῶν παίδων ἔρως seems to have been confined to grown-up men.

[9] It is also the view of Cobet, who punctuates accordingly in his ed. of Diogenes.

[1] Phaedr. p. 279 A.

when Isocrates would be justly described as "senior," a term which a Roman would not have applied to any one much under fifty years of age. At any rate, Cicero supposes a considerable interval to have elapsed between the imagined conversation and the actual composition of the Phaedrus; but the interval must have been very short, if the dialogue was written in Plato's youth. Of the accuracy of Cicero's statement I give no opinion; but I think we may fairly allow it to counterweigh that of Dicaearchus, or Aristoxenus, or whoever may have been Diogenes's authority for the story he has handed down.

If now we consider the internal evidence of the dialogue, we shall find that (with an exception hereafter to be mentioned[2]) it favours the later rather than the earlier date. We have already seen that the Phaedrus lays down the theory of a dialectical method, of which the Sophistes and Politicus contain elaborate examples. These dialogues profess to be a continuation of the Theaetetus, which we know from internal evidence to have been written at least six years after the death of Socrates, and the entire trilogy may have taken up some years in its composition[3]. The dialogue which, in another part of its contents, the Phaedrus most resembles, is the Symposium, and this is known, from internal but conclusive indications, to have been a somewhat late work[4]. The similar vein of Erotic speculation in these two dialogues indisposes us to separate them by any long interval of time. Whether we consider the topics handled or its general construction, the Phaedrus seems to class itself naturally with the Theaetetus[5], the Phaedo, the Symposium, and other considerable dialogues which occupied Plato's pen during the maturity of his manhood. Its place with reference to the Republic we cannot venture to fix; though, as the doctrine of the threefold division of the Soul, and the functions of the so-called irascible principle in the mental economy are clearly figured in the Erotic allegory, it seems highly probable that the Phaedrus was written at any rate after Plato's views on this subject had become known in philosophic circles.

Those, on the other hand, who hold to the tradition of the early date of the Phaedrus, have to explain the fact, that it is far superior as an effort of literary skill to the Lysis, the Laches, the Charmides, and even the Protagoras, which they as well as their opponents consider to have been written during the life of Socrates.

[2] See Appendix II.

[3] It probably did so. The Politicus is written in a "later manner" than the Theaetetus.

[4] See inter alia Stallbaum's Prolegomena ad Symp.

[5] If I may venture on a guess I should put it after the Theaetetus and before the other two.

They have also to explain how it is that in these dialogues Plato touches upon none of the topics which are handled in the Phaedrus, and which must have employed the mind of its author for some considerable time at least before he gave the result of his speculations to the world. The Lysis is a conversation on Friendship, the Laches, a treatise on Valour; but of both these the positive results are meagre, and the doctrines by no means characteristically Platonic, but rather such as Xenophon or any other follower of Socrates might have gleaned from the teaching of his master. In the Charmides, which is an advance upon the Lysis and Laches in point of composition, notions are put forward which are incompatible with Plato's later opinions—the virtue of σωφροσύνη, for instance, is handled in a manner far from satisfactory; and even the Protagoras, though the most perfect specimen of his early manner, conducts us to none but negative results. It leaves us dissatisfied with the Socratic theory of Virtue, but neither substitutes a better, nor indicates in what direction we are to look for it. In maintaining therefore the early date assigned to the Phaedrus by tradition we should be driven to suppose that Plato in his first published work had presented the world with ideas and speculations which he afterwards allowed to slumber for some twenty years; vouchsafing no explanation of allegories which are quite intelligible to us, but which must have seemed mere enigmas to those to whom his leading doctrines were unknown.

In this attempt to fix approximately the date of the Phaedrus, no account has been taken of the Pythagorean matter which is found in the Erotic Discourse. Stallbaum and others have built much on this; for it is a well-known tradition[6] that Plato owed the Pythagorean elements which enter into his scheme of philosophy, to his intercourse with the members of Pythagorean brotherhoods resident in Sicily and lower Italy; countries which he did not visit until some time after the death of Socrates. The argument hence derived is not without its weight, though it has been pressed somewhat too far by Stallbaum. It is, however, highly probable that the fondness for myth and allegory which appears nowhere in the purely Socratic—that is, as I venture to call them, the early—dialogues[7], but which eminently distinguishes those acknowledged to be later, was a taste which Plato derived from this ingenious and fantastic school. The cosmical speculations which are implied in the Erotic mythus

[6] Cic. de Republ. i. 10, 16. De Finn. v. 29, 87.

[7] The apologue put in the mouth of Protagoras is only a seeming exception; for no one can fail to perceive that it is a composition altogether different both in form and spirit from the true Platonic mythus.

are of Pythagorean origin, though in many of the details Plato seems to have introduced considerable variations.

Arguments have also been drawn from the notices of Lysias scattered in this dialogue, compared with what we know from other sources of the biography of that Orator. We should infer from four passages in the dialogue[8], that the reputation of Lysias as a λογογράφος had reached its highest point when the Phaedrus was written. He is styled "the ablest living writer," and appears to have been envied and decried in consequence. One of the public characters of the day having occasion to abuse him, had called him, says Phaedrus, λογογράφος. The word properly denoted one who composed for pay speeches to be delivered by others, particularly by plaintiffs or defendants in the law courts. Antiphon, of whom we read in the eighth book of Thucydides[9], was the first who adopted this practice, and it is well known that all the extant speeches of Lysias, save one, were composed to be spoken by others. There is no doubt that some discredit attached to this profession of a λογογράφος, at least sufficient to deter a man of wealth and good connexions from engaging in it. Now it is well known that Lysias, though a 'metœc,' was a member of a wealthy family. At the age of fifteen (B.C. 443) he had left Athens for Thurii, where he settled as a κληροῦχος, and resided in affluence until the year 411. In that year he was driven out by the oligarchal or Lacedaemonian party, which had been strengthened by the disastrous ending of the Sicilian expedition[1]. He returned direct to Athens, where his father Cephalus resided. There, as we learn from the opening page of the Republic, he made the acquaintance of Socrates and his friends, though he was not one of the Socratic circle, as his brother Polemarchus seems to have been. Living in affluence, as a member of a wealthy house, it is not likely that he would practise either as a teacher of rhetoric or as a writer of speeches, during the first years of his sojourn in Athens after his return. A man of literary tastes we may suppose him to have been, for we are told that, during his abode at Thurii, he had studied rhetoric under the Sicilian professor Tisias. He may, therefore, have written as an amateur (ὡς ἰδιώτης); but that alone would not have justified Plato in calling him δεινότατος τῶν νῦν γράφειν, still less in making him the prominent figure in an

[8] Λυσίας δεινότατος ὢν τῶν νῦν γράφειν (Phaedr. init. 228 A). Λυσίαν τὸν τοῦ λόγου πατέρα παῦε τῶν τοιούτων λόγων, ἐπὶ φιλοσοφίαν δέ, ὥσπερ ὁ ἀδελφὸς αὐτοῦ Πολέμαρχος τέτραπται, τρέψον (257 B). Λυσίαν τις τῶν πολιτικῶν ἐλοιδόρει, καὶ ἐκάλει λογογράφον (ib. C). εἴτε Λυσίας εἴτε τις ἄλλος πώποτ' ἔγραψεν ἢ γράψει ἰδίᾳ ἢ δημοσίᾳ νόμους τιθείς, σύγγραμμα πολιτικὸν γράφων (277 D).

[9] He was feared, says Thucydides, διὰ δόξαν δεινότητος. Compare Plato's δεινότατος τῶν νῦν γράφειν.

[1] Grote H. G. x. 530.

important dialogue like the Phaedrus. During the domination of the Thirty (B.C. 404) a change came over his fortunes. He was despoiled by them of a large portion of his property, of which however he retained enough to enable him to contribute nobly in aid of Thrasybulus and the exiles. It was after their return that he appeared for the first time in an Athenian court of justice. In the oration against Eratosthenes, spoken 403, he expresses great diffidence in his own powers, being, as he tells us, a novice in public business and public speaking[2], and he denies that either he or his father Cephalus had ever brought or defended an action. The speech is one of his best, and this leads to the conclusion that he had cultivated his talent of public speaking during his long residence at Thurii, where he appears to have been a considerable personage. But of his written speeches this against Eratosthenes appears to be the earliest. "Quarum aetatem cernere possumus eae omnes post XXXvirorum conficiebantur," says his biographer Taylor[3]. As Lysias was deprived of the rights of citizenship shortly after he had acquired them, he was prevented from mounting the bema or appearing in the law courts: hence he devoted himself to the composition of speeches for others, as the only means he had left of retrieving his fortunes. His fame as a Logographus was therefore acquired late in life; for he was fifty-five years of age at the trial of Eratosthenes, and fifty-nine at the trial of Socrates in 399. He worked at this profession during the last twenty-five years of his life, and died at the age of eighty (B.C. 378)[4].

These data are more consistent with the late than the early composition of this dialogue: at any rate, they seem to prove that Plato did not write the Phaedrus while still a stripling (*μειράκιον*), or about B.C. 406, when he was twenty years old; for at that date Lysias had not begun to employ himself as a Logographus, and could still less have risen to the head of that profession[5].

[2] §§ 3, 4, Bekk.

[3] The oration pro Polystrato was delivered in Ol. xcii. 1. B.C. 409. But its authenticity is denied. Comp. c. Eratosth. § 3, *οὔτ' ἐμαυτοῦ πώποτε οὔτε ἀλλότρια πράγματα πράξας νῦν ἠνάγκασμαι ... κατηγορεῖν*.

[4] Plato opened the Academy B.C. 388 or 386.

[5] We must therefore understand Plato's epithet *δεινότατος τῶν νῦν γράφειν*, as put in the mouth of Socrates, to be a *πρόληψις*—a liberty of which he would not have scrupled to avail himself in composing a dialogue the time of which was placed so far back as that of the Phaedrus must have been. To explain away the anachronisms of Plato, is a favourite amusement of his commentators—a task *πολλῆς σχολῆς δεόμενον*—and we may add, *οὐ πάνυ εὐτυχῶν ἀνδρῶν*.

ΠΛΑΤΩΝΟΣ ΦΑΙΔΡΟΣ.

ΤΑ ΤΟΥ ΔΙΑΛΟΓΟΥ ΠΡΟΣΩΠΑ

ΣΩΚΡΑΤΗΣ

ΦΑΙΔΡΟΣ

ΠΛΑΤΩΝΟΣ ΦΑΙΔΡΟΣ.

"a Happy Summer Day"
Wil Pl I

p. 227 Ὦ φίλε Φαῖδρε, ποῖ δὴ καὶ πόθεν;

ΦΑΙ. Παρὰ Λυσίου, ὦ Σώκρατες, τοῦ Κεφάλου. πορεύομαι δὲ πρὸς περίπατον ἔξω τείχους· συχνὸν γὰρ ἐκεῖ διέτριψα χρόνον καθήμενος ἐξ ἑωθινοῦ. τῷ δὲ σῷ καὶ ἐμῷ ἑταίρῳ πειθόμενος Ἀκουμενῷ κατὰ τὰς ὁδοὺς ποιοῦμαι τοὺς περιπάτους· φησὶ γὰρ ἀκοπωτέρους εἶναι
B τῶν ἐν τοῖς δρόμοις.

father]
physician
Symp

ΣΩ. Καλῶς γάρ, ὦ ἑταῖρε, λέγει. ἀτὰρ Λυσίας ἦν, ὡς ἔοικεν, ἐν ἄστει.

227. φησὶ—δρόμοις] 'he tells me that country exercise is more bracing than that taken in the public walks' ἄκοπα is a medical term, which Plato probably borrowed from Hippocrates, as ἐξάντης, p 244 E. It included all applications, external as well as internal, for removing lassitude and strengthening the nervous system, answering to our 'tonics.' For δρόμοις compare Eupolis ap Diog L. iii 7, ἐν εὐσκίοις δρόμοισιν Ἀκαδήμου θεοῦ Plut. Cim c. 13, τὴν δ' Ἀκαδημίαν ἐξ ἀνύδρου καὶ αὐχμηρᾶς κατάρρυτον ἀποδείξας ἄλσος, ἠσκημένον ὑπ' αὐτοῦ δρόμοις καθαροῖς καὶ συσκίοις περιπάτοις The word δρόμοι sometimes denotes the covered portico or cloister encompassing the great open court (ὕπαιθρον) of the palaestra or gymnasium These δρόμοι were used not only for walking exercise, but also in bad weather for foot-races and other sports which ordinarily took place in the open area They are also called ξυστοί, ξυστοὶ δρόμοι, κατάστεγοι δρόμοι Vitruv v 11 2, "Haec porticus ξυστὸς apud Graecos vocitatur, quod athletae per hyberna tempora in tectis stadiis exercentur" J. Poll 3 148, ξυστοὶ δρόμοι, ἐν οἷς αἱ ἀσκήσεις He elsewhere cites a line from Aristias, ἦν μοι παλαίστρα καὶ δρόμος ξυστὸς πέλας Xen Oecon xi 15, ἐγὼ δὲ περιπάτῳ χρῶμαι τῇ εἰς ἀγρὸν ὁδῷ, ἴσως ἄμεινον, ὦ Σώκρατες, ἢ εἰ ἐν τῷ ξυστῷ περιπατοίην Comp Euthyd p 273, εἰσελθόντες δὲ περιεπατείτην ἐν τῷ καταστέγῳ δρόμῳ, of the Lyceum, as appears from the context

B. ἐν ἄστει] Lysias probably resided with his father Cephalus, whose house, as we learn from the opening scene of the Republic, was in the Peiraeus, or he may have had a house of his own there. Epicrates is once, Morychus several times, mentioned by Aristophanes, the former as the possessor of an enviable beard, the latter as an eminent bon-vivant Eccles. 71, Ach 887, Pac 1008 In Vesp 506 Morychus is represented as ζῶν βίον γενναῖον, leading a life of gentlemanly ease and luxury Comp ib 1142 Epicrates, on the other hand, is described as a ῥήτωρ καὶ δημαγωγός, Schol. Eccles. l. l. He would seem to

ΦΑΙ. Ναί, παρ' Ἐπικράτει, ἐν τῇδε τῇ πλησίον τοῦ Ὀλυμπίου οἰκίᾳ τῇ Μορυχίᾳ.

ΣΩ Τίς οὖν δὴ ἦν ἡ διατριβή; ἢ δῆλον ὅτι τῶν λόγων ὑμᾶς Λυσίας εἱστία;

ΦΑΙ. Πεύσει, εἴ σοι σχολὴ προιόντι ἀκούειν.

ΣΩ Τί δαί; οὐκ ἂν οἴει με κατὰ Πίνδαρον καὶ ἀσχολίας ὑπέρτερον πρᾶγμα ποιήσασθαι τὸ σήν τε καὶ Λυσίου διατριβὴν ἀκοῦσαι,

ΦΑΙ. Πρόαγε δή. C

ΣΩ Λέγοις ἄν.

ΦΑΙ. Καὶ μήν, ὦ Σώκρατες, προσήκουσά γέ σοι ἡ ἀκοή· ὁ γάρ τοι λόγος ἦν, περὶ ὃν διετρίβομεν, οὐκ οἶδ' ὅντινα τρόπον ἐρωτικός. γέγραφε γὰρ δὴ ὁ Λυσίας πειρώμενόν τινα τῶν καλῶν, οὐχ ὑπ' ἐραστοῦ δέ, ἀλλ' αὐτὸ δὴ τοῦτο καὶ κεκόμψευται· λέγει γὰρ ὡς χαριστέον μὴ ἐρῶντι μᾶλλον ἢ ἐρῶντι.

ΣΩ Ὦ γενναῖος, εἴθε γράψειεν ὡς χρὴ πένητι μᾶλλον ἢ πλουσίῳ, καὶ πρεσβυτέρῳ ἢ νεωτέρῳ, καὶ ὅσα ἄλλα ἐμοί τε πρόσεστι καὶ τοῖς πολλοῖς ἡμῶν· ἦ γὰρ ἂν ἀστεῖοι καὶ D δημωφελεῖς εἶεν οἱ λόγοι. ἔγωγ' οὖν οὕτως ἐπιτεθύμηκα ἀκοῦσαι, ὥστ' ἐὰν βαδίζων ποιῇ τὸν περίπατον Μέγαράδε, καὶ κατὰ Ἡρόδικον προσβὰς τῷ τείχει πάλιν ἀπίῃς, οὐ μή σου ἀπολειφθῶ.

ΦΑΙ. Πῶς λέγεις, ὦ βέλτιστε Σώκρατες; οἴει με, ἃ Λυσίας | ἐν πολλῷ χρόνῳ κατὰ σχολὴν συνέθηκε, δεινότατος ὢν τῶν νῦν γράφειν, ταῦτα ἰδιώτην ὄντα ἀπομνημονεύσειν ἀξίως ἐκείνου, πολλοῦ γε δέω. καί τοι ἐβουλόμην γ' ἂν μᾶλλον ἤ μοι πολὺ χρυσίον γενέσθαι 228

have succeeded to the 'Morychian mansion,' possibly on the death of its former occupant. Hence the point of Socrates's question, ἢ δῆλον ὅτι τῶν λόγων ὑμᾶς Λυσίας εἱστία. The character of the entertainments had changed with the change of possessors.

κατὰ Πίνδαρον] The entire passage is to be found Isthm. i 1, Μᾶτερ ἐμά, τὸ τεόν, χρύσασπι Θήβα, πρᾶγμα καὶ ἀσχολίας ὑπέρτερον θήσομαι.

D ἦ γὰρ ἂν ἀστεῖοι] 'would indeed be charming and a boon to the public.' Cf. 242 E, ἡ εὐήθεια αὐτοῖν πάνυ ἀστεία, 'quite refreshing.' Stallbaum's idea of a double meaning is gratuitous.

Ἡρόδικον] Schol. ἰατρὸς ἦν καὶ τὰ γυμνάσια ἔξω τείχους ἐποιεῖτο, ἀρχόμενος ἀπό τινος διαστήματος οὐ μακροῦ ἀλλὰ συμμέτρου, ἄχρι τοῦ τείχους, καὶ ἀναστρέφων. In Protag. 316 D he is styled ὁ Σηλυμβριανός, τὸ δὲ ἀρχαῖον Μεγαρεύς, and is

ΣΩ. Ὦ Φαῖδρε, εἰ ἐγὼ Φαῖδρον ἀγνοῶ, καὶ ἐμαυτοῦ ἐπιλέλησμαι ἀλλὰ γὰρ οὐδέτερά ἐστι τούτων, εὖ οἶδα
ὅτι Λυσίου λόγον ἀκούων ἐκεῖνος οὐ μόνον ἅπαξ ἤκουσεν,
ἀλλὰ πολλάκις ἐπαναλαμβάνων ἐκέλευέν οἱ λέγειν· ὁ δὲ
B ἐπείθετο προθύμως. τῷ δὲ οὐδὲ ταῦτα ἦν ἱκανά, ἀλλὰ
τελευτῶν παραλαβὼν τὸ βιβλίον ἃ μάλιστα ἐπεθύμει
ἐπεσκόπει. καὶ τοῦτο δρῶν, ἐξ ἑωθινοῦ καθήμενος, ἀπει-
πὼν εἰς περίπατον ᾔει, ὡς μὲν ἐγὼ οἶμαι, νὴ τὸν κύνα,
ἐξεπιστάμενος τὸν λόγον, εἰ μὴ πάνυ τις ἦν μακρός.
ἐπορεύετο δ' ἐκτὸς τείχους, ἵνα μελετῴη ἀπαντήσας δέ
τῳ νοσοῦντι περὶ λόγων ἀκοήν, ἰδὼν μὲν ἰδὼν ἥσθη ὅτι
ἕξοι τὸν συγκορυβαντιῶντα, καὶ προάγειν ἐκέλευε δεο-
C μένου δὲ λέγειν τοῦ τῶν λόγων ἐραστοῦ, ἐθρύπτετο ὡς δὴ
οὐκ ἐπιθυμῶν λέγειν· τελευτῶν δὲ ἔμελλε, καὶ εἰ μή τις
ἑκὼν ἀκούοι, βίᾳ ἐρεῖν. σὺ οὖν, ὦ Φαῖδρε, αὐτοῦ δεήθητι,
ὅπερ τάχα πάντως ποιήσει, νῦν ἤδη ποιεῖν.

ΦΑΙ Ἐμοὶ ὡς ἀληθῶς πολὺ κράτιστόν ἐστιν οὕτως ὅπως δύναμαι λέγειν· ὥς μοι δοκεῖς σὺ οὐδαμῶς με ἀφήσειν πρὶν ἂν εἴπω ἁμῶς γέ πως.

ΣΩ Πάνυ γάρ σοι ἀληθῆ δοκῶ.

mode of treatment is satirically characterized in Rep III 406 A There was also an Herodicus of Leontini, a brother of Gorgias, a physician, like his namesake in the text Gorg 448 B

228 ἀλλὰ γὰρ—εὖ οἶδα] ἀλλὰ γὰρ are here equivalent to ἀλλ' ἐπεί, as in Eur Phoen 1307, Ἀλλὰ γὰρ Κρέοντα λεύσσω τόνδε δεῦρο συννεφῆ Πρὸς δόμους στείχοντα, παύσω τοὺς παρεστῶτας γόους, and in other passages quoted by Elmsley on Heracl 481 The ἐπαναλαμβάνων which follows is an instance of a participle used adverbially, 'repeatedly,' 'over and over again,' as τελευτῶν is presently used for εἰς τέλος

B For the ellipse in the clause ἃ μάλιστα ἐπεθύμει ἐπεσκόπει comp Symp 192 E, οἴοιτ' ἂν ἀκηκοέναι τοῦτο ὃ πάλαι ἄρα ἐπεθύμει, συνελθὼν τῷ ἐρωμένῳ ἐκ δυεῖν εἷς γενέσθαι Badham, ἐτεθαυμάκει, and in Symp ἀκηκοέναι τοῦ, οὗ πάλαι ἄρ' ἐπεθύμει Both conjectures seem to me unnecessary

ἀπαντήσας δέ τῳ] I have adopted the suggestion of Stephanus, notwithstanding Stallb's defence of the vulg τῷ νοσοῦντι as equiv to ἐμοί His explanation of the repeated ἰδὼν is ingenious and probably right εἶδον, εἶδον! may be supposed to have been the inward ejaculation of Phaedrus on meeting one who 'shared his enthusiasm' for literature At any rate this is better than to suppose with Steph that Plato wrote ἰδὼν μὲν ἰόντα, which is frigid in the extreme Synesius, Encom Calv, εἶδον γὰρ εἶδον εἰκόνας p 56, ed Turneb

C ἐθρύπτετο] Comp Xen Symp VIII 1, καὶ ὁ Σωκράτης ἐπισκώψας ὡς δὴ θρυπτόμενος, εἶπε, Μὴ νῦν μοι ἐν τῷ παρόντι ὄχλον πάρεχε ὡς σὺ γὰρ ὁρᾷς, ἄλλα πράττω and transl 'he coyly hung back,' like a prudish beauty Slightly different is the meaning of διαθρύπτεται in Theocr XV 99, Φθεγξεῖταί τι, σάφ οἶδα, καλόν, διαθρύπτεται ἤδη

σὺ οὖν] 'entreat him therefore yourself to do at once that which he will presently do whether or not'

δοκῶ] For δοκεῖ, as Rep 567 D quoted by Heind

ΦΑΙ. Οὑτωσὶ τοίνυν ποιήσω. τῷ ὄντι γάρ, ὦ Σώ- D
κρατες, παντὸς μᾶλλον τά γε ῥήματα οὐκ ἐξέμαθον· τὴν μέντοι διάνοιαν σχεδὸν ἁπάντων, οἷς ἔφη διαφέρειν τὰ τοῦ ἐρῶντος ἢ τὰ τοῦ μή, ἐν κεφαλαίοις ἐφεξῆς δίειμι, ἀρξάμενος ἀπὸ τοῦ πρώτου

ΣΩ. Δείξας γε πρῶτον, ὦ φιλότης, τί ἄρα ἐν τῇ ἀριστερᾷ ἔχεις ὑπὸ τῷ ἱματίῳ. τοπάζω γάρ σε ἔχειν τὸν λόγον αὐτόν. εἰ δὲ τοῦτό ἐστιν, οὑτωσὶ διανοοῦ περὶ ἐμοῦ, ὡς ἐγώ σε πάνυ μὲν φιλῶ, παρόντος δὲ καὶ Λυσίου
ἐμαυτόν σοι ἐμμελετᾶν παρέχειν οὐ πάνυ δέδοκται. ἀλλ' E
ἴθι, δείκνυ.

ΦΑΙ. Παῦε. ἐκκέκρουκάς με ἐλπίδος, ὦ Σώκρατες, ἣν εἶχον ἐν σοὶ ὡς ἐγγυμνασόμενος. ἀλλὰ ποῦ δὴ βούλει καθιζόμενοι ἀναγνῶμεν;

| ΣΩ. Δεῦρ' ἐκτραπόμενοι κατὰ τὸν Ἰλισσὸν ἴωμεν, 229
εἶτα ὅπου ἂν δόξῃ ἐν ἡσυχίᾳ καθιζησόμεθα.

ΦΑΙ. Εἰς καιρόν, ὡς ἔοικεν, ἀνυπόδητος ὢν ἔτυχον· σὺ μὲν γὰρ δὴ ἀεί. ῥᾷστον οὖν ἡμῖν κατὰ τὸ ὑδάτιον βρέχουσι τοὺς πόδας ἰέναι, καὶ οὐκ ἀηδές, ἄλλως τε καὶ τήνδε τὴν ὥραν τοῦ ἔτους τε καὶ τῆς ἡμέρας.

D διαφέρειν—ἢ] Comp Rep v 455 c, ταῦτα τὸ τῶν ἀνδρῶν γένος διαφερόντως ἔχει ἢ τὸ τῶν γυναικῶν So with other quasi comparatives, as ἐναντίον, ἔμπαλιν, and the like See Madvig, Gr Gr § 91

Δείξας—αὐτόν] 'yes, but first let me see what you are holding in your left hand beneath your cloak, I strongly suspect it is the very speech in question' Hirschig alters πρῶτον into πρότερον, following Hermeias, but comp Rep 338 c, ἐὰν μάθω γε πρῶτον τί λέγεις Phaedrus held the volume in his *left* hand, employing his right in holding together the folds of the himation which were flung over his left shoulder (ἀναβαλόμενος ἐπιδέξια ἐλευθέρως, according to the phrase in Theaet 175 E)

φιλότης] For φίλε, or φίλη κεφαλή, *abstr pro concreto*—a formula adopted by Plato's imitators, as Lucian, &c, but occurring nowhere else in extant Attic writers Eustathius however has ἀνὴρ Ἀττικὸς ἐροῖ ἂν καὶ σὺ φιλότης, p 1169, 58

ἐμαυτὸν—δέδοκται] 'I have no intention of hearing you rehearse your lesson'—ἐμμελετᾶν = to practise *upon* or *at the expense of* another Theocr III 36, ἐπεὶ τύ μοι ἐνδιαθρύπτῃ

E δείκνυ] V δείκνυε. I have followed Hirsch in restoring the Attic form, though with some hesitation The Hellenic δεικνύειν is used by Alexis, a poet of the middle comedy and Plato's contemporary Hence Cobet goes too far in saying that these forms "sub Menandri aetatem pullulant" Vv Lectt. p 317

Παῦε] 'have done,' act, not middle, according to Attic usage On the other hand παῦσαι in the aor, not παῦσον See Cobet, ibid pp 261, 5, who observes, "Semel mihi παύου apud antiquiores lectum est, apud Ephippum Athen VIII p 347 B ψυχρὸν τουτὶ παύου φυσῶν, Μακεδὼν ἄρχων, cui reddiderim παῦ' οὖν"

229 καθιζησόμεθα] Antiatt Bekk p 101, 2, καθιζησόμεθα ἀντὶ τοῦ καθεδούμεθα Πλάτων Φαίδρῳ

ΣΩ. Πρόαγε δή, καὶ σκόπει ἅμα ὅπου καθιζησόμεθα.

ΦΑΙ. Ὁρᾷς οὖν ἐκείνην τὴν ὑψηλοτάτην πλάτανον;

ΣΩ. Τί μήν;

B ΦΑΙ. Ἐκεῖ σκιά τ' ἐστὶ καὶ πνεῦμα μέτριον, καὶ πόα καθίζεσθαι ἤ, ἂν βουλώμεθα, κατακλιθῆναι.

ΣΩ. Προάγοις ἄν

ΦΑΙ. Εἰπέ μοι, ὦ Σώκρατες, οὐκ ἐνθένδε μέντοι ποθὲν ἀπὸ τοῦ Ἰλισσοῦ λέγεται ὁ Βορέας τὴν Ὠρείθυιαν ἁρπάσαι;

ΣΩ. Λέγεται γάρ.

ΦΑΙ. Ἆρ' οὖν ἐνθένδε; χαρίεντα γοῦν καὶ καθαρὰ καὶ διαφανῆ τὰ ὑδάτια φαίνεται, καὶ ἐπιτήδεια κόραις παίζειν παρ' αὐτά.

C ΣΩ. Οὔκ, ἀλλὰ κάτωθεν ὅσον δύ' ἢ τρία στάδια, ᾗ πρὸς τὸ τῆς Ἄγρας διαβαίνομεν· καί πού τίς ἐστι βωμὸς αὐτόθι Βορέου

ΦΑΙ. Οὐ πάνυ νενόηκα· ἀλλ' εἰπὲ πρὸς Διός, ὦ Σώκρατες· σὺ τοῦτο τὸ μυθολόγημα πείθει ἀληθὲς εἶναι;

ΣΩ. Ἀλλ' εἰ ἀπιστοίην, ὥσπερ οἱ σοφοί, οὐκ ἂν ἄτοπος εἴην· εἶτα σοφιζόμενος φαίην αὐτὴν πνεῦμα Βορέου κατὰ τῶν πλησίον πετρῶν σὺν Φαρμακείᾳ παίζουσαν ὦσαι, καὶ οὕτω δὴ τελευτήσασαν λεχθῆναι ὑπὸ τοῦ Βο-

D ρέου ἀνάρπαστον γεγονέναι. ἢ ἐξ Ἀρείου πάγου· λέγεται

B κατακλιθῆναι] So the Codd., κατακλινῆναι being the only form allowed by the stricter Atticists. See Cobet, N. Lectt. p. 310.

C διαβαίνομεν] Perhaps διεβαίνομεν. They are ascending the stream, which they probably crossed near the temple of Agra or Artemis Agrotera. Comp. the reply of Phaedr., οὐ πάνυ νενόηκα.

ὥσπερ οἱ σοφοί] There is much of this rationalizing vein in Euripides, derived perhaps from his contemporary Metrodorus, a friend and disciple of Anaxagoras, who had himself expressed an opinion that Homer's poetry was in a great measure allegorical. This view was carried by Metrodorus to extravagant lengths: he explained, for instance, Zeus, Hera, and Pallas as symbols of certain "physical substances or elemental arrangements" (φύσεως ὑποστάσεις καὶ στοιχείων διακοσμήσεις). Diog. Laert. B. ii. c. 3, § 11. This he did, ἐν τῷ περὶ Ὁμήρου—a book in which λίαν εὐήθως διείλεκται, πάντα εἰς ἀλληγορίαν μετάγων. It is probable that the sarcastic epithets in the text, λίαν δεινοῦ, κ.τ.λ., refer either to this author, or to some imitator who made the Attic myths his speciality. The explanation of the fable of Boreas is evidently a tempting one to a rationalist of this school.

D ἢ ἐξ Ἀρείου—ἡρπάσθη] This clause is not noticed by Hermeias in his paraphrase, and seems to Heindorf misplaced. Ast defends it on the ground that Plato meant to ridicule the arbitrary character of the rationalizing interpreta

γὰρ αὖ καὶ οὗτος ὁ λόγος, ὡς ἐκεῖθεν ἀλλ' οὐκ ἐνθένδε
ἡρπάσθη. ἐγὼ δέ, ὦ Φαῖδρε, ἄλλως μὲν τὰ τοιαῦτα χαρίεντα ἡγοῦμαι, λίαν δὲ δεινοῦ καὶ ἐπιπόνου καὶ οὐ
πάνυ εὐτυχοῦς ἀνδρός, κατ' ἄλλο μὲν οὐδέν, ὅτι δ' αὐτῷ
ἀνάγκη μετὰ τοῦτο τὸ τῶν Ἱπποκενταύρων εἶδος ἐπανορ-
θοῦσθαι, καὶ αὖθις τὸ τῆς Χιμαίρας. καὶ ἐπιρρεῖ δὲ
ὄχλος τοιούτων Γοργόνων καὶ Πηγάσων, καὶ ἄλλων ἀμη-
χάνων πλήθει τε καὶ ἀτοπίᾳ τερατολόγων τινῶν φύσεων· E
αἷς εἴ τις ἀπιστῶν προσβιβᾷ κατὰ τὸ εἰκὸς ἕκαστον, ἅτε
ἀγροίκῳ τινὶ σοφίᾳ χρώμενος, πολλῆς αὐτῷ σχολῆς δεήσει·
ἐμοὶ δὲ πρὸς αὐτὰ οὐδαμῶς ἐστι σχολή. τὸ δὲ αἴτιον, ὦ
φίλε, τούτου τόδε. οὐ δύναμαί πω κατὰ τὸ Δελφικὸν
γράμμα γνῶναι ἐμαυτόν· γελοῖον δή μοι φαίνεται | τοῦτο 230
ἔτι ἀγνοοῦντα [τὰ ἀλλότρια σκοπεῖν.] ὅθεν δὴ χαίρειν
ἐάσας ταῦτα, πειθόμενος δὲ τῷ νομιζομένῳ περὶ αὐτῶν,
ὃ νῦν δὴ ἔλεγον, σκοπῶ οὐ ταῦτα ἀλλὰ ἐμαυτόν, εἴτε τι

tions This however is no interpretation, but another version of the myth The words seem to me to be Plato's, whatever his object in introducing them, and I cannot think with Heind that they would stand better after the speech of Phaedrus (B, supra) beginning Εἰπέ μοι

ἐπανορθοῦσθαι] The office of the mythologer is humorously said to be to 'rectify,' or 'integrate' by restoring to their proper shape the monsters he has to do with In the seq I have preferred the dat sing to the vulg πλήθη τε καὶ ἀτοπίαι, which stand in most MSS The change is in reality no change as regards the letters, and relieves the otherwise cumbrous sentence πλήθει ἀμήχανον occurs Theaet 181 A, Tim 39 D

E προσβιβάζειν κατὰ τὸ εἰκός = to force into agreement with probability, προσβιβᾷ being of course fut

ἄγροικος σοφία seems to mean an untutored, ill regulated ingenuity, like that of certain modern interpreters of prophecy, hieroglyphics, Sinaitic inscriptions, &c &c

οὐ δύναμαί πω] "Pour les sages de l'antiquité le γνῶθι σεαυτὸν n'était guère qu'une maxime morale, une règle de conduite, un moyen de fonder et d'entretenir dans l'âme la justice et la tempérance ce n'était pas une méthode, dans l'acception philosophique du mot Ce n'est que dans les temps modernes que le 'Connais toi toi même' a été compris dans toute la portée de sa signification à la fois spéculative et pratique" C Waddington, Essais de Logique, p 310 This remark goes a little too far, for it can hardly be said that the author of the Theaetetus and the Republic was unaware of the speculative importance of a scientific psychology The self-knowledge of Socrates consisted in the rigorous examination of the *notions* of his own mind rather than of its operations and faculties, and chiefly of those notions which relate to moral distinctions, "primus a rebus occultis et ab ipsa natura involutis avocavit philosophiam et ad vitam communem adduxit" Cic Acad i 4 15

230 πειθόμενος δὲ τῷ νομιζομένῳ] 'acquiescing in the popular belief,' or, as Bp Thirlwall suggests, "complying with the common usage about them" Theologians have pointed to this passage as false and jesuitical, while others have gravely applauded it, as implying a pious preference of authority to reason in religious matters So true is it "que le sens commun n'est pas chose si commune qu'on le pense" The mythical matter in question is *harmless*, hence there is no inconsistency between this passage and those in the Republic and

θηρίον τυγχάνω Τυφῶνος πολυπλοκώτερον καὶ μᾶλλον ἐπιτεθυμμένον, εἴτε ἡμερώτερόν τε καὶ ἁπλούστερον ζῷον, θείας τινὸς καὶ ἀτύφου μοίρας φύσει μετέχον. Ἀτάρ, ὦ ἑταῖρε, μεταξὺ τῶν λόγων, ἆρ' οὐ τόδε ἦν τὸ δένδρον ἐφ' ὅπερ ἦγες ἡμᾶς;

B ΦΑΙ. Τοῦτο μὲν οὖν αὐτό.

ΣΩ. Νὴ τὴν Ἥραν, καλή γε ἡ καταγωγή. ἥ τε γὰρ

ἐπιτυφομαι burnt up, inflamed, furious LS

in strong affirmation LS yes indeed golden

GMT 778

elsewhere in which immoral myths are condemned.

πολυπλοκώτερον] With this compare Repub. ix 588 C, where the lower part of man's nature is compared to a "motley and many-headed monster, some of whose heads resemble those of tame, others those of wild creatures." Aesch. Prom. 353, ἑκατογκάρανον πρὸς βίαν χειρούμενον Τυφῶνα θοῦρον.

ἐπιτεθυμμένον—ἀτύφου] Plato's etymologizing vein breaks out here for the first time in the dialogue. As ἐπιτ. means inflamed, 'burning with pride or passion' (Ar. Lys. 222, ὅπως ἂν ἁνὴρ ἐπιτυφῇ μάλιστά μου), so ἄτυφος denotes modesty, unassuming simplicity, as in Plut. Mor. i 43 B, οἰήματος καὶ ἀλαζονείας ἀπολυθείς, εἰς βίον ἄτυφον καὶ ὑγιαίνοντα καταστήσεις σαυτόν. Id. de Genio Socr. c. 12, Σωκράτους, ἀνδρὸς ἀτυφίᾳ καὶ ἀφελείᾳ φιλοσοφίαν ἐξανθρωπίσαντος. Menander also uses the subst. ἀτυφία, explained by a grammarian as = ταπεινοφροσύνη.

μεταξὺ τῶν λόγων] "Gallorum *à propos*," Ast. Angl., 'by-the-bye.' Ast illustrates the formula from Lucian, with whom it is frequent. Dial. Mort. x. 912, ἀλλὰ μεταξὺ λόγων τίνες εἰσὶν οἱ πολεμοῦντες ἐκεῖνοι;

C

B καταγωγή] Called καταγώγιον 259 A. Both words are explained by the Greek Lexicographers in the same terms, κατάλυμα, πανδοκεῖον, ἀναπαύλη. Herod. i. 181, speaks of the landing-places (stazioni) in the tower of Belus, as καταγωγαί τε καὶ θῶκοι ἀμπαυστήριοι. The spot in question is easily discovered by the visitor at the present day; there is indeed but one place answering the conditions, and it answers them perfectly. On the left side, as one ascends the stream, the steep but not high banks retire and form an oval recess girt by rocks, in which are still visible certain small square niches, where doubtless stood the ἀγάλματα, little images of Pan and the Nymphs, like those which adorned one face of the rock of the Acropolis. The area thus enclosed is crossed by a thread of water issuing from a now nearly choked source (the πηγή of the text). A tree of by no means ample dimensions grows there. It is, if I mistake not, the only tree in the neighbourhood; and though the green turf has disappeared from the 'gentle slope,' the rocks still yield a grateful shelter from the sun. The Ilissus, in May 1856, contained quite sufficient water to 'wet the feet' of the pedestrian; in fact in this part of its course it was nowhere quite dry, though the season had been one of unusual drouth. Its rills (ὑδάτια) still answered to the description in the text: they were χαρίεντα καὶ καθαρὰ καὶ διαφανῆ, καὶ ἐπιτήδεια κόραις παίζειν παρ' αὐτά (sup. 229 B). Col. Leake, who does not notice this precise spot, remarks that "the most popular part of the worship of the terrene gods was that of Pan and the Nymphs, who presided over rivers, fountains, and caverns, and appear to have had many sanctuaries on the banks of the Ilissus." Athens i. p. 483. A temple of the Musae Ilissides stood some half-mile lower down the stream. The plane (represented now by a sorry poplar) seems to have disappeared in Cicero's time, as I understand him; he doubts its ever having existed, "mihi videtur non tam ipsa aquula quae describitur quam Platonis oratione crevisse." de Orat. i. § 28. This, one hopes, was an unreasonable sally of Academic scepticism, for no tree was more prized by the Athenians than the plane, which was planted even in the Agora, and magnificent specimens of which are still found in other parts of Greece, though the tree has ceased to exist in the neighbourhood of modern Athens. It usually grows near fountains and at river-heads, the huge roots being often laid bare by the gushing water which seems to issue from them, καλῇ ὑπὸ πλαταιίστῳ ὅθεν ῥέεν

πλάτανος αὕτη μάλ' ἀμφιλαφής τε καὶ ὑψηλή, τοῦ τε ἄγνου τὸ ὕψος καὶ τὸ σύσκιον πάγκαλον, καὶ ὡς ἀκμὴν ἔχει τῆς ἄνθης, ὡς ἂν εὐωδέστατον παρέχοι τὸν τόπον. ἥ τε αὖ πηγὴ χαριεστάτη ὑπὸ τῆς πλατάνου ῥεῖ μάλα ψυχροῦ ὕδατος, ὥς γε τῷ ποδὶ τεκμήρασθαι. Νυμφῶν τέ τινων καὶ Ἀχελώου ἱερὸν ἀπὸ τῶν κορῶν τε καὶ

ἄγλαον ὕδωρ The epithet ἀμφιλαφὴς answers to the "patulis diffusa ramis" of Cicero l. l.

τοῦ τε ἄγνου τὸ ὕψος] Suidas in v. ἄγνος, τοῦ τε ἄγνου δὲ τὸ ὕ, κ.τ.λ., quoting this passage. He cites two lines of a comic poet (Chionides)

καὶ μὴν μὰ τὸν Δί' οὐδὲν ἔτι γέ μοι δοκῶ
ἄγνου διαφέρειν ἐν χαράδρᾳ πεφυκότος

On which Meineke observes "Recte ἐν χαράδρᾳ. Dioscor. i. 136 ἄγνος ἢ λύγος παρὰ ποταμοῖς τραχέσι τε τόποις καὶ χαράδραις φυόμενος." The agnus castus or vitex is usually described as a φυτόν, not a δένδρον. But Pliny distinguishes two kinds. "Major in arborem salicis modo assurgit." "Non multum a salice . . . distat vitex, foliorum quoque aspectu, nisi odore gratior esset. . . . Prima album florem mittit cum purpureo, quae et candida vocatur, nigra quae tantum purpureum. Nascuntur in palustribus campis." "Graeci lygon vocant, alii agnon, quoniam matronae Thesmophoriis Atheniensium castitatem custodientes his foliis cubitus sibi sternunt." N. H. xxiv. 38. The plant would thus seem to owe its reputation to a false etymology.

καὶ ὡς ἀκμὴν—ὡς ἂν εὐωδέστατον] Commentators are at issue about the force of ὡς in each clause. The second ὡς, it is agreed, must be understood in the sense of 'quomodo,' as preceding παρέχοι ἄν, a potential, not a conjunctive. The first ὡς is regarded by Stallb. as exclamatory, by Ast as relative. The former translates thus "und wie steht er eben in der schönsten Blüthe in einer Weise, wie er den Ort im höchsten Grade mit Wohlgeruch zu erfüllen vermag." Ast, on the contrary, has the following: "Verba ita sunt intelligenda τοῦ τε ἄγνου τὸ ὕψος καὶ τὸ σύσκιον πάγκαλον καὶ (int. τοῦτο πάγκαλόν ἐστιν) ὡς (i. e. ὅτι οὕτως) ἀκμὴν ἔχει τῆς ἄνθης. Germ., und (suppl. gar schön ist auch dieses) dass es so in der höchsten Blüthe steht, dass es den Ort zum wohlduftendsten macht." In the latter case ὡς ἂν παρέχοι must = ὥστε παρέχειν, which is hardly possible. παρέχοι ἂν commonly means 'it will make'—'it cannot fail to make'—'it may well make,' and the clause in which it stands seems to form the *apodosis* to the former. In this there would be no difficulty, if the first ὡς could be understood as causal, or quasi causal, like the Lat. *ut* followed by *ita*. '*And being* (or, *as it is*) *at the height of its flowering* (ἄνθη Att. for ἄνθησις), *it cannot fail to make the spot the most fragrant imaginable*' (ὡς εὐωδέστατον). On the whole perhaps Stallb.'s rendering, cumbrous as it seems, and untranslatable as it is, will seem to most persons to give the true construction, though I confess I should be glad to see an analogous instance of an exclamatory followed by a relative ὡς. Heind.'s proposed emendations, ὡς ἀκμὴν . . ὣς ἄν, *ut* . . *ita*, or, καὶ οὕτως ἀκμὴν . . ὡς ἂν . ., seem to me equally inelegant. He however seems to think that the first ὡς may mean *ut*, and in that case there can be no great harshness in the suppression of the corresponding *ita*, which is all that is required in my version. Those who are still dissatisfied may if they please consult Ast's gigantic note, Comm. p. 212.

ὥς γε τῷ ποδὶ τεκμήρασθαι] 'judging by the foot' I dip into it. Most of the copies have ὥστε γε, but ὥς γε is given by one MS., and by Aristaenetus, in his almost literal citation of the entire passage, Ep. i. 3, p. 8, as quoted by Heind. Comp. Herod. ii. 135, μεγάλα ἐκτήσατο χρήματα, ὡς ἂν εἶναι Ῥοδῶπιν, ἀτὰρ οὐκ ὥς γε ἐς πυραμίδα τοιαύτην ἐξικέσθαι, and Rep. v. 475 D, ἀτοπώτατοί εἰσιν ὥς γ' ἐν φιλοσόφοις τιθέναι. Cicero refers to this passage in describing the coldness of a tributary of the river Liris. "Nec enim ullum hoc frigidius flumen attigi . . . ut vix pede tentare id possim, quod in Phaedro Platonis facit Socrates." Legg. ii. 3.

Ἀχελῴου] The personification of fresh

C ἀγαλμάτων ἔοικεν εἶναι εἰ δ' αὖ βούλει, τὸ εὔπνουν τοῦ
τόπου ὡς ἀγαπητὸν καὶ σφόδρα ἡδύ· θερινόν τε καὶ λι-
γυρὸν ὑπηχεῖ τῷ τῶν τεττίγων χορῷ. πάντων δὲ κομψό-
τατον τὸ τῆς πόας, ὅτι ἐν ἠρέμα προσάντει ἱκανὴ πέφυκε
κατακλινέντι τὴν κεφαλὴν παγκάλως ἔχειν. ὥστε ἄριστά
σοι ἐξενάγηται, ὦ φίλε Φαῖδρε.

ΦΑΙ Σὺ δέ γε, ὦ θαυμάσιε, ἀτοπώτατός τις φαίνει.
ἀτεχνῶς γάρ, ὃ λέγεις, ξεναγουμένῳ τινὶ καὶ οὐκ ἐπιχω-
D ρίῳ ἔοικας· οὕτως ἐκ τοῦ ἄστεος οὔτ' εἰς τὴν ὑπερορίαν
ἀποδημεῖς, οὔτ' ἔξω τείχους ἔμοιγε δοκεῖς τὸ παράπαν
ἐξιέναι.

ΣΩ Συγγίγνωσκέ μοι, ὦ ἄριστε. φιλομαθὴς γάρ
εἰμι. τὰ μὲν οὖν χωρία καὶ τὰ δένδρα οὐδέν μ' ἐθέλει
διδάσκειν, οἱ δ' ἐν τῷ ἄστει ἄνθρωποι. σὺ μέντοι δοκεῖς
μοι τῆς ἐμῆς ἐξόδου τὸ φάρμακον εὑρηκέναι. ὥσπερ γὰρ

water according to Herm, διὰ γὰρ τοῦ μεγίστου τούτου ποταμοῦ δηλοῦσι τὸν ἔφορον θεὸν τοῦ ποτίμου ὕδατος So frequently in the poets

ἀπὸ τῶν κορῶν τε καὶ ἀγαλμάτων] 'to judge by the puppets and the images' "κόρας Attici dicunt pupas ex cera argillave fictas, plangunculas" Ruhnken ad Tim L P s κοροπλάθοι These puppets or dolls (old Eng *babies*) were doubtless votive offerings, the ἀγάλματα were probably images of marble, like the small Pan which was brought from a shrine in the rock of the Acropolis, and now stands in the Fitzwilliam Museum at Cambridge

C ὑπηχεῖ] 'it answers' (either ὁ τόπος or impers) 'summer like and shrill to the quire of cicades' Eur Supp 710, ἔβρηξε δ' αὐδὴν ὥσθ' ὑπηχῆσαι χθόνα Plut Men 61 D, σαθρὸν ὑπηχεῖ καὶ ἀγεννές Comp Theaet 179 D, σαθρὸν φθέγγεται So in Lat, "sincerum sonere," Lucr. iii 886 and elsewhere Juv xii 293, "vestrum tonat," not "sonat," as quoted by Stallb

ἀτεχνῶς—ἔοικας] 'as you say, you are exactly like some stranger in the hands of a guide,' or 'cicerone' Ast quotes Lucian, Scyth § 1, σύ με παραλαβὼν ξενάγησον καὶ δεῖξον τὰ κάλλιστα τῶν Ἀθήνησιν

οὕτως, κ τ λ] Lat 'adeo' Eng 'this comes of your never absenting yourself, &c' That Socrates never set foot without the walls was not literally true, as the Lyceum, his favourite haunt, lay outside the city He also occasionally frequented the Academy, as we find from Lysis, init But these were exceptions which 'proved the rule' In the Crito he is said to have once attended the Isthmian festival His στρατεῖαι, being involuntary, were of course no exceptions

D τὰ μὲν οὖν—ἐθέλει διδάσκειν] 'the fields and trees you see won't teach me any thing,' that is, 'I can't get them to teach me,' as if they had the power of refusal Soph 252 L, τὰ μὲν ἐθέλει τὰ δὲ μὴ ξυμμίγνυσθαι, "some will blend, others refuse to blend," speaking of the εἴδη, a quasi impersonation This use of ἐθέλει is so common as hardly to need illustrating It is frivolous to dispute whether it is or is not equivalent to δύνασθαι in such cases

τῆς ἐμῆς ἐξόδου τὸ φάρμακον] 'the recipe which shall charm me out of town' "Antiphanes ap Stobaeum, ὁ δὲ λιμός ἐστιν ἀθανασίας φάρμακον φάρμακόν τινος utroque modo usurpatur, ut sit medicamentum vel *efficiendo bono* destinatum, vel *avertendo malo* τὰ γράμματα, Eurip, Pal fr 2, vocavit λήθης φ Plat Phaedr 274 E, μνήμης καὶ σοφίας φάρμακον" Wyttenbach ad Eunap v ii p 9, quoted by Dindorf on Steph Thes in v. φάρμακον

ὥσπερ γὰρ οἱ] If the οἱ is to stand, wo

μετάνοια Antiphon 5 91

οἱ τὰ πεινῶντα θρέμματα θαλλὸν ἤ τινα καρπὸν προσείοντες ἄγουσι, σὺ ἐμοὶ λόγους οὕτω προτείνων ἐν βιβλίοις τήν τε Ἀττικὴν φαίνει περιάξειν ἅπασαν καὶ ὅποι ἂν E ἄλλοσε βούλῃ. νῦν οὖν ἐν τῷ παρόντι δεῦρ' ἀφικόμενος ἐγὼ μέν μοι δοκῶ κατακείσεσθαι, σὺ δ' ἐν ὁποίῳ σχήματι οἴει ῥᾷστα ἀναγνώσεσθαι, τοῦθ' ἑλόμενος ἀναγίγνωσκε.

ΦΑΙ. Ἄκουε δή.

Περὶ μὲν τῶν ἐμῶν πραγμάτων ἐπίστασαι, καὶ ὡς νομίζω συμφέρειν ἡμῖν γενομένων τούτων ἀκήκοας· ἀξιῶ δὲ μὴ διὰ τοῦτο ἀτυχῆσαι | ὧν δέομαι, ὅτι οὐκ ἐραστὴς 231 ὤν σου τυγχάνω. ὡς ἐκείνοις μὲν τότε μεταμέλει ὧν ἂν εὖ ποιήσωσιν, ἐπειδὰν τῆς ἐπιθυμίας παύσωνται· τοῖς δὲ οὐκ ἔστι χρόνος ἐν ᾧ μεταγνῶναι προσήκει. οὐ γὰρ ὑπ' ἀνάγκης ἀλλ' ἑκόντες, ὡς ἂν ἄριστα περὶ τῶν οἰκείων βουλεύσαιντο, πρὸς τὴν δύναμιν τὴν αὑτῶν εὖ ποιοῦσιν. Ἔτι δὲ οἱ μὲν ἐρῶντες σκοποῦσιν ἅ τε κακῶς διέθεντο τῶν αὑτῶν διὰ τὸν ἔρωτα καὶ ἃ πεποιήκασιν εὖ, καὶ ὃν εἶχον πόνον προστιθέντες ἡγοῦνται πάλαι τὴν ἀξίαν ἀπο- B δεδωκέναι χάριν τοῖς ἐρωμένοις. τοῖς δὲ μὴ ἐρῶσιν οὔτε τὴν τῶν οἰκείων ἀμέλειαν διὰ τοῦτο ἔστι προφασίζεσθαι, οὔτε τοὺς παρεληλυθότας πόνους ὑπολογίζεσθαι, οὔτε τὰς πρὸς τοὺς προσήκοντας διαφορὰς †αἰτιάσασθαι†· ὥστε

Phaedo 114b

have a confusion of constructions ὥσπερ οἱ τὰ πεινῶντα θρέμματα ἄγοντες θαλλὸν . προσείοντες ἄγουσιν αὐτά. προσείειν τινί τι may mean either to *tempt* or to *scare* by waving an object before the eyes. Of the latter sense we have an instance in Thuc vi 86, οὐκ ἄλλον τινὰ προσείοντες φόβον, where however, as here, the object is to allure (ἐπαγαγέσθαι).

ἐγὼ μέν μοι δοκῶ κατακείσεσθαι] κατακεῖσθαι is the reading of the Bodl and some of the best MSS. Steph gives κατακείσεσθαι, and so Hirsch. The present used to be justified by Arist Vesp 177, ἀλλ' εἰσιών μοι τὸν ὄνον ἐξάγειν δοκῶ, "I have a mind to, &c," as if δοκεῖ μοι had been found. But this reading was condemned by Elmsl, and is now abandoned in consideration of the context. In Menand ap Mein iv p. 287, ἐξακεῖσθαί μοι δοκῶ τὸ δίκτυον, ἐξακεῖσθαι is an Attic future. In Arist Plut 1186, καταμενεῖν is now read for καταμένειν.

Περὶ μὲν τῶν ἐμῶν] Concerning this speech or epistle see the Introd.

231 ὡς ἐκείνοις μέν] Who the ἐκεῖνοι were had perhaps been explained in a previous communication. They are of course the ἐρῶντες, as contrasted with the writer, who describes himself as οὐκ ἐραστὴς ὤν.

ὡς ἂν—βουλεύσαιντο] 'in such sort as they will best provide, &c,' i e as the best way they know of promoting their own interests.

B αἰτιάσασθαι] There is no justification for the change of tense here. Dr Badham proposes ἐπαιτιᾶσθαι, comparing Ep vii p. 329, νῦν δ' ἄρα τὸ μῆκος τῆς πορείας ἐπαιτιώμενος οἴει δόξαν κακίας ἀποφευξεῖσθαί ποτε, and adding "ubi si ὑπολογιζόμενος scripsisset perinde fuisset." But αἰτιᾶσθαι might stand—'to allege,' i e in explanation of the neglect

περιῃρημένων τοσούτων κακῶν οὐδὲν ὑπολείπεται ἀλλ' ἢ ποιεῖν προθύμως ὅ τι ἂν αὐτοῖς οἴωνται πράξαντες χα-
C ριεῖσθαι. Ἔτι δὲ εἰ διὰ τοῦτο ἄξιον τοὺς ἐρῶντας περὶ πολλοῦ ποιεῖσθαι ὅτι τούτους μάλιστά φασι φιλεῖν ὧν ἂν ἐρῶσι, καὶ ἕτοιμοί εἰσι καὶ ἐκ τῶν λόγων καὶ ἐκ τῶν ἔργων τοῖς ἄλλοις ἀπεχθανόμενοι τοῖς ἐρωμένοις χαρίζεσθαι, ῥᾴδιον γνῶναι, εἰ ἀληθῆ λέγουσιν, ὅτι ὅσων ἂν ὕστερον ἐρασθῶσιν, ἐκείνους αὐτῶν περὶ πλείονος ποιήσονται, καὶ δῆλον ὅτι ἐὰν ἐκείνοις δοκῇ καὶ τούτους κακῶς ποιήσουσι. Καί τοι πῶς εἰκός ἐστι τοιοῦτον πρᾶγμα προέσθαι
D τοιαύτην ἔχοντι συμφοράν, ἣν οὐδ' ἂν ἐπιχειρήσειεν οὐδεὶς ἔμπειρος ὢν ἀποτρέπειν; καὶ γὰρ αὐτοὶ ὁμολογοῦσι νοσεῖν μᾶλλον ἢ σωφρονεῖν, καὶ εἰδέναι ὅτι κακῶς φρονοῦσιν, ἀλλ' οὐ δύνασθαι αὐτῶν κρατεῖν. ὥστε πῶς ἂν εὖ φρονήσαντες ταῦτα καλῶς ἔχειν ἡγήσαιντο, περὶ ὧν οὕτω διακείμενοι †βούλονται†. Καὶ μὲν δὴ εἰ μὲν ἐκ τῶν ἐρώντων τὸν βέλτιστον αἱροῖο, ἐξ ὀλίγων ἄν σοι ἡ ἔκλεξις εἴη· εἰ δ' ἐκ τῶν ἄλλων τὸν σαυτῷ ἐπιτηδειότατον, ἐκ
E πολλῶν. ὥστε πολὺ πλείων ἐλπὶς ἐν τοῖς πολλοῖς ὄντα τυχεῖν τὸν ἄξιον τῆς σῆς φιλίας. Εἰ τοίνυν τὸν νόμον τὸν καθεστηκότα δέδοικας, μὴ πυθομένων τῶν ἀνθρώ-

of which they are guilty after their passion has cooled (ἐπειδὰν τῆς ἐπιθυμίας παύσωνται). On the frequent confusion of infinitives in -ᾶσθαι with the aor. in -σασθαι, see Cobet, N. L. p. 629, who also suggests αἰτιᾶσθαι here. Ast calls attention to the ὁμοιοτέλευτα, προφασίζεσθαι — ὑπολογίζεσθαι — αἰτιάσασθαι. This artifice of style recurs frequently in the present speech. It is very common in Isocrates, and in the speeches of Thucydides, and Xenophon is somewhat too fond of it also.

C ἐκείνους — ποιήσονται] 'they will prize the new love more than the old.' The 'new love,' being less familiar to the apprehension, is denoted by the pronoun which implies distance. On the same principle, in 232 D, οὐκ ἂν τοῖς συνοῦσι φθονοῖεν, ἀλλὰ τοὺς μὴ ἐθέλοντας (συνεῖναι) μισοῖεν, ἡγούμενοι ὑπ' ἐκείνων μὲν ὑπερορᾶσθαι, ὑπὸ τῶν συνόντων δὲ ὠφελεῖσθαι,—ἐκείνων refers to the last-mentioned τοὺς μὴ ἐθέλοντας, as being less known than the former, οἱ συνόντες.

D εὖ φρονήσαντες] 'when they have returned to their right mind.' Either βούλονται at the end of the sentence is corrupt, or some lost infinitive went before it. "Patet loci sensum esse *qui vel insania laborantes de amore tam inique judicant*." Badh. βούλεσθαι περί τινος is scarcely Greek, and yields no sense. I had thought of ἀπολογοῦνται (supra αὐτοὶ ὁμολογοῦσι νοσεῖν), but this is too violent a change. Perhaps Heind.'s βεβούλευνται might stand, 'how in their saner mind can they approve of a course they have adopted in such a state as the one supposed,' i. e. in moments of aberration. Stallb.'s defence of βούλονται is inconclusive and his translation "quae ita affecti animo cupiunt" would require ἃ . . . βούλονται.

E τὸν νόμον τὸν καθεστηκότα] 'public opinion,' 'the established maxims of society.' Germ. tr., "die herrschende Meinung." Hermann, who also under-

πων ὄνειδός σοι γένηται, εἰκός ἐστι τοὺς μὲν ἐρῶντας,
οὕτως ἂν οἰομένους καὶ ὑπὸ τῶν ἄλλων ζηλοῦσθαι ὥσπερ 232
αὐτοὺς ὑφ' αὑτῶν, ἐπαρθῆναι τῷ λέγειν καὶ φιλοτιμουμένους ἐπιδείκνυσθαι πρὸς ἅπαντας ὅτι οὐκ ἄλλως αὐτοῖς
πεπόνηται· τοὺς δὲ μὴ ἐρῶντας, κρείττους αὑτῶν ὄντας,
τὸ βέλτιστον ἀντὶ τῆς δόξης τῆς παρὰ τῶν ἀνθρώπων
αἱρεῖσθαι. Ἔτι δὲ τοὺς μὲν ἐρῶντας πολλοὺς ἀνάγκη πυ-
T154 θέσθαι καὶ ἰδεῖν ἀκολουθοῦντας τοῖς ἐρωμένοις καὶ ἔργον τοῦτο ποιουμένους, ὥστε ὅταν ὀφθῶσι διαλεγόμενοι B
ἀλλήλοις, τότε αὐτοὺς οἴονται ἢ γεγενημένης ἢ μελλούσης
ἔσεσθαι τῆς ἐπιθυμίας συνεῖναι· τοὺς δὲ μὴ ἐρῶντας
οὐδ' αἰτιᾶσθαι διὰ τὴν συνουσίαν ἐπιχειροῦσιν, εἰδότες
ὅτι ἀναγκαῖόν ἐστιν ἢ διὰ φιλίαν τῳ διαλέγεσθαι ἢ δι'
ἄλλην τινὰ ἡδονήν. Καὶ μὲν δὴ εἴ σοι δέος παρέστηκεν
ἡγουμένῳ χαλεπὸν εἶναι φιλίαν συμμένειν, καὶ ἄλλῳ μὲν
τρόπῳ διαφορᾶς γενομένης κοινὴν ἀμφοτέροις καταστῆναι
τὴν συμφοράν, προεμένου δέ σου ἃ περὶ πλείστου ποιεῖ
μεγάλην ἄν σοι βλάβην γενέσθαι, εἰκότως ἂν τοὺς ἐρῶν- C
τας μᾶλλον ἂν φοβοῖο. πολλὰ γὰρ αὐτούς ἐστι τὰ λυ-
ποῦντα, καὶ πάντ' ἐπὶ τῇ αὑτῶν βλάβῃ νομίζουσι γίγνεσθαι. διόπερ καὶ τὰς πρὸς τοὺς ἄλλους τῶν ἐρωμένων
συνουσίας ἀποτρέπουσι, φοβούμενοι τοὺς μὲν οὐσίαν
κεκτημένους, μὴ χρήμασιν αὐτοὺς ὑπερβάλωνται, τοὺς δὲ
πεπαιδευμένους, μὴ συνέσει κρείττους γένωνται· τῶν δ'

stands νόμος to mean τὸ νενομισμένον, denies that any disgrace attached in public opinion to the relation in question, quoting Aesch c. Tim in proof that mercenary amours were alone infamous at Athens ὁ δὲ Σόλων ἐν τοῖς νόμοις τοῖς ἐλευθέροις τὸ ἐπιτήδευμα τετήρηκε, δοῦλον κωλύσας ἐρᾶν The speech of Aeschines alluded to is one of the foulest chapters in the record of Athenian depravity

232 ἐπαρθῆναι τῷ λέγειν] τὸ is found in a few MSS and approved by Buttmann and C F Hermann Badh with great ingenuity conj ἐ. τῷ ἔχειν, 'is elated by possession' Winckelmann's ὥστε λέγειν, though defensible in point of construction, does not commend itself to the ear, and λέγειν is itself flat Stallbaum's int. "eo quod dicunt" is sufficiently rigid, and can scarcely be got from the Greek ἐπαρθῆναι τῷ λέγειν, I apprehend, could only mean 'are excited by speaking' (dat instrum) The verb ἔχειν in re amatoria is common enough, and this is in my judgment the best reading hitherto proposed

καὶ φιλοτιμουμένους—πεπόνηται] 'and in the vanity of their hearts give all men to know that their labour has not been spent in vain'

B προεμένου δέ σου] 'when you have sacrificed or surrendered all you most prize.' Sup. 231 C, τοιοῦτον πρᾶγμα προέσθαι, i e honour

D ἄλλο τι κεκτημένων ἀγαθὸν τὴν δύναμιν ἑκάστου φυλάττονται. πείσαντες μὲν οὖν ἀπέχθεσθαί σε τούτοις εἰς ἐρημίαν φίλων καθιστᾶσιν· ἐὰν δὲ τὸ σεαυτοῦ σκοπῶν ἄμεινον ἐκείνων φρονῇς, ἥξεις αὐτοῖς εἰς διαφοράν. ὅσοι δὲ μὴ ἐρῶντες ἔτυχον, ἀλλὰ δι' ἀρετὴν ἔπραξαν ὧν ἐδέοντο, οὐκ ἂν τοῖς συνοῦσι φθονοῖεν, ἀλλὰ τοὺς μὴ ἐθέλοντας μισοῖεν, ἡγούμενοι ὑπ' ἐκείνων μὲν ὑπερορᾶσθαι, ὑπὸ τῶν συνόντων δὲ ὠφελεῖσθαι. ὥστε πολὺ πλείων ἐλπὶς
E φιλίαν αὐτοῖς ἐκ τοῦ πράγματος ἢ ἔχθραν γενήσεσθαι. Καὶ μὲν δὴ τῶν μὲν ἐρώντων πολλοὶ πρότερον τοῦ σώματος ἐπεθύμησαν ἢ τὸν τρόπον ἔγνωσαν καὶ τῶν ἄλλων οἰκείων ἔμπειροι ἐγένοντο, ὥστε ἄδηλον αὐτοῖς εἰ ἔτι τότε βουλήσονται φίλοι εἶναι, ἐπειδὰν τῆς ἐπιθυμίας παύσων-
233 ται· | τοῖς δὲ μὴ ἐρῶσιν, οἳ καὶ πρότερον ἀλλήλοις φίλοι ὄντες ταῦτα ἔπραξαν, οὐκ ἐξ ὧν ἂν εὖ πάθωσι ταῦτα εἰκὸς ἐλάττω τὴν φιλίαν αὐτοῖς ποιῆσαι, ἀλλὰ ταῦτα μνημεῖα καταλειφθῆναι τῶν μελλόντων ἔσεσθαι. Καὶ μὲν δὴ βελτίονί σοι προσήκει γενέσθαι ἐμοὶ πειθομένῳ ἢ ἐραστῇ. ἐκεῖνοι μὲν γὰρ καὶ παρὰ τὸ βέλτιστον τά τε λεγόμενα καὶ τὰ πραττόμενα ἐπαινοῦσι, τὰ μὲν δεδιότες μὴ ἀπέχθωνται, τὰ δὲ καὶ αὐτοὶ χεῖρον διὰ τὴν ἐπιθυμίαν
B γιγνώσκοντες. τοιαῦτα γὰρ ὁ ἔρως ἐπιδείκνυται· δυστυ-

D. πείσαντες, κ.τ.λ.] 'thus if they prevail with you to break with all these, you are left without a friend in the world, whereas if you are alive to your own interest, and have more sense than your advisers, you will have to quarrel with *them*.'

ὅσοι δὲ — ὠφελεῖσθαι] Those who never loved, but are indebted to their own merits for the success of their suit, so far from being jealous of those who seek the society of their favourite, will rather dislike those who shun it, deeming themselves slighted by *these last*, but benefited by the attentions of the former. See note on 231 D. The repeated use of ἐκεῖνοι in this refined sense, as in 231 A, 233 B, and elsewhere in this speech, savours of affectation.

E. τῶν ἄλλων οἰκείων] This use of ἄλλων is familiar enough, 'Before they were acquainted with *your* disposition and that of your connexions *as well*.'

233. ταῦτα ἔπραξαν] So ἔπραξαν ὧν ἐδέοντο, 232 D. (In 231 A, διαπραξάμενοι is used in the same sense.) In the next clause ταῦτα is the antecedent to ἐξ ὧν.

μνημεῖα] 'pledges, earnests.' "Μνημεῖον *monumentum* non solum refertur ad praeteritum tempus cujus memoriam conservat, sed etiam ad futurum, in quod memoria rei conservatur." So Ast, in reply to Heind., who conj. σημεῖα. He quotes Lys. de Rep. Ath. init., ἐνομίζομεν τὰς γεγενημένας συμφορὰς ἱκανὰ μνημεῖα τῇ πόλει καταλελεῖφθαι ὥστε μηδ' ἂν τοὺς ἐπιγιγνομένους ἑτέρας πολιτείας ἐπιθυμεῖν. The memory of past happiness is supposed to operate as an assurance of enjoyment to come.

B. τοιαῦτα γὰρ ὁ ἔρως ἐπιδείκνυται] 'the following are some of Love's feats,' performances by which he exhibits his power, the true sense of ἐπιδείκνυσθαι.

χοῦντας μέν, ἃ μὴ λύπην τοῖς ἄλλοις παρέχει, ἀνιαρὰ ποιεῖ νομίζειν· εὐτυχοῦντας δὲ καὶ τὰ μὴ ἡδονῆς ἄξια παρ' ἐκείνων ἐπαίνου ἀναγκάζει τυγχάνειν. ὥστε πολὺ μᾶλλον ἐλεεῖν τοῖς ἐρωμένοις ἢ ζηλοῦν αὐτοὺς προσήκει. ἐὰν δ' ἐμοὶ πείθῃ, πρῶτον μὲν οὐ τὴν παροῦσαν ἡδονὴν θεραπεύων συνέσομαί σοι, ἀλλὰ καὶ τὴν μέλλουσαν ὠφέλειαν ἔσεσθαι, οὐχ ὑπ' ἔρωτος ἡττώμενος ἀλλ' ἐμαυτοῦ C
κρατῶν, οὐδὲ διὰ σμικρὰ ἰσχυρὰν ἔχθραν ἀναιρούμενος ἀλλὰ διὰ μεγάλα βραδέως ὀλίγην ὀργὴν ποιούμενος, τῶν μὲν ἀκουσίων συγγνώμην ἔχων, τὰ δὲ ἑκούσια πειρώμενος ἀποτρέπειν· ταῦτα γάρ ἐστι φιλίας πολὺν χρόνον ἐσομένης τεκμήρια Εἰ δ' ἄρα σοι τοῦτο παρέστηκεν, ὡς οὐχ οἷόν τε ἰσχυρὰν φιλίαν γενέσθαι, ἐὰν μή τις ἐρῶν τυγχάνῃ, ἐνθυμεῖσθαι χρὴ ὅτι οὔτ' ἂν τοὺς υἱεῖς περὶ πολλοῦ D
ἐποιούμεθα οὔτ' ἂν τοὺς πατέρας καὶ τὰς μητέρας, οὔτ' ἂν πιστοὺς φίλους ἐκεκτήμεθα, οἳ οὐκ ἐξ ἐπιθυμίας τοιαύτης γεγόνασιν ἀλλ' ἐξ ἑτέρων ἐπιτηδευμάτων. Ἔτι δὲ εἰ χρὴ τοῖς δεομένοις μάλιστα χαρίζεσθαι, προσήκει καὶ τοῖς ἄλλοις μὴ τοὺς βελτίστους ἀλλὰ τοὺς ἀπορωτάτους εὖ ποιεῖν· μεγίστων γὰρ ἀπαλλαγέντες κακῶν πλείστην χάριν αὐτοῖς εἴσονται. καὶ μὲν δὴ καὶ ἐν ταῖς ἰδίαις δα-

but missed by the interpreters. Presently *εὐτυχοῦντας* is put absolutely. 'When Fortune smiles, Love makes things unpleasing in themselves to be approved by the objects of her favour.' *ἐκείνων* = *τῶν εὐτυχούντων*, the persons last named, and therefore nearer to the apprehension than the *δυστυχοῦντες*, whose case has been already considered.

ὥστε πολὺ μᾶλλον, κ τ λ.] *ἐλεεῖν* with a dat. is unheard of, though Hirsch interprets "quapropter miserari amasios magis oportet quam iis invidere." On the other hand, *ἐρωμένους*, the reading of Steph., has next to no MS authority. There seems, therefore, no alternative to Stallb.'s interpretation, "Quocirca in eos qui amantur multo potius convenit, ut eorum misereris, quam ut iis invideas," unless we accept Ast's hypothesis, that *τοῖς ἐρωμένοις* is a gloss. This is not very probable, though Ficinus omits the two words in his version. It is also remarkable that for *αὐτοὺς* some MSS have *αὐτοῖς*, a vacillation which seems to Ast to prove that the text is not intact. Dr. Badham suggests *τοῦ ἐρωμένου*, which he constructs with *ἐλεεῖν* and *ζηλοῦν*. But this would make the *lover* the object 'of compassion rather than of envy,' whereas it is evidently the beloved who suffers from the folly of his admirer, however the vulgar may 'envy' his supposed good fortune.

C *διὰ σμικρὰ ἰσχυράν, κ τ λ.*] Stallb. draws attention to the imperfect balance of this and the following clause. The balance was apparently intended to be perfect; I suspect therefore that *ταχέως* originally stood in the text between *σμικρὰ* and *ἰσχυράν*, corresponding to *μεγάλα βραδέως* in the following clause.

D *Ἔτι δὲ εἰ χρὴ—πλησμονῆς*] Observe the *reductio ad absurdum*—to Pagan apprehension doubtless a complete one.

καὶ μὲν δὴ καί] These particles occur in company Gorg. 458 D, and elsewhere

E πάναις οὐ τοὺς φίλους ἄξιον παρακαλεῖν, ἀλλὰ τοὺς προσαιτοῦντας καὶ τοὺς δεομένους πλησμονῆς· ἐκεῖνοι γὰρ καὶ ἀγαπήσουσι καὶ ἀκολουθήσουσι καὶ ἐπὶ τὰς θύρας ἥξουσι καὶ μάλιστα ἡσθήσονται καὶ οὐκ ἐλαχίστην χάριν εἴσονται καὶ πολλὰ ἀγαθὰ αὐτοῖς εὔξονται. ἀλλ' ἴσως προσήκει οὐ τοῖς σφόδρα δεομένοις χαρίζεσθαι, ἀλλὰ τοῖς μάλιστα ἀποδοῦναι χάριν δυναμένοις· οὐδὲ τοῖς ἐρῶσι
234 μόνον, ἀλλὰ τοῖς τοῦ πράγματος ἀξίοις· | οὐδὲ ὅσοι τῆς σῆς ὥρας ἀπολαύσονται, ἀλλ' οἵ τινες πρεσβυτέρῳ γενομένῳ τῶν σφετέρων ἀγαθῶν μεταδώσουσιν· οὐδὲ οἳ διαπραξάμενοι πρὸς τοὺς ἄλλους φιλοτιμήσονται, ἀλλ' οἵ τινες αἰσχυνόμενοι πρὸς ἅπαντας σιωπήσονται· οὐδὲ τοῖς ὀλίγον χρόνον σπουδάζουσιν, ἀλλὰ τοῖς ὁμοίως διὰ παντὸς τοῦ βίου φίλοις ἐσομένοις· οὐδὲ οἵ τινες παυόμενοι τῆς ἐπιθυμίας ἔχθρας πρόφασιν ζητήσουσιν, ἀλλ' οἳ παυ-
B σάμενοι τῆς ὥρας, τότε τὴν αὐτῶν ἀρετὴν ἐπιδείξονται. Σὺ οὖν τῶν τε εἰρημένων μέμνησο, καὶ ἐκεῖνο ἐνθυμοῦ, ὅτι τοὺς μὲν ἐρῶντας οἱ φίλοι νουθετοῦσιν ὡς ὄντος κακοῦ

E ἀγαπήσουσι] Hom. Od. XXI. 289, Οὐκ ἀγαπᾷς ὃ ἕκηλος ὑπερφιάλοισι μεθ' ἡμῖν Δαίνυσαι.

ἐπὶ τὰς θύρας ἥξουσι] This phrase, a frequent one in Plato, is used of those who seek advice, relief, or hospitality. Rep. 489 C, ἐπὶ ἰατρῶν θύρας ἰέναι. Ib. B, οὐ γὰρ ἔχει φύσιν τοὺς σοφοὺς ἐπὶ τὰς τῶν πλουσίων θύρας ἰέναι. Legg. XII. p. 953 D, ἴτω μὲν νῦν πᾶς ἀκέλευστος ὁ τοιοῦτος ἐπὶ τὰς τῶν πλουσίων καὶ σοφῶν θύρας, τοιοῦτος ἕτερος αὐτὸς ὤν. It denotes simple begging in Symp. 203 B, προσαιτήσουσα, οἷον δὴ εὐωχίας οὔσης, ἀφίκετο, καὶ ἦν περὶ τὰς θύρας. In Rep. 364 B, the religious quacks of the day—the ἀγύρται καὶ μάντεις—are said ἐπὶ πλουσίων θύρας ἰέναι. As an example of the custom at εὐωχίαι, we may take the case of Philippus the professed buffoon, who presents himself unbidden at the door of the men's apartment in the house of the rich Callias, νομίσας γελοιότερον εἶναι τὸ ἄκλητον ἢ τὸ κεκλημένον ἐλθεῖν ἐπὶ τὸ δεῖπνον. Xen. Conv. I. 13. An organized clientele, like that of the 'mane salutantes' at Rome, had no existence in Athens.

234 οὐδὲ οἵ τινες—ἐπιδείξονται] 'nor (will you grant favours) to those who, when their passion begins to abate, will seek to pick a quarrel, but rather to those who, when they have ceased to enjoy your charms will then display the virtue that is in them.' Such must be the sense if παυσάμενοι is retained. The ὥρα can only be that of the ἐρώμενος, the ἐραστὴς having long ceased to be ἐν ὥρᾳ. Comp. Plut. Ages. 34, ὥρα ἐν ᾗ τὸ ἥδιστον ἀνθοῦσιν ἄνθρωποι παριόντες εἰς ἄνδρας ἐκ παίδων. The difficulty of the passage consists in this unusual phrase παυσάμενοι τῆς ὥρας, as if he had said παυσάμενοι τῆς ἀπολαύσεως τῆς σῆς ὥρας. But is this more strange than to say παυομένης τῆς ὥρας for ληγούσης, which Stallb. has admitted into his text on the authority of one MS. and Ficinus? The conjectures πασάμενοι, ἐπαυράμενοι, γευσάμενοι, ἀπολαυσάμενοι do not give the required sense. The time referred to is not that succeeding fruition, but that which comes after fruition has entirely ceased. Godfrey Hermann, in the margin of his copy of Heind., proposes παυσαμένου, a conjecture (if any is required) better than the foregoing. Mr. Shilleto suggests παυομένου, which gives nearly the same sense, as does another conj. παυομένοις.

τοῦ ἐπιτηδεύματος, τοῖς δὲ μὴ ἐρῶσιν οὐδεὶς πώποτε τῶν οἰκείων ἐμέμψατο ὡς διὰ τοῦτο κακῶς βουλευομένοις περὶ ἑαυτῶν.

Ἴσως μὲν οὖν ἂν ἔροιό με εἰ ἅπασί σοι παραινῶ τοῖς μὴ ἐρῶσι χαρίζεσθαι. ἐγὼ δὲ οἶμαι οὐδ' ἂν τὸν ἐρῶντα πρὸς ἅπαντάς σε κελεύειν τοὺς ἐρῶντας ταύτην ἔχειν τὴν διάνοιαν. οὔτε γὰρ τῷ λόγῳ λαμβάνοντι χάριτος ἴσης C
ἄξιον, οὔτε σοὶ βουλομένῳ τοὺς ἄλλους λανθάνειν ὁμοίως δυνατόν· δεῖ δὲ βλάβην μὲν ἀπ' αὐτοῦ μηδεμίαν, ὠφέλειαν δὲ ἀμφοῖν γίγνεσθαι

Ἐγὼ μὲν οὖν ἱκανά μοι νομίζω τὰ εἰρημένα· εἰ δέ τι σὺ ποθεῖς, ἡγούμενος παραλελεῖφθαι, ἐρώτα.

Τί σοι φαίνεται, ὦ Σώκρατες, ὁ λόγος; οὐχ ὑπερφυῶς τά τε ἄλλα καὶ τοῖς ὀνόμασιν εἰρῆσθαι; D

ΣΩ. Δαιμονίως μὲν οὖν, ὦ ἑταῖρε, ὥς τέ με ἐκπλαγῆναι. καὶ τοῦτο ἐγὼ ἔπαθον διὰ σέ, ὦ Φαῖδρε, πρὸς σὲ ἀποβλέπων, ὅτι ἐμοὶ ἐδόκεις γάνυσθαι ὑπὸ τοῦ λόγου μεταξὺ ἀναγιγνώσκων. ἡγούμενος γὰρ σὲ μᾶλλον ἢ ἐμὲ ἐπαΐειν περὶ τῶν τοιούτων σοὶ εἱπόμην, καὶ ἑπόμενος συνεβάκχευσα μετὰ σοῦ τῆς θείας κεφαλῆς.

ΦΑΙ. Εἶεν· οὕτω δὴ δοκεῖ παίζειν;

ΣΩ. Δοκῶ γάρ σοι παίζειν καὶ οὐχὶ ἐσπουδακέναι;

ΦΑΙ. Μηδαμῶς, ὦ Σώκρατες, ἀλλ' ὡς ἀληθῶς εἰπὲ E
πρὸς Διὸς φιλίου, οἴει ἄν τινα ἔχειν εἰπεῖν ἄλλον τῶν Ἑλλήνων ἕτερα τούτων μείζω καὶ πλείω περὶ τοῦ αὐτοῦ πράγματος;

ΣΩ Τί δέ; καὶ ταύτῃ δεῖ ὑπ' ἐμοῦ τε καὶ σοῦ τὸν

C τῷ λόγῳ λαμβάνοντι] This is the reading of the Bodl and several other MSS Vulg, τῷ λαμβάνοντι λόγῳ λαμβάνειν is of frequent occurrence in Plato Legg i 634 C, οἱ λόγῳ τι λαβόντες ἐπιτήδευμα καὶ προθέμενοι ψέγειν ἢ ἐπαινεῖν Ib 653 B, μήπω δυναμένων λόγῳ λαμβάνειν said of children incapable as yet of reasoning. Here the words may mean, 'to him who takes a rational view of the matter' Comp Thuc iii 38, τὸ δρασθὲν ὄψει λαβόντες iv 17, λάβετε τοὺς λόγους μὴ πολεμίως. Plut Alcib c 18, ὀργῇ καὶ φόβῳ τὸ γεγονὸς λαμβάνοντες Badh's conj, τῷ γ' οὕτω λαμβάνοντι has much to recommend it, οὕτω implying, 'as one among many' τῷ λαμβάνοντι, 'to the recipient,' gives however all the sense absolutely required by the context

E Διὸς φιλίου] Schol Herm, φίλιος ὁ Ζεὺς λέγεται καὶ Ξένιος καὶ Κτήσιος (add Ἑρκεῖος, Soph Ant 487) More frequently Διὸς is omitted from the adjuration, as in Gorg 500 B, καὶ πρὸς φιλίου, ὦ Καλλίκλεις

λόγον ἐπαινεθῆναι, ὡς τὰ δέοντα εἰρηκότος τοῦ ποιητοῦ, ἀλλ' οὐκ ἐκείνῃ μόνον, ὅτι σαφῆ καὶ στρογγύλα καὶ ἀκριβῶς ἕκαστα τῶν ὀνομάτων ἀποτετόρνευται, εἰ γὰρ δεῖ, συγχωρητέον χάριν σήν, ἐπεὶ ἐμέ γε ἔλαθεν ὑπὸ τῆς ἐμῆς οὐδενίας· | τῷ γὰρ ῥητορικῷ αὐτοῦ μόνῳ τὸν νοῦν προσεῖχον· τοῦτο δὲ οὐδὲ αὐτὸν ᾤμην Λυσίαν οἴεσθαι ἱκανὸν εἶναι. καὶ δὴ οὖν μοι ἔδοξεν, ὦ Φαῖδρε, εἰ μή τι σὺ ἄλλο λέγεις, δὶς καὶ τρὶς τὰ αὐτὰ εἰρηκέναι, ὡς οὐ πάνυ εὐπορῶν τοῦ πολλὰ λέγειν περὶ τοῦ αὐτοῦ, ἢ ἴσως οὐδὲν αὐτῷ μέλον τοῦ τοιούτου· καὶ ἐφαίνετο δή μοι νεανιεύεσθαι ἐπιδεικνύμενος, ὡς οἷός τε ὢν ταὐτὰ ἑτέρως τε καὶ ἑτέρως λέγων ἀμφοτέρως εἰπεῖν ἄριστα.

B ΦΑΙ. Οὐδὲν λέγεις, ὦ Σώκρατες. αὐτὸ γὰρ τοῦτο καὶ

τοῦ ποιητοῦ] Herm *ποιητὴν κοινότερον λέγει τὸν ῥήτορα, ποιεῖ γὰρ καὶ οὗτος λόγους* Inf 236 D, *παρ' ἀγαθὸν ποιητὴν ἰδιώτης αὐτοσχεδιάζων*

ὅτι σαφῆ καὶ στρογγύλα καὶ ἀκριβῶς—ἀποτετόρνευται] 'every word comes oft his lathe clear and round and nicely polished' Arist. Thesm. v. 59, speaking of the poet Agathon, *τὰ δὲ τορνεύει, τὰ δὲ κολλομελεῖ* Hor Ep. ad Pis 441, male *tornatos* incudi reddere versus Propert iii 32 43, Incipe jam angusto versus includere *torno* Ast brackets the words *καὶ ἀκριβῶς*, on the ground that they are absent in Hermeias, and in the text quoted by Plutarch, de recta aud rat 15 A, (ὁ Πλάτων) *τὴν ἀπαγγελίαν αὐτοῦ (Λυσίου) ἐπαινεῖ, καὶ ὅτι τῶν ὀνομάτων σαφῶς καὶ στρογγύλως ἕκαστον ἀποτετόρνευται.* Heind also objects to the adv as coming somewhat flatly after two adjectives Badh 's conj *ἀποτετορνευμένα* is supported by Hermeias, who has *διὰ δὲ τὸ εἰπεῖν σαφῆ καὶ στρογγύλα καὶ ἀποτετορνευμένα δηλοῖ, κ τ λ* I agree, however, with Stallb in preferring the text as it stands Plato probably thought the *ἀκρίβεια* of Lysias excessive and pedantic. In the Theaet 184 B, he seems to apologize for the comparative negligence, as it may have seemed to his contemporaries, of his own style *τὸ δ' εὐχερὲς τῶν ὀνομάτων καὶ ῥημάτων καὶ μὴ δι' ἀκριβείας ἐξεταζόμενον τὰ μὲν πολλὰ οὐκ ἀγεννές, ἀλλὰ μᾶλλον τὸ τούτου ἐναντίον ἀνελεύθερον*

235 *τῷ γὰρ ῥητορικῷ*] "Ad eloquutionem tantum s orationis formam (*τὸ σαφῆ καὶ στρογγύλα, κ τ λ*) attendi, non ad sententiam *τοῦτο* refertur ad superiora, *τὸ τὰ δέοντα λέγειν*" Ast "My attention," says Socr, "was fixed on his style, the matter I did not suppose that Lysias himself deemed satisfactory." Perhaps *ἂν* should be inserted between *αὐτὸν* and *ᾤμην* Before and after such words as *νομίζω, οἶμαι*, and the like, *ἂν* is frequently omitted by the scribes, unconscious, it would seem, that the particle belongs not to the verbs in question, but to the infinitive which depends upon them

καὶ δὴ οὖν] 'nay, and by your leave, Phaedrus, he seemed to me to have said the same thing two or three times over, like one too barren of matter to be able to say many things on one subject' The reading *καὶ δὴ οὖν* is extracted from *δικαιοῦν, δίκαιον οὖν*, and other vagaries of the MSS Stallb 's *καὶ δὴ καὶ οὖν* is nearer to the orig But query as to the second *καί* *δὴ οὖν* come together not unfrequently, as inf. p 259 D, *πολλῶν δὴ οὖν ἕνεκα λεκτέον.* The formula of deprecation or apology *εἰ μή τι σὺ ἄλλο λέγεις* occurs Gorg 462 B, 513 C

νεανιεύεσθαι—ἄριστα] 'to make an ostentatious display of his skill by saying the same thing in two different ways, both equally excellent, as he flattered himself' I am unable to appreciate Stallb 's preference of the vulg *ταῦτα* to the *ταὐτὰ* of Heind adopted by the Zur and Hirschig

B *αὐτὸ γὰρ τοῦτο καὶ μάλιστα, κ τ λ*]

μάλιστα ὁ λόγος ἔχει. τῶν γὰρ ἐνόντων ἀξίως ῥηθῆναι ἐν τῷ πράγματι οὐδὲν παραλέλοιπεν, ὥστε παρὰ τὰ ἐκείνῳ εἰρημένα μηδέν' ἂν ποτε δύνασθαι εἰπεῖν ἄλλα πλείω καὶ πλείονος ἄξια.

ΣΩ. Τοῦτο ἐγώ σοι οὐκέτι οἷός τε ἔσομαι πείθεσθαι. παλαιοὶ γὰρ καὶ σοφοὶ ἄνδρες τε καὶ γυναῖκες περὶ αὐτῶν εἰρηκότες καὶ γεγραφότες ἐξελέγξουσί με, ἐάν σοι χαριζόμενος συγχωρῶ.

ΦΑΙ. Τίνες οὗτοι; καὶ ποῦ σὺ βελτίω τούτων C
ἀκήκοας;

ΣΩ. Νῦν μὲν οὕτως οὐκ ἔχω εἰπεῖν· δῆλον δὲ ὅτι τινῶν ἀκήκοα, ἤ που Σαπφοῦς τῆς καλῆς ἢ Ἀνακρέοντος τοῦ σοφοῦ ἢ καὶ συγγραφέων τινῶν. πόθεν δὴ τεκμαιρόμενος λέγω; πλῆρές πως, ὦ δαιμόνιε, τὸ στῆθος ἔχων αἰσθάνομαι παρὰ ταῦτ' ἂν ἔχειν εἰπεῖν ἕτερα μὴ χείρω. ὅτι μὲν οὖν παρά γε ἐμαυτοῦ οὐδὲν αὐτῶν ἐννενόηκα, εὖ οἶδα, συνειδὼς ἐμαυτῷ ἀμαθίαν. λείπεται δή, οἶμαι, ἐξ ἀλλοτρίων ποθὲν ναμάτων διὰ τῆς ἀκοῆς πεπληρῶσθαί D
με δίκην ἀγγείου· ὑπὸ δὲ νωθείας αὖ καὶ αὐτὸ τοῦτο ἐπιλέλησμαι ὅπως τε καὶ ὧν τινῶν ἤκουσα.

'if the speech has a merit, it is precisely that which you deny it of the topics implied in (naturally suggested by) the subject-matter, and capable of worthy treatment, there is not one which he has omitted' The latter clause may be analyzed thus ἅ τ' ἐνῆν τῷ πράγματι καὶ οἷς ἐνῆν ἀξίως ῥηθῆναι So in effect Ast, who quotes Thuc iv 59, τί ἄν τις πᾶν τὸ ἐνὸν ἐκλέγων ἐν εἰδόσι μακρηγοροίη. Aesch F. L p 122, ἴσως γὰρ οὐδὲν τῶν ἐνόντων εἰπεῖν, ὥς γ' οἶμαι, παρέλιπον

παλαιοὶ γὰρ καὶ σοφοί, κ τ λ] Gray has a good note on this passage "It is observable," he says, "that Socr whenever he would discourse affirmatively on any subject, or when he thought proper to raise or adorn his style, does it not in his own person, but assumes the character of another. Thus, for instance, he relates the beautiful fable of the choice] between Virtue and Pleasure, after Prodicus" (Xen Mem ii 1 21), "he treats of the miseries of human life in the words of the same Sophist; he describes the state of souls after death from the information of Gobryas, one of the Magi" (Axioch 371), "he makes a panegyric on Wine in the style of Gorgias" (Xen Symp ii 26?), "and here he does not venture to display his eloquence till the Nymphs and Muses have inspired him This is consistent with that character of simplicity and humility which he assumed" Works, ed Matth ii. p. 310. Add, among other instances, Crat 396 D, where Socr., wondering at his unwonted skill in etymology, pretends it has come to him from some mysterious source ἐξαίφνης νῦν οὑτωσὶ προσπέπτωκεν ἄρτι, οὐκ οἶδ' ὁπόθεν

C Νῦν μὲν οὕτως] 'without further consideration' The use of οὕτως with another adv as νῦν, ἁπλῶς, ἀτρέμα, ἐξαίφνης, is familiar to readers of Plato, who will find exx. in Ast's Lex Pl ii p 195

ἢ καὶ συγγραφέων τινῶν] 'or it may be from some prose writers'

ΦΑΙ. Ἀλλ', ὦ γενναιότατε, κάλλιστα εἴρηκας. σὺ γὰρ
ἐμοὶ ὧν τινῶν μὲν καὶ ὅπως ἤκουσας, μηδ' ἂν κελεύω
εἴπῃς, τοῦτο δὲ αὐτὸ ὃ λέγεις ποίησον· τῶν ἐν τῷ βιβλίῳ
βελτίω τε καὶ μὴ ἐλάττω ἕτερα ὑπόσχες [εἰπεῖν,] τούτων
ἀπεχόμενος. καί σοι ἐγώ, ὥσπερ οἱ ἐννέα ἄρχοντες, ὑπι-
E σχνοῦμαι χρυσῆν εἰκόνα ἰσομέτρητον εἰς Δελφοὺς ἀναθήσειν, οὐ μόνον ἐμαυτοῦ ἀλλὰ καὶ σήν.

D. μηδ' ἂν κελεύω εἴπῃς] Pherecr. ap. Athen. p. 335 A, μηδέποτ' ἰχθύν, ὦ Δευκαλίων, μηδ' ἢν αἰτῶ παραθῇς μοι. R. S.

ἕτερα ὑπόσχες] Bekk. after the Bodl., ἑτέρᾳ ὑποσχέσει εἰπεῖν, which is mere gibberish; others have ἕτερα. I have adopted Badh.'s suggestion, "quum verbum ὑπόσχες non intelligeret scriba, εἰπεῖν de suo adjecit." The final ει in ὑποσχέσει all admit to be a duplication of the initial syllable of εἰπεῖν. Stallb. imagines a *duplex lectio*, ὑπόστηθι (whence, he supposes, the ὑποσχέθητι of one or two MSS.) and ὑπόσχες εἰπεῖν, thinking it indifferent which we adopt. But ὑπόσχες εἰπεῖν cannot mean 'sustine dicere,' for which we should undoubtedly require the mid. ὑπόσχου. The active ὑπόσχες may mean 'submit to me as to a judge,' or simply, 'produce,' 'present us with, a better speech,' as if he had said πρότεινον. Arist. Pac. 874, ἀλλ' εὗρον ἄν σ' ὑπέχοντα τὴν ἐκεχειρίαν. The phrases ὑπέχειν λόγον, εὐθύνας, αἰτίαν, δίκην are familiar. In Gorg. 497 B, ὑπόσχες Σωκράτει ἐλέγξαι, ὑπ. = permitte. Except in this last sense, it would be difficult to find an instance of ὑπόσχες without an accus. following. Wex, in a long note on Soph. Antig. (ii. p. 77 seq.) seems first to have suggested ὑπόσχες εἰπεῖν, which he improperly translates, "sustine dicere, in te recipe dicere," in which Stallb. follows him. The barbarism ὑποσχέθητι of the vulg. is probably an old *interpretamentum* of ὑπόσχες which the scribe misunderstood for ὑπόσχου. The duplication of the ει may be compared with that of ου in 246 C, where for the vulg. πλαττομένου οὔτε Bekk. rightly reads πλάττομεν οὔτε.

καί σοι ἐγὼ—ἀναθήσειν] The oath of the nine archons, to which Phaedrus alludes, has perplexed writers on Attic antiquities. According to Plutarch (Solon, c. 25) every archon, before admission to office, took oath, εἴ τι παραβαίη τῶν θεσμῶν, ἀνδριάντα χρυσοῦν ἰσομέτρητον ἀναθήσειν ἐν Δελφοῖς. This statement can only mean that the slightest violation of law on the part of any of the archons was to be expiated by the erection of a statue of gold at Delphi of life size. Even this is improved upon by Suid., who makes the statues three instead of one, and represents them as portrait-statues of the delinquent (χρυσῆ εἰκών. ὤμνυον οἱ Ἀθήνησιν ἄρχοντες, ἄν τι παρέλθωσιν ἐφ' οἷς ἂν ἄρχωσιν, χρυσῆν εἰκόνα αὐτῶν ἀναθήσειν ἐν ἄστει, ἐν Πυθοῖ, ἐν Ὀλυμπίᾳ). Better accounts however are given by J. Pollux, viii. 86, and by Heraclides in his excerpts from the πολιτεῖαι of Aristotle; from whom it appears that only in the case of bribery was such punishment exacted—δῶρα μὴ λήψεσθαι, ἢ ἀνδριάντα χρυσοῦν ἀναθήσειν—where the omission of ἰσομέτρητον and αὐτοῦ is significant. It is not certain that in the passage before us either the word ἰσομέτρητον or αὐτοῦ is to be understood as quoted from the archon's oath. For besides that portrait-statues were not in use in the time of Solon (see the passage from Pliny quoted in the note next but one to this), it is very unlikely that the Delphians would have allowed their sacred peribolus to be defiled by the statue of a detected criminal. And if the penalty was intended to be enforced, the offering must needs have been of much more limited dimensions. It is therefore conceivable that both ἰσομέτρητον and αὐτοῦ were introduced by late writers into the text of the original oath, in order to make it conformable to the supposed meaning of Plato. If we assume the image to have been of definite but small size, which is all that the statements of Pollux and Heraclides necessitate, it is not impossible that it may also have been of solid gold. In a recent number of the Rhenish Museum (viii. p. 117), to which

ΣΩ. Φίλτατος εἶ καὶ ὡς ἀληθῶς χρυσοῦς, ὦ Φαῖδρε, εἴ με οἴει λέγειν ὡς Λυσίας τοῦ παντὸς ἡμάρτηκε, καὶ οἷόν τε δὴ παρὰ πάντα ταῦτα ἄλλα εἰπεῖν. τοῦτο δὲ οἶμαι οὐδ' ἂν τὸν φαυλότατον παθεῖν συγγραφέα. αὐτίκα περὶ οὗ ὁ λόγος, τίνα οἴει λέγοντα ὡς χρὴ μὴ ἐρῶντι μᾶλλον ἢ ἐρῶντι χαρίζεσθαι, παρέντα τοῦ μὲν | τὸ φρόνιμον 236 ἐγκωμιάζειν, τοῦ δὲ τὸ ἄφρον ψέγειν, ἀναγκαῖα γοῦν ὄντα, εἶτ' ἄλλ' ἄττα ἕξειν λέγειν; ἀλλ', οἶμαι, τὰ μὲν τοιαῦτα ἐατέα καὶ συγγνωστέα λέγοντι· καὶ τῶν μὲν τοιούτων οὐ

I am indebted for some of the above remarks, we are presented with a new solution of the difficulty, professing greater completeness than any that have preceded it The eminent scholar whose name is appended to the paper in question, contends that, the oath having originally had a bona fide purpose, it is necessary to suppose that the penalty was one within the power of an ex-archon to raise The dimensions of the statue were to equal, not those of the offender, but of the bribe received by him We know from Dinarchus (adv Demosth 60) that the punishment of bribery was a fine exceeding tenfold the money received by the offender the relative value of gold to silver at Athens in the time of Solon appears to have been as 10 1, hence the archon was required to set up an image of gold equalling in weight the sum supposed to have been received in silver In this case we must suppose *ἰσοστάσιον* to have originally stood in the text of the oath, and *ἰσομέτρητον* to have been substituted, apparently by Plato, in whose time the sanction had become a dead letter To me, I confess, the ingenuity of this hypothesis appears to exceed its credibility, but others may form a different opinion.

1 **αὐτίκα περὶ οὗ ὁ λόγος**] 'to begin with his thesis' So Gorg. 472 D, *αὐτίκα περὶ οὗ νῦν ὁ λόγος ἐστί*

τίνα οἴει λέγοντα, κ τ λ] 'who,' asks Socr, 'could argue that the cool is to be preferred to the impassioned suitor, without lauding the good sense of the former and censuring the absurdities of the latter or if he *did* overlook topics so trite and obvious, what else could he find to say? Of such commonplaces the less said the better They require no invention, but only the power of arrangement If a speaker would earn the praise of invention he must have something to say more recondite than platitudes like these' Struck by the justice of this criticism, Phaedr will allow Socr. to take for granted the truism that a man who is in love is in a less healthy state of mind than one who is free from that passion, 'but,' says he, 'produce arguments more and better than those contained in the remainder of the speech, and you shall stand in wrought gold at Olympia by the side of the great image set up by the Cypselidae' Of this image Hermeias says that it was actually erected by the sons of Periander, the son of Cypselus, on the occasion of recovering the tyranny of Corinth Better authorities, as Aristotle and Strabo, attribute the offering to Cypselus himself who, it is added, made his subjects pay a tax for ten years towards defraying the enormous expense The "golden statue" of Gorgias, at Delphi, Pausanias found to be a gilt one, though Pliny gravely assures us that "Hominum primus et auream statuam et solidam Gorgias Leontinus Delphis in templo sibi posuit lxx circiter Olympiade Tantus erat docendae artis oratoriae quaestus" N H xxxiii 24 Still more fabulous is the account in Valerius Max, viii ad fin, "Gorgiae Leontino . universa Graecia .. statuam solido in auro posuit cum caeterorum ad id tempus imaginas collocasset" The word *σφυρήλατος* (distinguished from *χοανευτός, cast*) does not necessarily imply more than a statue covered with plates of beaten gold, though we read of *ὁλόσφυρα* or *ὁλοσφύρητα ἀγάλματα* composed entirely of the precious metal, "nulla inanitate," as Pliny, l l expresses it Compare Muller, Handb der Archaol. §§ 210 2; 307

τὴν εὕρεσιν ἀλλὰ τὴν διάθεσιν ἐπαινετέον, τῶν δὲ μὴ ἀναγκαίων τε καὶ χαλεπῶν εὑρεῖν πρὸς τῇ διαθέσει καὶ τὴν εὕρεσιν.

ΦΑΙ. Συγχωρῶ ὃ λέγεις· μετρίως γάρ μοι δοκεῖς εἰρηκέναι. ποιήσω οὖν καὶ ἐγὼ οὕτως· τὸ μὲν τὸν ἐρῶντα
B τοῦ μὴ ἐρῶντος μᾶλλον νοσεῖν δώσω σοι ὑποτίθεσθαι, τῶν δὲ λοιπῶν ἕτερα πλείω καὶ πλείονος ἄξια εἰπὼν τῶν Λυσίου παρὰ τὸ Κυψελιδῶν ἀνάθημα σφυρήλατος ἐν Ὀλυμπίᾳ ἔσταθι.

ΣΩ. Ἐσπούδακας, ὦ Φαῖδρε, ὅτι σου τῶν παιδικῶν ἐπελαβόμην ἐρεσχηλῶν σε, καὶ οἴει δή με ὡς ἀληθῶς ἐπιχειρήσειν εἰπεῖν παρὰ τὴν ἐκείνου σοφίαν ἕτερόν τι ποικιλώτερον

ΦΑΙ. Περὶ μὲν τούτου, ὦ φίλε, εἰς τὰς ὁμοίας λαβὰς
C ἐλήλυθας. ῥητέον μὲν γάρ σοι παντὸς μᾶλλον οὕτως ὅπως οἷός τε εἶ, ἵνα μὴ τὸ τῶν κωμῳδῶν φορτικὸν πρᾶγμα ἀναγκαζώμεθα ποιεῖν, ἀνταποδιδόντες ἀλλήλοις, καὶ μὴ

236 B ἔσταθι] Vulg σταθήτι The true reading was restored by Cobet, V. Ll p 196, from a Scholium on this passage quoted in Photius's Lex, σφυρήλατος ἐν Ὀλυμπίᾳ ἐστάθη "Herod ii 141, καὶ νῦν ἕστηκε ἐν τῷ ἱρῷ λίθινος, sic et χρυσοῦς ἕστηκε dicitur et ἔστη et στήσεται, non item σταθῆναι et σταθήσεσθαι quae sunt Graecitatis languescentis et labentis" This, however, is saying too much Dinarch p 103—13, ἐν τῇ ἀγορᾷ χαλκοῦν σταθέντα Cf Virgil, Catal vi 9,

> Marmoreusque tibi, Dea, versicoloribus alis
> In morem picta *stabit* Amor pharetra

So Horace, Stabis marmoreus sub trabe citrea.

Ἐσπούδακας] 'you are seriously annoyed.' Ar Ran 812, ὡς ὅταν γ' οἱ δεσπόται Ἐσπουδάκωσι, κλαύμαθ' ἡμῖν γίγνεται.

ἐρεσχηλῶν σε] 'by way of teasing you' "ludificans, joco irritans" Steph. Bachmann, Anecd Gr ii p 323 11. "ἐπὶ τῶν φιλίως διαλεγομένων ἐρεσχηλεῖν. Nosti *necken*" Ast ἐρεσχελοῦντες, φλυαροῦντες ἐρεσχελεῖ. . ἐρεθίζει, ἀδολεσχεῖ, χλευάζει, παίζει, σκώπτει, διαμάχεται Hesych Hence perhaps corr ἐπὶ τῶν φιλίως διαμαχομένων in the Schol. quoted by Ast The long penult was adopted by Bekker from the Bodl and other MSS Vulg ἐρεσχελῶν

εἰς τὰς ὁμοίας λαβὰς ἐλήλυθας] 'you have laid yourself open to a like retort.' The metaphor in the Gr is "taken from the palaestra," as the Comm. observe. We say in like manner, 'You have given me a hold upon you' Phaedr might also have said τ. ὁ. λ. ἐνδέδωκας as Arist. Eq. 817, or δέδωκας, as ib 811.

C ἵνα μή] So the Bodl and the best MSS Vulg ἵνα δὲ μή, with a full stop after εἶ After ἀλλήλοις stood εὐλαβήθητι, a senseless interpolation, as Cobet observes, l. l. "magistello qui adscripsit reddendum, ut ἵνα μὴ pendeat a verbis ῥητέον παντὸς μᾶλλον"

τὸ τῶν κωμῳδῶν φορτικὸν πρᾶγμα] As a specimen of the kind of low wit in question, see Arist Eq 286 seq and 361 seq This ἀνταπόδοσις, or interchange of pleasantries, answers nearly to the 'tu quoque' of English school boys, and the 'Retourkutzsche' of German students Socr had said, ὦ Φαῖδρε, εἰ ἐγὼ Φαῖδρον ἀγνοῶ, καὶ ἐμαυτοῦ ἐπιλέλησμαι, p. 228, and Phaedr here threatens to 'pay him back' in his own coin

βούλου με ἀναγκάσαι λέγειν ἐκεῖνο τὸ εἰ ἐγώ, ὦ Σώκρατες, Σωκράτην ἀγνοῶ, καὶ ἐμαυτοῦ ἐπιλέλησμαι, καὶ ὅτι ἐπεθύμει μὲν λέγειν, ἐθρύπτετο δέ· ἀλλὰ διανοήθητι ὅτι ἐντεῦθεν οὐκ ἄπιμεν, πρὶν ἂν σὺ εἴπῃς ἃ ἔφησθα ἐν τῷ στήθει ἔχειν. ἐσμὲν δὲ μόνω ἐν ἐρημίᾳ, ἰσχυρότερος δὲ ἐγὼ καὶ νεώτερος, ἐκ δ' ἁπάντων τούτων ξύνες ὅ σοι λέγω, D καὶ μηδαμῶς πρὸς βίαν βουληθῇς μᾶλλον ἢ ἑκὼν λέγειν.

ΣΩ. Ἀλλ', ὦ μακάριε Φαῖδρε, γελοῖος ἔσομαι παρ' ἀγαθὸν ποιητὴν ἰδιώτης αὐτοσχεδιάζων περὶ τῶν αὐτῶν.

ΦΑΙ. Οἶσθ' ὡς ἔχει; παῦσαι πρός με καλλωπιζόμενος· σχεδὸν γὰρ ἔχω ὃ εἰπὼν ἀναγκάσω σε λέγειν.

ΣΩ. Μηδαμῶς τοίνυν εἴπῃς.

ΦΑΙ. Οὔκ, ἀλλὰ καὶ δὴ λέγω. ὁ δέ μοι λόγος ὅρκος ἔσται· ὄμνυμι γάρ σοι—τίνα μέντοι, τίνα θεῶν; ἢ βούλει τὴν πλάτανον ταυτηνί; ἦ μήν, ἐάν μοι μὴ εἴπῃς τὸν λόγον E ἐναντίον αὐτῆς ταύτης, μηδέποτέ σοι ἕτερον λόγον μηδένα μηδενὸς μήτ' ἐπιδείξειν μήτ' ἐξαγγελεῖν.

ΣΩ. Βαβαί, ὦ μιαρέ, ὡς εὖ ἀνεῦρες τὴν ἀνάγκην ἀνδρὶ φιλολόγῳ ποιεῖν ὃ ἂν κελεύῃς.

ΦΑΙ. Τί δῆτα ἔχων στρέφει;

ΣΩ. Οὐδὲν ἔτι, ἐπειδὴ σύ γε ταῦτα ὀμώμοκας. πῶς γὰρ ἂν οἷός τ' εἴην τοιαύτης θοίνης ἀπέχεσθαι;

| ΦΑΙ. Λέγε δή. 237

D. ξύνες ὅ σοι λέγω] A quotation with the change of τοὶ into σοὶ from a well-known frag of Pindar, Boeckh, No 71, which is parodied by Arist Av 941 In Menon 76 D we have ὅ τοι λέγω or ὅτι λέγω in the MSS

Ἀλλ', ὦ μακάριε] Socr affects reluctance (θρύπτεται, καλλωπίζεται), and on two grounds He is an ἰδιώτης, a plain man, whereas Lysias is a great author; moreover, the speech of Lysias had been composed at leisure, he, Socrates, being called upon to *extemporize* a discourse on the same thesis On ἰδιώτης see the note on 258 D

σχεδὸν γάρ] 'methinks I have that to say, &c,' nearly as ἴσως, 233 E

Οὔκ, ἀλλὰ καὶ δὴ λέγω] 'nay, but say it I must, and here you have it' This seems the force of the particles, καὶ δὴ often, as freq, a sense bordering on, but not to be confounded with, the hypothetical use of these particles For the use of the negative, comp Gorg 453 D, πείθει ἢ οὔ, Οὐ δῆτα ἀλλὰ πάντων μάλιστα πείθομαι.

ὁ δέ μοι λόγος] Hom Il. i 239, ὁ δέ τοι μέγας ἔσσεται ὅρκος

E ἐπιδείξειν] Not ἐπιδείξεσθαι, the speech not being his own, but another's Eng, 'let you see,' as ἐξαγγελεῖν = 'let you hear'

Τί δῆτα ἔχων στρέφει] 'then why all this shuffling?' For ἔχων comp Gorg 490 E, ποῖα ὑποδήματα φλυαρεῖς ἔχων, for στρέφει, Ar Ach 385, τί ταῦτα στρέφει, τεχνάζεις τε καὶ πορίζεις τριβάς, and Laches 196 B, ἀλλὰ στρέφεται ἄνω καὶ κάτω ἐπικρυπτόμενος τὴν αὑτοῦ σοφίαν, quoted by Ast in ann, who indulges in a lengthy speculation upon the origin of the idiomatic ἔχων

ΣΩ. Οἶσθ' οὖν ὡς ποιήσω;

ΦΑΙ. Τοῦ πέρι,

ΣΩ. Ἐγκαλυψάμενος ἐρῶ, ἵν' ὅ τι τάχιστα διαδράμω τὸν λόγον καὶ μή, βλέπων πρὸς σέ, ὑπ' αἰσχύνης διαπορῶμαι.

ΦΑΙ. Λέγε μόνον, τὰ δ' ἄλλα ὅπως βούλει ποίει.

ΣΩ. Ἄγετε δή, ὦ Μοῦσαι, εἴτε δι' ᾠδῆς εἶδος λίγειαι, εἴτε διὰ γένος μουσικὸν τὸ Λιγύων ταύτην ἔσχετ' ἐπωνυμίαν, ξύμ μοι λάβεσθε τοῦ μύθου, ὅν με ἀναγκάζει ὁ
B βέλτιστος οὑτοσὶ λέγειν, ἵν' ὁ ἑταῖρος αὐτοῦ, καὶ πρότερον δοκῶν τούτῳ σοφὸς εἶναι, νῦν ἔτι μᾶλλον δόξῃ

Ἦν οὕτω δὴ παῖς, μᾶλλον δὲ μειρακίσκος, μάλα καλός. τούτῳ δὲ ἦσαν ἐρασταὶ πάνυ πολλοί. εἷς δέ τις αὐτῶν αἱμύλος ἦν, ὃς οὐδενὸς ἧττον ἐρῶν ἐπεπείκει τὸν παῖδα ὡς οὐκ ἐρῴη. καί ποτε αὐτὸν αἰτῶν ἔπειθε τοῦτ' αὐτό, ὡς μὴ ἐρῶντι πρὸ τοῦ ἐρῶντος δέοι χαρίζεσθαι. ἔλεγέ τε ὧδε·

Περὶ παντός, ὦ παῖ, μία ἀρχὴ τοῖς μέλλουσι καλῶς

237 *διαπορῶμαι*] A deponent, not distinguishable in sense from *διαπορῶ* or the simple *ἀπορῶ*, for which *ἀποροῦμαι* is sometimes found We have also the true passives *ἀπορούμενον* in Soph 243 B, and *διηπορημένον*, ib 250 E, denoting the subject of a controversy or difficult investigation, *τὸ περὶ οὗ ἀπορεῖ τις.*

Ἄγετε δή, ὦ Μοῦσαι] The motive of this 'dithyrambic' invocation (inf 238 D) is of course to give a colour of probability to the artificial and stilted style of the prooem of the first speech of Socr., and still more to that of the second speech, the *μυθικὸς ὕμνος*, so alien from the ordinary simplicity of the speaker It is to this part of the dialogue that Aristotle alludes, Rhet iii 7 11, where he says that a high-flown poetical diction is admissible in prose, 1 when the feelings of the audience have been wrought to a high pitch by the speaker, or, 2 when such style is adopted *μετ' εἰρωνείας, ὅπερ Γοργίας ἐποίει, καὶ τὰ ἐν τῷ Φαίδρῳ* This criticism, for its taste and discernment, stands in favourable contrast with that of Dionysius of Halic., who is sorely scandalized by the "turbid and obscure, and disagreeably poetical style" which, as he thinks, is a grievous change for the worse from the gracefulness of the introductory scene

λίγειαι] A stereotyped epithet of the Muses Socr affects to doubt whether it was derived from the shrillness of their notes, or from the name of a race devoted to their service Herm *ἔθνος τῶν Λιγύων . οὕτως ἄγαν μουσικώτατόν ἐστιν, ὥστε μηδ' ἐν τοῖς πολέμοις πανστρατιᾳ μάχεσθαι, ἀλλὰ τὸ μέν τι τοῦ στρατεύματος ἀγωνίζεσθαι, τὸ δὲ ᾄδειν, πολεμοῦντος τοῦ λοιποῦ*,—a reputation, it is hardly necessary to say, which the Ligurians owe to the ingenuity of Greek etymologists The tmesis *ξύμ μοι λάβεσθε* is of course a designed poeticism

B *Ἦν οὕτω δή*] The conventional mode of beginning a fable, answering to our 'once upon a time' Aristoph. Vesp 1182, *οὕτω ποτ' ἦν μῦς καὶ γαλῆ*, where see the Schol Germ, 'Es war also einmal' Lysis 216 C, *τὸ μήτ' ἀγαθὸν μήτε κακὸν φίλον οὕτω ποτὲ γιγνόμενον τἀγαθοῦ*, 'that that which is neither good nor bad may *once in a way* become endeared to the good'

Περὶ παντός, κ.τ.λ.] This is the prooem

βουλεύεσθαι· εἰδέναι δεῖ περὶ οὗ ἂν ᾖ ἡ βουλή, ἢ παν- C
τὸς ἁμαρτάνειν ἀνάγκη. τοὺς δὲ πολλοὺς λέληθεν ὅτι οὐκ
ἴσασι τὴν οὐσίαν ἑκάστου· ὡς οὖν εἰδότες οὐ διομολο-
γοῦνται ἐν ἀρχῇ τῆς σκέψεως, προελθόντες δὲ τὸ εἰκὸς
ἀποδιδόασιν· οὔτε γὰρ ἑαυτοῖς οὔτε ἀλλήλοις ὁμολογοῦσιν.
ἐγὼ οὖν καὶ σὺ μὴ πάθωμεν ὃ ἄλλοις ἐπιτιμῶμεν, ἀλλ'
ἐπειδὴ σοὶ καὶ ἐμοὶ ὁ λόγος πρόκειται, πότερον ἐρῶντι
ἢ μὴ μᾶλλον εἰς φιλίαν ἰτέον, περὶ ἔρωτος, οἷόν τε ἔστι
καὶ ἣν ἔχει δύναμιν, ὁμολογίᾳ θέμενοι ὅρον, εἰς τοῦτο D
ἀποβλέποντες καὶ ἀναφέροντες τὴν σκέψιν ποιώμεθα,
εἴτε ὠφέλειαν εἴτε βλάβην παρέχει. Ὅτι μὲν οὖν δὴ ἐπι-

to a speech which professes, like that of Lysias, to uphold the thesis *ὡς μὴ ἐρῶντι πρὸ τοῦ ἐρῶντος δεῖ χαρίζεσθαι*. Instead of plunging in medias res, as Lysias had done, Socr. seeks in the first instance to define the terms of the question. What is *ἔρως*? All allow that it is an *ἐπιθυμία*—an appetite or desire. But this is an insufficient though a true description, for there are many *ἐπιθυμίαι*. Neither is it enough to add that Love is an *ἐπιθυμία τῶν καλῶν*, a desire of beautiful objects, for many desire beautiful objects who are not in love. How then are we to distinguish *ἔρως* from other *ἐπιθυμίαι τῶν καλῶν*, and what is its true differentia? Socr. sets about the inquiry thus. There are two principles of action in man, the desire of pleasure and the desire of excellence. Of these the first is innate, the second acquired; the second a rational, the first an unreasoning principle. When the rational principle predominates, the result is that state of mind which we call *σωφροσύνη*—temperance, or moderation, or self-government; when the appetite bears sway, its usurpation is branded with the name *ὕβρις*—licence or excess. But as *ὕβρις* is only *ἐπιθυμία* magnified, there are many *ὕβρεις* as there are many *ἐπιθυμίαι*, differing in nature or in name, according to the name and nature of their several objects. Thus the desire of food, when it becomes excessive, is styled *γαστριμαργία*, gluttony; the desire of drink under the same circumstances becomes a vice which all know. Love, it is assumed, is one of these forms of excess: it is the Excess which corresponds to the Desire of the Beautiful. Not however of *all* that is beautiful but especially of corporeal beauty. It is therefore the desire of beauty combined with carnal appetite, existing in such intensity as to triumph over all the restraints imposed by the antagonist principle. Its name corresponds to its nature: for the word *ἔρως* is near of kin to *ῥώμη*, *ῥώομαι*, and *ἐρρωμένως*,—one proof among many that names were given by those who saw deep into the nature of things (Crat. 401 B). Such seems the purport of this dialectico-dithyrambic *σκέψις*, in which jest and earnest are oddly but not inharmoniously blended. It is characteristic of Plato both in this particular and in the psychological distinction of the two *ἰδέα* or forms of mental being, upon which the definition is made to rest. Of this conception of *ἔρως*, we shall see hereafter what its author really thought: but meanwhile it answers its purpose: it is a true account of that passion against which Socr. is about to inveigh, and it is something less vile than the cold calculating desire, the 'passionless prurience,' recommended by the unloving suitor of Lysias.

C *τὸ εἰκὸς ἀποδιδόασιν*] The verb *ἀποδοῦναι* signifies to 'give back': hence to 'pay,' i.e. to give in consideration of a previous gift. In phrases like the present it denotes the relation between cause and consequence, a result answering to a foregone cause. 'They pay the natural penalty,' or, more generally, 'the natural result follows.' Cousin: "*Il en résulte ce qui était inévitable.*" Theaet. 175 D, *πάλιν αὖ τὰ ἀντίστροφα ἀποδίδωσι* = 'the tables are turned.'

θυμία τις ὁ ἔρως, ἅπαντι δῆλον· ὅτι δ' αὖ καὶ μὴ ἐρῶντες
ἐπιθυμοῦσι τῶν καλῶν, ἴσμεν τῷ δὴ τὸν ἐρῶντά τε
καὶ μὴ κρινοῦμεν; δεῖ αὖ νοῆσαι ὅτι ἡμῶν ἐν ἑκάστῳ
δύο τινέ ἐστον ἰδέα ἄρχοντε καὶ ἄγοντε, οἷν ἑπόμεθα ᾗ
ἂν ἄγητον, ἡ μὲν ἔμφυτος οὖσα ἐπιθυμία ἡδονῶν, ἄλλη
E δὲ ἐπίκτητος δόξα, ἐφιεμένη τοῦ ἀρίστου. τούτω δὲ ἐν
ἡμῖν τοτὲ μὲν ὁμονοεῖτον, ἔστι δὲ ὅτε στασιάζετον· καὶ
τοτὲ μὲν ἡ ἑτέρα, ἄλλοτε δὲ ἡ ἑτέρα κρατεῖ. δόξης μὲν
οὖν ἐπὶ τὸ ἄριστον λόγῳ ἀγούσης καὶ κρατούσης τῷ
238 κράτει σωφροσύνη ὄνομα· | ἐπιθυμίας δὲ ἀλόγως ἑλκούσης
ἐπὶ ἡδονὰς καὶ ἀρξάσης ἐν ἡμῖν τῇ ἀρχῇ ὕβρις ἐπωνο-
μάσθη. ὕβρις δὲ δὴ πολυώνυμον. πολυμελὲς γὰρ καὶ πολυειδές. καὶ τούτων τῶν ἰδεῶν ἐκπρεπὴς ἣ ἂν τύχῃ γενομένη, τὴν αὑτῆς ἐπωνυμίαν ὀνομαζόμενον τὸν ἔχοντα
παρέχεται, οὔ τέ τινα καλὴν οὔτε ἐπαξίαν κεκτῆσθαι
περὶ μὲν γὰρ ἐδωδὴν κρατοῦσα τοῦ τε λόγου τοῦ ἀρίστου
καὶ τῶν ἄλλων ἐπιθυμιῶν ἐπιθυμία γαστριμαργία τε, καὶ
τὸν ἔχοντα ταὐτὸν τοῦτο κεκλημένον παρέξεται· περὶ δ'
B αὖ μέθας τυραννεύσασα, τὸν κεκτημένον ταύτῃ ἄγουσα,
δῆλον οὗ τεύξεται προσρήματος· καὶ τἆλλα δὴ τὰ τούτων ἀδελφὰ καὶ ἀδελφῶν ἐπιθυμιῶν ὀνόματα, τῆς ἀεὶ
δυναστευούσης, ᾗ προσήκει καλεῖσθαι πρόδηλον. ἧς δ'

D *ἐπίκτητος δόξα, ἐφιεμένη τοῦ ἀρίστου*] Cous "*Le goût réfléchi du bien*" In 253 D the better horse is styled *ἀληθινῆς δόξης ἑταῖρος*

E *στασιάζετον*] The comparison of a mental struggle to a sedition or civil war is frequent in Plato as in Rep IV 442 E, (*φαμὲν τὸ θυμοειδὲς*) *ἐν τῇ τῆς ψυχῆς στάσει τίθεσθαι τὰ ὅπλα πρὸς τοῦ λογιστικοῦ*

238 *πολυμελές*] Vulg *πολυμερές πολυμελές*, which is the reading of the Bodl and others, is found also in Stobaeus, Flor II p 489 Gaist. The difference in sense is but slight Comp Politic 287 C, *κατὰ μέλη τοίνυν αὐτὰς οἷον ἱερεῖον διαιρώμεθα, ἐπειδὴ δίχα ἀδυνατοῦμεν*, where the speaker alludes to a classification similar to that which follows here.

καὶ τούτων—ἐκπρεπής, κ τ λ] "*Celle de ces formes qui se trouve le plus en évidence sert à qualifier la personne chez qui elle se manifeste*" Cous

ἐπαξίαν κεκτῆσθαι] Rep 367 C, *τῶν μεγίστων ἀγαθῶν, ἃ τῶν τε ἀποβαινόντων ἀπ' αὐτῶν ἕνεκα ἄξια κεκτῆσθαι, πολὺ δὲ μᾶλλον αὐτὰ αὑτῶν* Here ti 'no very valuable possession.' In the next clause *τῶν ἄλλων ἐπιθυμιῶν* means, of course, the appetites different from the 'ruling passion' which 'swallows all the rest' The 'reason of the best' nearly answers to the 'moral reason' of the moderns

B *τῆς ἀεὶ δυναστευούσης*] "Videtur requiri praepositio, ut ordo sit *πρόδηλον τὰ ὀνόματα καλεῖσθαι ἀπὸ τῆς ἀεὶ δυναστευούσης ᾗ προσήκει*" Buth Stallb., who adopts *ὃ* for *ᾗ* from a single MS of Stob considers the order to be, *πρόδηλον ὃ τῆς ἀεὶ δυναστευούσης (ὄνομα) προσήκει (τινὰ) καλεῖσθαι*, treating the former clause *καὶ τἆλλα δὴ τὰ τούτων ὀνόματα* as "absolute" If *ᾗ καλεῖσθαι* can be understood as *ὃ καλεῖσθαι* or

ἕνεκα πάντα τὰ πρόσθεν εἴρηται, σχεδὸν μὲν ἤδη φανερόν, λεχθὲν δὲ ἢ μὴ λεχθὲν πᾶν πως σαφέστερον. ἡ γὰρ ἄνευ λόγου δόξης ἐπὶ τὸ ὀρθὸν ὁρμώσης κρατήσασα ἐπιθυμία, πρὸς ἡδονὴν ἀχθεῖσα κάλλους, καὶ ὑπ' αὖ τῶν C
ἑαυτῆς συγγενῶν ἐπιθυμιῶν ἐπὶ σωμάτων κάλλος, ἐρρωμένως ῥωσθεῖσα νικήσασα ἀγωγῇ, ἀπ' αὐτῆς τῆς ῥώμης ἐπωνυμίαν λαβοῦσα, ἔρως ἐκλήθη.

Ἀτάρ, ὦ φίλε Φαῖδρε, δοκῶ τι σοί, ὥσπερ ἐμαυτῷ, θεῖον πάθος πεπονθέναι;

ΦΑΙ. Πάνυ μὲν οὖν, ὦ Σώκρατες, παρὰ τὸ εἰωθὸς εὔροιά τίς σε εἴληφεν.

ΣΩ. Σιγῇ τοίνυν μου ἄκουε. τῷ ὄντι γὰρ θεῖος ἔοικεν ὁ τόπος εἶναι. ὥστε ἐὰν ἄρα πολλάκις νυμφόληπτος προϊόν- D
τος τοῦ λόγου γένωμαι, μὴ θαυμάσῃς· τὰ νῦν γὰρ οὐκέτι πόρρω διθυράμβων φθέγγομαι.

ΦΑΙ. Ἀληθέστατα λέγεις.

ΣΩ. Τούτων μέντοι σὺ αἴτιος. ἀλλὰ τὰ λοιπὰ ἄκουε. ἴσως γὰρ κἂν ἀποτράποιτο τὸ ἐπιόν. ταῦτα μὲν οὖν θεῷ μελήσει, ἡμῖν δὲ πρὸς τὸν παῖδα πάλιν τῷ λόγῳ ἰτέον.

ὅπῃ καλεῖσθαι, perhaps τῆς ἀεὶ δυν. may be taken as epexegetic or limitary of the preceding ἐπιθυμιῶν, and equivalent to ἣ ἂν ἀεὶ δυναστεύῃ. The sense will thus be, 'there can be as little doubt as to the other names of the same class belonging to appetites akin to the two just mentioned, whichever of these may for the time be dominant, there can be no doubt, I say, how such names ought to be called,' "*quomodo nomina appellanda, h. e. ponenda sint*," as Ast renders it.

C. ἐρρωμένως ῥωσθεῖσα, κτλ] "In Trincav. Stob. abest ἐρρωμένως. Verba ἐρρωμένως κινήσασα (nam νικήσασα vitiosum est) interpretatio fuit participii ῥωσθεῖσα. Hesych. ῥώοντο· ὥρμουν, ἐρρωμένως ἐκινοῦντο." G. Hermann, MS. in mg. This is ingenious but not convincing. Hermeias reads nearly as in the text, but seems to have omitted ὑπ' αὖ and construed ἐπὶ σ. κάλλος with ἐρρωμένως ῥωσθεῖσα. For the sense see the paraphrase in note on 237 D.

D. ἐὰν ἄρα πολλάκις] 'if haply.' πολλάκις is frequently so used by Plato, with εἰ, εἰ δ' ἄρα, ἵνα μή, &c. So Thucyd. ii. 13, ὑποτοπήσας (ὁ Περικλῆς) μὴ πολλάκις (Ἀρχίδαμος) ἢ αὐτὸς ἰδίᾳ βουλόμενος χαρίζεσθαι τοὺς ἀγροὺς αὐτοῦ παραλίπῃ, κτλ.

νυμφόληπτος] On this and similar superstitions Lobeck remarks (Aglaoph. p. 641): "Horror quem vasti montes sylvaeque impenetrabiles, et solitudo ipsa errantibus offundere solent, in causa fuit, cur agrestia numina occursu suo obviam factos lymphare crederentur." He quotes J. Pollux i. 19, θεόληπτος, φοιβόληπτος, νυμφόληπτος, μουσόληπτος, ἐκ Πανὸς ἢ ἄλλου θεοῦ κάτοχος ἢ κατεχόμενος. Also Eur. Hipp. 141, σὺ γὰρ ἔνθεος, ὦ κούρα, εἴτ' ἐκ Πανός, κτλ. Festus identifies the νυμφόληπτοι with the Latin Lymphati, considering Lympha and Nympha to be the same. Hesych., in accordance with the present passage, has the gloss: Νυμφόληπτοι, οἱ κατεχόμενοι Νύμφαις, μάντεις δέ εἰσι καὶ ἐπιθειαστικοί. The Nymphs and Muses seem originally to have been the same. Hence the temple of the Muses Ilissides near the scene of this dialogue. Comp. infra, p. 278 B, and note.

ἀποτράποιτο] It is more proper to

Εἶεν, ὦ φέριστε. ὃ μὲν δὴ τυγχάνει ὂν περὶ οὗ βουλευτέον, εἴρηταί τε καὶ ὥρισται. βλέποντες δὲ δὴ πρὸς
E αὐτὸ τὰ λοιπὰ λέγωμεν, τίς ὠφέλεια ἢ βλάβη ἀπό τε ἐρῶντος καὶ μὴ τῷ χαριζομένῳ ἐξ εἰκότος συμβήσεται.

Τῷ δὴ ὑπὸ ἐπιθυμίας ἀρχομένῳ δουλεύοντί τε ἡδονῇ ἀνάγκη που τὸ ἐρώμενον ὡς ἥδιστον ἑαυτῷ παρασκευάζειν. νοσοῦντι δὲ πᾶν ἡδὺ τὸ μὴ ἀντιτεῖνον, κρεῖττον δὲ
239 καὶ ἴσον ἐχθρόν. οὔτε δὴ κρείττω | οὔτε ἰσούμενον ἑκὼν ἐραστὴς παιδικὰ ἀνέξεται, ἥττω δὲ καὶ ὑποδεέστερον ἀεὶ ἀπεργάζεται. ἥττων δὲ ἀμαθὴς σοφοῦ, δειλὸς ἀνδρείου, ἀδύνατος εἰπεῖν ῥητορικοῦ, βραδὺς ἀγχίνου. τοσούτων κακῶν καὶ ἔτι πλειόνων κατὰ τὴν διάνοιαν ἐραστὴν ἐρωμένῳ ἀνάγκη γιγνομένων τε καὶ φύσει ἐνόντων, τῶν μὲν ἥδεσθαι, τὰ δὲ παρασκευάζειν, ἢ στέρεσθαι τοῦ
B παραυτίκα ἡδέος. φθονερὸν δὴ ἀνάγκη εἶναι, καὶ πολλῶν μὲν ἄλλων συνουσιῶν ἀπείργοντα καὶ ὠφελίμων, ὅθεν ἂν μάλιστ' ἀνὴρ γίγνοιτο, μεγάλης αἴτιον εἶναι βλάβης, μεγίστης δὲ τῆς ὅθεν ἂν φρονιμώτατος εἴη. τοῦτο δὲ ἡ θεία φιλοσοφία τυγχάνει ὄν, ἧς ἐραστὴν παιδικὰ ἀνάγκη πόρ-

call this aor passive than middle Crat 395 B, ἡ πατρὶς αὐτοῦ ὅλη ἀνετράπετο So ἐσχόμην and its compounds are constantly used in strictly passive sense The general meaning is 'perhaps the madness with which I am threatened may even be averted,' as if by the agency of an ἀποτροπαῖος.

Εἶεν, ὦ φέριστε] Socr having settled with Phaedr to their mutual liking a definition of Love, proceeds to speculate on the probable results of such a passion to its object The Lover, according to the definition, is 'overmastered by lust and the bondslave of pleasure.' A person in this morbid condition will first try to extirpate all those nobler qualities and accomplishments which would be likely to indispose the beloved from hearkening to his suit He will tolerate no superiority, no equality even, in the object of his passion He will rather see him a dunce than a sage a coward than a hero; a stammerer rather than eloquent, slow rather than quick-witted 'So many and more besides are the mental defects which a lover must needs regard with pleasure if he see them implanted by nature in the beloved, and which, if acquired (γιγνομένων), he must seek to foster, or else forfeit the hope of present enjoyment.'

239 τῶν μὲν ἥδεσθαι] So Soph Phil 715, ὃς μηδ' οἰνοχύτου πώματος ἥσθη δεκέτει χρόνῳ, where Ellendt "Omnium optima interpretatio videtur ἀπέλαυσεν ὥστε ἥδεσθαι," which perhaps may be the force of the unusual construction here. I agree with Stallb in rejecting both the τοῖς μὲν of Heind and the κήδεσθαι of Hirschig G Herm. thinks that Plato meant to have written ἐνόντων ἥδεσθαι, and that τῶν μὲν was introduced on second thoughts to balance τὰ δὲ παρασκευάζειν Not in mg

B μεγίστης δέ, κ τ λ] An elliptical construction which may be thus supplied μεγίστης δέ (αἴτιον εἶναι βλάβης ἀπείργοντα) τῆς (συνουσίας) ὅθεν ἂν φρονιμώτατος εἴη The ἂν with εἴη is, as Stallb observes, indispensable 'that philosophic converse which will make him most intelligent' So βλαβερώτατος ἂν εἴη, 'he will be most mischievous,' i e. if the conditions named be complied with

ρωθεν εἴργειν, περίφοβον ὄντα τοῦ καταφρονηθῆναι· τά τε ἄλλα μηχανᾶσθαι ὅπως ἂν ᾖ πάντ' ἀγνοῶν καὶ πάντ' ἀποβλέπων εἰς τὸν ἐραστήν, οἷος ὢν τῷ μὲν ἥδιστος, ἑαυτῷ δὲ βλαβερώτατος ἂν εἴη. Τὰ μὲν οὖν κατὰ διά- C
νοιαν ἐπίτροπός τε καὶ κοινωνὸς οὐδαμῇ λυσιτελὴς ἀνὴρ ἔχων ἔρωτα.

Τὴν δὲ τοῦ σώματος ἕξιν τε καὶ θεραπείαν οἵαν τε καὶ ὡς θεραπεύσει οὗ ἂν γένηται κύριος, ὃς ἡδὺ πρὸ ἀγαθοῦ ἠνάγκασται διώκειν, δεῖ μετὰ ταῦτα ἰδεῖν. ὀφθήσεται δὲ μαλθακόν τινα καὶ οὐ στερεὸν διώκων, οὐδ' ἐν ἡλίῳ καθαρῷ τεθραμμένον ἀλλ' ὑπὸ συμμιγεῖ σκιᾷ, πόνων μὲν ἀνδρείων καὶ ἱδρώτων ξηρῶν ἄπειρον, ἔμπειρον δὲ ἁπαλῆς καὶ ἀνάνδρου διαίτης, ἀλλοτρίοις χρώμασι καὶ D
κόσμοις χήτει οἰκείων κοσμούμενον, ὅσα τε ἄλλα τούτοις ἕπεται, πάντα ἐπιτηδεύοντα. ἃ δῆλα· καὶ οὐκ ἄξιον περαιτέρω προβαίνειν, ἀλλ' ἓν κεφάλαιον ὁρισαμένους ἐπ' ἄλλο ἰέναι. τὸ γὰρ τοιοῦτον σῶμα ἐν πολέμῳ τε καὶ ἄλλαις χρείαις ὅσαι μεγάλαι οἱ μὲν ἐχθροὶ θαρροῦσιν, οἱ δὲ φίλοι καὶ αὐτοὶ οἱ ἐρασταὶ φοβοῦνται. Τοῦτο μὲν οὖν ὡς δῆλον ἐατέον.

C **Τὰ** *μὲν οὖν κατὰ διάνοιαν*] 'thus we see that in respect of his mental culture he can hardly have a less desirable guardian or companion (compare *ὁμιλία τε καὶ ἐπιτροπεία* inf. D) than a lover.' Having proved this, Socr. proceeds to show that the influence of a lover will be equally baneful as regards, 1. the physical condition, 2. the estate of the *παιδικά*. As regards the first, the lover will prefer an effeminate weakling to a manly and robust person—one bred in the chequered shade to a youth hardened by exposure to the clear sunshine, &c. Observe that the mark of effeminacy among the Greeks is intolerance of heat, not, as in more northern climates, of cold. Eur. Bacch. 456, *Λευκὴν δὲ χροιὰν εἰς παρασκευὴν ἔχεις Οὐχ ἡλίου βολαῖσιν, ἀλλ' ὑπὸ σκιᾶς, Τὴν Ἀφροδίτην καλλονῇ θηρώμενος*. Ast quotes Rep. VIII 556 D, *ὅταν* ... *ἰσχνὸς ἀνὴρ πένης, ἡλιωμένος, παραταχθεὶς ἐν μάχῃ πλουσίῳ ἐσκιατραφηκότι, πολλὰς ἔχοντι σάρκας ἀλλοτρίας, ἴδῃ ἄσθματός τε καὶ ἀπορίας μεστόν, κ.τ.λ.* and for *συμμιγεῖ σκιᾷ*, Pers. Sat. V 60 Tunc crassos transisse dies, *lucemque palustrem*, which however is hardly to the point. The modern Italians have a proverb, 'Dove non entra il sole, entra il medico.' On *συμμιγεῖ σκιᾷ* G. Herm. remarks, "oppositum *ἡλίῳ καθαρῷ*, ut solis lux commixta cum umbra intelligatur." MS. ubi supra.

ἱδρώτων ξηρῶν] Herm. *ἱδρῶτας ξηροὺς λέγει τοὺς ἀπὸ γυμνασίων* ... *εἶεν δ' ἂν ὑγροὶ ἱδρῶτες οἱ ἀπὸ λουτρῶν*. Hence the compound *ξηραλοιφεῖν* explained by Harpocrat. *τὸ χωρὶς λουτρῶν ἀλείφεσθαι*.

D *ἀλλοτρίοις χρώμασι*] 'with false or artificial colours and ornaments, for lack of such as are native.' Comp. Gorg. 165 B, *σχήμασι καὶ χρώμασι καὶ λειότησι καὶ ἐσθῆσιν ἀπατῶσα, ὥστε ποιεῖν ἀλλότριον κάλλος ἐφελκομένους τοῦ οἰκείου τοῦ διὰ τῆς γυμναστικῆς ἀμελεῖν*. *χήτει* (used only in the dative sing.) is a Homeric word first introduced into prose by Plato. Hesych., *χήτει, στερήσει, ἐνδείᾳ, σπάνει*. Plutarch (Mor. 51 D) quotes this passage from the Phaedr., substituting however *σχήμασιν* for the *κόσμοις* of the received text, apparently by a slip of memory.

Τὸ δ' ἐφεξῆς ῥητέον, τίνα ἡμῖν ὠφέλειαν ἢ τίνα βλάβην
E περὶ τὴν κτῆσιν ἡ τοῦ ἐρῶντος ὁμιλία τε καὶ ἐπιτροπεία παρέξεται. σαφὲς δὴ τοῦτό γε παντὶ μέν, μάλιστα δὲ τῷ ἐραστῇ, ὅτι τῶν φιλτάτων τε καὶ εὐνουστάτων καὶ θειοτάτων κτημάτων ὀρφανὸν πρὸ παντὸς εὔξαιτ' ἂν εἶναι τὸν ἐρώμενον. πατρὸς γὰρ καὶ μητρὸς καὶ ξυγγενῶν καὶ φίλων στέρεσθαι ἂν αὐτὸν δέξαιτο, διακωλυτὰς καὶ ἐπιτιμητὰς
240 ἡγούμενος τῆς ἡδίστης | πρὸς αὐτὸν ὁμιλίας. ἀλλὰ μὴν GP 34
οὐσίαν γ' ἔχοντα χρυσοῦ ἢ τινος ἄλλης κτήσεως οὔτ' εὐάλωτον ὁμοίως οὔτε ἁλόντα εὐμεταχείριστον ἡγήσεται. ἐξ ὧν πᾶσ' ἀνάγκη ἐραστὴν παιδικοῖς φθονεῖν μὲν οὐσίαν κεκτημένοις, ἀπολλυμένης δὲ χαίρειν. ἔτι τοίνυν ἄγαμον, ἄπαιδα, ἄοικον ὅ τι πλεῖστον χρόνον παιδικὰ ἐραστὴς εὔξαιτ' ἂν γενέσθαι, τὸ αὑτοῦ γλυκὺ ὡς πλεῖστον χρόνον καρποῦσθαι ἐπιθυμῶν.

B Ἔστι μὲν δὴ καὶ ἄλλα κακά, ἀλλά τις δαίμων ἔμιξε τοῖς πλείστοις ἐν τῷ παραυτίκα ἡδονήν. οἷον κόλακι, δεινῷ θηρίῳ καὶ βλάβῃ μεγάλῃ, ὅμως ἐπέμιξεν ἡ φύσις ἡδονήν τινα οὐκ ἄμουσον. καί τις ἑταίραν ὡς βλαβερὸν ψέξειεν ἄν, καὶ ἄλλα πολλὰ τῶν τοιουτοτρόπων θρεμμάτων τε καὶ ἐπιτηδευμάτων, οἷς τό γε καθ' ἡμέραν ἡδί-
C στοισιν εἶναι ὑπάρχει. παιδικοῖς δὲ ἐραστὴς πρὸς τῷ βλαβερῷ καὶ εἰς τὸ συνημερεύειν πάντων ἀηδέστατον. ἥλικα γὰρ καὶ ὁ παλαιὸς λόγος, τέρπειν τὸν ἥλικα· ἡ γάρ, οἶμαι, Diogen Cent Paroem p 253
χρόνου ἰσότης ἐπ' ἴσας ἡδονὰς ἄγουσα δι' ὁμοιότητα φιλίαν παρέχεται· ἀλλ' ὅμως κόρον γε καὶ ἡ τούτων συνου-

240 B Ἔστι μὲν δή, κ τ λ] Having shown that the relation of ἐραστής and παιδικὰ is injurious to the latter both in mind, body, and estate, Socr proceeds to show that it is attended with no compensating pleasures, like those which a κόλαξ or ἑταίρα may be supposed to offer An ἐραστής is in fact the most disgusting of all companions, &c

οἷον κόλακι, δεινῷ θηρίῳ καὶ βλάβῃ μεγάλῃ] Athen vi 254 C, (οἱ κόλακες) ζῶντας ἔτι τοὺς ἀγαθοὺς τῶν ἀνδρῶν κατεσθίουσι φησὶ γοῦν Ἀναξίλας· Οἱ κόλακές εἰσι τῶν ἐχόντων οὐσίας Σκώληκες, κ τ λ The κόλαξ of the old and middle comedy is identical with the παράσιτος of later times One of his qualifications was the possession of a ready wit So Eupolis (Κόλακες, ap Athen l. l. 236 F), δεῖ χαρίεντα πολλὰ Τὸν κόλακ' εὐθέως λέγειν, ἢ φέρεται θύραζε This is probably the ἡδονὴ οὐκ ἄμουσος to which Plato alludes

ἡδίστοισιν] This Ionic or old Attic dat occurs repeatedly in Plato as inf p 276, ἐν ἡμέραισιν ὀκτώ 278, ἄλλαισιν Inferior MSS frequently give the common form instead

C. ἥλικα γάρ] Schol τὸ τέλειον ἔχει Ἧλιξ ἥλικα τέρπε, γέρων δέ τε τέρπε γέροντα After γὰρ Stob inserts δή, and is followed by G Hermann

Isch

σία ἔχει. καὶ μὴν τό γε ἀναγκαῖον αὖ βαρὺ παντὶ περὶ πᾶν λέγεται· ὃ δὴ πρὸς τῇ ἀνομοιότητι μάλιστ' ἐραστὴς πρὸς παιδικὰ ἔχει. νεωτέρῳ γὰρ πρεσβύτερος συνὼν οὔθ' ἡμέρας οὔτε νυκτὸς ἑκὼν ἀπολείπεται, ἀλλ' ὑπ' ἀνάγκης τε καὶ οἴστρου ἐλαύνεται, ὃς ἐκείνῳ μὲν ἡδονὰς ἀεὶ διδοὺς D
ἄγει, ὁρῶντι, ἀκούοντι, ἁπτομένῳ καὶ πᾶσαν αἴσθησιν αἰσθανομένῳ τοῦ ἐρωμένου, ὥστε μεθ' ἡδονῆς ἀραρότως αὐτῷ ὑπηρετεῖν· τῷ δὲ δὴ ἐρωμένῳ ποῖον παραμύθιον ἢ τίνας ἡδονὰς διδοὺς ποιήσει τὸν ἴσον χρόνον συνόντα μὴ οὐχὶ ἐπ' ἔσχατον ἐλθεῖν ἀηδίας; ὁρῶντι μὲν ὄψιν πρεσβυτέραν καὶ οὐκ ἐν ὥρᾳ, ἑπομένων δὲ τῶν ἄλλων ταύτῃ, ἃ καὶ λόγῳ ἐστὶν ἀκούειν οὐκ ἐπιτερπές, μὴ ὅτι δὴ ἔργῳ E
ἀνάγκης ἀεὶ προσκειμένης μεταχειρίζεσθαι· φυλακάς τε δὴ καχυποτόπους φυλαττομένῳ διὰ παντὸς καὶ πρὸς ἅπαντας, ἀκαίρους τε ἐπαίνους καὶ ὑπερβάλλοντας ἀκούοντι, ὡς δ' αὔτως ψόγους νήφοντος μὲν οὐκ ἀνεκτούς, εἰς δὲ μέθην ἰόντος, πρὸς τῷ μὴ ἀνεκτῷ ἐπαισχεῖς, παρρησίᾳ κατακορεῖ καὶ ἀναπεπταμένῃ χρωμένου.

D *μὴ οὐχί*] These particles occur together in an interrogative sentence Phaed 72 D, *τίς μηχανὴ μὴ οὐχὶ πάντα καταναλωθῆναι εἰς τὸ τεθνάναι*, and Symp 197 A, *τίς ἐναντιώσεται μὴ οὐχὶ Ἔρωτος εἶναι σοφίαν* In all such cases the sentence is virtually negative

E *φυλακάς τε δὴ καχυποτόπους*] 'being ever watched with the most jealous vigilance' *καχυπόπτους* is preferred by Ast, who cites Rep. iii. 509 c But the Bodl and the majority of MSS support the reading in the text, which is further confirmed by the Lexicographers In Aristoph Ran 958, on the other hand, there can be little doubt that *κάχ' ὑποτοπεῖσθαι* is the true reading, not *καχυποτοπεῖσθαι*, as generally given, and as quoted here by Stallb

ἀκαίρους τε ἐπαίνους] Bodl *ἀκαίρους τε καὶ ἐπαίνους καὶ ὑπερβάλλοντας*, which Stallb., strange to say, admits into his text, not perceiving that the *καὶ* is a remnant of another reading *ἀκαίρους τε καὶ ἐγκαίρους ἐπαίνους*, found in five MSS With equal want of tact he rejects the excellent emendation of Heind., *ἐπαισχεῖς* for the vulg *ἐπ' αἴσχει*, which means next to nothing In this, however, he is supported by his own countrymen, and even by Hirschig The symmetry of the sentence is evidently incomplete without an epithet to answer to *οὐκ ἀνεκτούς*, and though *ἐπαισχής* is not found in any other extant Attic writer, it is acknowledged by Suid., who has the gloss, *ἐπαισχές, αἰσχύνης παραίτιον κἀμοὶ μὲν ἐπαισχές ἐστι τὸ πρᾶγμα καὶ βλαβερόν, κἀκείνῳ πολὺ αἴσχιον καὶ βλαβερώτερον, κ τ λ* The clause may be thus rendered 'He will likewise have to listen to taunts hard to bear even when the lover is sober, but when he gets drunk as indelicate as they are intolerable'

κατακορεῖ] 'fastidium movente,' like the "fastidiosa copia" of Horace Suid *ἀπλήστω.*

ἀναπεπταμένῃ] 'broad,' 'undisguised.' frequently used in this sense by Plutarch and other imitators of Plato "*παρρησία* dicitur *ἀναπεπταμένη* quae nihil non aperiens ipsa clandestina amoris gaudia effutit. Hinc *τὰ ἀναπεπτάμενα* in universum modestiae decoraeque temperantiae opponuntur, ut Xenoph. Mem ii 1 22, de muliere voluptaria *τὰ δὲ ὄμματα ἔχειν ἀναπεπτάμενα*" Ast. Comp Plut Sympos 712, *ἥ τε πρὸς τὰ σκώμματα καὶ βωμολοχίας εὐχέρεια, δεινῶς κατάκορος*

Καὶ ἐρῶν μὲν βλαβερός τε καὶ ἀηδής, λήξας δὲ τοῦ ἔρωτος εἰς τὸν ἔπειτα χρόνον ἄπιστος, εἰς ὃν πολλὰ καὶ μετὰ πολλῶν ὅρκων τε καὶ δεήσεων ὑπισχνούμενος, μόγις
241 κατεῖχε τὴν ἐν τῷ τότε | ξυνουσίαν ἐπίπονον οὖσαν φέρειν δι' ἐλπίδα ἀγαθῶν. τότε δὴ δέον ἐκτίνειν, μεταλαβὼν ἄλλον ἄρχοντα ἐν αὑτῷ καὶ προστάτην, νοῦν καὶ σωφροσύνην ἀντ' ἔρωτος καὶ μανίας, ἄλλος γεγονὼς λέληθε τὰ παιδικά. καὶ ὁ μὲν αὐτὸν χάριν ἀπαιτεῖ τῶν τότε, ὑπομιμνήσκων τὰ πραχθέντα καὶ λεχθέντα, ὡς τῷ αὐτῷ διαλεγόμενος· ὁ δὲ ὑπ' αἰσχύνης οὔτε εἰπεῖν τολμᾷ ὅτι ἄλλος γέγονεν, οὔθ' ὅπως τὰ τῆς προτέρας ἀνοήτου ἀρχῆς ὁρ-
B κωμόσιά τε καὶ ὑποσχέσεις ἐμπεδώσει ἔχει, νοῦν ἤδη ἐσχηκὼς καὶ σεσωφρονηκώς, ἵνα μὴ πράττων ταὐτὰ τῷ πρόσθεν ὅμοιός τε ἐκείνῳ καὶ ὁ αὐτὸς πάλιν γένηται. φυγὰς δὴ γίγνεται ἐκ τούτων, καὶ ἀπεστερηκὼς ὑπ' ἀνάγκης ὁ πρὶν ἐραστής, ὀστράκου μεταπεσόντος, ἵεται φυγῇ μετα-

καὶ ἀναπεπταμένη, καὶ γέμουσα ῥημάτων ἀκόσμων καὶ ἀκολάστων ὀνομάτων.

Καὶ ἐρῶν μέν, κ τ λ] Socr puts the finishing strokes to the picture, by describing the bad faith and ingratitude of the ἐραστὴς when his passion cools.

εἰς ὃν] 'for which (time) he had to make many a fair promise &c, and even so could with difficulty maintain an intimacy which even in those days was as much as the beloved could support, in consideration of future benefit.'

241 μεταλαβών] The MSS vary between μεταλαβὼν and μεταβαλών, as they very frequently do in the case of λαβεῖν, βαλεῖν, and their compounds. μεταλαβών, the reading of Bekk. and Ast, is abundantly defended by such passages as Thuc i 120, πόλεμον ἀντ' εἰρήνης μεταλαμβάνειν· Rep. iv 434 B, ὅταν τὰ ἀλλήλων ὄργανα μεταλαμβάνωσι. Theaet 172 D, λόγον ἐκ λόγου μεταλαμβάνομεν. On the other hand, μεταβαλὼν may be defended by Rep iv. 424 C, εἶδος καινὸν μουσικῆς μεταβάλλειν, &c, quoted by Stallb, who draws a distinction without much practical difference between the two verbs and their signification. The analogy of the Latin *muto* seems to extend to both.

οὔθ' ὅπως, κ τ λ] 'nor can he find the means of ratifying (redeeming) the solemn protestations and promises made under the old irrational régime,' "*sous l'empire de sa folle passion*." Cous. Comp supr μεταλαβὼν ἄλλον ἄρχοντα ἀντ' ἔρωτος καὶ μανίας. For ἐμπεδώσει the Bodl. and others have ἐμπεδώσῃ, which Stallb is inclined to adopt. But comp Soph O C 1739, ὅπως μολούμεθ' ἐς δόμους οὐκ ἔχω. Arist Plut 18, ἐγὼ μὲν οὖν οὐκ ἔσθ' ὅπως σιγήσομαι. These two passages are also sufficient to refute the arbitrary canon of Cobet, V. Ll. p. 105, "ὅπως, ὅστις, ὅτι, et sim habent conjunctivum ubi praecessit negatio," &c.

B ἀπεστερηκὼς ὑπ' ἀνάγκης] 'a constrained defaulter,' 'a traitor to his engagements,' 'a repudiator.' So Isocr Panath 283 D, τοὺς ἀποστεροῦντας τὰ συμβόλαια. ὁ πρὶν ἐραστής—he, the sometime lover. Hirsch's alteration ἀπεστυγηκὼς seems uncalled for, though it was anticipated by G. Hermann.

ὀστράκου μεταπεσόντος] The allusion is to the game called ὀστρακίνδα, described by Plato Comicus in the following fragm. quoted by Hermeias: Εἴξασιν γὰρ τοῖς παιδαρίοις τούτοις οἳ ἑκάστοτε γραμμὴν Ἐν ταῖσιν ὁδοῖς διαγράψαντες διανειμάμενοι δίχ' ἑαυτοὺς Ἑστᾶσ', αὐτῶν οἱ μὲν ἐκεῖθεν τῆς γραμμῆς, οἱ δ' ἄρ' ἐκεῖθεν. Εἷς δ' ἀμφοτέρων ὄστρακον αὐτοῖς εἰς μέσον ἑστὼς ἀνίησιν. Κἂν μὲν πίπτῃ τἄλλευκ' ἐπάνω, φεύγειν ταχὺ τοὺς ἑτέρους δεῖ, Τοὺς δὲ διώκειν. (I

βαλών· ὁ δὲ ἀναγκάζεται διώκειν ἀγανακτῶν καὶ ἐπιθεάζων, ἠγνοηκὼς τὸ ἅπαν ἐξ ἀρχῆς, ὅτι οὐκ ἄρα ἔδει ποτὲ ἐρῶντι καὶ ὑπ' ἀνάγκης ἀνοήτῳ χαρίζεσθαι, ἀλλὰ πολὺ C
μᾶλλον μὴ ἐρῶντι καὶ νοῦν ἔχοντι· εἰ δὲ μή, ἀναγκαῖον εἴη ἐνδοῦναι ἑαυτὸν ἀπίστῳ, δυσκόλῳ, φθονερῷ, ἀηδεῖ, βλαβερῷ μὲν πρὸς οὐσίαν, βλαβερῷ δὲ πρὸς τὴν τοῦ σώματος ἕξιν, πολὺ δὲ βλαβερωτάτῳ πρὸς τὴν τῆς ψυχῆς παίδευσιν, ἧς οὔτε ἀνθρώποις οὔτε θεοῖς τῇ ἀληθείᾳ τιμιώτερον οὔτε ἔστιν οὔτε ποτὲ ἔσται. Ταῦτά τε οὖν χρή, ὦ παῖ, ξυννοεῖν, καὶ εἰδέναι τὴν ἐραστοῦ φιλίαν, ὅτι οὐ μετ' εὐνοίας γίγνεται, ἀλλὰ σιτίου τρόπον, χάριν πλησμονῆς,

Ὡς λύκοι ἄρν' ἀγαπῶσ', ὣς παῖδα φιλοῦσιν ἐρασταί. D

Τοῦτ' ἐκεῖνο, ὦ Φαῖδρε, οὐκέτ' ἂν τὸ πέρα ἀκούσαις ἐμοῦ λέγοντος, ἀλλ' ἤδη σοι τέλος ἐχέτω ὁ λόγος.

ΦΑΙ. Καίτοι ᾤμην γε μεσοῦν αὐτόν, καὶ ἐρεῖν τὰ ἴσα περὶ τοῦ μὴ ἐρῶντος, ὡς δεῖ ἐκείνῳ χαρίζεσθαι μᾶλλον, λέγων ὅσ' αὖ ἔχει ἀγαθά. νῦν δὲ δή, ὦ Σώκρατες, τί ἀποπαύει;

ΣΩ. Οὐκ ᾔσθου, ὦ μακάριε, ὅτι ἤδη ἔπη φθέγγομαι, E
ἀλλ' οὐκέτι διθυράμβους, καὶ ταῦτα ψέγων, ἐὰν δ' ἐπαινεῖν τὸν ἕτερον ἄρξωμαι, τί με οἴει ποιήσειν; ἆρ' οἶσθ' ὅτι

have given τἄλλευκ', sc. τὰ ἔλλευκα, for the τὰ λευκὰ of Herm. See L. Dindorf in Steph. Lex. v. ἔλλευκος. Meineke gives πίπτησι τὰ λευκ'.)

ἐπιθεάζων] So Bekk. The Bodl. and several others have ἐπιθειάζων, adopted by Stallb. But ἐπιθεάζων is the true Attic form, as appears from Pherecrates, Com. ap. Suid., ὕστερον ἀρᾶται κἀπιθεάζει τῷ πατρί, as now read, instead of the unmetrical κἀπιθειάζει. Hesych. too and the Gramm. are generally in favour of this form. See Blomf. ad Choeph. 813. Hesych. ἐπιθεάζει· θεοὺς ἐπικαλεῖται.

C. εἰ δὲ μή, ἀναγκαῖον εἴη, κ. τ. λ.] 'else must he needs surrender himself to one as false as he is morose, jealous and disagreeable,' &c. εἴη is in the sermo obliquus dependent on the foregoing ὅτι.

ἀλλὰ σιτίου τρόπον, χάριν πλησμονῆς] These words, as Stallb. explains, are not to be taken with γίγνεται, but with the φιλοῦσιν of the following line. The same sentiment occurs Xen. Conv. viii. 15, ἅπερ πρὸς τὰ σιτία διὰ πλησμονὴν ἀνάγκη καὶ πρὸς τὰ παιδικὰ πάσχειν. The hexameter line is doubtless Plato's, as appears from the exclamation of Socr., τοῦτ' ἐκεῖνο! 'I told you so,' viz. that I was in danger of an access of νυμφοληψία: 'and behold already, not content with dithyrambs, I have got into heroics.' For τοῦτ' ἐκεῖνο comp. Ar. Ach. 41, τοῦτ' ἐκεῖν' οὑγὼ 'λεγον.

D. Ὡς λύκοι ἄρν' ἀγαπῶσ'] Hence the happy compound λυκοφιλία, by which the intercourse of Plato with Dionysius II. is characterized, Epist. iii. p. 318 E, τὴν ἐμὴν καὶ σὴν λυκοφιλίαν καὶ ἀκοινωνίαν.

E. ἤδη ἔπη φθέγγομαι, κ. τ. λ.] See Hom. Il. xxii. 262, 3.

ὑπὸ τῶν Νυμφῶν, αἷς με σὺ προὔβαλες ἐκ προνοίας, σαφῶς ἐνθουσιάσω, λέγω οὖν ἐνὶ λόγῳ ὅτι, ὅσα τὸν ἕτερον λελοιδορήκαμεν, τῷ ἑτέρῳ τἀναντία τούτων ἀγαθὰ πρόσεστι καὶ τί δεῖ μακροῦ λόγου, περὶ γὰρ ἀμφοῖν ἱκανῶς εἴρηται. καὶ οὕτω δὴ ὁ μῦθος, ὅ τι πάσχειν προσήκει αὐτῷ, τοῦτο πείσεται· κἀγὼ τὸν ποταμὸν | τοῦτον διαβὰς ἀπέρχομαι, πρὶν ὑπὸ σοῦ τι μεῖζον ἀναγκασθῆναι.

ΦΑΙ. Μήπω γε, ὦ Σώκρατες, πρὶν ἂν τὸ καῦμα παρέλθῃ. ἢ οὐχ ὁρᾷς ὡς σχεδὸν ἤδη μεσημβρία ἵσταται ἡ δὴ καλουμένη σταθερά; ἀλλὰ περιμείναντες, καὶ ἅμα περὶ τῶν εἰρημένων διαλεχθέντες, τάχ' ἐπειδὰν ἀποψυχῇ ἴμεν.

ΣΩ. Θεῖός γ' εἶ περὶ τοὺς λόγους, ὦ Φαῖδρε, καὶ ἀτεχνῶς θαυμάσιος. οἶμαι γὰρ ἐγὼ τῶν ἐπὶ τοῦ σοῦ βίου γεγονότων μηδένα πλείους ἢ σὲ πεποιηκέναι γεγενῆσθαι ἤτοι αὐτὸν λέγοντα ἢ ἄλλους ἐνί γέ τῳ τρόπῳ προσαναγκάζοντα Σιμμίαν Θηβαῖον ἐξαιρῶ λόγου· τῶν δὲ ἄλλων

σαφῶς ἐνθουσιάσω] Crat 396 D, *καὶ μὲν δή, ὦ Σώκρατες, ἀτεχνῶς γέ μοι δοκεῖς ὥσπερ οἱ ἐνθουσιῶντες ἐξαίφνης χρησμῳδεῖν* The verb *προβάλλειν*, p sup occurs in much the same sense in Eur Rhes 183, *ψυχὴν προβάλλων ἐν κύβοισι δαίμονος* Soph Oed T 754, *ἔοικ' ἐμαυτὸν εἰς ἀρὰς Δεινὰς προβάλλων ἀρτίως οὐκ εἰδέναι*

242 *μεσημβρία ἵσταται ἡ δὴ καλουμένη σταθερά*] The adj *σταθερὸς* being derived from *ἵστασθαι*, Heind is offended by the tautology, and ejects the words *ἡ δὴ καλουμένη στ* as a "Grammatici additamentum" To this Stallb replies (not without naiveté) that it is very common to find clauses in the text of Plato which have all the appearance of glosses I confess that Heind.'s suspicion appears to me but too probable, though I have not ventured, in the face of the testimonies appealed to by Ast, to bracket the questionable words *ἤδη μεσημβρία ἵσταται* means already, 'it is now high noon,' and *σταθερὰ* adds nothing to the idea Unless indeed we suppose that Plato fancies that *σταθερὸς* is derived from *σταθεύω*, a supposition not perhaps altogether inadmissible, considering the general character of his etymologies The word occurs Aesch fr *ψυχαγωγ*, quoted by Phot and Suid. *σταθεροῦ χεύματος*, which Phot exp by *στασίμου*, adding *καὶ Ἀριστοφάνης ἐν προαγῶνι Σταθερὰ δὲ κάλυξ νεαρᾶς ἥβης*, where it must mean 'full-blown,' rather than 'abiding,' *μονίμου*, as Phot interprets In Antimachus, as quoted *ibid*, we have *θέρεος σταθεροῖο* for 'midsummer,' or the 'summer *solstice*' "Graeci omnia quae nondum ad finem vel senectutem vergunt *ἵστασθαι* dicunt Hinc *σταθερὸς* *firmus, florens*, et *χρόνος ἱστάμενος* Nic Theriac, *ἠελίοιο θερειτάτη ἵσταται ἀκτίς*" Ruhnk ad Tim in v *σταθερά*, q v. Dind (in Steph Lex vii p 641) agrees with Ruhnk and Heind. in ejecting the obnoxious word

τάχ' ἐπειδὰν ἀποψυχῇ ἴμεν] Bekk Anecd i p 26, quoted by Ast, *ὅταν τὸ καῦμα λήγῃ καὶ εἰς ψῦχος τρέπηται Πλάτων ἐν Φαίδρῳ ἐπειδὰν ἀποψύχῃ ἄπιμεν* Some MSS have *ἀποψύξῃ*, and so Hirschig But *ἀποψυχῇ*, the 2nd aor conj is the true reading Hesych *ἀπεψύχη, ἀπεπνευματίσθη Αἰσχύλος Κερκύωνι σατ* Arist Nub 151, *ψυχείσῃ περιέφυσαν Περσικαί*, vulg *ψυγείσῃ* *τάχ' ἐπειδὰν* is equivalent to *ἐπειδὰν τάχιστα*

B *Σιμμίαν Θηβαῖον ἐξαιρῶ λόγου*] 'I strike out of the account,' i e make an

πάμπολυ κρατεῖς. καὶ νῦν αὖ δοκεῖς αἴτιός μοι γεγενῆσθαι λόγῳ τινὶ ῥηθῆναι.

ΦΑΙ. Οὐ πόλεμόν γε ἀγγέλλεις. ἀλλὰ πῶς δὴ καὶ τίνι τούτῳ;

ΣΩ. Ἡνίκ᾽ ἔμελλον, ὦ ᾽γαθέ, τὸν ποταμὸν διαβαίνειν, τὸ δαιμόνιόν τε καὶ τὸ εἰωθὸς σημεῖόν μοι γίγνεσθαι ἐγένετο—ἀεὶ δέ με ἐπίσχει, ὃ ἂν μέλλω πράττειν—, C
καί τινα φωνὴν ἔδοξα αὐτόθεν ἀκοῦσαι, ἥ με οὐκ ἐᾷ ἀπιέναι πρὶν ἂν ἀφοσιώσωμαι, ὥς τι ἡμαρτηκότα εἰς τὸ θεῖον. εἰμὶ δὴ οὖν μάντις μέν, οὐ πάνυ δὲ σπουδαῖος, ἀλλ᾽ ὥσπερ οἱ τὰ γράμματα φαῦλοι, ὅσον μὲν ἐμαυτῷ μόνον ἱκανός. σαφῶς οὖν ἤδη μανθάνω τὸ ἁμάρτημα,

exception in favour of, 'Simmias of Thebes' Theaet 162 D, (τοὺς θεούς) ἔκ τε τοῦ λέγειν καὶ τοῦ γράφειν περὶ αὐτῶν, ὡς εἰσὶν ἢ ὡς οὐκ εἰσίν, ἐξαιρῶ. The φιλολογία of Simmias is avowed by himself, Phaed 85 C, τὸ μέντοι τὰ λεγόμενα μὴ οὐχὶ παντὶ τρόπῳ ἐλέγχειν, καὶ μὴ προαφίστασθαι, πρὶν ἂν πανταχῇ σκοπῶν ἀπείπῃ τις, πάνυ μαλθακοῦ εἶναι ἀνδρός. In the Crito he is said to have offered a sum sufficient to procure the liberation of Socr, p 45 B. He and his inseparable friend Cebes are mentioned in the 13th Platonic Epistle, p. 363. They are both called νεάνισκοι in the Phaedo. The mention of Simmias in the Phaedrus may therefore be thought an argument against its early composition, for we can hardly suppose that he and Cebes visited Athens and became known to Socr before the termination of the Peloponnesian War, intercourse between Athens and Thebes being inconceivable during the continuance of hostilities.

γεγενῆσθαι] Badh. cj γενήσεσθαι. For the dat λόγῳ τινὶ comp Crat 116 D.

τὸ δαιμόνιόν τε καὶ τὸ εἰωθὸς σημεῖον] It is clear from this passage that the δαιμόνιον of Socr was a thing and not a person. The φωνὴ which he 'thought he heard' came αὐτόθεν, 'from the source in question,' viz. a supernatural source, divinitus exorta, as Apuleius, de Deo Socratis, expresses it. All the Platonic passages relating to the δαιμόνιον restrict it to the merely prohibitory action implied in the passage before ... μένη, ἣ ὅταν γένηται, ἀεὶ ἀποτρέπει με τούτου ὃ ἂν μέλλω πράττειν, προτρέπει δὲ οὔποτε. So Cic de Divin i. 54, "divinum quiddam quod daemonium appellat, cui semper ipse paruerit, nunquam impellenti, saepe revocanti." The clause ἀεὶ δέ μ᾽ ἐπίσχει ὃ ἂν μέλλω πράττειν, if taken literally, implies much more than this, and Heind and Hirsch would expel it accordingly. ἀεὶ may however have the sense of ἑκάστοτε, so that ὅταν γένηται shall be implied. 'Every time (it occurs) it restrains me from the thing, whatever it be, that I intend doing.' On the other hand, there seems no sufficient motive for this voluntary piece of information, and we may easily comprehend how the clause might be introduced by a copyist, mindful of the passage in the Apology from which the fabricator of the spurious Theages apparently took his circumstantial statement (Theag 128 D). There is some difficulty in reconciling the testimony of Plato and Xenophon on the subject of this δαιμόνιον. Those interested in the question will do well to consult Kuhner's preface to his edition of the Memorabilia, p. 18 seq. On the confusion of δαιμόνιον and δαίμων by later writers, the reader is referred to a note on A Butler's Lectures on Philosophy, vol i p 375.

C ἥ με οὐκ ἐᾷ] The voice, he says, forbade him to depart before he had made his peace with heaven. His own power of divination, though limited, was sufficient to reveal to him the nature of this offence. Herm, ἀφοσίωσις, ὁσι-[illegible] [illegible] ἀποπλήρωσις

ὡς δή τοι, ὦ ἑταῖρε, μαντικόν γέ τι καὶ ἡ ψυχή. ἐμὲ γὰρ ἔθραξε μέν τι καὶ πάλαι λέγοντα τὸν λόγον, καί πως
D ἐδυσωπούμην κατ' Ἴβυκον, μή τι παρὰ θεοῖς ἀμβλακὼν τιμὰν πρὸς ἀνθρώπων ἀμείψω· νῦν δ' ᾔσθημαι τὸ ἁμάρτημα.

ΦΑΙ. Λέγεις δὲ δὴ τί;

ΣΩ. Δεινόν, ὦ Φαῖδρε, δεινὸν λόγον αὐτός τε ἐκόμισας ἐμέ τε ἠνάγκασας εἰπεῖν.

ΦΑΙ. Πῶς δή;

ΣΩ. Εὐήθη καὶ ὑπό τι ἀσεβῆ· οὗ τίς ἂν εἴη δεινότερος;

ΦΑΙ. Οὐδείς, εἴ γε σὺ ἀληθῆ λέγεις.

ΣΩ. Τί οὖν; τὸν Ἔρωτα οὐκ Ἀφροδίτης καὶ θεόν τινα ἡγεῖ;

ΦΑΙ. Λέγεταί γε δή.

ΣΩ. Οὔ τι ὑπό γε Λυσίου, οὐδὲ ὑπὸ τοῦ σοῦ λόγου,
E ὃς διὰ τοῦ ἐμοῦ στόματος καταφαρμακευθέντος ὑπὸ σοῦ ἐλέχθη. εἰ δ' ἔστιν, ὥσπερ οὖν ἔστι, θεὸς ἤ τι θεῖον ὁ Ἔρως, οὐδὲν ἂν κακὸν εἴη· τὼ δὲ λόγω τὼ νῦν δὴ περὶ αὐτοῦ εἰπέτην ὡς τοιούτου ὄντος. ταύτῃ τε οὖν ἡμαρτανέτην περὶ τὸν Ἔρωτα, ἔτι τε ἡ εὐήθεια αὐτοῖν πάνυ ἀστεία, τὸ μηδὲν ὑγιὲς λέγοντε μηδὲ ἀληθὲς σεμνύνεσθαι
213 ὥς τι ὄντε, εἰ ἄρα | ἀνθρωπίσκους τινὰς ἐξαπατήσαντε

ὡς δή τοι, κ.τ.λ.] 'for, in point of fact, the soul herself is a creature endowed with the gift of prophecy.' Comp. Tim. 71 E, οἱ ξυστήσαντες ἡμᾶς . . . κατέστησαν ἐν τούτῳ (sc. τῷ ἥπατι) τὸ μαντεῖον.

καί πως ἐδυσωπούμην] 'I had a kind of misgiving.' Hesych.: δυσωπεῖσθαι· ὑφορᾶσθαι, φοβεῖσθαι. The line of Ibycus is quoted with slight variations in Suid. under the words ἀμπλάκημα, Ἰβύκειον, ῥησείδιον, and μή τοι παρ' θεοῖς probably stood in the original, and so Bergk, frag. Ibyc. 51. Socr. fears 'lest he should purchase honour from men at the price of offending heaven.' His speech had gratified Phaedr., but had given offence to Eros, by misrepresenting his character.

E σεμνύνεσθαι ὥς τι ὄντε] Cous. "de se donner l'air d'être quelque chose parcequ'ils imposeraient peut-être aux esprits frivoles et déroberaient leurs suffrages." For this folly and impiety combined Socr. knows of but one form of expiation: he must compose a palinode, as Stesichorus did in a parallel case. The first of the two poems of Stesichorus is usually cited under the title Ἰλίου πέρσις. The longest surviving fragment is that found in the Schol. to Eur. Orest. 243. In it Stesichorus asserts that Tyndareus the father of Helen having neglected to sacrifice to Aphrodite, the goddess wreaked her displeasure on his daughters Helen and Clytaemnestra, whom she caused to be διγάμους τε καὶ τριγάμους καὶ λιπεσάνορας. It was in these epithets, seemingly, that the offence lay, as we may

εὐδοκιμήσετον ἐν αὐτοῖς. ἐμοὶ μὲν οὖν, ὦ φίλε καθήρασθαι ἀνάγκη. ἔστι δὲ τοῖς ἁμαρτάνουσι περὶ μυθολογίαν καθαρμὸς ἀρχαῖος, ὃν Ὅμηρος μὲν οὐκ ᾔσθετο, Στησίχορος δέ. τῶν γὰρ ὀμμάτων στερηθεὶς διὰ τὴν Ἑλένης κακηγορίαν, οὐκ ἠγνόησεν ὥσπερ Ὅμηρος, ἀλλ' ἅτε μουσικὸς ὢν ἔγνω τὴν αἰτίαν, καὶ ποιεῖ εὐθὺς Οὐκ ἔστ' ἔτυμος λόγος οὗτος, οὐδ' ἔβας ἐν νηυσὶν εὐσέλμοις, οὐδ' ἵκεο Πέργαμα Τροίας. καὶ ποιήσας δὴ B πᾶσαν τὴν καλουμένην παλινῳδίαν, παραχρῆμα ἀνέβλεψεν. ἐγὼ οὖν σοφώτερος ἐκείνων γενήσομαι κατ' αὐτό γε τοῦτο. πρὶν γάρ τι παθεῖν διὰ τὴν τοῦ Ἔρωτος κακηγορίαν πειράσομαι αὐτῷ ἀποδοῦναι τὴν παλινῳδίαν, γυμνῇ τῇ κεφαλῇ, καὶ οὐχ ὥσπερ τότε ὑπ' αἰσχύνης ἐγκεκαλυμμένος

ΦΑΙ. Τουτωνί, ὦ Σώκρατες, οὐκ ἔστιν ἅττ' ἂν ἐμοὶ εἶπες ἡδίω.

ΣΩ. Καὶ γάρ, ὦ 'γαθὲ Φαῖδρε, ἐννοεῖς ὡς ἀναιδῶς C εἴρησθον τὼ λόγω, οὗτός τε καὶ ὁ ἐκ τοῦ βιβλίου ῥηθείς. εἰ γὰρ ἀκούων τις τύχοι ἡμῶν γεννάδας καὶ πρᾶος τὸ ἦθος, ἑτέρου δὲ τοιούτου ἐρῶν ἢ καὶ πρότερόν ποτε ἐρασθείς, λεγόντων ὡς διὰ σμικρὰ μεγάλας ἔχθρας οἱ ἐρασταὶ ἀναιροῦνται καὶ ἔχουσι πρὸς τὰ παιδικὰ φθονερῶς τε καὶ βλαβερῶς, πῶς οὐκ ἂν οἴει αὐτὸν ἡγεῖσθαι ἀκούειν ἐν ναύταις που τεθραμμένων καὶ οὐδένα ἐλεύθερον ἔρωτα

conjecture by comparing Isocr Encom Hel p 218 (§ 731 Bekk) ὅτε μὲν γὰρ ἀρχόμενος τῆς ᾠδῆς ἐβλασφήμησέ τι περὶ αὐτῆς, ἀνέστη (l ἀπέστη) τῶν ὀφθαλμῶν ἐστερημένος, ἐπειδὴ δὲ γνοὺς τὴν αἰτίαν τῆς συμφορᾶς τὴν καλουμένην παλινῳδίαν ἐποίησε, πάλιν αὐτὸν εἰς τὴν αὐτὴν φύσιν κατέστησε This 'palinode' is otherwise quoted as Ἑλένη or ἡ ὕστερον ᾠδή The version of Helen's story adopted by Euripides in the Helena was borrowed from this second ode of Stesichorus Comp Rep ix 586 c, τὸ τῆς Ἑλένης εἴδωλον ὑπὸ τῶν ἐν Τροίᾳ Στησίχορός φησι γενέσθαι περιμάχητον ἀγνοίᾳ τοῦ ἀληθοῦς According to Herodotus (ii 112, 113) this story was adopted by the priests at Memphis, who had doubtless learnt it from their Greek visitors Other references may be found collected [illegible]

Stesich fr 29 The whole story is allegorized by Hermeias in the most edifying strain of Neoplatonic piety It is critically examined by Geel in an Epistle to Welcker, Rh Museum, 1839, p 1

243 ἅτε μουσικὸς ὤν] Socr. in this playful passage takes advantage of the wide signification of μουσικός, which includes the lyric poet and the man of high mental culture, especially in philosophy He pretends that Stesichorus was more sagacious than Homer, who knew not either the cause or the remedy of his blindness A different turn is given to the relation between Helen and the Iliad by Isocrates in the Encom Hel § 71.

c. ἐν ναύταις που τεθραμμένων] The character of the ναυτικὸς ὄχλος (Arist Pol [illegible]) is well known Heind quotes

D ἑορακότων, πολλοῦ δ' ἂν δεῖν ἡμῖν ὁμολογεῖν ἃ ψέγομεν τὸν Ἔρωτα;

ΦΑΙ. Ἴσως νὴ Δί', ὦ Σώκρατες.

ΣΩ. Τοῦτόν γε τοίνυν ἔγωγε αἰσχυνόμενος, καὶ αὐτὸν τὸν Ἔρωτα δεδιώς, ἐπιθυμῶ ποτίμῳ λόγῳ οἷον ἁλμυρὰν ἀκοὴν ἀποκλύσασθαι. συμβουλεύω δὲ καὶ Λυσίᾳ ὅ τι τάχιστα γράψαι ὡς χρὴ ἐραστῇ μᾶλλον ἢ μὴ ἐρῶντι ἐκ τῶν ὁμοίων χαρίζεσθαι.

ΦΑΙ. Ἀλλ' εὖ ἴσθι ὅτι ἕξει τοῦθ' οὕτως· σοῦ γὰρ εἰπόντος τὸν τοῦ ἐραστοῦ ἔπαινον, πᾶσα ἀνάγκη Λυσίαν

E ὑπ' ἐμοῦ ἀναγκασθῆναι γράψαι αὖ περὶ τοῦ αὐτοῦ λόγον.

ΣΩ. Τοῦτο μὲν πιστεύω, ἕωσπερ ἂν ᾖς ὃς εἶ.

ΦΑΙ. Λέγε τοίνυν θαῤῥῶν.

ΣΩ. Ποῦ δή μοι ὁ παῖς πρὸς ὃν ἔλεγον; ἵνα καὶ τοῦτο ἀκούσῃ, καὶ μή, ἀνήκοος ὤν, φθάσῃ χαρισάμενος τῷ μὴ ἐρῶντι

ΦΑΙ. Οὗτος παρά σοι μάλα πλησίον ἀεὶ πάρεστιν, ὅταν σὺ βούλῃ.

ΣΩ. Οὑτωσὶ τοίνυν, ὦ παῖ καλέ, ἐννόησον, ὡς ὁ μὲν

244 πρότερος ἦν | λόγος Φαίδρου τοῦ Πυθοκλέους, Μυῤῥινουσίου ἀνδρός· ὃν δὲ μέλλω λέγειν, Στησιχόρου τοῦ Εὐφήμου, Ἱμεραίου. λεκτέος δὲ ὧδε, ὅτι Οὐκ ἔστ' ἔτυμος

Isocr de Pace, p 335, *εἰ τριήρεις πληροῖεν, τοὺς μὲν ξένους καὶ τοὺς δούλους εἰσεβίβαζον, τοὺς δὲ πολίτας μεθ' ὅπλων ἐξέπεμπον* Also Plat Legg IV 707, and Juv VIII 174, "Permixtum nautis et furibus et fugitivis."

D. *ποτίμῳ λόγῳ—ἀποκλύσασθαι*] Probably suggested by Eur. Hipp 653, *ἃ 'γὼ ῥυτοῖς νασμοῖσιν ἐξομόρξομαι Εἰς ὦτα κλύζων* Socr in like manner would fain purge his ears of the pestilent stuff he had heard by the infusion of more wholesome doctrine Presently *ἐκ τῶν ὁμοίων* answers to our 'caeteris paribus'

E *ἕωσπερ ἂν ᾖς ὃς εἶ*] "Pro ὃς cave corrigas *οἷος* Theaet 197 A, *ὤν γε ὃς εἰμι*" Heind "*A moins que tu ne cesses d'être Phèdre*" Cous

Οὗτος παρά σοι—πάρεστιν] Cobet, V L p. 119, somewhat rashly observes in reference to this passage "*Graecum est πάρειμί σοι, non πάρειμι παρά σοι* Scribe *πάρα σοι*, et apparebit quid sit verbo *πάρεστιν* faciendum." But in Soph Phil 1057 we find *ἐπεὶ πάρεστι μὲν Τεῦκρος παρ' ἡμῖν* *πάρα* for *πάρεστι* is hardly to be obtruded on an Attic *prose* writer on the strength of a (doubtful) reading of Lucian, as by Cobet, l l

244 *Φαίδρου τοῦ Πυθοκλέους*] All the proper names in this section are treated as significant. *Φαῖδρος* is the 'bright shiny one,' *Πυθοκλῆς* perhaps = *ὃς κλέους ἐπύθετο*, a hearkener to vulgar rumour or popular fallacy, *Μυῤῥινούσιος* quasi *ἐν μυῤῥίναις κατακλινείς* (Rep II 372 B), a lover of festivity, *Στησίχορος*, *Ἱμεραῖος*, and *Εὔφημος* explain themselves Accounts vary with respect to the name of the father of Stesichorus, no less than five names being mentioned by Suid, of which Socr has selected the most poetical

Οὐκ ἔστ' ἔτυμος, κ τ λ] It is a fallacy.

λόγος ὃς ἂν παρόντος ἐραστοῦ τῷ μὴ ἐρῶντι μᾶλλον φῇ δεῖν χαρίζεσθαι, διότι δὴ ὁ μὲν μαίνεται, ὁ δὲ σωφρονεῖ. εἰ μὲν γὰρ ἦν ἁπλοῦν τὸ μανίαν κακὸν εἶναι, καλῶς ἂν ἐλέγετο· νῦν δὲ τὰ μέγιστα τῶν ἀγαθῶν ἡμῖν γίγνεται διὰ μανίας, θείᾳ μέντοι δόσει διδομένης. Ἥ τε γὰρ δὴ ἐν Δελφοῖς προφῆτις αἵ τ' ἐν Δωδώνῃ ἱέρειαι μανεῖσαι B
μὲν πολλὰ δὴ καὶ καλὰ ἰδίᾳ τε καὶ δημοσίᾳ τὴν Ἑλλάδα εἰργάσαντο, σωφρονοῦσαι δὲ βραχέα ἢ οὐδέν. καὶ ἐὰν δὴ λέγωμεν Σίβυλλάν τε καὶ ἄλλους, ὅσοι μαντικῇ χρώμενοι ἐνθέῳ πολλὰ δὴ πολλοῖς προλέγοντες εἰς τὸ μέλλον ὤρθωσαν, μηκύνοιμεν ἂν δῆλα παντὶ λέγοντες τόδε μὴν ἄξιον ἐπιμαρτύρασθαι, ὅτι καὶ τῶν παλαιῶν οἱ τὰ ὀνόματα τιθέμενοι οὐκ αἰσχρὸν ἡγοῦντο οὐδὲ ὄνειδος μανίαν. οὐ γὰρ ἂν τῇ καλλίστῃ τέχνῃ, ᾗ τὸ μέλλον κρίνεται, αὐτὸ C
τοῦτο τοὔνομα ἐμπλέκοντες μανικὴν ἐκάλεσαν· ἀλλ' ὡς

says Socr., to argue that *because* the lover is mad, therefore the non-lover should have the preference. It might be so, were madness *per se* an evil; but this is not so. There is a divine as well as a human madness, and the divine madness is the choicest gift of heaven to man. Its kinds, or some of them, are then enumerated.

εἰ μὲν γὰρ ἦν ἁπλοῦν, κ.τ.λ.] 'had it been a simple proposition,' i.e. true without qualification, as Aristotle uses ἁπλῶς. So Symp. 206 A, ἆρ' οὖν οὕτως ἁπλοῦν ἐστι λέγειν ὅτι οἱ ἄνθρωποι τοῦ ἀγαθοῦ ἐρῶσιν—νῦν δέ 'but so far from that being the case,' &c. The entire passage from εἰ μὲν to καλὰ ἔργα, 245 B, is quoted by Aristides Rhetor, ed. Dind. vol. ii p. 15 (13 ed. Jebb).

B αἵ τ' ἐν Δωδώνῃ ἱέρειαι] No priestesses are mentioned by Homer as existing either at Delphi or Dodona. The latter oracle is tended by the Selli—ἀνιπτόποδες χαμαιεῦναι, Il. xvi. 235. He is equally ignorant of Sibylla, who is first named by Heraclitus, afterwards by Aristophanes and Plato, but always in the singular number. The 'Sibyls' were multiplied by later writers first to three and then to ten. The story of the Dodonaean ἱέρειαι, in Herod. ii. 54, is well known.

τῶν παλαιῶν οἱ τὰ ὀνόματα τιθέμενοι] Al. Rhet. τιθέμενοι. This notion that all names were originally significant (διδασκαλικὰ ὄργανα καὶ διακριτικὰ τῆς οὐσίας, Crat. p. 388) is developed at great length in the Cratylus. The etymological speculations in that dialogue present a singular mixture of acuteness and extravagance, sometimes bona fide, but sometimes with the design of parodying the ill-regulated ingenuity of Plato's predecessors in the same line, of whom Euthyphron is named, though others are doubtless intended. Perhaps the derivation of μαντικὴ may have been seriously meant. It was at any rate sufficiently plausible to have found favour with the Greeks of that day, as we know from Eustathius that it did in much later times. It also seems to have satisfied Cicero, Div. i. 1. If any refutation were necessary it would be found in the fact that the word μάντις is used by Homer, who was quite ignorant of the connexion between frenzy and the prophetic art. Yet Heind. censures Plato for not perceiving its connexion with μέμανται! The bad taste (ἀπειροκαλία) of those who inserted the ταῦ, is paralleled by the ἀτοπία of disguising the true origin of κάτοπτρον by encumbering the final syllable with a ρῶ! Crat. 414 C. The subsequent derivation of οἰωνιστική (οἴησις, νοῦς, ἱστορία) is in Plato's broadest style of banter.

καλοῦ ὄντος, ὅταν θείᾳ μοίρᾳ γίγνηται, οὕτω νομίσαντες ἔθεντο. οἱ δὲ νῦν ἀπειροκάλως τὸ ταῦ ἐπεμβάλλοντες μαντικὴν ἐκάλεσαν ἐπεὶ καὶ τήν γε τῶν ἐμφρόνων, ζήτησιν τοῦ μέλλοντος διά τε ὀρνίθων ποιουμένων καὶ τῶν ἄλλων σημείων, ἅτ' ἐκ διανοίας ποριζομένων ἀνθρωπίνῃ οἰήσει νοῦν τε καὶ ἱστορίαν, οἰονοιστικὴν ἐπωνόμασαν· ἣν
D νῦν οἰωνιστικὴν τῷ ὦ σεμνύνοντες οἱ νέοι καλοῦσιν. ὅσῳ δὴ οὖν τελεώτερον καὶ ἐντιμότερον μαντικὴ οἰωνιστικῆς, τό τε ὄνομα τοῦ ὀνόματος ἔργον τ' ἔργου, τόσῳ κάλλιον μαρτυροῦσιν οἱ παλαιοὶ μανίαν σωφροσύνης τὴν ἐκ θεοῦ τῆς παρ' ἀνθρώπων γιγνομένης. Ἀλλὰ μὴν νόσων γε καὶ πόνων τῶν μεγίστων, ἃ δὴ παλαιῶν ἐκ μηνιμάτων ποθὲν
E ἔν τισι τῶν γενῶν, ἡ μανία ἐγγενομένη καὶ προφητεύσασα οἷς ἔδει, ἀπαλλαγὴν εὕρετο, καταφυγοῦσα πρὸς θεῶν εὐχάς τε καὶ λατρείας, ὅθεν δὴ καθαρμῶν τε καὶ τελετῶν τυχοῦσα ἐξάντη ἐποίησε τὸν ἑαυτῆς ἔχοντα πρός τε τὸν παρόντα καὶ τὸν ἔπειτα χρόνον, λύσιν τῷ ὀρθῶς μανέντι
245 τε καὶ κατασχομένῳ τῶν παρόντων κακῶν εὑρομένῃ. | Τρίτη

C. ἐπεὶ καὶ τήν γε τῶν ἐμφρόνων] "Temuissem veterem lectionem *ποιουμένων*, ad quod liquet repetendum esse ex antegressis *τὴν ζήτησιν*, ita ut idem sit quod *ζητούντων*" Stallb The reading *ποιουμένην* is now displaced by *ποιουμένων* in the text of Ar Rhet But I confess that the construction appears to me clumsy and inelegant If we might venture on the change of a single letter, I should propose to read the passage as follows *ἐπεὶ καὶ τήν γε τῶν ἐμφρόνων* (sc *τέχνην* opposed to *τῇ καλλίστῃ τέχνῃ*, p sup) *ζήτησιν τοῦ μέλλοντος διά τε ὀρνίθων ποιουμένων καὶ τῶν ἄλλων σημείων, ἅτ' ἐκ διανοίας ποριζομένην ἀνθρ οἰήσει, κ τ λ* 'For even the art of the sane, who make research into futurity by the way of augury and the other well known signs, forasmuch as it is an art which derives insight and information from the reasoning faculty, by an effort of unaided human thought, they, the name-givers, have denominated *οἰονοιστική*

D τῷ ὦ σεμνύνοντες] Comp Crat 410 C, *ὧραι Ἀττικιστὶ ὡς τὸ παλαιὸν ὅραι*. When the *ω* was introduced into general use at Athens is uncertain It is found in no inscription previous to the archonship of Euclides (B C 403), but was probably used in literary compositions considerably earlier, perhaps soon after its reputed invention by Simonides This seems to follow from the *τὸ παλαιὸν* in the Cratylus l. l, where the word *Ἀττικιστὶ* also countenances the tradition of the Ionian origin of the letter The participle *σεμνύνοντες* is illustrated by the *τραγῳδεῖν* of Crat 414 C, *τὰ πρῶτα ὀνόματα τεθέντα κατακέχωσται ἤδη ὑπὸ τῶν βουλομένων τραγῳδεῖν αὐτά, κ τ λ.*

Ἀλλὰ μὴν—εὑρομένῃ] This curious and difficult passage has been ingeniously and on the whole satisfactorily explained by Lobeck, whose words I subjoin "Quia nonnunquam fit ubi morbus gravius exarserit, ut abstractus a corpore animus furoris afflatu occultas insidentis mali causas persentiscat, hunc Plato alterum genus divini furoris constituit ex praesagiis aegrotantium *ἀλλὰ μὴν* .. *ἔχοντα*, Phaedr 244 E, cujus loci interpretes sequi non possum Astius nomine *τῶν γενῶν* familias sacerdotales significari putat, quales Eumolpidae fuere aut Acestoridae Sed hi nunquam prophetandi et medicandi munere functi sunt, neque omnino *γένη* illa sunt eorum qui

δὲ ἀπὸ Μουσῶν κατοκωχή τε καὶ μανία, λαβοῦσα ἁπαλὴν καὶ ἄβατον ψυχήν, ἐγείρουσα καὶ ἐκβακχεύουσα κατά τε ᾠδὰς καὶ κατὰ τὴν ἄλλην ποίησιν, μυρία τῶν παλαιῶν ἔργα κοσμοῦσα τοὺς ἐπιγιγνομένους παιδεύει. ὃς δ' ἂν

aegrotantibus opitulantur, sed aegroti ipsi piacularium hominum posteri, quos nullius proprii delicti conscientia sed vis tacita avitae noxae exagitat. Haec autem non omnes ejusdem generis homines aequaliter affectat, sed modo intermittit, modo recrudescit, ut v c τῶν Ἐριννύων τοῦ Λαΐου καὶ Οἰδίποδος Τισαμενῷ μὲν οὐκ ἐγένετο μήνιμα, Αὐτεσίωνι δὲ τῷ Τισαμενοῦ, Paus ix 5 Ita vis illa hereditaria mali ἔν τισι τῶν γενῶν erumpit in apertum furorem, quo, ceu spiritu divino, tactus aliquis hujus funestae familiae et causas domesticae labis et remedia praesagit, adhibitisque piacularibus noxam a parentibus acceptam in omne tempus abolet Illa παλαιὰ μηνίματα sunt dirae ultrices sive parentum sive aliorum nefarie occisorum furiae temeratam domum diutina tabe urgentes, ἡ μῆνις τῶν τετελευτηκότων" Aglaophamus, p 636 seq What was the nature of the lustral rites (καθαρμοί) revealed to the favoured eye of madness, we learn generally from a passage of the Cratylus (405 A), in which are enumerated περιθειώσεις (fumigations), λουτρά, and περιρράνσεις, as the most efficacious means of moral as well as physical purification Compare a very curious passage in Aristides Rhetor, ἱερῶν λόγος β', i p 475, Dind The opinion that the maniac possessed a special insight into the causes and remedies of disease is paralleled in our own times by the belief in clairvoyance Among special difficulties presented by the passage, we may note—1 the clause ἃ δὴ παλαιῶν ἐκ μηνιμάτων ποθὲν ἔν τισι τῶν γενῶν, where C. F Hermann, offended by the absence of the verb, conjectures ἔν τισι τῶν γενῶν ᾖ, μανία, κ τ λ This however is but κακὸν κακῷ ἰᾶσθαι, for there is evidently no place for the conjunctive ᾖ If any alteration were necessary, it would be safer to substitute ἔνι (sc ἔνεστι) for ἐν. But the clause is suggested by a line of the Phoenissae quoted by Ast Κάδμου παλαιῶν Ἄρεος ἐκ μηνιμάτων, l 934, and the omission of the copula is a poeticism. 2 ἐξάντη is commonly but absurdly derived from ἔξω ἄτης Compare rather προσάντης, κατάντης with Passow The word means originally 'out of the way of,' 'exempt from,' hence 'safe and sound' frequently used with a gen., as in a line quoted in the Etym, ὦ Ζεῦ γενέσθαι τῆσδέ μ' ἐξάντη νόσου Hesych, ἐξάντες, ἐξ ἐναντίας ὅτε δὲ τὸ ὑγιές. So Hippocrates de Morbis, B 1 (Op. ed Kuhn, vol ii p 181), ἐξάντης τῆς τοιῆσδε νούσου γίνεται and without a case, ib B 3, p 295, ἢν δὲ ἄρα (ἐς τὰ ἑπτά) ἀφίκηται, ἐξάντης γίνεται, 'he gets well' Synesius περὶ ἐνυπν p 101, ed Turneb, καὶ ὅσοις ὕπνος ἰατρὸς ἐξάντη τὴν νόσον ἐποίησε, where ἐξάντης is transferred from the patient to the malady 3 τὸν ἑαυτῆς ἔχοντα I have retained this, the reading of by far the greater number of MSS, for which Ar Rhet has τὸν αὐτὴν ἔχοντα An attempt has been made to defend the reading of the MSS by Soph Oed. R 709, βρότειον οὐδὲν μαντικῆς ἔχον τέχνης But this passage, besides offering a solitary instance of ἔχειν with gen, is not really in point Its true meaning, as Hermann pointed out, is not, '*nemo mortalium particeps est divinationis*,' but rather '*nihil rerum humanarum ex vatum arte pendet*' Nor are the analogies given in Matth Gr Gr § 321, to which Ast and Stallb. appeal, to be relied on It is indeed just possible that this may be an affected poeticism, suggested to Plato by the line in the Oedipus, as he quotes παλαιῶν ἐκ μηνιμάτων in a sense somewhat different from that which the words bear in the original Even so, why the reflexive pronoun? I think there is much to be said in favour of the suggestion of Dr Badham, who observes, "Postremam vocem (ἔχοντα) libenter eximam, utpote a dittographia ortam, τὸν ἑαυτῆς / ἔχοντα" 4 κατασχομένῳ this epic use of the aor 2 mid for the passive is universally adopted by the Attics in the case of ἐσχόμην and its compounds See note to 238 D

215 κατοκωχῇ] Ar Rhet and vulg κατοχή But four or five MSS give the true form

ὃς δ' ἂν — ἠφανίσθη] 'whoso,' says Socr, 'knocks at the doors of Poesy untouched with the Muses' frenzy—

ἄνευ μανίας Μουσῶν ἐπὶ ποιητικὰς θύρας ἀφίκηται, πεισθεὶς ὡς ἄρα ἐκ τέχνης ἱκανὸς ποιητὴς ἐσόμενος, ἀτελὴς αὐτός τε καὶ ἡ ποίησις ὑπὸ τῆς τῶν μαινομένων ἡ τοῦ σωφρονοῦντος ἠφανίσθη.

B Τοσαῦτα μέν σοι καὶ ἔτι πλείω ἔχω μανίας γιγνομένης ἀπὸ θεῶν λέγειν καλὰ ἔργα. ὥστε τοῦτό γε αὐτὸ μὴ φοβώμεθα, μηδέ τις ἡμᾶς λόγος θορυβείτω δεδιττόμενος, ὡς πρὸ τοῦ κεκινημένου τὸν σώφρονα δεῖ προαιρεῖσθαι φίλον· ἀλλὰ τόδε πρὸς ἐκείνῳ δείξας φερέσθω τὰ νικητήρια, ὡς οὐκ ἐπ' ὠφελείᾳ ὁ ἔρως τῷ ἐρῶντι καὶ τῷ ἐρωμένῳ ἐκ θεῶν ἐπιπέμπεται. ἡμῖν δὲ ἀποδεικτέον αὖ τοὐναντίον, ὡς ἐπ' εὐτυχίᾳ τῇ μεγίστῃ παρὰ θεῶν ἡ

C τοιαύτη μανία δίδοται. ἡ δὲ δὴ ἀπόδειξις ἔσται δεινοῖς μὲν ἄπιστος, σοφοῖς δὲ πιστή. δεῖ οὖν πρῶτον ψυχῆς φύσεως

fondly persuading himself that art alone will make him a thorough poet,—neither he nor his works will ever attain perfection, but are destined, for all their cold propriety, to be eclipsed by the effusions of the inspired madman.' Compare Proclus, Polit p 365, l 16, ὃς γὰρ ἄν, φησίν, ἄνευ μουσῶν μανίας ἐπὶ ποιητικῆς θύρας ἀφίκηται, καὶ αὐτὸς ἀτελής ἐστι καὶ ποίησις αὐτοῦ, κ τ λ This more intelligible reading ποιητικῆς is patronized by Ast and by Badh, who also quotes Synesius in defence of it But the MSS are unanimous in favour of ποιητικάς, which is also the reading of Ar Rhet, and Seneca has "frustra *poeticas fores* compos sui pepulit," de Tranquill. An c. 16 It is a question whether Plato borrowed from Democritus this now sufficiently trite sentiment Cic Div i. 37, "negat sine furore Democritus quemquam poetam magnum esse posse, quod idem dicit Plato" Hor A P 295, "excludit sanos Helicone poetas Democritus" Aristotle means much the same thing, Probl xxx I, when he asks, διὰ τί οἱ εὐφυεῖς μελαγχολικοί, a passage referred to by Cic Tusc. i 33 80, "Aristoteles ait omnes ingeniosos melancholicos esse" In the proverb ἄφθονοι Μουσῶν θύραι the metaphor is preserved though the sentiment differs In illustration of ἀτελὴς compare inf 248 B, ἀτελεῖς τῆς τοῦ ὄντος θέας ἀπέρχονται, and especially the trigm of Pind, ἀτελῆ σοφίας καρπὸν δρέπει, quoted in Rep v 457 B. Boeckh, fr 227 Of the poetic fury Plato elsewhere speaks disrespectfully enough, when he has not, as here, his singing garments on Compare the Ion, esp p 533 E seq, and Meno 99 C, ὀρθῶς ἂν καλοῖμεν θείους τε οὓς νῦν δὴ ἐλέγομεν χρησμῳδοὺς καὶ μάντεις καὶ τοὺς ποιητικοὺς ἅπαντας, κ τ λ

πεισθεὶς ὡς ἄρα—ἐσόμενος] So Rep 560 D, μετριότητα δὲ καὶ κοσμίαν δαπάνην ὡς ἀγροικίαν καὶ ἀνελευθερίαν οὖσαν πείθοντες

B δεδιττόμενος, ὡς] Stallb. appositely quotes Demosth contra Symm 185 5, εἰ πάντες οἱ ἐνταυθὶ λέγοντες φοβοῖεν ὡς ἥξει βασιλεύς, κ τ λ The deponent verb δεδίττομαι is borrowed by Plato and the Attics from the Homeric δειδίσσομαι They never use it in the sense of δεδιέναι, as Homer and after him Hippocrates sometimes do, but always transitively See Lobeck, Phryn p 320

τῷ ἐρῶντι] Ar. Rhet τῷ ποθοῦντι

C. δεινοῖς μὲν ἄπιστος, σοφοῖς δὲ πιστή] The σοφοί are those trained to high speculation, as in the Pythagorean and Academic schools, the δεινοί may include the litigants of the courts and agora, as well as the Eristic and empirical sects. The latter will see no cogency in the argument, as they will reject or fail to comprehend the theory of the soul on which it is based This theory Socr proceeds to expound, borrowing, in the early part of his exposition, the dogmatic and oracular tone of the earlier speculators, Anaxagoras, Heraclitus, and the Pythagoreans

If it, a beginning came from something, it would not come from that as a beginning. But all becomes from a beginning (D 2) therefore it does not become?

πέρι θείας τε καὶ ἀνθρωπίνης, ἰδόντα πάθη τε καὶ ἔργα, τἀληθὲς νοῆσαι. ἀρχὴ δὲ ἀποδείξεως ἥδε.

Ψυχὴ πᾶσα ἀθάνατος. τὸ γὰρ ἀεικίνητον ἀθάνατον· τὸ δ' ἄλλο κινοῦν καὶ ὑπ' ἄλλου κινούμενον, παῦλαν ἔχον κινήσεως, παῦλαν ἔχει ζωῆς. μόνον δὴ τὸ αὐτὸ κινοῦν, ἅτε οὐκ ἀπολεῖπον ἑαυτό, οὔ ποτε λήγει κινούμενον, ἀλλὰ καὶ τοῖς ἄλλοις ὅσα κινεῖται τοῦτο πηγὴ καὶ ἀρχὴ κινή- D σεως. ἀρχὴ δὲ ἀγένητον. ἐξ ἀρχῆς γὰρ ἀνάγκη πᾶν τὸ γιγνόμενον γίγνεσθαι, αὐτὴν δὲ μηδ' ἐξ ἑνός· εἰ γὰρ ἔκ του ἀρχὴ γίγνοιτο, οὐκ ἂν ἐξ ἀρχῆς γίγνοιτο. ἐπειδὴ δὲ ἀγένητόν ἐστι, καὶ ἀδιάφθορον αὐτὸ ἀνάγκη εἶναι. ἀρχῆς γὰρ δὴ ἀπολομένης οὔτε αὐτή ποτε ἔκ του οὔτε ἄλλο ἐξ ἐκείνης γενήσεται, εἴπερ ἐξ ἀρχῆς δεῖ τὰ πάντα γίγνεσθαι. οὕτω δὴ κινήσεως μὲν ἀρχὴ τὸ αὐτὸ αὑτὸ κινοῦν. τοῦτο δὲ οὔτ' ἀπόλλυσθαι οὔτε γίγνεσθαι δυνατόν, ἢ πάντα τε οὐρανὸν πᾶσάν τε γένεσιν συμπεσοῦσαν στῆναι καὶ μή- E ποτε αὖθις ἔχειν ὅθεν κινηθέντα γενήσεται. ἀθανάτου

Ψυχὴ πᾶσα] Not 'every soul,' but rather 'all soul,' i.e. the vital principle in general. The argument amounts to this, that organization depends on soul, not soul on organization, as will be shown more at length in the excursus on the Erotic Discourses of Socrates.

D *εἰ γὰρ ἔκ του ἀρχὴ γίγνοιτο, οὐκ ἂν ἐξ ἀρχῆς γίγνοιτο*] "Recte monuit supplendum esse *τουτ'*" (sc. post *γίγνοιτο*). "Sic enim ratiocinatur: '*Si principium ab aliqua re oritur, res ea non poterit oriri ex principio; atqui jam concessum erat omnem rem a principio oriri oportere*.'" Bädh. Praef. p. vi. Acutely, as usual: but is not the same thing implied in the text as it stands, and as Ficinus renders it, "ex principio utique non oriretur," i.e. a first principle must in that case derive its existence from something which is *not* a first principle, as if he had said, *ἐξ οὐκ ἀρχῆς γίγνοιτ' ἄν*, a perfect reductio ad absurdum? G. Herm. explains differently: "Hoc ipsum, *πᾶν τὸ γιγνόμενον*, ex praecedentibus repetendum est. Id, si principium aliunde gigneretur, *οὐκ ἂν ἐξ ἀρχῆς γίγνεσθαι* dicit." Ann. in marg. Cicero, who translates this proof in the 6th book of his Repub. c. 25, and repeats his translation in T [illegible]

rendering of this passage to have read *ἀρχὴ* for *ἐξ ἀρχῆς*. His words are: "Ipsum (principium) nulla ex re alia nasci potest, *nec enim esset id principium* quod gigneretur aliunde." Schleiermacher, I observe, has anticipated Bädh.'s *τουτ'*. "Hinter dem ersten oder zweiten *γίγνοιτο* sehr leicht kann *τοῦτο* ausgefallen sein, da man denn übersetzen muss 'denn wenn der Anfang aus etwas entstände, so entstände dies nicht aus dem Anfange.'" But I confess that the comparative difficulty of the MS. reading is with me an argument of its genuineness, and in the second *ἀρχή*, if it ever existed, I can see only a conjecture of some ingenious glossator. The passage in Theodoret, Therap. ii. p. 36, 12 Sylb. (Gaisf. p. 100) is a quotation from the pseudo-Timaeus, not from the Phaedrus directly, as Stallb. seems to imagine. From that source probably came the *ἀρχή*, which would entail the further change of *γίγνοιτο* into *εἴη*, or *ἦν* as in Tim. Locr. 1. 1, *εἰ γὰρ ἐγένετο, οὐκ ἂν ἦν ἔτι ἀρχά, ἀλλ' ἐκεῖνα ἐξ ἇς ἀρχὰ ἐγένετο*.

τοῦτο δὲ οὔτ' ἀπόλλυσθαι—γενήσεται] In like strain, *mutatis mutandis*, argues a great physicist of our own day. "To limit that force may be destructible, or

δὲ πεφασμένου τοῦ ὑφ' ἑαυτοῦ κινουμένου, ψυχῆς οὐσίαν
τε καὶ λόγον τοῦτον αὐτόν τις λέγων οὐκ αἰσχυνεῖται.
πᾶν γὰρ σῶμα ᾧ μὲν ἔξωθεν τὸ κινεῖσθαι, ἄψυχον, ᾧ
δὲ ἔνδοθεν αὐτῷ ἐξ αὐτοῦ, ἔμψυχον, ὡς ταύτης οὔσης
φύσεως ψυχῆς. εἰ δ' ἔστι τοῦτο οὕτως ἔχον, μὴ ἄλλο τι
246 εἶναι τὸ αὐτὸ ἑαυτὸ κινοῦν | ἢ ψυχήν, ἐξ ἀνάγκης ἀγένη-
τόν τε καὶ ἀθάνατον ψυχὴ ἂν εἴη. Περὶ μὲν οὖν ἀθανασίας αὐτῆς ἱκανῶς.

Περὶ δὲ τῆς ἰδέας αὐτῆς ὧδε λεκτέον· οἷον μέν ἐστι, πάντῃ πάντως θείας εἶναι καὶ μακρᾶς διηγήσεως, ᾧ δὲ

can altogether disappear, would be to admit that matter could be uncreated, for we know matter only by its forces" Faraday, on the Conservation of Force After *στῆναι* we must understand, not *δυνατόν*, but some other word, as *δεῖ* or *ἀναγκαῖον* 'Else must all heaven and all created nature collapse and become fixed, having no source of fresh movement or growth remaining'

E *ψυχῆς οὐσίαν τε καὶ λόγον*] Comp Legg x 895 E, *ᾧ δὴ ψυχὴ τοὔνομα, τίς τούτου λόγος, ἔχομεν ἄλλον πλὴν τὸν νῦν δὴ ῥηθέντα, τὴν δυναμένην αὐτὴν αὑτὴν κινεῖν κίνησιν*, ibid supra, *ἆρ' οὐκ ἂν ἐθέλοις περὶ ἕκαστον τρία νοεῖν—ἓν μὲν τὴν οὐσίαν, ἓν δὲ τῆς οὐσίας τὸν λόγον, ἓν δὲ ὄνομα* where *λόγος*, as here, is equivalent to *ὅρος* or *ὁρισμός*, of which *οὐσία* is the objective counterpart Socr had shown that motion or change must have an *ἀρχή*, and that this *ἀρχὴ* must have the source of its motion in itself, &c. He now proceeds to show that soul only is such an *ἀρχή*, and that, being such, it is uncreate and immortal, *ἀεικινησία* being implied in *αὐτοκινησία* — *τοῦτον αὐτὸν* is used by an ordinary attraction for *τοῦτ' αὐτό*, namely *τὸ ὑφ' ἑαυτοῦ κινούμενον*

246 *Περὶ δὲ τῆς ἰδέας*] 'concerning its form,' or 'type,' or generally, 'concerning its nature,' *ἰδέα* being frequently equivalent to *φύσις* The *θεία καὶ μακρὰ διήγησις* which Socr declines is developed in the Republic and Timaeus the views which are there reasoned out being here presented in the form of an allegory For nothing can be more true than Stallb 's remark "Philosophus quo tempore Phaedrum scripsit, jam eandem de animi humani natura sententiam animo suo informatam tenuit quam in libris de Republica copiosius illustravit" All commentators, ancient and modern, have recognized in the Charioteer and his pair of steeds the well-known triple division of the soul into the reasoning, the passionate, and the appetent principles (*λογιστικόν, θυμικόν, ἐπιθυμητικόν*), which lies at the root of Plato's ethical doctrine See Galen de Hippocrate et Plat. (Opp v 5, p 302, ed Kuhn) *ὃν γὰρ ἱππεὺς πρὸς ἵππον, ἢ κυνηγέτης πρὸς κύνα λόγον ἔχουσιν, τοῦτον ὁ λογισμὸς πρὸς θυμὸν συμβαίνει δ' οὐκ ἀεὶ νόμῳ φύσεως διοικεῖσθαι τὴν συζυγίαν, ἀλλ' ἵππος μὲν ἐνίοτε δυσπειθὴς οὐ κατὰ κόσμον ἐκφερόμενος συναπήνεγκεν αὑτῷ τὸν ἀναβάτην*, κ τ λ And again, p 493, *ὅτι τὸ θυμαινόμενον ἕτερόν ἐστι τοῦ ἐπιθυμοῦντος, καὶ ὡς τὸ θυμαινόμενον οὐδέποτε συμμαχεῖ τῷ ἐπιθυμητικῷ, δι' ἑνὸς ἐνεδείξατο (ὁ Πλάτων) τοῦδε τοῦ προειρημένου παραδείγματος*, alluding to the anecdote of Leontius in Repub iv 439 E Observe, Plato asserts only that where the reason and the appetites are at variance, the *θυμὸς* naturally takes part with the former (*ἐν τῇ τῆς ψυχῆς στάσει ὅπλα τίθεται πρὸς τοῦ λογιστικοῦ*) He nowhere denies that a feud may spring up between the *θυμὸς* and the reason The *θυμὸς* is *in itself* good and of heavenly extraction, but in excess it may disturb the equipoise of the soul, and so produce evil Whereas the natural tendency of the lower appetites is evil and degrading to human nature, and they are therefore figured here by the low-bred and ill conditioned steed, as the *θυμὸς* is said to be 'noble and good and of noble and good parentage'

ἔοικεν, ἀνθρωπίνης τε καὶ ἐλάττονος. ταύτῃ οὖν λέγωμεν. Ἐοικέτω δὴ ξυμφύτῳ δυνάμει ὑποπτέρου ζεύγους τε καὶ ἡνιόχου. θεῶν μὲν οὖν ἵπποι τε καὶ ἡνίοχοι πάντες αὐτοί τε ἀγαθοὶ καὶ ἐξ ἀγαθῶν, τὸ δὲ τῶν ἄλλων μέμικται. καὶ πρῶτον μὲν ἡμῶν ὁ ἄρχων ξυνωρίδος B
ἡνιοχεῖ, εἶτα τῶν ἵππων ὁ μὲν αὐτῷ καλός τε καὶ ἀγαθὸς καὶ ἐκ τοιούτων, ὁ δὲ ἐξ ἐναντίων τε καὶ ἐναντίος. χαλεπὴ δὴ καὶ δύσκολος ἐξ ἀνάγκης ἡ περὶ ἡμᾶς ἡνιόχησις. Πῇ δὴ οὖν θνητόν τε καὶ ἀθάνατον ζῷον ἐκλήθη, πειρατέον εἰπεῖν. πᾶσα ἡ ψυχὴ παντὸς ἐπιμελεῖται τοῦ ἀψύχου, πάντα δὲ οὐρανὸν περιπολεῖ, ἄλλοτ' ἐν ἄλλοις εἴδεσι γιγνομένη. τελέα μὲν οὖν οὖσα καὶ ἐπτερωμένη μετεωρο- C
πορεῖ τε καὶ πάντα τὸν κόσμον διοικεῖ· ἡ δὲ πτερορρυήσασα φέρεται, ἕως ἂν στερεοῦ τινὸς ἀντιλάβηται, οὗ κατοικισθεῖσα, σῶμα γήινον λαβοῦσα, αὐτὸ αὑτὸ δοκοῦν κινεῖν διὰ τὴν ἐκείνης δύναμιν, ζῷον τὸ ξύμπαν ἐκλήθη, ψυχὴ καὶ σῶμα παγέν, θνητόν τ' ἔσχεν ἐπωνυμίαν· ἀθάνατον δὲ οὐδ' ἐξ ἑνὸς λόγου λελογισμένου, ἀλλὰ πλάττομεν οὔτε ἰδόντες οὔτε ἱκανῶς νοήσαντες θεόν, ἀθάνατόν

B Πῇ δὴ οὖν, κ τ λ] Socr. now endeavours to explain the meaning of the terms 'mortal' and 'immortal animal' respectively. Stallb unnecessarily supplies ψυχὴ to be the understood subject of ἐκλήθη

πᾶσα ἡ ψυχή] Soul in its entirety, the soul of the universe, which is also a providence (ἐπιμελεῖται), regulating matter and animating its various forms. This soul is not to be regarded as a personality excluding all finite personalities, but rather as *including* them, as forming the sum total of the separate intelligences. "Alles Geistige wird hier offenbar als eins betrachtet, ohne Unterschied des Ranges und der Persönlichkeit." Schleierm, Anm. Hermeias, Comm p. 130, λέγει ὅτι πᾶν μόριον τοῦ παντὸς πάντως ὑπό τινος ψυχῆς ἐπιτροπεύεται, ὥστε πᾶν ὑπὸ πασῶν

C ἡ δὲ πτερορρυήσασα, κ τ λ] Certain souls fall from their high estate, and become incarnate upon the earth, when they take to them an earthy body, earth being the heaviest of the elements. The heavenly bodies, according to the ancient physicist ... and lighter than those which make up our planet. Having stated the fact of this *lapsus animarum*, Socr proceeds (mythically) to set forth its causes

λελογισμένου] Badh proposes λελογίσμεθα, on the ground that the perf. of λογίζομαι is never used passively. Stallb makes no reply to the objection, but translates λόγος λ by "ratio apte conclusa" I apprehend that λελογισμένου is *not* passive here, any more than in Eur Iph A 386, τὸ λελογισμένον παρείς, where λελ is much the same as εὔλογον or as τὸ ἐντεθυμημένον in Crat. 404, where see Heind. "Immortal it cannot be called on any principle of sound reason,"—ἔσχον ἐπωνυμίαν being supplied from the foregoing clause. A similar perfect is παρημελημένη (negligent, remiss), Ar Eth N. x. 1 10. The only tense of λογίζομαι which the Attics use passively seems to be the aor 1, ἐλογίσθην

ἀλλὰ πλάττομεν] 'but though we never saw nor have adequately conceived him, we figure a God as a kind of immortal animal, possessing both a soul and a body ... united in a unity which is to last for

D τι ζῷον, ἔχον μὲν ψυχήν, ἔχον δὲ σῶμα, τὸν ἀεὶ δὲ χρόνον ταῦτα ξυμπεφυκότα. Ἀλλὰ ταῦτα μὲν δή, ὅπῃ τῷ θεῷ φίλον, ταύτῃ ἐχέτω τε καὶ λεγέσθω. τὴν δ' αἰτίαν τῆς τῶν πτερῶν ἀποβολῆς, δι' ἣν ψυχῆς ἀποῤῥεῖ, λάβωμεν. ἔστι δέ τις τοιάδε

Πέφυκεν ἡ πτεροῦ δύναμις τὸ ἐμβριθὲς ἄγειν ἄνω μετεωρίζουσα, ᾗ τὸ τῶν θεῶν γένος οἰκεῖ. κεκοινώνηκε δέ πῃ μάλιστα τῶν περὶ τὸ σῶμα τοῦ θείου. τὸ δὲ θεῖον καλόν, σοφόν, ἀγαθὸν καὶ πᾶν ὅ τι τοιοῦτον. τού-
E τοις δὴ τρέφεταί τε καὶ αὔξεται μάλιστά γε τὸ τῆς ψυχῆς πτέρωμα, αἰσχρῷ δὲ καὶ κακῷ καὶ τοῖς ἐναντίοις φθίνει τε καὶ διόλλυται. ὁ μὲν δὴ μέγας ἡγεμὼν ἐν οὐρανῷ Ζεύς, ἐλαύνων πτηνὸν ἅρμα, πρῶτος πορεύεται, διακοσμῶν πάντα καὶ ἐπιμελούμενος· τῷ δ' ἕπεται στρατιὰ
247 θεῶν τε καὶ δαιμόνων, κατὰ ἕνδεκα μέρη | κεκοσμημένη.

ever' In the Timaeus the created gods are compounded of body and soul, which can only be put asunder by the will of the supreme Deity In the δαίμονες or inferior divinities, the union is essentially dissoluble In the tenth of the Laws, on the other hand, Plato inclines to the notion that even the created gods may be incorporeal (Laws, p. 899 A) Possibly the words in the text are to be understood as conveying an apology for his temerity in speculating upon the subject at all

D Πέφυκεν ἡ πτ.] It is the nature of all plumage to raise heavenward the body to which it is attached · so that of all bodily instruments it may be said to have most affinity with the divine, for we conceive the gods as dwelling on high Hence the upward tendencies of the soul may be aptly symbolized by feathers. These tendencies which are the soul's plumage are fostered by all that is fair, wise, good—in a word, by that which is divine. Such is the obvious meaning of this passage, in which, for the purposes of the allegory, the sign and the thing signified are intentionally fused Compare Plutarch, Plat Quaest vi, οὐκ ἀπὸ τρόπου πτερὸν προσηγόρευσε (τὴν διανοητικήν) ὡς τὴν ψυχὴν ἀπὸ τῶν ταπεινῶν καὶ θνητῶν ἀναφέρουσαν After τοῦ θείου the MSS give ψυχή, a gloss which Heind., on the authority of Plutarch l l, properly exterminated

E ὁ μὲν δὴ μέγας, κ.τ.λ.] The grand Miltonic pomp of this passage exceeded the comprehension of Dionysius of Halicarnassus, whose criticisms on Plato and on Thucydides are of nearly equal frigidity (De admirabili vi dicendi in Demosth p 971, Reiske). The language was probably suggested by Soph Elect 175, ἔστι μέγας ἐν οὐρανῷ Ζεὺς ὃς ἐφορᾷ πάντα καὶ κρατύνει, but it seems hypercritical with Groen v Prinsterer to object to ἡγεμὼν as an interpolation. See inf 252 E, σκοποῦσιν (οἱ τοῦ Διός) εἰ ἡγεμονικὸς τὴν φύσιν Zeus is here as elsewhere, the impersonation of intelligence (νοῦς, σοφία, φρόνησις) Comp Phileb p 30 D, οὐκοῦν ἐν μὲν τῇ τοῦ Διὸς ἐρεῖς φύσει βασιλικὴν μὲν ψυχὴν βασιλικὸν δὲ νοῦν ἐγγίγνεσθαι ἐν δ' ἄλλοις (sc θεοῖς) ἄλλα καλά, καθ' ὃ φίλον ἑκάστοις λέγεσθαι Of the 'other gods,' three are enumerated inf 252 The δαίμονες represent the as yet unfallen spirits, marshalled under their respective patron-deities (ib) Plotinus, Enn v 8 c 10, seems to distinguish between δαίμονες and ψυχαὶ in this passage, but this is a needless refinement

τῷ δ' ἕπεται] G Hermann's note on this is amusing "Poetarum verba legere te putares τῷ δ' ἕπεται στρατιή τε θεῶν καὶ δαίμονες ἁγνοί—Ἡγεῦνται κατὰ τάξιν (κόσμον) ὅπως τάχθησαν ἕκαστοι Et trimetrum μένει γὰρ Ἑστία 'ν θεῶν οἴκῳ μόνη" (!)

μένει γὰρ Ἑστία ἐν θεῶν οἴκῳ μόνη· τῶν δὲ ἄλλων ὅσοι ἐν τῷ τῶν δώδεκα ἀριθμῷ τεταγμένοι θεοὶ ἄρχοντες, ἡγοῦνται κατὰ τάξιν ἣν ἕκαστος ἐτάχθη. πολλαὶ μὲν οὖν καὶ μακάριαι θέαι τε καὶ διέξοδοι ἐντὸς οὐρανοῦ, ἃς θεῶν γένος εὐδαιμόνων ἐπιστρέφεται, πράττων ἕκαστος

217 *μένει γὰρ Ἑστία—μόνη*] In this clause Plato has availed himself of a Pythagorean philosophism Aristotle tells us that "the Pythagoreans place a fire in the centre of the universe, round which they suppose the earth to revolve, as the other planets do." Among the planets they enumerate the Sun and Moon this central fire is therefore distinct from the Sun, and there is no foundation for the opinion, repeated in a recent treatise on Egyptian Astronomy (Rawlinson's Herodotus, vol ii p 330), that Pythagoras was acquainted with the true theory of the solar system The Pythagoreans named this Central Fire *Διὸς φυλακή*, *Διὸς πυργός*, *Διὸς οἶκος*, and lastly *ἑστία τοῦ παντός* Comp Arist de Caelo ii 13, with Stob Ecl i p. 188

πολλαὶ μὲν οὖν, κ τ λ] It is true, says Plato, that *within* the circumference of the heavenly sphere there is no lack of glorious spectacles and goodly highways, which the gods traverse as they go about their every-day avocations, but besides these there is a route which they tread only on their high feast days—a route uphill from first to last, leading to the very apex of the arch which supports the vault of heaven, and there opening upon its outer circumference, whence they can feast their eyes upon the glories of the super celestial region—*θεωροῦσι τὰ ἐκτὸς τοῦ οὐρανοῦ*—which far exceed the *θέαι ἐντὸς οὐρανοῦ* in beauty, as the road which leads to them exceeds in difficulty the beaten highways on which the gods ordinarily go to and fro Such, after much consideration, I believe to be Plato's meaning in this grand but obscure passage The sense I have given to *διέξοδοι* seems justified by Thuc ii 98, *ἐς τὴν ὕλην ἐσφερομένους, ὅθεν οὐκ ἦσαν διέξοδοι*, compared with Herod i 199 *σχοινοτενέες δὲ διέξοδοι πάντα τρόπον ὁδῶν ἔχουσι διὰ τῶν γυναικῶν, δι' ὧν οἱ ξεῖνοι διεξιόντες ἐκλέγονται* The word is sometimes used for the orbits described by the heavenly bodies, as in Epin 977 B, *στρέφων ἄστρα πάσας διεξόδους* sometimes also for the evolutions of an army, as Legg vii 813 E In this place however the *διέξοδοι* seem to be roads leading *through* and *out of* the spheres of the several planets, included in the great sphere of the fixed stars, which to the ancients formed the boundary of the *κόσμος* or *οὐρανός*. So a recent German translator, "gar manche den Himmel durchschneidende Bahn" *ἁψίς*, which I have rendered 'arch,' properly denotes the orbit of a wheel Here I take it to mean a zone or 'rib,' supporting the vault of heaven Proclus, Theol iv c 4, gives the following explanation *ἔπειτα εἰς τὴν ὑπουράνιον ἁψῖδα, προσεχῶς ὑπεζωκυῖαν τὸν οὐρανόν, καὶ ἐν αὐτῷ περιεχομένην, καὶ μετὰ ταύτην εἰς αὐτὸν τὸν οὐρανὸν καὶ τὸ τοῦ οὐρανοῦ νῶτον.* The word *ὑπεζωκυῖαν* shows that he understands *ἁψίς* to mean the undermost of two or more coats or shells of which the heavenly sphere consists Comp Galen de Hipp et Plat, p. 190, Kuhn *εἰς τὸν ὑπεζωκότα τὰς πλευρὰς χιτῶνα*, 'to the coat or membrane which lines the ribs' If *ἁψίς* can mean a vault or spherical arch (fornix coeli, coeli convexa, as the interpr render it), there is no objection to this view, which Stallb adopts Mine however is more in accordance with the classical use of *ἁψίς*, and it seems to me that the idea of such a zone may easily have been suggested by the phenomenon of the milky way. I suppose this *ἁψίς* to touch the under surface of the *οὐρανός*, as Procl supposes his *ὑπόζωμα* to do and both interpretations explain *ὑπὸ* and *ὑπουράνιον*, the readings supported by the best MSS. The position of *ἄκραν* in the sentence shows it to be a secondary predicate 'up to its summit or vertex' Comp Arist Av 390, *παρ' αὐτὴν τὴν χύτραν ἄκραν ὁρῶντες ἐγγύς* The variant *ἐπὶ* for *ὑπὸ* removes some difficulties, and so does *οὐράνιον* for *ὑπουράνιον*, but in an obscure passage like this it seems the safer course to hold to the reading for which there is preponderant authority Proclus has much to say upon the inner meaning of the mythos, but nothing worth attending to

αὐτῶν τὸ αὑτοῦ. ἕπεται δὲ ὁ ἀεὶ ἐθέλων τε καὶ δυνάμενος· φθόνος γὰρ ἔξω θείου χοροῦ ἵσταται. ὅταν δὲ δὴ
B πρὸς δαῖτα καὶ ἐπὶ θοίνην ἴωσιν, ἄκραν ὑπὸ τὴν ὑπουράνιον ἁψῖδα πορεύονται πρὸς ἄναντες ἤδη. τὰ μὲν θεῶν ὀχήματα ἰσοῤῥόπως εὐήνια ὄντα ῥᾳδίως πορεύεται, τὰ δὲ ἄλλα μόγις· βρίθει γὰρ ὁ τῆς κάκης ἵππος μετέχων, ἐπὶ τὴν γῆν ῥέπων τε καὶ βαρύνων ᾧ μὴ καλῶς ᾖ τεθραμμένος τῶν ἡνιόχων. ἔνθα δὴ πόνος τε καὶ ἀγὼν ἔσχατος ψυχῇ πρόκειται. αἱ μὲν γὰρ ἀθάνατοι καλούμεναι, ἡνίκ' ἂν πρὸς ἄκρῳ γένωνται, ἔξω πορευ-
C θεῖσαι ἔστησαν ἐπὶ τῷ τοῦ οὐρανοῦ νώτῳ, στάσας δὲ αὐτὰς περιάγει ἡ περιφορά, αἱ δὲ θεωροῦσι τὰ ἔξω τοῦ οὐρανοῦ. τὸν δὲ ὑπερουράνιον τόπον οὔ τέ τις ὕμνησέ πω τῶν τῇδε ποιητὴς οὔ τέ ποθ' ὑμνήσει κατ' ἀξίαν. ἔχει δὲ ὧδε. τολμητέον γὰρ οὖν τό γε ἀληθὲς εἰπεῖν,

φθόνος γὰρ ἔξω θείου χοροῦ ἵσταται] A bye-blow at the vulgar notion, *ὅτι τὸ θεῖον πᾶν φθονερόν*. Compare Arist. Metaph. I. 2. 13, *εἰ δὴ λέγουσί τι οἱ ποιηταὶ καὶ πέφυκε φθονεῖν τὸ θεῖον, ἐπὶ τούτου συμβαίνει μάλιστα εἰκὸς καὶ δυστυχεῖς εἶναι πάντας τοὺς περιττούς. ἀλλ' οὔτε τὸ θεῖον φθονερὸν ἐνδέχεται εἶναι, ἀλλὰ καὶ κατὰ τὴν παροιμίαν πολλὰ ψεύδονται ἀοιδοί, οὔτε τῆς τοιαύτης* (*ἐπιστήμης*) *ἄλλην χρὴ νομίζειν τιμιωτέραν*.

πρὸς δαῖτα καὶ ἐπὶ θοίνην] The pleonasm is in harmony with the general grandiloquence of the passage. Inf. 250 B, *ὄψιν τε καὶ θέαν*. The incident is of course suggested by Hom. Il. i. 123, *Ζεὺς γὰρ ἐς Ὠκεανὸν μετ' ἀμύμονας Αἰθιοπῆας χθιζὸς ἔβη κατὰ δαῖτα, θεοὶ δ' ἅμα πάντες ἕποντο*, on which Ast observes: "Homerus poeta Jovem cum reliquis dîs ad *epulas* facit proficiscentem, Plato philosophus ad rerum divinarum spectationes, quae animi sunt epulae. (Vid. inf. p. 247 A.)"

B. *τὰ μὲν θεῶν, κ. τ. λ.*] The asyndeton is harsh and scarcely defensible. To avoid it, Ast proposed the omission of *πορεύονται*, and the substitution of a comma for a fuller stop after *ἤδη*. Badh. takes the same view, objecting also to the "putida repetitio" of *πορεύεται* after *πορεύονται*. Some few MSS. have *τὰ μὲν οὖν θ. ὀχ.* I should rather incline to the omission of *πορεύεται* and the retention of *πορεύονται*. The passage will in that case run thus: *ἄκραν ὑπὸ τὴν ὑπουράνιον ἁψῖδα πορεύονται πρὸς ἄναντες ἤδη, τὰ μὲν θεῶν ὀχήματα, ἰσοῤῥόπως εὐήνια ὄντα, ῥᾳδίως, τὰ δὲ ἄλλα μόγις*. 'The teams of the gods easily, being evenly poised and held well in hand, but those of the other spirits with difficulty, for the vicious steed goes heavily, by his earthward inclination depressing the driver, in case he have not thoroughly broken him.' Another expedient is that of G. Hermann, l. l., who, following Schneider, proposes to read *πρὸς ἄναντες, ᾗ δὴ τὰ θεῶν, κ. τ. λ.*

ᾧ μὴ καλῶς ᾖ] Lit. 'in the case of any driver who may have a steed not properly trained.' This is the reading of the best MSS., and is confirmed by Firmus "*cuicunque aurigarum equus non bonus*" (he read *καλὸς* with one MS.) "*nutritus fuerit*." Two MSS. give *ἦν* for *ᾖ*, which Stallb. and Ast prefer, but the best are in favour of the text I have adopted, which is also found without variation in the Schol. on Synesius, *περὶ ἐνυπνίων*, p. 105, Turneb. Herm. inserts *ἂν* after *ᾧ*, but perhaps the omission of the particle may be tolerated in a semi-poetical composition like the present.

C. *τολμητέον γὰρ οὖν*] We must dare to speak the truth, says Socr., above all

ἄλλως τε καὶ περὶ ἀληθείας λέγοντα. ἡ γὰρ ἀχρώματός
τε καὶ ἀσχημάτιστος καὶ ἀναφὴς οὐσία, ὄντως οὖσα,
ψυχῆς κυβερνήτῃ μόνῳ θεατὴ νῷ, περὶ ἣν τὸ τῆς ἀληθοῦς ἐπιστήμης γένος, τοῦτον ἔχει τὸν τόπον. ἅτ' οὖν D
θεοῦ διάνοια νῷ τε καὶ ἐπιστήμῃ ἀκηράτῳ τρεφομένη,
καὶ ἁπάσης ψυχῆς, ὅσῃ ἂν μέλλῃ τὸ προσῆκον δέξεσθαι,
ἰδοῦσα διὰ χρόνου τὸ ὂν ἀγαπᾷ τε καὶ θεωροῦσα τἀληθῆ
τρέφεται καὶ εὐπαθεῖ, ἕως ἂν κύκλῳ ἡ περιφορὰ εἰς
ταὐτὸν περιενέγκῃ. ἐν δὲ τῇ περιόδῳ καθορᾷ μὲν αὐτὴν
δικαιοσύνην, καθορᾷ δὲ σωφροσύνην, καθορᾷ δὲ ἐπιστήμην, οὐχ ᾗ γένεσις πρόσεστιν, οὐδ' ἥ ἐστί που ἑτέρα E
ἐν ἑτέρῳ οὖσα ὧν ἡμεῖς νῦν ὄντων καλοῦμεν, ἀλλὰ τὴν
ἐν τῷ ὅ ἐστιν ὂν ὄντως ἐπιστήμην οὖσαν· καὶ τἆλλα

when truth itself is our theme For the region in question is the abode of that Essence which is the subject-matter of science truly so called,—an Essence hueless, formless, intangible, in the strictest sense real, though visible only to the eye of pure intelligence The text was formerly embarrassed by an interpolated *χρῆται* (*θεατῇ νῷ χρῆται*), a reading which Bekk has unaccountably retained, though *χρῆται* is absent from the Bodl and other MSS of good repute The text given above seems to me to be open to no objection, and is fully supported by MS authority. For the sense compare Phileb 62 E, *ἐπιστήμη ἐπιστήμης διάφορος, ἡ μὲν ἐπὶ τὰ γιγνόμενα καὶ ἀπολλύμενα ἀποβλέπουσα, ἡ δὲ ἐπὶ τὰ μήτε γιγνόμενα μήτε ἀπολλύμενα, κατὰ ταὐτὰ δὲ καὶ ὡσαύτως ὄντα ἀεί ταύτην εἰς τὸ ἀληθὲς ἐπισκοπούμενοι, ἡγησάμεθα ἐκείνης ἀληθεστέραν εἶναι.*

D *ἅτ' οὖν θεοῦ διάνοια, κ τ λ*] For *ἡ οὖν θ διάνοια, ἅτε τρεφομένη* One might conj with G Herm *ἥ τ' οὖν*, but *ἅτε* is so placed in Tim 24 D, *ἅτ' οὖν φιλοπόλεμός τε καὶ φιλόσοφος ἡ θεὸς οὖσα, κ τ λ*, and elsewh For *ἀκηράτῳ τρεφομένη* Stallb, offended by the recurrence of *τρέφεται*, has restored the old reading *ἀκήρατος στρεφομένη*, which is found in most MSS, and which he thus translates "*Ubi ipse igitur dei ratio* (Christ) propter mentem et scientiam *sese vertens* puram et intaminatam," &c, an interpretation which greatly needs an interpreter I think there can be no doubt that Hermann was right in receiving *τρεφομένη* on the authority of a Vienna, supported by other MSS Others have *ἀκηράτως*, which leads to *ἀκηράτῳ* The mind of a god feeds, says Socr, on pure intelligence and pure science, so does every soul, though not divine, which is destined to receive what rightfully belongs to it (i e to enter on its rightful inheritance, the truth, in distinction from those less fortunate spirits which accident, or the headstrong violence of the unruly steed, prevents from reaching the *ἀληθείας πεδίον* presently named) Every such favoured soul welcomes, after long absence, the sight of the Essential, it feeds on and revels in the contemplation of the True, until the rotation of the great celestial sphere brings it round again to the point of its departure *εὐπαθεῖ* is nearly equivalent to *ἡδυπαθεῖ*, 'enjoys itself'

ὅσῃ ἂν μέλλῃ] Bodl *ὅσηι* G. Herm conj *ὅσῃ ἂν μέλῃ*

οὐχ ᾗ γένεσις πρόσεστιν] The object of the highest science is not the phenomenal, but the real—not the concrete, but the abstract This highest and truest science is, in Plato's view, Dialectic Comp Phileb 57 E, *ἡμᾶς ἀπαξιοῖ ἂν ἡ τοῦ διαλέγεσθαι δύναμις εἴ τινα πρὸ αὐτῆς ἄλλην κρίναιμεν τὴν γὰρ περὶ τὸ ὂν καὶ τὸ ὄντως, καὶ τὸ κατὰ ταὐτὸν ἀεὶ πεφυκὸς πάντως ἔγωγε οἶμαι ἡγεῖσθαι ξύμπαντας, ὅσοις νοῦ καὶ σμικρὸν προσήρτηται, μακρῷ ἀληθεστάτην εἶναι γνῶσιν*

E. *ἐπιστήμην οὖσαν*] This science is said to be *real* (*οὖσαν*) as the *ὂν* which

ὡσαύτως τὰ ὄντα ὄντως θεασαμένη καὶ ἑστιαθεῖσα, δῦσα πάλιν εἰς τὸ εἴσω τοῦ οὐρανοῦ, οἴκαδε ἦλθεν. ἐλθούσης δὲ αὐτῆς ὁ ἡνίοχος πρὸς τὴν φάτνην τοὺς ἵππους στήσας παρέβαλεν ἀμβροσίαν τε καὶ ἐπ' αὐτῇ νέκταρ ἐπότισε.
248 καὶ οὗτος μὲν θεῶν βίος. αἱ δὲ ἄλλαι ψυχαί, | ἡ μὲν ἄριστα θεῷ ἑπομένη καὶ εἰκασμένη ὑπερῆρεν εἰς τὸν ἔξω τόπον τὴν τοῦ ἡνιόχου κεφαλήν, καὶ συμπεριηνέχθη τὴν περιφοράν, θορυβουμένη ὑπὸ τῶν ἵππων καὶ μόγις καθορῶσα τὰ ὄντα· ἡ δὲ τοτὲ μὲν ἦρε, τοτὲ δ' ἔδυ, βιαζομένων δὲ τῶν ἵππων τὰ μὲν εἶδε, τὰ δ' οὔ. αἱ δὲ δὴ ἄλλαι γλιχόμεναι μὲν ἅπασαι τοῦ ἄνω ἕπονται, ἀδυνατοῦσαι δὲ ὑποβρύχιαι ξυμπεριφέρονται, πατοῦσαι ἀλλήλας
B καὶ ἐπιβάλλουσαι, ἑτέρα πρὸ τῆς ἑτέρας πειρωμένη γενέσθαι. θόρυβος οὖν καὶ ἅμιλλα καὶ ἱδρὼς ἔσχατος γίγνεται. οὗ δὴ κακίᾳ ἡνιόχων πολλαὶ μὲν χωλεύονται, πολλαὶ δὲ πολλὰ πτερὰ θραύονται· πᾶσαι δέ, πολὺν ἔχουσα πόνον, ἀτελεῖς τῆς τοῦ ὄντος θέας ἀπέρχονται, καὶ ἀπελθοῦσαι τροφῇ δοξαστῇ χρῶνται. οὗ δ' ἕνεχ' ἡ πολλὴ σπουδὴ τὸ ἀληθείας ἰδεῖν πεδίον οὗ ἐστίν, ἥ τε δὴ προσήκουσα

it contemplates. Other sciences have to do with the *οὐσίας μετέχοντα*, which are called *ὄντα* in virtue of this *μέθεξις*, but have no independent reality. They are *ὄντα πῃ* or *κατά τι*, but not *ὄντως* nor *αὐτὰ καθ' αὑτὰ ὄντα*. Compare Sophist. 241 D.

τοὺς ἵππους στήσας] Il. v. 368, Ἔνθ' ἵππους ἔστησε ποδήνεμος ὠκέα Ἶρις, Λύσασ' ἐξ ὀχέων, παρὰ δ' ἀμβρόσιον βάλεν εἶδαρ.

αἱ δὲ ἄλλαι ψυχαί] The gods, we have seen, stand on the outer surface (*νώτῳ*) of heaven. Of the other souls, those which most resemble gods can only partially emerge into the outer region. Their heads being above water, or whatever be the element of which the great sphere is composed, they are able to view the Essences, though with some difficulty, for their steeds confuse and trouble them. A second order of souls is less favoured: they see but in part, for ever and anon the restiveness of their teams causes them to dip below the surface. The majority are unable to struggle up into the higher region at all, but are carried round with the rest, immersed in the liquid element. Hom. Hymn 33. 11, ἐπ' ἀκρωτήρια βάντες Πρύμνης· τὴν δ' ἄνεμός τε μέγας καὶ κῦμα θαλάσσης Θῆκαν ὑποβρυχίην. Apollodor. III. 15. 8. 3 (ap. Steph. Lex.), τὴν κόρην τῆς πρύμνης τῶν ποδῶν ἐκδήσας ὑποβρύχιον ἐποίησε. Her. I. 189, ὑποβρύχιον οἰχώκεε φέρων (sc. ὁ ποταμὸς τὸν ἵππον).

218 B *ἀτελεῖς*] "Quasi initiationis expertes," Ast. The mysteries were called *τέλη*, *τελεταί*, the adepts *τετελεσμένοι*, as is well known. Those who depart frustrated and disappointed of the wished-for spectacle, are fain to feed henceforth upon the chaff and husks of opinion, instead of the pure nectar and ambrosia of exact truth, as the steeds of the gods, and, we may suppose, their drivers also, were wont to do: sup. 247 E.

οὗ δ' ἕνεχ'—ἥ τε δή, κ. τ. λ.] This reading, restored by Bekk. after careful collation of MSS (see his V. Ll.), is not, I think, to be disturbed. Badh. conjectures ὧν δ' ἕνεχ' .... δύ' ἐστόν, ἥ τε δὴ .... ἥ τε τοῦ

ψυχῆς τῷ ἀρίστῳ νομὴ ἐκ τοῦ ἐκεῖ λειμῶνος τυγχάνει οὖσα, ἥ τε τοῦ πτεροῦ φύσις, ᾧ ψυχὴ κουφίζεται, τούτῳ C
τρέφεται. θεσμός τε Ἀδραστείας ὅδε, ἥτις ἂν ψυχὴ θεῷ ξυνοπαδὸς γενομένη κατίδῃ τι τῶν ἀληθῶν, μέχρι τε τῆς ἑτέρας περιόδου εἶναι ἀπήμονα, κἂν ἀεὶ τοῦτο δύνηται ποιεῖν, ἀεὶ ἀβλαβῆ εἶναι· ὅταν δὲ ἀδυνατήσασα ἐπισπέσθαι μὴ ἴδῃ, καί τινι συντυχίᾳ χρησαμένη, λήθης τε καὶ κακίας πλησθεῖσα βαρυνθῇ, βαρυνθεῖσα δὲ πτερορρυήσῃ τε καὶ ἐπὶ τὴν γῆν πέσῃ, τότε νόμος ταύτην μὴ φυτεῦσαι εἰς μηδεμίαν θηρείαν φύσιν ἐν τῇ πρώτῃ γενέ- D
σει, ἀλλὰ τὴν μὲν πλεῖστα ἰδοῦσαν εἰς γονὴν ἀνδρὸς γε-

πτ, κ τ λ The old reading was οὗ δὴ ἕνεχ', for which Ast plausibly suggested τοῦ (sc. τίνος) δὴ ἕνεχ' οὗ ἐστίν. The reason, says Socr., why the souls exhibit this exceeding eagerness to behold the Fields of Truth, is that pasturage is found there suited to the pure intellect, the best and noblest part of the soul, and to the growth of the plumage from which the soul derives her lightness and buoyancy Where, we may observe, the sign and thing signified are represented as two independent facts, for the 'plumage' of the soul is simply the same thing with τὸ ἄριστον τῆς ψυχῆς. This is one of many artifices by which Plato obliges his readers to keep in mind the inner meaning of his allegory. The ἀληθείας πεδίον is a new feature in the scenery of the mythus Possibly Plato found the phrase in some Orphic poet, possibly also in some Pythagorean book It is used by the author of the Axiochus (371 B) to denote the place where Minos and Rhadamanthus hold their court Analogous phrases are ἀρετῆς λείμων in Orph Lith 81, Ἄτης λείμων in Empedocles v 23, Karst, λήθης πεδίον in Republ x. 621 Plutarch, de Defect Orac, uses ἀληθείας πεδίον in a sense half mathematical half mystical, and savouring strongly of a Pythagorean source The periphrasis ἡ τοῦ πτεροῦ φύσις is analogous to τὸ τῆς ἀληθοῦς ἐπιστήμης γένος, sup 247 D

C θεσμός τε Ἀδραστείας ὅδε] Adrasteia, the Inevitable, is an epithet of Ἀνάγκη, and her mystical name in the Orphic theology (Lob Aglaoph p 185) In Aesch Prom 972, Adrasteia is identified with ...

to be in the popular creed Auct Rhesi 468, ξὺν δ' Ἀδραστείᾳ λέγω Republ. 451 A, προσκυνῶ δὲ Ἀδράστειαν On this occasion the mystical sense is adopted by Plato, who, according to Olympiodorus, πανταχοῦ παρῳδεῖ τὰ Ὀρφέως, and nowhere more than in this mythus. θεσμὸς Ἀδραστείας is simply the 'law of destiny,' according to which those spirits which in the course of the divine progress have seen somewhat, i e some considerable measure, of truth, shall remain unharmed until the *next* great revolution, and so on each time in succession. Those whose powers are unequal to the effort, and who, through mishap or fault of their own, shed their plumage and fall to the earth in consequence, are in their first earthly genesis incarnated as men, never as beasts, this last degradation being apparently the result of a perverse choice deliberately made by the soul itself at a subsequent period (inf 249 B) Human destiny would seem therefore to be partly the result of choice, partly of necessity—and we have here a metaphysical problem clothed in a mythical dress

D τὴν μὲν πλεῖστα—τυραννικός] For this curious classification 'in order of merit' we are not obliged to seek any more occult motive than Plato's private predilections. Empedocles, in a passage relating to the Metempsychosis, had given the precedence to μάντεις τε καὶ ὑμνοπόλοι καὶ ἰητροί, Karst πρόμοι 381, Karst But in Plato's estimation the φιλόσοφος naturally holds the first rank, the 'lover of beauty' and 'the musical and erotic man' meaning much ... than ... φιλοσοφίας οὔσης

νησομένου φιλοσόφου ἢ φιλοκάλου ἢ μουσικοῦ τινὸς καὶ ἐρωτικοῦ, τὴν δὲ δευτέραν εἰς βασιλέως ἐννόμου ἢ πολεμικοῦ καὶ ἀρχικοῦ, τρίτην εἰς πολιτικοῦ ἤ τινος οἰκονομικοῦ ἢ χρηματιστικοῦ, τετάρτην εἰς φιλοπόνου ἢ γυμνα-
E στικοῦ ἢ περὶ σώματος ἴασίν τινα ἐσομένου, πέμπτην μαντικὸν βίον ἤ τινα τελεστικὸν ἕξουσαν· ἕκτῃ ποιητικὸς ἢ τῶν περὶ μίμησίν τις ἄλλος ἁρμόσει, ἑβδόμῃ δημιουργικὸς ἢ γεωργικός, ὀγδόῃ σοφιστικὸς ἢ δημοτικός, ἐννάτῃ τυραννικός. ἐν δὴ τούτοις ἅπασιν ὃς μὲν ἂν δι-

μεγίστης μουσικῆς, Phaed 61 A. In assigning a low position to the 'soothsayer or ritualist,' and also to the poetic or mimetic genius, he somewhat maliciously corrects Empedocles, and at the same time aims a blow at the superstitious pietism and literary sentimentalism of his own day For Plato's view of *μίμησις* we may compare a curious passage in the tenth book of the Repub init to p 608 His estimate of the *μαντικὸν γένος* may be gathered from a striking description ibid ii 364 C seq, fully explaining the *μαντικὸς βίος ἢ τελεστικὸς* of the text The 'sophist and people's man' are placed where we should expect to find them, just above the worst and most irredeemable of monsters, the tyrant So in the Republic the *δημοκρατικὸς* is raised but one step above the *τυραννικός* Rep 559 comp with 562 Of the first four kinds we may remark that they represent some more or less dignified and useful employment, while of the four which follow, three denote, in Plato's view, some variety of imposture, the class of 'mechanics and tillers of the soil' being placed thus low in the scale partly for the purpose of depressing their associates It may surprise us to find the *χρηματιστικὸς* placed so high, and the physician no higher in the scale, especially as a physician (Hippocrates) is almost the only one of his contemporaries, out of his own circle, of whom Plato speaks in terms of unqualified admiration But Hippocrates, as we are told inf 270 C, was one of the few who combined physic and physics, the study of the human frame with that of natural philosophy. *He* may therefore be classed with the *φιλόσοφοι*, and we do not find that Plato speaks with much respect of any other member of the medical faculty It may be observed that in the Politicus, 259 C, the *βασιλικὸς οἰκονομικὸς* and *πολιτικὸς* are *identified*, a discrepancy which I mention for the benefit of those critics who maintain, on grounds hardly stronger than this, that the Politicus was the work of an anonymous opponent of Plato * It will be observed that I have followed Badh in inserting ἢ after *φιλοπόνου* The members of this higher class being all arranged in triplets (for *μουσικὸς καὶ ἐρωτικὸς* form only one sub-genus), symmetry requires that the *φιλόπονος* should be distinguished from his compeers

E *δημοτικός*] This is the reading of the Bodl and other MSS of good note Bekk retains the vulg *δημοκοπικός*— 'the life of the hunter for popularity,' the *captator popularis aurae* This, however, in a description of recognized human professions is too vituperative, and blunts the edge of Plato's satire Every public man in a democracy is *δημοτικός*, only the worst specimens of the class are *δημοκοπικοί* Besides, the word *δημοκόπος* and its derivatives seem to have come into use at a much later period

τυραννικός] Either one who has usurped or one who seeks to usurp the supreme power by unconstitutional means, or perhaps, more generally, the man who in his own sphere acts solely with a view to self, as the tyrant does in his. So the *τυραννικὸς ἀνὴρ* of the Republic denotes one under the sway of some one passion which tyrannizes over his whole being

ἐν δὴ τούτοις, κ τ λ] The destiny of

---

* In the Republic the *βασιλικὸς* is identified with the *φιλόσοφος*

καίως διαγάγῃ, ἀμείνονος μοίρας μεταλαμβάνει, ὃς δ' ἂν ἀδίκως, χείρονος. εἰς μὲν γὰρ τὸ αὐτὸ ὅθεν ἥκει ἡ ψυχὴ ἑκάστη, οὐκ ἀφικνεῖται ἐτῶν μυρίων· οὐ γὰρ πτεροῦται πρὸ τοσούτου χρόνου, | πλὴν ἡ τοῦ φιλοσοφήσαν- 249
τος ἀδόλως ἢ παιδεραστήσαντος μετὰ φιλοσοφίας. αὗται δὲ τρίτῃ περιόδῳ τῇ χιλιετεῖ, ἐὰν ἕλωνται τρὶς ἐφεξῆς τὸν βίον τοῦτον, οὕτω πτερωθεῖσαι τρισχιλιοστῷ ἔτει ἀπέρχονται. αἱ δὲ ἄλλαι, ὅταν τὸν πρῶτον βίον τελευτήσωσι, κρίσεως ἔτυχον. κριθεῖσαι δέ, αἱ μὲν εἰς τὰ ὑπὸ

the soul after death is determined solely by the life it had led on earth, without reference to the ante-natal state How a *σοφιστὴς* or a *τύραννος* can be said *δικαίως διάγειν* we are not informed, and the *τούτοις ἅπασιν* must therefore probably be taken with a grain of allowance. It is however noteworthy, that in its *first* genesis, the soul's condition is fixed according to an *intellectual* standard (*τὴν μὲν πλεῖστα ἰδοῦσαν*), whereas its doom after leaving the body depends on moral considerations (*ὃς ἂν δικαίως διαγαγῇ*)

εἰς μὲν γὰρ τὸ αὐτό] i e *εἰς τὴν τοῦ ξυννόμου οἴκησιν ἄστρου* Tim 42 B Comp Virg G. iv 226, "viva volare Sideris in numerum atque alto succedere coelo"

οὐκ ἀφικνεῖται ἐτῶν μυρίων] This 'genitive of time' is usually accompanied with *πρὸ* or *ἐντός* But the prep is frequently omitted, as in a Law ap Dem Mid p 529, *οἱ δὲ θεσμοθέται εἰσαγόντων εἰς τὴν ἡλιαίαν τριάκοντα ἡμερῶν ἀφ' ἧς ἂν ἡ ἡ γραφή* Herod vi 58, *ἀγορὴ δέκα ἡμερέων οὐκ ἵσταταί σφι* Similarly in reference to past time, Arist Plut 98, *πολλοῦ γὰρ αὐτοὺς οὐχ ἑόρακά πω χρόνου* It would be vain to inquire into Plato's reasons for fixing this precise number of years An 'annus magnus,' at the end of which the planets recover the relative positions they occupied at its commencement was a device of the Egyptian astronomers, but there is no proof that Plato thought of it here Besides, the Egyptian cycle was fixed at 36,525 years Other cycles are enumerated by Ideler, Chronol i 182 seq, none of which are of the length of a myriad years. It is more probable that Plato took the hint from Empedocles, whom [illegible]

sings thus *Ἔστιν Ἀνάγκης χρῆμα, θεῶν ψήφισμα παλαιόν* (comp. *θεσμὸς Ἀδραστείας*, p sup) *Ἀΐδιον, πλατέεσσι κατεσφρηγισμένον ὅρκοις Εὖτε τις ἀμπλακίῃσι φόνῳ φίλα γυῖα μιήνῃ, (Δαίμονες οἵτε βίοιο λελόγχασι μακραίωνος,) Τρίς μιν μυρίας ὥρας ἀπὸ μακάρων ἀλάλησθαι Γεινόμενον παντοῖα διὰ χρεῶ εἴδεα θνητῶν Τῶν* (f *τῷ*) *καὶ ἐγὼ νῦν εἰμὶ φυγὰς θεόθεν καὶ ἀλήτης* whereas in Plato the human soul, before its fall, is ranked among the *δαίμονες* Krische (Phaedr p 66) will have it that by *ὥρα* Empedocles meant the third part of a year If there be any truth in this notion, the *μύρια ἔτη* of Plato and the *τρὶς μυρίαι ὧραι* of Empedocles will denote the same period of time But this is probably a needless refinement, the numbers three and ten being both 'sacred' numbers, and therefore naturally suggesting themselves to a mind of a mystical turn like that of Empedocles, and indeed of Plato in his mythopoeic moods

249] The soul of the true philosopher is excused from seven of the ten millennial probations through which the rest have to pass This is probably an Orphico-Pythagorean idea Pindar, who borrows largely from such sources, has the well-known lines *ὅσοι δ' ἐτόλμασαν ἐς τρὶς Ἑκατέρωθι μείναντες ἀπὸ πάμπαν ἀδίκων ἔχειν ψυχάν, ἔτειλαν Διὸς ὁδὸν παρὰ Κρόνου τύρσιν ἔνθα μακάρων νᾶσος* κ.τ.λ Ol. ii 68 Compare also the curious statement of Herodotus (ii 123), who speaks of a *περιήλυσις τρισχιλίων ἐτῶν* as a feature in the Egyptian metempsychosis, which he accuses his own countrymen of plagiarizing *τούτῳ τῷ λόγῳ εἰσὶ οἳ Ἑλλήνων ἐχρήσαντο, οἱ μὲν πρότερον οἱ δὲ ὕστερον, ὡς ἰδίῳ ἑωυτῶν ἐόντι· τῶν ἐγώ, εἰδὼς τὰ οὐνόματα, οὐ γράφω* The *αἵρεσις βίων*, which takes place at the end of each millennial pe-

γῆς δικαιωτήρια ἐλθοῦσαι δίκην ἐκτίνουσιν, αἱ δ' εἰς τοὐ-
B ρανοῦ τινὰ τόπον ὑπὸ τῆς δίκης κουφισθεῖσαι διάγουσιν
ἀξίως οὗ ἐν ἀνθρώπου εἴδει ἐβίωσαν βίου. τῷ δὲ χιλιο-
στῷ ἀμφότεραι ἀφικνούμεναι ἐπὶ κλήρωσίν τε καὶ αἵρεσιν
τοῦ δευτέρου βίου, αἱροῦνται ὃν ἂν ἐθέλῃ ἑκάστη ἔνθα
καὶ εἰς θηρίου βίον ἀνθρωπίνη ψυχὴ ἀφικνεῖται, καὶ ἐκ
θηρίου, ὅς ποτε ἄνθρωπος ἦν, πάλιν εἰς ἄνθρωπον. οὐ
γὰρ ἥ γε μή ποτε ἰδοῦσα τὴν ἀλήθειαν εἰς τόδε ἥξει τὸ
σχῆμα. δεῖ γὰρ ἄνθρωπον ξυνιέναι κατ' εἶδος λεγόμενον,
ἐκ πολλῶν ἰόντ' αἰσθήσεων εἰς ἓν λογισμῷ ξυναιρούμενον.
C τοῦτο δέ ἐστιν ἀνάμνησις ἐκείνων, ἅ ποτ' εἶδεν ἡμῶν ἡ
ψυχὴ συμπορευθεῖσα θεῷ καὶ ὑπεριδοῦσα ἃ νῦν εἶναί
φαμεν, καὶ ἀνακύψασα εἰς τὸ ὂν ὄντως. διὸ δὴ δικαίως

riod, is described circumstantially in the mythus, Rep x 617

δικαιωτήρια] *βασανιστήρια*, 'places of torment,' is Pollux's interpretation of the word Comp Gorg 523 B, *τὸ τῆς δίκης δεσμωτήριον, ὃ δὴ Τάρταρον καλοῦσι*

B *ἐπὶ κλήρωσίν τε καὶ αἵρεσιν*] These words are explained by Rep x 617 F, where the souls are made to draw lots for the first choice and then *πρῶτος ὁ λαχὼν πρῶτος αἱρείται βίον*—a mythical mode of reconciling freedom and necessity—choice being left free, but under limiting conditions

ἔνθα καί] Where too,—at this stage in its history,—the human soul is permitted to migrate into a bestial state of existence, or vice versâ It had before been stated that in its first *γένεσις* the soul invariably animates a *human* form (sup 248 D) From the two passages compared, it would appear that *every* soul had caught at least *some* dim glimpse of the truth in its heavenly progress, as is stated below, 249 E *πᾶσα ἀνθρώπου ψυχὴ φύσει τεθέαται τὰ ὄντα*

δεῖ γὰρ ἄνθρωπον—ξυναιρούμενον] It is a law of the human understanding that it can only act by the way of general notions, 'the form so called' ascending from the manifold impressions of sense to a unity collected by a process of reason or reflection In other words, sensibles are *per se* unintelligible; we can only understand a thing by referring it to a class or general notion This, Plato goes on to say, is neither more nor less than an act of reminiscence (*ἀνάμνησις*), these general forms of the understanding reminding us of their transcendent prototypes—the ideas presented to the gaze of the unbodied soul in the ante-natal state It will be observed that I have adopted for the vulg. *ἰὸν* Badh's correction *ἰόντ'* This will be thought over bold, in face of a consensus of MSS. But to speak of the *εἶδος* itself as *ἰόν*—proceeding or advancing to a 'unity,' itself *being* that 'unity' which is the result of the process—is a licence of bad writing in which it is difficult to believe that Plato would indulge. Neither can we speak of an *εἶδος* as *ξυναιρούμενον εἰς ἕν*, which is equally tautological It is evidently the man, the generalizing mind, which can alone be said *ἰέναι εἰς ἓν λογισμῷ ξυναιρούμενον*, or in other words, *ἐκ πολλῶν αἰσθήσεων εἰς ἓν εἶδος* Comp Rep x 596 A, *εἶδος γάρ πού τι ἓν ἕκαστον εἰώθαμεν τίθεσθαι περὶ ἕκαστα τὰ πολλὰ οἷς ταὐτὸν ὄνομα ἐπιφέρομεν* This generalizing process, the primary law of the human understanding, is briefly expressed in the Platonic formula *ἓν καὶ πολλά* Phileb 16 C is a 'locus classicus' on this subject

C *διὸ δὴ δικαίως*] The intellect of the philosopher obeys the same laws as other minds, it too can only arrive at truth by collecting generals from particulars but the philosopher does that systematically and perseveringly, which

μόνη πτεροῦται ἡ τοῦ φιλοσόφου διάνοια· πρὸς γὰρ ἐκείνοις ἀεί ἐστι μνήμῃ κατὰ δύναμιν, πρὸς οἷσπερ θεὸς ὢν θεῖός ἐστι. τοῖς δὲ δὴ τοιούτοις ἀνὴρ ὑπομνήμασιν ὀρθῶς χρώμενος, τελέους ἀεὶ τελετὰς τελούμενος, τέλεος ὄντως μόνος γίγνεται. ἐξιστάμενος δὲ τῶν ἀνθρωπίνων D
σπουδασμάτων, καὶ πρὸς τῷ θείῳ γιγνόμενος, νουθετεῖται μὲν ὑπὸ τῶν πολλῶν ὡς παρακινῶν, ἐνθουσιάζων δὲ λέληθε τοὺς πολλούς.

[Ἔστι δὴ οὖν δεῦρο ὁ πᾶς ἥκων λόγος περὶ τῆς τετάρ-

ordinary men do in a purposeless and intermitting manner Hence the soul of the sage alone recovers its lost plumage, the symbol and earnest of its divinity 'For it is *always* dwelling in memory upon that Essence, by dwelling on which it is that even a god is divine,' i e to the contemplation of which a god owes his divinity, as if he had said θεὸς θεῖός ἐστι διότι πρὸς τοῖς οὖσίν ἐστι For the phrase πρός τινι εἶναι comp Phaed 84 c, αὐτὸς πρὸς τῷ εἰρημένῳ λόγῳ ἦν ὁ Σωκράτης, 'defixus est in' So paul inf we have, πρὸς τῷ θείῳ γιγνόμενος

πρὸς οἷσπερ θεὸς ὢν θεῖός ἐστι] Hermeias tells us that there were no less than four readings of this clause ἢ πρὸς οἷσπερ θεὸς ὢν θεός ἐστιν, ἢ πάλιν θεῖός ἐστιν, ἢ μετὰ τοῦ ἄρθρου, πρὸς οἷσπερ ὁ θεὸς ὢν θεός ἐστιν, ἢ πάλιν θεῖός ἐστιν The second of these is found in the Bodl and Vat, and is much the best ὁ θεὸς could only mean the supreme Deity, a meaning which would clash with the conventional theology of the Mythus Θεὸς without the article denotes any one of the twelve gods or rather of the eleven before alluded to, for we are left to conjecture what the spiritual nutriment of Hestia may have been, wings being evidently inappropriate to so sedentary a deity

ὑπομνήμασιν] The εἴδη, it would seem, are not themselves ὄντα, but only 'memoranda' suggestive of ὄντα This Ast has perceived, comm p 132 "haec veri comprehensio recordatio dicitur, quia ipsum verum quod in superiore vita spectavimus (h e ἰδέα, proprio sensu ita dicta, ut distinguatur ab eo quod εἶδος, h e notio universi vel genus, vocatur) hac comprehensione revocatur" In modern language, it is by meditating 'aright'

philosopher arrives at exact scientific ideas ὀρθῶς implies that this must be done methodically, i. e according to the principles of a true dialectic I think the distinction between εἶδος and ἰδέα is here not to be overlooked, though the two words are in most cases interchangeable All men understand according to an εἶδος, more or less, according to their several capacities, the philosopher alone ascends to ὄντα or ἰδέαι,—τῇ τοῦ ὄντος ἀεὶ διὰ λογισμῶν προσκείμενος ἰδέᾳ (Soph 254) The mysteries in which the sage is ever undergoing initiation are called τέλεοι, as presently we read of τῶν τελετῶν ἣν θέμις εἰπεῖν μακαριωτάτην (250 B) In Phileb 67 the absolute Good is styled ἡ τοῦ ἱκανοῦ καὶ τελέου δύναμις, and distinguished by three predicates from the νοῦς which contemplates it. The philosopher is thus the subject of a true ἐνθουσιασμός, of which the emotions of the awe stricken mystae at Eleusis are but a type. Compare also Rep viii. 560 E, τελουμένου ψυχὴν μεγάλοισι τέλεσι

D ὡς παρακινῶν] Properly the compound means to 'move amiss,' as in Arist. Ran 615, σκοπεῖ νῦν ἤν με παρακινήσαντ' ἴδῃς, where παρακ. is now substituted on MS. authority for the vulg ὑποκινήσαντ'. The same correction seems to be required in Rep ix 573 C, μαινόμενος καὶ ὑποκεκινηκώς As a synonym of μαίνεσθαι, the intransitive παρακινεῖν is usual, not παρακινεῖσθαι, which is first used by late writers Com. ap Harpocr p. 23 συνέπινε παρακινοῦσι καὶ μεμηνόσιν So an old dotard is called παρακεκινηκὼς ὑφ' ἡλικίας by a comic poet ap J. Poll Mein Com Gr iv 680

Ἔστι δὴ οὖν δεῦρο] Socr. in these words reminds Phaedr of the drift of the brilliant episode just concluded It

της μανίας, ἣν ὅταν τὸ τῇδέ τις ὁρῶν κάλλος, τοῦ ἀληθοῦς ἀναμιμνησκόμενος, πτερῶταί τε καὶ [ἀναπτερούμενος] προθυμούμενος ἀναπτέσθαι, ἀδυνατῶν δέ, ὄρνιθος δίκην
E βλέπων ἄνω, τῶν κάτω δὲ ἀμελῶν, αἰτίαν ἔχει ὡς μανικῶς διακείμενος, ὡς ἄρα αὕτη πασῶν τῶν ἐνθουσιάσεων

was designed as a picture of the 'fourth Madness,' that of Love, or rather as a theory of the philosophic habit of mind of which Love is the symbol The point really attained is, that the philosopher is the subject of an 'enthusiasm,' a rapt and passionate yearning after a truth higher and purer than either the senses or the understanding reflecting on the objects of sense can furnish Why is this enthusiasm to be styled Love, and what have the two states of consciousness in common with each other? This is the question which is now to be attacked, and to which Plato proceeds with much skill and ingenuity to elaborate an answer 'Beauty' furnishes the connecting link. Beauty, the object of Love, is one of the Ideas, and it is that one of which alone the world of sense presents a vivid and approximately adequate resemblance The transition from ideal truth in general to this particular variety, in other words from τὸ ὂν to τὸ καλόν, had been prepared by the vivid imagery of the ὑπερουράνιος πορεία, and the speaker is able to slip in the word κάλλος at the very commencement of this portion of the discourse, as if it were synonymous with τὸ ὄν, and had formed the subject of the foregoing episode, when in fact it has never once been mentioned With regard to the construction of the sentence, which is irregular in more respects than one, we may observe (1) That the apodosis to δεῦρο is contained in the words, ὡς ἄρα αὕτη γίγνεται, καὶ ὅτι . καλεῖται, the intervening clauses being parenthetical from ἣν to διακείμενος incl (2) This parenthetical sentence is itself anacoluthic, in two respects The relative ἥν, sc μανίαν (for which Ast conj ἧ), is a 'pendent' accusative, referring to αἰτίαν ἔχει ὡς μανικῶς διακείμενος, though not grammatically constructed with it In the next place ὅταν would naturally have been followed by a second subjunctive, instead of which we have the three participles ἀδυνατῶν, βλέπων, ἀμελῶν We might have had ἀδυνατῇ δὲ followed by βλέπων and ἀμελῶν, or ἀδυνατῶν δὲ . βλέπῃ ἀμελῇ The clause ὅταν . . ἀμελῶν is in effect an epexegesis of ἥν, and serves as a *résumé* of the foregoing description of the philosophic enthusiasm The difficulty of rendering this in English is skilfully surmounted in Mr Wright's translation of Phaedr. p 40.

ὄρνιθος δίκην βλέπων ἄνω] 'bird-like, casts many an upward glance, regardless of things below' Ar. Av 50 χὠ κολοιὸς οὑτοσὶ Ἄνω κέχηνεν Socr. alludes to the vulgar prejudice against philosophers is described Theaet 174 A. Compare the ludicrous incident in the Nubes, 171 The passage quoted by Ast from Plut Epict. vii 318, ἐγὼ μὲν βλέπων ἔξω, καθάπερ ὄρνις ποθῶν πόθεν ἀναπτέσθαι, illustrates, but may hardly be regarded as an imitation of, the present Still less can I see that in the present passage "homines amoris corporei appetentes irridentur"! It would have been more correct to say 'homines amore divino instincti adumbrantur' They expose themselves to the jeers of the vulgar by their habits of rapt abstraction, longing as they do, like caged birds, to escape from their fleshly incumbrances.

E. ὡς ἄρα αὕτη, κ.τ.λ.] This, the philosophic, is said to be the best of all the enthusiasms, or θεῖαι μανίαι, both in itself and in its origin and antecedents, it is best for its possessor, and for him who shares it with him, for the sage, that is, and for his youthful disciple whom he infects with his own sacred frenzy. The φιλόσοφος had already (248 D) been placed in the same category with the φιλόκαλος and ἐρωτικός, and (249) we read of the παιδεραστῶν μετὰ φιλοσοφίας We were thus prepared for the identification, for the purposes of this discussion, of the sage and the lover which is effected in the next clause. The madman, it is said, of this philosophic type, who falls in love with a beautiful human being is under such circumstances called ἐραστής.

ἀρίστη τε καὶ ἐξ ἀρίστων τῷ τε ἔχοντι καὶ τῷ κοινωνοῦντι αὐτῆς γίγνεται, καὶ ὅτι ταύτης μετέχων τῆς μανίας ὁ ἐρῶν τῶν καλῶν ἐραστὴς καλεῖται. καθάπερ γὰρ εἴρηται, πᾶσα μὲν ἀνθρώπου ψυχὴ φύσει τεθέαται τὰ ὄντα, ἢ οὐκ ἂν ἦλθεν εἰς τόδε τὸ ζῶον, | ἀναμιμνήσκεσθαι 250
δ' ἐκ τῶνδε ἐκεῖνα οὐ ῥᾴδιον ἁπάσῃ, οὔτε ὅσαι βραχέως εἶδον τότε τἀκεῖ, οὔτε αἳ δεῦρο πεσοῦσαι ἐδυστύχησαν, ὥστε ὑπό τινων ὁμιλιῶν ἐπὶ τὸ ἄδικον τραπόμεναι λήθην ὧν τότε εἶδον ἱερῶν ἔχειν. ὀλίγαι δὴ λείπονται αἷς τὸ τῆς μνήμης ἱκανῶς πάρεστιν. αὗται δέ, ὅταν τι τῶν ἐκεῖ ὁμοίωμα ἴδωσιν, ἐκπλήττονται καὶ οὐκέθ' αὑτῶν γίγνονται, ὃ δ' ἔστι τὸ πάθος ἀγνοοῦσι διὰ τὸ μὴ ἱκανῶς διαισθάνεσθαι. δικαιοσύνης μὲν οὖν καὶ σωφροσύ- B

καθάπερ γὰρ εἴρηται] Sup 218 D. comp with 219 B

ἢ οὐκ ἂν ἦλθεν, κ τ λ] 'else had it never entered the animal called man.' *ἤ*, *alioquin*, as sup 237 C. It would seem to follow from this that every man is potentially a philosopher, as the slave-boy in the Meno is shown to be an unconscious geometer. There are very few however who realize their own capacities, *ἀναμιμνήσκεσθαι δ' ἐκ τῶνδε ἐκεῖνα οὐ ῥᾴδιον ἁπάσῃ*. This may be owing to their ill luck either in the former or in the present state of existence. In the latter case evil associations may have turned them from the right path and clouded their memory, so that they quite forget the 'sacred objects' they beheld on the solemn occasion of their initiation. The force of *ἱερὰ* will appear more fully in the sequel

250 *αὗται δέ, κ τ λ*] As the ideas are *παραδείγματα τῶν ἐνθάδε*, so the phenomenal is *ὁμοίωμα τῶν ἐκεῖ* Comp Tim 29 B, 48 E, *ἓν μὲν ὡς παραδείγματος εἶδος ὑποτεθέν, νοητὸν καὶ ἀεὶ κατὰ ταὐτὸν ὄν, μίμημα δὲ παραδείγματος δεύτερον, γένεσιν ἔχον καὶ ὁρατόν* Parm 132 D, *καταφαίνεται τὰ μὲν εἴδη ταῦτα ὥσπερ παραδείγματα ἑστάναι ἐν τῇ φύσει, τὰ δὲ ἄλλα τούτοις ἐοικέναι καὶ εἶναι ὁμοιώματα καὶ ἡ μέθεξις αὕτη τοῖς ἄλλοις γίγνεσθαι τῶν εἰδῶν οὐκ ἄλλη τις ἢ εἰκασθῆναι αὐτοῖς* The phraseology of the ideal theory is pretty fully illustrated by A Butler, Lectt. ii. 127 fol

ἐκπλήτ[illegible] γί-γνονται] The latter of these phrases is hardly to be distinguished in sense from the former, *ἐκπλήττεσθαι* being equivalent to *ἐξίστασθαι* (Schol Nub 811, *ἐκπεπληγμένοι· ἐξεστηκότες*), and this again, with or without *φρενῶν*, to *οὐκέθ' αὑτοῦ γίγνεσθαι* In Charm 155 D we have the still more idiomatic phrase *οὐκέτ' ἐν ἐμαυτοῦ ἦν*, answering to the Lat *apud me*. So Ar Vesp 612 *σκορδινᾶται κἄστιν οὐκ ἐν αὑτοῦ* In Xen. Anab i 5 17, we find *ἀκούσας ταῦτα ὁ Κλέαρχος ἐν ἑαυτῷ ἐγένετο*, 'recovered himself,' where probably *ἑαυτοῦ* was the original reading, as it seems to have been in Soph Phil 950, *ἀλλὰ νῦν ἔτ' ἐν σαυτοῦ γενοῦ*, though both Herm and Dind adhere to the vulg *σαυτῷ*, the latter alleging that the idiom *ἐν σαυτοῦ* is too familiar for the language of tragedy. It seems more likely that copyists have changed the forgotten Attic into the commoner form.

B *δικαιοσύνης μὲν οὖν, κ τ λ*] 'now of justice, of temperance, and of all the other ideas which to souls are precious, there is no lustre in the counterfeits here below, indeed, so dull are the organs through which men apprehend the copies of such ideas, that but few are able, and that with difficulty, to behold in the imitation the features of the original' By *ὅσα τίμια ψυχαῖς* he seems to mean *moral* ideas (comp inf. *τἆλλα ὅσα ἐραστά*), among which he afterwards proceeds to show that beauty also has its clear antitype on earth

νης, καὶ ὅσα ἄλλα τίμια ψυχαῖς, οὐκ ἔνεστι φέγγος οὐδὲν ἐν τοῖς τῇδε ὁμοιώμασιν, ἀλλὰ δι' ἀμυδρῶν ὀργάνων μόγις αὐτῶν καὶ ὀλίγοι ἐπὶ τὰς εἰκόνας ἰόντες θεῶνται τὸ τοῦ εἰκασθέντος γένος. κάλλος δὲ τότ' ἦν ἰδεῖν λαμπρόν, ὅτε σὺν εὐδαίμονι χορῷ μακαρίαν ὄψιν τε καὶ θέαν, ἑπόμενοι μετὰ μὲν Διὸς ἡμεῖς, ἄλλοι δὲ μετ' ἄλλου

In the words *μόγις αὐτῶν καὶ ὀλίγοι*, *αὐτῶν* is to be construed with *εἰκόνας*, and referred to *δικαιοσύνης, κ.τ.λ.*, as Stallb observes. In that case there is no difficulty in the position of *μόγις*

μετὰ μὲν Διὸς ἡμεῖς] That is, *we philosophers*, of whom Zeus, the symbol of the highest reason, is the especial patron Comp. Phileb 30 D The passage which follows is full of phrases borrowed from the Eleusinian rites From this we must not infer that Plato countenances the notion that a purer and more philosophic faith was communicated to the initiated at Eleusis, a fancy which still lingers in some minds even after the triumphant exposure of its baselessness effected by Lobeck in his greatest work. The contrary, in fact, follows from the language of Plato, for how could the mysteries have served the purpose of metaphorical illustration had they possessed a philosophic meaning of their own? When the figure and the thing figured are both *in eodem genere*, we have no metaphor but only confusion and it were scarcely less absurd to argue from the image of the chariot and pair that the Olympic games had a philosophic meaning, than to use the passage before us in support of the Warburtonian theory At the same time it is more than probable that this portion of the Phaedr, and others in which the same metaphor occurs, have helped to produce the opinion alluded to So far as we can make out the nature of the *ἱερὰ μυστικὰ* or *μυστήρια* shown to the initiated in the *μυστοδόκος δόμος* (Ar Nub 303), or great hall of the Eleusinian temple, they consisted partly in images of Demeter and her *σύνναοι* Iacchus and Persephone, and partly in relics, 'priscae religionis monumenta,' like those shown to the devout in Romish churches at the present day These objects, *φάσματα*, were exhibited *ἐν αὐγῇ καθαρᾷ*, under the 'clear effulgence' of blazing torches, and the *μύησις* or *ἐποπτεία* (for the distinction between the two words, as if they implied, the one an earlier, the other a more advanced stage of initiation, was a later refinement) consisted in the fruition of the dazzling scene presented to the eye of the worshipper Comp Plut Mor. i 312, Wytt, *ὡς οἱ τελούμενοι κατ' ἀρχὰς ἐν θορύβῳ καὶ βοῇ πρὸς ἀλλήλους συνίασι, δρωμένων δὲ καὶ δεικνυμένων τῶν ἱερῶν προσέχουσιν ἤδη μετὰ φρίκης* (int. p. 251) *καὶ σιωπῆς, οὕτω καὶ φιλοσοφίας ἐν ἀρχῇ . . πολὺν θόρυβον ὄψει . ὁ δὲ ἐντὸς γενόμενος καὶ φῶς μέγα ἰδών, οἷον ἀνακτόρων ἀνοιγομένων, κ τ λ* (ap Lob Aglaoph p 61). Also Arist Ran 340, *ἔγειρε φλογέας λαμπάδας ἐν χερσὶ τινάσσων, Ἴακχ', ὦ Ἴακχε, Νυκτέρου τελετῆς φωσφόρος ἀστήρ*, where the Schol observes, *ἐν νυκτὶ ἄγεται τὰ μυστήρια* If we accept this view, which Lobeck supports with a profusion of learning and argument, the passage before us is perfectly intelligible "Etenim Plato in Phaedr quum docere vellet quantum oblectationis habeat inquisitio et investigatio veri (*ἡ τῶν ὄντως ὄντων θέα*) exemplum sumit a mysteriis, contenditque animos e rerum superarum immutabiliumque cognitione plus voluptatis capere, quam divinae species initiatis afferunt *εἶδον* (animi a corporibus secreti et liberi) *καὶ ἐτελοῦντο ἐποπτεύοντες* quae ab Eleusiniis translata esse recte judicat Hermeias" Lob l l p 57. The initiation of the philosophic soul is said to be *μακαριωτάτη*, the most blissful of all initiations, not excepting that of Eleusis —'so we may without impiety style it' (*θέμις λέγειν*) *μάκαρ* and *εὐδαίμων* were technical predicates of the initiated, *εὐδαιμονία* being the last stage—the consummation of the whole initiatory process Theon Math p. 18 So Eurip Bacch 72, *Ὦ μάκαρ ὅστις εὐδαίμων τελετὰς θεῶν εἰδώς, κ τ λ* The *φάσματα* displayed to the soul in the *ὑπερουράνιος τόπος* are of course *τὰ ὄντως ὄντα*, the

θεῶν, εἶδόν τε καὶ ἐτελοῦντο τῶν τελετῶν ἣν θέμις λέγειν μακαριωτάτην, ἣν ὠργιάζομεν ὁλόκληροι μὲν αὐτοὶ C ὄντες καὶ ἀπαθεῖς κακῶν ὅσα ἡμᾶς ἐν ὑστέρῳ χρόνῳ ὑπέμενεν, ὁλόκληρα δὲ καὶ ἁπλᾶ καὶ ἀτρεμῆ καὶ εὐδαίμονα φάσματα μυούμενοί τε καὶ ἐποπτεύοντες ἐν αὐγῇ καθαρᾷ, καθαροὶ ὄντες καὶ ἀσήμαντοι τούτου ὃ νῦν σῶμα περιφέροντες ὀνομάζομεν, ὀστρέου τρόπον δεδεσμευμένοι. ταῦτα μὲν οὖν μνήμῃ κεχαρίσθω, δι' ἣν πόθῳ

ideas or archetypal forms. To these perhaps, rather than to the Eleusinian images, the epithets ὁλόκληρα καὶ ἁπλᾶ καὶ ἀτρεμῆ καὶ εὐδαίμονα properly belong, though it is probable that there is some reference to the serene beauty of the colossal statues which decorated the mystic temple. Witness the grandeur of the fragment preserved in our own University, which is certainly 'simple and full of repose,' though, alas! far from 'entire' (See below 251 B, εἶδεν αὐτὴν . ἐν ἁγνῷ βάθρῳ βεβῶσαν). The ideas are ὁλόκληρα καὶ ἁπλᾶ, because seen as they are in themselves, αὐτὰ καθ' αὐτά, not in the concrete (κατακεκερματισμένα, διεσπαρμένα, Soph 258 D, 260 B). They are also ἀτρεμῆ because ἀεὶ κατὰ ταὐτὰ ὡσαύτως ἔχοντα, μεταβολὴν μηδ' ἡντινοῦν ἐνδεχόμενα (Phaed 78 D). The word ὁλόκληρος occurs in Tim. 44 C, ὁλόκληρος ὑγιής τε παντελῶς, τὴν μεγίστην ἀποφυγὼν νόσον, γίγνεται, where it answers to our 'whole' as opposed to 'sick'. For the epithet εὐδαίμονα (effect predicated of the cause, as μακαριωτάτη is transferred from the spectator to the θέα) compare the 'Beatific Vision' of Christian Theology. μυούμενοι and ἐποπτεύοντες are not to be distinguished here, except in so far as the latter word defines the sense of the former. Properly speaking μύησις is the generic term for the entire process, including the ἐποπτεία, or state of the epopt or adept, who after due previous instructions and the like is admitted into the adytum to behold the αὐτοπτικὰ ἀγάλματα (Iambl Myst. ii 10, 53). So Symp. 209 E, ταῦτα μὲν οὖν τὰ ἐρωτικὰ κἂν σὺ μυηθείης· τὰ δὲ τέλεα καὶ ἐποπτικὰ ὧν ἕνεκα καὶ ταῦτ' ἔστιν, ἐάν τις ὀρθῶς μετίῃ οὐκ οἶδ' εἰ οἷός τ' ἂν εἴης, where after εἴης we must supply μυηθῆναι, a sufficient proof that μύησις is not [illegible]

stage. A difficulty has been raised about the use of ὑπέμενεν, for which Hirsch ventures to substitute περιέμενεν. If he is right, it will be necessary also to alter Xen Anab. iv 1 21, διὰ ταῦτά σε οὐχ ὑπέμενον, φθάσαι βουλόμενος, where the compound has the same sense which it bears here. Comp also Polyb i 81 3, quoted by Stallb., ἡ κόλασις ὑπομένει αὐτόν.

C καθαροὶ ὄντες καὶ ἀσήμαντοι—δεδεσμευμένοι] Of the two epithets καθαροὶ has reference to the ceremonial and legal purity presupposed in the ἐπόπται, as indeed in worshippers generally, "quum *omnis praefatio sacrorum eos quibus non sint purae manus, sacris arceat*" (Liv. xlv 5, ap Lob I 1 p. 17). ἀσήμαντοι has evidently a double meaning, which it is impossible to express by one word in English. It means (1) 'unmarked,' i e unpolluted, and (2) 'unentombed,' 'unimprisoned,' according to the two senses of σῆμα. Hence tr 'free from the bondage and pollution of that which *now* we call σῶμα,' instead of σῆμα, which, there is reason to suppose, was the original name of the body, καὶ γὰρ σῆμά τινές φασιν αὐτὸ εἶναι τῆς ψυχῆς (Crat. 400 C). Comp Gorg 493. The notion and etymology are both Orphic, as Plato states in the former of the passages quoted, in which other etyma are mentioned and discussed with laudable impartiality. This fleshly prison we 'bear about with us, bound in its chains as the oyster is fastened to his shell.' For the Pythagorean, as well as Orphic, theory of the penal incarceration of the soul in the body, see also Phaed 62 B and the interpreters. Also ib 82 E, τὴν ψυχὴν ἀτεχνῶς διαδεδεμένην ἐν τῷ σώματι καὶ προσκεκολλημένην, ὥσπερ δι' εἱργμοῦ, κ τ λ.

ταῦτα μὲν οὖν μνήμῃ κεχαρίσθω] 'let this then serve by way of tribute to

τῶν τότε νῦν μακρότερα εἴρηται. περὶ δὲ κάλλους, ὥσπερ
D εἴπομεν, μετ' ἐκείνων τε ἔλαμπεν ὄν, δεῦρό τε ἐλθόντες
κατειλήφαμεν αὐτὸ διὰ τῆς ἐναργεστάτης αἰσθήσεως τῶν
ἡμετέρων στίλβον ἐναργέστατα. ὄψις γὰρ ἡμῖν ὀξυτάτη
τῶν διὰ τοῦ σώματος ἔρχεται αἰσθήσεων, ᾗ φρόνησις
οὐχ ὁρᾶται. δεινοὺς γὰρ ἂν παρεῖχεν ἔρωτας, εἴ τι τοιοῦτον ἑαυτῆς ἐναργὲς εἴδωλον παρείχετο εἰς ὄψιν ἰόν,
καὶ τἆλλα ὅσα ἐραστά. νῦν δὲ κάλλος μόνον ταύτην ἔσχε
E μοῖραν, ὥστ' ἐκφανέστατον εἶναι καὶ ἐρασμιώτατον. ὁ
μὲν οὖν μὴ νεοτελὴς ἢ διεφθαρμένος οὐκ ὀξέως ἐνθένδε
ἐκεῖσε φέρεται πρὸς αὐτὸ τὸ κάλλος, θεώμενος αὐτοῦ
τὴν τῇδε ἐπωνυμίαν. ὥστε οὐ σέβεται προσορῶν, ἀλλ'
ἡδονῇ παραδοὺς τετράποδος νόμον βαίνειν ἐπιχειρεῖ καὶ
251 παιδοσπορεῖν, καὶ ὕβρει προσομιλῶν | οὐ δέδοικεν οὐδ'

memory, for she is the cause of this too long digression, which was prompted by a fond yearning for the glories of a past state of existence.' He then reverts to the subject of beauty and its relation to love, taking up the argument interrupted 219 E.

D ὄψις γὰρ ἡμῖν ὀξυτάτη, κ τ λ] This passage is thus translated by Cicero, Finn. ii 16 52 "*Oculorum*, inquit Plato, *est in nobis sensus acerrimus, quibus sapientiam non cernimus Quam illa ardentes amores excitaret sui, si videretur!*" It is imitated De Off i 5 "Formam honesti video . quae si oculis cerneretur, mirabiles amores excitaret" On the superiority of sight over the other senses see Tim. 47, ὄψις δὴ κατὰ τὸν ἐμὸν λόγον αἰτία τῆς μεγίστης ὠφελείας γέγονεν ἡμῖν, κ τ λ Here ὀξυτάτη may be rendered 'the most acute and penetrating,' though it might also bear the meaning 'swiftest,' ἐπεὶ τὸ ἀκουστὸν ὑπὸ τοῦ ὁρατοῦ πέφυκε φθάνεσθαι (Pseud-Arist de Mundo 4 18) After τοιοῦτον παρείχετο we must understand οἷον κάλλος παρέχεται Before καὶ τἆλλα ὅσα ἐραστὰ Butt supposes οἷον to have been dropped by the copyists, "absorbed" by ἰόν But this is needless τἆλλα ὅσα ἐραστὰ are the τίμια ψυχαῖς before mentioned, δικαιοσύνη, σωφροσύνη, &c Tr 'so, too, would the other forms which are fitted to inspire love,' if they, like beauty, had their visible counterparts

νῦν δέ] 'as it is, however, Beauty alone is privileged to be at once most lustrous and most loveable.'

E ὁ μὲν οὖν μὴ νεοτελής, κ τ λ.] It is only minds fresh from the initiatory rite, or those which have not yet been spoilt, that pass rapidly from the visible to the invisible or ideal Beauty, when they 'behold her earthly namesake' In Parm 133 D, sensible phenomena, τὰ παρ' ἡμῖν ταῦτα, are said to be ὁμώνυμα ἐκείνοις, homonymous with the corresponding ideas In the same sense Socr speaks in Phaed 103 B, ἐπονομάζοντες αὐτὰ τῇ ἐκείνων ἐπωνυμίᾳ, sc τὰ καθ' ἕκαστα τῇ τῶν εἰδῶν

ἡδονῇ παραδούς] i q εἴξας ἐνδιδόναι is frequently used in this intransitive way, as Rep viii. 567, ἐνδοὺς τοῖς πολεμίοις frequently also with the reflexive pronoun, αὑτὸν or the like

ὕβρει προσομιλῶν] A periphrasis for ὑβρίζων Soph Trach 591, πείρᾳ δ' οὐ προσωμίλησά πω Tim 88 C, γυμναστικῇ προσομιλοῦντα So inf 253 E, the unruly steed is called ὕβρεως καὶ ἀλαζονείας ἑταῖρος Here tr 'addicting himself to excess,' ὕβρις being the ὑπερβολὴ of ἐπιθυμία, as explained, sup 238 A Rationalized, this whole passage may be taken to mean that to the pure only all things are pure that the enthusiastic love of moral or ideal beauty can alone prevent corporeal beauty from becoming a snare and a source of defilement to those who are susceptible of its

αἰσχύνεται παρὰ φύσιν ἡδονὴν διώκων. ὁ δὲ ἀρτιτελής, ὁ τῶν τότε πολυθεάμων, ὅταν θεοειδὲς πρόσωπον ἴδῃ κάλλος εὖ μεμιμημένον, ἤ τινα σώματος ἰδέαν, πρῶτον μὲν ἔφριξε, καί τι τῶν τότε ὑπῆλθεν αὐτὸν δειμάτων, εἶτα προσορῶν ὡς θεὸν σέβεται, καὶ εἰ μὴ ἐδεδίει τὴν τῆς σφόδρα μανίας δόξαν, θύοι ἂν ὡς ἀγάλματι καὶ θεῷ τοῖς παιδικοῖς. ἰδόντα δὲ αὐτόν, οἷον ἐκ τῆς φρίκης, μεταβολή τε καὶ ἱδρὼς καὶ θερμότης ἀήθης λαμ- B
βάνει. δεξάμενος γὰρ τοῦ κάλλους τὴν ἀπορροὴν διὰ τῶν ὀμμάτων, ἐθερμάνθη ᾗ ἡ τοῦ πτεροῦ φύσις ἄρδεται.

influence, as 'men of genius' usually are The enthusiasm of the ἀρτιτελὴς is next described Not *mere* poetical or artistic sensibility, but the possession of a poetico-philosophical temperament is implied in the description, which agrees with the epithets φιλόσοφος ἢ φιλόκαλος ἢ μουσικός τις καὶ ἐρωτικός, sup 248 D No better description could be given of Plato's own idiosyncrasy.

251 ἐδεδίει] Vulg δεδίει Bodl δεδίει ἤ, supported by three others which give δεδιείη. This form Bekk has adopted into the text The only objection to the reading in the text (which is but the vulg. with the necessary addition of the augment) is the questionable tense in the apodosis θύοι ἂν for ἔθυεν ἄν To this however neither Cobet, nor Butt, a better syntactical authority, take exception. Both agree that δεδιείη is repugnant to analogy. If we had a perf opt it would rather be δεδιοίη, thinks Butt "Indispensable analogy requires δεδιοίη, like πεφευγοίη, ἐληλυθοίη, ἐδηδοκοίη, πεποιθοίη." Butt Irreg Verbs, tr p 59, note This δεδιοίη calls forth from Cobet a shriek of horror, and it certainly seems as bad, if not worse than δεδιείη

οἷον ἐκ τῆς φρίκης] 'as is natural after his cold fit' sup πρῶτον μὲν ἔφριξε The first effect of love on the highest natures is to abash and dismay, then to kindle the imagination and stimulate the intellectual faculties Both φρίκη and ῥῖγος are used by Hippocrates to denote the cold fit of a fever

B δεξάμενος — ἄρδεται] Socr here presses into his service the well known theory of Emanations, by which Empedocles [illegible]

problem of perception. γνῶθ' ὅτι πάντων εἰσὶν ἀπορροαὶ ὅσσ' ἐγένοντο, v 267 Karst coll Plat Menon 76 C, οὐκοῦν λέγετε ἀπορροάς τινας τῶν ὄντων κατ' Ἐμπεδοκλέα, Σφόδρα γε. Καὶ πόρους εἰς οὓς καὶ δι' ὧν αἱ ἀπορροαὶ πορεύονται, Πάνυ γε Καὶ τῶν ἀπορροῶν τὰς μὲν ἁρμόττειν ἐνίοις τῶν πόρων, τὰς δ' ἐλάττους ἢ μείζους εἶναι, Ἔστι ταῦτα. Οὐκοῦν καὶ ὄψιν καλεῖς τι, Ἔγωγε. Ἐκ τούτων δὴ ξύνες ὅ τοι λέγω, ἔφη Πίνδαρος ἔστι γὰρ χροὰ ἀπορροὴ σχημάτων ὄψει σύμμετρος καὶ αἰσθητός, κ τ λ These ἀπορροαὶ consisted of minute particles momentarily thrown off from all corporeal substances alike, which found their way through equally minute pores in the human body, *whither* Empedocles does not say, but according to Socr, to the soul, 'whereby (ᾗ) her native plumage is watered' By the twofold operation of heat and moisture 'the parts lying about the quill-sprouts are dissolved,' having previously been long pinched and shut up, so as to prevent the feathers from shooting Such is the evident meaning, whether the text is perfectly sound I hesitate to decide, as I cannot but feel with Ast that there is an awkwardness in the position of the clause ᾗ ἡ τοῦ πτεροῦ φύσις ἄρδεται We should have expected θερμανθέντος to have immediately followed ἐθερμάνθη, nor is the inelegance of the interposed clause diminished by translating ᾗ by '*qua ratione*,' with Stallb instead of referring it to ἀπορροὴν with Ast Still I do not see that the words can be dispensed with, and I have left them accordingly without any note of doubtfulness A remedy however is proposed by Ast, who observes "Verba haec tam importuno

θερμανθέντος δὲ ἐτάκη τὰ περὶ τὴν ἔκφυσιν, ἃ πάλαι ὑπὸ σκληρότητος συμμεμυκότα εἶργε μὴ βλαστάνειν. ἐπιῤῥυείσης δὲ τῆς τροφῆς ᾤδησέ τε καὶ ὥρμησε φύεσθαι ἀπὸ τῆς ῥίζης ὁ τοῦ πτεροῦ καυλὸς ὑπὸ πᾶν τὸ τῆς ψυχῆς εἶδος· πᾶσα γὰρ ἦν τὸ πάλαι πτερωτή. ζεῖ οὖν ἐν
C τούτῳ ὅλη καὶ ἀνακηκίει, καὶ ὅπερ τὸ τῶν ὀδοντοφυούντων πάθος περὶ τοὺς ὀδόντας γίγνεται ὅταν ἄρτι φύωσι, κνῆσίς τε καὶ ἀγανάκτησις περὶ τὰ οὖλα, ταὐτὸν δὴ πέπονθεν ἡ τοῦ πτεροφυεῖν ἀρχομένου ψυχή· ζεῖ τε καὶ ἀγανακτεῖ καὶ γαργαλίζεται φύουσα τὰ πτερά ὅταν μὲν οὖν βλέπουσα πρὸς τὸ τοῦ παιδὸς κάλλος, ἐκεῖθεν

loco posita sunt ut pro insitivis haberi possint, quanquam egregie sensum adjuvant Quocirca videndum an non verbis sic positis, τὴν ἀποῤῥοὴν διὰ τῶν ὀμμάτων, ᾗ ἡ τοῦ πτεροῦ φύσις ἄρδεται, ἐθερμάνθη, θερμανθέντος δέ, κ τ λ, locus egregius restituatur." He adds an illustrative quotation from Origen, c Cels vi p 666 c μεταλαμβάνειν τοῦ ζῶντος ἄρτου καὶ τοῦ ἀληθινοῦ ποτοῦ, ἀφ' ὧν τρεφόμενον καὶ ἀρδόμενον ἐπισκευάζεται τὸ πτερόν

ἐπιῤῥυείσης δέ, κ τ λ] 'no sooner does the fertilizing moisture descend upon the soul than over her entire surface the stump of each feather swells and strives to grow from the root upwards' For ὑπὸ Gray conjectures ἐπὶ πᾶν τὸ τῆς ψυχῆς εἶδος. Stallb. "subter universam animi speciem." Ast, "intra universam, &c" But Ficin "per animae speciem totam." ὑπὸ seems to be used as in ὑποπλησθῇ, inf 253 E. The aor ἐπιῤῥυείσης is in accordance with the practice of Attic prose authors, who never write ἐῤῥευσα, but ἐῤῥύην, ῥυῆναι, ῥυείς, and so in compounds also Phot, προσεῤῥύη, οὐ προσέῤῥευσε (ap Lob Phryn 739, q v.) So also ῥυήσομαι in preference to ῥεύσομαι

ζεῖ οὖν—καὶ ἀνακηκίει] 'hence in this condition of things she (the soul) ferments and throbs (bubbles) all over' ἀνακηκίει, ἀναπηδᾷ, Tim. Lex Hom Il vii 262, ἀνεκήκιεν αἷμα· ib xiii 705, ἀνακηκίει ἱδρώς Said of springing water in Apoll Rhod. iii 227 (ap Ruhnk ad Tim), κοίλης ἀνεκήκιε πέτρης κηκὶς denotes any kind of exsudation or moisture bursting forth See the Lexx in v ἀνακηκίειν seems also to have been used by Hippocrates and the medical writers (Steph. Lex. i 2, p 103). The penult is long in Attic Soph Phil 784, φοίνιον τόδ' ἐκ βυθοῦ Κηκῖον αἷμα

C φύωσι] Bekk and Zur. φυῶσι. But the transitive present is preferable. ὅταν ἄρτι φύωσιν ὀδόντας οἱ ὀδοντοφυοῦντες and so Ast and Stallb With φυῶσι, ὀδόντες would have to be supplied, but the aorist does not suit the sense, though right in form, for though the Attics say ἔφυν, not ἐφύην, they borrow the conjunctive from the passive aorist Tr 'when they are just beginning to have teeth'

ζεῖ τε καὶ ἀγανακτεῖ] 'is in a state of ferment and general irritability and titillation' (γαργαλ) The two words occur in connexion, Plut Symp viii. 10. 1, οὐ γὰρ τὸν οἶνον εἰκός ἐστι μόνον ζεῖν καὶ ἀγανακτεῖν We find ἀγανακτεῖν said of the intestines in Hippocrates (or Pseudo-Hippocrates?) de usu liquid, ἡ κοιλίη κρατουμένη ὑπὸ τοῦ ψυχροῦ μάλιστα ἀγανακτεῖ καὶ θαναιοῖ (ii 158, ed. Kuhn). Compare also Phileb. 17 A, γαργαλίζει τε καὶ ἠρέμα ἀγανακτεῖν ποιεῖ

ὅταν μὲν οὖν—γέγηθεν] We have here another of those fanciful etymologies with which Plato amused himself and readers. ἵμερος is supposed to be derived from ἰέναι μέ-ρη and ῥεῖν, as in the Cratylus he pretends to get it from ἱέμενος ῥεῖ . διὰ τὴν ἕσιν τῆς ῥοῆς (p 120) In the same vein he proceeds ἔρως δὲ ἀπὸ τοῦ ἐσρεῖν ἔξωθεν ἔσρος τὸ παλαιὸν ἐκαλεῖτο (ibid n). Ast very improbably contends that the words μέρη . . . καλεῖται are interpolated With more reason the Zur. Edd. bracket τὸν

μέρη ἐπιόντα καὶ ῥέοντα, ἃ δὴ διὰ ταῦτα ἵμερος καλεῖται, δεχομένη [τὸν ἵμερον] ἄρδηταί τε καὶ θερμαίνηται, λωφᾷ τε τῆς ὀδύνης καὶ γέγηθεν· ὅταν δὲ χωρὶς γένηται D
καὶ αὐχμήσῃ, τὰ τῶν διεξόδων στόματα, ᾗ τὸ πτερὸν

ἵμερον as unnecessary Stallb defends both The words *ἐπιόντα καὶ ῥέοντα* are found in the best MSS, but three give *ἐπιῤῥέοντα καὶ ἰόντα*, whence Badh conj *ἰόντα καὶ ἐπιῤῥέοντα*, and so, I suspect, Plato wrote. Kirsche conj that the word *λωφᾶν* was suggested by Empedocl Carm 121, *οὔποτε δειλαίων ἀχέων λωφήσετε θυμόν*, but this seems idle, as *λωφᾶν νόσου* or *ἀπὸ νόσου* (Thuc vi 12) is found both in popular and medical Greek (Hippocr ii 517, Kuhn, *ποιεῖ λωφᾶν τῆς νούσου* So λ *χόλου, ξυμφορᾶς*, &c). The popular etym of *λωφᾶν* from *λόφ-ος* is ridiculous, but it may possibly be connected with the Germ *laben*, 'to refresh,' it being not very unfrequently used transitively, as in Emped 1 1, Aesch Prom 27, *ὁ λωφήσων γὰρ οὐ πέφυκέ πω* and by Apoll Rhod

D *ὅταν δὲ χωρὶς γένηται, κ τ λ*] 'when the soul is parted from her beloved, and her moisture fails, then the mouths of the passages, or pores, where the feather is shooting shrivel up, and so close and intercept the nascent germ Every such germ, imprisoned thus below the surface, along with the infused desire (*ἵμερος*), throbs like a pulsing artery, and knocks at its proper outlet so that the soul tingles and smarts all over, and is maddened with pain and anguish' This description has all the gravity of a medical diagnosis, and some part at least of its phraseology is borrowed from medical authors e. g. we find *μύσας στόμα* in Hippocr i 376, ed K, *συναυαίνεται* ib. ii 110, 207, 795, *ξυμμύει τὸ στόμα* ib 791, *ἀποκλεισθέντων* ib *σφύζειν* ib iii 161, *οὗ ἂν ἡ φλὲψ ἡ ἐν τῷ ἀγκῶνι σφύζῃ μανικός*, where Galen observes, *ἔνδηλός ἐστι τὸ σφύζειν ἐπὶ τῆς μεγάλης οὕτω καὶ σφοδρᾶς κινήσεως τῶν ἀρτηριῶν ἐπιφέρων* But *σφύζειν* is also said of any throbbing *σφυγμὸς ἐν τοῖς ἕλκεσιν*, Hipp Aph. 7 21 Hence in this place *τὰ σφύζοντα, sc. μέρη*, may be rendered, 'those parts of the body which throb violently' *διέξοδοι* and *ἐγχρίειν* are also medical terms, though I have no example *in promptu* where they occur in the senses they bear here. For *διεξ.* comp Timaeus 84 C, where *διεξόδους* = air-passages Hesych, *ἐγχρίει-τύπτει, ἐγκεντρίζει* Herm, *ἐγχρίει ἀντὶ τοῦ κεντεῖ καὶ ἐμπίπτει* Comp Ruhnk and Tim Lex v *ἐγχρίμπτει* Pors ad Eur Or 900 So much for the phraseology of the passage, which might be much more copiously illustrated The readings about which there is any dispute are three I have written *ἀποκλῄει* for the vulg *ἀποκλείει*—two MSS giving *ἀποκλύει*. Similarly for *ἀποκεκλῃμένη*,—*ἀποκεκλεισμένη, ἀποκεκλειμένη, ἀποκεκλιμένη* are found The Bodl and a few others have *αποκεκλημένη*, whence Bekk rightly restored *ἀποκεκλημένη*, and so subsequent edd, who however inconsistently retain *ἀποκλείει* It is now pretty generally acknowledged that *κλῄω, κλῄσω, κέκλῃκα*, &c are the true and only Attic forms So Dind (in Steph Lex v *κλείω*) now admits, and he gives citations from the grammarians establishing the point, which is made yet clearer by Cobet, V v L l p 159 "Antiquae scripturae quam grammaticorum auctoritas tuetur, passim in libris paulo melioribus aut certa exempla comparent, aut manifesta vestigia in antiquis corruptelis, quae *proxime a vero abesse solent*, ut in Eccles 120, *ἢν δ' ἀποκλείῃ τῇ θύρᾳ*, *Ravennas* dedit *ἀποκλίνῃ* levi errore pro *ἀποκλῄῃ* (IN pro HI), seq" So in Rep. viii 560 E, *κλῄσαντες* has been restored from the oldest Paris MS for *κλείσαντες* For the vulg *ἑκάστῃ* I have given *ἑκάστη*, sc *βλάστη*, in obedience to the suggestion of Ast *βλάστη* is here = *βλαστὸς* rather than *βλάστησις*,—a sprout or germ, rather than a 'sprouting' (cf sup *ὁ τοῦ πτεροῦ καυλός*) Both senses are acknowledged by the Lexx, though the latter is the more common of the two In the preceding clause one *πτεροῦ βλάστη* is put as a specimen of all, and afterwards *each* is said to graze, rub, or prick against its own orifice The Zur. also gives *ἑκάστη*, but Stallb adheres to the MSS, which vary so much in the matter of ι's subscript, that their authority is of little weight in the present case

ὁρμᾷ, συναυαινόμενα μύσαντα ἀποκλῄει τὴν βλάστην τοῦ πτεροῦ. ἡ δ' ἐντὸς μετὰ τοῦ ἱμέρου ἀποκεκλῃμένη, πηδῶσα οἷον τὰ σφύζοντα, τῇ διεξόδῳ ἐγχρίει ἑκάστη τῇ καθ' αὑτήν, ὥστε πᾶσα κεντουμένη κύκλῳ ἡ ψυχὴ οἰστρᾷ καὶ ὀδυνᾶται. μνήμην δ' αὖ ἔχουσα τοῦ καλοῦ γέγηθεν. ἐκ δ' ἀμφοτέρων μεμιγμένων ἀδημονεῖ τε τῇ ἀτοπίᾳ τοῦ πάθους καὶ ἀποροῦσα λυττᾷ, καὶ ἐμμανὴς οὖσα οὔτε νυκτὸς δύναται καθεύδειν οὔτε μεθ' ἡμέραν οὗ ἂν ᾖ μένειν, θεῖ δὲ ποθοῦσα ὅπου ἂν οἴηται ὄψεσθαι τὸν ἔχοντα τὸ κάλλος. ἰδοῦσα δὲ καὶ ἐποχετευσαμένη ἵμερον ἔλυσε μὲν τὰ τότε συμπεφραγμένα, ἀναπνοὴν δὲ λαβοῦσα κέντρων τε καὶ ὠδίνων ἔληξεν, ἡδονὴν δ' αὖ ταύτην γλυκυτάτην ἐν τῷ παρόντι καρποῦται. | ὅθεν δὴ ἑκοῦσα εἶναι οὐκ ἀπολείπεται, οὐδέ τινα τοῦ καλοῦ περὶ πλείονος ποιεῖται, ἀλλὰ μητέρων τε καὶ ἀδελφῶν καὶ ἑταίρων πάντων λέλησται, καὶ οὐσίας δι' ἀμέλειαν ἀπολλυμένης παρ' οὐδὲν τίθεται, νομίμων δὲ καὶ εὐσχημόνων, οἷς

ἐκ δ' ἀμφοτέρων μεμιγμένων] The states of feeling 'mixed of pleasure and pain' are described less poetically but with equal truth and vivacity in Phileb. 46 seq, a passage which the student should by all means compare with the present.

ἀδημονεῖ] She is sore troubled by the strangeness of her sensations. *ἀδημονεῖν* occurs in company with *ἀπορεῖν*, also in Theaet 175 D, *ὑπὸ ἀηθείας ἀδημονῶν καὶ ἀπορῶν* The etymology and consequently the original meaning of the word are uncertain Buttm in Lexil derives it from *δῆμος*, and compares the Germ 'nicht daheim seyn,' 'unheimlich,' expressions to which we have the counterpart in English But this is unlikely, in my opinion Others comp the Homeric *ἀδδηκότες* The adj *ἀδήμων* is supposed by Buttm to be a figment, but *ἀδημονέστερος* is attested by Suid Phot, *ἀδημονεῖν κυρίως τὸ ἀπορεῖν καὶ ἀμηχανεῖν ἔν τινι δήμῳ ἢ χώρᾳ.* The latter part of the explanation may be dismissed, but the synonyms are rightly chosen In Demosth F L p 402 the agitation of a modest female pressed to sing at a riotous party is described by this verb

E *ἐποχετευσαμένη ἵμερον*] 'having refreshed (irrigated) herself with the love shower,' or 'effluence of beauty,' before described, 251 B One MS has *ἀποχετευσαμένη*, which is also not amiss But *ἐποχ* occurs Gorg 493 E, Crit 117 B Presently for *ὠδίνων* Badh conj *ὀδυνῶν* cf sup *κεντουμένη ὀδυνᾶται.* The confusion of the two words is common In Tim 84 E, *ὀδύνας* is the reading of the Bodl, Bekk *ὠδῖνας*, not so well So too ib 86 C, *ὀδύνας* ought not to have been disturbed, as it is the true antitheton to the foregoing *ἡδονάς.*

252 *ὅθεν δή*] 'and this, you will observe, is the reason why she never willingly quits the presence of the fair one' Symp 192 D, *ὥστε καὶ νύκτα καὶ ἡμέραν μὴ ἀπολείπεσθαι ἀλλήλων.*

νομίμων δὲ] 'she makes light too of the laws of custom and etiquette, on the observance of which she once piqued herself, and is prepared to resign her freedom, and to couch (slave-like) as near as they will let her to her love' An allusion possibly to the custom of lodging servants in the vestibule of the house Comp Symp 203 D, *ἐπὶ θύραις καὶ ἐν ὁδοῖς ὑπαίθριος κοιμώμενος* *πόθος* is put 'abstract for concrete,' as *'Αφροδίτην* for *ἐρωμένην* in Eur Ion 1103 "Sir Bion,

πρὸ τοῦ ἐκαλλωπίζετο, πάντων καταφρονήσασα δουλεύειν ἑτοίμη καὶ κοιμᾶσθαι ὅπου ἂν ἐᾷ τις ἐγγυτάτω τοῦ πόθου· πρὸς γὰρ τῷ σέβεσθαι τὸν τὸ κάλλος ἔχοντα ἰατρὸν εὕρηκε μόνον τῶν μεγίστων πόνων. τοῦτο δὲ τὸ πάθος, B ὦ παῖ καλέ, πρὸς ὃν δή μοι ὁ λόγος, ἄνθρωποι μὲν Ἔρωτα ὀνομάζουσι, θεοὶ δὲ ὃ καλοῦσιν ἀκούσας εἰκότως

i 53, πόθος δέ μοι ὡς ὕδαρ ἔπτη Catull ii 5, Quum desiderio meo nitenti Carum nescio quid lubet jocari" Ast Comp the use of ἔρως presently τόν τε οὖν Ἔρωτα . . ἐκλέγεται.

πρὸς γὰρ τῷ σέβεσθαι] 'not only does she worship the possessor of the Beauty, but in him she has found the sole physician of her exceeding woes'

B πρὸς ὃν δή μοι ὁ λόγος] 'to whom I am supposed to be speaking' Sup. 213 F, ποῦ δή μοι ὁ παῖς πρὸς ὃν ἔλεγον.

θεοὶ δὲ ὃ καλοῦσιν] Hom. Il xx 74, ὃν Ξάνθον καλέουσι θεοὶ ἄνδρες δὲ Σκάμανδρον i. 404, ὃν Βριάρεων καλέουσι θεοὶ ἄνδρες δέ τε πάντες Αἰγαίων': xiv. 291, Χαλκίδα κικλήσκουσι θεοὶ ἄνδρες δὲ Κύμινδιν In all these cases the more significant name is said to be used by the gods, the unmeaning one by men Crat. 391 D, δῆλον ὅτι οἵ γε θεοὶ αὐτὰ καλοῦσι πρὸς ὀρθότητα ἅπερ ἐστὶ φύσει ὀνόματα In this passage, as Lobeck observes, "Plato Amoris nomen significantius manifesto diis tribuit, ita etiam e ceteris exx apparet divina vocabula tum ornatiora esse humanis, tum rebus ipsis accommodatiora" (Aglaoph pp. 860—63) According to the same authority the ἀπόθετα ἔπη are simply "apocryphal" lines or poems known to the few, but not found in the current books or editions. Suid, βιβλίων σπουδαίων καὶ ἀνακεχωρηκότων, ἀντὶ τοῦ ἀποκρύφων (in v ἀνακεχ) Id, ἀπόθετον· τὸ ἀποτεθησαυρισμένον Themist Orat. iv. 60, στῖφος ἀρχαίας σοφίας οὐ κοινῆς οὐδὲ ἐν μέσῳ καλινδουμένης, ἀλλ . . . πανίου καὶ ἀποθέτου Such ἀπόθετα were frequently fathered upon celebrated authors—were in fact forgeries Onomacritus, it will be remembered, was banished from Athens for this offence (Herod. vii 6) The same Onomacritus had the credit of being the composer of all—properly of the more ancient—poems which bore the pseudonyms of Orpheus and Musaeus. [illegible] originating about the time of Pisistratus, Plato frequently appeals with a kind of mock solemnity, as if it contained hidden treasures of ancient wisdom. Comp Gorg 493 A D with Crat 400 C. To this Orphic school the two lines here quoted may possibly have belonged "Hos versus non a Platone confictos puto, qui quum a poetica minime alienus et in omni genere dicendi potentissimus esset, haud dubie meliores finxisset, sed ex alio poeta sumtos, et leni quadam mutatione ad praesentem causam accommodatos. Nam quum ille (ut exemplum ponam) hoc modo scripsisset Τὸν δ' ἤτοι θνητοὶ μὲν Ἔρωτα καλοῦσι ποτηνόν, Ἀθάνατοι δ' ἀλαῶπα δι' ἠλεόφοιτον ἀνάγκην, Plato, qui jam multa de alis dixerat, πτέρωτα et πτερόφοιτον substituit, distichumque ita a se concinnatum ὑβριστικὸν καὶ οὐ σφόδρα ἔμμετρον vocat, quorum prius de sententia valet, alterum de modulatione versuum" Lob ibid 861. The alternative supposition, that Plato invented the lines which he pretends to quote, is upheld by Ast, and seems to me not so incredible for Plato could doubtless have written bad lines if it had suited his purpose, and in the harshness for which he apologizes may lurk a sarcasm upon the spurious literature of which they are, on this hypothesis, a parody Herm, τοῖς ἀποθέτοις Ὁμήρου ἔξεστι πείθεσθαι εἰ βούλοιτό τις, τοῦτο δὲ εἶπεν, ἐπειδὴ δοκεῖ αὐτὸς αὐτὰ πλάσαι In calling the second line ὑβριστικὸν πάνυ Plato does not refer to any supposed lewd meaning, as Ast and Stallb dream, but simply to the extravagance of the conception and the words in which it is embodied, esp πτέρωτα,—just as we speak of 'licentiousness' in style or expression This sense comes out clearly in the following passages Crat 426 B, ἃ μὲν τοίνυν ἐγὼ ᾔσθημαι περὶ τῶν πρώτων ὀνομάτων πάνυ μοι δοκεῖ ὑβριστικὰ εἶναι καὶ γελοῖα, 'extravagant and ridiculous' Longinus ap Theodoret Therap 714 2, Ζήνωνι μὲν γοῦν καὶ Κλεάνθει νεμεσήσειεν ἄν τις

διὰ νεότητα γελάσει. λέγουσι δέ, οἶμαι, τινὲς Ὁμηριδῶν ἐκ τῶν ἀποθέτων ἐπῶν δύο ἔπη εἰς τὸν Ἔρωτα, ὧν τὸ ἕτερον ὑβριστικὸν πάνυ καὶ οὐ σφόδρα τι ἔμμετρον. ὑμνοῦσι δὲ ὧδε,

> τὸν δ' ἤτοι θνητοὶ μὲν Ἔρωτα καλοῦσι ποτηνόν,
> C ἀθάνατοι δὲ Πτέρωτα, διὰ πτεροφύτορ' ἀνάγκην.

τούτοις δὴ ἔξεστι μὲν πείθεσθαι, ἔξεστι δὲ μή· ὅμως δὲ ἥ γε αἰτία καὶ τὸ πάθος τῶν ἐρώντων τοῦτο ἐκεῖνο τυγχάνει ὄν. τῶν μὲν οὖν Διὸς ὀπαδῶν ὁ ληφθεὶς ἐμβριθέστερον δύναται φέρειν τὸ τοῦ πτερωνύμου ἄχθος· ὅσοι δὲ Ἄρεώς τε θεραπευταί, καὶ μετ' ἐκείνου περιεπόλουν, ὅταν ὑπ' Ἔρωτος ἁλῶσι καί τι οἰηθῶσιν ἀδικεῖσθαι ὑπὸ

δικαίως, οὕτω σφόδρα ὑβριστικῶς περὶ τῆς ψυχῆς διαλεχθεῖσιν. ἄμφω γὰρ τοῦ στερεοῦ σώματος εἶναι τὴν ψυχὴν ἀναθυμίασιν ἔφασαν. In the same sense Callias the versifying grammarian is said by Athenaeus to have written certain lines (which he quotes) ἀκολαστότερον κατὰ τὴν διάνοιαν, x. 454 A. Hermeias understands ὑβριστικὸν in the same sense, but conceives the ὕβρις to lie solely in the audacious violation of metre: τὸ δὲ πάνυ ὑβριστικὸν ἡρμήνευσε διὰ τοῦ εἰπεῖν οὐ σφόδρα τι ἔμμετρον· ἄμετρον γάρ ἐστι τὸ ἔπος.

C. ἀθάνατοι—ἀνάγκην] The ἀμετρία for which Plato apologizes consists in the shortening of the δὲ before two consonants, and in the lengthening of the ῡ in πτεροφύτορα. That πτεροφύτορ' and not πτερόφοιτον is the true reading, follows clearly from the context, in which the growth of the feathers and the attendant phenomena are dwelt upon. The reading is preserved in three MSS., also in Stob. Ecl. Phys. p. 23 [103 ed. Gaisf.], and is adopted by Bekker. This is corrupted into πτερόφυτον in the Bodl. and most others, whence the further corruption into πτερόφοιτον adopted by Steph. from one MS. The 'tendency,' or 'necessity, which gives birth to plumage' is, according to the mythus, the cause of love and of its symptoms, ἥ γε αἰτία καὶ τὸ πάθος τῶν ἐρώντων τοῦτ' ἐκεῖνο τυγχάνει ὄν. Ast and Stallb., who retain πτερόφοιτον, revel in a licence of interpretation truly *hybristic*. The simple φύτωρ is acknowledged by Hesych. and restored to the text of Soph. Trach. 1031 by Dind. in place of the vulg. φύσαντ'. See his comm. on Sophocles, ed. Oxon. p. 270, where he thus corrects the hitherto unmetrical text:

> ὦ Παλλάς, Παλλάς, τόδε μ' αὖ λωβᾶται, ἰὼ παῖ,
> τὸν φύτορ' οἰκτείρας ἀνεπίφθονον εἴρυσον ἔγχος.

To deny the short quantity of the penult. of φύτωρ is a paradox to me unaccountable, though maintained by Stallb. and apparently by Lobeck also.

ἐμβριθέστερον] 'with greater constancy or sedateness,' as beseems the followers of Zeus, compared with those of less intellectual deities. Ast compares Theaet. 144 B, οἱ ἐμβριθέστεροι νωθροί πως ἀπαντῶσι πρὸς τὰ μαθήματα (opposed to ὀξεῖς sup.). Ep. vii. 328 B, τὸ δὲ Δίωνος ἠπιστάμην τῆς ψυχῆς πέρι φύσει τε ἔμβριθες ὂν ἡλικίας τε ἤδη μετρίως ἔχον. In Plut. Coriol. 220 D ἔμβριθες is coupled with πρᾷον. Herm., κατεσταλμένον καὶ οὐ σφόδρα κεκινημένον. Synonymous with βλοσυρὸς and βέβαιος, Rep. vii. 535 A B, where the legislator, in selecting the members of the ruling class, is directed to look out for τοὺς βεβαιοτάτους καὶ ἀνδρειοτάτους, and again, for youths, γενναίους τε καὶ βλοσυροὺς τὰ ἤθη.

ὅσοι δὲ Ἄρεώς τε, κ.τ.λ.] Herm., οἱ κάτοχοι τοῦ Διὸς σταθεροί εἰσιν, οἱ δὲ τοῦ Ἄρεος [illegible]

τοῦ ἐρωμένου, φονικοὶ καὶ ἕτοιμοι καθιερεύειν αὐτούς τε καὶ τὰ παιδικά. καὶ οὕτω καθ' ἕκαστον θεόν, οὗ ἕκα- D
στος ἦν χορευτής, ἐκεῖνον τιμῶν τε καὶ μιμούμενος εἰς τὸ δυνατὸν ζῇ, ἕως ἂν ᾖ ἀδιάφθορος καὶ τὴν τῇδε πρώτην γένεσιν βιοτεύῃ, καὶ τούτῳ τῷ τρόπῳ πρός τε τοὺς ἐρωμένους καὶ πρὸς τοὺς ἄλλους ὁμιλεῖ τε καὶ προσφέρεται. τόν τε οὖν Ἔρωτα τῶν καλῶν πρὸς τρόπου ἐκλέγεται ἕκαστος, καὶ ὡς θεὸν αὐτὸν ἐκεῖνον ὄντα ἑαυτῷ, οἷον ἄγαλμα τεκταίνεταί τε καὶ κατακοσμεῖ, ὡς τιμήσων τε καὶ ὀργιάσων. οἱ μὲν δὴ οὖν Διὸς Δίιόν τινα εἶναι E

D ἕως ἂν ᾖ ἀδιάφθορος] i e 'so long as he retains his pristine purity,' undebauched by evil associates, &c Comp sup 250 E, ὁ μὲν οὖν μὴ νεοτελὴς ἢ διεφθαρμένος For βιοτεύῃ in the next clause the codd give βιοτεύει, which Heind corrected

καὶ τούτῳ τῷ τρόπῳ, κ τ λ] 'and in this wise (sc κατὰ τὸν ἑαυτοῦ θεόν) he demeans himself in his intercourse both with the objects of his passion and with the rest of mankind.'

τόν τε οὖν Ἔρωτα, κ τ λ,] 'hence each man in selecting his love from the ranks of beauty follows his own peculiar bent,' his choice being determined by a kind of complexional necessity, the doctrine of 'temperaments' being thus early, it would seem, connected with the notion of a 'ruling deity.' πρὸς τρόπου is here equiv to πρὸς τοῦ οἰκείου τρόπου So Legg ii 721 E, πρὸς τοῦ Λακωνικοῦ τρόπου It is more usually adverbial, as Rep v 470 E, πρὸς τρόπου λέγω (rite), and opposed to ἀπὸ τρόπου, which occurs inf 278 D So πρὸς λόγου, Gorg 459 C, if the reading is correct Presently τεκταίνεται, 'moulds or fashions,' is explained by ῥυθμίζοντες, inf. 253 B

τιμήσων τε καὶ ὀργιάσων] Equiv to ὀργίοις τιμήσων. ὀργιάζειν θεῷ is the usual construction, but in later writers we have also ὀργ θεόν, 'to celebrate with mystic rites'

E οἱ μὲν δὴ οὖν Διὸς Δίιόν τινα, κ τ λ] 'hence it comes that the followers of Jove are curious that he they love shall be of the Jovial type of soul,' i e one in whom intellect is predominant The reading Δίιον is well supported by MS authority, the Bodl δι' ὃν being only [illegible] by H [illegible] Procl Alcib i (p 310 Cousin, ὁ τοίνυν δίιος καὶ ἡγεμονικὸς τὴν φυσιν), who elsewhere speaks of Δίιος ζωή (Comm in Tim 45 F, 319 D), using also the adverbs διίως and ἡραίως, 'Jovialiter' and 'Junonice.' Suid, Δίιος ὀργὴ καὶ Δίιος Βωμός Themist Or. xiii 165 C, ἀμφοῖν ἀγαθοῖν μὲν καὶ ἀτεχνῶς διίοιν (ap Piers ad Moerid p 186, q v) We have also Δίιος as a proper name in Plut Mor 421 E Stallb and the Zur Ed give Δῖον, which has but one considerable MS in its favour For the idea, which was afterwards adopted and improved upon by Neo-Platonists ancient and modern, compare Horace's Mercurialium custos virorum. Also Shakspeare, Cymbeline iv 2, "His foot Mercurial, his Martial thigh The brawns of Hercules but his Jovial face?" ib v. 4, "Our Jovial star reigned at his birth" Spenser, F Q ii 12, st 51, "Thereto the heavens always Jovial Lookt on them lovely" explained by "under the aspect of the planet Jupiter" It is an interesting question how much of the 'occult science,' so popular at the time of the Renaissance, may be traced up to the Platonic myths We have clear traces of the doctrine of planetary influence in Proclus, and in the Neo-platonic treatises which bear the name of Hermes Trismegistus, to which Cornelius Agrippa frequently appeals The curious are referred to the Occulta Philosophia of the latter, B ii. c 59, De septem mundi Gubernatoribus planetis, ib c 60, fin, a passage which seems suggested by 253 A of this dialogue, read, of course, through Neoplatonic glasses B iii c 38, treats of the question "Quae divina dona homo desuper a singulis coelorum et intelligentiarum ordinibus accipiat Compare

ζητοῦσι τὴν ψυχὴν τὸν ὑφ' αὑτῶν ἐρώμενον. σκοποῦσιν οὖν εἰ φιλόσοφός τε καὶ ἡγεμονικὸς τὴν φύσιν, καὶ ὅταν αὐτὸν εὑρόντες ἐρασθῶσι, πᾶν ποιοῦσιν ὅπως τοιοῦτος ἔσται. ἐὰν οὖν μὴ πρότερον ἐμβεβῶσι τῷ ἐπιτηδεύματι, τότε ἐπιχειρήσαντες μανθάνουσί τε ὅθεν ἄν τι δύνωνται καὶ αὐτοὶ μετέρχονται. ἰχνεύοντες δὲ παρ' ἑαυτῶν ἀνευ-
253 ρίσκειν τὴν τοῦ σφετέρου θεοῦ φύσιν, | εὐποροῦσι διὰ τὸ συντόνως ἠναγκάσθαι πρὸς τὸν θεὸν βλέπειν, καὶ ἐφαπτόμενοι αὐτοῦ τῇ μνήμῃ, ἐνθουσιῶντες, ἐξ ἐκείνου λαμβάνουσι τὰ ἔθη καὶ τὰ ἐπιτηδεύματα, καθ' ὅσον δυνατὸν θεοῦ ἀνθρώπῳ μετασχεῖν. καὶ τούτων δὴ τὸν ἐρώμενον

also ib c 46 seq for the four kinds of 'furor divinus,' also Proclus in Timaeum, p 45 E, 319 D,—both curious passages, as showing the astrological interpretation put by his Greek commentators upon Plato's mythical psychology Among the εἴδη ζωῆς enumerated by Proclus, are the Κρόνιον (according to him the highest type of all), the Δῖον, Ἡλιακόν, Σεληνιακόν, Ἀρεικόν, Ἀφροδισιακόν, Ἑρμαικόν, on each of which he spends a great deal of fanciful ingenuity The following passage contains a résumé of the Neo-platonic theory of astral influence on human character ὅθεν καὶ λέγειν τινὲς εἰώθασιν ὡς τὸ μὲν νοερὸν αὐτοῦ (sc τοῦ ἀνθρώπου) τῇ ἀπλανεῖ (sc σφαίρᾳ) τέτακται ἀνὰ λόγον, τοῦ δὲ λόγου τὸ μὲν θεωρητικὸν τῷ Κρόνῳ, τὸ δὲ πολιτικὸν τῷ Διΐ, τοῦ δὲ ἀλόγου τὸ μὲν θυμοειδὲς Ἄρει, τὸ δὲ φωνητικὸν Ἑρμῇ, τὸ δὲ ἐπιθυμητικὸν Ἀφροδίτῃ, τὸ δὲ αἰσθητικὸν Ἡλίῳ, τὸ δὲ φυτικὸν Σελήνῃ, (ib 348 A) This preference of the Saturnine temperament seems grounded on the dictum of Aristotle, ὅτι οἱ εὐφυεῖς μελαγχολικοί.

εἶναι ζητοῖσι] Inf 253 B, ζητοῦσι πεφυκέναι: Rep ii. 375 E, οὐ παρὰ φύσιν ζητοῦμεν τοιοῦτον εἶναι τὸν φύλακα

καὶ ὅταν αὐτόν, κ τ λ] The true ἐραστής, unlike the selfish lover described in the former Socratic speech, sup 239 B, uses every effort to develope the faculties of the ἐρώμενος, and to make him φιλόσοφός τε καὶ ἡγεμονικός. The latter word is of course used in its esoteric sense, Ζεὺς being the symbol of the universal Reason, the μέγας ἡγεμὼν ἐν οὐρανῷ In the next sentence Plato seems to intimate [illegible] Zeus' is in some cases unconscious of his high vocation until stimulated by the converse of a kindred spirit If the lover have not previously been grounded in the study of philosophy, he sets about it now, and in addition to his own researches he has recourse to every accessible source of knowledge. τῷ ἐπιτηδεύματι is equiv to τῇ φιλοσοφίᾳ, as Heind remarks

ἰχνεύοντες δέ, κ τ λ] The idea of 'tracking' is implied in the foregoing μετέρχονται (inf. 276 D, τῷ ταὐτὸν ἴχνος μετιόντι). In endeavouring to detect by traces in his own nature the true character of the god to whom he belongs,—the Lover finds his search facilitated by the very necessity he feels of gazing intently upon that god The obscurity of this passage escapes the comm πρὸς τὸν θεὸν seems to refer both to Zeus, and to his incarnate image in the person of the beloved, which, mystically speaking, may be looked upon as one and the same. Comp. sup. καὶ ὡς θεὸν αὐτὸν ἐκεῖνον ὄντα ἑαυτῷ It is the Jovial element in the loved one, which produces an ἀνάμνησις of the archetypal Zeus just as the contemplation of sensible beauty recalls the τὸ καλὸν itself In other words, the philosophic genius of the beloved reminds the Lover of his own vocation, and makes him long to bring his manners and pursuits into conformity with the highest reason To teach and to learn are, in the Socratic view, but parts of the same process,—master and pupil being συνθιασῶται of the same god

253. θεοῦ ἀνθρώπῳ μετασχεῖν] This [illegible] s in

αἰτιώμενοι ἔτι τε μᾶλλον ἀγαπῶσι, κἂν ἐκ Διὸς ἀρύτωσιν
ὥσπερ αἱ βάκχαι, ἐπὶ τὴν τοῦ ἐρωμένου ψυχὴν ἐπαν-
τλοῦντες ποιοῦσιν ὡς δυνατὸν ὁμοιότατον τῷ σφετέρῳ
θεῷ. ὅσοι δ' αὖ μεθ' Ἥρας εἵποντο, βασιλικὸν ζητοῦσι, B
καὶ εὑρόντες περὶ τοῦτον πάντα δρῶσι τὰ αὐτά. οἱ δὲ
Ἀπόλλωνός τε καὶ ἑκάστου τῶν θεῶν οὕτω κατὰ τὸν
θεὸν ἰόντες ζητοῦσι τὸν σφέτερον παῖδα πεφυκέναι, καὶ
ὅταν κτήσωνται, μιμούμενοι αὐτοί τε καὶ τὰ παιδικὰ
πείθοντες καὶ ῥυθμίζοντες εἰς τὸ ἐκείνου ἐπιτήδευμα καὶ
ἰδέαν ἄγουσιν, ὅση ἑκάστῳ δύναμις, οὐ φθόνῳ οὐδ' ἀνε-
λευθέρῳ δυσμενείᾳ χρώμενοι πρὸς τὰ παιδικά, ἀλλ' εἰς
ὁμοιότητα αὐτοῖς καὶ τῷ θεῷ, ὃν ἂν τιμῶσι, πᾶσαν πάντως C
ὅ τι μάλιστα πειρώμενοι ἄγειν οὕτω ποιοῦσι. προθυμία

Theaet 176 B, ὁμ. θεῷ κατὰ τὸ δυνατόν· ὁμοίωσις δὲ δίκαιον καὶ ὅσιον μετὰ φρονήσεως γενέσθαι. So created things are sometimes spoken of as μετέχοντα, sometimes as μιμήματα τῶν ὄντων

κἂν ἐκ Διὸς ἀρύτωσιν ὥσπερ αἱ βάκχαι] "Reason being the Zeus in man," says Krische, "Plato may have mythically denoted the act of pure thought as a drawing draughts from Zeus himself, a process which he happily compares with that of the Bacchic women," who are represented by Euripides as causing water to burst from the rock, and wine, honey, and milk from the dry ground. Bacch 142, 704 seq This entire passage is well illustrated by a fragment of Aeschines Socraticus, ap Aristid. Rhet ii p 23, Dind (to which Stallb. also refers, as well as to Ion 534) ἐγὼ δὲ διὰ τὸν ἔρωτα ὃν ἐτύγχανον ἐρῶν Ἀλκιβιάδου οὐδὲν διάφορον τῶν Βακχῶν ἐπεπόνθειν καὶ γὰρ αἱ Βάκχαι ἐπειδὰν ἔνθεοι γένωνται, ὅθεν οἱ ἄλλοι ἐκ τῶν φρεάτων οὐδὲ ὕδωρ δύνανται ὑδρεύεσθαι, ἐκεῖναι μέλι καὶ γάλα ἀρύονται (l ἀρύτονται) καὶ δὴ καὶ ἐγὼ οὐδὲν μάθημα ἐπιστάμενος ὃ διδάξας ἄνθρωπον ὠφελήσαιμ' ἄν, ὅμως ᾤμην ξυνὼν ἂν ἐκείνῳ διὰ τὸ ἐρᾶν βελτίω ποιῆσαι

ὅσοι δ' αὖ μεθ' Ἥρας] Hera is the symbol of the practical as Zeus of the speculative intellect Her votaries are not philosophers, but rather men born for empire · βασιλεῖς ἔννομοι ἢ πολεμικοὶ καὶ ἀ[illegible] Ἥρα [illegible] βασιλική The MSS give the whimsical variant μεθ' ἡμέρας

B οἱ δὲ Ἀπόλλωνος] It is not clear whether poets come under this category. Probably not all, but only the lyrical It may also include the seer and the physician. Aesch Eum 62, ἰατρόμαντις δ' ἐστὶ καὶ τερασκόπος Καὶ τοῖσιν ἄλλοις δωμάτων καθάρσιος

οὕτω κατὰ τὸν θεὸν ἰόντες] οὕτω belongs here to πεφυκέναι, the next clause being epexegetic, "dei sui exemplum sectantes" (Stallb) The use of ἔρως as an engine of education was no new idea in Greece Compare Eurip Med. 844 with Frag inc. 889, Nauck, παίδευμα δ' ἔρως σοφίας ἀρετῆς Πλεῖστον ὑπάρχει and Dictys, 342 (Frag viii Dind)

καὶ τὰ παιδικὰ πείθοντες] Herm., τέλος γὰρ τῆς ἐρωτικῆς τὸ ἀντέρωτα γεννῆσαι ῥυθμίζοντες, shaping or conforming them to the mode of life and the moral standard proper to the god they serve.

οὐ φθόνῳ] This, as Hermeias remarks, has reference to the φθόνος attributed to the ἐραστὴς in the Speech of Lysias οὐ δυσμενοῦντες ὡς οἱ νόθοι ἐρασταί. ὃ γὰρ βούλονται ἑαυτοῖς, τοῦτο καὶ τοῖς ἐρωμένοις μία γάρ ἐστιν ἡ ζωὴ αὐτῶν τοιοῦτοι δὲ ἦσαν καὶ οἱ Πυθαγόρειοι ὅθεν καὶ φέρεται Πυθαγορείου τινὸς τοῦτο τὸ ῥῆμα τὸ Τί ἐστι φίλος, ἄλλος ἐγώ (p 166, Ast).

[illegible] location [illegible] in Phaedr [illegible] παρασκευάζονθ'

μὲν οὖν τῶν ὡς ἀληθῶς ἐρώντων καὶ τελετή, ἐάν γε
διαπράξωνται ὃ προθυμοῦνται, ἥν λέγω, οὕτω καλή τε
καὶ εὐδαιμονικὴ ὑπὸ τοῦ δι' ἔρωτα μανέντος φίλου τῷ
φιληθέντι γίγνεται, ἐὰν αἱρεθῇ. ἁλίσκεται δὲ δὴ ὁ αἱρεθεὶς
τοιῷδε τρόπῳ.

Καθάπερ ἐν ἀρχῇ τοῦδε τοῦ μύθου τριχῇ διείλομεν
D ψυχὴν ἑκάστην, ἱππομόρφω μὲν δύο τινὲ εἴδη, ἡνιοχι-
κὸν δὲ εἶδος τρίτον, καὶ νῦν ἔτι ἡμῖν ταῦτα μενέτω.
τῶν δὲ δὴ ἵππων ὁ μέν, φαμέν, ἀγαθός, ὁ δ' οὔ. ἀρετὴ
δὲ τίς τοῦ ἀγαθοῦ ἢ κακοῦ κακία, οὐ διείπομεν, νῦν δὲ

ἑαυτὸν ἐν τῷ βίῳ ὅτι ἐγγυτάτω ὄντα τοῦ τεθνάναι οὕτω ζῆν, as if he had said οὕτω ζῆν ὥστε παρασκευάζειν. Comp. Gorg. 507 D, πάντα εἰς τοῦτο . . ξυντείνοντα οὕτω πράττειν.

προθυμία μὲν οὖν, κ τ λ] Such, says Socr., is the high object the true lover strives after, so glorious and so fraught with bliss to the beloved the secret rites celebrated by his love-frenzied admirer if he be successful in his suit. ἥν λέγω is to be taken with οὕτω according to Ast, as if we had found οὕτως, ὡς λέγω, καλή. He quotes Gorg 173 E, ὅταν τοιαῦτα λέγῃς ἃ οὐδεὶς ἂν φήσειεν. But query? Stallb.'s ᾗ λέγω, which he takes with διαπρ., is perhaps better than the vulg. The change had been recommended by Heind., with the remark "ipsum quoque admodum friget." The τελετὴ is the initiation into the mysteries of philosophy—the ἐπιτήδευμα δῖον—for though those of other deities have been mentioned, it is this study which Socr has principally in view. For γε διαπραξ., the reading of most MSS and Bekk. is γ' ἐνδιαπράξωνται. διαπράξωνται is adopted by Stallb and the Zur., and is found also in Hermeias, who omits the γ'. The old reading will give the sense 'if they succeed in working in the beloved the effect they desire to produce.' But this seems more and less than the context requires. The force of γε is—'a τελετή, as in truth it is, if the lover achieve his object.' διαπράξωνται is here used in the spiritual as before, 234 A and elsewh., in the vulgar sense. ἐὰν αἱρεθῇ is an explanatory repetition of ἐὰν διαπράξωνται ὃ προθυμοῦνται. For the use of the verb comp Lys. 206 A, οὐκ ἐπαινεῖ τὸν ἐρώμενον πρὶν ἂν ἕλῃ. Obs that ἑάλω ἑάλωκα are the usual Attic passives of αἱρεῖν, ᾑρέθην ᾕρημαι being commonly the passives of αἱρεῖσθαι, eligere. But exceptions occur, as Phileb. 66, περὶ μέτρον καὶ τὸ μέτριον . . τὴν ἀΐδιον ᾑρῆσθαι φύσιν, where, if ᾑρῆσθαι be interpreted 'captam esse,' in allusion to the foregoing chase (τὸ ἀγαθὸν θηρεῦσαι, 64 F), there is no necessity for the emend. εὑρῆσθαι suggested by Badh., and which I once approved.

Καθάπερ ἐν ἀρχῇ] Socr now proceeds to make the ends of his discourse meet, by showing (1) the relation between the doctrine of ἀνάμνησις and that of the tripartite soul, sup. 246; and (2) the relation of both doctrines to the phenomena of Love.

διείλομεν] MSS διειλόμην, corr. Heind. Later edd. perversely restore the evidently vicious reading of the MSS. Compare Soph. 220 B, where the same corruption occurs, διελοίμην for διέλοιμεν. Socr has throughout spoken in the plural, and continues to do so both here and in the dialogue quoted. It is a part of his εἰρωνεία to represent the mythus as a joint performance. Ast however defends διειλόμην by 245 B, τοσαῦτα μέν σοι καὶ ἔτι πλείω ἔχω μανίας γιγνομένης ἀπὸ θεῶν λέγειν καλὰ ἔργα· ὥστε τοῦτό γε αὐτὸ μὴ φοβώμεθα, μηδέ τις ἡμᾶς λόγος θορυβείτω. But here we must remember Socr is engaged in a dialogue with an imaginary παῖς καλός, πρὸς ὃν δὴ ὁ λόγος—a personage of whom he has by this time lost sight. εἴδη is an Attic dual, for the common εἴδεε, as we have φύση in Rep. 410 E, and πόλη in Isocr. Paneg. 54.

λεκτέον. ὁ μὲν τοίνυν αὐτοῖν ἐν τῇ καλλίονι στάσει ὢν

D ὁ μὲν τοίνυν αὐτοῖν ἐν τῇ καλλίονι στάσει ὢν] i.e. ὁ ἐν δεξιᾷ, the off horse being usually the better, as the epith δεξιόσειρος implies In the description of the two steeds there is an evident parallelism but in some of the details a certain liberty has been taken Thus, while ὀρθὸς and σκόλιος, ἐπίγρυπος and σιμοπρόσωπος, λευκὸς ἰδεῖν and μελάγχρως answer literally to each other, the relation of the other contrasted features is rather essential than verbal. For instance, to διηρθρωμένος, 'clean-limbed,' 'with joints well defined,' respond two epithets, πολύς (= nimius, lumbering, over-large, or, as our jockeys say, 'too much of a horse') and εἰκῇ συμπεφορημένος, ill-made, as if thrown together at hap hazard Again, μελανόμματος answers to γλαυκόμματος ὕφαιμος, 'with grey and bloodshot eyes' J Poll 2 62, ὕφαιμον βλέποντες ὀφθαλμοί This is better than Stallb's "sanguineus," referring to the general temperament. For there is nothing to answer to this in the former catalogue, and the restive horse would scarcely have been called 'sanguine,' but rather 'phlegmatic,' or 'choleric' The necessity for two epithets, κρατεραυχὴν and βραχυτράχηλος, answering to the single ὑψαυχήν, is not so manifest, and the antithesis between τιμῆς ἐραστὴς μετὰ σωφροσύνης τε καὶ αἰδοῦς on the one hand, and ὕβρεως καὶ ἀλαζονείας ἑταῖρος on the other, seems complete without the addition of the words καὶ ἀληθινῆς δόξης ἑταῖρος to the former ἀληθινῆς δόξης is interpreted "verae opinionis" but it may well be doubted whether this is possible ἀληθὴς δόξα has a definite sense in Plato, but where does he use ἀληθινή in such connexion? 'Veritable opinion' would rather denote δόξα as distinguished from ἐπιστήμη, and in this case the epithet would be the reverse of laudatory. It is remarkable that Hermeias takes no notice of this clause, and this aggravates its suspicious appearance. Lastly, in the description of the bad steed, the clauses περὶ ὦτα λάσιος, κωφός, answer to nothing very definite in the portrait of his yokefellow If περὶ ὦτα λάσιος simply mean 'stupid,' 'senseless' (see Photius, quoted presently), and κωφὸς be taken with the succeeding clause, we have a kind of antithesis to ἀληθινῆς δόξης ἑταῖρος, suppos[illegible] f these words to stand. But I cannot consent to separate μετὰ σωφροσύνης καὶ αἰδοῦς from τιμῆς ἐραστής, as in that case the opposition to ὕβρ καὶ ἀλαζονείας ἑταῖρος would be incomplete As regards the text, it may be observed that besides βαρυτράχηλος for βραχυτρ. there is no considerable variant in the MS readings as given by Bekk, with the remarkable exception λασιόκωφος, which the Bodl and some others have Porson, who examined the Bodl before it went to Oxford, seems to have adopted this compound in lieu of the vulg λάσιος, κωφός, and he is supported by Phot in Lex λασιόκωφος· ὁ λίαν κωφός, οἷον λάσια τὰ ὦτα ἔχων ὡς συγκεκωφῶσθαι καὶ ἀναισθητεῖν, evidently referring to this passage, to which the reference is still more explicit in Synesius, Encom Calv. 67 D, εἰ δὲ καὶ Πλάτων τὸν ἄδικον ἵππον περὶ ὦτα λασιόκωφον λέγει Add Hesych, λασιοκώφους τοὺς κωφούς The reading is therefore not derived from the Bodl as Stallb thinks, but is of high antiquity, and the temptation to receive it would have been great, were it not that the still more ancient 'Homeric Allegories' of Heraclitus (hitherto called Heraclides) rather countenance the vulg We there read περιωτάλσιος ὑπόκωφος (comp Ar Eq 43, γερόντιον Ὑπόκωφον). The entire passage is quoted by Heraclitus, cap xvii p 36, ed Mehler He gives besides the v. ll. τό τ' εἶδος for the vulg τότε omits ἀληθινῆς before δόξης, as does the Cod Vat, inspected by Cobet, for κελεύματι μόνον καὶ λόγῳ he gives κελεύσματι καὶ λόγῳ μόνῳ for βραχυτράχηλος, πολυτράχηλος for μελάγχρως, μελανόχρως· and for μόγις, μόλις Amid this discrepancy of authorities I have not ventured to alter the received text, though by no means satisfied with it —The description of the better horse is illustrated by Virg Georg iii 79, Illi ardua cervix, Argutumque caput, brevis alvus, obesaque terga Luxuriatque toris animosum pectus Also by Shaksp, Venus and Adonis, "Round-hoofed, short-jointed, fetlocks shag and long Broad breast, full eyes, small head and nostril wide High crest, short ears, straight legs and passing strong Thin mane, thick tail, broad buttock, tender hide" For ὑψαύχην compare Xen Eq i 8, ἀπὸ τοῦ στέρνου ὁ μὲν αὐχὴν αὐτοῦ μὴ ὥσπερ κάπρου προπετὴς πεφύκοι (th[illegible] eems to

τό τ' εἶδος ὀρθὸς καὶ διηρθρωμένος, ὑψαύχην, ἐπίγρυπος, λευκὸς ἰδεῖν, μελανόμματος, τιμῆς ἐραστὴς μετὰ σωφροσύνης τε καὶ αἰδοῦς, καὶ ἀληθινῆς δόξης ἑταῖρος, ἄπληκτος, κελεύματι μόνον καὶ λόγῳ ἡνιοχεῖται· ὁ δ'
E αὖ σκολιός, πολύς, εἰκῇ συμπεφορημένος, κρατεραύχην, βραχυτράχηλος, σιμοπρόσωπος, μελάγχρως, γλαυκόμματος, ὕφαιμος, ὕβρεως καὶ ἀλαζονείας ἑταῖρος, περὶ ὦτα λάσιος, κωφός, μάστιγι μετὰ κέντρων μόγις ὑπείκων. ὅταν δ' οὖν ὁ ἡνίοχος ἰδὼν τὸ ἐρωτικὸν ὄμμα, πᾶσαν αἰσθή-

countenance the v. l. βαρυτράχηλος in the second portrait) ἀλλ' ὥσπερ ἀλεκτρυόνος ὀρθὸς πρὸς τὴν κορυφὴν ἥκοι.

ἐπίγρυπος] 'hook-nosed,'—a feature of a serviceable though hardly of a handsome steed, but in a man a sign of dignity and good descent. Ast quotes Rep. 474 D, τοῦ δὲ τὸ γρυπὸν βασιλικόν φατε εἶναι. J. Poll. ii. 73, ῥὶν ἐπίγρυπος, ὃν καὶ βασιλικὸν οἴονται.

λευκὸς ἰδεῖν] Virg. Georg. iii. color deterrimus albis,—a difference of opinion which it is hardly necessary to discuss. Comp. Conington in loc. Probably Plato is thinking of the inward purity of which whiteness is the symbol, as in the following epithets, τιμῆς ἐραστής, κ.τ.λ. he speaks of human rather than equine qualities. In ἄπληκτος . . . ἡνιοχεῖται he mixes both natures in the description, λόγῳ being applicable only to men.

E βραχυτράχηλος] The v. l. πολυτράχηλος is supported by Xen. Eq. i. 8, λαγαρὸς δὲ εἴη (ὁ αὐχήν) τὰ κατὰ τὴν συγκαμπήν, as βαρυτράχηλος is by the passage quoted sup. But a 'short throat,' combined with a thick neck, would *cause* a horse to be προπετὴς ὥσπερ καπρός, as Xen. expresses it. A fanciful etymologist might be inclined to connect the verb 'to bore,' used of a horse who carries his head low, with this phrase of Xenophon's, and to spell it accordingly.

σιμοπρόσωπος] This, in a stage-mask, was a physiognomy proper to menials. J. Poll. iv. 151, τὸ οἰκουρὸν γραΐδιον σιμόν. So Herm., εὐτελής, χαμαιπετὴς καὶ οὐχὶ βασιλικός. Others explain τὸ σιμὸν as a sign of λαγνεία.

γλαυκόμματος, ὕφαιμος] Ast suggests καὶ ὕφαιμος. I have already said that the latter word refers to the eyes, as γλαῦκος alone sometimes means 'grey-eyed,' Lat. *caesius*. In this there seems to me no difficulty, but Badh., more fastidious, leaves the meaning of the word in doubt, thinking that it is the antitheton of τιμῆς ἐραστής. I confess I do not see how this can be the case; unless we press into the service a phrase in the Physiognomonica attributed to Aristotle (c. 3, p. 807, Bekk.), where among the ἀναιδοῦς σημεῖα occurs τὸ χρῶμα ὕφαιμον. But in the same place we also read βλέφαρα ὕφαιμα καὶ παχέα. It is curious that the early Greek physiognomists found their art on a comparison between the bestial and human. Thus Aeschylus uses both ἱππογνώμων and προβατογνώμων in reference to *human affairs*. It is not to be supposed that Plato was the first who speculated in this tempting field.

ὅταν δ' οὖν ὁ ἡνίοχος, κ.τ.λ.] The mind, in the first instance, through the channel of the senses, apprehends the beauty of the ἐρώμενος, but the effect of this perception is not confined to the rational, but extends to the entire soul, both in its emotive and concupiscent region. This is evidently Plato's meaning, allegorically it is the driver who 'espies the amatory (love-inspiring) spectacle, and by sense diffuses a glow through the whole soul,' whereby he is himself 'filled with titillation and the stings of desire.' The two horses, we find, are, each in his own way, affected with the passion of Love. So too is the rational soul, which from the aspect of sensible conceives an uneasy yearning for ideal beauty. Without the aid of the senses, which are the ministers of the understanding, neither the affections nor the appetites could be warmed and excited. The νοῦς therefore, in its wider sense, may justly be said πᾶσαν αἰσθήσει

σει διαθερμήνας τὴν ψυχήν, γαργαλισμοῦ τε καὶ πόθου
κέντρων ὑποπλησθῇ, | ὁ μὲν εὐπειθὴς τῷ ἡνιόχῳ τῶν 254
ἵππων, ἀεί τε καὶ τότε αἰδοῖ βιαζόμενος, ἑαυτὸν κατέχει
μὴ ἐπιπηδᾶν τῷ ἐρωμένῳ· ὁ δὲ οὔτε κέντρων ἡνιοχικῶν
οὔτε μάστιγος ἔτι ἐντρέπεται, σκιρτῶν δὲ βίᾳ φέρεται,
καὶ πάντα πράγματα παρέχων τῷ σύζυγί τε καὶ ἡνιόχῳ
ἀναγκάζει ἰέναι τε πρὸς τὰ παιδικὰ καὶ μνείαν ποιεῖσθαι
τῆς τῶν ἀφροδισίων χάριτος. τὼ δὲ κατ' ἀρχὰς μὲν ἀντι-
τείνετον ἀγανακτοῦντε, ὡς δεινὰ καὶ παράνομα ἀναγκα- B
ζομένω· τελευτῶντε δέ, ὅταν μηδὲν ᾖ πέρας κακοῦ, πο-
ρεύεσθον ἀγομένω, εἴξαντε καὶ ὁμολογήσαντε ποιήσειν τὸ
κελευόμενον. καὶ πρὸς αὐτῷ τ' ἐγένοντο καὶ εἶδον τὴν
ὄψιν τὴν τῶν παιδικῶν ἀστράπτουσαν. ἰδόντος δὲ τοῦ
ἡνιόχου ἡ μνήμη πρὸς τὴν τοῦ κάλλους φύσιν ἠνέχθη,
καὶ πάλιν εἶδεν αὐτὴν μετὰ σωφροσύνης ἐν ἁγνῷ βάθρῳ

διαθερμαίνειν τὴν ψυχήν Comp inf 255, τὸ ῥεῦμα . . διὰ τῶν ὀμμάτων ἰόν, ᾗ πέφυκεν ἐπὶ τὴν ψυχὴν ἰέναι These considerations seem to remove the difficulty with regard to αἰσθήσει, and prevent us from yielding to Stallb.'s proposal of substituting διαθερμῆναι for διαθερμήνας,—a change in every point of view undesirable Presently, 254 C, the ἀγαθὸς ἵππος in his turn ἱδρῶτι πᾶσαν ἔβρεξε τὴν ψυχήν The psychology of the passage is Platonic, if not in all points unexceptionable Particularly striking is the description of passionate love, as distinguished from mere lust The 'obedient steed' is restrained by shame from violence, true passion being always united with sexual modesty, ἀεί τε καὶ τότε, 'then as always' Compare with the entire passage 251 C, ὅταν μὲν οὖν, βλέπουσα πρὸς τὸ τοῦ παιδὸς κάλλος . . θερμαίνηται, and ibid. B, δεξάμενος τοῦ κάλλους τὴν ἀποῤῥοὴν διὰ τῶν ὀμμάτων, ἐθερμάνθη, κ τ λ The use of ὄμμα for ὄψιν is poetical, and frequent in tragedy For ὑποπλησθῇ comp Protag init, πώγωνος ἤδη ὑποπιμπλάμενος sup 251 B, ὑπὸ πᾶν τὸ τῆς ψυχῆς εἶδος

254. τῷ σύζυγί τε καὶ ἡνιόχῳ] Observe that the article affects both nouns, though relating to different subjects In such cases τε occurs usually before καί, but not always Eur Herc. Fur 1 10, τὸν Ἡράκλειον πατέρα καὶ ξυνάορον, 'the sire and [illegible]'

τὼ δὲ κατ' ἀρχὰς μὲν ἀντιτείνετον] The *two* are of course the λογικὸν and the θυμοειδὲς μέρος τῆς ψυχῆς, which combine to resist the mere animal appetite. Presently we find that the driver 'brings both horses on their haunches' but there is this difference, that the better horse makes no resistance So in Rep IV 440 B, ταῖς ἐπιθυμίαις αὐτὸν (τὸν θυμὸν) κοινωνήσαντα, αἱροῦντος λόγου μὴ δεῖν τι πράττειν, οἶμαί σε οὐκ ἂν φάναι γενομένου ποτὲ ἐν σεαυτῷ τοῦ τοιούτου αἰσθέσθαι, οἶμαι δ' οὐδ' ἐν ἄλλῳ

B τελευτῶντε δέ, κ τ λ] Ultimately, when they are weary of resisting, the driver and his ally are fain to come to terms with the refractory steed They yield for a while, but so soon as they come in presence of the beloved, the aspect of his beauty awakens the repugnance of the driver by reviving the memory of the absolutely Beautiful (αὐτὴν τὴν τοῦ κάλλους μνήμην) Comp with this passage one of Galen, de Hippocr et Platone, VI 510, Kühn, πολλάκις μὲν ἕπεται τῷ θυμοειδεῖ τὰ λοιπὰ δύο, πολλάκις δὲ τῷ ἐπιθυμητικῷ, καθάπερ ἑλκόμενα καὶ συρόμενα παραπλήσιον τρόπον ὡσεὶ καὶ ξυνωρίδες ἵππων, κ τ λ

ἐν ἁγνῷ βάθρῳ] 'on a holy pedestal,'—an allusion doubtless to the images in the adytum at Eleusis Paus III 19 3, τοῦ δὲ ἀγάλματος τὸ βάθρον παρέχεται βωμοῦ σχῆμα Etym M., βάθρον βῆμα ἢ βάσις τοῦ ἀνδριάντος So also Hesych

βεβῶσαν. ἰδοῦσα δὲ ἔδεισέ τε καὶ σεφθεῖσα ἀνέπεσεν
C ὑπτία, καὶ ἅμα ἠναγκάσθη εἰς τοὐπίσω ἑλκύσαι τὰς ἡνίας
οὕτω σφόδρα, ὥστε ἐπὶ τὰ ἰσχία ἄμφω καθίσαι τὼ ἵππω,
τὸν μὲν ἑκόντα διὰ τὸ μὴ ἀντιτείνειν, τὸν δὲ ὑβριστὴν
μάλα ἄκοντα. ἀπελθόντε δὲ ἀπωτέρω, ὁ μὲν ὑπ' αἰσχύνης τε καὶ θάμβους ἱδρῶτι πᾶσαν ἔβρεξε τὴν ψυχήν, ὁ
δέ, λήξας τῆς ὀδύνης ἣν ὑπὸ τοῦ χαλινοῦ τε ἔσχε καὶ
τοῦ πτώματος, μόγις ἐξαναπνεύσας ἐλοιδόρησεν ὀργῇ,
πολλὰ κακίζων τόν τε ἡνίοχον καὶ τὸν ὁμόζυγα ὡς δειλίᾳ
D τε καὶ ἀνανδρίᾳ λιπόντε τὴν τάξιν καὶ ὁμολογίαν. καὶ
πάλιν οὐκ ἐθέλοντας προσιέναι ἀναγκάζων μόγις συνε-
χώρησε, δεομένων εἰσαῦθις ὑπερβαλέσθαι. ἐλθόντος δὲ
τοῦ συντεθέντος χρόνου, [οὗ] ἀμνημονεῖν προσποιουμένω
ἀναμιμνήσκων, βιαζόμενος, χρεμετίζων, ἕλκων ἠνάγκασεν
αὖ προσελθεῖν τοῖς παιδικοῖς ἐπὶ τοὺς αὐτοὺς λόγους.
καὶ ἐπειδὴ ἐγγὺς ἦσαν, ἐγκύψας καὶ ἐκτείνας τὴν κέρκον,
ἐνδακὼν τὸν χαλινόν, μετ' ἀναιδείας ἕλκει. ὁ δ' ἡνίοχος

σεφθεῖσα] Hesych., ἐσέφθην· ἐσεβάσθην, ἡσυχάσας ᾐσχύνθην· Σοφοκλῆς Δαιδάλῳ (Frag. 175, Dind.) This deponent aor. formed contrary to analogy from σέβομαι, is noted by other grammarians as occurring only twice, here and in Soph. l. l. The MSS have the variants στεφθεῖσα, στρεφθεῖσα, στραφεῖσα, ὀφθεῖσα. Comp. Ellendt, Lex. Soph. in v. σέβω.

C. ὡς—λιπόντε τὴν τάξιν καὶ ὁμολογίαν] As guilty of λιποτάξιον in breaking the terms of the agreement. The τε which Badh. would insert seems unnecessary. Hipp. Maj. 293 D, ἐλεήσας μου τὴν ἀπειρίαν καὶ ἀπαιδευσίαν.

D. καὶ πάλιν, κ.τ.λ.] 'after one more attempt to force his unwilling companions to draw nigh to the beloved, he has to yield a reluctant assent to their prayer for further delay.' The aorists in this passage and the context are illustrated by Phaed. 73 D (quoted by Heind.), οὐκοῦν οἶσθα, ὅτι οἱ ἐρασταὶ ὅταν ἴδωσι λύραν ἢ ἱμάτιον ἢ τι ἄλλο οἷς τὰ παιδικὰ αὐτῶν εἴωθε χρῆσθαι, πάσχουσι τοῦτο, ἔγνωσάν τε τὴν λύραν, καὶ ἐν τῇ διανοίᾳ ἔλαβον τὸ εἶδος τοῦ παιδός, οὗ ἦν ἡ λύρα. For ὑπερβαλέσθαι the Attic verb in use is ἀναβαλέσθαι. This is possibly one of the Ionicisms of which Plato, according to the grammarians, was fond. Herod. ix. 45, ἢν ὑπερβάληται τὴν συμβολὴν Μαρδόνιος. But Lucian, perhaps imitating Plato, has ἐς αὔριον ὑπερβαλώμεθα τὴν συνουσίαν. Later writers frequently use ὑπερτίθεσθαι in the same sense. The gen. abs. δεομένων—'though they pray' or 'because they pray'—needs neither alteration nor apology, though Heind.'s conj. δεομένοιν is not in itself improbable, the substitution of a plural for a dual being a common error in MSS. Presently οὗ is found in all the MSS after χρόνου, evidently by an error of the scribes, who have repeated the last syllable of χρόνου. Heind. seems first to have called attention to this error.

καὶ ἐπειδὴ ἐγγὺς ἦσαν—ἕλκει] The tense changes from past to present, as in the passage of the Phaedo just quoted it changes from present to past.

ἐγκύψας καὶ ἐκτείνας τὴν κέρκον] 'with head down, and tail stretched out.' Xen. Eq. i. 8, οὐ γὰρ ἐγκάμπτοντες, ἀλλ' ἐκτείναντες τὸν τράχηλον καὶ τὴν κεφαλὴν βιάζεσθαι οἱ ἵπποι ἐπιχειροῦσι.

ἔτι μᾶλλον ταὐτὸν πάθος παθών, ὥσπερ ἀπὸ ὕσπληγος E
ἀναπεσών, ἔτι μᾶλλον τοῦ ὑβριστοῦ ἵππου ἐκ τῶν ὀδόντων βίᾳ ὀπίσω σπάσας τὸν χαλινόν, τήν τε κακηγόρον γλῶτταν καὶ τὰς γνάθους καθῄμαξε καὶ τὰ σκέλη τε καὶ τὰ ἰσχία πρὸς τὴν γῆν ἐρείσας ὀδύναις ἔδωκεν. ὅταν δὲ ταὐτὸν πολλάκις πάσχων ὁ πονηρὸς τῆς ὕβρεως λήξῃ, ταπεινωθεὶς ἕπεται ἤδη τῇ τοῦ ἡνιόχου προνοίᾳ, καὶ ὅταν ἴδῃ τὸν καλόν, φόβῳ διόλλυται. ὥστε ξυμβαίνει τότ' ἤδη τὴν τοῦ ἐραστοῦ ψυχὴν τοῖς παιδικοῖς αἰδουμένην τε καὶ δεδιυῖαν ἕπεσθαι. | ἅτ' οὖν πᾶσαν θεραπείαν ὡς ἰσόθεος 255
θεραπευόμενος οὐχ ὑπὸ σχηματιζομένου τοῦ ἐρῶντος, ἀλλ' ἀληθῶς τοῦτο πεπονθότος, καὶ αὐτὸς ὢν φύσει φίλος [εἰς ταὐτὸν ἄγει τὴν φιλίαν] τῷ θεραπεύοντι, ἐὰν ἄρα καὶ ἐν

ταὐτὸν πάθος παθών] i e *δείσας καὶ σεφθείς*, paul sup. The next clause is epexegetic, and therefore the copula is dispensed with

E *ὥσπερ ἀπὸ ὕσπληγος*] As racers fall back at the barrier which their eager team strives to force *ὕσπληξ*, for which the commoner form is *ὕσπληγξ*, is mentioned by J Poll (iii 147), with its synonyms *ἄφεσις, γραμμή, βαλβίς* It is distinguished from the last term in the Lex Rhet *βαλβίς ξύλα δύο τῶν δρομέων, ἀφ' ὧν σχοινίον τι διατέταται* This *σχοίνιον* seems to be the *ὕσπληξ* proper, which is accordingly explained by Steph as "funis obtentus cursoribus, i e *τοῖς ἱπποδραμοῦσι*, quo laxato dejectoque curriculum ingrederentur" On the other hand Pausanias seems to deny that the *ὕσπληξ* was a rope Speaking of the hippodrome at Olympia, he says, *διήκει πρὸ αὐτῶν καλώδιον ἀντὶ ὕσπληγγος* (vi 20, § 7) The entire passage is thus translated by Mr Wright · "Backward he falls like racers at the barrier, and with a wrench still more violent than before pulls back the bit from the teeth of the restive horse, thereby drenching his jaws and riotous tongue with blood, and bruising against the ground his legs and haunches, consigns him to anguish" *ὀδύναις ἔδωκεν* is a poeticism found elsewhere in Plato The comm quote Hom Od xviii. 567, *ὀδύνῃσιν ἔδωκεν*, ib. xix 167, *ἀχέεσσί γε δώσεις* also Rep ix 574 c, *πληγαῖς δοῦναι* So Ovid, Exitio terras quum dabit una dies But the passage which suggested the phrase to Plato was probably Eurip frag Antig, *Τίς γὰρ πετραῖον σκόπελον οὐτάζων δορὶ Ὀδύναισι δώσει*, (No 176, Nauck)

φόβῳ διόλλυται] The extinction of gross appetite by the actual presence of beauty coveted in absence, is a remarkable feature in the psychology of this passage

255 *ἅτ' οὖν—ὁμιλίαν*] The construction of this sentence presents no difficulty, if the bracketed words be ejected. They are absent from the Bodl and several other MSS The *δὲ* after *προϊόντος* is *in apodosi* Though the *ἐρώμενος* have been induced by the prejudices early imbibed from schoolmates or others to repel the advances of the *ἐραστής*, yet as time wears on, &c *διαβεβλημένος* must mean "deceptus," as Heind interprets. Arist Av 1648, *διαβάλλεταί σ' ὁ θεῖος, ὦ πονηρὲ σύ* ib Thesm 1214, *διέβαλέ μ' ἁ γραῦς* The more usual Attic sense of *διαβάλλω*, 'to set at variance,' does not apply to the present passage, in which reference is made to prejudices against the practice of keeping company with an *ἐραστής*, not to any repugnance felt towards a particular admirer. *προσέσθαι*, 'to admit,' is the emendation of Heind for the vulg *προέσθαι* The consent of the Bodl seems to be assumed by Bekk and subsequent edd, though no notice is taken of the variant by Gaisford in his collation of that codex with Steph's text

τῷ πρόσθεν ὑπὸ ξυμφοιτητῶν ἤ τινων ἄλλων διαβεβλημένος ᾖ, λεγόντων ὡς αἰσχρὸν ἐρῶντι πλησιάζειν, καὶ διὰ
τοῦτο ἀπωθῇ τὸν ἐρῶντα· προιόντος δὲ ἤδη τοῦ χρόνου
ἥ θ' ἡλικία καὶ τὸ χρεὼν ἤγαγεν εἰς τὸ προσέσθαι αὐτὸν
B εἰς ὁμιλίαν. οὐ γὰρ δήποθ' εἵμαρται κακὸν κακῷ φίλον
οὐδ' ἀγαθὸν μὴ φίλον ἀγαθῷ εἶναι. προσεμένου δὲ
καὶ λόγον καὶ ὁμιλίαν δεξαμένου, ἐγγύθεν ἡ εὔνοια
γιγνομένη τοῦ ἐρῶντος ἐκπλήττει τὸν ἐρώμενον, διαισθανόμενον ὅτι οὐδ' οἱ ξύμπαντες ἄλλοι φίλοι τε καὶ οἰκεῖοι
μοῖραν φιλίας οὐδεμίαν παρέχονται πρὸς τὸν ἔνθεον φίλον.
ὅταν δὲ χρονίζῃ τοῦτο δρῶν καὶ πλησιάζῃ μετὰ τοῦ
C ἅπτεσθαι ἔν τε γυμνασίοις καὶ ἐν ταῖς ἄλλαις ὁμιλίαις,
τότ' ἤδη ἡ τοῦ ῥεύματος ἐκείνου πηγή, ὃν ἵμερον Ζεὺς
Γανυμήδους ἐρῶν ὠνόμασε, πολλὴ φερομένη πρὸς τὸν
ἐραστήν, ἡ μὲν εἰς αὐτὸν ἔδυ, ἡ δ' ἀπομεστουμένου ἔξω
ἀποῤῥεῖ· καὶ οἷον πνεῦμα ἤ τις ἠχὼ ἀπὸ λείων τε καὶ

B *οὐ γὰρ δήποθ' εἵμαρται*] 'for it cannot surely be in the order of destiny.' I have followed Hirsch in writing *δήποθ'* as one word in place of the received *δή ποτε*. The particle has no temporal significance here, but is equivalent to *δήπου*, as in Soph. Trach. 876, *οὐ δήποθ' ὡς θανοῦσα*. *εἵμαρται* is an echo of the foregoing *χρεών*.

προσεμένου] Vulg. *προεμένου*. Corr. Heind.

διαισθανόμενον] 'clearly as he discerns that all others his friends and kindred taken together have no affection to offer comparable in degree to that felt for him by his heaven-inspired friend.' Comp. the speech of Lysias, p. 233 C, where the contrary view is upheld.

τοῦτο δρῶν] Apparently we must understand *ὁμιλῶν*, implied in *ὁμιλίαν δεξαμένου*, paul. sup.

C *ἡ τοῦ ῥεύματος—πηγή*] i. e. *ἡ τοῦ κάλλους ἀποῤῥοή*, sup. 251 B.

ὃν ἵμερον Ζεὺς—ὠνόμασε] Plato here attributes to the highest authority the whimsical etymology of *ἵμερος* given above (p. 252 C), *ἐκεῖθεν μέρη ἐπιόντα καὶ ῥέοντα, ἃ δὴ διὰ ταῦτα ἵμερος καλεῖται*, where see the note. There is an equally fanciful etymology of the name *Γανυμήδης* in the Symposium of Xenophon (viii. 30). In the Laws Plato attributes the invention of the fable of Ganymede to the Cretans: *Κρητῶν τὸν περὶ τὸν Γανυμήδη μῦθον κατηγοροῦμεν . . τοῦτον δὴ τὸν μῦθον προστεθεικέναι κατὰ τοῦ Διός, ἵνα ἑπόμενοι δὴ τῷ θεῷ καρπῶνται καὶ ταύτην τὴν ἡδονήν* (p. 636 D). If Plato is in earnest, his accusation is disproved by Hom. Il. xx. 232, a version of the story entirely free from impurity. But perhaps it is only meant that the Cretans gave a vile meaning to the more ancient tradition. Eusebius, Praep. Evang. xiii. 709 C, quotes this entire passage of the Phaedrus from *ὅταν δὲ χρονίζῃ* to *εἰπεῖν οὐκ ἔχει*, and again from *ἐπιθυμεῖ δὲ* to *κόσμιοι ὄντες*, p. 256, and from *ἐὰν δὲ δὴ διαίτῃ φορτικωτέρᾳ* to *ἡ παρ' ἐραστοῦ φιλία*, ib. E. He proceeds to quote Levit. xx. 13 to show the greater strictness and purity of the Mosaic institutes.

ἀπομεστουμένου] 'as he fills up and brims over.'

καὶ οἷον πνεῦμα, κ.τ.λ.] 'and as a wind or a sound, rebounding from smooth and solid bodies, travels back to the point of its departure, so the stream of beauty returns through the eyes to its source, the beautiful youth, and when it has reached his soul through that the appointed channel of communication, and quickened and excited him, it waters the passages of the feathers and sets them sprouting.'

στερεῶν ἁλλομένη πάλιν ὅθεν ὡρμήθη φέρεται, οὕτω τὸ
τοῦ κάλλους ῥεῦμα πάλιν εἰς τὸν καλὸν διὰ τῶν ὀμμάτων
ἰόν, ᾗ πέφυκεν ἐπὶ τὴν ψυχὴν ἰέναι ἀφικόμενον καὶ
ἀναπτερῶσαν, τὰς διόδους τῶν πτερῶν ἄρδει τε καὶ ὥρμησε πτεροφυεῖν τε, καὶ τὴν τοῦ ἐρωμένου αὖ ψυχὴν D
ἔρωτος ἐνέπλησεν. ἐρᾷ μὲν οὖν, ὅτου δέ, ἀπορεῖ· καὶ οὔθ'
ὅ τι πέπονθεν οἶδεν οὐδ' ἔχει φράσαι, ἀλλ' οἷον ἀπ'
ἄλλου ὀφθαλμίας ἀπολελαυκὼς πρόφασιν εἰπεῖν οὐκ ἔχει,
ὥσπερ δὲ ἐν κατόπτρῳ [ἐν] τῷ ἐρῶντι ἑαυτὸν ὁρῶν λέληθε.
καὶ ὅταν μὲν ἐκεῖνος παρῇ, λήγει κατὰ ταὐτὰ ἐκείνῳ τῆς
ὀδύνης· ὅταν δὲ ἀπῇ, κατὰ ταὐτὰ αὖ ποθεῖ καὶ ποθεῖ-
ται, εἴδωλον ἔρωτος ἀντέρωτα ἔχων· καλεῖ δὲ αὐτὸν καὶ
οἴεται οὐκ ἔρωτα ἀλλὰ φιλίαν εἶναι. ἐπιθυμεῖ δὲ ἐκείνῳ E
παραπλησίως μέν, ἀσθενεστέρως δέ, ὁρᾶν, ἅπτεσθαι,

Such seems to be the proper arrangement of this somewhat cumbrous sentence With Ast I refer ἀναπτερῶσαν to αὐτόν, sc τὸν καλόν. Others punctuate after ἀφικόμενον. Heind. conjectures ἀνα-πληρῶσαν, Schneider in Lex ἀναστομῶσαν, both referring the participle to τὰς διόδους

D ὀφθαλμίας ἀπολελαυκώς] Herm, ἀναπίμπλαται ὀφθαλμίας. The accusative is more usual in such cases, but in Rep iii 395 C we find ἵνα μὴ ἐκ τῆς μιμήσεως τοῦ εἶναι ἀπολαύσωσιν "Credebant autem veteres lippitudinem per ipsum aspectum communicari" (Ast) The medical writers do not seem to have endorsed this superstition, in illustration of which Ast quotes Porphyry de Abstinentia, i 28

ὥσπερ δὲ ἐν κατόπτρῳ [ἐν] τῷ ἐρῶντι] Cobet, Vv. Ll. p 165, insists on the omission of the second ἐν So read, the passage is both more harmonious to the ear and more idiomatic He quotes, among other passages, Protag 337 E, ὥσπερ ὑπὸ διαιτητῶν ἡμῶν Tim 79 A, ῥεῖν ὥσπερ δι' αὐλῶνος τοῦ σώματος· and in Rep viii 553 B would read πταίσαντα ὥσπερ πρὸς ἕρματι τῇ πόλει for πρὸς τῇ πόλει. I add Eur Cycl 433, ὥσπερ πρὸς ἰξῷ τῇ κύλικι λελημμένος. It is highly probable that a construction of this kind would be tampered with by copyists, but there are passages in Plato where the second preposition can hardly be dispensed with, e g Phaed [illegible]

τούτου σκοπεῖσθαι τὰ ὄντα ib 109, ὥσπερ περὶ τέλμα μύρμηκας ἢ βατράχους περὶ τὴν θάλατταν οἰκοῦντας

κατὰ ταὐτὰ—ἔχων] Aesch Ag 544 τῶν ἀντερώντων ἱμέρῳ πεπληγμένος K Ποθεῖν ποθοῦντα τήνδε γῆν στρατὸν λέγεις The word ἀντέρως, in the sense of 'love returned,' Germ 'Gegenliebe,' occurs nowhere but in Plato or his imitators, though the passage quoted from Aesch shows that the conception must have been familiar to the poets The word too must have been in common use, for statues were erected to Eros and Anteros at Elis Pausan Eliac c 23, καὶ Ἔρωτος καὶ ὃν Ἠλεῖοι καὶ Ἀθηναῖοι κατὰ ταὐτὰ Ἠλείοις Ἀντέρωτα ὀνομάζουσι ib init, ἔχει δὲ ὁ μὲν φοίνικος ὁ Ἔρως κλάδον ὁ δὲ ἀφελέσθαι πειρᾶται τὸν φοίνικα ὁ Ἀντέρως From another passage (Attic c 29) we learn that it was the province of Anteros to avenge as an ἀλάστωρ the wrongs of slighted lovers. This would follow, according to mythological etiquette, from his being the patron of mutual passion There is therefore no such contradiction, as Ast supposes, between the popular idea of Anteros and that of Plato in the text Here Anteros is called an 'image' or reflection of Eros, in accordance with the previous figure of a mirror. Herm, τὰ δεύτερα δὲ προσάπτει τῷ ἀντέρωτι, ἐπειδὴ καὶ πρωτουργὸν αἴτιόν ἐστι τοῦ ἀντέρωτος ὁ ἔρως.

φιλεῖν, συγκατακεῖσθαι. καὶ δή, οἷον εἰκός, ποιεῖ τὸ
μετὰ τοῦτο ταχὺ ταῦτα. ἐν οὖν τῇ συγκοιμήσει τοῦ μὲν
ἐραστοῦ ὁ ἀκόλαστος ἵππος ἔχει ὅ τι λέγῃ πρὸς τὸν ἡνίο-
256 χον, καὶ ἀξιοῖ ἀντὶ πολλῶν πόνων σμικρὰ ἀπολαῦσαι· | ὁ
δὲ τῶν παιδικῶν ἔχει μὲν οὐδὲν εἰπεῖν, σπαργῶν δ᾽ καὶ
ἀπορῶν περιβάλλει τὸν ἐραστὴν καὶ φιλεῖ, ὡς σφόδρ᾽
εὔνουν ἀσπαζόμενος, ὅταν τε συγκατακέωνται, οἷός ἐστι
μὴ ἂν ἀπαρνηθῆναι τὸ αὑτοῦ μέρος χαρίσασθαι τῷ
ἐρῶντι, εἰ δεηθείη τυχεῖν. ὁ δὲ ὁμόζυξ αὖ μετὰ τοῦ ἡνιόχου πρὸς ταῦτα μετ᾽ αἰδοῦς καὶ λόγου ἀντιτείνει. ἐὰν
μὲν δὴ οὖν εἰς τεταγμένην τε δίαιταν καὶ φιλοσοφίαν
νικήσῃ τὰ βελτίω τῆς διανοίας ἀγαγόντα, μακάριον μὲν
B καὶ ὁμονοητικὸν τὸν ἐνθάδε βίον διάγουσιν, ἐγκρατεῖς
αὑτῶν καὶ κόσμιοι ὄντες, δουλωσάμενοι μὲν ᾧ κακία ψυχῆς ἐνεγίγνετο, ἐλευθερώσαντες δὲ ᾧ ἀρετή· τελευτήσαντες
δὲ δή, ὑπόπτεροι καὶ ἐλαφροὶ γεγονότες, τῶν τριῶν παλαισμάτων τῶν ὡς ἀληθῶς Ὀλυμπιακῶν ἓν νενικήκασιν,

1 ἔχει ὅ τι λέγῃ] The MSS as usual vary between λέγει, λέγοι, and λέγῃ, of which the last only is admissible. Ar. Vesp. 915, ἀλλ᾽ οὐκ ἔχειν οὗτός γ᾽ ἔοικεν ὅτι λέγῃ. Isocr. Paneg. 49, ἀλλ᾽ ἑκατέρους ἔχειν ἐφ᾽ οἷς φιλοτιμηθῶσιν. In the affirmative sentence the future indic. is more usual, but not more legitimate.

256 ὁ δὲ ὁμόζυξ] Herm., τουτέστι, τὸ θυμικόν.

ἐὰν μὲν δὴ οὖν, κ.τ.λ.] If in this inward battle the two higher principles triumph over the lower, and bring the pair of lovers to submit to a strict and philosophic life, then are their days here on earth full of harmony and bliss, they are masters of self, orderly and tranquil: 'having brought into subjection that part of the soul which was the nursery of vice, and liberated that in which were the seeds of virtue.' For τεταγμένην comp. Gorg. 504, ἕως ἂν τὸ ἅπαν συστήσηται τεταγμένον τε καὶ κεκοσμημένον πρᾶγμα... τοῖς δὲ τῆς ψυχῆς τάξεσί τε καὶ κοσμήσεσι νόμιμόν τε καὶ νόμος (ὄνομά ἐστιν) ὅθεν καὶ νόμιμοι γίγνονται καὶ κόσμιοι· ταῦτα δ᾽ ἔστι δικαιοσύνη τε καὶ σωφροσύνη. In Rep. III 404 we read of the τεταγμένη δίαιτα—the 'strict régime' to which athletes were confined by their trainers. With δουλωσάμενοι comp. the still more energetic language of St Paul, 1 Cor. IX 27, ὑπωπιάζω μου τὸ σῶμα καὶ δουλαγωγῶ.

B τῶν τριῶν παλαισμάτων τῶν ὡς ἀληθῶς Ὀλυμπιακῶν] 'of the three rounds of a combat in the truest sense Olympian.' The victorious lovers are votaries of Zeus the Olympian, the patron of those who φιλοσοφοῦσιν ἀδόλως καὶ παιδεραστοῦσι μετὰ φιλοσοφίας (sup. 248 E), called Διὸς ὀπαδοὶ 252 C. These have but three periods of probation to pass through (τρίτῃ περιόδῳ τῇ χιλιετεῖ, ἐὰν ἕλωνται τρὶς ἐφεξῆς τὸν βίον τοῦτον, οὕτω πτερωθεῖσαι τρισχιλιοστῷ ἔτει ἀπέρχονται, p. 249), and in this respect they resemble the wrestlers at Olympia, who were crowned after thrice throwing their antagonists. The lovers who in this the first stage of their corporeal existence (τὴν τῇδε πρώτην γένεσιν βιοτεύοντες,—252 D) remain true to their high philosophic vocation until parted by death, are in the position of a combatant who has won one of the three παλαίσματα required. To this Olympic usage allusions are frequent in Greek literature. See Aesch. Eum. 559, with Mr Paley's note. Also Rep. IX 583 B. The reward of the victorious soul consists in its perfect freedom, after death, from the en-

οὗ μεῖζον ἀγαθὸν οὔτε σωφροσύνη ἀνθρωπίνη οὔτε θεία
μανία δυνατὴ πορίσαι ἀνθρώπῳ. ἐὰν δὲ δὴ διαίτῃ φορ- C
τικωτέρᾳ τε καὶ ἀφιλοσόφῳ, φιλοτίμῳ δὲ χρήσωνται, τάχ'
ἄν που ἐν μέθαις ἢ τινι ἄλλῃ ἀμελείᾳ τὼ ἀκολάστω αὐτοῖν ὑποζυγίω λαβόντε τὰς ψυχὰς ἀφρούρους, ξυναγα-
γόντε εἰς ταὐτόν, τὴν ὑπὸ τῶν πολλῶν μακαριστὴν αἵρεσιν εἱλέτην τε καὶ διεπράξαντο· καὶ διαπραξαμένω τὸ

cumbrance of the lower appetites (ἐλαφροὶ γεγονότες), and in its power of soaring fully plumed to the highest regions of intellectual contemplation. Mere human or prudential virtue has no boon to confer which is comparable to this, the best result of god-given madness in its highest manifestation.

C ἐὰν δὲ δὴ διαίτῃ] Having fixed the destiny of the philosophic lovers, Plato proceeds to discuss the case of the 'philotimic' or those who, though actuated by a generous ambition and a love of glory, fall short of the refined standard of excellence aimed at by the Δῖοι or votaries of Zeus, and of philosophic truth. Probably he has in his mind the character so vividly portrayed in the eighth book of the Republic—a man with the virtues and failings proper to what we should call the *aristocratic*, and what Plato styles the *timocratic* type (l. l. p. 549). In that passage as in this the φιλότιμος is put second in order of excellence to the φιλόσοφος. According to the Platonic psychology he is one in whom the θυμικὸν predominates, proud, high spirited, and generous, a votary, we may suppose, of the queenly and imperious Hera, πολεμικὸς καὶ ἀρχικὸς rather than φιλόκαλος καὶ φιλόσοφος (248 D). Such characters are naturally impulsive and unguarded, liable therefore to be surprised by the senses, and hurried into excesses which their better judgment disapproves. Doubtless many of Plato's near connexions and dearest friends would supply the materials for this typical class, a consideration not to be lost sight of in judging of a passage which is in many respects revolting to our moral taste. If we compare Plato's lenient view of these transgressors and their doom, with the hard measure which Dante metes out to his less guilty Paolo and Francesca, we shall obtain a not unfair gauge of the difference [illegible] the theological standard of purity. The passage, it may be observed, is mentioned with grave reprobation by Theodoret (Therap. ix. 53), who, however, misrepresents Plato's meaning in more respects than one.

τάχ' ἄν] Here τάχ' ἂν has the force of a single particle, not communicating its conditional sense, as usually, to the leading verb. Comp. Arist. Vesp. 281, τάχα δ' ἂν διὰ τὸν χθιζινὸν ἄνθρωπον . . διὰ τοῦτ' ὀδυνηθείς, εἶτ' ἴσως κεῖται πυρέττων. Soph. Oed. C. 965, θεοῖς γὰρ ἦν οὕτω φίλον Τάχ' ἄν τι μηνίουσιν εἰς γένος πάλαι. The ἂν in these cases affects the sense of the participle just as little as it does that of the leading verb; yet Ellendt, Lex. Soph., says it is "added to the participle" in this and similar passages which he quotes. If this were so, μηνίουσιν ἂν would mean, 'who would be incensed against the race,' whereas the participle is evidently causal: 'it may be because they, the gods, harboured some old resentment,' &c. See inf. p. 265 B, ἴσως μὲν ἀληθοῦς τινος ἐφαπτόμενοι, τάχα δ' ἂν καὶ ἄλλοσε παραφερόμενοι . . προσεπαίσαμεν, κ. τ. λ.

τὴν ὑπὸ τῶν πολλῶν—εἱλέτην τε καὶ διεπράξαντο] I cannot but wish that the reading in Eusebius, εἱλέσθην (which Heind. has adopted), were supported by some one of the Platonic MSS. But Eusebius also reads διεπραξάσθην, and this gives to both variants the air of a critical emendation. The received reading yields the following sense: 'They seize, and consummate a choice which the vulgar esteem the height of bliss'—'choice' being put *per euphemismum* for the thing chosen, the gratification of appetite. Herm., τὴν αἰσχρὰν ἡδονὴν λέγει. Of the coupling of duals and plurals in the same clause Stallb. gives many instances. One of these, Phaedr. 261 B, appears doubtful, though there can be no doubt as to others.

λοιπὸν ἤδη χρῶνται μὲν αὐτῇ, σπανίᾳ δέ, ἅτε οὐ πάσῃ
δεδογμένα τῇ διανοίᾳ πράττοντες. φίλω μὲν οὖν καὶ
D τούτω, ἧττον δὲ ἐκείνων, ἀλλήλοιν διά τε τοῦ ἔρωτος καὶ
ἔξω γενομένω διάγουσι, πίστεις τὰς μεγίστας ἡγουμένω
ἀλλήλοιν δεδωκέναι τε καὶ δεδέχθαι, ἃς οὐ θεμιτὸν εἶναι
λύσαντας εἰς ἔχθραν ποτὲ ἐλθεῖν. ἐν δὲ τῇ τελευτῇ ἄπτεροι
μέν, ὡρμηκότες δὲ πτεροῦσθαι ἐκβαίνουσι τοῦ σώματος,
ὥστε οὐ σμικρὸν ἆθλον τῆς ἐρωτικῆς μανίας φέρονται·
εἰς γὰρ σκότον καὶ τὴν ὑπὸ γῆς πορείαν οὐ νόμος ἐστὶν
ἔτι ἐλθεῖν τοῖς κατηργμένοις ἤδη τῆς ὑπουρανίου πορείας,
E ἀλλὰ φανὸν βίον διάγοντας εὐδαιμονεῖν μετ' ἀλλήλων
πορευομένους, καὶ ὁμοπτέρους ἔρωτος χάριν, ὅταν γένωνται, γενέσθαι.

Ταῦτα τοσαῦτα, ὦ παῖ, καὶ θεῖα οὕτω σοι δωρήσεται ἡ παρ' ἐραστοῦ φιλία. ἡ δὲ ἀπὸ τοῦ μὴ ἐρῶντος οἰκειότης, σωφροσύνῃ θνητῇ κεκραμένη, θνητά τε καὶ φειδωλὰ οἰκονομοῦσα, ἀνελευθερίαν ὑπὸ πλήθους ἐπαινουμένην ὡς

χρῶνται μὲν αὐτῇ] Sc τῇ αἱρέσει, as if he had written ἡδονῇ.

D διά τε τοῦ ἔρωτος καὶ ἔξω γενομένω] 'both while their passion lasts and after they have escaped from its influence' (got over it)

ὡρμηκότες δὲ πτεροῦσθαι] Sup 255 C, ὥρμησε πτεροφυεῖν 'With their plumage in act to shoot,' or, as Krische gives it, "mit dem Triebe sich zu befiedern" The perf ὥρμηκα is always intransitive and scarcely distinguishable in sense from ὥρμημαι

ὑπουρανίου] The MSS vacillate as usual between ἐπουρανίου, οὐρανίου, and ὑπουρανίου, but the last is the best supported It is also found in all the copies of Eusebius Comp 219, αἱ δὲ ἄλλαι (ψυχαί) ὅταν τὸν πρῶτον βίον τελευτήσωσι κρίσεως ἔτυχον κριθεῖσαι δέ, αἱ μὲν εἰς τὰ ὑπὸ γῆς δικαιωτήρια ἐλθοῦσαι δίκην ἐκτίνουσιν, αἱ δ' εἰς τοὐρανοῦ τινα τόπον ὑπὸ τῆς δίκης κουφισθεῖσαι, διάγουσιν ἀξίως οὗ ἐν ἀνθρώπου εἴδει ἐβίωσαν βίου See also the note on ὑπουρανία ἁψίς, p. 247 B The souls sojourn in some region of the οὐρανός, or space enclosed by the great outermost sphere, that of the fixed stars They do not, of course, mount to the outer surface, the ἀληθείας πεδίον, not being ὑπόπτεροι like the more highly gifted spirits

E φανὸν βίον διάγοντας] Comp Aesch Prom 510, φαναῖς θυμὸν ἀλδαίνουσαν ἐν εὐφροσύναις

ὅταν γένωνται] 'sooner or later,' 'in due time' So Heind, who quotes Euthyphr 7 D, ἐχθροὶ ἀλλήλοις γιγνόμεθα ὅταν γιγνώμεθα also Euthyd 280 B, Phileb 31 B In all these cases ὅταν or ὁπόταν has the full sense of 'whenever,' as we say, 'whenever that may be' or 'happen'

οἰκειότης] 'familiarity,' not true and disinterested φιλία

σωφρ θνητῇ κεκρ.] 'alloyed with worldly and self-seeking prudence,' in allusion to the lover who is not in love, lauded by Lysias

οἰκονομοῦσα, κ τ λ] 'dispensing,' or 'doling out, a scant measure of worldly benefits, and so breeding in that soul of thine those vulgar qualities which the populace applaud and take for virtues, will cause it to flit, a senseless shade, for nine millenniums over the surface of this earth and beneath it' ἄνουν, which Badh obelizes, is explained by Tim 44 A, κατ' ἀρχὰς ἄνους ψυχὴ γίγνεται τὸ πρῶτον ὅταν εἰς σῶμα ἐνδεθῇ θνητόν, and by the context, which strikingly illus-

ἀρετὴν τῇ φίλῃ ψυχῇ ἐντεκοῦσα, ἐννέα χιλιάδας ἐτῶν | περὶ 257
γῆν κυλινδουμένην αὐτὴν καὶ ὑπὸ γῆς ἄνουν παρέξει.

Αὕτη σοι, ὦ φίλε Ἔρως, εἰς ἡμετέραν δύναμιν ὅ τι καλλίστη καὶ ἀρίστη δέδοταί τε καὶ ἐκτέτισται παλινῳδία, τά τε ἄλλα καὶ τοῖς ὀνόμασιν ἠναγκασμένη ποιητικοῖς τισὶ διὰ Φαῖδρον εἰρῆσθαι. ἀλλὰ τῶν προτέρων τε συγγνώμην καὶ τῶνδε χάριν ἔχων, εὐμενὴς καὶ ἵλεως τὴν ἐρωτικήν μοι τέχνην, ἣν ἔδωκας, μήτε ἀφέλῃ μήτε πηρώσῃς δι' ὀργήν, δίδου δ' ἔτι μᾶλλον ἢ νῦν παρὰ τοῖς
καλοῖς τίμιον εἶναι. τῷ πρόσθεν δ' εἴ τι λόγῳ σοι ἀπηνὲς B
εἴπομεν Φαῖδρός τε καὶ ἐγώ, Λυσίαν τὸν τοῦ λόγου πατέρα αἰτιώμενος παῦε τῶν τοιούτων λόγων, ἐπὶ φιλοσο-

trates the present passage For κυλινδ., a word co-extensive in meaning with the Lat *versari*, comp Phaed 81 C, ψυχὴ περὶ τὰ μνήματα καὶ τοὺς τάφους κυλινδουμένη, where see Wyttenbach's note In other passages of Plato the variant καλινδεῖσθαι is found in some of the MSS, as Theaet. 172 C, οἱ ἐν δικαστηρίοις καὶ τοῖς τοιούτοις ἐκ νέων καλινδούμενοι, or κυλινδ The same variation of form exists in other writers, early and late In illustration of the sentiment the comm quote the well-known fragment of a Pindaric threne preserved by Clem Alex, Ψυχαὶ δ' ἀσεβέων ὑπουράνιοι Γαίᾳ πωτῶνται ἐν ἄλγεσι φονίοις Ὑπὸ ζευγλαῖς ἀφύκτοις κακῶν. Εὐσεβέων δ' ἐπουράνιοι νάοισαι Μολπαῖς μάκαρα μέγαν ἀείδοντ' ἐν ὕμνοις (No 97, Boeckh), where πωτῶνται answers to the κυλινδ of the text

257. Αὕτη σοι, ὦ φίλε Ἔρως] Socr had offended the majesty of Eros in his former discourse, by confounding him with a baser power The speech just concluded is to be understood as a palinode or recantation of the first See above, pp 212, 213 He adds an apology for the poetic diction, to which, he says, he was fain to resort 'on account of Phaedrus' In a spirit of banter he repeats the words of Phaedrus, 234 C, τί σοι φαίνεται, ὦ Σώκρατες, ὁ λόγος (ὁ τοῦ Λυσίου). οὐχ ὑπερφυῶς τά τε ἄλλα καὶ τοῖς ὀνόμασιν εἰρῆσθαι. Whether by the words διὰ Φαῖδρον we are to understand that the poetic grandiloquence referred to was adopted in accommodation to the youthful taste of his hearer, or whether [illegible] Socr an affected disclaimer of poetic genius, like that in p 238 C, is a question on which the comm are not agreed. To the former view it is enough to reply, that the diction and spirit of the Socratic are in studied contrast to the prosaic trimness of the Lysiac discourse, with which Phaedrus had professed himself enraptured

B ἀπηνές] 'harsh and repulsive' Legg 950 B, ἄγριον καὶ ἀπηνὲς φαίνοιτ' ἂν τοῖς ἄλλοις ἀνθρώποις, sc ἡ ξενηλασία. Hermeias appears to have read ἀπηχές, 'grating,' 'discordant,' and so two MSS. in Bekk But there seems to be no classical authority for this word

Λυσίαν τὸν τοῦ λόγου πατέρα, κ τ λ] In this prayer for the conversion of Lysias those who adopt the tradition of the early composition of this dialogue seem to discover a strong confirmation of their opinion How, it is urged, could Plato have hoped for so blessed a result, if, at the time he wrote, Lysias had been already a hoary offender? But this argument involves a confusion between the pretended date of the colloquy and the date of the actual composition of the dialogue A prayer in behalf of the middle-aged orator may fairly be interpreted as a satire on the unreclaimed offender of advanced years, between whom and Plato it is likely that no love was lost Polemarchus, the brother of Lysias, was probably a member of the Socratic clique He bears a part in the discussion with Socr. concerning Justice, in the First Book of the Republic (331 D), and it was in his house that the discussion took place (ib 328 B). Another

φίαν δέ, ὥσπερ ἀδελφὸς αὐτοῦ Πολέμαρχος τέτραπται, τρέψον, ἵνα καὶ ὁ ἐραστὴς ὅδε αὐτοῦ μηκέτι ἐπαμφοτερίζῃ καθάπερ νῦν, ἀλλ' ἁπλῶς πρὸς Ἔρωτα μετὰ φιλοσόφων λόγων τὸν βίον ποιῆται.

ΦΑΙ. Συνεύχομαί σοι, ὦ Σώκρατες, εἴπερ ἄμεινον
C ταῦθ' ἡμῖν εἶναι, ταῦτα γίγνεσθαι. τὸν λόγον δέ σου πάλαι θαυμάσας ἔχω, ὅσῳ καλλίω τοῦ προτέρου ἀπειργάσω. ὥστε ὀκνῶ μή μοι ὁ Λυσίας ταπεινὸς φανῇ, ἐὰν ἄρα καὶ ἐθελήσῃ πρὸς αὐτὸν ἄλλον ἀντιπαρατεῖναι. καὶ γάρ τις αὐτόν, ὦ θαυμάσιε, ἔναγχος τῶν πολιτικῶν τοῦτ' αὐτὸ λοιδορῶν ὠνείδιζε, καὶ διὰ πάσης τῆς λοιδορίας ἐκάλει λογογράφον. τάχ' οὖν ἂν ὑπὸ φιλοτιμίας ἐπίσχοι ἡμῖν ἂν τοῦ γράφειν.

ΣΩ. Γελοῖόν γ', ὦ νεανία, τὸ δόγμα λέγεις, καὶ
D τοῦ ἑταίρου συχνὸν διαμαρτάνεις, εἰ αὐτὸν οὕτως ἡγεῖ τινὰ ψοφοδεᾶ. ἴσως δὲ καὶ τὸν λοιδορούμενον αὐτῷ οἴει νομίζοντα λέγειν ἃ ἔλεγεν.

brother, Euthydemus, is named ibid., who is not to be confounded with Euthydemus the Sophist, or with Euthydemus the son of Diocles, though he too is named among the Σωκράτους ἐρασταί, Symp. 222 B. Polemarchus ὁ φιλόσοφος is mentioned by Plutarch as having fallen a victim to the cruelty of the Thirty, with "Niceratus, the son of Nicias, and Theramenes the Strategus" (De Esu Carn. ii. c. 4). From his appearance in such company we may conclude that Polemarchus was a person of some consideration, at any rate in literary circles.

ἐραστής] Simply 'admirer,' i. e. τῆς τοῦ Λυσίου σοφίας. So Gorgias is said ἐραστὰς ἐπὶ σοφίᾳ εἰληφέναι Ἀλευαδῶν τοὺς πρώτους (Meno, init.).

μηκέτι ἐπαμφοτερίζῃ] 'may no longer waver,' or 'halt between two courses.'

Συνεύχομαί σοι] Phaedr. joins his prayers to those of Socr., professing to have found his second discourse much more beautiful than the former. He even fears that Lysias' may appear tame and prosaic in comparison,—if indeed he should consent to enter the lists against Socr., which Phaedr. doubts, for he has lately heard Lysias taunted by a man in political life for addicting himself to a pursuit so mean as that of writing speeches. So that perhaps vanity may keep him from writing any more. Socr. answers that he is amused by his young friend's simplicity. Lysias is not so easily frightened as he supposes. Perhaps, he adds, you think that his assailant really meant all he said. To which Phaedr. rejoins, that the speaker was to all appearance thoroughly in earnest; in fact it was quite common for men high in political life to shrink from writing speeches, lest, if any of their literary productions survived them, they should become known to posterity by the dreaded name of Sophists or littérateurs. All very fine, replies Socr., but there is a certain proverb, γλυκὺς ἀγκών, which Phaedr. is not aware of, and which imports that people frequently affect to like what they hate, and to hate what they secretly hanker after. The great men in question are in reality more fond of authorship than their inferiors, otherwise they would not be so extravagantly fond of seeing their own names and those of their admirers prefixed to documents of state.

ΦΑΙ. Ἐφαίνετο γάρ, ὦ Σώκρατες. καὶ σύνοισθά που καὶ αὐτὸς ὅτι οἱ μέγιστον δυνάμενοί τε καὶ σεμνότατοι ἐν ταῖς πόλεσιν αἰσχύνονται λόγους τε γράφειν καὶ καταλείπειν συγγράμματα ἑαυτῶν, δόξαν φοβούμενοι τοῦ ἔπειτα χρόνου, μὴ σοφισταὶ καλῶνται.

ΣΩ. Γλυκὺς ἀγκών, ὦ Φαῖδρε, λέληθέ σε ὅτι ἀπὸ τοῦ μακροῦ ἀγκῶνος τοῦ κατὰ Νεῖλον ἐκλήθη· καὶ πρὸς E
τῷ ἀγκῶνι λανθάνει σε ὅτι οἱ μέγιστον φρονοῦντες τῶν πολιτικῶν μάλιστα ἐρῶσι λογογραφίας τε καὶ καταλείψεως συγγραμμάτων, οἵ γε καὶ ἐπειδάν τινα γράφωσι λόγον,

D. Γλυκὺς ἀγκών] This proverb is said by Meineke (Com Gr ii 677) to be "unum omnium ad explicandum difficillimum" The text of Plato seems to offer an explanation but it is only one amongst many The nearest English equivalent appears to be the proverbial 'Sour grapes' In Libanius, Epist xlvi, it has evidently this meaning An old man is there made to say, that ὃ τοῖς ἄλλοις εἰς τέρψιν ἔρχεται, τοῦτ' ἐμοὶ γλυκὺς ἀγκὼν διὰ τὴν ἀσθένειαν, that youthful pleasures are to him but 'sour grapes,' by reason of his enfeebled powers Accordingly, the Paroemiographers tell us that the phrase is used ἐπὶ τῶν κατειρωνευομένων, or as the gloss in Hesych. runs, ἐπὶ τῶν αἰσχρόν τι δοκιμαζόντων, ἐπαινούντων δὲ ὡς καλόν, ἢ τοῦ ἐναντίου, σπουδαῖον μὲν ἡγουμένων, χλευαζόντων δὲ ὡς φαῦλον So, too, the Scholl in loc including Hermeias The words have evidently this sense in Plato, and the interpretation he offers is found also in Hesych and the Paroemiographers The μακρός, or as some would read, πικρὸς ἀγκὼν in question appears to have been the same as that bend or 'elbow' of the Nile below Memphis, which Herodotus tells us the Persians dammed up, after cutting a new and shorter channel (ii 99) Comp Paroem Gr ii 66, Leutsch, τόπος δέ ἐστιν ἐν τῇ Μεμφίδι Ἀγκὼν [leg γλυκὺς Ἀγκών] προσαγορευόμενος ὑπὸ τῶν πλεόντων κατ' ἀντίφρασιν ἴσως, διὰ τὸ δυσχερές A very different explanation is given in Athenaeus (xii 516) upon the authority of Clearchus, who asserts that the name γλυκὺς ἀγκὼν or γυναικῶν ἀγκών (or ἀγών ?) was bestowed by the Lydians in mockery upon a certain secluded region of their [illegible] sale shame and wickedness had been perpetrated by the contrivance of their queen Omphale. The same Lydian story is repeated by Eustathius on the Iliad, p 1082, and by Hesych and others in connexion with γλυκὺς ἀγκών. Eustath. adds that there was a place in Samos dedicated in like manner by Polycrates to purposes of shameful licentiousness Hence, according to Plutarch, the similar ὑποκόρισμα or euphemism· Σαμίων ἄνθη or Σαμιακὴ λαύρα (Plut Prov. lxi). Comp Lob Aglaoph p. 1022 A third explanation of the proverb, widely different from the foregoing, is given in Suidas, v. γλυκὺς ἀγκών, from which we might infer that the phrase had a serious as well as an ironical meaning The passage, however, adduced in Suid from the Phaon of Plato Comicus, is too fragmentary to enable us to judge of the correctness of the interpretation put upon it Heind positively denies that the explanation in the text can have come from Plato's pen He would therefore strike out the words ὅτι ἀπὸ τοῦ ... ἐκλήθη, which, he says, "Grammatici esse possunt, Platonis esse non possunt" This appears to me too bold an expedient, though it does seem improbable that the ἀγκὼν in question should have become so familiar to the Greek sailors before the conquest of Egypt by Cambyses, as to have given occasion to a phrase of such general application as γλυκὺς ἀγκὼν seems to have been Neither is it quite in Plato's manner to interpret his own pleasantries The true origin of the phrase, like those of many other proverbial expressions, we must be content to leave *in ambiguo*.

Erbse P.

οὕτως ἀγαπῶσι τοὺς ἐπαινέτας, ὥστε προσπαραγράφουσι πρώτους οἳ ἂν ἑκασταχοῦ ἐπαινῶσιν αὐτούς

ΦΑΙ. Πῶς λέγεις τοῦτο ; οὐ γὰρ μανθάνω.

258 ΣΩ. Οὐ μανθάνεις ὅτι | ἐν ἀρχῇ ἀνδρὸς πολιτικοῦ συγγράμματι πρῶτος ὁ ἐπαινέτης γέγραπται ;

ΦΑΙ. Πῶς.

ΣΩ. Ἔδοξέ πού φησι τῇ βουλῇ ἢ τῷ δήμῳ ἢ ἀμφοτέροις. καὶ ὃς εἶπε, τὸν αὐτὸν δὴ λέγων μάλα σεμνῶς καὶ ἐγκωμιάζων ὁ συγγραφεύς· ἔπειτα λέγει δὴ μετὰ τοῦτο, ἐπιδεικνύμενος τοῖς ἐπαινέταις τὴν ἑαυτοῦ σοφίαν,
B ἐνίοτε πάνυ μακρὸν ποιησάμενος σύγγραμμα. ἢ σοι ἄλλο τι φαίνεται τὸ τοιοῦτον ἢ λόγος συγγεγραμμένος ;

ΦΑΙ. Οὐκ ἔμοιγε.

ΣΩ. Οὐκοῦν ἐὰν μὲν οὗτος ἐμμένῃ, γεγηθὼς ἀπέρ-

392, 52.4; PPetr 3 p 267 (I III)

E προσπαραγράφουσι] Demosth. c. Boeot 997, προσπαραγράψουσι νὴ Δία τὸν ἐκ Πλαγγόνος, ἐὰν σὲ ἐγγράφωσιν (οἱ ἄρχοντες sc) The word is used specially in the case of public documents, as its cognate παράγραμμα, ibid 'They add a clause containing the names of their approvers,' i e not content with the παράγραμμα, Δημοσθένης or ὁ δεῖνα εἶπε, they further name the senate and people, one or both, πρώτους, at the very commencement of the bill

Οὐ μανθάνεις ὅτι ἐν ἀρχῇ, κ τ λ] 'are you not aware that in any work penned by a statesman the approver is first named in the opening clause?' σύγγραμμα means usually a work written for publication but it has also a political application See Gorg 451 B Socr here takes advantage of the ambiguity

258 Ἔδοξέ πού φησι] 'he' (the συγγραφεὺς presently mentioned) 'says, methinks, Resolved by the senate,' &c ποὺ is transposed from its proper place as an enclitic after φησί, as in Phileb 34 E, διψῇ που λέγομεν ἑκάστοτέ τι, 'we say, do we not so and so is thirsty' Other instances are given by Ast and Stallb. of the transposition of enclitic particles and pronouns

καὶ ὃς εἶπε—συγγραφεύς] '"And he moved"—our author with all solemnity mentioning and lauding his worthy self' With καὶ ὃς comp Protag 312 A, καὶ ὃς εἶπεν ἐρυθριάσας Symp 201 E, καὶ ἥ, Οὐκ εὐφημήσεις, ἔφη So in the formula ἦ δ' ὅς Yet I rather incline to Winckelmann's conj ὃς καὶ ὅς, 'so and so' Herod iv 68, ὡς τὰς βασιληΐας ἱστίας ἐπιόρκηκεν ὃς καὶ ὅς

τὸν αὐτόν] The article is not unfrequently prefixed to the personal pronouns, as in Sophist 239 A, τὸν μὲν τοίνυν ἔμεγε τί τις ἂν λέγοι. Theaet 166 A, γέλωτα δὴ τὸν ἐμὲ . ἀπέδειξεν Herm. τὸν ἑαυτὸν δή τὸ τὸν προέθηκε διὰ τὸ μέγα φρονεῖν αὐτούς. The irony is here increased by the added δή, scilicet Probably Stallb is right in supposing that ὁ συγγραφεὺς is a kind of iteration of the unexpressed subject of φησί,—'he, our author, I mean' He punctuates after ἐγκωμιάζων to indicate this So is to be explained Theocr xiv 56 οὔτε κάκιστος, Οὔτε πρᾶτος ἴσως ὁμαλὸς δέ τις ὁ στρατιώτας

B ἐὰν μὲν οὗτος ἐμμένῃ] Perhaps we may supply τῇ σανίδι See Aeschines c. Ctes p 59, § 39 Bekk, ἀναγεγραφότας ἐν σανίσιν, κ τ λ It was the business of the thesmothetae to revise or codify the mass of Athenian legislation καθ' ἕκαστον ἐνιαυτόν, striking out (ἐξαλείφοντας, ἀναιροῦντας) contradictory or unconstitutional enactments Comp Aesch l l with Andocides de Myst p. 11 'If the speech or motion in question stand, then the poet leaves the theatre in high glee' "Concita est more antiquorum non raro oratio in hanc sententiam γεγηθὼς ἀπέρχεται ὁ συγ-

χεται ἐκ τοῦ θεάτρου ὁ ποιητής· ἐὰν δὲ ἐξαλειφθῇ καὶ ἄμοιρος γένηται λογογραφίας τε καὶ τοῦ ἄξιος εἶναι συγγράφειν, πενθεῖ αὐτός τε καὶ οἱ ἑταῖροι.

ΦΑΙ. Καὶ μάλα.

ΣΩ. Δῆλόν γε ὅτι οὐχ ὡς ὑπερφρονοῦντες τοῦ ἐπιτηδεύματος, ἀλλ' ὡς τεθαυμακότες.

ΦΑΙ. Πάνυ μὲν οὖν.

ΣΩ. Τί δέ; ὅταν ἱκανὸς γένηται ῥήτωρ ἢ βασιλεύς,
ὥστε λαβὼν τὴν Λυκούργου ἢ Σόλωνος ἢ Δαρείου δύναμιν ἀθάνατος γενέσθαι λογογράφος ἐν πόλει, ἆρ' οὐκ C
ἰσόθεον ἡγεῖται αὐτός τε αὑτὸν ἔτι ζῶν, καὶ οἱ ἔπειτα
γιγνόμενοι ταὐτὰ ταῦτα περὶ αὐτοῦ νομίζουσι, θεώμενοι
αὐτοῦ τὰ συγγράμματα;

ΦΑΙ. Καὶ μάλα.

ΣΩ. Οἴει τινὰ οὖν τῶν τοιούτων, ὅστις καὶ ὁπωστιοῦν δύσνους Λυσίᾳ, ὀνειδίζειν αὐτὸ τοῦτο ὅτι συγγράφει;

ΦΑΙ. Οὔκουν εἰκός γε ἐξ ὧν σὺ λέγεις· καὶ γὰρ ἂν τῇ ἑαυτοῦ ἐπιθυμίᾳ, ὡς ἔοικεν, ὀνειδίζοι.

γραφεὺς ἐκ τῆς ἐκκλησίας, ὥσπερ ποιητὴς ἐκ τοῦ θεάτρου" (Heind.), unless we suppose γεγηθὼς ἀπέρχεται ὁ ποιητὴς to have been a proverbial phrase to denote joy at success.

ἐξαλειφθῇ] I have restored the reading of the great majority of MSS in place of ἐξαλιφῇ, which Bekk. and his successors have adopted on the authority of the Bodl. The 2 aor. occurs nowhere else, and is at best a doubtful form. 'If his discourse be rubbed out (his motion lost, or afterwards rescinded) and he thereby be excluded from the profession of a λογογράφος and the coveted dignity of an author, he puts on mourning, and all his friends with him.'

ἢ Δαρείου] Darius Hystaspes on his accession recast the Persian empire. He is therefore compared as a revolutionary legislator to Solon and Lycurgus. Plat. Legg. 695 C, Δαρεῖος γὰρ βασιλέως οὐκ ἦν υἱὸς παιδείᾳ τε οὐ διατρυφώσῃ τεθραμμένος, ἐλθὼν δ' εἰς τὴν ἀρχὴν καὶ λαβὼν αὐτὴν ἕβδομος διείλετο ἑπτὰ μέρη τεμόμενος, ὧν καὶ νῦν ἔτι σμικρὰ ὀνείρατα λέλειπται, καὶ νόμους ἠξίου θέμενος οἰκεῖν ἰσότητά [illegible] πορίζων καὶ κοινωνίαν πᾶσι Πέρσαις, χρήμασι καὶ δωρεαῖς τὸν Περσῶν δῆμον προσαγόμενος. In Epist. vii. 332 Darius is praised for the wisdom of his legislation ἔδειξε παράδειγμα οἷον χρὴ τὸν νομοθέτην καὶ βασιλέα τὸν ἀγαθὸν γίγνεσθαι· νόμους γὰρ διασκευάσας, ἔτι καὶ νῦν διασέσωκε τὴν Περσῶν ἀρχήν. He was therefore ἀθάνατος λογογράφος ἐν πόλει, as the politician spoken of in the text would fain become.

C. Οἴει τινὰ οὖν—λόγους] The object of Plato in the foregoing argument has been to vindicate the dignity of literary pursuits against the sneers of professed politicians. He has shown, or seemed to show, that their disdain was hollow and affected, for that they too were in love with literary celebrity of a certain kind. In reproaching Lysias they were virtually censuring themselves, and holding up to contempt their own favourite pursuit. Authorship, per se, neither is nor is seriously believed by any one to be disgraceful. It is not to writing, but only to bad writing that disgrace really attaches.

D ΣΩ. Τοῦτο μὲν ἄρα παντὶ δῆλον, ὅτι οὐκ αἰσχρὸν αὐτό γε τὸ γράφειν λόγους.

ΦΑΙ. Τί γάρ;

ΣΩ. Ἀλλ' ἐκεῖνο οἶμαι αἰσχρὸν ἤδη, τὸ μὴ καλῶς λέγειν τε καὶ γράφειν ἀλλ' αἰσχρῶς τε καὶ κακῶς.

ΦΑΙ. Δῆλον δή.

ΣΩ. Τίς οὖν ὁ τρόπος τοῦ καλῶς τε καὶ μὴ γράφειν; δεόμεθά τι, ὦ Φαῖδρε, Λυσίαν τε περὶ τούτων ἐξετάσαι καὶ ἄλλον ὅστις πώποτέ τι γέγραφεν ἢ γράψει, εἴτε πολιτικὸν σύγγραμμα εἴτε ἰδιωτικόν, ἐν μέτρῳ [ὡς ποιητής], ἢ ἄνευ μέτρου [ὡς ἰδιώτης];

D. *Τίς οὖν ὁ τρόπος τοῦ καλῶς τε καὶ μὴ γράφειν*] To this question the remainder of the dialogue supplies the answer. But before he proceeds to discuss the principles of rhetoric, Socr. sounds Phaedr., to ascertain whether he is inclined to enter on an inquiry which may occupy a considerable time and involve some effort. Phaedrus is indignant at the doubt implied in the question, and Socr. invents a myth by way of encouraging his philosophic ardour.

ἐν μέτρῳ [ὡς ποιητής], ἢ ἄνευ μέτρου [ὡς ἰδιώτης]] "*ἰδιώτης* oppositum *ποιητῇ* pervulgati est usus. De Legg. p. 800 A, *ταῦτ' ἐστὶν ἅπαντα ἀνδρῶν σοφῶν . . ἰδιωτῶν τε καὶ ποιητῶν*" (Heind.) Add Symp. 178 D, *ὑπ' οὐδενὸς οὔτε ἰδιώτου οὔτε ποιητοῦ*. *ἰδιώτης* is the general antitheton to *ὁ τέχνην ἔχων*—whatever the *τέχνη* may be. Soph. 221 C, *καὶ μὴν ἐκεῖνό γ' ἦν τὸ ζήτημα πρῶτον, πότερον ἰδιώτην ἤ τινα τέχνην ἔχοντα θετέον εἶναι τὸν ἀσπαλιευτήν*. The English word which comes nearest in extent of application is 'layman.' See an apposite instance in Carew's Poems:

"Thus while you deal your body 'mongst
  your friends,
 And fill their circling arms my glad
  soul sends
 This her embrace: thus we of Delphi
  greet—
 As *laymen* clasp their hands, so we
  our feet."

Upon Master W. Montague
his return from travel.

So also Sir P. Sidney, Sonnet 74:

"The Muses scorn with vulgar brains
  to dwell—
 Poor *layman* I, for sacred rites unfit."

The distinction between metrical and unmetrical compositions may seem at first sight out of place here. But in 277 E, a passage written with direct reference to the present, *λόγοι ἐν μέτρῳ* and *λόγοι ἄνευ μέτρου* are distinguished in the same manner. Comp. also 278 C, *Λυσίᾳ τε καὶ εἴ τις ἄλλος συντίθησι λόγους, καὶ Ὁμήρῳ καὶ εἴ τις ἄλλος αὖ ποίησιν ψιλὴν ἢ ἐν ᾠδῇ συντέθεικε, τρίτον δὲ Σόλωνι καὶ ὅστις ἐν πολιτικοῖς λόγοις, νόμους ὀνομάζων, συγγράμματα ἔγραψεν*. The remarkable feature in the passage before us is the use of *ἰδιωτικὸν* in one sense followed immediately by *ἰδιώτης* in another. Certainly the words *ὡς ποιητής, ὡς ἰδιώτης* are not indispensable to the sense, and it is strange to find Plato subdividing *ἰδιωτικοὶ λόγοι* into *ἰδιωτικοὶ* and *ποιητικοί*. On referring to the Commentary of Hermeias, we find no traces of *ὡς ποιητής, ὡς ἰδιώτης*, either in the Lemmata or their interpretation, though he is careful to paraphrase the remainder of the sentence: *ὅρα πῶς καθολικὸν ποιεῖται λόγον· οὐ γὰρ μόνον περὶ τοῦ Λυσίου εἶπεν, ἀλλ' εἴτε πολιτικὸν εἴτε ἰδιωτικόν, εἴτε μετὰ μέτρου εἴτε ἄνευ μετρου. οὕτω δῆλόν ἐστιν, ὅτι περὶ τῶν καθόλου λόγων καὶ συγγραφῶν ὁ παρὼν ἔστι λόγος. πολιτικὸν λέγει τὸν νομοθετικὸν ἢ συμβουλευτικόν, ἰδιωτικὸν δὲ τὸν δικαστικὸν ἢ δικανικόν* (Herm. Comm. p. 177, ed. Ast). For these reasons I have bracketed the words in question as doubtful, though

777 ΦΑΙ. Ἐρωτᾷς εἰ δεόμεθα; τίνος μὲν οὖν ἕνεκα κἂν E
τις ὡς εἰπεῖν ζῴη, ἀλλ' ἢ τῶν τοιούτων ἡδονῶν ἕνεκα; οὐ γάρ που ἐκείνων γε ὧν προλυπηθῆναι δεῖ ἢ μηδὲ ἡσθῆναι, ὃ δὴ ὀλίγου πᾶσαι αἱ περὶ τὸ σῶμα ἡδοναὶ ἔχουσι· διὸ καὶ δικαίως ἀνδραποδώδεις κέκληνται.

ΣΩ. Σχολὴ μὲν δή, ὡς ἔοικε. καὶ ἅμα μοι δοκοῦσιν ὡς ἐν τῷ πνίγει ὑπὲρ κεφαλῆς ἡμῶν οἱ τέττιγες ᾄδοντες

the doubt does not appear to have occurred to any editor before Hirsch and Badh., the latter of whom extends the query to the entire clause from *ἐν* to *ἰδιώτης*. This scepticism however goes too far, as the parallel passages abundantly prove.

E *οὐ γάρ που—προλυπηθῆναι δεῖ*] This distinction between pure and mixed pleasures is developed in the Philebus with great force and clearness (Phileb p. 31 to p. 55). The results of this long investigation seem to be taken for granted in the present passage. Phaedr. assumes that intellectual pleasures are *nearly* the only pleasures which are unmixed with pain—*almost* (*ὀλίγου*) all corporeal pleasures imply a foregoing uneasiness. Phaedr. does not specify the excepted cases, which are however carefully enumerated in the Philebus (50 E to 52 B). *κατὰ φύσιν τοίνυν μετὰ τὰς μιχθείσας ἡδονὰς ὑπὸ δή τινος ἀνάγκης ἐπὶ τὰς ἀμίκτους πορευοίμεθ' ἂν ἐν τῷ μέρει . . Ἀληθεῖς δ' αὖ τίνας, ὦ Σώκρατες, ὑπολαμβάνων ὀρθῶς τις διανοοῖτ' ἄν, Τὰς περί τε τὰ καλὰ λεγόμενα χρώματα καὶ περὶ τὰ σχήματα, καὶ τῶν ὀσμῶν τὰς πλείστας καὶ τὰς τῶν φθόγγων, καὶ ὅσα, τὰς ἐνδείας ἀναισθήτους ἔχοντα καὶ ἀλύπους, τὰς πληρώσεις αἰσθητὰς καὶ ἡδείας καθαρὰς λυπῶν παραδίδωσιν . . Ἔτι δὴ τοίνυν τούτοις προσθῶμεν τὰς περὶ τὰ μαθήματα ἡδονάς, εἰ ἄρα δοκοῦσιν ἡμῖν αὗται πείνας μὲν μὴ ἔχειν τοῦ μανθάνειν, μηδὲ διὰ μαθημάτων πείνην ἀλγηδόνας ἐξ ἀρχῆς γενομένας*. The dramatic propriety of putting so refined a sentiment in the mouth of Phaedr. has been questioned, very hypercritically, as I think, by Heind. "Ex meo quidem sensu nihil hic inferri poterit languidius et jejunius, nihil Phaedri persona dialogique tenore alienius, nihil denique magis *ἀπροσδιόνυσον*." He is obliged, however, as he well might be, to admit that he is unable to detect "the faintest vestige of fraud" in the passage. It is indeed clear from the sequel of the dialogue that Phaedr. was by no means such a fool as Heind. supposes; his very vanity would impel him to parade the recent acquisition of a philosophical refinement known to few: and so far from conceding that Plato was half-asleep ("dormitasse") when he wrote this passage, I conceive that there is no part of the dialogue written with more entire propriety.

διὸ καὶ δικ. ἀνδραποδώδεις κέκληνται] The pleasures 'justly called servile' are those of which even *ἀνδράποδα* are capable, whereas those of the intellect are proper to *τοῖς ἐναντίως ἢ ὡς ἀνδραπόδοις τραφεῖσιν*, sc. *τοῖς ἐλευθέροις* (Theaet. 175 D). Comp. Phileb. 52 B, *ταύτας τοίνυν τὰς τῶν μαθημάτων ἡδονὰς ἀμίκτους τε εἶναι λύπαις ῥητέον, καὶ οὐδαμῶς τῶν πολλῶν ἀνθρώπων ἀλλὰ τῶν σφόδρα ὀλίγων*. This oligarchic spirit reigns through the entire ethical philosophy of Plato, and in a less degree of Aristotle also. Heind. aptly compares Eth. N. iii. 10. 21, *περὶ τὰς τοιαύτας ἡδονὰς ἡ σωφροσύνη καὶ ἡ ἀκολασία ἐστίν, ὧν καὶ τὰ λοιπὰ ζῷα κοινωνεῖ, ὅθεν ἀνδραποδώδεις καὶ θηριώδεις φαίνονται*. Also Plat. Epist. vii. 335 A, *τὴν ἀνδραποδώδη καὶ ἀχάριστον ἀφροδίσιον λεγομένην οὐκ ὀρθῶς ἡδονήν*.

Σχολὴ μὲν δὴ—καὶ ἅμα μοι δοκοῦσιν, κ.τ.λ.] The little episode which follows reminds the reader of the scenery of the dialogue, while it forms a natural transition from the mythic raptures of the second Socratic discourse to the lighter but still poetical style of the sequel. It also furnishes a dramatic motive to a discussion sustained under unfavourable circumstances, by persons one of whom at least may be supposed not to have been superior to the sleep-persuading influences of the place and time.

259 | καὶ ἀλλήλοις διαλεγόμενοι καθορᾶν εἰ οὖν ἴδοιεν καὶ νῷ καθάπερ τοὺς πολλοὺς ἐν μεσημβρίᾳ μὴ διαλεγομένους ἀλλὰ νυστάζοντας καὶ κηλουμένους ὑφ' αὑτῶν δι' ἀργίαν τῆς διανοίας, δικαίως ἂν καταγελῷεν, ἡγούμενοι ἀνδράποδ' ἄττα σφίσιν ἐλθόντα εἰς τὸ καταγώγιον ὥσπερ προβάτια μεσημβριάζοντα περὶ τὴν κρήνην εὕδειν· ἐὰν δὲ ὁρῶσι διαλεγομένους καὶ παραπλέοντάς σφας ὥσπερ Σειρῆνας ἀκηλήτους, ὃ γέρας παρὰ θεῶν ἔχουσιν ἀνθρώποις
B διδόναι, τάχ' ἂν δοῖεν ἀγασθέντες.

ΦΑΙ. Ἔχουσι δὲ δὴ τί τοῦτο; ἀνήκοος γάρ, ὡς ἔοικε, τυγχάνω ὤν.

ΣΩ. Οὐ μὲν δὴ πρέπει γε φιλόμουσον ἄνδρα τῶν τοιούτων ἀνήκοον εἶναι. λέγεται δ' ὥς ποτ' ἦσαν οὗτοι ἄνθρωποι τῶν πρὶν Μούσας γεγονέναι. γενομένων δὲ Μουσῶν καὶ φανείσης ᾠδῆς, οὕτως ἄρα τινὲς τῶν τότε ἐξεπλάγησαν ὑφ' ἡδονῆς, ὥστε ᾄδοντες ἠμέλησαν σίτων
C τε καὶ ποτῶν, καὶ ἔλαθον τελευτήσαντες αὑτούς. ἐξ ὧν τὸ τεττίγων γένος μετ' ἐκεῖνο φύεται, γέρας τοῦτο παρὰ Μουσῶν λαβόν, μηδὲν τροφῆς δεῖσθαι γενόμενον, ἀλλ' ἄσιτόν τε καὶ ἄποτον εὐθὺς ᾄδειν, ἕως ἂν τελευτήσῃ, καὶ μετὰ ταῦτα ἐλθὸν παρὰ Μούσας ἀπαγγέλλειν τίς τίνα αὐτῶν τιμᾷ τῶν ἐνθάδε. Τερψιχόρᾳ μὲν οὖν τοὺς ἐν τοῖς χοροῖς τετιμηκότας αὐτὴν ἀπαγγέλλοντες ποιοῦσι

259 καθορᾶν] Intrans, 'to look down' Plato has here adopted a Homeric usage, of which I can find no other example in an Attic writer Hom Il xi 336, Ἔνθα σφι κατὰ ἶσα μάχην ἐτάνυσσε Κρονίων, Ἐξ Ἴδης καθορῶν This and similar passages from Homer are brought forward by Stallb as a triumphant reply to Badh's question, "Quis unquam verbum καθορᾶν sine casu usurpari vidit?" His triumph would have been more complete, had he been able to produce a parallel instance from a prose author of the Attic period He is right, however, in rejecting Badh's ingenious suggestion, δοκοῖσι νῷ (for δοκοῦσιν ὡς), which is forbidden by the καὶ νῷ of the sentence following ὡς ἐν τῷ πνίγει = ut solent 'sole sub ardenti' a habit which Stallb rather unnecessarily demonstrates by a long array of authorities extending from Aristophanes to Themistius This heavy artillery is levelled at Dr Badham, whom Stallb justly regards as an emissary of the archfiend of Leyden

εἰς τὸ καταγώγιον] Above, 230 B, καλή γε ἡ καταγωγή

B τῶν πρὶν Μούσας γεγονέναι] An abbreviated construction for the usual τῶν ὅσοι ἐγένοντο πρίν, κ τ λ Protag 320 D, τῶν ὅσα πυρὶ καὶ γῇ κεράννυται

C ἔλαθον τελευτήσαντες αὑτούς] 'died ere they felt themselves to be dying'

γενόμενον] Badh proposes a transposition. μηδὲν τροφῆς δεῖσθαι, ἀλλ' ἄσιτόν τε καὶ ἄποτον εὐθὺς γενόμενοι ᾄδειν

προσφιλεστέρους, τῇ δὲ Ἐρατοῖ τοὺς ἐν τοῖς ἐρωτικοῖς, D
καὶ ταῖς ἄλλαις οὕτω, κατὰ τὸ εἶδος ἑκάστης τιμῆς. τῇ δὲ πρεσβυτάτῃ Καλλιόπῃ καὶ τῇ μετ' αὐτὴν Οὐρανίᾳ τοὺς ἐν φιλοσοφίᾳ διάγοντάς τε καὶ τιμῶντας τὴν ἐκείνων μουσικὴν ἀγγέλλουσιν, αἳ δὴ μάλιστα τῶν Μουσῶν περί τε οὐρανὸν καὶ λόγους οὖσαι θείους τε καὶ ἀνθρωπίνους ἱᾶσι καλλίστην φωνήν. πολλῶν δὴ οὖν ἕνεκεν λεκτέον τι καὶ οὐ καθευδητέον ἐν τῇ μεσημβρίᾳ.

ΦΑΙ. Λεκτέον γὰρ οὖν.

ΣΩ. Οὐκοῦν, ὅπερ νῦν προὐθέμεθα, σκέψασθαι τὸν E
λόγον ὅπῃ καλῶς ἔχει λέγειν τε καὶ γράφειν καὶ ὅπῃ μή, σκεπτέον.

τῇ δὲ Ἐρατοῖ] Ovid, Ar. Amat. ii 15, Nunc mihi, siquando, puer et Cytherea, favete, Nunc Erato, nam tu nomen amoris habes

D κατὰ τὸ εἶδος ἑκάστης τιμῆς] τουτέστι, κατὰ τὰ ἰδιώματα ἑκάστης Θεοῦ. Herm.

Καλλιόπῃ] This is one of the Pythagorisms which Plato has scattered over the face of the present Dialogue δεῖ δὲ ἄλλης Μούσης ἀνδρικωτέρας, ἣν Ὅμηρος μὲν Καλλιόπην ὀνομάζων χαίρει, ὁ Πυθαγόρας δὲ φιλοσοφίαν (Max Tyr., Diss. vii 2 63, quoted by Ast). Hermeias has the gloss, Καλλιόπη δὲ ἐκλήθη παρὰ τὴν ὄπα, τοὺς ἐν λόγοις οὖν αὐτὴν τετιμηκότας ἀπαγγέλλουσι· τῇ δὲ Οὐρανίᾳ τοὺς ἀστρονομήσαντας

τὴν ἐκείνων μουσικήν] Phaed 61 A, ὡς φιλοσοφίας οὔσης τῆς μεγίστης μουσικῆς Comp Legg iii 689 D, ἡ καλλίστη καὶ μεγίστη τῶν ξυμφωνιῶν μεγίστη δικαιότατ' ἂν λέγοιτο μουσική, κ τ.λ.

ἱᾶσι καλλίστην φωνήν] καὶ λέγεται (ὅτι) ὁ Πυθαγόρας ᾔσθετο τῆς οὐρανίας φωνῆς καί τινες δὲ τα ὀνόματα τῶν χορδῶν ἐκ τῶν οὐρανίων σφαιρῶν ὠνόμασαν οἷον ὅτι Προσλαμβανομένη ἐστὶν ἡ τοῦ Κρόνου σφαῖρα, καὶ ἐπὶ τῶν ἄλλων ὁμοίως ἄλλας χορδὰς εἶπον (Herm) This, though not directly in point, is curious as being probably a genuine Pythagorism προσλαμβανομένη or -ος is explained as "nomen soni musici, respondens ei quem hodierni A appellant " Steph Thes vi 1959, Dind

οὖν ἕνεκεν] So the Bodl Bekk has unaccountably adopted the poetic οὕνεκεν (v [illegible] MSS In Attic prose, the only legitimate forms of this prep are ἕνεκα and ἕνεκεν. οὕνεκα is found in Aristoph

E Οὐκοῦν—σκεπτέον] I have retained the punctuation of Bekk and Stallb. Ast places a comma after σκέψασθαι But σκεπτέον may more naturally be taken with ὃ προὐθέμεθα, as if he had written, ποιητέον ὃ προὐθ τοῦτ' ἔστι, τὸ σκέψασθαι, κ τ λ So, in effect, Stallb The redundancy is in Plato's manner.

ὅπῃ καλῶς ἔχει] Socr. now enters in earnest upon the investigation of a true Rhetoric He begins by proposing the question, whether a really good speech does not presuppose on the part of the speaker an accurate knowledge of the subject he proposes to handle Phaedr replies to this with the well-known paradox of the rhetoricians, that a speaker has no need to know the actual right or wrong or the good or evil of the matter in hand, but only that which is likely to approve itself as right or wrong, good or evil, to his audience The final cause of speaking is persuasion, and this is produced not by truth but by seeming truth. Socr. receives this answer with mock respect, and then proceeds to examine how much of truth it contains Comp Gorg 454 E, ἡ ῥητορική, ὡς ἔοικε, πειθοῦς δημιουργός ἐστι πιστευτικῆς ἀλλ' οὐ διδασκαλικῆς περὶ τὸ δίκαιόν τε καὶ ἄδικον . . Ναί οὐδ' ἄρα διδασκαλικὸς ὁ ῥήτωρ ἐστὶ δικαστηρίων τε καὶ τῶν ἄλλων ὄχλων δικαίων τε περὶ καὶ ἀδίκων, ἀλλὰ πιστικὸς μόνον, κ τ.λ

ΦΑΙ. Δῆλον.

ΣΩ. Ἆρ' οὖν οὐχ ὑπάρχειν δεῖ τοῖς εὖ γε καὶ καλῶς ῥηθησομένοις τὴν τοῦ λέγοντος διάνοιαν εἰδυῖαν τἀληθὲς ὧν ἂν ἐρεῖν πέρι μέλλῃ;

ΦΑΙ. Οὑτωσὶ περὶ τούτου ἀκήκοα, ὦ φίλε Σώκρατες,
260 οὐκ εἶναι ἀνάγκην | τῷ μέλλοντι ῥήτορι ἔσεσθαι τὰ τῷ ὄντι δίκαια μανθάνειν, ἀλλὰ τὰ δόξαντα ἂν πλήθει οἵπερ δικάσουσιν, οὐδὲ τὰ ὄντως ἀγαθὰ ἢ καλά, ἀλλ' ὅσα δόξει· ἐκ γὰρ τούτων εἶναι τὸ πείθειν, ἀλλ' οὐκ ἐκ τῆς ἀληθείας.

ΣΩ Οὔτοι ἀπόβλητον ἔπος εἶναι δεῖ, ὦ Φαῖδρε, ὃ ἂν εἴπωσι σοφοί, ἀλλὰ σκοπεῖν μή τι λέγωσι. καὶ δὴ καὶ τὸ νῦν λεχθὲν οὐκ ἀφετέον.

ΦΑΙ. Ὀρθῶς λέγεις.

ΣΩ. Ὧδε δὴ σκοπῶμεν αὐτό.

ΦΑΙ. Πῶς;

B ΣΩ. Εἴ σε πείθοιμι ἐγὼ πολεμίους ἀμύνειν κτησάμενον ἵππον. ἄμφω δὲ ἵππον ἀγνοοῖμεν, τοσόνδε μέντοι τυγχάνοιμι εἰδὼς περὶ σοῦ, ὅτι Φαῖδρος ἵππον ἡγεῖται τὸ τῶν ἡμέρων ζῴων μέγιστα ἔχον ὦτα—

ΦΑΙ. Γελοῖόν γ' ἄν, ὦ Σώκρατες, εἴη.

ΣΩ. Οὔπω γε· ἀλλ' ὅτε δὴ σπουδῇ σε πείθοιμι, συντιθεὶς λόγον ἔπαινον κατὰ τοῦ ὄνου, ἵππον ἐπονομάζων καὶ λέγων ὡς παντὸς ἄξιον τὸ θρέμμα οἴκοι τε κεκτῆσθαι καὶ ἐπὶ στρατείας, ἀποπολεμεῖν τε χρήσιμον

260 Οὔτοι ἀπόβλητον] Il ii 361, οὔτοι ἀπόβλητον ἔπος ἔσσεται, ὅττι κεν εἴπω The ironical σοφοί probably includes all the τεχνογράφοι from Corax and Tisias downwards

μή τι λέγωσι] 'lest there should be truth in what they say,' or 'whether what they say may not be true' Protag 339 C, ἐφοβούμην μή τι λέγοι If the present λέγουσι had been used, it would have been correct to transl 'whether what they say is true, and this is rather what we should have expected here But see Soph 212 B, ἐπισκέψασθαι (ἀναγκαῖον) μή πῃ τεταραγμένοι μὲν ὦμεν περὶ ταῦτα, ῥᾳδίως δ' ἀλλήλοις ὁμολογῶμεν ὡς εὐκρινῶς ἔχοντες. Winckelm s conj. εἴ πή τι λέγουσιν is perfectly gratuitous.

B Εἴ σε πείθοιμι] Socr here puts a particular case corresponding to the general formula under review. The formula, being found to break down when applied to a simple case, must be surrendered as untenable

Οὔπω γε] The Bodl and others have οὔποτε, which has no meaning οὔπω γε = "not just yet," implying that Phaedr. is premature in saying that the case is absurd, the absurdity having yet to be developed.

ἀποπ τε χρήσιμον] 'good to fight from,' i e to ride into battle The next phrase, προσενεγκεῖν σκεύη, is interpreted "apportare utensilia" But query

καὶ † προσενεγκεῖν † δυνατὸν σκεύη καὶ ἄλλα πολλὰ ὠφέλιμον. C

ΦΑΙ. Παγγέλοιόν γ' ἂν ἤδη εἴη.

ΣΩ. Ἆρ' οὖν οὐ κρεῖττον γελοῖον καὶ φίλον ἢ δεινόν τε καὶ ἐχθρὸν [εἶναι] ;

ΦΑΙ. Φαίνεται

ΣΩ. Ὅταν οὖν ὁ ῥητορικὸς ἀγνοῶν ἀγαθὸν καὶ κακόν, λαβὼν πόλιν ὡσαύτως ἔχουσαν πείθῃ, μὴ περὶ ὄνου σκιᾶς ὡς ἵππου τὸν ἔπαινον ποιούμενος, ἀλλὰ περὶ κακοῦ ὡς ἀγαθοῦ, δόξας δὲ πλήθους μεμελετηκὼς πείσῃ κακὰ πράττειν ἀντ' ἀγαθῶν, ποῖόν τιν' ἂν οἴει μετὰ ταῦτα τὴν ῥητορικὴν καρπὸν ὧν ἔσπειρε θερίζειν ;

as to this use of *προσφέρειν* I conj *καὶ πρός γ' ἐνεγκεῖν δυνατὸν σκεύη* Soph 234 E, *φημί, καὶ πρός γε θαλάττης (ποιητήν) καὶ οὐρανοῦ καὶ θεῶν καὶ τῶν ἄλλων ἁπάντων* *προσφέρειν σκεύη* would naturally mean 'to apply instruments to a purpose,' a matter beyond the powers of ass or horse. *ἀχθοφορεῖν* is the gloss of Hermeias The illustration in the text was probably suggested by a current proverb, *ἀφ' ἵππων ἐπ' ὄνον ἐπὶ τῶν ἀπὸ σεμνῶν ἐπὶ τὰ ἄσεμνα ἡκόντων* Paroem Gr. ii p 320, Leutsch

C *Ἆρ' οὖν οὐ κρεῖττον γελοῖον καὶ φίλον, κ τ λ*] I have adopted this reading from a scholium of Hermeias, which has hitherto escaped the notice of the edd It runs thus, with a slight but necessary change in the punctuation of Ast *Ἆρ' οὖν διαιρετικὸν διπλοῦν προσήνεγκεν ἆρα, φησίν, οὐ κρεῖττον γελοῖον καὶ φίλον ἢ δεινὸν καὶ ἐχθρόν, αἱρετώτερον γάρ. τὸ γελοῖον καὶ φίλον τὸ ἐπὶ τοῦ ὄνου ὡς ἵππον τὸ δὲ δεινὸν καὶ ἐχθρὸν τὸ ἐπὶ τῶν δικαίων καὶ ἀγαθῶν ὡς ἀδίκων καὶ κακῶν* (Herm Comm p 182, Ast) If we return the *εἶναι*, which Herm does not notice, we obtain the sense, Is it not better to be ridiculous and a friend (as I am when I advise you in good truth [*σπουδῇ*], to ride an ass, &c) than to be clever and a foe (as he is who for purposes of his own persuades an audience that right is wrong)? *εἶναι* however is not necessary to the sense, and perhaps the Greek is more idiomatic without it but with this c [illegible] the reading of a passage which as given in the MSS, has been a stumbling-block to editors The great majority of codices give, *ἆρ' οὖν οὐ κρεῖττον γελοῖον ἢ δεινόν τε καὶ ἐχθρὸν εἶναι ἢ φίλον*, One Parisian cod omits *εἶναι ἢ φίλον*, and three, according to Bekk, omit *ἢ* only This last is the reading adopted by Heind and the Zur But it involves the harsh and here pointless oxymoron, *ἐχθρὸν φίλον*,—much harsher than the *κακὸς φίλος* quoted from Soph. Oed Tyr. 582

μὴ περὶ ὄνου σκιᾶς] The word *σκιᾶς* is added *augendae invidiae gratiâ*, *ὄνου σκιὰ* being a proverbial phrase denoting that which is beneath contempt A comedy of Archippus was known indifferently by the titles *Ὄνος* and *Ὄνου σκιά* See Meineke, Com Gr i 208, and comp Arist Vesp 191, *Περὶ τοῦ μαχεῖ νῷν δῆτα, Περὶ ὄνου σκιᾶς.* Yet Hirsch, following Heind, brackets *σκιᾶς*, most unnecessarily, as I think The argument is, How much worse to deceive in matters of the highest moment, than in mere trifles such as that in the case supposed, the mistake of one brute or its shadow for another.

δόξας—πλήθους μεμελετηκώς] 'having made a special study of popular notions and prejudices'

ποῖόν τιν' ἂν οἴει, κ τ λ] 'what manner of harvest, think you, will Rhetoric thereafter reap from the evil seed she sowed?' I have not scrupled to adopt Hirsch's *τιν' ἂν* for the vulg. *τινα* Nothing is more common than this throwing back of *ἂν* in sentences where [illegible]

ὄνου σκιά

App 4.21

D ΦΑΙ. Οὐ πάνυ γε ἐπιεικῆ.

ΣΩ. Ἆρ' οὖν, ὦ 'γαθέ, ἀγροικότερον τοῦ δέοντος λελοιδορήκαμεν τὴν τῶν λόγων τέχνην; ἡ δ' ἴσως ἂν εἴποι· Τί ποτ', ὦ θαυμάσιοι, ληρεῖτε; ἐγὼ γὰρ οὐδέν' ἀγνοοῦντα τἀληθὲς ἀναγκάζω μανθάνειν λέγειν, ἀλλ', εἴ τις ἐμὴ ξυμβουλή, κτησάμενος ἐκεῖνο, οὕτως ἐμὲ λαμβάνειν· τόδε δ' οὖν μέγα λέγω, ὡς ἄνευ ἐμοῦ τῷ τὰ ὄντα εἰδότι οὐδέν τι μᾶλλον ἔσται πείθειν τέχνῃ.

E ΦΑΙ. Οὐκοῦν δίκαια ἐρεῖ, λέγουσα ταῦτα;

ΣΩ. Φημί, ἐὰν οἵ γ' ἐπιόντες αὐτῇ λόγοι μαρτυρῶσιν εἶναι τέχνη. ὥσπερ γὰρ ἀκούειν δοκῶ τινῶν προσιόντων καὶ διαμαρτυρομένων λόγων ὅτι ψεύδεται καὶ οὐκ

οἴεσθαι, ἡγεῖσθαι, νομίζειν, &c are followed by an infinitive See by all means Cobet, Novv Lectt. p. 362. The copyists, not perceiving that the ἂν in such cases belongs to the infinitive, perpetually omit it in transcription Even Stallb, in his note, acknowledges the necessity of the particle to the sense For the sentiment comp. Aesch Pers. 821, "Ὕβρις γὰρ ἐξανθοῦσ' ἐκάρπωσε στάχυν Ἄτης, ὅθεν πάγκλαυτον ἐξαμᾷ θέρος Krische ingeniously suggests a direct reference to a dictum of Gorgias preserved Arist Rhet iii 3 4, οἷον Γοργίας "χλωρὰ καὶ ἔναιμα (al ἄναιμα) τὰ πράγματα σὺ δὲ ταῦτα αἰσχρῶς μὲν ἔσπειρας, κακῶς δὲ ἐθέρισας" ποιητικῶς γὰρ ἄγαν But the phrase was proverbial, as we might infer from Aesch l c Herm p 182 καὶ τοῦτο δὲ ἀπὸ παροιμίας εἴρηται, ὅτι Ὁ κακὰ σπείρων κακὰ θερίζει.

D Οὐ πάνυ γε ἐπιεικῆ] 'a most indifferent (harvest)' Not satisfied with the easy assent of Phaedr, Socr professes to be afraid that his attack on Rhetoric had been too coarse and sweeping He accordingly produces her in person to make her own apology *She* never used the language imputed to her professors, nor insisted on ignorance of truth as a qualification for successful orators What she does insist on is this that knowledge is not sufficient of itself to work persuasion, unless it be united to accomplishments which she and she alone can impart If her advice is to go for any thing (si quid valet meum consilium), the student will first furnish his mind with knowledge, and then proceed to acquire the art of using it successfully For ἐμὴ ξυμβουλή, the MSS. have ἐμῇ ξυμβουλῇ, after which Heind. inserts χρῆται. Plato would rather have written εἴ τις ἐμοὶ συμβούλῳ χ Hermeias supplies πείθεται, not however as part of the text For the vulg εἴ τις the Bodl has εἴ τι, 'if my advice is worth any thing' Many of the edd give λαμβάνει, for which we should expect λαμβανέτω Godf Herm reads λαμβάνειν, referring to Phaed 87. C, and Seidler ad Eur El. 533 If this stands, the infinitive will depend formally on ἀναγκάζω, really on a verb suppressed And this seems the best solution of the difficulty This portion of the dialogue may be intended to qualify the sweeping denunciations of Rhetoric contained in the Gorgias, to which dial. there is a more undisguised allusion in the immediate sequel Possibly Plato meant to answer the unfriendly criticisms of Isocrates or some other of his censors

E Φημί, ἐὰν οἵ γ' ἐπιόντες αὐτῇ λόγοι, κ τ λ] 'yes' if only the on-coming arguments bear her witness that she is really an Art' The 'arguments' or reasonings here personified, under the figure of a party of fresh witnesses in the cause, are doubtless those which triumphed over Gorgias and Polus Gorg. 463 B, οὐκ ἔστι τέχνη ἀλλ' ἐμπειρία τε καὶ τριβή 501 A, κομιδῇ ἀτέχνως ἔρχεται ἀλόγως τε παντάπασιν, ὡς ἔπος εἰπεῖν τριβὴ καὶ ἐμπειρία Comp int 270 B

ἔστι τέχνη ἀλλ' ἄτεχνος τριβή. τοῦ δὲ λέγειν, φησὶν ὁ Λάκων, ἔτυμος τέχνη ἄνευ τοῦ ἀληθείας ἧφθαι οὔτ' ἔστιν οὔτε μή ποθ' ὕστερον γένηται.

| ΦΑΙ. Τούτων δεῖ τῶν λόγων, ὦ Σώκρατες· ἀλλὰ 261
δεῦρο αὐτοὺς παράγων, ἐξέταζε τί καὶ πῶς λέγουσιν.

ΣΩ. Πάριτε δή, θρέμματα γενναῖα, καλλίπαιδά τε Φαῖδρον πείθετε, ὡς ἐὰν μὴ ἱκανῶς φιλοσοφήσῃ, οὐδὲ ἱκανός ποτε λέγειν ἔσται περὶ οὐδενός. ἀποκρινέσθω δὴ ὁ Φαῖδρος.

ΦΑΙ. Ἐρωτᾶτε.

τοῦ δὲ λέγειν, φησὶν ὁ Λάκων] See Rep. ix 575 E, *μητρίδα τε, Κρῆτές φασι, καὶ πατρίδα ἕξει τε καὶ θρέψει* Epist vii 345, *ἴττω Ζεύς, φησὶν ὁ Θηβαῖος*. These apophthegms are sometimes quoted in the original Doric, but sometimes, as in Aristotle, Rhet iii 18 6, they are paraphrased in good Attic. In the present passage the poetic *ἔτυμος* is the only remnant of the original dictum, whatever it may have been. The passage has been much criticized, as by Schleierm., Voegelein (in Praef. ed Baiter p xii), and by a writer in the Rhenish Mus xii. p. 404. Some have recommended the mutilation, others the entire excision of the sentence but the last-named writer's suggestion is more ingenious—*φησὶν ὁ λαχών*, i. e *ὁ ἀγορεύειν λαχών*, "the spokesman of the party" But why this *λῆξις* here? Stallb. is said by its author to have approved of this clever, but, I think, uncalled for alteration The passage quoted from the Rhetoric will be found sufficient to justify the present text The collector of Laconian apophthegms, whether Plutarch or some other, gives the sentiment in nearly the same words, but with a prefatory *νὴ τὼ σιώ* Plut. Mor p 233 B, *Μεγαλυνομένου τινὸς ἐπὶ τῇ ῥητορικῇ τέχνῃ, εἶπέ τις Λάκων, Ἀλλά, νὴ τὼ σιώ, τέχνη ἀνεὺ τοῦ ἀληθείας ἧφθαι οὔτε ἐστὶν οὔτε μήποτε γένηται* No one however regards this as an independent testimony The phrase *ἀληθείας ἧφθαι* betrays Plato's hand (Phaed 65 B, Theaet 186 D, *οὐσίας καὶ ἀληθείας ἅψασθαι* and elsewh) *φησὶν ὁ Λάκων* seems to have been a usual formula of citation, when these *ῥηματίσκια*, of which the Athenians seem to [illegible] to season their discourse For the Laconian dislike of rhetoric comp Sext Empir, Math ii § 21, *τὸν ἐπὶ ξένης ῥητορικὴν ἐκπονήσαντα νεανίαν, ἐπανελθόντα ἐκόλασαν οἱ Ἔφοροι προσθέντες . ὡς δολεροὺς λόγους ἐπὶ παρακρούσει τᾶς Σπάρτας ἐμελέτησεν* Perhaps the dictum in the text may have been connected with this story, which no comm notices

261 *δεῖ*] Vulg *δή* The *δεῖ* is but a makeshift reading, taken from a limited number of MSS The alternative is to suppose that a verb has been dropped, such as *δεόμεθα* or perhaps *δεῖ* after *λόγων*

Πάριτε δή] 'approach, ye gentle creatures, and try to convince the prolific Phaedrus that without a due tincture of philosophy he will never be able to speak on any subject as he ought to speak' Hermeias's interpretation of *θρέμματα* is a curiosity *τοὺς λόγους θρέμματα καλεῖ· οἱ γὰρ λόγοι τῆς ψυχῆς θρέμματά εἰσιν, οἱ οὐσιώδεις καὶ ἀληθεῖς καὶ ἀποδεικτικοί*. He is more successful in his gloss on *καλλίπαιδα ἢ αὐτὸν τὸν Φ καλὸν παῖδα, ἢ καλοὺς παῖδας τίκτοντα, τοὺς λόγους*. The latter is the sense generally adopted, as by Plutarch, Mor. p 1000, quoted by Heind., *τῶν ἐρωτικῶν λόγων πατέρα Φαῖδρον ἐν Συμποσίῳ προσεῖπεν εἰσηγήτην αὐτὸν γενόμενον, ἐν δὲ τῷ ὁμωνύμῳ διαλόγῳ καλλίπαιδα* (for the vulg *καλλιπίδην*) Aesch Ag 761, *οἴκων εὐθυδίκων καλλίπαις πότμος ἀεί* But we have it in the former sense in Eur. Or. 964, *ὃν ἔλαχ' ἁ κατὰ χθονὸς νερτέρων καλλίπαις θεά*, sc Persephone Socr uses a poetic phrase to humour his companion's love of fine writing.

Ἐρωτᾶτε] Herm, *ὡς πρὸς τὰ θρέμματα* [illegible]

ΣΩ. Ἆρ' οὖν οὐ τὸ μὲν ὅλον ἡ ῥητορικὴ ἂν εἴη τέχνη ψυχαγωγία τις διὰ λόγων, οὐ μόνον ἐν δικαστηρίοις καὶ ὅσοι ἄλλοι δημόσιοι σύλλογοι, ἀλλὰ καὶ ἐν ἰδίοις,
B ἡ αὐτὴ σμικρῶν τε καὶ μεγάλων πέρι; καὶ οὐδὲν ἐντιμότερον τό γε ὀρθὸν περὶ σπουδαῖα ἢ περὶ φαῦλα γιγνόμενον; ἢ πῶς σὺ ταῦτ' ἀκήκοας;

ΦΑΙ. Οὐ μὰ τὸν Δί' οὐ παντάπασιν οὕτως, ἀλλὰ μάλιστα μέν πως περὶ τὰς δίκας λέγεταί τε καὶ γράφεται τέχνῃ, λέγεται δὲ καὶ περὶ δημηγορίας· ἐπὶ πλέον δὲ οὐκ ἀκήκοα.

ΣΩ. Ἀλλ' ἦ τὰς Νέστορος καὶ Ὀδυσσέως τέχνας

Ἆρ' οὖν οὐ, κ.τ.λ.] As a step towards the proof of the position, that a philosophic training is necessary to the rhetor, the Λόγοι begin *secundum artem* by defining the art of Rhetoric. Rhetoric is 'a winning or working upon the soul by means of discourses,' and this description holds good whatever the matter in which Rhetoric works, or whatever the occasion on which she exerts her powers: for, in strictness, the dignity or meanness of the subject-matter does not affect her greatness as an art. For this broad view of the scope of Rhetoric Phaedr. is not prepared. The treatises he has read restrict her functions to the law-courts and the popular assemblies,—a restriction which Socr. proceeds to reason away by examples.

ψυχαγωγία τις] This definition puts in a more philosophical form the well-known Ῥητορικὴ πειθοῦς δημιουργός, attributed to Corax and Tisias. The verb ψυχαγωγεῖν is common. Arist. Poet. 6. 17, τὰ μέγιστα οἷς ψυχαγωγεῖ ἡ τραγῳδία τοῦ μύθου μέρη ἐστίν, αἵ τε περιπέτειαι καὶ ἀναγνωρίσεις. Sext. Empir. adv. Gramm. 297, οἱ μὲν τοῦ ἀληθοῦς στοχάζονται, οἱ δὲ ἐκ παντὸς ψυχαγωγεῖν ἐθέλουσι· ψυχαγωγεῖ δὲ μᾶλλον τὸ ψεῦδος ἢ τἀληθές. Also in the orators, Lycurg. c. Leocr. 933, τίνας δὲ δυνατὸν εἶναι δοκεῖ τοῖς λόγοις ψυχαγωγῆσαι, καὶ τὴν ὑγρότητα αὐτῶν τοῦ ἤθους τοῖς δακρύοις εἰς ἔλεον προαγαγέσθαι; τοὺς δικαστάς. Cic. de Orat. ii. c. 21, Tantam vim habet illa quae recte a bono poeta dicta est, *Flexanima atque omnium regina rerum oratio*. It is uncertain whether Plato invented the substantive or found it ready to his hand.

ἐν ἰδίοις] The ἴδιοι σύλλογοι are private meetings or conversazioni for the purposes of eristic debate on abstract questions. They are more explicitly mentioned Soph. 232 C: ἔν γε ταῖς ἰδίαις ξυνουσίαις, ὁπόταν γενέσεως τε καὶ οὐσίας πέρι κατὰ πάντων λέγηταί τι, ξύνισμεν ὡς αὐτοί τε ἀντειπεῖν δεινοὶ τούς τε ἄλλους ποιοῦσιν ἅπερ αὐτοὶ δυνατούς. Socr. includes in his definition of Rhetoric the ἀντιλογικὴ τέχνη, as it is called in the same passage. This agrees with the assertion in the Gorgias, ὅτι σοφιστὴς καὶ ῥήτωρ ταὐτόν, ἢ ἐγγύς τι καὶ παραπλήσιον. This will appear further in the sequel.

B. μάλιστα μέν πως] Phaedr. replies that the technical lectures and treatises on Rhetoric relate chiefly to the forensic branch, some of the former including also the eloquence of the assembly. These two kinds were designated as δικανικοὶ and συμβουλευτικοὶ λόγοι. Aristotle, too, makes it matter of complaint that the technographers preceding his time had confined their attention chiefly to the former. Rhet. i. 1. 10, διὰ τοῦτο τῆς αὐτῆς οὔσης μεθόδου περὶ τὰ δημηγορικὰ καὶ δικανικά, καὶ καλλίονος καὶ πολιτικωτέρας τῆς δημηγορικῆς πραγματείας οὔσης, περὶ μὲν ἐκείνης οὐδὲν λέγουσιν, περὶ δὲ τοῦ δικάζεσθαι πάντες πειρῶνται τεχνολογεῖν. He proceeds to explain the cause of this preference in a manner not complimentary to the professors of rhetoric. Isocrates enlarges on the same topic with his wonted querulousness (*Contra Sophistas*, § 22, p. 295).

Ἀλλ' ἦ τὰς Νέστορος, κ.τ.λ.] What, says Socr., is it possible that you have

μόνον [περὶ] λόγων ἀκήκοας, ἃς ἐν Ἰλίῳ σχολάζοντε συνεγραψάτην, τῶν δὲ Παλαμήδους ἀνήκοος γέγονας;

ΦΑΙ. Καὶ ναὶ μὰ Δί' ἔγωγε τῶν Νέστορος, εἰ μὴ Γοργίαν Νέστορά τινα κατασκευάζεις, ἤ τινα Θρασύμαχόν τε καὶ Θεόδωρον Ὀδυσσέα.

ΣΩ. Ἴσως. ἀλλὰ γὰρ τούτους ἐῶμεν· σὺ δ' εἰπέ, ἐν δικαστηρίοις οἱ ἀντίδικοι τί δρῶσιν; οὐκ ἀντιλέγουσι μέντοι; ἢ τί φήσομεν;

ΦΑΙ. Τοῦτ' αὐτό.

only heard of the technical treatises of Nestor and Ulysses, and have never been informed of those of Palamedes? By these heroic worthies it is afterwards hinted that Gorgias, Thrasymachus and Theodorus, one or both, and Zeno of Elea are respectively meant The question is therefore equivalent to this 'Have you heard only of the professed Rhetors, and not also of the people called Eristics, of whom Zeno is the father?' Gorgias is called Nestor partly on account of his great age, and partly because τοῦ καὶ ἀπὸ γλώσσης μέλιτος γλυκίων ῥέεν αὐδή. Of Thrasymachus and Theodorus we shall hear more anon Zeno is well represented by Palamedes, the 'sophist' of the heroic times, distinguished for his inventive genius. Philostr. Heroicus x 1 αὐτομαθῆ ἀφικέσθαι (τὸν Παλαμήδην) καὶ σοφίας ἤδη γεγυμνασμένον, καὶ πλείω γιγνώσκοντα ἢ ὁ Χείρων His discoveries were ὧραι, μηνῶν κύκλος, ἐνιαυτός, νόμισμα, σταθμά, μέτρα, ἀριθμεῖν In the text, περὶ before λόγων is probably interpolated

C εἰ μὴ—κατασκευάζεις, κ τ λ] 'unless you are dressing up, let us say, a Gorgias in the garb of Nestor, or a Thrasymachus or Theodorus in that of Ulysses,' or, 'unless the mask of Nestor conceals a Gorgias,' &c Aristotle, in his work De Sophisticis Elenchis, seems to imply that Gorgias wrote no technical treatise on Rhetoric, but lent his pupils model speeches (communes loci) to learn by heart instead The first technographer, he says, was Tisias, then came Thrasymachus, and thirdly Theodorus So in the Gorgias, p 462 B, we read of a written τέχνη of *Polus*, but not of one by Gorgias On the other hand, it is not to be supposed with Spengel (Art. Scriptt. p 83) that Plato would cause Phaedr. to make a wrong guess, or that Γοργίαν τινὰ can possibly mean 'Gorgias or somebody else like him,' for who but Gorgias can be represented by Nestor, or what doubt can there be of Plato's meaning when he makes that hero as well as Ulysses employ his long leisure at Troy in composing (συνεγραψάτην) a τέχνη? Compare also 267 A, where Gorgias is coupled with the acknowledged technographer Tisias. Either Plato wrote carelessly in the present passage, or—what is more probable—Gorgias wrote a τέχνη, but found or thought it useless for educational purposes That Aristotle's catalogue of the earliest technographers l. l is not complete, follows from a passage of the *Rhetorice ad Alexandrum* (1 17), in which a τέχνη of Corax, the predecessor of Tisias, is expressly mentioned If, as many think, Anaximenes was the author of the work quoted, his testimony to a fact of literary history is not inferior to Aristotle's, who indeed himself speaks of a τέχνη of Corax, Rhet ii 24 11 From another passage, ib iii 18 7, it follows that Gorgias was at any rate the author of rhetorical precepts, and not a mere writer of speeches, as indeed Spengel admits The byename of Nestor, as we learn from Syrianus, ap Spengel l l. p 113, was afterwards given to Isocrates

οὐκ ἀντιλέγουσι μέντοι] Sup 229 B, εἰπέ μοι, οὐκ ἐνθένδε μέντοι . λέγεταί ὁ Βορέας τὴν Ὠρειθυῖαν ἁρπάσαι. inf 267 C. Socr. is now showing that the controversies of the law-court, the assembly, and the schools are all conducted on the same principles, and amenable to the same rules of art.

ΣΩ. Περὶ τοῦ δικαίου τε καὶ ἀδίκου;

ΦΑΙ. Ναί.

ΣΩ. Οὐκοῦν ὁ τέχνῃ τοῦτο δρῶν ποιήσει φανῆναι τὸ αὐτὸ τοῖς αὐτοῖς τοτὲ μὲν δίκαιον, ὅταν δὲ βούληται, ἄδικον;

ΦΑΙ. Τί μήν;

D ΣΩ. Καὶ ἐν δημηγορίᾳ δὴ τῇ πόλει δοκεῖν τὰ αὐτὰ τοτὲ μὲν ἀγαθά, τοτὲ δ' αὖ τἀναντία;

ΦΑΙ. Οὕτως.

ΣΩ. Τὸν οὖν Ἐλεατικὸν Παλαμήδην λέγοντα οὐκ ἴσμεν τέχνῃ, ὥστε φαίνεσθαι τοῖς ἀκούουσι τὰ αὐτὰ ὅμοια καὶ ἀνόμοια, καὶ ἓν καὶ πολλά, μένοντά τε αὖ καὶ φερόμενα;

ΦΑΙ. Μάλα γε.

ΣΩ Οὐκ ἄρα μόνον περὶ δικαστήριά τέ ἐστιν ἡ ἀντιλογικὴ καὶ περὶ δημηγορίαν, ἀλλ', ὡς ἔοικε, περὶ πάντα E τὰ λεγόμενα μία τις τέχνη, εἴπερ ἔστιν, αὕτη ἂν εἴη ᾗ τις οἷός τ' ἔσται πᾶν παντὶ ὁμοιοῦν τῶν δυνατῶν καὶ οἷς δυνατόν, καὶ ἄλλου ὁμοιοῦντος καὶ ἀποκρυπτομένου εἰς φῶς ἄγειν.

ΦΑΙ. Πῶς δὴ τὸ τοιοῦτον λέγεις;

Οὐκοῦν ὁ τέχνῃ, κ τ λ.] 'and he who conducts such a controversy (ὁ ἀντιλέγων περὶ δικαίου καὶ ἀδίκου) scientifically will cause a given action to appear in either light—just, or, when he chooses, unjust—to the same jury at two different times, will he not?'

D τὸν οὖν Ἐλεατικὸν Παλαμήδην] Schol, Ζήνωνα φησὶ τὸν Παρμενίδου ἑταῖρον That the father of the Eristic sects is here meant, the context proves to demonstration The various reading Ἐλαΐτην derived from Quintilian, Inst. iii 1 10 (meaning the rhetor Alcidamas), is entitled to no consideration, as it destroys the point and purpose of the passage Diog L ix 25, ὁ δ' αὐτὸς ἐν τῷ Φαίδρῳ καὶ Ἐλεατικὸν Παλαμήδην αὐτὸν (sc τὸν Ζήνωνα) καλεῖ Zeno's paradoxes on the subjects of the One and Many, of Rest and Motion, &c, which Socr. here alludes to, may be learned from any history of philosophy. The dialogue called Sophista was written to overthrow this 'Antilogic' method, in order to make way for a rational Logic

Οὐκ ἄρα μόνον, κ τ λ] The art of controversy is therefore not confined to oratory forensic or popular, but, so far as appears, it must be an art, if art it really is, applicable to all kinds of discourse without exception—an art capable of making any thing appear like any thing else within the limits of possibility, also of exposing every attempt on the part of an adversary to perform the same feat without detection. Socr proceeds to argue that a man who has this power must know whether one thing is like another or not that in order to impose on others and to detect imposition in them, he must himself be undeceived A science of truth (ὄντος) is consequently implied in the science of seeming (δοκοῦντος) Comp. Arist Rhet i 1 12, quoted p 262 inf.

ΣΩ. Τῇδε δοκῶ ζητοῦσι φανεῖσθαι. ἀπάτη πότερον ἐν πολὺ διαφέρουσι γίγνεται μᾶλλον ἢ ὀλίγον ;

ΦΑΙ. Ἐν τοῖς ὀλίγον. 262

ΣΩ. Ἀλλά γε δὴ κατὰ σμικρὸν μεταβαίνων μᾶλλον λήσεις ἐλθὼν ἐπὶ τὸ ἐναντίον ἢ κατὰ μέγα.

ΦΑΙ. Πῶς δ' οὔ ;

ΣΩ. Δεῖ ἄρα τὸν μέλλοντα ἀπατήσειν μὲν ἄλλον, αὐτὸν δὲ μὴ ἀπατήσεσθαι τὴν ὁμοιότητα τῶν ὄντων καὶ ἀνομοιότητα ἀκριβῶς διειδέναι.

ΦΑΙ. Ἀνάγκη μὲν οὖν.

ΣΩ. Ἦ οὖν οἷός τ' ἔσται, ἀλήθειαν ἀγνοῶν ἑκάστου, τὴν τοῦ ἀγνοουμένου ὁμοιότητα σμικράν τε καὶ μεγάλην ἐν τοῖς ἄλλοις διαγιγνώσκειν ;

ΦΑΙ. Ἀδύνατον. B

ΣΩ. Οὐκοῦν τοῖς παρὰ τὰ ὄντα δοξάζουσι καὶ ἀπατωμένοις δῆλον ὡς τὸ πάθος τοῦτο δι' ὁμοιοτήτων τινῶν εἰσεῤῥύη.

ΦΑΙ. Γίγνεται γοῦν οὕτως.

ΣΩ. Ἔστιν οὖν ὅπως τεχνικὸς ἔσται μεταβιβάζειν κατὰ σμικρὸν διὰ τῶν ὁμοιοτήτων ἀπὸ τοῦ ὄντος ἑκάστοτε ἐπὶ τοὐναντίον ἀπάγων, ἢ αὐτὸς τοῦτο διαφεύγειν, ὁ μὴ ἐγνωρικὼς ὃ ἔστιν ἕκαστον τῶν ὄντων ,

ΦΑΙ. Οὐ μή ποτε.

ΣΩ. Λόγων ἄρα τέχνην, ὦ ἑταῖρε, ὁ τὴν ἀλήθειαν μὴ

262. Ἦ οὖν οἷός τ' ἔσται] 'suppose a man to be ignorant of the truth of any given thing, how is he, in other things, to detect a resemblance to that of which by the hypothesis he is ignorant, or to discern whether such resemblance is great or small?'

B Οὐκοῦν τοῖς παρὰ τὰ ὄντα] 'consequently where people are deceived, and their notions are at variance with the realities, it is plain that such illusions slid into their minds by means of certain resemblances' τὸ πάθος τοῦτο = τὸ ἀπατᾶσθαι

Ἔστιν οὖν] Without a familiarity with truth, argues Socr., it is impossible for a speaker either to mislead his hearer [illegible] or to avoid being himself misled For μεταβιβάζειν the vulg had μεταβιβάζων The correction is supplied by Galen, Hipp. et Plat. p 331 (v p 729, Kuhn) Bodl, μεταβιβάζει. No further alteration seems necessary The rhetor ἀπάγει ἀπὸ τοῦ ὄντος and μεταβιβάζει κατὰ σμικρὸν ἐπὶ τοὐναντίον, κ τ λ, leads his audience away from the truth, and brings them round insensibly to the opposite of the truth, effecting this by means of resemblances or artful counterfeits as when, says Herm, τὸν ὑδράργυρον ἄργυρον (νομίσαι ποιῇ) ἢ τὸν χαλκὸν χρυσόν, καὶ ἐπὶ ζῴων τὴν φάτταν περιστεράν, ἐπὶ ἐπιτηδευμάτων δὲ τὸν γόητα τελέστην.

C εἰδώς, δόξας δὲ τεθηρευκὼς γελοίαν τινά, ὡς ἔοικε, καὶ ἄτεχνον παρέξεται.

ΦΑΙ. Κινδυνεύει.

ΣΩ. Βούλει οὖν, ἐν τῷ Λυσίου λόγῳ ὃν φέρεις καὶ ἐν οἷς ἡμεῖς εἴπομεν ἰδεῖν τι ὧν φαμὲν ἀτέχνων τε καὶ ἐντέχνων εἶναι;

ΦΑΙ. Πάντων γέ που μάλιστα, ὡς νῦν γε ψιλῶς πως λέγομεν, οὐκ ἔχοντες ἱκανὰ παραδείγματα.

ΣΩ. Καὶ μὴν κατὰ τύχην γέ τινα, ὡς ἔοικεν, ἐρρη-
D θήτην τὼ λόγω ἔχοντέ τι παράδειγμα, ὡς ἂν ὁ εἰδὼς τὸ ἀληθὲς προσπαίζων ἐν λόγοις παράγοι τοὺς ἀκούοντας. καὶ ἔγωγε, ὦ Φαῖδρε, αἰτιῶμαι τοὺς ἐντοπίους θεούς· ἴσως δὲ καὶ οἱ τῶν Μουσῶν προφῆται οἱ ὑπὲρ κεφαλῆς ᾠδοὶ ἐπιπεπνευκότες ἂν ἡμῖν εἶεν τοῦτο τὸ γέρας. οὐ γάρ που ἔγωγε τέχνης τινὸς τοῦ λέγειν μέτοχος.

ΦΑΙ. Ἔστω ὡς λέγεις· μόνον δήλωσον ὃ φῄς.

ΣΩ. Ἴθι δή μοι ἀνάγνωθι τὴν τοῦ Λυσίου λόγου ἀρχήν.

E ΦΑΙ. Περὶ μὲν τῶν ἐμῶν πραγμάτων ἐπίστασαι, καὶ ὡς νομίζω συμφέρειν ἡμῖν τούτων γενομένων, ἀκήκοας. ἀξιῶ δὲ μὴ διὰ τοῦτο ἀτυχῆσαι ὧν δέομαι, ὅτι οὐκ

C δόξας—τεθηρευκώς] Angl., 'a master of claptrap.' Germ. Tr., "der Meinungen nachjagt." τεθηρευκώς, Galen and Bodl. for the vulg. τεθηρακώς. Plato never uses θηρᾶν either literally or metaphorically, but always θηρεύειν or θηρεύεσθαι. Xenophon employs both forms.

ὧν φαμὲν ἀτέχνων τε καὶ ἐντέχνων εἶναι] For the constr. comp. 217 E, ὧν ἡμεῖς νῦν ὄντων καλοῦμεν. The MSS. give ἄτεχνον, ἔντεχνον: corr. Heind. Socr. proposes to illustrate his principle by reference to the discourse of Lysias, and to his own two discourses. To this Phaedr. gladly agrees, for, says he, we are at present reasoning too abstractedly—ψιλῶς. Comp. Theaet. 165 A, ἐκ τῶν ψιλῶν λόγων πρὸς τὴν γεωμετρίαν—'we left abstract dialectics for geometry,' which uses paradigms. In 278 C ποίησις ψιλή = poetry unaccompanied with music. Legg. ii. 669 D, λόγοι ψιλοὶ denotes prose as distinguished from metrical composition.

Καὶ μὴν κατὰ τύχην] The connexion between the two main portions of the dialogue is here plainly indicated. The speeches are patterns—παραδείγματα—illustrative of the theoretical principles developed in the second half of the work. Socr. affects to believe that this advantage is accidental, if it be not rather due to the inspiration of the local divinities or the Μουσῶν προφῆται, the sweet singers overhead.

D ὡς ἂν—παράγοι] 'how one who knows the truth may play upon and mislead his hearers.' Euthyd. 278 B, φημὶ ἐγώ σοι τούτους προσπαίζειν—'amuse themselves at your expense.'

Ἔστω ὡς λέγεις] Phaedr. is impatient of the frequent allusions to these insects: a dramatic touch this of great delicacy. Socr. takes the hint, and introduces them no more.

ἐραστὴς ὢν σοῦ τυγχάνω. ὡς ἐκείνοις μὲν τότε μεταμέλει—

ΣΩ. Παῦσαι τί δὴ οὖν οὗτος ἁμαρτάνει καὶ ἄτεχνον ποιεῖ; λεκτέον, | ἦ γάρ; 263

ΦΑΙ. Ναί.

ΣΩ. Ἆρ' οὖν οὐ παντὶ δῆλον τό γε τοιόνδε, ὡς περὶ μὲν ἔνια τῶν ὄντων ὁμονοητικῶς ἔχομεν, περὶ δ' ἔνια στασιωτικῶς;

ΦΑΙ. Δοκῶ μὲν ὃ λέγεις μανθάνειν, ἔτι δ' εἰπὲ σαφέστερον.

ΣΩ. Ὅταν τις ὄνομα εἴπῃ σιδήρου ἢ ἀργύρου, ἆρ' οὐ τὸ αὐτὸ πάντες διενοήθημεν;

ΦΑΙ. Καὶ μάλα.

ΣΩ. Τί δ' ὅταν δικαίου ἢ ἀγαθοῦ; οὐκ ἄλλος ἄλλῃ φέρεται, καὶ ἀμφισβητοῦμεν ἀλλήλοις τε καὶ ἡμῖν αὐτοῖς;

ΦΑΙ. Πάνυ μὲν οὖν.

ΣΩ. Ἐν μὲν ἄρα τοῖς συμφωνοῦμεν, ἐν δὲ τοῖς οὔ. B

ΦΑΙ. Οὕτως.

ΣΩ. Ποτέρωθι οὖν εὐαπατητότεροί ἐσμεν, καὶ ἡ ῥητορικὴ ἐν ποτέροις μεῖζον δύναται;

ΦΑΙ. Δῆλον ὅτι ἐν οἷς πλανώμεθα.

ΣΩ. Οὐκοῦν τὸν μέλλοντα τέχνην ῥητορικὴν μετιέναι

263. περὶ μὲν ἔνια τῶν ὄντων] Vulg τοιούτων The reading ὄντων is taken from Cod Γ, and is certainly right, in my judgment

ἀμφισβητοῦμεν ἀλλήλοις] This distinction of ἀμφισβητήσιμα καὶ μή is illustrated by Arist Rhet. i 1.12 τἀναντία δεῖ δύνασθαι πείθειν καθάπερ καὶ ἐν τοῖς συλλογισμοῖς, οὐχ ὅπως ἀμφότερα πράττωμεν (οὐ γὰρ δεῖ τὰ φαῦλα πείθειν) ἀλλ' ἵνα μήτε λανθάνῃ πῶς ἔχει, καὶ ὅπως ἄλλου χρωμένου τοῖς λόγοις μὴ δικαίως αὐτοὶ λύειν ἔχωμεν. τῶν μὲν οὖν ἄλλων τεχνῶν οὐδεμία τἀναντία συλλογίζεται, ἡ δὲ διαλεκτικὴ καὶ ἡ ῥητορικὴ τοῦτο ποιοῦσιν ὁμοίως γάρ εἰσιν ἀμφότεραι τῶν ἐναντίων Here τὸ δίκαιον is the special subject of the forensic, τὸ ἀγαθὸν of the deliberative rhetoric

B Οὐκοῦν τὸν μέλλοντα] Having shown that rhetoric is chiefly conversant with debatable terms Socr. proceeds to argue that a complete theory of Rhetoric presupposes a methodical division of the things which are and of those which are not debatable or ambiguous The word ὁδῷ (via et arte, Cic.) excludes a mere popular (εἰκῇ), or verbal, as distinguished from a scientific and natural διαίρεσις So Aristotle uses ὁδοποιεῖν, Rhet init., in the sense 'to systematize,' or 'methodize' (for ὁδὸς = μέθοδος), and he begins his treatise by defining the object-matter of the art he is about to handle. It is remarkable that Lysias himself is not mentioned by Plato in the list of technographers, whom he treats so roughly in the sequel Cicero indeed says, on the authority of Aristotle, Lysiam primo profiteri solitum artem esse dicendi, deinde quod Theodorus esset in arte subtilior, in orationibus autem ieiunior, orationes eum scribere aliis coepisse, artem removisse (Brut. 12

πρῶτον μὲν δεῖ ταῦτα ὁδῷ διῃρῆσθαι, καὶ εἰληφέναι τινὰ χαρακτῆρα ἑκατέρου τοῦ εἴδους, ἐν ᾧ τε ἀνάγκη τὸ πλῆθος πλανᾶσθαι καὶ ἐν ᾧ μή.

C ΦΑΙ. Καλὸν γοῦν ἄν, ὦ Σώκρατες, εἶδος εἴη κατανενοηκὼς ὁ τοῦτο λαβών.

ΣΩ. Ἔπειτά γε οἶμαι πρὸς ἑκάστῳ γιγνόμενον μὴ λανθάνειν, ἀλλ' ὀξέως αἰσθάνεσθαι, περὶ οὗ ἂν μέλλῃ ἐρεῖν, ποτέρου ὂν τυγχάνει τοῦ γένους.

ΦΑΙ. Τί μήν;

ΣΩ. Τί οὖν; τὸν Ἔρωτα πότερον φῶμεν εἶναι τῶν ἀμφισβητησίμων ἢ τῶν μή;

ΦΑΙ. Τῶν ἀμφισβητησίμων δή που. ἢ οἴει ἄν σοι συγχωρῆσαι εἰπεῖν ἃ νῦν δὴ εἶπες περὶ αὐτοῦ, ὡς βλάβη

D τέ ἐστι τῷ ἐρωμένῳ καὶ ἐρῶντι, καὶ αὖθις ὡς μέγιστον τῶν ἀγαθῶν τυγχάνει;

48) Quintilian attributes to Lysias the opinion that Rhetoric "observationem quandam esse non artem" (Inst ii c 17) This was probably the judgment of his riper years, when the change in his practice alluded to by Cicero had taken place. It would be unsafe to conclude from such authorities as the pseudo-Plutarch and Suidas that his treatise, if he published one, survived him Krische's inference that the τεχνη of Lysias was written after the ἐρωτικός, which Plato here criticizes, is palpably unsound It would be equally fair to argue that the work had disappeared from circulation before the Phaedrus was written, or that Plato had never seen it. But the words of Cicero by no means prove the existence of a *written* τέχνη by Lysias. His instruction in the art of Rhetoric may have been comprised in oral lectures, as must have been the case in other instances Compare what Phaedr says, sup 261 B λέγεταί τε καὶ γράφεται τέχνῃ, λέγεται δὲ καὶ περὶ δημηγορίας, and the note

C Καλὸν γοῦν ἄν] As we might say, 'a very pretty generalization this, if you can carry it out' Herm, ὁ εἰδὼς τὴν διαιρετικὴν μέθοδον ἄριστα ἔχει This 'diaeretic method' is further explained in the sequel, p. 265 C.

Ἔπειτά γε οἶμαι] In the second place, when he comes in contact with either of the two classes, the Disputable or the Indisputable, he ought not to be baffled by it, but should be able to discern at a glance to whether of the two the matter he has to speak about does properly belong

ἢ οἴει ἄν σοι συγχωρῆσαι] 'else do you suppose he would have let you say of him,' &c, τὸν Ἔρωτα being understood I prefer this to Badh's ἐγχωρῆσαι On the omission of ὢν with τυγχάνει, &c, see Lob ad Phryn. p. 277, "Neque fas duco, etsi in proclivi emendatio, tot tamque gravia testimonia in dubitationem devocare: τυγχάνει καλή, Plato Hipp. i. 300," &c Also Heind on the present passage, who quotes Isocr Archid p. 256, μεθ' ὧν (sc. τῶν νόμων) οἰκοῦντες, εὐδαιμονέστατοι τῶν Ἑλλήνων ἐτύγχανον For the other side of the question, see Porson on Eur Hec. 782, with Scholefield's note Homer gives the first example of this construction, Od x 87, ὂν πέρι πέτρη Ἠλίβατος τετύχηκε διαμπερὲς ἀμφοτέρωθεν. Porson allowed it in the tragedies, but doubted its admissibility in comedy or prose But the passages from the Hippias and Isocrates are not easily altered Hence I have not thought it right to meddle with the text here, though it would be easy to conjecture μέγιστον ὂν with Heind, or, with Hirsch, ἀγαθῶν ὂν τ. Of the passages adduced from Aristoph.

ΣΩ. Ἄριστα λέγεις. ἀλλ' εἰπὲ καὶ τόδε—ἐγὼ γάρ τοι διὰ τὸ ἐνθουσιαστικὸν οὐ πάνυ μέμνημαι—εἰ ὡρισάμην ἔρωτα ἀρχόμενος τοῦ λόγου.

ΦΑΙ. Νὴ Δί' ἀμηχάνως γε ὡς σφόδρα.

ΣΩ. Φεῦ, ὅσῳ λέγεις τεχνικωτέρας Νύμφας τὰς Ἀχελῴου καὶ Πᾶνα τὸν Ἑρμοῦ Λυσίου τοῦ Κεφάλου πρὸς λόγους εἶναι. ἢ οὐδὲν λέγω, ἀλλὰ καὶ ὁ Λυσίας ἀρχόμενος τοῦ ἐρωτικοῦ ἠνάγκασεν ἡμᾶς ὑπολαβεῖν τὸν Ἔρωτα ἕν τι τῶν ὄντων, ὃ αὐτὸς ἐβουλήθη, καὶ πρὸς τοῦτο ἤδη
συνταξάμενος πάντα τὸν ὕστερον λόγον διεπεράνατο; E
βούλει πάλιν ἀναγνῶμεν τὴν ἀρχὴν αὐτοῦ;

ΦΑΙ. Εἰ σοί γε δοκεῖ· ὃ μέντοι ζητεῖς, οὐκ ἔστ' αὐτόθι.

ΣΩ. Λέγε, ἵν' ἀκούσω αὐτοῦ ἐκείνου.

ΦΑΙ. Περὶ μὲν τῶν ἐμῶν πραγμάτων ἐπίστασαι, καὶ ὡς νομίζω συμφέρειν ἡμῖν τούτων γενομένων, ἀκήκοας.
ἀξιῶ δὲ μὴ διὰ | τοῦτο ἀτυχῆσαι ὧν δέομαι, ὅτι οὐκ 264
ἐραστὴς ὢν σοῦ τυγχάνω. ὡς ἐκείνοις μὲν τότε μεταμέλει ὧν ἂν εὖ ποιήσωσιν, ἐπειδὰν τῆς ἐπιθυμίας παύσωνται.

ΣΩ Ἦ πολλοῦ δεῖν ἔοικε ποιεῖν ὅδε γε ὃ ζητοῦμεν, ὃς οὐδὲ ἀπ' ἀρχῆς ἀλλ' ἀπὸ τελευτῆς ἐξ ὑπτίας ἀνάπαλιν

that from Av 760 is ambiguous, and of Eccles 1137 Porson suggests the emendation κεἰ τῶν θεατῶν ὤν τις εὔνους τυγχάνει, for καὶ . εἴ τις

D διὰ τὸ ἐνθουσιαστικόν] Sc τῆς διανοίας. Transl οὐ πάνυ μέμνημαι, 'I have quite forgotten'

ἀμηχάνως γε ὡς σφόδρα] Alluding to the elaborate definitions in 237 B seq and 211 seq

ἠνάγκασεν ἡμᾶς ὑπολαβεῖν] 'did he force us to conceive of Love as some definite entity selected by himself? Did he, I say, compose the ensuing discourse from first to last in due subordination to this idea?'

264 Ἦ πολλοῦ δεῖν] Hence, says Hermeias, later critics say of Lysias, ὅτι τίκτειν δυνατὸς ἐγένετο, τάξαι δὲ οὔ, διὰ τὸ εὑρετικὸν αὐτοῦ καὶ ἄτακτον τοῦ λόγου If Lysias could have been heard in reply, he would have said that his ἐραστής had the best of reasons for not defining [illegible] address

ὃς οὐδὲ ἀπ' ἀρχῆς] "Lysias," says Krische, "begins where he should have ended, inasmuch as he assumes as known the particulars concerning the person and personal relations of the suitor, and gives them precedence of that which is general" (περὶ μὲν τῶν ἐμῶν πραγμάτων ἐπίστασαι, κ τ λ.). Plato is apparently aware that this was done of set purpose, and as a stroke of art, and he compares the trick to the feat of swimming on the back. For the expression comp. Rep vii 529 C, κἂν ἐξ ὑπτίας νέων ἐν γῇ ἢ ἐν θαλάττῃ μανθάνῃ, a curious passage, in which Plato ridicules the popular notion that the study of astronomy has an elevating tendency Comp also Parmen. 137 A, διανεῦσαι τοιοῦτόν τε καὶ τοσοῦτον πλῆθος λόγων Herm, οὕτως οὖν ἔγραφε τὸν λόγον ὡς ἐξ ὑπτίας νέων (πλέων, ed Ast), ἐπ' ἐξουσίας ἔχων καὶ ἀφ' ἑαυτοῦ διατιθέμενος τὸν λόγον [illegible] τοὺς χρόνους [illegible] καὶ παρὰ διανεῖν ἐπιχειρεῖ τὸν λόγον, καὶ ἄρχεται ἀφ' ὧν πεπαυμένος ἂν ἤδη ὁ ἐραστὴς λέγοι πρὸς τὰ παιδικά. ἢ οὐδὲν εἶπον, Φαῖδρε, φίλη κεφαλή;

B ΦΑΙ. Ἔστι γέ τοι δή, ὦ Σώκρατες, τελευτή, περὶ οὗ τὸν λόγον ποιεῖται.

ΣΩ. Τί δὲ τἆλλα; οὐ χύδην δοκεῖ βεβλῆσθαι τὰ τοῦ λόγου; ἢ φαίνεται τὸ δεύτερον εἰρημένον ἔκ τινος ἀνάγκης δεύτερον δεῖν τεθῆναι, ἤ τι ἄλλο τῶν ῥηθέντων; ἐμοὶ μὲν γὰρ ἔδοξεν, ὡς μηδὲν εἰδότι, οὐκ ἀγεννῶς τὸ ἐπιὸν εἰρῆσθαι τῷ γράφοντι· σὺ δ' ἔχεις τινὰ ἀνάγκην λογογραφικήν, ᾗ ταῦτα ἐκεῖνος οὕτως ἐφεξῆς παρ' ἄλληλα ἔθηκεν;

C ΦΑΙ. Χρηστὸς εἶ, ὅτι με ἡγεῖ ἱκανὸν εἶναι τὰ ἐκείνου οὕτως ἀκριβῶς διιδεῖν.

ΣΩ. Ἀλλὰ τόδε γε οἶμαί σε φάναι ἄν, δεῖν πάντα λόγον ὥσπερ ζῷον συνεστάναι σῶμά τι ἔχοντα αὐτὸν αὐ-

φύσιν, ὡς οἱ κολυμβῶντες ὕπτιοι Lysias doubtless plumed himself on his skill in plunging thus *in medias res*, instead of commencing *ab ovo*, as a novice might think it his duty to do And even the confusion of which Plato complains he might justify on practical grounds the entire speech being an example of rhetorical insinuation, where more is meant than meets or is fit to meet the ear. But it does not suit Plato's purpose to place himself on the 'Standpunkt' of his victim

πεπαυμένος] Sc τοῦ λόγου.

Φαῖδρε, φίλη κεφαλή] An imitation of the Homeric Τεῦκρε, φίλη κεφαλή (Il viii 281), as Ast and Stallb observe One MS gives ὦ Φαῖδρε, a reading which I am surprised to see that Hirsch. and Badh patronize

B *Ἔστι γέ τοι δή*] 'That of which he speaks (in the exordium) is, I grant you, a termination' rather than a beginning

χύδην 'helter skelter,' like rubbish shot from a cart

ἐμοὶ μὲν γάρ 'I, who am but a novice, could not help being struck by the audacity of the writer, in blurting out the first thing that came into his head' The phrases οὐκ ἀγεννῶς, πάνυ γενναίως, πάνυ νεανικῶς are frequent in the ironical sense Exactly in point is Gorg. 492 D, οὐκ ἀγεννῶς γε, ὦ Καλλίκλεις, ἐπεξέρχει τῷ λόγῳ παρρησιαζόμενος

σὺ δ' ἔχεις τινὰ ἀνάγκην] 'are *you* aware of any cogent literary or rhetorical reason which can have induced the writer to string his topics together thus?' To which Phaedr. replies 'you do me too much honour in supposing that I am clever enough to penetrate his motives so exactly' χρηστὸς εἶ, ἡδὺς εἶ are well-known ironical formulas, like our 'thank you,' 'you are very kind,' &c

C *δεῖν πάντα λόγον ὥσπερ ζῷον*] This comparison of a well-arranged discourse to a living organism occurs again, Phileb. 64 B. ἐμοὶ μὲν γὰρ καθαπερεὶ κόσμος τις ἀσώματος ἄρξων καλῶς ἐμψύχου σώματος ὁ νῦν λόγος ἀπειργάσθαι φαίνεται. It is also implied inf 268 D, καταγελῷεν ἂν εἴ τις οἴεται τραγῳδίαν ἄλλο τι εἶναι ἢ τὴν τούτων σύστασιν, πρέπουσαν ἀλλήλοις καὶ τῷ ὅλῳ συνισταμένην Comp Politicus, p 277 B, ἀλλ' ἀτεχνῶς ὁ λόγος ἡμῶν ὥσπερ ζῷον, κ τ λ, where, however, the ζῷον is γεγραμμένον Aristotle borrows the illustration from Plato in his remarks on Epic poetry, Poet 23 1 περὶ δὲ τῆς διηγηματικῆς καὶ ἐν μέτρῳ μιμητικῆς, ὅτι δεῖ τοὺς μύθους καθάπερ ἐν ταῖς τραγῳδίαις συνιστάναι δραματικούς.

τοῦ, ὥστε μήτε ἀκέφαλον εἶναι μήτε ἄπουν, ἀλλὰ μέσα τε ἔχειν καὶ ἄκρα, πρέποντ' ἀλλήλοις καὶ τῷ ὅλῳ γεγραμμένα.

ΦΑΙ. Πῶς γὰρ οὔ;

ΣΩ. Σκέψαι τοίνυν τὸν τοῦ ἑταίρου σου λόγον, εἴθ' οὕτως εἴτε ἄλλως ἔχει· καὶ εὑρήσεις τοῦ ἐπιγράμματος οὐδὲν διαφέροντα, ὃ Μίδᾳ τῷ Φρυγί φασί τινες ἐπιγε- D
γράφθαι.

ΦΑΙ. Ποῖον τοῦτο, καὶ τί πεπονθός;

ΣΩ. Ἔστι μὲν τοῦτο τόδε,

> χαλκῆ παρθένος εἰμί, Μίδα δ' ἐπὶ σήματι κεῖμαι.
> ὄφρ' ἂν ὕδωρ τε νάῃ καὶ δένδρεα μακρὰ τεθήλῃ,
> αὐτοῦ τῇδε μένουσα πολυκλαύτου ἐπὶ τύμβου,
> ἀγγελέω παριοῦσι Μίδας ὅτι τῇδε τέθαπται.

ὅτι δὲ οὐδὲν διαφέρει αὐτοῦ πρῶτον ἢ ὕστατόν τι λέγε- E
σθαι, ἐννοεῖς που, ὡς ἐγῷμαι.

καὶ περὶ μίαν πρᾶξιν ὅλην καὶ τελείαν, ἔχουσαν ἀρχὴν καὶ μέσον καὶ τέλος, ἵν' ὥσπερ ζῷον ἓν ὅλον ποιῇ τὴν οἰκείαν ἡδονήν, δῆλον Otherwise, he says, we find the same defects of construction as the ordinary histories present, in which γίνεται θάτερον μετὰ θατέρου, ἐξ ὧν ἓν οὐδὲν γίνεται τέλος This is in effect the application to literary criticism of the Platonic formula ἓν καὶ πολλά Heirm, ἐπειδὴ παντὶ πράγματι τὸ καλὸν καὶ τὸ εὖ ἀπὸ τοῦ ενὸς ἐπιλάμπεται, . οὕτως καὶ τὸ κάλλος οὐκ ἔστι καλόν, εἰ μὴ ἕνωσις γένηται πάντων τῶν μορίων It is for want of this natural coherence of parts that the Lysianic discourse resembles nothing so much as the celebrated epigram said to have been graven on the tomb of Midas, in which every line is independent of every other, both in sense and metre, so that the poem yields much the same meaning in whatever order the lines are read This epigrammatic *jeu d'esprit* was attributed, as we learn from Diog Lacrt, to Cleobulus of Lindus, one of the seven sages. It was censured by Simonides in an ode, of which Laertius favours us with a fragment (l i c 6, § 2) τὸ ἐπίγραμμά τινες τὸ ἐπὶ Μίδᾳ τοῦτον (Κλεόβουλον) φασὶ ποιῆσαι Χαλκῆ παρθένος εἰμί, Μίδα δ' ἐπὶ σήματι κεῖμαι Ἔστ' ἂν ὕδωρ τε νάῃ καὶ δένδρεα μακρὰ τεθήλῃ Ἠέλιός τ' ἀνιὼν λάμπῃ λαμπρά τε σελήνη, Καὶ ποταμοί γε ῥέωσιν, ἀνακλύζῃ τε θάλασσα, Αὐτοῦ τῇδε, κ.τ.λ φέρουσι δὲ μαρτύριον Σιμωνίδου ᾆσμα ὅπου φησί Τίς κεν αἰνήσειε νόῳ πίσυνος Λίνδου ναέταν Κλεόβουλον, κ τ λ. (Bergk, Lyr. Gr, Simon. 6) The epigram, adds Diog, could not have been Homer's, for he preceded Midas by many years! The German translators compare the Monkish lines called 'versus cancrini,' which will scan both backwards and forwards, as, "Otto tenet mappam madidam mappam tenet Otto" Plato, it will be observed, omits two of the lines quoted by Diog, as they would have interfered with his criticism of the epigram and its satirical application to Lysias Simonides in his reply seems to forget that the "Maiden" was of bronze, and not of marble · λίθον δὲ καὶ βρότεοι παλάμαι θραύοντι (v 5) It is also curious that Hermeias speaks of the epigram as consisting of three lines only, adding, ὅθεν τινὲς τὰ τοιαῦτα ἐπιγράμματα τρίγωνα καλοῦσιν, ἐπειδὴ ὅθεν ἂν ἐθέλῃς δύνασαι ἄρξασθαι Can the first line have been wanting in the older MSS? It certainly interferes with the interchangeability of the lines. The reading ἔστ' ἂν for ὄφρ' ἂν is also found in Thom. Magist. Encom Gregorii, p 101

ΦΑΙ. Σκώπτεις τὸν λόγον ἡμῶν, ὦ Σώκρατες.

ΣΩ. Τοῦτον μὲν τοίνυν, ἵνα μὴ σὺ ἄχθῃ, ἐάσωμεν— καί τοι συχνά γε ἔχειν μοι δοκεῖ παραδείγματα, πρὸς ἅ τις βλέπων ὀνίναιτ' ἄν, μιμεῖσθαι αὐτὰ ἐπιχειρῶν μὴ πάνυ τι—εἰς δὲ τοὺς ἑτέρους λόγους ἴωμεν. ἦν γάρ τι ἐν
265 αὐτοῖς, ὡς δοκῶ, προσῆκον ἰδεῖν τοῖς βουλο|μένοις περὶ λόγων σκοπεῖν.

ΦΑΙ. Τὸ ποῖον δὴ λέγεις;

ΣΩ. Ἐναντίω που ἤστην· ὁ μὲν γάρ, ὡς τῷ ἐρῶντι, ὁ δ' ὡς τῷ μὴ δεῖ χαρίζεσθαι, ἐλεγέτην.

ΦΑΙ. Καὶ μάλ' ἀνδρικῶς. Ar. Eq 599, Vesp 153 al

ΣΩ. Ὤιμην σε τἀληθὲς ἐρεῖν, ὅτι μανικῶς. ὃ μέντοι ἐζήτουν, ἐστὶν αὐτὸ τοῦτο. μανίαν γάρ τινα ἐφήσαμεν εἶναι τὸν Ἔρωτα. ἢ γάρ;

ΦΑΙ. Ναί.

ΣΩ. Μανίας δέ γε εἴδη δύο, τὴν μὲν ὑπὸ νοσημάτων ἀνθρωπίνων, τὴν δὲ ὑπὸ θείας ἐξαλλαγῆς τῶν εἰω-
B θότων νομίμων γιγνομένην.

F. παραδείγματα] Herm., ἁμαρτήματα λέγει.

μιμεῖσθαι αὐτὰ ἐπιχειρῶν μὴ πάνυ τι] We may supply ἀλλὰ πολὺ μᾶλλον φεύγειν. There are many things in the speech of Lysias, says Socr., which may serve as useful examples to the learner if he endeavours—I do not say to imitate them—far from that. The aposiopesis is adopted out of deference to Phaedr. The only difficulty in the passage is the position of the words μὴ πάνυ τι. They seem however to be introduced παρ' ὑπόνοιαν, and certainly no proposed change is for the better. Ast suggests πρὸς ἅ τις βλέπων μὲν ὀνίναιτ' ἄν, μιμεῖσθαι δὲ ἐπιχειρῶν, μὴ πάνυ τι (sc. ὀνίναιτ' ἄν), "in quae si quis intueatur inde proficiat aliquid, sin imitari ea conetur nihil proficiat." But in that case we must have οὐ πάνυ τι, which it is strange that Ast should not have perceived. Winckelm.'s μὴ πάνυ τι ἀφυὴς ἂν hardly needs discussion. Herm., πρὸς ταῦτα τὰ παραδείγματα καὶ τὰ ἁμαρτήματα τοῦ Λυσίου λόγου βλέπων τις καὶ μὴ χρώμενος ὠφελοῖτο. Socr. then turns to his own discourses, which, as they were given him by inspiration, it is no breach of modesty to prefer to that of Lysias. There was one feature in them, he thinks, which it concerns every speculator on rhetoric to give heed to.

265 ἤστην] So all the MSS and Hermeias. The form occurs frequently in Plato, as inf. 273 B, and twice or three times in Aristoph., as we include or not Aves 19, τὼ δ' οὐκ ἄρ' ἤστην οὐδὲν ἄλλο πλὴν δάκνειν, where Porson prefers ᾔστην, Cobet ἤστην.

Μανίας δέ γε] Socr. had pointed out a glaring omission in the speech of Lysias. The orator had discoursed fluently of Love, but had forgotten to explain what he meant by the term. His own speeches present a favourable contrast in this respect. Not only had he 'compelled his hearers to conceive of Love' under the more general idea of Madness, but by dividing and subdividing, he had determined the particular variety of Madness to which Love corresponds. In order to this he had first adopted the obvious distinction of divine and human, showing that beside the ordinary morbid madness, there was one caused by a divine influence emancipating the soul from the yoke of usage

ΦΑΙ. Πάνυ γε.

ΣΩ. Τῆς δὲ θείας τεττάρων θεῶν τέτταρα μέρη διελόμενοι, μαντικὴν μὲν ἐπίπνοιαν Ἀπόλλωνος θέντες, Διονύσου δὲ τελεστικήν, Μουσῶν δ' αὖ ποιητικήν, τετάρτην δὲ Ἀφροδίτης καὶ Ἔρωτος, ἐρωτικὴν μανίαν ἐφήσαμέν τε ἀρίστην εἶναι, καὶ οὐκ οἶδ' ὅπῃ τὸ ἐρωτικὸν πάθος ἀπεικάζοντες, ἴσως μὲν ἀληθοῦς τινὸς ἐφαπτόμενοι, τάχα δ' ἂν καὶ ἄλλοσε παραφερόμενοι, κεράσαντες οὐ παντάπασιν ἀπίθανον λόγον, μυθικόν τινα ὕμνον προσε- C
παίσαμεν μετρίως τε καὶ εὐφήμως τὸν ἐμόν τε καὶ σὸν δεσπότην Ἔρωτα, ὦ Φαῖδρε, καλῶν παίδων ἔφορον.

ΦΑΙ. Καὶ μάλα ἔμοιγε οὐκ ἀηδῶς ἀκοῦσαι.

ΣΩ. Τόδε τοίνυν αὐτόθεν λάβωμεν, ὡς ἀπὸ τοῦ ψέγειν πρὸς τὸ ἐπαινεῖν ἔσχεν ὁ λόγος μεταβῆναι.

ΦΑΙ. Πῶς δὴ οὖν αὐτὸ λέγεις;

ΣΩ. Ἐμοὶ μὲν φαίνεται τὰ μὲν ἄλλα τῷ ὄντι παιδιᾷ πεπαῖσθαι· τούτων δέ τινων ἐκ τύχης ῥηθέντων δυοῖν

and convention (sup. 252 A, *νομίμων δὲ καὶ εὐσχημόνων, κ.τ.λ.*) This divine Madness he had parcelled into four, &c. Above, p 244 seq

B *τάχα δ' ἄν*] On this use of *ἂν* in coalition with *τάχα*, see the note on 237 C

παραφερόμενοι] Herm., *ἐπειδὴ καὶ τὰς ἀποπτώσεις τοῦ ἔρωτος εἶπε* This passage has evidently an apologetic purpose, though it is not quite clear whether Plato means to apologize for the dubious morality of portions of his *ἐρωτικὸς λόγος*, or only for its high flights of mythical speculation

κεράσαντες] 'having mixed a not unpalatable discourse,' as men mix a *κρατὴρ* for libation

μυθικόν τινα ὕμνον προσεπ.] 'we chanted for the solace of Eros a mythic hymn in strain meet and pious' "*προσεπαίσαμεν* per synesin dictum, idem est quod *προσπαίζοντες ὑμνήσαμεν*" (Stallb.) The verb is sometimes used in the same sense with a dative Plut Erot. c 20, *τὰ μὲν οὖν πολλὰ ποιηταὶ προσπαίζοντες ἐοίκασι τῷ θεῷ γράφειν περὶ αὐτοῦ καὶ ᾄδειν ἐπικωμάζοντες, ὀλίγα δ' εἴρηται μετὰ σπουδῆς αὐτοῖς.* *παίζειν* and its derivatives *παιδιά*, &c., are not unfrequently [illegible] or choral celebrations. Arist Ran. 318, *οἱ μεμυημένοι Ἐνταῦθά που παίζουσιν, οὓς ἔφραζε νῷν, Ἄιδουσι γοῦν τὸν Ἴακχον.* Ib Lysist 700, *ὥστε καχθὲς θἠκάτῃ ποιοῦσα παιγνίαν ἐγώ* (where perhaps *παιδιὰν* should be restored, the Attics usually writing *παίγνιον*, but not *παιγνία*. Later writers seem only to have used *ἔπαιξα παιγνία*, &c., and hence the freq variations in MSS) Plat Crat 406 C, *φιλοπαίσμονες οἱ θεοί* It is more important to observe that in the Timaeus Plato extends the term *παιδιὰ* to all mythical presentments of speculative ideas, especially in Physics, the region, in his view, of probability and plausible conjecture Tim 59 C, *τὴν τῶν εἰκότων μύθων μεταδιώκοντα ἰδέαν, ἣν ὅταν τις ἀναπαύσεως ἕνεκα τοὺς περὶ τῶν ὄντων ἀεὶ καταθέμενος λόγους, τοὺς γενέσεως πέρι διαθεώμενος εἰκότας ἀμεταμέλητον ἡδονὴν κτᾶται, μετρίαν ἂν ἐν τῷ βίῳ παιδιὰν καὶ φρόνιμον ποιοῖτο* This explains Socr.'s meaning, when he declares presently that, *ἐμοὶ μὲν φαίνεται τὰ μὲν ἄλλα τῷ ὄντι παιδιᾷ πεπαῖσθαι*

C *παιδιᾷ πεπαῖσθαι*] Galen gives the non attic *πεπαῖχθαι*

τούτων δὲ τίνων] Equiv. to *ἐν δὲ* [illegible] *τινῶν ἐκ τύχης ῥηθεῖσι δύο τιν'* [illegible]

D εἴδοιν, εἰ αὐτοῖν τὴν δύναμιν τέχνῃ λαβεῖν δύναιτό τις, οὐκ ἄχαρι.

ΦΑΙ. Τίνων δή;

ΣΩ. Εἰς μίαν τε ἰδέαν συνορῶντα ἄγειν τὰ πολλαχῇ

εἴδη ἤτην, ὧν εἴ τις τὴν δύναμιν, κ.τ.λ. 'Among these, so to speak, chance utterances' (alluding to the two speeches) 'there were implied two forms of procedure, of which it were gratifying if one could obtain a clear technical description.' This is Ast's view of this somewhat difficult passage. He says "Genitivi autem *τούτων* . *ῥηθέντων δυοῖν εἰδοῖν* non sunt *duae harum orationum casu quodam dictarum species*, sed objective, quod dicunt, accipiendi sunt *duae species quas invenimus vel conspicimus in his orationibus*, sic enim genitivum a Graecis poni constat ut patrio eum sermone praepositione *an* vel *in* exprimere possimus" (Comm maj. p 515). The genitives *τούτων ῥηθέντων* will thus depend on *εἰδοῖν*, which itself depends virtually on *δύναμιν*, *αὐτοῖν* being interpolated to prevent ambiguity. Those who think the interpretation too subtle, will perhaps be disposed to acquiesce in Ast's earlier view, as shown in his version "horum autem fortuito memoratorum generum, si quis ipsam (*αὐτὴν* ut vulg. pro *αὐτοῖν*) vim arte percipere possit haud ingratum." And so Galen probably understood it, for he gives *εἰδῶν* and *αὐτήν*. Plato *had* alluded to the two processes, without explaining them technically, but rather *ἐκ τύχης*, (paul. sup. *μανίαν γάρ τινα ἐφήσαμεν εἶναι τὸν Ἔρωτα*, and, *μανίας δέ γε εἴδη δύο*, the first being a generalization, the second a 'division'—the very two processes referred to here.) For *τίνων* I had thought of *τοι νῷν*, but I lay no stress upon this conjecture. The 'two forms of procedure' are, according to Herm., the *ὁριστική* and *διαιρετική*, according to Galen, the *συνθετική* and *διαιρετικὴ μέθοδος* respectively. *συναγωγική* and *διαιρετική* would better correspond to Plato's language. Modern interpreters, not very correctly, render *διαιρ.* by "analytic," a term usually applied by the ancients (as pseudo Perictyone, ap. Stob. Anth. i p. 7, *ὅστις ἂν ἀναλῦσαι οἷός ἐστι πάντα γένη ὑπὸ μίαν ἀρχάν*) to the former or generalizing process, which Aristotle denotes by *ἐπαγωγή*. Topic. viii 1. 18, *δι' ἐπαγωγῆς ἀπὸ τῶν καθ' ἕκαστα τὸ καθόλου λαμβάνεται*. 'Collection' and 'division' are the terms which answer most nearly to *συναγωγή* and *διαίρεσις*, and should be used in translating them. The 'divisive' definition is called by Sext. Emp. *ὁ ἐξ ἐπισυνθέσεως ὅρος* (adv. Math. ii 2). The scholastic term is Division, and Abelard has left a treatise under the title of Divisio Divisionum, in which he shows in how many different ways the process may be effected. The Socratic definitions, it may be observed, were founded on a *συναγωγή*, or collection of particulars, the *ἐπακτικοὶ λόγοι* of Aristotle. The method of division, on the other hand, is always attributed to Plato, as by Galen in his work De Hippocrate et Platone. It is in one point of view supplementary to the simpler Socratic process, being designed to fix the 'differentia' of the thing to be defined with the greatest possible exactitude. The emphasis with which it is here introduced favours the belief that it was a novelty in the Athenian schools at the time when the Phaedrus was written or published, though from Xen. Mem. iv 5. 12 we should infer that it had presented itself in an elementary form to Socr. Galen insists particularly on the value of this 'diacritic method' in the classification of diseases, and professes to believe that it was first suggested by the works of Hippocrates, with which he rightly supposes that Plato was familiar. The "Practick" of the physician was "the mistress," according to Galen, to the philosopher's "Theorick." But probably he overrates the obligation of one of his favourite authors to the other.

D *Εἰς μίαν τε ἰδέαν*] He here describes the process from the many to the one. Comp. sup. 249 B, *δεῖ γὰρ ἄνθρωπον ξυνιέναι κατ' εἶδος λεγόμενον, ἐκ πολλῶν ἰόντ' αἰσθήσεων εἰς ἓν λογισμῷ ξυναιρούμενον*. The word *συνορῶντα* is illustrated by Legg. xii 965, *πρὸς τὸ ἓν συντάξασθαι πάντα συνορῶντα*. The first method, says Socr., consists in taking a comprehensive view of the multitude of scattered particulars and bringing them

διεσπαρμένα, ἵν' ἕκαστον ὁριζόμενος δῆλον ποιῇ περὶ οὗ ἂν ἀεὶ διδάσκειν ἐθέλῃ. ὥσπερ τὰ νῦν δὴ περὶ Ἔρωτος, ὃ ἔστιν, ὁρισθέν, εἴτ' εὖ εἴτε κακῶς ἐλέχθη. τὸ γοῦν σαφὲς καὶ τὸ αὐτὸ αὑτῷ ὁμολογούμενον διὰ ταῦτ' ἔσχεν εἰπεῖν ὁ λόγος.

ΦΑΙ. Τὸ δ' ἕτερον δὴ εἶδος τί λέγεις, ὦ Σώκρατες; E

ΣΩ. Τὸ πάλιν κατ' εἴδη δύνασθαι τέμνειν, κατ' ἄρθρα, ᾗ πέφυκε, καὶ μὴ ἐπιχειρεῖν καταγνύναι μέρος μηδέν, κακοῦ μαγείρου τρόπῳ χρώμενον. ἀλλ' ὥσπερ ἄρτι

under one general form or notion, for the purpose of defining and so placing out of doubt the nature of the particular subject you wish to give instruction in. In the next clause τὰ νῦν δὴ is a 'pendent,' ὁρισθὲν an 'absolute' nominative. The latter may be illustrated from Thuc. iv 125, ἀμφοτέροις μὲν δοκοῦν ἀναχωρεῖν . . κυρωθὲν δὲ οὐδὲν . νυκτός τε ἐπιγενομένης, οἱ μὲν Μακεδόνες . ἐχώρουν ἐπ' οἴκου. (See Greg. Corinth p. 38, Ἀττικὸν τὸ εὐθεῖαν ἀντὶ γενικῆς, κ τ λ) Transl., 'as in our recent discourse on Love—it having been defined what Love is—whether correctly or not I do not say, but however that may be, it is certain that the discourse owed to such definition all that it possessed both of clearness and consistency.' For τὸ αὐτὸ αὑτῷ ὁμ. Hirsch. quite wrongly gives ταὐτὸν αὑτῷ.

F. Τὸ πάλιν κατ' εἴδη] On this concise description of the 'diaeretic method,' or way of passing from the One down to the Many, the best commentary is furnished by the dialogues called the Sophist and the Statesman, the former of which at least no student of Plato or of the Greek language should leave unread. The passage is quoted, as far as χρώμενον, by Galen, de Hippocr. et Plat. (v 753, ed. Kuhn, 331, ed. Basil), with the context from ἐμοὶ δὲ φαίνεται incl. With the exception of διατέμνειν for τέμνειν (in which Stobaeus agrees, Eclog. ii c 2) his MSS present no variant from those of Plato. τέμνειν is found in the Bodl. and Paris Δ.

κατ' ἄρθρα, ᾗ πέφυκε, κ τ λ] The importance of a natural and not merely arbitrary system of classification is insisted on by all men of science, modern as well as ancient, however little credit some of them may be disposed to allow to Plato for the use he makes of his principle. The phrase ᾗ πέφυκε is illustrated by Crat. 386 E, δῆλον δὴ ὅτι αὐτὰ αὑτῶν οὐσίαν ἔχοντά τινα βέβαιόν ἐστι τὰ πράγματα, οὐ πρὸς ἡμᾶς οὐδὲ ὑφ' ἡμῶν, ἑλκόμενα ἄνω καὶ κάτω τῷ ἡμετέρῳ φαντάσματι, ἀλλὰ καθ' αὑτὰ πρὸς τὴν αὑτῶν οὐσίαν ἔχοντα ᾗπερ πέφυκε. And again 387, πότερον ἡμῖν τμητέον ἕκαστον ὡς ἂν ἡμεῖς βουλώμεθα καὶ ᾧ ἂν βουληθῶμεν, ἢ ἐὰν μὲν κατὰ τὴν φύσιν βουληθῶμεν ἕκαστον τέμνειν τοῦ τέμνειν τε καὶ τέμνεσθαι καὶ ᾧ πέφυκε, τεμοῦμέν τε καὶ πλέον τι ἡμῖν ἔσται καὶ ὀρθῶς πράξομεν τοῦτο, ἐὰν δὲ παρὰ φύσιν, ἐξαμαρτησόμεθά τε καὶ οὐδὲν πράξομεν. These passages are important, as showing that the method owed its value in Plato's eyes not merely to the ingenuity it calls forth (though on that too he elsewhere insists, Polit. 286 D), but to its power as an engine of positive discovery, and as a means of revealing the thought or plan in Nature which underlies all her phenomena. If we remember this, we shall not wonder at the enthusiasm with which Socr. presently speaks of the able dialectician.

καταγνύναι] "Cic. de Finibus ii 9 26, Hoc est non dividere sed *frangere*. Sen. Epist. 89, § 2, Faciam ergo quod exigis, et philosophiam in partes non in *frusta* dividam. dividi enim illam non concidi utile est" (Ast). In Polit. 262 D, we have specimens of this chopping method held up for avoidance.

μαγείρου] The functions of the ancient μάγειρος seem to have been manifold, including those of the butcher and dissector, as well as those ordinarily assigned to the cook, plain or ornamental. So in the Cyclops of Euripides the κακὸς Ἅιδου μάγειρος slaughters his victims before he roasts or boils them. And in Plutarch,

Euthy 301 d Laws 849

347

τὼ λόγω τὸ μὲν ἄφρον τῆς διανοίας ἕν τι κοινῇ εἶδος
266 *ἐλαβέτην, | ὥσπερ δὲ σώματος ἐξ ἑνὸς διπλᾶ καὶ ὁμ-*
ώνυμα πέφυκε, σκαιά, τὰ δὲ δεξιὰ κληθέντα, οὕτω καὶ
τὸ τῆς παρανοίας ὡς ἓν ἐν ἡμῖν πεφυκὸς εἶδος ἡγησα-
μένω τὼ λόγω, ὁ μὲν τὸ ἐπ' ἀριστερὰ τεμνόμενος μέρος,
πάλιν τοῦτο τέμνων οὐκ ἐπανῆκε, πρὶν ἐν αὐτοῖς ἐφευ-
ρὼν ὀνομαζόμενον σκαιόν τινα ἔρωτα ἐλοιδόρησε μάλ'
ἐν δίκῃ, ὁ δ' εἰς τὰ ἐν δεξιᾷ τῆς μανίας ἀγαγὼν ἡμᾶς,
ὁμώνυμον μὲν ἐκείνῳ, θεῖον δ' αὖ τιν' ἔρωτα ἐφευρών,

Mor 175 D, we read of *βοῦν σφαττόμενον ὑπὸ μαγείρου*

ἀλλ' ὥσπερ ἄρτι τὼ λόγω] Understand *τέμνειν ὥσπερ ἄρτι, κ τ λ.* The two discourses presented each a specimen of diaeresis Each assumed the general idea denoted by madness or aberration of mind, but finding that the idea naturally divided itself into two, either discourse took a moiety for the purpose of further dissection. The *λόγω* are here personified as in 260 E

266 *σώματος ἐξ ἑνὸς διπλᾶ*] Herm, *ὥσπερ ἡ φύσις τισὶ δύο διαστήμασι διεῖλε τὰ ζῷα, τὰ μὲν δεξιά, τὰ δὲ ἀριστερὰ ποιήσασα, καὶ ἑκάτερον τῶν μορίων τοῖς αὐτοῖς ὀνόμασι καλεῖται, οἷον ὀφθαλμὸς καὶ ὀφθαλμός, χεὶρ καὶ χείρ, πλὴν ὅτι ἡ μὲν δεξιά, ἡ δὲ ἀριστερά, οὕτω καὶ αὕτη* (f. *αὐτή*) *ἡ παραφροσύνη καὶ μανία διττὴ οὖσα, ἡ μὲν ἐπὶ τὰ ἀριστερὰ ἡ δὲ ἐπὶ τὰ δεξιὰ ἔνευσεν* This pairwise arrangement in living organisms is alleged here in justification of the dichotomy on which Plato lays so much stress in other dialogues But that *τὸ δίχα τέμνειν*, though in most cases the natural, is not the only legitimate form of diaeresis, he fully admits in Phileb. 16 D, and indeed in the instance here alluded to he had dissected the right-hand moiety of *μανία*, not into two, but into four subdivisions of co ordinate importance Probably Hermeias is in the right when he says that Plato's dichotomies were suggested by the well-known *συστοιχίαι* or tables of contraries devised by the Pythagoreans *ἀπὸ τῶν Πυθαγορείων ὁ Πλάτων ὠφεληθεὶς τὰς συστοιχίας οὕτως ἔλαβεν ἐνταῦθα.*

σκαιά, τὰ δὲ δεξιά] So the Bodl and Stob Polit 291 E, *δυὸ παρεχομένην εἴδη δυοῖν ὀνόμασι, τυραννίδι τὸ δὲ βασιλικῇ*—where, as in the present passage, we find the variant *τὸ μὲν τυραννίδι.* In such cases it is nearly certain that the more idiomatic is the true reading The vulg *σκαιὰ τάδε ἢ δεξιὰ* proves that the idiom puzzled the copyists, and hence their efforts to emend or explain it No doubt rests on the reading in Soph 248, *γένεσιν, τὴν δὲ οὐσίαν χωρίς που διελόμενοι λέγετε.* Inf. 270 D, *ἁπλοῦν ἢ πολυειδές ἐστι*, where some MSS give *πότερον ἁπλοῦν*, doubtless *ex manu interpretis*

τεμνόμενος] The middle is also found Legg 695 C, *διείλετο* (*τὴν ἀρχήν*) *ἑπτὰ μέρη τεμόμενος* (*ὁ Δαρεῖος*) And we have the compound *ἀποτεμόμενος*, Phileb. 42 C. So *διελεῖν* and *διελέσθαι* seem to be used indiscriminately.

οὐκ ἐπανῆκε] The interpp give "non prius destitit," or "remisit" *ἐπανίημι* is used both with and without a case Xen Cyneg vii 1, *ἐπανιέντα τῶν πόνων* ib iv 5, *διωκέτωσαν* (pot *διωκόντων*) *ἐρρωμένως καὶ μὴ ἐπανιεῖσαι.* Stobaeus gives *ἀνῆκε*, which Hirsch is inclined to adopt. But the change is needless, and besides mars the dactylic rhythm of the clause The dissector's efforts were not relaxed until among the parts into which he had divided the left-hand moiety, he detected a left hand or sinister species of Love, as it may be called, which he railed at in terms answering to its demerits There seems to be no necessity for altering *ἐν αὐτοῖς* "Refertur *αὐτοῖς* per synesin ad *τὸ ἐπ' ἀριστερὰ μέρος*, in quo multitudinis notio comprehensa est" (Stallb) The 'synesis' would be a little less harsh if we could read *τεμνόμενον μέρος*, but even so we should rather have expected *αὐτόθι*, 'in the portion in question' The rhythm however is most favourable to the received reading.

[καὶ] προτεινάμενος ἐπῄνεσεν ὡς μεγίστων αἴτιον ἡμῖν B
ἀγαθῶν.

ΦΑΙ. Ἀληθέστατα λέγεις.

ΣΩ. Τούτων δὴ ἔγωγε αὐτός τε ἐραστής, ὦ Φαῖδρε,
τῶν διαιρέσεων καὶ συναγωγῶν, ἵν' οἷός τε ὦ λέγειν τε
καὶ φρονεῖν· ἐάν τέ τιν' ἄλλον ἡγήσωμαι δυνατὸν εἰς ἓν
καὶ ἐπὶ πολλὰ πεφυκόθ' ὁρᾶν, τοῦτον διώκω κατόπισθε
μετ' ἴχνιον ὥστε θεοῖο. καὶ μέντοι καὶ τοὺς δυναμένους
αὐτὸ δρᾶν εἰ μὲν ὀρθῶς ἢ μὴ προσαγορεύω, θεὸς οἶδε,
καλῶ δὲ οὖν μέχρι τοῦδε διαλεκτικούς. τὰ δὲ νῦν παρὰ C
σοῦ τε καὶ Λυσίου μαθόντας εἰπὲ τί χρὴ καλεῖν. ἢ τοῦτο
ἐκεῖνό ἐστιν ἡ λόγων τέχνη, ᾗ Θρασύμαχός τε καὶ οἱ
ἄλλοι χρώμενοι σοφοὶ μὲν αὐτοὶ λέγειν γεγόνασιν, ἄλλους

B προτεινάμενος] 'having held out to view,' 'exhibited,' as an anatomist to his pupils. So ἐπιδεῖξαι is used Sophist. 264 E, πάλιν τοίνυν ἐπιχειρῶμεν, σχίζοντες διχῇ τὸ προτεθὲν γένος, πορεύεσθαι κατὰ τοὐπὶ δεξιὰ ἀεὶ μέρος τοῦ τμηθέντος ἐχόμενοι τῆς τοῦ σοφιστοῦ κοινωνίας, ἕως ἂν αὐτοῦ τὰ κοινὰ πάντα περιελόντες, τὴν οἰκείαν λιπόντες φύσιν ἐπιδείξωμεν μάλιστα μὲν ἡμῖν αὐτοῖς, ἔπειτα δὲ καὶ τοῖς ἐγγυτάτω γένει τῆς τοιαύτης μεθόδου πεφυκόσιν,—a passage exactly parallel to the present. Ib 247 D, σκόπει προτεινομένων ἡμῶν ἆρ' ἐθέλοιεν ἂν δέχεσθαι καὶ ὁμολογεῖν τοιόνδ' εἶναι τὸ ὄν. In the same dialogue, 235 B, we find ἀποφῆναι τὴν ἄγραν—another metaphor for the same thing. Before προτεινάμενος Badh brackets καί, I think rightly. 'When he has found what he seeks, he holds it up to view, and,' &c.

Τούτων δὴ ἔγωγε—φρονεῖν] Socr is not only greatly addicted to these 'divisions' and 'collections' in his own practice, and with a view to his improvement as a speaker and a thinker, but, &c. A like educational effect is attributed to these dialectical exercises in the Politicus, 285 D, 287, where their tediousness and seeming pedantry is justified on the ground that they make men διαλεκτικώτεροι καὶ εὑρετικώτεροι.

εἰς ἓν καὶ ἐπὶ πολλὰ πεφυκόθ'] The best MSS and Stob have πεφυκός, a few πεφυκότα as in the vulg. Stallb πεφυκόθ', which I have adopted. πεφυκὸς may have arisen from the not unfrequent [illegible] of C and Θ.—He whose view embraces both a One and a Many, as they exist in nature (comp. ᾗ πέφυκε and ἓν ἐν ἡμῖν πεφυκός), has for Socr. the greatest attraction—he is prepared 'to follow close behind him as a god.' κατόπισθε and the foll words are not quoted from any existing line of Homer: the nearest is Od v 193, ὁ δ' ἔπειτα μετ' ἴχνια βαῖνε θεοῖο. Heind aptly compares, for the sense, Dion. Hal Rhet (p. 407, Reiske), ἡ γὰρ τέχνη τῆς διαιρέσεως, ὥς φησιν ὁ Πλάτων, διαιρέσεις καὶ συναγωγαί, δεῖξαι τὰ εἴδη πόσα ἐστὶ καὶ πόσας ἔχει τομάς, καὶ πάντα συναγαγεῖν εἰς ταὐτό· τοῦτο γάρ ἐστι διαιρέσεως τέχνη, ἓν πολλά, πολλὰ ἕν.

C διαλεκτικούς] In antithesis to ἀντιλογικοὺς or ἐριστικούς, who refuse to see the Many in the One. Repub v. 451, ἡ γενναία, ἦν δ' ἐγώ, ὦ Γλαύκων, ἡ δύναμις τῆς ἀντιλογικῆς τέχνης. Τί δή; Ὅτι, εἶπον, δοκοῦσί μοι εἰς αὐτὴν καὶ ἄκοντες πολλοὶ ἐμπίπτειν, καὶ οἴεσθαι οὐκ ἐρίζειν ἀλλὰ διαλέγεσθαι, διὰ τὸ μὴ δύνασθαι κατ' εἴδη διαιρούμενοι τὸ λεγόμενον ἐπισκοπεῖν, ἀλλὰ κατ' αὐτὸ τὸ ὄνομα διώκειν τοῦ λεχθέντος τὴν ἐναντίωσιν, ἔριδι, οὐ διαλέκτῳ πρὸς ἀλλήλους χρώμενοι. This description applies to Zeno and his followers, and to some of the minor Socratic sects, especially the Megaric and Cynic.

τὰ δὲ νῦν] Socr proceeds ironically to inquire whether the art of dialectic as he had described it was the art professed and taught by the rhetors, Lysias and Thrasymachus.

τε ποιοῦσιν, οἳ ἂν δωροφορεῖν αὐτοῖς ὡς βασιλεῦσιν ἐθέλωσιν;

ΦΑΙ. Βασιλικοὶ μὲν ἄνδρες, οὐ μὲν δὴ ἐπιστήμονές γε ὧν ἐρωτᾷς. ἀλλὰ τοῦτο μὲν τὸ εἶδος ὀρθῶς ἔμοιγε δοκεῖς καλεῖν, διαλεκτικὸν καλῶν· τὸ δὲ ῥητορικὸν δοκεῖ μοι διαφεύγειν ἔθ' ἡμᾶς.

D ΣΩ. Πῶς φής, καλόν πού τι ἂν εἴη ὃ τούτων ἀπολειφθὲν ὅμως τέχνῃ λαμβάνεται; πάντως δ' οὐκ ἀτιμαστέον αὐτὸ σοί τε καὶ ἐμοί. λεκτέον δὲ τί μέντοι καὶ ἔστι τὸ λειπόμενον τῆς ῥητορικῆς.

ΦΑΙ. Καὶ μάλα που συχνά, ὦ Σώκρατες, τά γ' ἐν τοῖς βιβλίοις τοῖς περὶ λόγων τέχνης γεγραμμένοις.

ΣΩ. [Καὶ] καλῶς γ' ὑπέμνησας. προοίμιον μὲν οἶμαι πρῶτον ὡς δεῖ τοῦ λόγου λέγεσθαι ἐν ἀρχῇ. ταῦτα λέγεις

E —ἦ γάρ;—τὰ κομψὰ τῆς τέχνης;

ΦΑΙ. Ναί.

ΣΩ. Δεύτερον δὲ δὴ διήγησίν τινα μαρτυρίας τ' ἐπ'

δωροφορεῖν] Alluding of course to the mercenary character of the paid teachers of rhetoric

ὡς βασιλεῦσιν] Hesiod, ap. Plat. Rep. 390 E, *δῶρα θεοὺς πείθει, δῶρ' αἰδοίους βασιλῆας*. Arist. Av. 507, *εἴ τις καὶ βασιλεύοι Ἐπὶ τῶν σκήπτρων ἐκάθητ' ὄρνις, μετέχων ὅ τι δωροδοκοίη*. Some codd. have *δορυφορεῖν*, which would be good if *δωροφορεῖν* were not better.

Βασιλικοὶ μὲν ἄνδρες] The codd. all give *ἄνδρες*, which the Zur. retains. But in this and similar cases the MSS. carry no weight. Stallb. makes *ἄνδρες* the predicate, in which I cannot agree. The men are like kings, it is true, says Phaedr., but for all their grandeur they know nothing of the methods you have explained. To which Socr. rejoins that rhetoric must be a very fine thing indeed, if it can be taught as an art without any admixture of dialectic. What *is* rhetoric, what remains of it, when thus denuded? Phaedr. replies that there is a great deal indeed left, if we take into account all that is written about it in the current treatises or *τέχναι*.

D [*καὶ*] *καλῶς γ' ὑπέμνησας*] I have followed Stallb. and Hirsch. in bracketing *καί*, which has no particular force. Socr. thanks Phaedr. for reminding him, and proceeds to give a list of the *κομψὰ τῆς τέχνης*—the niceties or subtleties (technicalities, we should say) of the Rhetorician, to which he presumes that Phaedr. alludes. Comp. Cic. Orat. 12. 39, Quo magis sunt Herodotus Thucydidesque admirabiles, quorum aetas, cum in eorum tempora, quos nominavi, incidisset, longissime tamen ipsi a talibus *deliciis* vel potius ineptiis afuerunt. He had mentioned Thrasymachus, Gorgias, and Theodorus, "quorum satis *arguta* multa, sed ut modo primumque nascentia, minuta." These *κομψὰ τῆς τέχνης* are the *ῥητορικὰ κεφάλαια* of later technographers—the heads or main divisions of a speech.

E *διήγησίν τινα*] A so called enarration (statement of facts), supported by evidence. *τεκμήρια* is explained by the author of the Rhet. ad Alex. c. 10, *τεκμήρια δ' ἐστὶν ὅσα ἂν ἐναντίως ᾖ πεπραγμένα τῷ περὶ οὗ ὁ λόγος, καὶ ὅσα ὁ λόγος αὐτὸς ἑαυτῷ ἐναντιοῦται· τῶν γὰρ ἀκουόντων οἱ πλεῖστοι τοῖς συμβαίνουσι περὶ τὸν λόγον ἢ τὴν πρᾶξιν ἐναντιώμασι τεκμαίρονται μηδὲν ὑγιὲς εἶναι μήτε τῶν λεγομένων μήτε τῶν πραττομένων*. This kind of indirect evidence would take the

αὐτῇ, τρίτον τεκμήρια, τέταρτον εἰκότα· καὶ πίστωσιν οἶμαι καὶ ἐπιπίστωσιν λέγειν τόν γε βέλτιστον λογοδαίδαλον Βυζάντιον ἄνδρα.

ΦΑΙ. Τὸν χρηστὸν λέγεις Θεόδωρον;

ΣΩ. Τί μήν; καὶ ἔλεγχόν γε καὶ | ἐπεξέλεγχον ὡς 267 ποιητέον ἐν κατηγορίᾳ τε καὶ ἀπολογίᾳ. τὸν δὲ κάλλιστον Πάριον Εὔηνον εἰς μέσον οὐκ ἄγομεν, ὃς ὑποδήλωσίν

form, ψεύδεται ὁ δεῖνα—τεκμήριον δέ—οὐ γὰρ ἂν τάδε ἢ τάδε ἐποίησεν ἢ εἶπεν Ibid 8 3, εἰκὸς μὲν οὖν ἐστίν, οὗ λεγομένου παραδείγματα ἐν ταῖς διανοίαις ἔχουσιν οἱ ἀκούοντες, κ τ λ εἰκότα are therefore arguments drawn from the general experience of mankind, τεκμήρια from the known antecedents of an individual. Whether this is the meaning of the term here it is impossible to say, but it seems probable that the author quoted has preserved in this, as in other instances, the traditions of the more ancient schools. A different explanation of τεκμήρια is suggested by Ammonius, p 127, Valck. (quoted in Spengel, Artt Scriptt p 117), σημεῖον καὶ τεκμήριον διαφερει 'Αντίφων ἐν τῇ τέχνῃ, τὰ παρῳχημένα σημείοις πιστοῦσα, τὰ δὲ μέλλοντα τεκμηρίοις.

πίστωσιν—καὶ ἐπιπίστωσιν] The distinction is explained Rhet ad Alex 8, εἰσὶ δὲ δύο τρόποι τῶν πίστεων γίνονται γὰρ αἱ μὲν ἐξ αὐτῶν τῶν λόγων καὶ τῶν πράξεων καὶ τῶν ἀνθρώπων, αἱ δ' ἐπίθετοι τοῖς λεγομένοις ἢ πραττομένοις τὰ μὲν γὰρ εἰκότα καὶ παραδείγματα καὶ τεκμήρια καὶ ἐνθυμήματα καὶ γνῶμαι καὶ τὰ σημεῖα καὶ οἱ ἔλεγχοι πίστεις ἐξ αὐτῶν τῶν λόγων καὶ τῶν ἀνθρώπων καὶ τῶν πραγμάτων εἰσίν, ἐπίθετοι δὲ μαρτυρίαι ὅρκοι βάσανος Here ἐπίθετοι πίστεις seem equivalent to the ἐπιπίστωσις of the text

λογοδαίδαλον] Cicero refers to this expression in the Orator, 1 1, Theodorum Byzantium, multosque alios quos λογοδαιδάλους appellat in Phaedro Socrates It denotes a master of rhetorical artifice, a 'cunning speech wright,' and refers doubtless to the multiplicity and subtlety of his rules of art By ἔλεγχος καὶ ἐπεξέλεγχος a distinction analogous to that between πίστωσις and ἐπιπίστωσις is probably meant 'proof or confutation primary and secondary,' or 'subsidiary' What kind of πίστις is technical [illegible]

quite clear—probably a *reductio ad absurdum*. Comp Arist Rhet. ii. 22. 14, ἔστι γὰρ τῶν ἐνθυμημάτων εἴδη δύο τὰ μὲν γὰρ δεικτικά ἐστιν ὅτι ἔστιν ἢ οὐκ ἔστιν, τὰ δὲ ἐλεγκτικά καὶ διαφέρει ὥσπερ ἐν τοῖς διαλεκτικοῖς ἔλεγχος καὶ συλλογισμός. ἔστι δὲ τὸ μὲν δεικτικὸν ἐνθύμημα τὸ ἐξ ὁμολογουμένων συνάγειν, τὸ δὲ ἐλεγκτικὸν τὸ τὰ ἀνομολογούμενα συνάγειν, with the instances given in the Rhet ad Alex 14 2, all of which involve inconsistency or contradiction Thus to prove an alibi would, according to this author, be an ἔλεγχος, or in a case of alleged robbery, to show that the article said to have been carried away was too heavy for the thief to lift. The inventions of Theodorus are enumerated by Aristotle, Rhet. iii 13 5· ἔσται οὖν, ἄν τις ταῦτα διαιρῇ, ὅπερ ἐποίουν οἱ περὶ Θεόδωρον, διήγησις ἕτερον καὶ ἐπιδιήγησις καὶ προδιήγησις καὶ ἔλεγχος καὶ ἐπεξέλεγχος (al ἐπέλεγχος) Aristotle himself distinguishes between διηγεῖσθαι and παραδιηγεῖσθαι, ib. 16 5 A very singular technical term is attributed to a Theodorus (possibly him of Byzantium) by the author of the treatise περὶ ὕψους, § 5 5 τούτῳ παράκειται τρίτον τι κακίας εἶδος ἐν τοῖς παθητικοῖς, ὅπερ ὁ Θεόδωρος παρένθυρσον ἐκάλει ἔστι δὲ πάθος ἄκαιρον καὶ κενόν, ἔνθα μὴ δεῖ πάθους, κ τ λ

267 Πάριον Εὔηνον] This sophist-poet is named as living *temp* Socr in Phaed 60 D, Apol 20 B His poetical fragments are collected in Bergk, Poet Lyr p 436 The present is, I believe, the only passage in which he is mentioned among the technographers, though he is probably included tacitly by the author of the Rhet. ad Alex (1. 16) in his sweeping censure of the 'Parian Sophists' See Cope, Journal of Phil iii 258 seq Plato's tone in speaking of Evenus is always one of mock-respect Comp σοφὸς γὰρ ἀνὴρ with Apol and Phaed. l. l. His elegiac remains are not desti-

τε πρῶτος εὗρε καὶ παρεπαίνους; οἱ δ' αὐτὸν καὶ παραψόγους φασὶν ἐν μέτρῳ λέγειν, μνήμης χάριν· σοφὸς γὰρ ἀνήρ. Τισίαν δὲ Γοργίαν τε ἐάσομεν εὕδειν, οἳ πρὸ τῶν ἀληθῶν τὰ εἰκότα εἶδον ὡς τιμητέα μᾶλλον, τά τε αὖ σμικρὰ μεγάλα καὶ τὰ μεγάλα σμικρὰ φαίνεσθαι ποιοῦσι διὰ ῥώμην λόγου, καινά τε ἀρχαίως τά τ' ἐναντία και-
B νῶς, συντομίαν τε λόγων καὶ ἄπειρα μήκη περὶ πάντων ἀνεῦρον; ταῦτα δὲ ἀκούων ποτέ μου Πρόδικος ἐγέλασε,

tute of point and neatness, and some of his γνῶμαι have been much quoted, e g a line, called "iambic" by Hermeias, Ἢ δέος ἢ λύπη παῖς πατρὶ πάντα βίον. —ὑποδήλωσιν, explained by the verb from which it comes Arist Thesm 1011, ἀλλά μοι Σημεῖον ὑπεδήλωσε Περσεὺς ἐκδραμών, Ὅτι δεῖ με γίγνεσθ' Ἀνδρομέδαν—'telegraphed to me,' 'conveyed a secret intimation' Hence the substantive may mean 'hint,' 'insinuation,' 'covert allusion,' as of one who "just hints a fault, and hesitates dislike." παρέπαινος and παράψογος may be varieties of ὑποδήλωσις, but as the words nowhere recur, it is impossible to be quite sure of this 'Indirect compliment' or 'censure' seems to express what is meant by the terms. παράψογος answers to our 'side-thrust' Mr Cope doubts whether the metrical παράψογοι of the text were in the nature of precepts or examples. The latter would accord best with the words of Plato, and, I apprehend, with the practice of the schools, for, the metre apart, there was nothing new in furnishing learners with pattern instances of the different rhetorical σχήματα.

Τισίαν δὲ Γοργίαν τε, κ τ λ] Gorgias was accompanied by his reputed master Tisias, on the occasion of his visit to Athens, A B P I They are here made jointly responsible for the opinion that to the orator the Probable is of more value than the True, and also, it would seem, for the σχηματισμοὶ which follow A parallel passage is quoted from Isocrates, Paneg p 12 c (written B.C 380) A comparison of the two illustrates the difference of style in the two authors ἐπειδὴ δ' οἱ λόγοι τοιαύτην ἔχουσι τὴν φύσιν, ὥσθ' οἷόν τ' εἶναι περὶ τῶν αὐτῶν πολλαχῶς ἐξηγήσασθαι, καὶ τά τε μεγάλα ταπεινὰ ποιῆσαι καὶ τοῖς μικροῖς μέγεθος περιθεῖναι, καὶ τὰ παλαιὰ καινῶς διελθεῖν καὶ περὶ τῶν νεωστὶ γεγενημένων ἀρχαίως εἰπεῖν, κ τ λ Possibly some similar vaunt had occurred in one of the public ἐπιδείξεις of Gorgias, known both to Isocrates and Plato. In the Vitae X Rhet (838 F) μικρὰ μεγάλα ποιεῖν τὰ δὲ μεγάλα μικρὰ is given as Isocrates' definition of Rhetoric The words καινά τ' ἀρχαίως τά τ' ἐναντία καινῶς seem to stand in no regular constructional relation either to those which precede or to those which follow Heind supposes an ellipse of λέγουσι or some equivalent verb, but does not conceal his suspicion that the text is faulty Ast, on the other hand, joins ἀρχαίως and καινῶς with φαίνεσθαι, adding "fit enim saepenumero ut adverbia loco adjectivorum ponantur" In his larger commentary this explanation is not repeated, nor is any other substituted for it Stallb would supply λέγειν διδάσκουσι, which may be Plato's meaning, though one sees not how these words can be "understood from the foregoing ποιοῦσι διὰ ῥώμην λόγου" The governing verb, it seems to me, should rather be supplied from the sequel for it is not to be supposed that the text is defective, no insertion being conceivable which would not spoil the rhythm of the passage It is as if Plato had meant after καινῶς, to add συντομώτατά τε λέγειν καὶ εἰς μῆκος ἀνεῦρον, instead of the accusatives he actually uses The meaning of the words is suggested by the quotation from Isocrates, who understands by καινά, τὰ νεωστὶ γεγενημένα (more properly, things strange and novel), which the orator was to dignify by the use of antique phrases and allusions, while τἀναντία, i.e. τὰ ἀρχαῖα, things trite and stale, were to be enlivened by a novelty of treatment, the καινολογία with which Dion Hal tells us that Gorgias used to "astonish the vulgar" (De Lysia, p 458, Reiske)

καὶ μόνος αὐτὸς εὑρηκέναι ἔφη ὧν δεῖ λόγων τέχνῃ· δεῖν δὲ οὔτε μακρῶν οὔτε βραχέων, ἀλλὰ μετρίων.

ΦΑΙ. Σοφώτατά γε, ὦ Πρόδικε.

ΣΩ. Ἱππίαν δὲ οὐ λέγομεν; οἶμαι γὰρ ἂν σύμψηφον αὐτῷ καὶ τὸν Ἠλεῖον ξένον γενέσθαι.

ΦΑΙ. Τί δ' οὔ;

ΣΩ. Τὰ δὲ Πώλου πῶς φράσωμεν αὖ μουσεῖα λό-

For συντομίαν τε λόγων, κ τ λ, comp. the boast of Gorgias in Gorg 449 C with Protag 334 E, where Socr attributes similar accomplishments to the Abderite professor

B ὧν δεῖ λόγων τέχνῃ] The MSS. have τέχνην, but the sense seems to demand τέχνῃ, the reading of Steph The meaning is not, 'those speeches which art wants,' but rather, 'what speeches, on principles of art, are right and desirable' τέχνῃ is quasi-adverbial, as 261 B, γράφεται τέχνῃ C, ὁ τέχνῃ τοῦτο δρῶν. D, λέγοντα οὐκ ἴσμεν τέχνῃ, and elsewhere

Σοφώτατά γε, ὦ Πρόδικε] Phaedr evidently perceives Socr's ironical drift, in repeating the platitude of Prodicus Ast, who represents Phaedrus as an idiot, supposes the exclamation to be uttered in good faith Prodicus and Hippias probably agreed in jealousy of the Sicilian school and dislike of their meretricious ornaments, while Plato seems to have entertained an impartial contempt for the minute pedantry of Prodicus and the frothy magniloquence of Gorgias

Τὰ δὲ Πώλου—εὐεπείας] Polus not only invented a number of technical terms, but borrowed others from his friend or master Licymnius. What these latter were, Aristotle tells us, Rhet iii 13 5, where he condemns the use of unnecessary technical distinctions δεῖ δὲ εἶδός τι λέγοντα καὶ διαφορὰν ὄνομα τίθεσθαι· εἰ δὲ μή, γίγνεται κενὸν καὶ ληρῶδες, οἷον Λικύμνιος ποιεῖ ἐν τῇ τέχνῃ, ἐπούρωσιν ὀνομάζων καὶ ἀποπλάνησιν καὶ ὄζους The characteristic of this school seems to have been εὐέπεια—*fine* in contradistinction to accurate writing, the ὀρθοέπεια on which Protagoras prided himself, and it was in order to the creation of such an ornate style that these technicalities were devised Such is the received view of the meaning of this passage, which however present [illegible]

scend to particulars First among these is the phrase μουσεῖα λόγων This, Heind thinks, was the title of a work by Polus, but he grounds his opinion on a misunderstood Schol of Hermeias on the words μ λ. ἐκεῖνος γὰρ (sc Polus) ἐξεῦρε τὰ πάρισα, διὸ καὶ μουσεῖα λόγων ἐκάλεσεν (sc Plato) ἐπειδὴ ἐδόκει τῇ καλλιλεξίᾳ πάνυ [κατακόρως?] κοσμεῖν τὸν λόγον Had Heim meant that Polus gave the name to his own figures of speech, ἐκάλει, not ἐκάλεσεν, would have been used. It is far more likely that the name is given in banter by Plato, but whether to the figures of speech enumerated, or to the book treating of them may fairly be doubted The word μουσεῖον, originally a τέμενος of the Muses (inf. p 278 B), seems already to have acquired secondary meanings. Aeschines, c Timarch p 2, speaks of μουσεῖα, small chapels of the Muses, as existing in every public school and hence μουσεῖον came to mean figuratively a haunt of learned or refined leisure, as when the comic poet called Athens the μουσεῖον Ἑλλάδος In accordance with this view Spengel renders μουσεῖα λόγ *Tummelplätze von Λόγοι* —'gymnasia,' 'exercise grounds' In Euripides χελιδόνων μουσεῖα is said of an ivy bush, as a haunt or concert-room of twittering swallows; and in the Helena, v 1106, μουσεῖα happily expresses the leafy bower of the nightingale. To translate the word by 'repository,' as of curiosities, &c, would involve an anachronism, as that sense is, I apprehend, of modern origin The same false association is suggested by Ast's "Blumenlesen," otherwise not an unhappy rendering In any case the metaphor is obscure, but that the καλλιλεξία, the affected prettinesses of Polus, is what Plato meant to ridicule, there is, I think, no reasonable doubt These he calls, with an affectation parodying that of the [illegible] 'shrines of

c γων, ὡς διπλασιολογίαν καὶ γνωμολογίαν καὶ εἰκονολογίαν, ὀνομάτων τε Λικυμνίων ἃ ἐκείνῳ ἐδωρήσατο πρὸς ποίησιν εὐεπείας;

ΦΑΙ. Πρωταγόρεια δέ, ὦ Σώκρατες, οὐκ ἦν μέντοι τοιαῦτ' ἄττα;

ΣΩ. Ὀρθοέπειά γέ τις, ὦ παῖ, καὶ ἄλλα πολλὰ καὶ

learned speech' Mr Cope's view (Journ. Phil. iii. 253 and note), that the words refer to a "collection of speeches for the use of Polus' school, similar to Gorgias' *laudes et vituperationes*, and Protagoras' *communes loci*, in which these new figures of speech were illustrated," does not, I confess, seem to me so probable as that of the old Greek commentator, though, of course, τὰ πάρισα or παρισώσεις are not the only figures to which the words apply. I think also with Spengel, that in the word λόγων itself there may be a mocking allusion to the termination -λογια in διπλασιολογία, &c. Comp 272, βραχυλογίας καὶ ἐλεινολογίας . . ἑκάστων τε ὅσ' ἂν εἴδη μάθῃ λόγων. Mr Cope differs from me further in retaining Bekker's ὃς for the ὡς of the Bodl. In this I should be glad to agree with him, if I could reconcile myself to the ellipse of εὗρεν which he supposes, for the use of ὡς in the sense of οἷον, 'veluti,' is certainly not common. If ὃς were established, I should be strongly moved to accept the conj. of Cornarius, and read προσεποίησεν, taking εὐεπείας as an acc. pl. with the gen. ὀνομάτων, 'nominum venustates' προσεποίησεν might, I conceive, mean 'annexed,' 'added,' i. e. to the previously existing rhetorical figures: it certainly could not have the meaning 'arrogavit' (as if we had found προσεποιήσατο), as Stallb., who adopts the conj. in his last ed., seems to think. By διπλασιολογία Stallb. supposes that Polus meant τὰ πάρισα, that is, balanced clauses in which the changes are rung on a couple of words, as in the well-known passage of Gorg. 448 c, ἐκ τῶν ἐμπειριῶν ἐμπείρως εὑρημέναι, κ.τ.λ. The explanation of the Schol. has, at any rate, the merit of simplicity: οἷον τὸ φεῦ, φεῦ. He might have quoted the οὐκ ἔστιν, οὐκ ἔστιν ὅπως ἡμάρτετε of Demosthenes. The next word, γνωμολογία (comp. γνωμοτυπικός, Ar. Eq. 1378), seems to mean the 'style sententious' (ὡς τὸ "δεινὸν ἡ πονηρία," Schol.), while εἰκονολογία may denote the free use of metaphor or simile, as when Gorgias called vultures 'living tombs.' The 'Licymnian names' are explained by the passage quoted from the Rhetoric, which is carefully discussed by Mr. Cope, l. l. p. 255. The genitive must depend on μουσεῖα, and ἐδωρήσατο is constructed with Λικύμνιος, understood from the derivative adj. For Λικυμνίων Ast would read Λικυμνείων, of which there is the trace in the corrupt reading of one MS λυκυμνείων. But Lobeck, the great authority on such questions, considers Λικύμνιος equally legitimate. "Possessivorum quae a propriis in -ιος exeuntibus derivantur, terminatio duplex est, una omnibus partibus expressa, Ναυπλίειος, Ἡλίειος, altera concisior, δόλος Ναύπλιος, Phalar. Ep. ix. τὸ Ἥλιον, τὰ Ἥλια." Pathol. Serm. Gr. I. 310.

c εὐεπείας] Dion. Hal. de Isocr. p. 538, ὁ γὰρ ἀνὴρ οὗτος (sc. Ἰσοκράτης) τὴν εὐέπειαν ἐκ παντὸς διώκει, καὶ τοῦ γλαφυρῶς λέγειν στοχάζεται μᾶλλον ἢ τοῦ ἀφελῶς.

Πρωταγόρεια — μέντοι τοιαῦτ' ἄττα] 'were there not, as I fancy there were, some similar coinages of Protagoras?' For μέντοι in interrogat. see above, 261 c.

Ὀρθοέπεια] 'correct diction,' the title, as some think, of a grammatical work of Protagoras, whom we know from Crat. 391 c to have speculated upon the ὀρθότης ὀνομάτων. It appears certain that Protagoras wrote a work on Grammar, in which the moods of verbs and genders of nouns were enumerated, perhaps for the first time. See Frei Quaestt. Protagg. p. 130 fol., Spengel, Artt. Script. p. 40, and Cope, Journ. Phil. iii. 48. The explanation of Hermeias is different. He supposes the word to denote the simple and straightforward style which Protagoras adopted in preference to the affected Sicilian rhetoric: ὀρθοέπειά γέ τις· τουτέστι, κυριολεξία· διὰ γὰρ τῶν κυρίων ὀνομάτων μετήρχετο ὁ Πρωταγόρας τὸν λόγον, καὶ οὐ διὰ παραβολῶν

καλά. τῶν γε μὴν οἰκτρογόων ἐπὶ γῆρας καὶ πενίαν ἑλκομένων λόγων κεκρατηκέναι τέχνῃ μοι φαίνεται τὸ τοῦ Χαλκηδονίου σθένος. ὀργίσαι τε αὖ πολλοὺς ἅμα δεινὸς ἀνὴρ γέγονε, καὶ πάλιν ὠργισμένοις ἐπᾴδων κηλεῖν, ὡς D
ἔφη· διαβάλλειν τε καὶ ἀπολύσασθαι διαβολὰς ὁθενδὴ κράτιστος. τὸ δὲ δὴ τέλος τῶν λόγων κοινῇ πᾶσιν ἔοικε συνδεδογμένον εἶναι, ᾧ τινὲς μὲν ἐπάνοδον, ἄλλοι δὲ ἄλλο τίθενται ὄνομα.

ΦΑΙ. Τὸ ἐν κεφαλαίῳ ἕκαστα λέγεις ὑπομνῆσαι ἐπὶ τελευτῆς τοὺς ἀκούοντας περὶ τῶν εἰρημένων.

ΣΩ. Ταῦτα λέγω, καὶ εἴ τι σὺ ἄλλο ἔχεις εἰπεῖν λόγων τέχνης πέρι.

ΦΑΙ. Σμικρά γε καὶ οὐκ ἄξια λέγειν.

ΣΩ. Ἐῶμεν δὴ τά γε σμικρά· ταῦτα δὲ | ὑπ' αὐγὰς 268
μᾶλλον ἴδωμεν, τίνα καί ποτ' ἔχει τὴν τῆς τέχνης δύναμιν

καὶ ἐπιθέτων. This sense of the word certainly agrees better with that which it bears in Dion Hal de Demosth p 1035, where Plato is called the κανὼν ὀρθοεπείας, in reference to his purity of style Besides, if the ὀρθοέπεια of Protagoras was purely grammatical, we should hardly expect to find it noticed in the Phaedrus. On the whole, I incline to the opinion that the ὀρθότης ὀνομάτων of the Cratylus was something different from the ὀρθοέπεια of this passage What the ἄλλα πολλὰ καὶ καλὰ may have been, we know not.

τῶν γε μήν] Thrasymachus was a master of the art of composing pathetic commonplaces, applicable to the sorrows of age and penury This meaning Plato has purposely wrapt in pompous poetic diction, in mockery of the 'mighty man of Chalcedon' The dactylic, or rather choriambic, rhythm of the passage is remarkable For ἑλκομένων ἐπὶ comp inf 271, εἵλκυσεν ἐπὶ τὴν τῶν λόγων τέχνην τὸ πρόσφορον Spengel's notion that ἐπὶ is separated from ἑλκομένων by tmesis, though ingenious, is untenable, as the middle ἐφέλκεσθαι could bear no sense suitable to the passage, as the act ἐφέλκειν would Possibly allusion is made to the practice of bringing into court the aged and destitute, young children, &c Hermi, ὁ γὰρ Χαλκηδόνιος, τουτέστιν, ὁ Θρασύμ[illegible] οἶκτον ἐγεῖραι τὸν δικαστήν, καὶ ἐπισπᾶσθαι ἔλεον, γῆρας, πενίαν, τέκνα ἀποδυρόμενον (sic Speng, codd ἀποδυρόμενα) For an instance of a moving tale of age and penury, accompanied by the appearance of their victim in person, see Aeschines adv Timarchum, c 104, Bekk From Aristotle, Rhet. iii, 1, we learn that Thrasymachus wrote Ἔλεοι, apparently a treatise, accompanied with examples, on the best mode of exciting compassion To this Plato alludes, and from the sequel we are tempted to conjecture that Thrasymachus may have composed a similar work on the passion of anger, unless indeed his ἔλεοι had a wider scope than their name would indicate.

D ὁθενδή] 'on any or no grounds' i e under circumstances most unfavourable to himself ἀπολύεσθαι διαβολήν, to wipe off an aspersion, is a common phrase

ἄλλο—ὄνομα] According to the interp the terms omitted are ἐπίλογος or ἀνακεφαλαίωσις ἐπάνοδος, 'recapitulation,' is recognized by Arist Rhet iii 13. 3

268. ὑπ' αὐγάς] See Ruhnken on Tim. Lex, in v, and add to his instances Eur. Hec 1136, Pors, ᾖνουν θ', ὑπ' αὐγὰς τούσδε λεύσσουσαι πέπλους, Socr proposes to submit the wares of Thrasymachus to a searching scrutiny, holding them up to the light, as purchasers in the [illegible] market hold the [illegible] offered

ΦΑΙ. Καί μάλα ἐῤῥωμένην, ὦ Σώκρατες, ἔν γε δὴ
πλήθους συνόδοις.

ΣΩ. Ἔχει γάρ ἀλλ', ὦ δαιμόνιε, ἰδὲ καὶ σὺ εἰ ἄρα
καὶ σοὶ φαίνεται διεστηκὸς αὐτῶν τὸ ἠτρίον ὥσπερ ἐμοί.

ΦΑΙ. Δείκνυ μόνον.

ΣΩ. Εἰπὲ δή μοι· εἴ τις προσελθὼν τῷ ἑταίρῳ σου
Ἐρυξιμάχῳ ἢ τῷ πατρὶ αὐτοῦ Ἀκουμενῷ εἴποι ὅτι Ἐγὼ
ἐπίσταμαι τοιαῦτ' ἄττα σώμασι προσφέρειν, ὥστε θερμαί-
B νειν τ' ἐὰν βούλωμαι καὶ ψύχειν, καὶ ἐὰν μὲν δόξῃ μοι,
ἐμεῖν ποιεῖν, ἐὰν δ' αὖ, κάτω διαχωρεῖν, καὶ ἄλλα πάμ-
πολλα τοιαῦτα· καὶ ἐπιστάμενος αὐτὰ ἀξιῶ ἰατρικὸς εἶναι
καὶ ἄλλον ποιεῖν ᾧ ἂν τὴν τούτων ἐπιστήμην παραδῶ·
τί ἂν οἴει ἀκούσαντας εἰπεῖν;

ΦΑΙ. Τί γε ἄλλο ἢ ἐρέσθαι εἰ προσεπίσταται καὶ
οὕστινας δεῖ καὶ ὁπότε ἕκαστα τούτων ποιεῖν, καὶ μέχρι
ὁπόσου;

ΣΩ. Εἰ οὖν εἴποι ὅτι Οὐδαμῶς· ἀλλ' ἀξιῶ τὸν ταῦτα
C παρ' ἐμοῦ μαθόντα αὐτὸν οἷόν τ' εἶναι ποιεῖν ἃ ἐρωτᾷς;

ΦΑΙ Εἴποιεν ἄν, οἶμαι, ὅτι μαίνεται ἄνθρωπος, καὶ
ἐκ βιβλίου ποθὲν ἀκούσας ἢ περιτυχὼν φαρμακίοις ἰατρὸς
οἴεται γεγονέναι, οὐδὲν ἐπαΐων τῆς τέχνης.

for sale, in order to ascertain whether the texture is sound or defective

διεστηκὸς—τὸ ἠτρίον] 'if they show the weft' is, I believe, the corresponding English phrase This would be the case, if the warp (ἠτρίον) had διαστήματα, gaps or faults in its texture The metaph is preserved in δείκνυ μόνον.

τῷ ἑταίρῳ σου] Phaedr and Eryximachus are together in the house of Callias (Protag 315 c), and at Agathon's table in the Symposium For Acumenus, see the commencement of this dial.

B κάτω διαχωρεῖν] Hippocrates uses διαχωρεῖν and ὑποχωρεῖν indifferently of the excretions Aphorism 7 67, τὰ διὰ τῆς κύστιος διαχωρέοντα ὁρῆν δεῖ, εἰ οἷα τοῖς ὑγιαίνουσι ὑποχωρέεται Xen Anab VIII 20, καὶ ἤμουν καὶ κάτω διεχώρει αὐτοῖς Here διαχωρεῖν is probably transitive, as freq in the medical writers

C αὐτόν] 'of himself,' i e. 'unassisted,' or, as we say, 'by the light of nature.' W

αὐτοὺς παρ' ἑαυτῶν

Εἴποιεν ἄν] MSS εἴποι But I have little doubt that Plato wrote εἴποιεν, as Steph conj. The instances adduced in defence of the MS reading are not in point The following ἂν or preceding εἴποι would account for the error in transcription. εἴποι ἂν Ἐρυξίμαχός τε καὶ Ἀκουμενὸς would be good Greek, but εἴποι ἂν without a case cannot mean 'they would say'

περιτυχὼν φαρμακίοις] 'having picked up a nostrum or two' Compare Dryden's invective against the 'apothecary tribe,'

"From files a random recipe they take,
And many deaths of one prescription make"

To John Dryden, Esq

Sext Emp Math II 41, ἀλλ' ὃν λόγον ἔχει φαρμακοπώλης πρὸς ἰατρόν, τοῦτον

ΣΩ. Τί δ' εἰ Σοφοκλεῖ αὖ προσελθὼν καὶ Εὐριπίδῃ τις λέγοι, ὡς ἐπίσταται περὶ σμικροῦ πράγματος ῥήσεις παμμήκεις ποιεῖν καὶ περὶ μεγάλου πάνυ σμικράς, ὅταν τε βούληται, οἰκτρὰς καὶ τοὐναντίον αὖ φοβερὰς καὶ ἀπειλητικάς, ὅσα τ' ἄλλα τοιαῦτα, καὶ διδάσκων αὐτὰ D τραγῳδίας ποίησιν οἴεται παραδιδόναι;

ΦΑΙ. Καὶ οὗτοι ἄν, ὦ Σώκρατες, οἶμαι, καταγελῷεν, εἴ τις οἴεται τραγῳδίαν ἄλλο τι εἶναι ἢ τὴν τούτων σύστασιν, πρέπουσαν ἀλλήλοις τε καὶ τῷ ὅλῳ συνισταμένην.

ΣΩ. Ἀλλ' οὐκ ἂν ἀγροίκως γε, οἶμαι, λοιδορήσειαν, ἀλλ' ὥσπερ ἂν μουσικὸς ἐντυχὼν ἀνδρὶ οἰομένῳ ἁρμονικῷ εἶναι, ὅτι δὴ τυγχάνει ἐπιστάμενος ὡς οἷόν τε ὀξυτάτην καὶ βαρυτάτην χορδὴν ποιεῖν, οὐκ ἀγρίως εἴποι ἂν Ὦ E μοχθηρέ, μελαγχολᾷς, ἀλλ' ἅτε μουσικὸς ὢν πρᾳότερον, ὅτι Ὦ ἄριστε, ἀνάγκη μὲν καὶ ταῦτ' ἐπίστασθαι τὸν μέλλοντα ἁρμονικὸν ἔσεσθαι, οὐδὲν μὴν κωλύει μηδὲ σμικρὸν ἁρμονίας ἐπαΐειν τὸν τὴν σὴν ἕξιν ἔχοντα· τὰ γὰρ πρὸ ἁρμονίας ἀναγκαῖα μαθήματα ἐπίστασαι, ἀλλ' οὐ τὰ ἁρμονικά.

ΦΑΙ. Ὀρθότατά γε.

| ΣΩ. Οὐκοῦν καὶ ὁ Σοφοκλῆς τόν σφισιν ἐπιδεικνύμενον τὰ πρὸ τραγῳδίας ἂν φαίη ἀλλ' οὐ τὰ τραγικά, 269 καὶ ὁ Ἀκουμενὸς τὰ πρὸ ἰατρικῆς ἀλλ' οὐ τὰ ἰατρικά.

ΦΑΙ. Παντάπασι μὲν οὖν.

ΣΩ. Τί δέ; τὸν μελίγηρυν Ἄδραστον οἰόμεθα ἢ καὶ

D *τὴν τούτων σύστασιν*] This apt reply of Phaedr is evidently inconsistent with Ast's mean opinion of his understanding. Accordingly we are informed that the remark is plagiarized from Socr., sup 264 C, *δεῖν πάντα λόγον ὥσπερ ζῷον συνεστάναι, κ.τ.λ.* This grouping or consistence of parts is essential to every *λόγος*, whether metrical or not, and to every art and science pretending to theoretical completeness

πρέπουσαν—συνισταμένην] "*πρέπουσαν* per prolepsin quandam dictum, ut idem valent quod *ὥστε πρέπειν ἀλλήλοις τε καὶ τῷ ὅλῳ*" Stallb.

ὡς οἷόν τε ὀξυτάτην] Herm., *τὸ ἐπιτείνειν* [illegible]

269 *τὰ πρὸ τραγῳδίας*] The *μαθήματα* which precede tragedy, and are necessary to its production, its *προγυμνάσματα*, or preliminaries Skill in these does not of itself constitute a tragic poet, but is a *sine qua non* towards becoming one

τὸν μελίγηρυν Ἄδραστον] The epithet was probably suggested by Tyrtaeus *γλῶσσαν δ' Ἀδρήστου μειλιχόγηρυν ἔχοι* (Fr 8, v 8, Bergk). The mythic king seems to have owed this epithet to the skill with which he worked on the feelings of Theseus on the occasion which forms the subject of the Supplices of Euripides. The opinion of Ast, that, as "Gorgias wears the mask of Nestor, and Thrasymachus or Theodorus that of

Περικλέα, εἰ ἀκούσειαν ὧν νῦν δὴ ἡμεῖς διῇμεν τῶν παγ-
κάλων τεχνημάτων, βραχυλογιῶν τε καὶ εἰκονολογιῶν καὶ
ὅσα ἄλλα διελθόντες ὑπ' αὐγὰς ἔφαμεν εἶναι σκεπτέα,
B *πότερον χαλεπῶς ἂν αὐτούς, ὥσπερ ἐγώ τε καὶ σύ, ὑπ'*
ἀγροικίας ῥῆμά τι εἰπεῖν ἀπαίδευτον εἰς τοὺς ταῦτα γε-
γραφότας τε καὶ διδάσκοντας ὡς ῥητορικὴν τέχνην, ἢ
ἅτε ἡμῶν ὄντας σοφωτέρους κἂν νῷν ἐπιπλῆξαι, εἰπόν-
τας Ὦ Φαῖδρέ τε καὶ Σώκρατες, οὐ χρὴ χαλεπαίνειν
ἀλλὰ συγγιγνώσκειν εἴ τινες μὴ ἐπιστάμενοι διαλέγεσθαι
ἀδύνατοι ἐγένοντο ὁρίσασθαι τί ποτ' ἔστι ῥητορική, ἐκ
δὲ τούτου τοῦ πάθους τὰ πρὸ τῆς τέχνης ἀναγκαῖα μα-
C *θήματ' ἔχοντες ῥητορικὴν ᾠήθησαν εὑρηκέναι, καὶ ταῦτα*

Ulysses" (p 261 c), so by Adrastus some contemporary orator is here meant, and that this can only be Antiphon Rhamnusius, is supported by the following arguments (1) We should expect a pair of orators answering to the pairs of poets and of physicians just introduced, and as the latter were real personages, there is a presumption that Adrastus, as well as Pericles, would be so too (2) Antiphon, as we know from the Pseudo-Plutarch (Vitt X Oratt p 311, Wytt) and Philostratus (V. Sophist. 915), got the bye-name of Nestor from his powers of persuasion, but as the disguise of Nestor had been used already, it was natural for Plato to substitute another 'honey-tongued' hero to personate another contemporary orator (3) The fame of Antiphon's defence (Thuc iv 68), said to have been the finest effort of the kind that the men of that day had heard, may seem to justify his being coupled with Pericles, as Euripides with Sophocles Against these considerations, however, may be set the fact, that Antiphon's style was noted by the ancient critics *for its deficiency in sweetness*, an impression also conveyed by the existing remains (Dion Hal de Comp. Verb. p 52, Reiske; ib p 250, where he is classed with Aeschylus, Thucydides, and the other well known representatives of the *αὐστηρὰ λέξις*) In the Menexenus, moreover, Plato's allusion to Antiphon is not complimentary *ἀλλὰ καὶ ὅστις ἐμοῦ κάκιον ἐπαιδεύθη, μουσικὴν μὲν ὑπὸ Λάμπρου παιδευθείς, ῥητορικὴν δὲ ὑπ' Ἀντιφῶντος τοῦ Ῥαμνουσίου* (p 236) There is also force in Heind's remark, that the *καὶ* before *Περικλέα* implies a difference, "seu aetate seu genere," between the two orators mentioned Lastly, from the magnificent terms in which Plato presently speaks of Pericles, it is probable that he looked upon him as standing quite alone among Athenian orators, as one, in fact, whose parallel could only be found in the heroic age If this view is correct, we should mar a graceful compliment by refusing to take the passage in its literal sense, as referring to a hero familiar in Attic tradition.

οἰόμεθα] Hirsch conj *οἰόμεθ' ἂν*—not improbably, as the double *ἂν* is common in cases where the verb is distant in the sentence, as paul sup, *ὥσπερ ἂν μουσικὸς ἐντυχὼν . . . οὐκ ἀγρίως εἴποι ἄν.* Before and after *οἶμαι*, *ἂν* is frequently suppressed by the scribes, who probably thought it a solecism, not being aware that in such cases it belongs to the following infinitive.

B. *ὥσπερ ἐγώ τε καὶ σύ*] The *ῥῆμα ἀπαίδευτον* probably refers to the *ἄτεχνος τριβὴ* of p 261 E, for which Socr, in his present courteous mood, indirectly apologizes.

μὴ ἐπιστάμενοι διαλέγεσθαι] Being no scientific dialecticians, the old rhetors were unaware of the importance of strict definition and of the mode of obtaining it Hence they were ignorant of the true scope of their own science, and by consequence of the relation of its various parts to the whole and to each other A true definition of rhetoric (such as the *ψυχαγωγία διὰ λόγων*, p 261) would have enlightened them on these points

δὴ διδάσκοντες ἄλλους ἡγοῦνταί σφισι τελέως ῥητορικὴν δεδιδάχθαι, τὸ δ' ἕκαστα τούτων πιθανῶς λέγειν τε καὶ τὸ ὅλον συνίστασθαι, οὐδὲν ἔργον, αὐτοὺς δεῖν παρ' ἑαυτῶν τοὺς μαθητάς σφων πορίζεσθαι ἐν τοῖς λόγοις.

ΦΑΙ. Ἀλλὰ μήν, ὦ Σώκρατες, κινδυνεύει τοιοῦτόν τι εἶναι τὸ τῆς τέχνης, ἣν οὗτοι οἱ ἄνδρες ὡς ῥητορικὴν διδάσκουσί τε καὶ γράφουσι· καὶ ἔμοιγε δοκεῖς ἀληθῆ εἰρηκέναι. ἀλλὰ δὴ τὴν τοῦ τῷ ὄντι ῥητορικοῦ τε καὶ D
πιθανοῦ τέχνην πῶς καὶ πόθεν ἄν τις δύναιτο πορίσασθαι;

ΣΩ. Τὸ μὲν δύνασθαι, ὦ Φαῖδρε, ὥστε ἀγωνιστὴν τέλεον γενέσθαι, εἰκός, ἴσως δὲ καὶ ἀναγκαῖον, ἔχειν ὥσπερ τἆλλα. εἰ μέν σοι ὑπάρχει φύσει ῥητορικῷ εἶναι, ἔσει ῥήτωρ ἐλλόγιμος, προσλαβὼν ἐπιστήμην τε καὶ μελέτην· ὅτου δ' ἂν ἐλλίπῃς τούτων, ταύτῃ ἀτελὴς ἔσει. ὅσον δὲ

C οὐδὲν ἔργον] Hermeias reads ὡς οὐδὲν ἔργον ὄν, and so two MSS. But the omission of ὂν seems justified by Gorg 507 E, οὐκ ἐπιθυμίας ἐῶντα ἀκολάστους εἶναι καὶ ταύτας ἐπιχειροῦντα πληροῦν, ἀνήνυτον κακόν, λῃστοῦ βίον ζῶντα Of the other passages quoted by Ast there is scarce one in which the participle does not seem to have been absorbed by a preceding word ending in -ον In Crat. 386 E, οὐ πρὸς ἡμᾶς οὐδὲ ὑφ' ἡμῶν, ὄντα is *not* understood, but the words are constructed with ἔχοντα ἐστὶν οὐσίαν to be repeated from the foregoing clause. The phrases οὐ σμικρόν, οὐκ ὀλίγον, οὐ μέγ' ἔργον, are familiar, and οὐδὲν ἔργον occurs in Philippides Comicus (ap Meineke, iv. 471)—Πύκτῃ τ' ἐπιτιμᾶν οὐδὲν ἔργον μαχομένῳ, Αὐτὸν μάχεσθαι δ' οὐκέτ' ἐστὶ ῥᾴδιον, in the same sense as here, not, as more freq., with the force 'non opus' That which the teachers of rhetoric regarded as a mere nothing, which their pupils were to extemporize at pleasure, was in truth the most difficult thing of all viz the judgment to use the different figures of speech impressively, joined with the skill to combine the parts of a discourse—its proem, its exegesis, &c—into an harmonious whole.

D Τὸ μὲν δύνασθαι, κ τ λ] As for the power, says Socr - if you mean that of becoming a finished performer—it will, or rather must follow universal analogy: if you are blessed with a natural faculty for speaking, and improve it by science and assiduous practice, you will be a considerable orator This became a commonplace among the rhetoricians. Isocr Antid § 200, Bekk , λέγομεν ὡς δεῖ τοὺς μέλλοντας διοίσειν ἢ περὶ τοὺς λόγους ἢ περὶ τὰς πράξεις ἢ περὶ τὰς ἄλλας ἐργασίας, πρῶτον μὲν πρὸς τοῦτο πεφυκέναι καλῶς ὃ ἂν προῃρημένοι τυγχάνωσιν, ἔπειτα παιδευθῆναι καὶ λαβεῖν τὴν ἐπιστήμην, ἥτις ἂν ᾖ περὶ ἑκάστου, τρίτον ἐντριβεῖς γενέσθαι καὶ γυμνασθῆναι περὶ τὴν χρείαν καὶ τὴν ἐμπειρίαν αὐτῶν ἐκ τούτων γὰρ ἐν ἁπάσαις ταῖς ἐργασίαις τελείους γίγνεσθαι καὶ πολὺ διαφέροντας τῶν ἄλλων This reads like Plato diluted, but on the other hand we might suspect that Plato had himself borrowed the sentiment from the oration c Sophistas 294 D, a passage which he seems also to have had before him when he wrote Gorg. 463 D An author, professing to be earlier than either, has the same sentiment· χρὴ γὰρ ὅστις μέλλει ἰητρικῆς ξύνεσιν ἀτρεκέως ἁρμόζεσθαι, τῶνδέ μιν ἐπήβολον γενέσθαι φυσιος, διδασκαλίης, τρόπου εὐφυέος, παιδομαθίης, φιλοπονίης, χρόνου, κ τ λ Hippocratis Lex (i 4, Kuhn) But the genuineness of the piece is open to suspicion.

ὅσον δὲ αὐτοῦ τέχνη] 'for as much of it as is technical' This clause is in opposition to τὸ μὲν δύνασθαι, precepts of art being contrasted with natural genius

αὐτοῦ τέχνη, οὐχ ᾗ Λυσίας τε καὶ Θρασύμαχος πορεύεται δοκεῖ μοι φαίνεσθαι ἡ μέθοδος. >

ΦΑΙ. Ἀλλὰ πῇ δή;

E ΣΩ. Κινδυνεύει, ὦ ἄριστε, εἰκότως ὁ Περικλῆς πάντων τελεώτατος εἰς τὴν ῥητορικὴν γενέσθαι.

ΦΑΙ. Τί δή;

ΣΩ. Πᾶσαι ὅσαι μεγάλαι τῶν τεχνῶν, προσδέονται
270 ἀδολεσχίας καὶ μετεωρολογίας φύσεως πέρι· τὸ γὰρ ὑψηλόνουν τοῦτο καὶ πάντη τελεσιουργὸν ἔοικεν ἐντεῦθέν ποθεν εἰσιέναι. ὃ καὶ Περικλῆς πρὸς τῷ εὐφυὴς εἶναι

The present professors, says Socr., are on a wrong track: we must look in a different direction if we would discover the true way of handling rhetoric as an art. The correction Τισίαν for Λυσίαν, adopted from Schaefer by Spengel and Stallb., is plausible, but far from certain: see below, 272 c, εἴ τινά πη βοήθειαν ἔχεις ἐπακηκοὼς Λυσίου ἢ τινος ἄλλου. The scribes disfigure the name Τισίας in almost every instance, but they never seem to confound it with Λυσίας. The emendation is supported by Krische, p. 113 and note, but with more subtlety than soundness. Why should not Plato single out Lysias as an instance of what he considered vicious practice, as Thrasymachus was an example of empirical theory?

E. Κινδυνεύει—εἰσιέναι] He now proceeds to show that a philosophic training is a necessary condition of attaining the highest excellence as a speaker. To prepare Phaedr. for a view so different from any to which he had been accustomed, the imposing example of Pericles is appealed to. It was to his frequent converse with Anaxagoras, that the great master of rhetoric owed his immense superiority. For, says Socr., no really great art can attain perfection without endless discussion and high speculative discourse upon nature. It is by that door that the loftiness of thought, the all-sided completeness which characterize such arts would seem to enter, and those qualities Pericles acquired, and added them to his great natural endowments. The 'great arts' here spoken of are opposed to βαναυσίαι, which rely solely on τριβὴ or ἐμπειρία and imply no scientific insight. Rhetoric belongs to one class or the other, according to the spirit in which it is pursued, and the capacity or incapacity of its professors.—The word ἀδολεσχία—endless chatter, garrulity—applied by the vulgar in contempt to philosophic διάλεξις, is accepted by Plato and paraded with a kind of defiance. Thus in the Parmenides the youthful Socrates is exhorted to exercise and improve his powers, διὰ τῆς δοκούσης ἀχρήστου εἶναι καὶ καλουμένης ὑπὸ τῶν πολλῶν ἀδολεσχίας: else, it is added, σὲ διαφεύξεται ἡ ἀλήθεια (135 D). And in Crat. 401 B, μετεωρολόγοι καὶ ἀδολέσχαι are laudatory epithets—κινδυνεύουσιν οἱ πρῶτοι τὰ ὀνόματα τιθέμενοι οὐ φαῦλοι εἶναι ἀλλὰ μ. καὶ ἀ. τινές. This usage, though echoed by later writers, seems originally to have been peculiar to Plato. It is characteristic of the proud humility which formed so considerable an element in the Socratic εἰρωνεία, for such epithets were bestowed with especial liberality upon Socr. and his clique. See Arist. Nub. 1485, 360. And in the next generation they were found equally convenient by the assailants of the Platonists: comp. Isocr. c. Soph. 292 C D, νομίζουσιν ἀδολεσχίαν καὶ μικρολογίαν ἀλλ' οὐ τῆς ψυχῆς ἐπιμέλειαν εἶναι τὰς τοιαύτας διατριβάς (a passage which probably reflects pretty fairly the prevailing opinion). In opposition to this prejudice, Plato asserts that such studies have a direct tendency to promote grandeur of conception and completeness of execution, whether in an orator, a physician, or any other of the higher class of τεχνῖται. The epithets ὑψηλ. καὶ τελεσ., it will be observed, are not restricted to Pericles, though most felicitous as applied to him. Of his ἀδολεσχία a curious instance is given by Plutarch, V. Per. c. 36.

ἐκτήσατο· προσπεσὼν γάρ, οἶμαι, τοιούτῳ ὄντι Ἀναξαγόρᾳ, μετεωρολογίας ἐμπλησθεὶς καὶ ἐπὶ φύσιν νοῦ τε καὶ ἀνοίας ἀφικόμενος, ὧν δὴ πέρι τὸν πολὺν λόγον ἐποιεῖτο Ἀναξαγόρας, ἐντεῦθεν εἵλκυσεν ἐπὶ τὴν τῶν λόγων τέχνην τὸ πρόσφορον αὐτῇ.

270 *προσπεσὼν—Ἀναξαγόρᾳ*] A different estimate of Anaxagoras is formed in the Phaedo (p 97 B), as of Pericles in the Gorgias It is not, however, difficult to account for the seeming discrepancy In the Gorgias Plato speaks of Pericles from an ethico-political, in the Phaedrus from an artistic point of view, while the defect in the Anaxagorean system pointed out in the Phaedo need not be supposed to have blinded Plato to its striking originality and superiority to the efforts of earlier speculators. We may well believe that he would cheerfully have accorded the praise of a *ὑψηλόνους* and *τελεσιουργὸς* to a philosopher who, according to Aristotle, in comparison with the random guesses of his predecessors, might be said to speak words of truth and soberness *οἷον νήφων ἐφάνη παρ' εἰκῇ λέγοντας τοὺς πρότερον* (Met. i 4 16)

μετεωρολογίας—αὐτῇ] It was from converse with Anaxagoras, says Socr, that Pericles 'stored his mind with lofty speculations, and was able to penetrate to the essential nature of Intelligence and Unintelligence—the theme on which Anaxagoras chiefly loved to descant, and from that source he borrowed, for the behoof of his own art, all that could be made available for it' The *νοῦς καὶ ἄνοια* of the text are the intelligent and unintelligent principles in Nature, which Anaxagoras was the first to place in sharp antithesis to each other (Herm, *ἄνοιαν λέγει τὴν ὕλην*) Thus his celebrated *βιβλίον* commenced with the words, *ὁμοῦ πάντα χρήματα, εἶτα Νοῦς ἐλθὼν διεκόσμησε.* On this account, says Plutarch, *Ἀναξαγόραν οἱ τότ' ἄνθρωποι Νοῦν προσηγόρευον*, either, he adds, from admiration of his profound physiological genius, or because he was the first to dethrone Chance or Necessity and set up pure Intelligence in their room as the principle of law and order in the universe —*ἐν μεμιγμένοις πᾶσι τοῖς ἄλλοις ἀποκρίνοντα τὰς ὁμοιομερείας* (Vit. Pericl c 1) He adds, *τοῦτον ὑπερφυῶς τὸν ἄνδρα θαυμάσας ὁ Περικλῆς, καὶ τῆς λεγομένης μετεωρολογίας καὶ μεταρσιολογίας ὑποπιμπλάμενος, . . ὡς ἔοικε, τὸ φρόνημα σοβαρὸν καὶ τὸν λόγον ὑψηλὸν εἶχε καὶ καθαρὸν ὀχλικῆς καὶ πανούργου βωμολοχίας* To the same cause Plutarch attributes the superiority of Pericles to the vulgar *δεισιδαιμονία* which arises from ignorance of physical causation All this is intelligible and not improbable, but Plato seems to say considerably more than this, viz that it was to the lessons of Anaxagoras, especially on *νοῦς* and *ἄνοια*, that Pericles owed his deep knowledge of human nature (*τὸ διελέσθαι φύσιν ψυχῆς*, inf) Now it is pretty certain that nothing of the kind was to be learnt from Anaxagoras, whose theory of a cosmical Intelligence had nothing to do with the theory of human nature On the other hand, it is impossible either to understand the passage in an ironical sense, or to treat it as a mere rhetorical flourish. Plato's meaning was probably this Pericles, having become familiar with the Anaxagorean distinction between the Rational and Irrational principles as exhibited on a great scale in Nature (*ἐν τῇ ὅλῃ φύσει*, inf), found it easy to apply the same distinction to that department of nature (the mind of man) with which as an orator and statesman he had to do He would know how to distinguish between the *λόγον ἔχον* and the *ἄλογον*—the reasoning and unreasoning principle in his audience—and to address himself successfully to each in its turn (compare sup 246 B, *πᾶσα ἡ ψυχὴ παντὸς ἐπιμελεῖται τοῦ ἀψύχου*) It is thus, apparently, that Cicero understands the passage—Orat iv. 11 Nam nec latius nec copiosius de magnis variisque rebus sine philosophia potest quisquam dicere si quidem etiam in Phaedro Platonis hoc Periclem praestitisse caeteris dicit oratoribus Socrates, quod is Anaxagorae physici fuerit auditor · a quo censet eum, quum alia praeclara quaedam et magnifica didicisset, uberem et fecundum fuisse, gnarumque (quod est eloquentiae maximum) *quibus orationis modis quaeque animorum partes pellerentur* The same view is more vaguely expressed in the Brutus

ΦΑΙ. Πῶς τοῦτο λέγεις;

B ΣΩ. Ὁ αὐτός που τρόπος τέχνης ῥητορικῆς, ὅσπερ καὶ ἰατρικῆς.

ΦΑΙ. Πῶς δή;

ΣΩ. Ἐν ἀμφοτέραις δεῖ διελέσθαι φύσιν, σώματος μὲν ἐν τῇ ἑτέρᾳ, ψυχῆς δ' ἐν τῇ ἑτέρᾳ, εἰ μέλλεις μὴ τριβῇ μόνον καὶ ἐμπειρίᾳ ἀλλὰ τέχνῃ τῷ μὲν φάρμακα καὶ τροφὴν προσφέρων ὑγίειαν καὶ ῥώμην ἐμποιήσαι, τῇ δὲ λόγους τε καὶ ἐπιτηδεύσεις νομίμους πειθὼ ἣν ἂν βούλῃ καὶ ἀρετὴν παραδώσειν.

ΦΑΙ. Τὸ γοῦν εἰκός, ὦ Σώκρατες, οὕτως.

C ΣΩ. Ψυχῆς οὖν φύσιν ἀξίως λόγου κατανοῆσαι οἴει δυνατὸν εἶναι ἄνευ τῆς τοῦ ὅλου φύσεως;

ΦΑΙ. Εἰ μὲν Ἱπποκράτει γε τῷ τῶν Ἀσκληπιαδῶν

(xi 41) Pericles primus adhibuit doctrinam quae quamquam tunc erat nulla dicendi, tamen, ab Anaxagora physico eruditus, exercitationem mentis a reconditis abstrusisque rebus ad causas forenses popularesque facile traduxit

B Ὁ αὐτός που τρόπος, κ.τ.λ.] In modern language, Rhetoric is to be based on Psychology, in the same way as Medicine on Physiology, otherwise both are alike empirical. The parallel between ἀρετὴ and ὑγίεια is familiar in Plato More remarkable is the statement that the final cause of rhetoric is to improve the morals and institutions of a people. Comp Polit 301, ῥητορεία, πείθουσα τὸ δίκαιον, ξυνδιακυβερνᾷ [τῇ βασιλικῇ] τὰς ἐν ταῖς πόλεσι πράξεις See also the Introduction.

C Ψυχῆς οὖν φύσιν] The soul being a part of Nature, Psychology must needs be a branch of general Physics. This view is universal in Greek Philosophy.

Εἰ μὲν—γε] The MSS have εἰ μὲν Ἱπποκράτει τε. Galen, in quoting this passage (Opp xv. 4, Kuhn), reads εἰ μὲν οὖν Ἱπποκράτει τῷ, κ.τ.λ. The reading in the text is that adopted by Stallb, Ast, and Hirschig The Zurich Edd have εἰ μὲν οὖν γε, but μὲν οὖν would imply a modified dissent, which is out of place here.

Ἱπποκράτει γε] Protag 311 B, Ἱπποκράτη τὸν Κῷον τὸν τῶν Ἀσκληπιαδῶν Concerning this medical caste, order, or corporation, see Grote, H G i. 218, Sprengel, Gesch. der Arzneikunde, i 237, Littré, Hippocrate, t i. c. 1. According to Galen (or Pseudo-Galen), Isagog p 677, Kuhn, the Asclepiads belonged to the Methodic, as distinguished from the Empirical, sect in medicine One of their maxims was, ὑφηγήσεως ἀρχὴ ἡ φυσικὴ θεωρία—'nay,' it is added, ἁπλῶς καὶ Ἱπποκράτης ἔφη, "ἀρχὴ τοῦ ἐν ἰατρικῇ λόγου ἡ φύσις πρώτη" In the Comm in Hippocr de Natura Hominis (xv 12, Kuhn), Galen infers the genuineness of the treatise on which he is commenting from this passage of the Phaedrus for the sentiment (οὐδὲ περὶ τοῦ σώματος, κ τ λ) is to be found, he says, οὐ καθ' ἓν ἄλλο παρὰ τὸ προκείμενον ἡμῖν σύγγραμμα τὸ περὶ φύσιος ἀνθρώπου The object of this work of Hippocrates is to show that the human body is not a homogeneous substance, as certain physicians, following the Ionic physiologists, had affirmed, but composed of four elements—αἷμα, φλέγμα, χολὴ ξανθή, and χολὴ μέλαινα, whence the old doctrine of temperaments (κράσεις) was derived In § 13, we find the words, ἀνάγκη τοίνυν τῆς φύσιος τοιαύτης ὑπαρχούσης καὶ τῶν ἄλλων ἁπάντων καὶ τῆς τοῦ ἀνθρώπου, μὴ ἓν εἶναι τὸν ἄνθρωπον, ἀλλ' ἕκαστον τῶν στοιχείων τῶν ξυμβαλλομένων εἰς τὴν γένεσιν ἔχειν τινὰ δύναμιν ἐν τῷ σώματι οἵηνπερ ξυνεβάλετο And this is probably the passage to which we must understand Plato to refer, for it pronounces clearly in favour of the view ὅτι

δεῖ τι πείθεσθαι, οὐδὲ περὶ σώματος ἄνευ τῆς μεθόδου ταύτης.

ΣΩ. Καλῶς γάρ, ὦ ἑταῖρε, λέγει. χρὴ μέντοι πρὸς τῷ Ἱπποκράτει τὸν λόγον ἐξετάζοντα σκοπεῖν εἰ συμφωνεῖ.

ΦΑΙ. Φημί.

ΣΩ. Τὸ τοίνυν περὶ φύσεως σκόπει τί ποτε λέγει Ἱπποκράτης τε καὶ ὁ ἀληθὴς λόγος. ἆρ' οὐχ ὧδε δεῖ διανοεῖσθαι περὶ ὁτουοῦν φύσεως; πρῶτον μέν, ἁπλοῦν D
ἢ πολυειδές ἐστιν, οὗ πέρι βουλησόμεθα εἶναι αὐτοὶ τεχνικοὶ καὶ ἄλλον δυνατοὶ ποιεῖν, ἔπειτα δέ, ἐὰν μὲν ἁπλοῦν ᾖ, σκοπεῖν τὴν δύναμιν αὐτοῦ, τίνα πρὸς τί πέφυκεν εἰς

τὸ σῶμα πολυειδές ἐστι Compare also § 3, εἰ ἓν ἦν ὁ ἄνθρωπος, οὐδέποτ' ἂν ἤλγεεν, κ τ λ. Possibly, too, he may refer to the first section of the treatise, which contains a protest against the hasty generalizations of contemporary physiologists, and may therefore be construed into an acknowledgment of the importance to the physician of a sounder method, and this is the colour put upon it by Galen However this may be, Plato would naturally sympathize with the strong aversion expressed in the tract to the one-sidedness of the early physicists, seeing in Hippocrates' method a practical anticipation of his own principle, τὸ ἓν πολλά, τὰ πολλὰ ἕν The medical precepts in Charm. 156 C are probably borrowed from Hippocrates or his school, and to a certain extent illustrate the passage before us

οὐδὲ περὶ σώματος] i e δυνατόν ἐστι κατανοῆσαι. The genitive with περὶ is a not uncommon periphrasis for the accusative, as Ast observes. inf 271 C, εἰδότες ψυχῆς πέρι παγκάλως Gorg 512 8, ἐπιτρέψαντα περὶ τούτων τῷ θεῷ The variation from the preceding constr, ψυχὴν κατανοῆσαι, is designed We have κατανοεῖν περὶ τούτων in Xen Cyr i 6 20, quoted by Heind In the next speech ὁ λόγος is personified, as throughout this dialogue For ἐξετάζοντα Galen read ἐξετάζοντας

ἄνευ τῆς μεθόδου ταύτης] μέθοδος means either 'investigation' (going in quest), or a particular mode of investigation, our 'Method' The μέθοδος here intended would seem to be that which connects any particular branch of inquiry with ge[illegible]

stand Plato, if his words are to be taken *au pied de la lettre.* But when he comes to the application, we look in vain for any such general theory of nature The scheme of psychology he presently traces out rests solely on the observation of *human* nature, and is as inductive as Bacon himself could desire And equally so is the method of Hippocrates, which Plato justly regards as parallel with his own. Both conform equally to the requirements of a sound dialectic, both equally eschew fanciful *a priori* reasonings This difficulty, which seems to have escaped the commentators, is felt and clearly stated by M Littré in the Introduction to his elaborate edition of Hippocrates (tom i p 295 fol) But I confess that his solution is not to me satisfactory In the passage from the Hippocratean treatise de Victus ratione (i. 627, Kuhn), which M Littré supposes to be that referred to sup c, Dietetics are made to depend on the facts of human, not general physiology, precisely as Plato connects Rhetoric with those of human psychology. What if, after all, Plato means nothing more by ἡ τοῦ ὅλου φύσις than the general law of the One in Many, which holds alike in Nature and in Thought?

D ἐὰν μὲν ἁπλοῦν ᾖ] If it (the substance on which art is to be exerted) be simple and uniform, we are to study its powers, both active and passive, also on what substances it can act, and by what it is acted upon τίνα (sc δύναμιν) πέφυκεν ἔχον is equiv to τίνα φύσει ἔχει, and there is no necessity for altering [illegible] as Steph proposed and

τὸ δρᾶν ἔχον ἢ τίνα εἰς τὸ παθεῖν ὑπὸ τοῦ; ἐὰν δὲ πλείω εἴδη ἔχῃ, ταῦτα ἀριθμησάμενον, ὅπερ ἐφ' ἑνός, τοῦτ' ἰδεῖν ἐφ' ἑκάστου, τῷ τί ποιεῖν αὐτὸ πέφυκεν ἢ τῷ τί παθεῖν ὑπὸ τοῦ;

ΦΑΙ. Κινδυνεύει, ὦ Σώκρατες.

ΣΩ. Ἡ γοῦν ἄνευ τούτων μέθοδος ἐοίκοι ἂν ὥσπερ
E τυφλοῦ πορείᾳ. ἀλλ' οὐ μὴν ἀπεικαστέον τόν γε τέχνῃ μετιόντα ὁτιοῦν τυφλῷ οὐδὲ κωφῷ, ἀλλὰ δῆλον ὡς ἄν τῳ τις τέχνῃ λόγους διδῷ, τὴν οὐσίαν δείξει ἀκριβῶς τῆς φύσεως τούτου πρὸς ὃ τοὺς λόγους προσοίσει· ἔσται δέ που ψυχὴ τοῦτο.

ΦΑΙ. Τί μήν;

271 ΣΩ. Οὐκοῦν ἡ ἅμιλλα αὐτῷ τέταται | πρὸς τοῦτο πᾶσα. πειθὼ γὰρ ἐν τούτῳ ποιεῖν ἐπιχειρεῖ. ἢ γάρ;

ΦΑΙ. Ναί.

ΣΩ. Δῆλον ἄρα ὅτι ὁ Θρασύμαχός τε καὶ ὃς ἂν ἄλλος

Heind. read ἔχον is found in all the MSS. and in Galen, and may be defended by Xen. Symp. iv. 54, τὸν χρῶτα τοιοῦτον φῦναι ἔχοντα, which Ast quotes, observing that πεφυκέναι with the inf. has the sense "natura ita comparatum esse ut faciat." There is a clear distinction between πέφυκεν ἔχον here and ποιεῖν πέφυκεν in the next sentence, where ποιεῖν answers to εἰς τὸ δρᾶν, not to ἔχον. If the substance in question be not uniform, we are to count its different forms or manifestations, and repeat the process described in each instance: asking ourselves, as before, in what part (τῷ) its powers active and passive reside, what these powers are, and what the causes by which they are acted upon.

ἀριθμησάμενον] This reading is found in Galen, and adopted by Heind. The vulg. ἀριθμησάμενος is defended by Ast and Stallb. on the ground that anacoluthiae are common in Plato. The question is, however, whether in the present case such an anacoluthia as a nom. immediately preceding an inf. is tolerable or not; and I cannot believe that Plato would have thought it so. It is clear from his writing ἰδεῖν that he intended the clause to be dependent on the foregoing δεῖ, whereas an anacoluthia implies that an author has inadvertently changed the structure of his sentence. No one, I presume, will contend that ἰδεῖν is used imperatively.

E. ἀλλὰ δῆλον ὡς] 'we must not doubt,' says Socr., 'that a rhetor who professes to furnish his pupil (τῷ) with speeches framed *secundum artem*, will exhibit to him the essential nature of that substance to which he will have to apply such speeches; which substance, if I mistake not, will prove to be Soul.' In other words, a scientific Rhetoric must be founded on Psychology. In the text τῷ is omitted by the Bodl. Compare τέχνην ῥητορικὴν διδῷ in the sequel. προσφέρειν λόγους is analogous to προσφέρειν φάρμακα.

Οὐκοῦν] 'Hence in Soul all his efforts centre, for it is in that he essays to work conviction.'

271. Δῆλον ἄρα] The rhetorician will (1) ascertain whether the soul is uniform and homogeneous, or whether it contains a variety of εἴδη, answering to the parts or elements of our bodily frame. εἴδη is explained by μόρια . . . οἷον ὅτι ἔχει φανταστικὸν θυμικὸν ὀρεκτικόν, καὶ τὰ τοιαῦτα (Herm.). In the Timaeus Plato fixes the abode of each of these εἴδη, or principles: placing the reasonable soul in the brain, the irascible in the heart, the concupiscent in the liver, &c. Aris-

σπουδῇ τέχνην ῥητορικὴν διδῷ, πρῶτον πάσῃ ἀκριβείᾳ γράψει τε καὶ ποιήσει ψυχὴν ἰδεῖν, πότερον ἓν καὶ ὅμοιον πέφυκεν ἢ κατὰ σώματος μορφὴν πολυειδές. τοῦτο γάρ φαμεν φύσιν εἶναι δεικνύναι.

ΦΑΙ. Παντάπασι μὲν οὖν.

ΣΩ. Δεύτερον δέ γε, ὅτῳ τί ποιεῖν ἢ παθεῖν ὑπὸ τοῦ πέφυκεν.

ΦΑΙ. Τί μήν;

ΣΩ. Τρίτον δὲ δὴ διαταξάμενος τὰ λόγων τε καὶ B
ψυχῆς γένη καὶ τὰ τούτων παθήματα, δίεισι τὰς αἰτίας, προσαρμόττων ἕκαστον ἑκάστῳ, καὶ διδάσκων οἵα οὖσα ὑφ᾽ οἵων λόγων δι᾽ ἣν αἰτίαν ἐξ ἀνάγκης ἡ μὲν πείθεται, ἡ δὲ ἀπειθεῖ.

ΦΑΙ. Κάλλιστα γοῦν ἄν, ὡς ἔοικ᾽, ἔχοι οὕτως.

totle, on the other hand, made the heart the centre of the entire consciousness, while the Stoic Chrysippus discarded the distinction of εἴδη altogether (οὔτε τὴν θυμοειδῆ συγχωρήσας ὑπάρχειν οὔτε τὴν ἐπιθυμητικήν), but agreed with Aristotle in placing the reason and will (προαίρεσιν) in the heart. Galen de Plat et Hipp. vi 1 al

σπουδῇ] 'in earnest,' not as a mere amateur or ἰδιώτης, but *ex cathedra* διδόναι τ. ῥητ. probably refers to the practice of placing in the hands of their pupils manuals called τέχναι, which seems to have been nearly universal among the teachers of rhetoric

Δεύτερον δέ γε] Having determined the constituent parts of the Soul, the philosophic rhetorician will proceed (2) to enumerate their modes of action, and the affections to which they are respectively subject ὅτῳ, as τῷ paul sup., denotes the μόριον ψυχῆς 'in' or 'by which' any particular functions are exercised This part of Rhetoric and that which follows are handled by Aristotle in his inimitable second book

τρίτον δὲ δή] His third and last step will be to classify, διατάξασθαι, the different modifications of Soul and the various kinds of discourse, arranging them, as it were, in parallel tables for the purpose of pairing them according to their mutual correspondences such a kind o … … tion

emotive, such another for the rational part, &c. Nor will the theory be complete, unless he further show the causes of this compatibility,—why a soul so constituted is necessarily wrought on by discourses of such and such a kind, but insensible to those of a different description Just as in Medicine, the ideal Physician knows how to adapt his treatment to different κράσεις or temperaments, as well as to the different parts of the body, and can explain the physical reasons which determine his choice of remedies in every case. The λόγων γένη enumerated by Hermeias are, λ. ἀποδεικτικοί, δικανικοί, ἐγκωμιαστικοί. He adds, οἷον ὁ τῷ ὀρθῷ λόγῳ ἑπόμενος τοῖς ἀποδεικτικοῖς λόγοις χαίρει, ὁ δὲ κατ᾽ ἐπιθυμίαν ζῶν τοῖς κολακικοῖς καὶ ἐγκωμιαστικοῖς Aristotle goes, of course, much deeper than this (Rhet ii 12—17)

B. Κάλλιστα γοῦν] I admit, says Phaedr., that the way you point out will be the best. Socr., dissatisfied with this concession, tells him there is no other method possible: this alone is in accordance with the idea of what art should be, no matter what the subject-matter to which the method may be applied The existing technographers, he pretends, know this well, but are crafty enough to keep their psychological lore to themselves The method of συναγωγὴ and διαίρεσις (p 266) is therefore … to Plato equally ap-

ΣΩ. Οὔτοι μὲν οὖν, ὦ φίλε, ἄλλως ἐνδεικνύμενον ἢ λεγόμενον τέχνῃ ποτὲ λεχθήσεται ἢ γραφήσεται οὔτε τι ἄλλο οὔτε τοῦτο. ἀλλ' οἱ νῦν γράφοντες, ὧν σὺ ἀκήκοας, τέχνας λόγων πανοῦργοί εἰσι καὶ ἀποκρύπτονται,
C εἰδότες ψυχῆς πέρι παγκάλως. πρὶν ἂν οὖν τὸν τρόπον τοῦτον λέγωσί τε καὶ γράφωσι, μὴ πειθώμεθ' αὐτοῖς τέχνῃ γράφειν.

ΦΑΙ. Τίνα τοῦτον;

ΣΩ. Αὐτὰ μὲν τὰ ῥήματα εἰπεῖν οὐκ εὐπετές· ὡς δὲ δεῖ γράφειν, εἰ μέλλει τεχνικῶς ἔχειν καθ' ὅσον ἐνδέχεται, λέγειν ἐθέλω.

ΦΑΙ. Λέγε δή.

ΣΩ. Ἐπειδὴ λόγου δύναμις τυγχάνει ψυχαγωγία οὖσα, τὸν μέλλοντα ῥητορικὸν ἔσεσθαι ἀνάγκη εἰδέναι
D ψυχὴ ὅσα εἴδη ἔχει. ἔστιν οὖν τόσα καὶ τόσα, καὶ τοῖα καὶ τοῖα· ὅθεν οἱ μὲν τοιοίδε, οἱ δὲ τοιοίδε γίγνονται. τούτων δὲ δὴ διῃρημένων, λόγων αὖ τόσα καὶ τόσα ἔστιν εἴδη, τοιόνδε ἕκαστον. οἱ μὲν οὖν τοιοίδε ὑπὸ τῶν

plicable to all arts and sciences. This supports the view that ἡ τοῦ ὅλου φύσις refers, not to positive physical science, but to the principles which should regulate physical research. For Nature creates, as our minds conceive, according to genera and species. The One in Many is both a condition of thought and a law of things.

C μὴ πειθώμεθ' αὐτοῖς τέχνῃ γράφειν] 'let us not believe them that they write *secundum artem*, i. e. let them not persuade us that,' &c.

ψυχαγωγία τις] Not the only, but one special mode of acting upon the Soul (sup. 261). Legislation, music, religion, are also forms of 'psychagogy' according to Plato and Aristotle. Poetry, so far as it is designed to act on the Will, may be classed as a branch of Rhetoric, which, like it, is a ψυχαγωγία διὰ λόγων (261 A). In the elegant passage which follows, Plato sketches the ground plan of an ideal philosophical Rhetoric—a plan upon which the treatise of Aristotle was afterwards constructed. The εἴδη ψυχῆς are, as before, the λόγον ἔχον and the ἄλογον, with their subdivisions—the faculties, the passions, the appetites, &c. It is from the combinations of these elements that we get the varieties of character (ὅθεν οἱ μὲν τοιοίδε, κ.τ.λ.) and when these are determined (approximately, we may suppose) it will be time to make a corresponding list of the 'kinds of discourse' ("orationis modi"—Cic. Brut. 41), showing that 'persons of a given description are from such particular causes easily wrought upon by such and such modes of address, while persons of a different complexion are, for certain reasons, insusceptible of such influence.' This is evidently an application to Rhetoric of the general Method of Division sketched in p. 265 D fol., as indeed Galen points out, Hipp. et Plat., Opp. tom. v. p. 754, Kuhn. He cites the present passage from ἐπειδὴ to ὁ μὴ πειθόμενος κρατεῖ, and proceeds to illustrate the subject further by a passage from the Philebus (18 B), where the diaeretic method is applied to the science of Grammar.

D τοιόνδε ἕκαστον] Galen, τοιόνδε δὲ ἕκαστον.

τοιῶνδε λόγων διὰ τήνδε τὴν αἰτίαν εἰς τὰ τοιάδε εὐπει-
θεῖς, οἱ δὲ τοιοίδε διὰ τάδε δυσπειθεῖς. δεῖ δὴ ταῦτα
ἱκανῶς νοήσαντα, μετὰ ταῦτα θεώμενον αὐτὰ ἐν ταῖς
πράξεσιν ὄντα τε καὶ πραττόμενα, ὀξέως τῇ αἰσθήσει δύνασθαι ἐπακολουθεῖν, ἢ μηδὲν εἶναί πω πλέον αὐτῷ E
ὧν τότε ἤκουε λόγων ξυνών. ὅταν δὲ εἰπεῖν τε ἱκανῶς
ἔχῃ οἷος ὑφ' οἵων πείθεται, παραγιγνόμενόν τε δυνατὸς
ᾖ διαισθανόμενος ἑαυτῷ ἐνδείκνυσθαι ὅτι οὗτός ἐστι | καὶ 272
αὕτη ἡ φύσις, περὶ ἧς τότε ἦσαν οἱ λόγοι, νῦν ἔργῳ
παροῦσά οἱ, ᾗ προσοιστέον τούσδε ὧδε τοὺς λόγους ἐπὶ
τὴν τῶνδε πειθώ,—ταῦτα δὲ ἤδη πάντα ἔχοντι, προς-

δεῖ δὴ ταῦτα] A theoretical knowledge of the varieties of human character is not enough the student must have his senses sharpened to detect their manifestations in actual life and practice, 'or be thus far none the better or wiser for all the lessons he heard in the days of his pupillage' The MSS give ἢ μηδέ (εἰ μὴ Bodl) εἰδέναι πω πλέον αὐτῶν (Bodl αὐτῷ) ὧν τότε ἤκουε λόγων ξυνών. In the text I have adopted, which is Ast's, εἶναι is taken from the MSS of Galen, μηδὲν from Gal and Hermeias, αὐτῷ from the Bodl. and some other MSS. Heind and after him Bekk. adhere to the vulg, which would give the sense, 'or know no more than the mere (αὐτῶν) lectures he heard from his teachers' But the amended text gives, in my judgment, a more pointed meaning Plato would say that without tact and experience the labour of the schools is labour lost The only objection to my rendering is grounded on the absence of a preposition before ὧν λόγων "πλέον γίγνεσθαι vel εἶναί τινι ἐκ τινὸς Graeci vulgo dicunt, πλέον εἶναί τινός τινι, quod sciam, non dicunt" (Heind) To evade this objection, Ast resolves ὧν ἤκουε λόγων into λόγους ὧν ἤκουε, supposing λόγους to be the subject of εἶναι "alioquin nihildum utilitatis afferre quae tum audiverit praecepta" But this seems to me harsher than to suppose an ellipse of the preposition, in which we are completely justified by Isocr Antid 315 D, ὧν οὐδέν μοι πλέον γέγονεν, 'from all which performances I have reaped no benefit' Hence in Euthyd 290 B, for οὐδεμία τῆς θηρευτικῆς αὐτῆς ἐπὶ πλέον ἐστὶν ἢ ὅσον θηρεῦσαι καὶ χειρώσασθαι we should perhaps read οὐδὲν . ἐπὶ πλέον ἐστίν. 'Of the art of hunting nothing comes except ' The Zur Edd read with Ast, Hirsch adheres to the vulg.

τότε—ξυνὼν = τότε, ὅτε ξυνῆν τῷ διδασκάλῳ Gorg 455 D, τί ἡμῖν, ὦ Γοργία, ἔσται ἐάν σοι ξυνῶμεν, where he might have said τί ἡμῖν πλέον ἔσται.

E. ὅταν δὲ εἰπεῖν τε] The particles τε—τε are emphatic 'So soon as the student is not merely qualified to tell us what sort of men are influenced by such and such discourses, but able also to single out an individual hearer, and satisfy himself that the character of that man then present to him in the court or assembly answers to the description given in the lecture-room, &c , when, I say, his attainments have reached this point, and he has also learnt when to speak and when to refrain, and can discern when the various rhetorical styles and figures—brevity, pathos, exaggeration, or what not—are in or out of season, then, and not till then, is he a perfect master of his craft'

272 ταῦτα δὲ ἤδη] Gal ταῦτα δή, which Hirsch has adopted Both readings are good, but that of the MSS seems the more idiomatic This is the form noted by Buttm "in qua particula δὲ apodosin occupat, non per oppositionem ad protasin, sed ita ut mera sit repetitio alius δὲ quod est in protasi" (Mid p 152) Here the δὲ after ὅταν is repeated before ἤδη πάντ' ἔχοντα by way of connecting the various conditions enumerated, and contrasting more vividly the entire description of the perfect artist with that of the mere schoolman.

λαβόντι καιροὺς τοῦ πότε λεκτέον καὶ ἐπισχετέον, βραχυλογίας τε αὖ καὶ ἐλεινολογίας καὶ δεινώσεως ἑκάστων τε ὅσ' ἂν εἴδη μάθῃ λόγων, τούτων τὴν εὐκαιρίαν τε καὶ ἀκαιρίαν διαγνόντι, καλῶς τε καὶ τελέως ἐστὶν ἡ τέχνη ἀπειργασμένη, πρότερον δ' οὔ· ἀλλ' ὅ τι ἂν αὐτῶν τις
B ἐλλείπῃ λέγων ἢ διδάσκων ἢ γράφων, φῇ δὲ τέχνῃ λέγειν, ὁ μὴ πειθόμενος κρατεῖ. τί δὴ οὖν, φήσει ἴσως ὁ συγγραφεύς, ὦ Φαῖδρέ τε καὶ Σώκρατες, δοκεῖ οὕτως ἢ ἄλλως πως ἀποδεκτέον λεγομένης λόγων τέχνης;

ΦΑΙ. Ἀδύνατόν που, ὦ Σώκρατες, ἄλλως· καί τοι οὐ σμικρόν γε φαίνεται ἔργον.

ΣΩ. Ἀληθῆ λέγεις. τούτου τοι ἕνεκα χρὴ πάντας τοὺς λόγους ἄνω καὶ κάτω μεταστρέφοντα ἐπισκοπεῖν εἴ τίς
C πῃ ῥᾴων καὶ βραχυτέρα φαίνεται ἐπ' αὐτὴν ὁδός, ἵνα μὴ μάτην πολλὴν ἀπίῃ καὶ τραχεῖαν, ἐξὸν ὀλίγην τε καὶ λείαν. ἀλλ' εἴ τινά πῃ βοήθειαν ἔχεις ἐπακηκοὼς Λυσίου ἤ τινος ἄλλου, πειρῶ λέγειν ἀναμιμνησκόμενος.

Buttm. quotes Phaed. 80 D, ἡ δὲ ψυχὴ ἄρα, τὸ ἀειδὲς . . . αὕτη δὲ ἡμῖν . . . εὐθὺς διαπεφύσηται: add inf. p. 277 E, ὁ δέ γε ἐν μὲν τῷ γεγραμμένῳ λόγῳ . . . οὗτος δὲ ὁ τοιοῦτος ἀνὴρ κινδυνεύει, κ.τ.λ. (where after οὗτος some few codd. give δή).

ἐλεινολογίας] Vulg. ἐλεεινολογίας. Galen's text preserves the Attic form.

δεινώσεως] J. Poll. iv. 33, ὑπερβολαί, δεινώσεις, δεινολογίαι (apparently meant for synonyms). So the author of the περὶ ὕψους, § 11. 2, mentions δείνωσις as an ἰδέα αὐξήσεως. Ib. § 12. 5, ἔν τε ταῖς δεινώσεσι καὶ τοῖς σφοδροῖς πάθεσι, καὶ ἔνθα δεῖ τὸν ἀκροατὴν τὸ σύνολον ἐκπλῆξαι.

B. ὁ μὴ πειθόμενος κρατεῖ] 'he who refuses to believe him, has the better case,' i.e. we have a right to say, I don't believe you. A proverbial phrase for οὐ πειστέον, as Heind. suggests. The version of Serranus is amusing: "is nimirum pervicacia non ratione vincit." Epist. vii. 343 D, ὁ βουλόμενος τῶν δυναμένων ἀνατρέπειν κρατεῖ. Tim. 51, ἐκεῖνος οὐκ ἐχθρὸς ὢν ἀλλὰ φίλος κρατεῖ.

ὁ συγγραφεύς] That is, the ideal teacher of rhetoric described 271 A as one ὃς ἂν σπουδῇ τέχνην ῥητορικὴν διδῷ. Socr. had just said that the conditions laid down were equally binding upon the public speaker, the oral instructor, and the writer on rhetoric (λέγων ἢ διδάσκων ἢ γράφων).

ἀποδεκτέον λεγομένης] 'are we to accept (acquiesce in) this account of rhetoric or some others in preference?' ἀποδέχεσθαι *cum gen. rei* is very rare, if indeed it ever occurs (Alc. ii. 150 C is not in point); and we are therefore to regard λεγομένης τέχνης as a gen. absol. He might have written ἀποδεκτέον, ἐὰν οὕτως λέγηται ἡ τῶν λόγων τέχνη, or ἀποδεκτέον οὕτως λεγομένην λ. τέχνην, or ἀποδ. οὕτως λεγόντων λ. τέχνην.

C. πολλὴν ἀπίῃ] Of ἀπιέναι so used with accus. I have no other instance at hand. Badh. conj. περιίῃ, observing, "Ridiculum est ἀπίῃ: vid. infra περιιτέον, περίοδος" (p. 274). Hirsch. accordingly reads περιίῃ. Nor is the change in reality so great as it appears. περιίῃ might easily degenerate into πίῃ, and this be mistaken for ἀπίῃ. Bast. Ep. Crit. p. 928, Schaef., gives an instance of a mistake arising from the abbreviated way of writing περί, viz. as π with a small ε over it. C. F. Hermann, with curious infelicity, proposes αἱρῇ: Stallb. ἀνίῃ. I retain the vulg., to which there is no theoretical objection. Compare Lobeck on Soph. Aj. v. 20.

ΦΑΙ. Ἕνεκα μὲν πείρας ἔχοιμ' ἄν, ἀλλ' οὔτι νῦν γ' οὕτως ἔχω.

ΣΩ. Βούλει οὖν ἐγώ τιν' εἴπω λόγον ὃν τῶν περὶ ταῦτά τινων ἀκήκοα;

ΦΑΙ. Τί μήν; D

ΣΩ. Λέγεται γοῦν, ὦ Φαῖδρε, δίκαιον εἶναι καὶ τὸ τοῦ λύκου εἰπεῖν.

ΦΑΙ. Καὶ σύ γε οὕτω ποίει.

ΣΩ. Φασὶ τοίνυν οὐδὲν οὕτω ταῦτα δεῖν σεμνύνειν οὐδ' ἀνάγειν ἄνω μακρὰν περιβαλλομένους· παντάπασι γάρ, ὃ καὶ κατ' ἀρχὰς εἴπομεν τοῦδε τοῦ λόγου, ὅτι οὐδὲν ἀληθείας μετέχειν δέοι δικαίων ἢ ἀγαθῶν πέρι πραγμάτων, ἢ καὶ ἀνθρώπων γε τοιούτων φύσει ὄντων ἢ τροφῇ, τὸν E μέλλοντα ἱκανῶς ῥητορικὸν ἔσεσθαι. τὸ παράπαν γὰρ οὐδὲν ἐν τοῖς δικαστηρίοις τούτων ἀληθείας μέλειν οὐδενί, ἀλλὰ τοῦ πιθανοῦ. τοῦτο δ' εἶναι τὸ εἰκός, ᾧ δεῖν προσέχειν τὸν μέλλοντα τέχνῃ ἐρεῖν. οὐδὲ γὰρ αὖ τὰ πραχθέντα

Ἕνεκα μὲν πείρας] If 'trying' would avail, says Phaedr., he might perhaps remember,—but at the moment he can think of nothing.

νῦν γ' οὕτως = without further assistance or consideration.

D. τὸ τοῦ λύκου] The adage implies that even the worse cause should have a fair hearing. Our 'give the devil his due' expresses a similar feeling. The Greek comm. suppose the proverb to be derived from the Æsopian fable of the wolf and the shepherds, told thus by Plutarch: λύκος ἰδὼν ποιμένας ἐσθίοντας ἐν σκηνῇ πρόβατον, ἐγγὺς προσελθών, Ἡλίκος ἂν ἦν ὑμῖν θόρυβος εἰ ἐγὼ τοῦτο ἐποίουν (Sept. Sap. Conv. 156 A). Hence perhaps the proverb λύκου ῥήματα. We are reminded of the ecclesiastical 'Advocatus diaboli'—the wolf frequently supplying the place of the latter personage, as in the adage, εἰ καὶ λύκου ἐμνήσθης, equiv. to the Lat. 'lupus in fabula' and our 'talk of the devil' &c.

Φασὶ τοίνυν] Having propounded his new scheme of a philosophical Rhetoric, Socr. proceeds to examine the objections which the popular teachers will probably bring against it. 'No more,' they will say, '[illegible] this roundabout way of dealing with a simple matter. Probability, we repeat, and not truth—not the verum, but the veri-simile—is the province of the rhetor.' For μακρὰν περιβαλλ. comp. Symp. 222 C, οὕτω κομψῶς κύκλῳ περιβαλλόμενος. The usage is rare, and confined apparently to Plato and his later imitators. It may have come from the military sense of περιβάλλειν, to send round a detachment for the purpose of taking an enemy in the flank or rear. περιβάλλεσθαι is passive in form, but virtually neuter.

ὅτι οὐδὲν—δέοι] The sentence, as Heind. observes, wants its apodosis, ὅτι δέοι referring formally to ὃ εἴπομεν, but virtually taking the place of δεῖν after φασί. The connexion is re-established by μέλειν in the next sentence.

E. τοῦ πιθανοῦ] The persuasive, the objector goes on to say, is another word for the probable, which ought to occupy the attention of the skilled orator, if he would deserve that title. Hence even the facts are to be suppressed if they happen to be unlikely. For οὐδὲ γὰρ αὖ τὰ πρ., Heind. conj. οὐδὲ γὰρ αὐτὰ τὰ πρ., i.e. τὰ τῷ ὄντι πρ. But αὖ can hardly be spared in this connexion.

δεῖν λέγειν ἐνίοτε, ἐὰν μὴ εἰκότως ᾖ πεπραγμένα, ἀλλὰ τὰ εἰκότα, ἔν τε κατηγορίᾳ καὶ ἀπολογίᾳ· καὶ πάντως λέγοντα τὸ δὴ εἰκὸς διωκτέον εἶναι, πολλὰ εἰπόντα χαίρειν τῷ
73 ἀληθεῖ. | τοῦτο γὰρ διὰ παντὸς τοῦ λόγου γιγνόμενον τὴν ἅπασαν τέχνην πορίζειν.

ΦΑΙ. Αὐτά γε, ὦ Σώκρατες, διελήλυθας ἃ λέγουσιν οἱ περὶ τοὺς λόγους τεχνικοὶ προσποιούμενοι εἶναι. ἀνεμνήσθην γὰρ ὅτι ἐν τῷ πρόσθεν βραχέως τοῦ τοιούτου ἐφηψάμεθα, δοκεῖ δὲ τοῦτο πάμμεγα εἶναι τοῖς περὶ ταῦτα.

ΣΩ. Ἀλλὰ μὴν τόν γε Τισίαν αὐτὸν πεπάτηκας ἀκριβῶς. εἰπέτω τοίνυν καὶ τόδε ἡμῖν ὁ Τισίας, μή τι ἄλλο λέγει τὸ εἰκὸς ἢ τὸ τῷ πλήθει δοκοῦν.

B ΦΑΙ. Τί γὰρ ἄλλο;

ΣΩ. Τοῦτο δή, ὡς ἔοικε, σοφὸν εὑρὼν ἅμα καὶ

καὶ πάντως] That is, not only in the practice of the law-court, in which *κατηγορία* and *ἀπολογία* have place, but also in that of the *ἀγορά* Sup 261 B, *μάλιστα μὲν περὶ τὰς δίκας λέγεταί τε καὶ γράφεται τέχνῃ, λέγεται δὲ καὶ περὶ δημηγορίας* Whatever be the occasion, the speaker should keep probability in view, without troubling himself about the truth The double accus after the verbal *διωκτέον* is too trite a usage to require illustration.

273 *Αὐτά γε*] Badh recasts the parts thus —Φ *Αὐτά γε, ὦ Σώκρατες, διελήλυθας ἃ λέγουσιν οἱ περὶ τοὺς λόγους τεχνικοὶ προσποιούμενοι εἶναι* Σ *Ἀνεμνήσθην γὰρ ὅτι ἐν τῷ πρόσθεν βραχέως τοῦ τοιούτου ἐφηψάμεθα δοκεῖ δὲ τοῦτο πάμμεγα εἶναι τοῖς περὶ ταῦτα* Φ *Ἀλλὰ μὴν τόν γε Τισίαν αὐτὸν πεπάτηκας ἀκριβῶς* Σ *Εἰπέτω τοίνυν καὶ τόδε ἡμῖν ὁ Τισίας, κ.τ λ.* This arrangement has the advantage of explaining the tense of *ἀνεμνήσθην*, and the use of *γάρ* 'I have given the precepts of the rhetors word for word (*αὐτά*),' says Socr, '*because* I bethought me that we had already touched briefly on the subject, and I know what importance is attached to it by the professional teachers' On the other hand *ἀλλὰ μὴν* and *τοίνυν* seem to be hardly the particles required from the speakers in Badh's arrangement Socr would not have passed over without comment his companion's assertion that he was familiar with the *τέχνη* of Tisias. He would have owned the impeachment or disowned it In the former case, *ἴσως*, or some equivalent, would have preceded *εἰπέτω τοίνυν*

ἐν τῷ πρόσθεν] Sup. 259 E, *οὐκ εἶναι ἀνάγκην τῷ μέλλοντι ῥήτορι ἔσεσθαι τὰ τῷ ὄντι δίκαια μανθάνειν, ἀλλὰ τὰ δόξαντ' ἂν πλήθει, κ τ λ*

τόν γε Τισίαν αὐτὸν πεπάτηκας] 'you have, at all events, read up your Tisias carefully' *αὐτὸν* = in his own book So Ar Av. 471, *οὐδ' Αἴσωπον πεπάτηκας*, 'nor have you conned—are you at home in Aesop' Hermeias strangely mistakes the meaning *τουτέστιν, ἔδειξας μηδὲν ὄντα τὸν Τισίαν.*

B *Τοῦτο δή, ὡς ἔοικε*] The instance of a *suppressio veri* which follows is doubtless extracted from the *τέχνη* of Tisias, which Phaedr has at his fingers' ends. 'If a weak but courageous man be tried for beating a powerful but cowardly one, and robbing him of his cloak or the like, neither party is to state the precise truth. The coward is to pretend that the brave man was not alone when he thrashed him, while the other should first try to prove that no one else was by, and then make the most of the argument, How can a poor creature like me be supposed to have assaulted so fine a man? The other, we are told, will not avow his own cowardice, but will try to invent some other falsehood, whereby, if

τεχνικὸν ἔγραψεν, ὡς ἐάν τις ἀσθενὴς καὶ ἀνδρικὸς ἰσχυρὸν καὶ δειλὸν συγκόψας, ἱμάτιον ἤ τι ἄλλο ἀφελόμενος, εἰς δικαστήριον ἄγηται, δεῖ δὴ τἀληθὲς μηδέτερον λέγειν, ἀλλὰ τὸν μὲν δειλὸν μὴ ὑπὸ μόνου φάναι τοῦ ἀνδρικοῦ συγκεκόφθαι, τὸν δὲ τοῦτο μὲν ἐλέγχειν ὡς μόνω ἤστην, ἐκείνῳ δὲ καταχρήσασθαι τῷ πῶς δ' ἂν ἐγὼ τοιόσδε C τοιῷδε ἐπεχείρησα; ὁ δ' οὐκ ἐρεῖ δὴ τὴν ἑαυτοῦ κάκην, ἀλλά τι ἄλλο ψεύδεσθαι ἐπιχειρῶν τάχ' ἂν ἔλεγχόν πῃ παραδοίη τῷ ἀντιδίκῳ. καὶ περὶ τἆλλα δὴ τοιαῦτ' ἄττ' ἐστὶ τὰ τέχνῃ λεγόμενα. οὐ γάρ, ὦ Φαῖδρε;

ΦΑΙ Τί μήν;

ΣΩ. Φεῦ, δεινῶς γ' ἔοικεν ἀποκεκρυμμένην τέχνην ἀνευρεῖν ὁ Τισίας ἢ ἄλλος ὅστις δή ποτ' ὢν τυγχάνει καὶ ὁπόθεν χαίρει ὀνομαζόμενος. ἀτάρ, ὦ ἑταῖρε, τούτῳ ἡμεῖς πότερον λέγωμεν ἢ μὴ— D

ΦΑΙ. Τὸ ποῖον,

ΣΩ. Ὅτι, ὦ Τισία, πάλαι ἡμεῖς, πρὶν καὶ σὲ παρελθεῖν, τυγχάνομεν λέγοντες ὡς ἄρα τοῦτο τὸ εἰκὸς τοῖς πολλοῖς δι' ὁμοιότητα τοῦ ἀληθοῦς τυγχάνει ἐγγιγνόμενον· τὰς δὲ ὁμοιότητας ἄρτι διήλθομεν ὅτι πανταχοῦ ὁ τὴν

it so happen, he will give his antagonist a fair chance of refuting him' The impotent conclusion of these elaborate mystifications was not, we may presume, contemplated by Tisias, but is maliciously added by Socr

C. φεῦ, δεινῶς γ'] 'bless me' what a dreadfully recondite artifice' whether Tisias has the merit of its discovery, or some one else, whoever he may be, or whencesoever it is his pleasure to be named' Doubtless a mocking allusion to Corax and his ill-omened name So Herm., τοῦτο εἶπεν ἴσως διὰ τὸν κόρακα, ἐπειδὴ ἐλέγετο ὁ Κόραξ Τισίου μαθητὴς (not διδάσκαλος) εἶναι Comp the prov κακοῦ κόρακος κακὸν ᾠόν (Paroem Gr. ii. p 166, ed Leutsch, where for Σιτίαν read Τισίαν). The irony is increased by the circumstance that the formula ὁπόθεν χ. ὀν was used in solemn prayer Crat 400 E, ὥσπερ ἐν ταῖς εὐχαῖς νόμος ἐστὶν ἡμῖν εὔχεσθαι, οἵτινές τε καὶ ὁπόθεν χαίρουσιν ὀνομαζόμενοι (οἱ θεοί) So Heind ὁπόθεν here refers to the practice of giving the gods epithets taken from their favourite abodes. Δήλιε, Πύθιε, or the like

τούτῳ] If τούτῳ could be dispensed with we should be tempted by Heind 's τοῦτο, which τὸ ποῖον in the next sentence appears to presuppose. In every instance that I can find, τὸ ποῖον, or τὰ ποῖα, refers to some definite antecedent Inf 277 D, ἆρ' οὐ δεδήλωκε τὰ λεχθέντα ὀλίγον ἔμπροσθεν τὰ ποῖα, Phil 34 B, ἆρ' οὖν οὐ τόδε τὸ ποῖον, In the present case three or four MSS give τοῦτο Perhaps Plato wrote τοῦτ' αὐτῷ.

D πάλαι ἡμεῖς] Socr informs Tisias that his objection has already been refuted, referring of course to p 262 A, δεῖ ἄρα τὸν μέλλοντα ἀπατήσειν μὲν ἄλλον, αὐτὸν δὲ μὴ ἀπατήσεσθαι τὴν ὁμοιότητα τῶν ὄντων καὶ ἀνομοιότητα ἀκριβῶς διειδέναι, κ τ λ Likeness and unlikeness to truth can only be apparent to one who knows what the truth itself is.

ἀλήθειαν εἰδὼς κάλλιστα ἐπίσταται εὑρίσκειν. ὥστ' εἰ μὲν
ἄλλο τι περὶ τέχνης λόγων λέγεις, ἀκούοιμεν ἄν· εἰ δὲ
μή, οἷς νῦν δὴ διήλθομεν πεισόμεθα, ὡς ἐὰν μή τις
E τῶν τε ἀκουσομένων τὰς φύσεις διαριθμήσηται, καὶ κατ'
εἴδη τε διαιρεῖσθαι τὰ ὄντα καὶ μιᾷ ἰδέᾳ δυνατὸς ᾖ καθ'
ἓν ἕκαστον περιλαμβάνειν, οὔ ποτ' ἔσται τεχνικὸς λόγων
πέρι καθ' ὅσον δυνατὸν ἀνθρώπῳ. ταῦτα δὲ οὐ μή ποτε
κτήσηται ἄνευ πολλῆς πραγματείας· ἣν οὐχ ἕνεκα τοῦ
λέγειν καὶ πράττειν πρὸς ἀνθρώπους δεῖ διαπονεῖσθαι
τὸν σώφρονα, ἀλλὰ τοῦ θεοῖς κεχαρισμένα μὲν λέγειν δύνασθαι, κεχαρισμένως δὲ πράττειν τὸ πᾶν εἰς δύναμιν.
οὐ γὰρ δὴ ἄρα, ὦ Τισία, φασὶν οἱ σοφώτεροι ἡμῶν,
274 ὁμοδούλοις | δεῖ χαρίζεσθαι μελετᾶν τὸν νοῦν ἔχοντα, ὅ τι
μὴ πάρεργον, ἀλλὰ δεσπόταις ἀγαθοῖς τε καὶ ἐξ ἀγαθῶν.

ὥστ'—λέγεις] Galen, who quotes this passage, from *ὥστ' εἰ* to *δυνατὸν ἀνθρώπῳ*, gives *λέγοις*, and so Bekk from some MSS. But *ἀκούοιμεν ἂν* having the force of a future, as *πεισόμεθα* in the next clause, the indic is better. Presently Galen's MSS give *ἀδύνατος* for *δυνατός*, and *οὔπω ἔσται* for *οὔποτ'* (ed. Kuhn, v p 756). What Socr desiderates in a speaker is, (1) a dialectical training, enabling him to 'divide' and to 'collect,' and (2) the power of applying his dialectical science to human nature and its varieties. *διαριθμεῖσθαι* means much the same as *διατάξασθαι*, sup 271 B, to 'enumerate in order to classification.' The limitation *καθ' ὅσον δυνατὸν ἀνθρώπῳ* is freq introduced by Plato when speaking of things of high and difficult attainment, either in this form or with a preposition, as Rep. vi. 500 D, *θεῖος εἰς τὸ δυνατὸν ἀνθρώπῳ γίγνεται*. Tim 16 C, *τὴν τοῦ ἀρίστου κατὰ τὸ δυνατὸν ἰδέαν ἀποτελῶν*. So presently, *εἰς δύναμιν*.

E *κτήσηται*] So the Bodl. Bekk gives *κτήσεται* on comparatively slender authority.

θεοῖς κεχαρισμένα] The sentiment is in conformity with Plato's celebrated dictum, *πάντων χρημάτων μέτρον θεός*, Legg iv 716 C. "How many," asks Stallb, "of our writers on pulpit-eloquence" (*homileticen*) "treat this branch of theology in so lofty a spirit?"

φασὶν οἱ σοφώτεροι ἡμῶν] Probably he alludes to the elder Pythagoreans, who, according to Proclus, Theol i 5, p 13, are described Phileb. 16 C, in the words, *οἱ παλαιοὶ κρείττονες ἡμῶν καὶ ἐγγυτέρω θεῶν οἰκοῦντες*. So Hermeias understands *οἱ σοφ.* *οἷον οἱ Πυθαγόρειοι*. The sentiment which follows, that all men are fellow-slaves under the superintendence of divine taskmasters, is found, as Heind observes, in Phaed 62 B. *τόδε γέ μοι δοκεῖ εὖ λέγεσθαι, τὸ θεοὺς εἶναι ἡμῶν τοὺς ἐπιμελουμένους καὶ ἡμᾶς τοὺς ἀνθρώπους ἓν τῶν κτημάτων τοῖς θεοῖς εἶναι*. Ib 85 B, Socr speaks of himself as *ὁμόδουλος τῶν κύκνων καὶ ἱερὸς τοῦ αὐτοῦ θεοῦ*. The word *ὁμόδουλος* occurs Theaet. 172 D in a different connexion, but still with reference to oratory. *οἱ δὲ λόγοι ἀεὶ περὶ ὁμοδούλου πρὸς δεσπότην καθήμενον*, the 'master' in this case being the dicast. Before *ὁμοδούλοις* the best MSS, including the Bodl, give *ἤ*, others *μή*. But nothing can be made of either, unless we admit the improbable supposition that some other substantive has been lost before *ὁμοδούλοις*.

274 *ὅ τι μὴ πάρεργον*] Herm, *ὅ τι μὴ πάρεργον, ἀντὶ τοῦ, εἰ μὴ πάρεργον, τουτέστι, κατὰ συμβεβηκός*. Eng 'except incidentally,' or 'as a secondary consideration.' *ὅστις μὴ* and *ὅ τι μὴ* are of freq. occurrence, as Gorg 522 E, *οὐδεὶς φοβεῖται ὅστις μὴ παντάπασιν ἄνανδρός ἐστι*, 'unless he be a very coward.'

ὥστ' εἰ μακρὰ ἡ περίοδος, μὴ θαυμάσῃς· μεγάλων γὰρ ἕνεκα περιιτέον, οὐχ ὧν σὺ δοκεῖς. ἔσται μήν, ὡς ὁ λόγος φησίν, ἐάν τις ἐθέλῃ, καὶ ταῦτα κάλλιστα ἐξ ἐκείνων γιγνόμενα.

ΦΑΙ. Παγκάλως ἔμοιγε δοκεῖ λέγεσθαι, ὦ Σώκρατες, εἴπερ οἷός τέ τις εἴη.

ΣΩ. Ἀλλὰ καὶ ἐπιχειροῦντί τοι τοῖς καλοῖς καλὸν καὶ πάσχειν ὅ τι ἄν τῳ ξυμβῇ παθεῖν.

ΦΑΙ. Καὶ μάλα. B

ΣΩ. Οὐκοῦν τὸ μὲν τέχνης τε καὶ ἀτεχνίας λόγων πέρι ἱκανῶς ἐχέτω.

ΦΑΙ. Τί μήν;

ΣΩ. Τὸ δ' εὐπρεπείας δὴ γραφῆς πέρι καὶ ἀπρεπείας, πῇ γιγνόμενον καλῶς ἂν ἔχοι καὶ ὅπῃ ἀπρεπῶς, λοιπόν. ἦ γάρ;

ΦΑΙ. Ναί.

ΣΩ. Οἶσθ' οὖν ὅπῃ μάλιστα θεῷ χαριεῖ λόγων πέρι πράττων ἢ λέγων;

ὥστ' εἰ μακρά] 'marvel not, therefore, if the way be long and circuitous; it is for great ends, not for such as you imagine, that we are to take the winding road,' i.e. it is to please the gods, not, as you think, to gratify men, that we adopt the arduous and scientific in preference to the easy and empirical method. Heind.'s conj., *ὧν* for *ὡς*, which I have adopted, seems necessary in order to furnish an antecedent to *ταῦτα* in the following clause: 'not but what, as our reasoning shows, these ordinary purposes (*ἃ σὺ δοκεῖς*, sc. *τὸ εἰκός, τὸ πιθανόν*) may, if one has a mind, be attained, and in the best possible manner, as following out of the first.' He had before said that the best way of ascertaining the probable was first to learn the true. (Herm. explains *ἐξ ἐκείνων* by *ἐκ τῶν θεῶν*. Read *ἐκ τῶν θείων*, a good gloss, *ταῦτα* being equiv. to *τἀνθρώπινα*. So 246 A, *θεία καὶ μακρὰ διήγησις* is opposed to *ἀνθρωπίνη καὶ ἐλάττων*.) Phaedr. admits that the Socratic way is in theory excellent, but doubts its practicability. To which Socr. replies, that, practicable or not, it is noble to aim at noble ends, even though the attempt should end in failure. And with these words he dismisses the question of art or no art.

B. *Τὸ δ' εὐπρεπείας δὴ γραφῆς πέρι*] At the commencement of the discussion following the last Erotic Discourse, Socr. had exposed the futility of the prejudice against authorship in general, and caused Phaedr. to admit *ὅτι οὐκ αἰσχρὸν αὐτό γε τὸ γράφειν λόγους* (258 D). This done, he makes the admission (ib. E) that there is a difference between *τὸ καλῶς τε καὶ μὴ γράφειν*, and proposes, as the theme of the day's discussion, the question *ὅπῃ καλῶς ἔχει λέγειν τε καὶ γράφειν καὶ ὅπῃ μή* (259 E). The discussion however has to wait until the preliminary question (commencing 260 E) of *τέχνη τε καὶ ἀτεχνία* is disposed of: hence the present passage is, in form at least, a resumption of the thread of the dialogue, after a long parenthetic interruption. In commencing the art-discussion, he had roused the attention of Phaedr., by introducing a company of imaginary *Λόγοι*, uttering pretended Laconian apophthegms. Here he puts in the mouth of an Egyptian deity paradoxes redolent of an Attic phrontisterium.

ΦΑΙ. Οὐδαμῶς. σὺ δέ;

C ΣΩ. Ἀκοήν γ' ἔχω λέγειν τῶν προτέρων, τὸ δ' ἀληθὲς αὐτοὶ ἴσασιν. εἰ δὲ τοῦτο εὕροιμεν αὐτοί, ἆρά γ' ἂν ἔθ' ἡμῖν μέλοι τι τῶν ἀνθρωπίνων δοξασμάτων;

ΦΑΙ. Γελοῖον ἤρου. ἀλλ' ἃ φῂς ἀκηκοέναι, λέγε.

ΣΩ. Ἤκουσα τοίνυν περὶ Ναύκρατιν τῆς Αἰγύπτου γενέσθαι τῶν ἐκεῖ παλαιῶν τινὰ θεῶν, οὗ καὶ τὸ ὄρνεον [τὸ] ἱερόν, ὃ δὴ καλοῦσιν Ἶβιν· αὐτῷ δὲ ὄνομα τῷ δαίμονι εἶναι Θεύθ· τοῦτον δὲ πρῶτον ἀριθμόν τε καὶ λογισμὸν εὑρεῖν καὶ γεωμετρίαν καὶ ἀστρονομίαν, ἔτι δὲ
D πεττείας τε καὶ κυβείας, καὶ δὴ καὶ γράμματα. βασιλέως δ' αὖ τότε ὄντος Αἰγύπτου ὅλης Θαμοῦ περὶ τὴν μεγάλην πόλιν τοῦ ἄνω τόπου, ἣν οἱ Ἕλληνες Αἰγυπτίας Θήβας καλοῦσι, καὶ τὸν θεὸν Ἄμμωνα, παρὰ τοῦτον ἐλθὼν ὁ Θεὺθ τὰς τέχνας ἐπέδειξε, καὶ ἔφη δεῖν διαδοθῆναι τοῖς ἄλλοις Αἰγυπτίοις. ὁ δὲ ἤρετο ἥντινα ἑκάστη ἔχοι ὠφέλειαν. διεξιόντος δέ, ὅ τι καλῶς ἢ μὴ καλῶς δοκοίη λέγειν,

C Ναύκρατιν] This was a Greek emporium in Egypt, originally, according to Herod ii 179, the only foreign port Theuth or Thôth, the Egyptian Hermes, is again mentioned in Phileb 18 B He was one of the twelve gods of second rank, and called by the Aegyptians 'the scribe of the gods,' the 'lord of the divine word,' the 'writer of truth' So Bunsen, Aegypten i. 462, from Lepsius. He was also the Moon-god Herod. (ii 67) informs us that the dead ibis was always taken for burial to Hermopolis, the city of Thoth (see Sir G Wilkinson's note in Rawlinson's ed) being, as Plato says, sacred to that god (Aelian, N. H x 29) The second article before ἱερόν admits, of course, of explanation, but probability would be much in favour of the emended reading of Heind., Ast, and Hirsch, οὗ καὶ τὸ ὄρνεον ἱερόν, even if we did not find it in the comm of Hermeias (who by the way gives a mystical reason of surpassing absurdity for the relation of the bird to the god, Schol Herm 199, Ast)

ἀριθμόν τε καὶ λογισμόν] The words recur, Rep vii 522 C ἀριθμὸς for Arithmetic is common Aesch Prom 459, ἀριθμὸν ἔξοχον σοφισμάτων, and a poet (prob Euripides) in Stobaeus: πρῶτα μὲν τὸν πάνσοφον Ἀριθμὸν εὕρηκ' ἔξοχον σοφισμάτων

D. Θαμοῦ] It is impossible to say where Plato found this word, which seems a corruption or variety of Ἀμοῦς, Ἀμοῦν, the Egyptian name, according to Herodotus, of Zeus (Her ii 42) Accordingly his name heads the list of the eight superior deities. This Amon or Amn was besides in an especial sense the god of Thebes, hence styled by Herod. ibid Ζεὺς Θηβαιεύς He was the Zeus Ammon of the Greeks, his image being κριοπρόσωπον, ib Hence Thebes itself was styled Dio-polis With the anacoluthia ἣν . . . καλοῦσι, καὶ τὸν θεὸν Ἄμμωνα compare a similar sup 258 E, ὧν προλυπηθῆναι δεῖ ἢ μηδὲ ἡσθῆναι· τὸν θεὸν is, of course, the Thamus just mentioned For ἥν, the reading received by all edd. since Heind, all the MSS but one have ὅν

ἐπέδειξε] So the Bodl, the majority of codd, and Hermeias. Bekk edits ἀπέδειξε from eight MSS But ἐπέδειξε is better 'exhibited,' or as Stallb 'ostentavit"

δοκοίη] Vulg δοκοῖ, al δοκεῖ The Attic form is preserved in Stobaeus.

τὸ μὲν ἔψεγε, τὸ δ' ἐπῄνει. πολλὰ μὲν δὴ περὶ ἑκάστης E
τῆς τέχνης ἐπ' ἀμφότερα Θαμοῦν τῷ Θεὺθ λέγεται ἀποφήνασθαι, ἃ λόγος πολὺς ἂν εἴη διελθεῖν. ἐπειδὴ δὲ ἐπὶ τοῖς γράμμασιν ἦν, Τοῦτο δέ, ὦ βασιλεῦ, τὸ μάθημα, ἔφη ὁ Θεύθ, σοφωτέρους Αἰγυπτίους καὶ μνημονικωτέρους παρέξει· μνήμης τε γὰρ καὶ σοφίας φάρμακον εὑρέθη. ὁ δ' εἶπεν Ὦ τεχνικώτατε Θεύθ, ἄλλος μὲν τεκεῖν δυνατὸς τὰ τῆς τέχνης, ἄλλος δὲ κρῖναι τίν' ἔχει μοῖραν βλάβης
τε καὶ ὠφελείας τοῖς μέλλουσι χρῆσθαι. | καὶ νῦν σύ, 275
πατὴρ ὢν γραμμάτων, δι' εὔνοιαν τοὐναντίον εἶπες ἢ δύναται. τοῦτο γὰρ τῶν μαθόντων λήθην μὲν ἐν ψυχαῖς παρέξει, μνήμης ἀμελετησίᾳ, ἅτε διὰ πίστιν γραφῆς ἔξωθεν ὑπ' ἀλλοτρίων τύπων, οὐκ ἔνδον αὐτοὺς ὑφ' αὑτῶν ἀναμιμνησκομένους. οὔκουν μνήμης ἀλλ' ὑπομνήσεως φάρμακον εὗρες. σοφίας δὲ τοῖς μαθηταῖς δόξαν, οὐκ ἀλήθειαν πορίζεις· πολυήκοοι γάρ σοι γενόμενοι ἄνευ

E. ἐπ' ἀμφότερα] 'for and against.' ἐπὶ τοῖς γράμμασιν ἦν, 'when he got upon the subject of written characters.' Polit. 271 B, ἐπ' αὐτῷ νῦν ἐσμὲν ἤδη.

μνήμης—φάρμακον] 'a specific for the memory and the wit.' So above, 230 D, σὺ μέντοι δοκεῖς μοι τῆς ἐξόδου τὸ φάρμακον εὑρηκέναι. A more usual form would have been λήθης καὶ ἀμαθίας φάρμακον, as we find in Eurip. Fr. Palam. 2, Dind., τὰ τῆς γε λήθης φάρμακ' ὀρθώσας μόνος Ἄφωνα καὶ φωνοῦντα, κ.τ.λ. But Synesius, π. ἐνυπν. p. 110, τὰς ἐλπίδας ἐνέχεεν ὁ Προμηθεύς, διαμονῆς φάρμακον.

275 καὶ νῦν σὺ—δύναται] 'so, in the present instance, you, who are the father of letters, have, out of tenderness for your offspring, attributed to them a power (or tendency), the contrary of that which they really possess.' ἢ δύναται for ἢ ὃ δύναται, or better οὗ or ὧν δύναται, is confirmed by Phileb. 35 A, ἐπιθυμεῖ τῶν ἐναντίων ἢ πάσχει, and by several other passages cited by Stallb. in his ann.

τοῦτο γάρ] Theuth's invention would impair the memory, by tempting men to neglect practising it. They would rely on written memoranda, and so get the habit of referring to outward symbols impressed on alien material, rather than to those stamped on the tablets of the brain. Hence writing is an aid, not to memory, but to reminiscence; helping us not to retain impressions but to recover them. The commentators quote largely in illustration of this passage Quint. Inst. xi. 2. 9, quamquam invenio apud Platonem, obstare memoriae usum literarum: videlicet quod illa, quae scriptis reposuimus, velut custodire desinimus, et ipsa securitate dimittimus: where the annotators refer to Caesar, B. G. vi. 14, to show the existence of a similar prejudice among the Druids, who forbade their lore to be committed to writing: "quod neque in vulgum disciplinam efferri velint, neque eos qui discant, litteris confisos, minus memoriae studere." To these Stallb. adds Senec. Ep. 88. 28. An anecdote is related by Hermeias of a disciple of Plato, who, πάντα τὰ λεγόμενα παρ' αὐτοῦ ἀπογραψάμενος ἀπέπλευσεν, καὶ ναυαγίᾳ περιπεσὼν πάντα ἀπώλεσε, καὶ ὑπέστρεψε πρὸς τὸν διδάσκαλον, ἔργῳ πειραθεὶς ὅτι οὐ δεῖ ἐν βιβλίοις ἀποτίθεσθαι τὰ νοήματα, ἀλλ' ἐν τῇ ψυχῇ. This may have been suggested by a saying of Aristippus, of whom we are told ὅτι παρεκελεύετο τοῖς νέοις τοιαῦτα ἐφόδια κτᾶσθαι, ἅ τινα αὐτοῖς καὶ ναυαγήσασι συνεκκολυμβήσει (Stob. Anthol. Append. p. 66).

πολυήκοοι γάρ σοι γενόμενοι] 'your

διδαχῆς, πολυγνώμονες εἶναι δόξουσιν, ἀγνώμονες ὡς
B ἐπὶ τὸ πλῆθος ὄντες, καὶ χαλεποὶ ξυνεῖναι, δοξόσοφοι γεγονότες ἀντὶ σοφῶν.

ΦΑΙ. Ὦ Σώκρατες, ῥᾳδίως σὺ Αἰγυπτίους καὶ ὁποδαποὺς ἂν ἐθέλῃς λόγους ποιεῖς.

ΣΩ. Οἱ δέ γ', ὦ φίλε, ἐν τῷ τοῦ Διὸς τοῦ Δωδωναίου ἱερῷ δρυὸς λόγους ἔφησαν μαντικοὺς πρώτους γενέσθαι. τοῖς μὲν οὖν τότε, ἅτε οὐκ οὖσι σοφοῖς ὥσπερ ὑμεῖς οἱ νέοι, ἀπέχρη δρυὸς καὶ πέτρας ἀκούειν ὑπ' εὐηθείας, εἰ μόνον ἀληθῆ λέγοιεν· σοὶ δ' ἴσως διαφέρει τίς ὁ λέγων
C καὶ ποδαπός. οὐ γὰρ ἐκεῖνο μόνον σκοπεῖς, εἴτε οὕτως εἴτε ἄλλως ἔχει.

ΦΑΙ. Ὀρθῶς ἐπέπληξας. καί μοι δοκεῖ περὶ γραμμάτων ἔχειν ᾗπερ ὁ Θηβαῖος λέγει.

pupils will be well informed without being well taught, hence they will be thought very knowing, though, with few exceptions, perfectly ignorant,—overbearing too in society, as having acquired the conceit of wisdom instead of the reality. With χαλεποὶ ξυνεῖναι compare Theaet 210 C, ἧττον ἔσει βαρὺς τοῖς ξυνοῦσι καὶ ἡμερώτερος, σωφρόνως οὐκ οἰόμενος εἰδέναι ἃ μὴ οἶσθα With the sentiment comp. the aphorism of Heraclitus πολυμαθίη νόον οὐ διδάσκει.

B. Ὦ Σώκρατες] A warning to the reader not to take Socr at his word, when he pretends to have received an edifying recital from ancient tradition (ἀκοὴ τῶν προτέρων) The comm think that Αἰγυπτίους implies in itself something of contempt, the verb αἰγυπτιάζειν having the derived sense πανουργεῖν Arist Thesm 920, οἴμ' ὡς πανοῦργος καὐτὸς εἶναί μοι δοκεῖς, Καὶ τοῖσδέ τις ξύμβουλος οὐκ ἔτος πάλαι 'Ηιγυπτιάζετ' Hesych., Αἰγυπτιάζειν τὸ ὕπουλα πράττειν. But this relates to the character of the Egyptians, not to the truth of their legends Phaedr merely means to say you will not impose on me by affecting to lay the scene of your romances in Egypt or any other foreign country, we know how little it costs you to invent fables like that we have just heard. Whereupon Socr, partly ignoring his meaning, reproves him for thinking more of the nationality of a speaker than of the truth of what he says; a reproof to which Phaedr. good-humouredly submits 'The priests,' says Socr, 'in the sanctuary of Zeus, at Dodona, declared that the first oracles issued from an oak: the men of that day being so simple as to be content to hearken to tree and rock, if they spake but truth'

δρυὸς καὶ πέτρας] Socr had only mentioned an oak, but he adds καὶ πέτρας for the sake of the adage So (260 c) he says, περὶ ὄνου σκιᾶς ὡς ἵππου, when the ὄνος itself had been in question The proverb is sufficiently trite Hom Od xix 163, οὐ γὰρ ἀπὸ δρυός ἐσσι παλαιφάτου οὐδ' ἀπὸ πέτρης, i e you had human parents, like other people. Hence Socr in the Apol 34 D, ἐμοί εἰσι μέν πού τινες καὶ οἰκεῖοι καὶ γὰρ τοῦτ' αὐτὸ τὸ τοῦ Ὁμήρου, οὐδ' ἐγὼ ἀπὸ δρυὸς οὐδ' ἀπὸ πέτρας πέφυκα. 'I am not literally a "terrae filius."' Rep viii. 544 D, ἢ οἴει ἐκ δρυός ποθεν ἢ ἐκ πέτρας τὰς πολιτείας γίγνεσθαι, ἀλλ' οὐχὶ ἐκ τῶν ἠθῶν τῶν ἐν ταῖς πόλεσιν. Cic Acad Pr ii. 31 100, Non enim est e saxo sculptus aut e robore dolatus; habet corpus; habet animum, &c The proverb is learnedly discussed by G G Nitzsch, Rhein Mus 1857, p 106 Its meaning in the present passage is faithfully given by Hermeias as cited above The προσήγοροι δρύες of Dodona are sufficiently well known—nor need we suppose that there is any allusion here to the Δελφὶς πέτρα, which was vocal only in a figure.

ΣΩ. Οὐκοῦν ὁ τέχνην οἰόμενος ἐν γράμμασι καταλιπεῖν καὶ αὖ ὁ παραδεχόμενος, ὥς τι σαφὲς καὶ βέβαιον ἐκ γραμμάτων ἐσόμενον, πολλῆς ἂν εὐηθείας γέμοι καὶ τῷ ὄντι τὴν Ἄμμωνος μαντείαν ἀγνοοίη, πλέον τι οἰόμενος εἶναι λόγους γεγραμμένους τοῦ τὸν εἰδότα ὑπομνῆσαι περὶ ὧν ἂν ᾖ τὰ γεγραμμένα. D

ΦΑΙ. Ὀρθότατα.

ΣΩ. Δεινὸν γάρ που, ὦ Φαῖδρε, τοῦτ' ἔχει γραφή, καὶ ὡς ἀληθῶς ὅμοιον ζωγραφίᾳ. καὶ γὰρ τὰ ἐκείνης ἔκγονα ἕστηκε μὲν ὡς ζῶντα, ἐὰν δ' ἀνέρῃ τι, σεμνῶς πάνυ σιγᾷ. ταὐτὸν δὲ καὶ οἱ λόγοι· δόξαις μὲν ἂν ὥς τι φρονοῦντας αὐτοὺς λέγειν, ἐὰν δέ τι ἔρῃ τῶν λεγομένων βουλόμενος μαθεῖν, ἕν τι σημαίνει μόνον ταὐτὸν ἀεί. ὅταν δὲ ἅπαξ γραφῇ, κυλινδεῖται μὲν πανταχοῦ πᾶς λόγος ὁμοίως παρὰ τοῖς ἐπαΐουσιν, ὡς δ' αὔτως παρ' οἷς οὐδὲν E
προσήκει, καὶ οὐκ ἐπίσταται λέγειν οἷς δεῖ τε καὶ μή. πλημμελούμενος δὲ καὶ οὐκ ἐν δίκῃ λοιδορηθεὶς τοῦ πατρὸς ἀεὶ δεῖται βοηθοῦ· αὐτὸς γὰρ οὔτ' ἀμύνασθαι οὔτε βοηθῆσαι δυνατὸς αὑτῷ.

ΦΑΙ. Καὶ ταῦτά σοι ὀρθότατα εἴρηται.

C. *Οὐκοῦν ὁ τέχνην*] Socr applies the pretended oracle of Ammon to the subject in hand. A written manual of rhetoric will not of itself make its readers skilful orators, its only value is to remind those who use it of what they knew already

ἀγνοοίη] Of this reading we have trace in the *ἀγνοοῖν* of one cod Vulg *ἀγνοοῖ*

πλέον τι—εἶναι λόγους γεγραμμένους] There is no necessity to substitute *ἔχειν* for *εἶναι* as Heind, or *ποιεῖν* as Stallb suggests. *εἶναι* is here used idiomatically in the sense of *δύνασθαι* Arist. Ran 227, *οὐδὲν γάρ ἐστ' ἀλλ' ἢ κοάξ* Aves 19, *τὼ δ' οὐκ ἄρ' ἤστην οὐδὲν ἄλλο πλὴν δάκνειν* (which is perhaps better than Porson's *ᾔστην*) Amphis ap Diog Laert. iii § 28, *ὦ Πλάτων Ὡς οὐδὲν ᾔσθα πλὴν σκυθρωπάζειν μόνον.* Vulg. *οἶσθα*, Cod Arund *ᾔσθα*, Cobet *ἦσθα*

D *Δεινὸν γάρ που*] There is one inconvenience in written speech, which is, in fact, incident to printing also The creator [illegible] stand upright as if they were alive, if you ask them a question, will preserve a solemn silence

δόξαις μὲν ἄν] 'you might fancy they had some conception of the meaning of what they say, but if you ask them, &c, they still tell the same unvarying tale' So in the Protag 347 E, the reading of the poets is denounced as unprofitable, and for a like reason, *οὓς οὔτε ἀνερέσθαι οἷόν τ' ἐστὶ περὶ ὧν λέγουσιν, κ τ λ*

κυλινδεῖται μέν] 'is handed about,' or 'circulates' *πλημμελούμενος*, 'being sinned against,' i e. subjected to ill-usage or indignity. Decret. ap Demosth. Cor. p. 279, *ὅπως μὴ περιίδῃ ὑπὸ τῶν ἀσεβῶν Ἀμφισσέων τὸν θεὸν πλημμελούμενον*

E. *οἷς δεῖ τε*] Vulg *δεῖ γε* Corr Hirschig.

τοῦ πατρός] Theaet. 164 E, *οὔτι ἄν, οἶμαι, εἴπερ γε ὁ πατὴρ τοῦ ἑτέρου μύθου ἔζη, ἀλλὰ πολλὰ ἂν ἤμυνε νῦν δὲ ὀρφανὸν ὄντα αὐτὸν ἡμεῖς προπηλακίζομεν. καὶ γὰρ οὐδ' οἱ ἐπίτροποι οὓς Πρωταγ κατέλιπε βοηθεῖν ἐθέλουσιν* Another

276 ΣΩ. Τί δ'; ἄλλον ὁρῶμεν | λόγον τούτου ἀδελφὸν γνήσιον, τῷ τρόπῳ τε γίγνεται, καὶ ὅσῳ ἀμείνων καὶ δυνατώτερος τούτου φύεται;

ΦΑΙ. Τίνα τοῦτον, καὶ πῶς λέγεις γιγνόμενον;

ΣΩ. Ὃς μετ' ἐπιστήμης γράφεται ἐν τῇ τοῦ μανθάνοντος ψυχῇ, δυνατὸς μὲν ἀμῦναι ἑαυτῷ, ἐπιστήμων δὲ λέγειν τε καὶ σιγᾶν πρὸς οὓς δεῖ.

ΦΑΙ. Τὸν τοῦ εἰδότος λόγον λέγεις ζῶντα καὶ ἔμψυχον, οὗ ὁ γεγραμμένος εἴδωλον ἄν τι λέγοιτο δικαίως.

B ΣΩ. Παντάπασι μὲν οὖν. τόδε δή μοι εἰπέ· ὁ νοῦν ἔχων γεωργός, ὧν σπερμάτων κήδοιτο καὶ ἔγκαρπα βούλοιτο γενέσθαι, πότερα σπουδῇ ἂν θέρους εἰς Ἀδώνιδος κήπους ἀρῶν χαίροι θεωρῶν καλοὺς ἐν ἡμέραισιν ὀκτὼ γιγνομένους, ἢ ταῦτα μὲν δὴ παιδιᾶς τε καὶ ἑορτῆς χάριν δρῴη ἄν, ὅτε καὶ ποιοίη· ἐφ' οἷς δὲ ἐσπούδακε, τῇ γεωργικῇ χρώμενος ἂν τέχνῃ, σπείρας εἰς τὸ προσῆκον, ἀγαπῴη ἂν ἐν ὀγδόῳ μηνὶ ὅσα ἔσπειρε τέλος λαβόντα;

and very elegant instance of Plato's fondness for personifying the *λόγος*

276 *τούτου ἀδελφὸν γνήσιον*] The written *λόγος* is therefore the *νόθος ἀδελφὸς* of the spoken The distinction between the living and dead word which follows is analogous to the Christian antithesis of "letter" and "spirit," of which the one "killeth," but the other "giveth life" The Neo-platonists, from Philo downwards, express the distinction by *λόγος ἐνδιάθετος* and *λόγος προφορικός*, the words used by Hermeias in commenting on this passage

B *ὁ νοῦν ἔχων γεωργός*] 'would a husbandman of any intelligence take seeds which he cared for and wished to bear fruit, and in sober seriousness plant them during the heat of summer in gardens of Adonis, and then rejoice as he watched them coming up in full beauty ere they had been eight days sown?' Hesych., *Ἀδώνιδος κῆποι. ἐν τοῖς Ἀδωνίοις εἴδωλα ἐξάγουσιν καὶ κήπους ἐπ' ὀστράκων, καὶ παντοδαπὴν ὀπώραν οἷον ἐκ μοράθρων καὶ θριδάκων παρασκευάζουσιν αὐτῷ τοὺς κήπους καὶ γὰρ ἐν θριδακίναις αὐτὸν κατακλινθῆναι ὑπὸ Ἀφροδίτης φασίν* The glosses of the paroemiographers are to the same effect *Ἀδ κῆπ ἐπὶ τῶν ἀώρων καὶ μὴ ἐρριζωμένων Ἐπειδὴ γὰρ Ἄδωνις ἐρώμενος ὤν, ὡς ὁ μῦθος, Ἀφροδίτης, πρὸ ἥβης τελευτᾷ, οἱ ταύτῃ ὀργιάζοντες, κήπους εἰς ἀγγεῖά τινα φυτεύοντες ἢ φυτεύουσαι, ταχέως ἐκείνων διὰ τὸ μὴ ἐρριζῶσθαι μαραινομένων, Ἀδώνιδος αὐτοὺς ἐκάλουν* Theocritus xv. 111, *Ἀρσινόα πάντεσσι καλοῖς ἀτιτάλλει Ἄδωνιν Πὰρ μέν οἱ ὥρια κεῖται ὅσα δρυὸς ἄκρα φέροντι, Πὰρ δ' ἁπαλοὶ κᾶποι, πεφυλαγμένοι ἐν ταλαρίσκοις Ἀργυρέοις, Συρίω δὲ μύρω χρύσει' ἀλάβαστρα, κ τ λ* The use of *ἀροῦν* for *σπείρειν*, or *φυτεύειν*, is not uncommon in poetry Soph Frag Ion, *Ἐν Διὸς κήποις ἀροῦσθαι μόνον εὐδαίμονας ὄλβους* So Oed R 1485, *πατὴρ ἐφάνθην ἔνθεν αὐτὸς ἠρόθην*, for which we find, v. 1498, *ὅθενπερ αὐτὸς ἐσπάρη* The occurrence of the word here is a poeticism, not out of keeping with the general colour of the passage

ἐφ' οἷς δὲ ἐσπούδακε] 'where he is really in earnest, the cultivator will proceed on true principles of agriculture, he will sow his grain in fitting soil, and be well content if it come to maturity within eight months' The MSS show some confusion in the placing of the conditional particles some giving *ἂν* thrice. I have kept Bekk.'s text, as on

ΦΑΙ. Οὕτω που, ὦ Σώκρατες, τὰ μὲν σπουδῇ, τὰ C
δὲ ὡς ἑτέρως ἄν, ᾗ λέγεις, ποιοίη.

ΣΩ. Τὸν δὲ δικαίων τε καὶ καλῶν καὶ ἀγαθῶν ἐπιστήμας ἔχοντα τοῦ γεωργοῦ φῶμεν ἧττον νοῦν ἔχειν εἰς τὰ ἑαυτοῦ σπέρματα;

ΦΑΙ. Ἥκιστά γε.

ΣΩ. Οὐκ ἄρα σπουδῇ αὐτὰ ἐν ὕδατι γράψει μέλανι σπείρων διὰ καλάμου μετὰ λόγων ἀδυνάτων μὲν αὑτοῖς λόγῳ βοηθεῖν, ἀδυνάτων δὲ ἱκανῶς τἀληθῆ διδάξαι.

ΦΑΙ. Οὔκουν δὴ τό γ' εἰκός.

ΣΩ. Οὐ γάρ· ἀλλὰ τοὺς μὲν ἐν γράμμασι κήπους, D
ὡς ἔοικε, παιδιᾶς χάριν σπερεῖ τε καὶ γράψει, ὅταν γράφῃ, ἑαυτῷ τε ὑπομνήματα θησαυριζόμενος, εἰς τὸ λήθης γῆρας ἐὰν ἵκηται, καὶ παντὶ τῷ ταὐτὸν ἴχνος μετιόντι, ἡσθήσεταί τε αὐτοὺς θεωρῶν φυομένους ἁπαλούς· ὅταν δὲ ἄλλοι παιδιαῖς ἄλλαις χρῶνται, συμποσίοις τε ἄρδοντες αὑτοὺς ἑτέροις τε ὅσα τούτων ἀδελφά, τότ' ἐκεῖνος, ὡς ἔοικεν, ἀντὶ τούτων οἷς λέγω παίζων διάξει.

the whole the best. The former ἂν is, of course, a mere anticipation of that after ἀγαπῴη, to which verb both particles belong.

C. Οὐκ ἄρα σπουδῇ] The philosopher who has true scientific views of the Just, the Fair, and the Good, will surely deal as intelligently with this precious grain, the produce of his inner self, as the farmer does with his seeds. To commit them to paper would be like writing them in water; for what else is it to 'sow them in ink through a reed in the form of Discourses, as incapable of defending themselves logically, as they are of conveying an exact impression of the truth.' This, therefore, he will not do in his serious moods (σπουδῇ), but only by way of sport and recreation (παιδιᾶς χάριν).

ἐν ὕδατι γράψει] Another instance of Plato's way of sliding in a proverbial phrase by way of additional illustration. See 275 D. "ἐν ὕδατι s. καθ' ὕδατος enim γράφειν vel σπείρειν, ut Latinorum in vento et aqua scribere (Catull. lxx. 4), proverbialiter dicitur is, qui nihil quidquam facit, ἐπὶ τῶν μάτην πονούντων, ut Suidas [illegible]" (s. v.). "Here he com whose name was written in water" is the well-known inscription over the grave of an English poet. So, in verses attributed to Bacon:

"Who then to frail mortality shall trust,
But limns the water, or but writes in dust!"
Works, vii. p. 271. Spedding.

D. ὑπομνήματα] The use of literature is to preserve memorials of oral discussion; also to furnish an innocent substitute for the grosser kinds of pastime. εἰς τὸ λήθης γῆρας ἐὰν ἵκηται, 'should the writer ever reach oblivious eld.' As Heind. observes, "verba haec poetam sapiunt," and possibly they are a literal quotation. This is at any rate more likely than Winckelmann's wild or rather perhaps tame emendation. ἑαυτῷ τε ὑπ. θησ. εἰς τὸ γῆρας, λήθης φάρμακα, καὶ παντί, κ. τ. λ. The πᾶς ὁ ταὐτὸν ἴχνος μετιών, is of course the philosopher who adopts the Socratic method, literally, 'who hunts the same trail.'

ἀντὶ τούτων οἷς λέγω] The οἷς is explained by the following ἐν λόγοις. 'The philosopher will divert himself with the amusements I am describing, rather than

E ΦΑΙ. Παγκάλην λέγεις παρὰ φαύλην παιδιάν, ὦ Σώκρατες, τοῦ ἐν λόγοις δυναμένου παίζειν, δικαιοσύνης τε καὶ ἄλλων ὧν λέγεις πέρι μυθολογοῦντα.

ΣΩ. Ἔστι γάρ, ὦ φίλε Φαῖδρε, οὕτω· πολὺ δ', οἶμαι, καλλίων σπουδὴ περὶ αὐτὰ γίγνεται, ὅταν τις τῇ διαλεκτικῇ τέχνῃ χρώμενος, λαβὼν ψυχὴν προσήκουσαν, φυτεύῃ τε καὶ σπείρῃ μετ' ἐπιστήμης λόγους, οἳ ἑαυτοῖς
277 τῷ τε φυτεύσαντι βοηθεῖν ἱκανοὶ | καὶ οὐχὶ ἄκαρποι ἀλλὰ ἔχοντες σπέρμα, ὅθεν ἄλλοι ἐν ἄλλοις ἤθεσι φυόμενοι τοῦτ' ἀεὶ ἀθάνατον παρέχειν ἱκανοί, καὶ τὸν ἔχοντα εὐδαιμονεῖν ποιοῦντες εἰς ὅσον ἀνθρώπῳ δυνατὸν μάλιστα.

ΦΑΙ. Πολὺ γὰρ τοῦτ' ἔτι κάλλιον λέγεις.

ΣΩ. Νῦν δὴ ἐκεῖνα ἤδη, ὦ Φαῖδρε, δυνάμεθα κρίνειν, τούτων ὡμολογημένων.

with those of the vulgar. The old reading was οἷς λέγων, for which Heind. suggested ἐν οἷς λέγω. Bekk. found οἷς λέγω in the margin of one MS., and rightly adopted it. Heind.'s ἐν, though good in other respects, would mar the rhythm of the clause. Both are better than Ast's οἷα λέγω.

E Παγκάλην — παρὰ φαύλην] 'the recreation you describe, that of him, &c., is as excellent as the other is contemptible.' Comp. the speech of Phaedr., 258 E, so strangely objected to by Heind.

μυθολογοῦντα] Heind. forbids us to restrict this word to mythical discourse. No doubt it will bear the more general sense 'fabulari,' 'sermocinari,' as μῦθος is not unfrequently used for λόγος: but I think that here at least Plato had a special view to the myths with which he delights to embellish his dialogues. His own form of composition was as nearly as possible an imitation of the process described so vividly in the next ῥῆσις: and he seems to have thought it the best attainable substitute for the oral διάλεξις which he extols. This being the case, the written copy could hardly be contrasted with the spoken original; the less so, as Plato, in his dialogues, takes pains to diminish the distance between the two, as by making his λόγοι not only able to defend themselves and crush their antagonists, but also careful to convey a right impression of the mind of their parent, and of the truth. If this view be correct, we have in this and the succeeding passage an apology for the Platonic method of composition, both on its mythical and its dramatic side; the latter, however, rather by implication than expressly. In his larger commentary Ast seems to hint something of the same kind.

πολὺ δ', οἶμαι, καλλίων σπουδή] Rhetoric, at its very best, is inferior to pure Dialectic, which, when it works in minds of suitable capacity, is the surest method of propagating fruitful truths, and preserving them from extinction. The λόγοι thus sown owe their vitality to the circumstance, that they grow up, not all in the same kind of soil, in which case they would soon degenerate, but ἄλλοι ἐν ἄλλοις ἤθεσι.

277 τοῦτ' ἀεὶ ἀθάνατον] Referred by Ast to σπέρμα (better to τὸ ἔχειν σπέρμα). Heind., from whom I dissent, understands τὸ βοηθεῖν ἑαυτοῖς τῷ τε φυτεύσαντι.

Νῦν δὴ ἐκεῖνα] Having established, parenthetically, the superiority of oral to written speech, Socr. reverts to the subject proposed 274 B—τὸ εὐπρεπείας δὴ γραφῆς πέρι καὶ ἀπρεπείας, πῇ γιγνόμενον καλῶς ἂν ἔχοι, κ.τ.λ. The object of the dialogue, he says, had been twofold: (1) to ascertain the justice or injustice of the reproach implied in the term λογογράφος (sup. 257 C), and (2) to determine the conditions of a technical

ΦΑΙ. Τὰ ποῖα;

ΣΩ. Ὧν δὴ πέρι βουληθέντες ἰδεῖν ἀφικόμεθα εἰς τόδε, ὅπως τὸ Λυσίου τε ὄνειδος ἐξετάσαιμεν τῆς τῶν λόγων γραφῆς πέρι, καὶ αὐτοὺς τοὺς λόγους οἳ τέχνῃ καὶ B
ἄνευ τέχνης γράφοιντο. τὸ μὲν οὖν ἔντεχνον καὶ μὴ δοκεῖ μοι δεδηλῶσθαι μετρίως.

ΦΑΙ. Ἔδοξέ γε δή. πάλιν δὲ ὑπόμνησόν με πῶς.

ΣΩ Πρὶν ἄν τις τό τε ἀληθὲς ἑκάστων εἰδῇ περὶ ὧν λέγει ἢ γράφει, κατ' αὐτό τε πᾶν ὁρίζεσθαι δυνατὸς γένηται, ὁρισάμενός τε πάλιν κατ' εἴδη μέχρι τοῦ ἀτμήτου τέμνειν ἐπιστηθῇ· περί τε ψυχῆς φύσεως διιδὼν κατὰ ταὐτά, τὸ προσαρμόττον ἑκάστῃ φύσει εἶδος ἀνευρίσκων, οὕτω τιθῇ καὶ διακοσμῇ τὸν λόγον, ποικίλῃ μὲν ποικίλους C
ψυχῇ καὶ παναρμονίους διδοὺς λόγους, ἁπλοῦς δὲ ἁπλῇ, οὐ πρότερον δυνατὸν τέχνῃ ἔσεσθαι καθ' ὅσον πέφυκε μεταχειρισθῆναι τὸ λόγων γένος, οὔτε τι πρὸς τὸ διδάξαι οὔτε τι πρὸς τὸ πεῖσαι, ὡς ὁ ἔμπροσθεν πᾶς μεμήνυκεν ἡμῖν λόγος.

ΦΑΙ. Παντάπασι μὲν οὖν τοῦτό γε οὕτω πως ἐφάνη.

ΣΩ. Τί δ' αὖ περὶ τοῦ καλὸν ἢ αἰσχρὸν εἶναι τὸ D

or scientific Rhetoric The second head having been satisfactorily disposed of, he is now in a condition to discuss the former This intention is interfered with by Phaedr, who wishes to be reminded of the results arrived at in the course of the art discussion These are accordingly enumerated by Socr in a passage of singular pregnancy and neatness

B. **Πρὶν ἄν τις, κ τ λ**] It has been shown, says Socr, that it will not be possible for speeches, whether didactic or persuasive, to be constructed technically, so far as it is in their nature to admit of such handling, unless the following conditions be fulfilled (1) unless the speaker or writer have been thoroughly trained in dialectic, so as to be able to define any general term he may make use of, and then conversely to dissect it into its constituent species, until he reach the point when such dissection is no longer possible (2) unless he can look with the discerning eye of a dialectician at Soul and its species, so as to find out what manner of speeches suit the several varieties of mental character, and plan and adjust his discourse accordingly, providing simple speeches for the simple soul, but for minds of more varied development discourses of varied range, and of intricate but harmonious structure For *ἔσεσθαι* we should rather have looked for *ἔσται*, but the inf depends virtually on *δεδηλῶσθαι δοκεῖ*. Notwithstanding this, Plato adds the clause *ὡς ὁ ἔμπροσθεν μεμήνυκεν ἡμῖν λόγος*, just as he would have done had the sentence not been oblique.

D **Τί δ' αὖ περὶ τοῦ καλὸν ἢ αἰσχρόν**] The original question which has been so long delayed, is now shown by Socr. to have been virtually disposed of in the course of the foregone discussions. Speech-writing is disgraceful if the writer use terms he cannot explain, especially if such terms involve important moral distinctions, whereas, if the author know how to appraise his art at its true value and no higher, being master of the noble art of writing his thoughts on receptive and congenial

λόγους λέγειν τε καὶ γράφειν, καὶ ὅπῃ γιγνόμενον ἐν δίκῃ λέγοιτ' ἂν ὄνειδος ἢ μή, ἆρα οὐ δεδήλωκε τὰ λεχθέντα ὀλίγον ἔμπροσθεν.

ΦΑΙ. Τὰ ποῖα;

ΣΩ. Ὡς εἴτε Λυσίας ἤ τις ἄλλος πώποτε ἔγραψεν ἢ γράψει, ἰδίᾳ ἢ δημοσίᾳ, νόμους τιθείς, σύγγραμμα πολιτικὸν γράφων, καὶ μεγάλην τινὰ ἐν αὐτῷ βεβαιότητα ἡγούμενος καὶ σαφήνειαν, οὕτω μὲν ὄνειδος τῷ γράφοντι,
E εἴτε τίς φησιν εἴτε μή. τὸ γὰρ ἀγνοεῖν ὕπαρ τε καὶ ὄναρ δικαίων τε καὶ ἀδίκων πέρι καὶ κακῶν καὶ ἀγαθῶν οὐκ ἐκφεύγει τῇ ἀληθείᾳ μὴ οὐκ ἐπονείδιστον εἶναι, οὐδὲ ἂν ὁ πᾶς ὄχλος αὐτὸ ἐπαινέσῃ.

ΦΑΙ. Οὐ γὰρ οὖν.

ΣΩ. Ὁ δέ γε ἐν μὲν τῷ γεγραμμένῳ λόγῳ περὶ ἑκάστου παιδιάν τε ἡγούμενος πολλὴν ἀναγκαῖον εἶναι, καὶ οὐδένα πώποτε λόγον ἐν μέτρῳ οὐδ' ἄνευ μέτρου μεγάλης ἄξιον σπουδῆς γραφῆναι, οὐδὲ λεχθῆναι ὡς οἱ ῥαψῳδού-
278 μενοι ἄνευ ἀνακρίσεως καὶ διδαχῆς πειθοῦς ἕνεκα | ἐλέχθησαν, ἀλλὰ τῷ ὄντι αὐτῶν τοὺς βελτίστους εἰδότων

souls—in that case 'he will go near to be one whom both Socr. and his friend would heartily pray to be like' (278 B)

νόμους τιθείς, σύγγραμμα πολιτικὸν γράφων] 'proposing laws, and so being the author of a political treatise' The text is perfectly sound, Plato meaning to say that the public man is essentially an author, however much he may repudiate the title So presently 278 C, *ὅς τις ἐν πολιτικοῖς λόγοις, νόμους ὀνομάζων, συγγράμματα ἔγραψεν* Comp sup 257 E fol Heind objects that an accurate writer would have used *συγγράμματα* rather than *σύγγραμμα*, and therefore, with Ast and Schleierm, condemns *νόμους τιθείς* as a gloss On the other hand, an elegant writer would hardly have put *γράφων* so soon after *γράψει*, as Plato would have done if *νόμους τιθείς* had not intervened 'In his capacity of lawgiver, the statesman is in effect an author,' would be our modern way of expressing the meaning of the passage So Stallb, "Indem er Gesetze gebend eine Staatschrift verfasst."

1 *ὕπαρ τε καὶ ὄναρ*] 'waking or sleeping,' i e under all circumstances or conditions of mind 'To have no knowledge, clear or confused, of justice and injustice, &c, cannot but be a reproach to a writer, though the multitude with one voice applaud such ignorance' Phileb 65 E, *οὐδεὶς πώποτε οὔθ' ὕπαρ οὔτ' ὄναρ αἰσχρὸν οὔτ' εἶδεν οὔτ' ἐπενόησεν.*

ὡς οἱ ῥαψῳδούμενοι] 'as the speeches recited by rhapsodes have been spoken with a view to persuasion, and without any attempt at questioning or teaching.' See below 278 C, *καὶ Ὁμήρῳ καὶ εἴ τις ἄλλος ποίησιν ψιλὴν συντέθεικε*, whence it follows that *οἱ ῥαψῳδούμενοι (λόγοι)* is to be understood literally, and not as Stallb and Heind suppose, of the declamations of sophists *ἀνάκρισις* is met with in non-technical sense in Charm ad fin, *Βιάσει ἄρα, ἦν δ' ἐγώ, καὶ οὐδ' ἀνάκρισίν μοι δώσεις*, where, as here, the reference is to Socrates' interrogatory method There is therefore no occasion for Heind 's conj *ἄνευ κρίσεως* For *ὡς οἱ* Schleierm. conj *ὅσοι*

ὑπόμνησιν γεγονέναι, ἐν δὲ τοῖς διδασκομένοις καὶ μα-
θήσεως χάριν λεγομένοις καὶ τῷ ὄντι γραφομένοις ἐν
ψυχῇ περὶ δικαίων τε καὶ καλῶν καὶ ἀγαθῶν, ἐν μόνοις
τό τε ἐναργὲς εἶναι καὶ τέλεον καὶ ἄξιον σπουδῆς· δεῖν
δὲ τοὺς τοιούτους λόγους αὑτοῦ λέγεσθαι οἷον υἱεῖς γνη-
σίους εἶναι, πρῶτον μὲν τὸν ἐν ἑαυτῷ, ἐὰν εὑρεθεὶς ἐνῇ,
ἔπειτα εἴ τινες τούτου ἔκγονοί τε καὶ ἀδελφοὶ ἅμα ἐν B
ἄλλαισιν ἄλλων ψυχαῖς κατ' ἀξίαν ἐνέφυσαν· τοὺς δὲ
ἄλλους χαίρειν ἐῶν—οὗτος δὲ ὁ τοιοῦτος ἀνὴρ κινδυνεύει,
ὦ Φαῖδρε, εἶναι οἷον ἐγώ τε καὶ σὺ εὐξαίμεθ' ἂν σέ τε καὶ
ἐμὲ γενέσθαι.

ΦΑΙ. Παντάπασι μὲν οὖν ἔγωγε βούλομαί τε καὶ
εὔχομαι ἃ λέγεις.

ΣΩ. Οὐκοῦν ἤδη πεπαίσθω μετρίως ἡμῖν τὰ περὶ
λόγων· καὶ σύ τε ἐλθὼν φράζε Λυσίᾳ, ὅτι νῷ καταβάντε
εἰς τὸ Νυμφῶν νᾶμά τε καὶ μουσεῖον ἠκούσαμεν λόγων,
οἳ ἐπέστελλον λέγειν Λυσίᾳ τε καὶ εἴ τις ἄλλος συντίθησι C
λόγους, καὶ Ὁμήρῳ καὶ εἴ τις ἄλλος αὖ ποίησιν ψιλὴν
ἢ ἐν ᾠδῇ συντέθεικε, τρίτον δὲ Σόλωνι καὶ ὅστις ἐν

278 *ἐν μόνοις*] We must either read with Heind *ἐν μόνοις τούτοις*, or eject *ἐν*, with Hirsch and Stallb The former expedient seems to me preferable.

ἐὰν εὑρεθεὶς ἐνῇ] Not equiv to *εὑρεθῇ ἐνών*, but rather to *ἐὰν ὁ ἐνὼν λόγος ὑφ' αὐτοῦ εὑρεθῇ*—the word within, if it have been discovered by himself, or, as it were, self-sown, and not transplanted from some other mind

B *ἄλλαισιν*] This Ionic or rather old Attic form is freq in Plato. See instances, p. 210 B, note On this archaism see Bentley, Dissert. on Phalaris, § xiii. (vol ii p 6, Dyce)

οὗτος δὲ] Some MSS give *δή*, but see above, p 272 A

εἰς τὸ Νυμφῶν νᾶμά τε καὶ μουσεῖον] Alluding to the recess on the banks of the Ilissus, described in the opening scene of the dialogue, which was sacred to Pan and the Nymphs, and decorated with images inserted in niches carven on the rocks. Strictly speaking this was a *Πανεῖον* or *Νυμφαῖον*, Pan and the Nymphs being inseparable in such localities But the Musae Ilissides, to whom an elegant temple was dedicated on the opposite side of the stream, were in fact river-nymphs See Servius ad Virg Ecl. vii 21 "*Nymphae, noster amor, Libethrides* Libethros fons est ubi coluntur Musae, et sic ait *Libethrides*, ac si diceret *Hippocrenides* a fonte Hippocrene, ut autem poetae invocent Nymphas, sicut hoc loco etiam in fine (Ecl x 1), *Extremum hunc, Arethusa, mihi concede laborem*, haec ratio est, quod secundum Varronem ipsae sint Nymphae quae et Musae, nam et in aqua consistere dicuntur, quae de fontibus manat," &c. Aristides Rhet. ii p 708, Dind, *ἀνεμιμνήσκομεν δὲ τῶν ποιητῶν, ὅτι Νύμφας καὶ Μούσας ἀεί πως συνάγουσιν* So also Hesych, *Νύμφαι Μοῦσαι θεαί* It is curious that there is no trace of this connexion in Homer; from which however we are not to infer that it was a later invention See Welck Gr Götterlehre, i 705 By *νᾶμα* is meant, not the Ilissus, but the fountain *μάλα ψυχροῦ ὕδατος* described 230 B, which flowed into the stream

C. *ποίησιν ψιλὴν ἢ ἐν ᾠδῇ*] This distinction is explained by Legg 669 D, which the comm quote *ταῦτα γὰρ*

πολιτικοῖς λόγοις νόμους ὀνομάζων συγγράμματα ἔγραψεν· εἰ μὲν εἰδὼς ᾗ τἀληθὲς ἔχει συνέθηκε ταῦτα, καὶ ἔχων βοηθεῖν, εἰς ἔλεγχον ἰὼν περὶ ὧν ἔγραψε, καὶ λέγων αὐτὸς δυνατὸς τὰ γεγραμμένα φαῦλα ἀποδεῖξαι, οὔ τι τῶνδε D ἐπωνυμίαν ἔχοντα δεῖ λέγεσθαι τὸν τοιοῦτον, ἀλλ' ἐφ' οἷς ἐσπούδακεν ἐκείνων.

ΦΑΙ. Τίνας οὖν τὰς ἐπωνυμίας αὐτῷ νέμεις;

ΣΩ. Τὸ μὲν σοφόν, ὦ Φαῖδρε, καλεῖν ἔμοιγε μέγα

ὁρῶσι πάντα κυκώμενα καὶ ἔτι διασπῶσιν οἱ ποιηταί, ῥυθμὸν μὲν καὶ σχήματα μέλους χωρίς, λόγους ψιλοὺς εἰς μέτρα τιθέντες, μέλος δ' αὖ καὶ ῥυθμοὺς ἄνευ ῥημάτων, ψιλῇ κιθαρίσει τε καὶ αὐλήσει προσχρώμενοι whence it appears that the dialogue of tragedy would be ranked as ποίησις ψιλή. In the passage of the Laws Plato seems to regret the divorce between poetry and music, as a sign of declining Art

ὅς τις ἐν πολιτικοῖς λόγοις] 'whoever, under the form of political discourses, which he names laws, has composed written treatises,' and so committed himself to an act of authorship Schleierm.'s συλλόγοις for λόγοις is plausible, but needless

λέγων αὐτὸς δυνατὸς — φαῦλα ἀποδεῖξαι] 'able, by his own *viva voce* efforts, to demonstrate the inferiority of written speech to oral' Previously (277 E) one condition of a first-rate (i. e. a philosophical) writer was stated to be a disposition to disparage writing καὶ οὐδένα πώποτε λόγον—μεγάλης ἄξιον σπουδῆς γραφῆναι The meaning is not that the philosopher will give a formal proof of the inferiority of writing, but that, by the skill with which he conducts a *viva voce* inquiry, he will leave that impression on the minds of his hearers Stallb quotes in illustration of this use of ἀποδεῖξαι, Phaed. 72 C τελευτῶντα πάντα λῆρον τὸν Ἐνδυμίωνα ἀποδείξειεν

οὔ τι τῶνδε—ἀλλ' ἐφ' οἷς ἐσπούδακεν ἐκείνων] He who fulfils the conditions last enumerated who employs no terms which he is not prepared to define, and makes no statements which he cannot defend, &c., must not on any account receive a designation proper to any of the above named pursuits, but must be named after those which form the serious business of his life In other words, he is not to be classed as λόγων συγγραφεὺς with Lysias as ποιητὴς with Homer, or as νομογράφος with Solon, but with the sincere investigators of truth as a Philosopher. The former names may serve for the author who has nothing in him greater or more glorious than the phrases which he has put on paper, or delivered in the form of a set speech, whatever pains he may have taken in the arrangement and combination of the parts

D Τὸ μὲν σοφὸν —θεῷ μόνῳ πρέπειν] The comm quote Parmen 134 C, οὐκοῦν εἴπερ τι ἄλλο αὐτῆς ἐπιστήμης μετέχει, οὐκ ἄν τινα μᾶλλον ἢ θεὸν φαίης ἔχειν τὴν ἀκριβεστάτην ἐπιστήμην The terms φιλόσοφος and φιλοσοφία are traditionally said to have been invented by Pythagoras (Cic Tusc Qu V 3) At what time they came into general use in Athens may be a question Probably, however, not before the time of Socrates, from whom Isocrates may have conceived the idea of appropriating them, as he frequently does, to himself and his occupation Of the comic poets Aristophanes is the first who uses φιλόσοφος, but in a late play, the Ecclesiazusae * (v 571) A passage in Aristides, Rhet ii 407, Dind, is illustrative of the history of the word, and indirectly of the passage before us He protests against the restriction of the term to any particular class or sect of thinkers or writers, maintaining that in the best times φιλοσοφία meant φιλοκαλία τις καὶ διατριβὴ περὶ λόγους, καὶ οὐχ ὁ νῦν τρόπος οὗτος, ἀλλὰ παιδεία κοινῶς This general sense, he says, is attested by "Demosthenes and thousands of others," including Plato himself, who uses the term both in its popular and its restricted acceptation The same passage reviews the history of the word σοφιστής, which in the days of

* Where, however, W Dindorf proposes φιλόδημον, metri causa Meineke adheres to the received reading, which is much more suitable to the context

εἶναι δοκεῖ καὶ θεῷ μόνῳ πρέπειν· τὸ δὲ ἢ φιλόσοφον ἢ τοιοῦτόν τι μᾶλλόν τε ἂν αὐτῷ ἁρμόττοι καὶ ἐμμελεστέρως ἔχοι.

ΦΑΙ. Καὶ οὐδέν γε ἄπο τρόπου.

ΣΩ. Οὐκοῦν αὖ τὸν μὴ ἔχοντα τιμιώτερα ὧν συνέθηκεν ἢ ἔγραψεν ἄνω κάτω στρέφων ἐν χρόνῳ, πρὸς ἄλληλα κολλῶν τε καὶ ἀφαιρῶν, ἐν δίκῃ που ποιητὴν ἢ E
λόγων συγγραφέα ἢ νομογράφον προσερεῖς ;

ΦΑΙ. Τί μήν ;

ΣΩ. Ταῦτα τοίνυν τῷ ἑταίρῳ φράζε.

ΦΑΙ. Τί δὲ σύ ; πῶς ποιήσεις ; οὐδὲ γὰρ οὐδὲ τὸν σὸν ἑταῖρον δεῖ παρελθεῖν.

ΣΩ. Τίνα τοῦτον ;

ΦΑΙ. Ἰσοκράτη τὸν καλόν. ᾧ τί ἀπαγγελεῖς, ὦ Σώκρατες ; τίν᾽ αὐτὸν φήσομεν εἶναι ;

ΣΩ. Νέος ἔτι, ὦ Φαῖδρε, Ἰσοκράτης· ὃ μέντοι μαντεύομαι | κατ᾽ αὐτοῦ, λέγειν ἐθέλω. 279

the Empire had lost much of its invidious meaning Lysias, we are told, called not only Aeschines Socraticus, but Plato himself, a Sophist (possibly in his speech against the former, of which we have a short but curious fragment) Isocrates, too, not only calls the Eristics (τοὺς περὶ τὴν ἔριν) Sophists, but those too who would have called themselves dialecticians Plato, says Aristides, τὸν σοφιστὴν δοκεῖ μέν πως κακίζειν ἀεί, καὶ ὅ γε δὴ μάλιστα ἐπαναστὰς τῷ ὀνόματι Πλάτων εἶναί μοι δοκεῖ "The cause of this was his contempt for the vulgar, and for his own contemporaries generally" Yet even Plato, he says, on one occasion could use this invidious name as a title of honour, "when he called the God of all wisdom and truth a τέλεος σοφιστής" The plain truth seems to be, that when σοφιστής had become a term of reproach, φιλόσοφος or some equivalent became indispensable 'Philosopher' was then, as it has remained to this day, a prized and honoured name, and no sect or profession, literary or scientific, willingly renounced the pretension to wear it The subsequent recognition of the superior claim of the speculative sects was owing partly to the imposing character and vast ability of Plato and Aristotle partly also to the extinction of political life, which impaired the value of rhetoric in public estimation

ἐν δίκῃ] So Bekk, though the Bodl and others give δίκῃ without the preposition. But it is doubtful whether δίκῃ alone can have the force of the Lat 'jure,' and the prep may easily have been absorbed by the preceding word

E Ἰσοκράτη τὸν καλόν] The epithet in cases like the present does not imply personal beauty · Epist. ii 314 c, Σωκράτους νέου καὶ καλοῦ γεγονότος Nor youth Athen 505 E, ἥκει ἡμῖν ὁ καλός τε καὶ χρυσοῦς Γοργίας—where Plato is the supposed speaker In the instances quoted by Heind, on Hipp. i. init, it is applied to a variety of persons —Philebus, Callias, Euthydemus, Critias —who seem to have had nothing in common but the taste for letters or philosophy 'Gentle' or 'accomplished' would convey something like the same associations The reading Ἰσοκράτη is in the Bodl and other first-rate codd Vulg Ἰσοκράτην So Ἱπποκράτη, Protag 328 D

Νέος ἔτι] Isocr was six or seven years older than Plato, hence thirty-five or thirty-six at the death of Socr (B C

ΦΑΙ. Τὸ ποῖον δή;

ΣΩ. Δοκεῖ μοι ἀμείνων ἢ κατὰ τοὺς περὶ Λυσίαν εἶναι λόγους τὰ τῆς φύσεως, ἔτι τε ἤθει γεννικωτέρῳ κεκρᾶσθαι· ὥστε οὐδὲν ἂν γένοιτο θαυμαστὸν προϊούσης τῆς ἡλικίας εἰ περὶ αὐτούς τε τοὺς λόγους, οἷς νῦν ἐπιχειρεῖ, πλέον ἢ παίδων διενέγκοι τῶν πώποτε ἁψαμένων λόγων, εἴτε εἰ αὐτῷ μὴ ἀποχρήσαι ταῦτα, ἐπὶ μείζω [δέ] τις αὐτὸν ἄγοι ὁρμὴ θειοτέρα. φύσει γάρ, ὦ φίλε,
B ἔνεστί τις φιλοσοφία τῇ τοῦ ἀνδρὸς διανοίᾳ. ταῦτα δὴ

399). The dramatic or fictitious date of the Phaedr. falls after the return of Lysias from Thurii (B.C. 411); and we may therefore suppose Isocr. to be under thirty when the remark is supposed to be made. He was two and twenty years the junior of Lysias.—This entire passage is translated by Cicero in the Orator, xiii. 41: Est enim quasi in extrema pagina Phaedri his ipsis verbis loquens Socrates: "Adolescens etiam nunc, o Phaedre, Isocrates est, sed quid de illo augurer, lubet dicere. Quid tandem?" inquit ille. "Majore mihi ingenio videtur esse quam ut cum orationibus Lysiae comparetur. Praeterea ad virtutem major indoles: ut minime mirum futurum sit, si, quum aetate processerit, aut in hoc orationum genere cui nunc studet, tantum, quantum pueris, reliquis praestet omnibus, qui unquam orationes attigerunt: aut (εἴτε), si contentus his non fuerit, divino aliquo animi motu majora concupiscat. Inest enim natura philosophia in hujus viri mente quaedam." Haec de adolescente Socrates auguratur. At ea de seniore scribit Plato, et scribit aequalis, et quidem, exagitator omnium rhetorum, hunc miratur unum. Me autem, qui Isocratem non diligunt, una cum Socrate et cum Platone errare patiantur.

279. ἔτι τε ἤθει γεννικωτέρῳ κεκρᾶσθαι] The phraseology is borrowed from the medical writers and their doctrine of temperament. "The elements were kindlier mixed" in Isocr. than in Lysias. Comp. Epist. vii. 326 C, οὐχ οὕτω θαυμαστῇ φύσει κραθήσεται, where φύσις, as in the clause preceding this passage, refers to intellectual endowments, not moral (ἤθει). Legg. xi. 930 A, εἰκὸς εἶναι τοὺς τοιούτους μὴ πραέσιν ἤθεσι κεκραμένους.

πλέον ἢ παίδων διενέγκοι] Epist. vii. 326 C, προσήκει πλέον ἢ παίδων τῶν ἄλλων ἀνθρώπων διαφέρειν.

εἴτε εἰ αὐτῷ μὴ ἀποχρήσαι] Vulg. ἔτι τε. I have restored to the text the reading of the Bodl. and first Vatican, supported by several other codd. of note, and by Cicero, l. l., who omits in his version the δὲ of the following clause. This omission is not noticed by Spengel, who was the first to call attention to the importance of the variant adopted in the text. (See Appendix II.) Socrates would not be surprised if Isocrates should *either*, as a speech-writer, distance all his rivals in that profession, *or* should be dissatisfied with this his present employment, and borne by a diviner impulse to higher things. Herm., μὴ ἀποχρήσαι ταῦτα, τουτέστι, τὸ λογογραφεῖν, ἀλλὰ τραπηθείη κατ' εὐμοιρίαν τινὰ εἰς φιλοσοφίαν. In other words, two courses were before him: that of persevering in his present employment, in which case Socr. augurs that he will throw all other logographers into the shade; secondly, that of abandoning the rhetorical and adopting the philosophic profession. Isocr., as we know, chose the former alternative. If the Vulgate reading ἔτι δὲ be retained, the meaning will rather be, that Isocr. will add to his eminence in the λόγοι οἷς νῦν ἐπιχειρεῖ some further accomplishments of a higher kind; that without ceasing to be a λογογράφος, he will infuse into his rhetorical exercises an element of philosophic speculation. A favourable critic might say that the prediction, thus understood, was verified in his practice. But it is difficult to believe that the shreds of philosophy with which Isocr. garnishes his orations would have excited the admiration of Plato; and the less so, as the rhetorician omits no opportunity of disparaging that very science of dia-

οὖν ἐγὼ μὲν παρὰ τῶνδε τῶν θεῶν ὡς ἐμοῖς παιδικοῖς Ἰσοκράτει ἐξαγγέλλω, σὺ δ᾽ ἐκεῖνα ὡς σοῖς Λυσίᾳ.

ΦΑΙ. Ταῦτα ἔσται. ἀλλὰ ἴωμεν, ἐπειδὴ καὶ τὸ πνῖγος ἠπιώτερον γέγονεν.

ΣΩ. Οὐκοῦν εὐξαμένω πρέπει τοῖσδε πορεύεσθαι;

ΦΑΙ. Τί μήν;

ΣΩ. Ὦ φίλε Πάν τε καὶ ἄλλοι ὅσοι τῇδε θεοί, δοίητέ μοι καλῷ γενέσθαι τἄνδοθεν· ἔξωθεν δ᾽ ὅσα ἔχω, τοῖς ἐντὸς εἶναί μοι φίλια. πλούσιον δὲ νομίζοιμι τὸν σοφόν. C
τὸ δὲ χρυσοῦ πλῆθος εἴη μοι ὅσον μήτε φέρειν μήτε ἄγειν δύναιτ᾽ ἄλλος ἢ ὁ σώφρων.
Ἔτι ἄλλου του δεόμεθα, ὦ Φαῖδρε; ἐμοὶ μὲν γὰρ μετρίως ηὖκται.

ΦΑΙ. Καὶ ἐμοὶ ταῦτα συνεύχου· κοινὰ γὰρ τὰ τῶν φίλων.

ΣΩ. Ἴωμεν.

lectic, which it is the object of the Phaedr to exalt above all others

B τοῖσδε] Of course to the θεοὶ and δαίμονες ἐντόπιοι (262 D), to Pan, Achelous, and the Ilissian Muses or Nymphs, whose ἀγάλματα are mentioned in the opening scene, p. 230 B.

δοίητέ μοι καλῷ γενέσθαι τἄνδοθεν] Socr prays—(1) that he may be 'made beautiful in the inward parts,' (2) that such outward advantages as he possesses may not interfere with his soul's health, (3) that he may count the wise wealthy; and (lastly) that the amount of gold at his disposal may be such as the temperate man, and he only, can 'bear and carry' The last clause of the prayer is ambiguous, for the temperate man, the man of well regulated mind, can 'bear and carry' more gold than another without injury to his moral being he can also dispense with money and money's worth better than others And this ambiguity seems intentional, implying that Socrates neither prays for wealth with the worldling, nor deprecates it with the Cynic Both the sentiment and language of this petition derive illustration from a fine passage of the Critias, where, in describing the spirit and temper of the citizens of his Atlantis, Plato says, διὸ πλὴν ἀρετῆς πάντα ὑπερορῶντες σμικρὰ ἡγοῦντο τὰ παρόντα, καὶ ῥᾳδίως ἔφερον οἷον ἄ … τῶν ἄλλων κτημάτων ὄγκον, ἀλλ᾽ οὐ μεθύοντες ὑπὸ τρυφῆς διὰ πλοῦτον ἀκράτορες αὑτῶν ὄντες ἐσφάλλοντο (p. 120 E) The Commentators seem to me to mistake Plato's drift, when they quote as in point the speech of Antisthenes in Xenophon's Banquet iv. 34 The Cynic thinks τοὺς ἀνθρώπους οὐκ ἐν τῷ οἴκῳ τὸν πλοῦτον καὶ τὴν πενίαν ἔχειν ἀλλ᾽ ἐν ταῖς ψυχαῖς, and so far agrees with Socr in the text, but the remainder of his speech is an ἐγκώμιον πενίας going far beyond the moderate views of Plato. Of the phrase ἄγειν καὶ φέρειν used sensu bono, as they say, Heind. gives one other instance from Plato, Legg 817 A ἐάν τινες (τῶν περὶ τραγῳδίαν ποιητῶν) ἐπανερωτήσωσιν οὑτωσί πως Ὦ ξένοι, πότερον φοιτῶμεν ὑμῖν εἰς τὴν πόλιν τε καὶ χώραν ἢ μή, καὶ τὴν ποίησιν φέρωμέν τε καὶ ἄγωμεν, i e 'may we have free ingress and egress with our poetical wares?' But in this passage of the Phaedr it is rather equiv to 'manage,' 'administer,' as in Plutarch, de Frat Amore, 486 E ὁ ἀδελφὸς ἄγει καὶ φέρει πάντα, καὶ θαυμάζεται καὶ θεραπεύεται σοὶ δὲ οὐδεὶς πρόσεισιν Both senses are to be distinguished from the much more familiar usage of ἄγειν καὶ φέρειν in the sense of 'plundering' or 'harrying' an enemy's country, or 'sacking' a captured town

APPENDIX I.

ON THE EROTIC DISCOURSES OF SOCRATES.

THE FIRST DISCOURSE OF SOCRATES.

Of the two speeches put into the mouth of Socrates in this dialogue, the first is a homily on the evil effects and inherent baseness of the practice of παιδεραστία as it was understood by Lysias and followed by the Athenians of his day. The arguments adduced by Lysias had all been founded on considerations of expediency: the ἐρώμενος would gain more in fortune and lose less in reputation by complying with the entreaties of a suitor who had no real affection for him than he would by yielding to a truly impassioned admirer: he is advised, in short, to consent to dishonour for the sake of worldly advantage. Socrates artfully suppresses his indignation on hearing sentiments so cynical and immoral, pretending to have paid attention only to the style and arrangement (τὸ ῥητορικόν) of the discourse, without heeding its subject-matter. His own counter-speech is confined to establishing the first of Lysias's topics, "that it is not good to show favour to a suitor who is in love." His arguments, like those of his predecessor, professedly appeal to self-interest, but to a self-interest more enlightened, comprehensive and far-sighted. The vulgar ἐραστὴς is, he insists, of all companions the most disagreeable and the most pernicious. By yielding to his importunities the ἐρώμενος will deliver himself body and soul into the power of a jealous and capricious, a selfish and brutal tyrant: he will surrender all he holds most dear without an equivalent either of pleasure or profit. The pleasure, such as it is, will be reaped by the ἐραστὴς alone, while the consequences to the ἐρώμενος will be the probable wreck of his worldly prospects and bodily health, and the certain deterioration of his mental culture, "the thing which is of all most precious in the eyes of gods and men," 241 c. Incidentally, and as if unintentionally, Socrates paints in the blackest and we may add the truest colours that passion which was the bane of Athenian society. In Athens the list of "things, of which it is a shame even to speak," was briefer than with us, and Socrates would have been untrue to his calling had he been deterred by prudery or fastidiousness from approaching a subject of which poets sang, men of letters wrote, and fine gentlemen in their "noctes coenaeque deum" delighted to reason. The sanctity of Socrates is not the less to be acknowledged, because unalloyed with sanctimoniousness and those who are inclined to be sceptical as to the unblemished purity of his sentiments and teaching upon this to us offensive subject, ought to have their doubts dispelled when they find the literal and not over-refined Xenophon uniting his testimony with that of Plato. Xenophon was under no temptation to represent his master as a loftier thinker or purer moralist than he really was: if his picture of Socrates is unfaithful it is either because he purposely throws into the shade the more unpopular of his characteristics—those qualities in fact which stood in the most marked contrast to the maxims and usages of his time and country or because he occasionally sacrifices general effect to accuracy of detail. It is the more satisfactory that in the discourse on Love, put into the mouth of Socrates in Xenophon's Banquet[1], we find arguments which so strikingly resemble those in the speech under our review, as to make it very probable that in both we have the actual sentiments of Socrates represented—we may even say reproduced—by his rival disciples. From both we rise with the feelings expressed by the

[1] c. viii. There is this difference between the two speeches that Plato's is addressed to the ἐρώμενος, Xenophon's to Callias, who was in the condition of an ἐραστής. But allowing for this, the train of reasoning is substantially the same, and the resemblance in certain passages striking. Compare, for instance, the following:—

Xen. § 21, οὐ μὴν ὅτι γε ὡραῖος ἀώρῳ οὐδ' ὅτι γε καλὸς οὐκέτι καλῷ καὶ ἐρῶντι οὐκ ἐρῶν ὁμιλεῖ, φιλήσει αὐτόν	Plato, 210 C, νεωτέρῳ γὰρ πρεσβύτερος συνών, κ τ λ. Ib. D. ὁρῶντι μὲν ὄψιν πρεσβυτέραν καὶ οὐκ ἐν ὥρᾳ
§ 23, ἀεὶ γάρ τοι προσαιτῶν καὶ προσδεόμενος ἢ φιλήματος ἢ ἄλλου τινὸς ψηλαφήματος παρακολουθεῖ	Ib., ὁρῶντι ἀκούοντι ἁπτομένῳ καὶ πᾶσαν αἴσθησιν αἰσθανομένῳ τοῦ ἐρωμένου, ὥστε μεθ' ἡδονῆς ἀραρότως αὐτῷ ὑπηρετεῖν
§ 33, ὅτι ἄνευ φιλίας συνουσία οὐδεμία ἀξιόλογος πάντες ἐπιστάμεθα . . τῶν δὲ τοῦ σώματος ἐπιθυμούντων πολλοὶ μισοῦσι τὸν ἐρώμενον . . καὶ μὴν ἐν μὲν τῇ τοῦ σώματος χρήσει ἔνεστί τις κόρος, ὥστε ἅπερ καὶ πρὸς τὰ σιτία διὰ πλησμονὴν ταῦτα ἀνάγκη καὶ πρὸς τὰ παιδικὰ πάσχειν	211 C, ταῦτά τε οὖν χρή, ὦ παῖ, ξυννοεῖν καὶ εἰδέναι τὴν ἐραστοῦ φιλίαν, ὅτι οὐ μετ' εὐνοίας γίγνεται, ἀλλὰ σιτίου τρόπον χάριν πλησμονῆς, . ὡς λύκοι ἄρν' ἀγαπῶσ' ὡς παῖδα φιλοῦσιν ἐρασταί

Lycon of Xenophon (c. 9. 1), νὴ τὴν Ἥραν, ὦ Σώκρατες, καλός τε κἀγαθὸς δοκεῖς μοι ἄνθρωπος εἶναι

Concerning this first discourse of Socrates, we may further observe, that it is accompanied with a brief prefatory exposition of the Passion of Love. This preface, it must be allowed, does not either in matter or manner harmonize with the impressive exhortation which follows it. This Plato seems to have felt, for he has separated the preface from the main body of the discourse by a dramatic interlude. Its purpose is, however, clear. Plato meant to intimate that the ἔρως of which the first discourse treats is the son not of Venus Urania, but rather of Venus Pandemus[2]. It is an appetite for pleasure combined with a sensibility to beauty just sufficient to create a personal preference, but insufficient to elevate or purify the compound emotion of which it is an ingredient Itself feeble, the Love of Beauty derives its strength and fire from its baser but more powerful companion. It is when the delight in beauty is thus alloyed with appetite and strengthened by the alloy, that to the irresistible passion resulting from the combination the name of Love is ordinarily assigned This is probably the meaning of the very obscure etymological definition of ἔρως which concludes the prefatory exposition referred to (p. 238 c)

We have seen that Socrates in this speech confines himself to one of the two topics handled by Lysias. He proves convincingly ὅτι οὐ χρὴ τῷ ἐρῶντι χαρίζεσθαι; but he omits to show ὅτι χρὴ χαρίζεσθαι τῷ μὴ ἐρῶντι. His motives for this omission are to us obvious, but it is not his way to explain his true motives Accordingly he affects an exceeding horror at his own impiety, and deep contrition for the wrong he has done to one of the Immortals "Is not Eros," he exclaims, "a god and a son of Aphrodite?" "So we are told," replies Phaedrus "Lysias does not tell us so, nor does that discourse which fell indeed from my lips, but represents your views of the nature of Eros rather than my own, for you bewitched me, and I spoke under a spell." In other words, your views of Love and those of Lysias are unworthy and ignoble· there is another and purer passion of which you reck not, a passion alone entitled to the sacred name which you abuse[3].

[2] Compare Xen Symp c. viii. §§ 9, 10

[3] This passage conveys a bitter reflection upon the ἐρωτικοὶ λόγοι of Lysias, and perhaps upon other popular compositions of the day Whether it is fair to read in it a sweeping condemnation of the so-called sophists is another matter So far as we know, Lysias was the first to commit to writing discourses of this description and it is an injustice to Protagoras and Prodicus and Hippias to make them accomplices in the offence That the speech of Lysias is in a very legitimate sense of the word sophistical we may freely grant, but that Plato produces it as a specimen of

This sudden outburst of pious remorse will surprise no one who has studied either the Socrates of Plato or the Socrates of Xenophon. Though something of irony is mixed with it, it is not wholly ironical. Socrates never affected to have shaken off the religious prejudices of his time and country: he even added to them some private fancies of his own. Though the δαιμόνιον, the voice or inward monitor of which he often speaks, was not, as later and particularly Christian writers have assumed, a natal Genius or familiar Demon, he doubtless supposed it to come from some external and supernatural source. And as regards the god Eros in particular, he repeatedly avows himself his servant and votary. On this point his language is so strong as to have laid him open to grave misapprehensions on the part of his contemporaries. In Xenophon's Banquet he calls himself a θιασώτης of Eros[4], an adept in all Love's mysteries, and declares that he cannot remember the time at which he was not in love with some one or other—οὐκ ἔχω χρόνον εἰπεῖν ἐν ᾧ οὐκ ἐρῶν τινος διατελῶ. In the Theages again he tells us that the only science he is thoroughly acquainted with is the Erotic[5] (σμικροῦ τινος μαθήματος)—"a poor thing, but his own." Neither must we forget the eloquent peroration of his speech in Plato's Symposium[6]—καὶ αὐτὸς τιμῶ τὰ ἐρωτικά, καὶ διαφερόντως ἀσκῶ, καὶ τοῖς ἄλλοις παρακελεύομαι, καὶ νῦν τε καὶ ἀεὶ ἐγκωμιάζω τὴν δύναμιν καὶ ἀνδρείαν τοῦ Ἔρωτος καθ' ὅσον οἷός τ' εἰμί. In the same dialogue he names Alcibiades as the object of his then ruling passion. We know how Alcibiades had misunderstood him, and how he had been undeceived. No one now-a-days puts so gross a meaning upon the words of Socrates, but there is another misconception against which we shall do well to guard. The ἔρως of Socrates is not that mystical emotion which Plato paints in the highly imaginative mythical discourse which we shall presently consider. If less exalted and poetical, it was more unequivocally pure. It was not the beauty of Alcibiades, but his splendid mental endowments, his great capacity for good or for evil, which excited the admiration and the solicitude of Socrates. Οἱ εὐεργετοῦντες μᾶλλον φιλοῦσι τῶν εὐεργετουμένων is the deep and true remark of Aristotle, and it was the memory of what he had done and suffered for his brilliant but erring friend which warmed the heart of Socrates towards Alcibiades, and prompted him to ever greater efforts in his behalf. This affection was not diminished by

the general teaching of those whom he would have styled Sophists, is an assumption which none but loose or prejudiced thinkers will be disposed to make. The bearing of this last observation will be intelligible to those who have been in the habit of reading their Plato by the light of Stallbaum's notes.

[4] Xen. Conv. viii. 2. [5] p. 128. [6] p. 212 B.

the grievous faults in the character of its object, and would have remained equally strong had Alcibiades been as ugly as a Satyr, as indeed Theaetetus, another of his ἐρώμενοι, seems to have been[7]. For an attachment like this, φιλία seemed and was too cold a word: Socrates could find no other name for it than ἔρως, and he represents himself as the ἐραστὴς of Alcibiades accordingly. In like manner, Euripides does not scruple to denote by the same terms the passionate love of a son for a tender and noble mother—

> ἐρᾶτε μητρὸς παῖδες, οὐ γὰρ ἔστ' ἔρως
> τοιοῦτος ἄλλος ὅστις ἡδίων ἐρᾶν[8]

That Socrates was to this extent serious in professing himself the votary of Eros there can be little doubt. But with this seriousness was mixed in large measure that humorous affectation of qualities the opposite of his own which the Greeks knew as the εἰρωνεία of Socrates. Intellectually the acutest man of his age, he represents himself in all companies as the dullest person present. Morally the purest, he affects to be the slave of passion, and borrows the language of gallantry to describe a benevolence too exalted for the comprehension of his contemporaries. He is by turns an ἐραστής, a προαγωγός, a μαστροπός[9], a μαιευτικός[1], disguising the sanctity of his true vocation by names suggestive of vile or ridiculous images. The same spirit of whimsical paradox leads him, in Xenophon's Banquet[2], to argue that his own satyr-like visage was superior in beauty to that of the handsomest man present. That this irony was to some extent calculated is more than probable; it disarmed ridicule by anticipating it, it allayed jealousy and propitiated envy: and it possibly procured him admission into gay circles from which a more solemn teacher would have been excluded. But it had for its basis a real greatness of soul, a hearty and unaffected disregard of popular opinion, a perfect disinterestedness, an entire abnegation of self. He made himself a fool that others by his folly might be made wise: he humbled himself to the level of those among whom his work lay that he might raise some few among them to his own level: he was "all things to all men, if by any means he might win some." "Of you who are present," says Alcibiades in the Symposium[3], "there is not one who understands Socrates: but I will unfold to you his true character. You all see or think you see that Socrates is a pas-

[7] Theaet. 143 E. How austere his view of the duties of an ἐραστὴς we see from Lysis 210 E, ταπεινοῦντα καὶ συστέλλοντα, κ.τ.λ. He is to "minish and keep low" his παιδικά.

[8] Erecth. 360.

[9] Xen. Symp. iii. 10.

[1] Theaet. 161 E al.

[2] Cap. v.

[3] p. 216 c, foll.

sionate admirer of beautiful persons, that he is ever in their company, and professes to be enslaved by their charms: again, his ignorance is boundless—he knows absolutely nothing. Yet all this is counterfeit: it is but the grotesque Silenus-mask which conceals the features of the god within: for if you remove the covering, how shall I describe to you, my friends and boon companions, the excellent virtue you will find within. I assure you that if a youth be ever so handsome, his beauty is nothing to Socrates: he looks upon it with a contempt you cannot fathom. So too if a man be rolling in wealth, or be remarkable for any other attribute which the vulgar admire and envy—all such advantages he counts as dross, and their possessors as mere cyphers. Thus does he spend his whole life dissembling and playing with the rest of mankind. Whether any of you have seen him in his serious mood, when he has thrown aside the mask and disclosed the divine features beneath it, is more than I know. But I have seen them, and I can tell you that they seemed to me glorious and marvellous and truly godlike in their beauty."

This splendid éloge[4], artfully put by Plato in the mouth of Alcibiades, doubtless represents the feelings with which Socrates was regarded by the philosopher himself. But his picture of Socrates as a man was more faithful than his picture of Socrates as a philosopher. Plato was not content, like Xenophon, with reproducing from memory or from written memoranda, the doctrines which actually fell from his master's lips. When Socrates died, the philosophical education of Plato had but completed its first stage. The acquaintance with other more ambitious systems which his travels enabled him to acquire or to perfect[5], though it never disturbed his reverence for the teacher of his youth, greatly enlarged his views of philosophy and the philosophic calling: and as, in his earlier compositions, Socrates had ever been the νοῦς τῆς διατριβῆς[6], the ruling and informing spirit of the dialogue, he continued in his later writings to credit his first master with all the results of thought and study with which his own researches or the conversation of others from time to time enriched him. The alternative course would have been to have spoken in his own person or in that of some other philosopher. And this he has occasionally done, as in the Timaeus, where a Pythagorean, and in the Sophistes and Politicus, where an Eleatic Philosopher conducts the dialogue, to say nothing of his

[4] I have ventured to call it so, in spite of the foolish and ill-natured remark of Theodoret, ἃ δὲ Ἀλκιβιάδης ἐν τῷ Συμποσίῳ περὶ Σωκράτους ἔφη Πλάτων μὲν ἔγραψεν, ἐγὼ δὲ φειδοῖ τοῦ Σωκράτους εἰπεῖν οὐκ ἀνέξομαι. De Virt. activ. p. 174.

[5] A locus classicus on this subject is Cic. de Repub. i. 10. 16.

[6] The terms by which, as is well known, Plato denoted the young Aristotle

latest work, the Laws, in which Plato himself appears in the thin disguise of a "Stranger from Athens." But these are exceptional instances; and in the majority of the works written during his maturity, Socrates occupies the same place of honour as in the more juvenile dialogues.

THE SECOND DISCOURSE OF SOCRATES.

This Discourse is a striking instance of the "quidlibet audendi potestas" which Plato assumed in his character of a philosophic artist. The doctrines it is intended to convey were specially and exclusively his own; they are not only non-Socratic, but they are precisely those in which the distinction between Platonism and pure Socraticism is to be looked for and indeed is affirmed by Aristotle to reside. The imagery under which those doctrines are conveyed is drawn from the most various sources, Eleatic, Pythagorean, Orphic: but the doctrines themselves are his own, and may be traced with sufficient distinctness through the many-coloured veil of their allegorical presentment[7].

In endeavouring to analyze this speech, we should perhaps consult clearness by taking the philosophical before the mythical, the thing signified before the sign. The two are, however, so interwoven that it is no easy task to keep them entirely apart. It was Plato's design in this discourse to construct a psychological theory of the passion of Love: to analyze it into its constituent elements, and to refer each of such elements to that region of the human soul to which it rightfully belonged. In order to this, he presents us with a statement of the divine origin and antecedent as well as prospective existence of the soul: of its threefold nature, and of the relation *de jure* as well as *de facto* of the inferior to the higher faculties. Plato's Ethical theory is based upon Psychology, as indeed all sound Ethical science must be: it was therefore in his view impossible to consider Love in its moral until it had been viewed in its psychological aspect; and as it was not his way to isolate the various branches of philosophy, but rather to consider them in their vital connexion with each other and with their common root, we must not be surprised if we are presented at an early stage of the discourse with a concise exposition of the nature and true conception of the soul or vital principle. This investigation is prefaced by a discussion on Madness. It had been assumed in the former speeches that the Lover was mad. The position is granted, but that, it is

[7] At a later stage of the discussion Plato represents Socrates as attributing the speeches he had uttered to the direct inspiration of the local deities, &c., καὶ ἔγωγε ὦ Φ. αἰτιῶμαι τοὺς ἐντοπίους θεούς, κ.τ.λ. 262 D.

urged, is no reason for slighting the Lover in comparison with his cool and sane rival. Madness is not *per se* an evil[8] There is a madness of heavenly, as there is one of earthly origin. one which raises a man above, as well as one which sinks him below his normal self There is a madness of the seer, a madness of the priest, a madness of the poet[9], and from these three manifestations of madness have flowed the choicest blessings to mankind. Love too is an ecstasy, a sacred rapture, a madness inspired by heaven Its origin is divine, its result the highest bliss[1] This, says Socrates, it will be our business to demonstrate, and our proof will be such as to satisfy the educated philosopher, however it may fail of convincing the disputer of the law courts or the wrangler of the schools[2] But a proof satisfactory to the philosopher must not rest on mere popular principles. Love being a condition of the Soul, we must first inquire what soul is, and what are its *ἔργα καὶ πάθη*, the functions, active and passive, of which it is capable.

In the theory of Love hereafter to be developed, the antecedent immortality of the Soul is postulated This position accordingly Socrates begins the second part of his discourse by affirming. His reasoning is *σοφοῖς πιστή*, in other words it would have been accepted as satisfactory by minds trained in the loftier schools of Grecian speculation, as in that of Pythagoras, from which the technical terms employed seem to have come[3]. It is assumed, as self-evident, that soul or life is the first cause of all motion, matter its opposite being capable of receiving and propagating, but not of originating, motion But if it is the first cause of motion, Soul moves itself, otherwise we must assume a cause of motion earlier than the first, which is a contradiction Moreover, motion or activity being of the essence of Soul, it cannot cease to move without ceasing to be And if it cease to be, the course of Nature must stand still. Neither, as *γένεσις* is a form of *κίνησις*, can Soul ever have come into being. It is *ἀγεννητὸν* as well as *ἀδιάφθορον*, antecedently as well as prospectively immortal To sum up its definition (*οὐσία, λόγος*) in brief,

[8] p. 214 A. [9] p 215

[1] *ἐπ' εὐτυχίᾳ τῇ μεγίστῃ παρὰ θεῶν ἡ τοιαύτη μανία δίδοται* 215 B

[2] *δεινοῖς μὲν ἄπιστος σοφοῖς δὲ πιστή* 215 C The word *δεινὸς* is applied both to the *ῥήτωρ* and the eristic sophist—and here perhaps includes both. It denotes cleverness without wisdom, talent without insight, acuteness without depth. *δεινοί* is moreover a term perpetually applied by Plato to his opponents, philosophical or otherwise, and perhaps in this place is equivalent to the 'plebeii philosophi' of whom Cicero speaks in his well-known comment on this passage Tusc c 23, Licet concinnant plebeii omnes philosophi, sic enim ii qui a Platone et Socrate et ab ea familia dissident appellandi videntur

[3] *ἀεικίνατος* is found in the fragments of Philolaus, who also defined the soul as an *αὐτοκίνατος ἀριθμός* It may be observed that the remains of this Philosopher's writings are accepted as genuine by most historians of philosophy, all the Pythagorean fragments besides his being either certainly or probably spurious

Soul is an essence self-moved and self-moving, without beginning and without end of existence.

This argument, oracular in its tone and dogmatic in its method, is not, as Plato admits, sufficient of itself to convince the gainsayer and sceptic. It assumes, on the part of the reader, a familiarity with such dialectical investigations as we meet with, for instance, in the Phaedo. To an audience thus prepared, the σοφοί of whom he speaks, this argument, he thinks, is convincing. We must therefore regard it as a résumé of principles and results, thrown into the form of an *à priori* demonstration, of which the premisses are assumed rather than proved. But with this allowance, there is nothing to which exception can fairly be taken. The brief authoritative tone is an echo of the earlier philosophers, such as Anaxagoras and the Pythagoreans, and the exordium is pitched in the same key as the sequel of the Discourse. In such compositions, which "fill up the intervals of severer investigation," Plato himself tells us that analogy and probability (the εἰκότων μύθων ἰδέα[4]) are admissible and if we interpret ψυχή to mean Soul in the abstract, the animating principle of the universe, most persons will assent both to the premisses and the conclusion of the argument.

But between the eternity of the animating principle and the individual immortality of the Souls of Gods and men, there is plainly a wide interval, which Plato cannot be said to have bridged over, at least in this Discourse. The steps that are wanting seem to be supplied in a passage of the Laws[5], though after a fashion not satisfactory to the modern mind. From this curious passage, occurring in the gravest and most dogmatic of his works, we gather Plato's deliberate opinion[6], that the rational soul by which the material universe is informed and governed is distributed into a number of distinct divine personalities, to each of which is assigned the government of some one or other of the heavenly bodies. Whether these divine or "angelic" souls are linked each to its own material body, or whether, unfettered by matter, they guide the stars in their orbits by the exercise of some marvellous powers transcending human analogy, is an alternative which the philosopher proposes without determining[7]. He seems however in this place of the Laws

[4] Timaeus 59 c

[5] Book x 896 A, where the λόγος ψυχῆς is said to be, ἡ δυναμένη αὐτὴ αὑτὴν κινεῖν κίνησις

[6] At least the opinion of his old age, for in the Laws the mythical matter of earlier dialogues is recast in a dogmatic form. Dialectic and Poetry seem to blend in Metaphysic, losing their vitality in the process. The Mythus of Plato's mature life thus forms a transition from his early dialectical scepticism to the dogmatism of his declining years

[7] 899 A. ἢ τρίτον, αὐτὴ ψιλὴ σώματος οὖσα (ἡ ψυχή) ἔχουσα δὲ δυνάμεις ἄλλας τινὰς ὑπερβαλλούσας θαύματι ποδηγεῖ

to lean to the latter supposition, and what is more curious still, we find him attributing to unbodied Soul the possession of passions and feelings, to the exercise of which, from other parts of his writings, we should rather have inferred that he deemed a corporeal investiture indispensable[8]

However this be, the tripartition of the Soul into νοῦς θυμὸς and ἐπιθυμία which is lucidly set forth in the Republic, and is here figured by the charioteer and his pair of steeds—is predicated both of the Divine Spirits who lead, and of the as yet in one sense unbodied Souls who accompany them in the heavenly journey. Neither the created Gods, nor the souls formed in their image, are pure intelligences. Both are the subjects of analogous passions, both moved by anger and desire, by impulse and appetite, for by these terms the θυμὸς and ἐπιθυμία, figured by the two horses, may in their greatest generality be most aptly denoted But as we gather from the mythical account of the Creation given in the Timaeus (p. 30 foll), the Gods were the handiwork of the supreme Artificer of the Universe, who delegated to these subordinate divinities the task of forming the inferior orders of the rational creation To this end God, we are told, created a certain definite number of Souls or distinct personalities, which he "sowed" (ἔσπειρε) among the stars[9], assigning to each soul its proper habitation The God to whom each particular heavenly body belonged, attached these souls to perishable bodies, endued with organs of sense, and with limbs capable of moving in all directions through space. The souls of men and animals, it would seem, have all at one time animated a celestial body, which they are enabled to re-enter after the completion of a millennial cycle, and so to return εἰς τὴν τοῦ συννόμου οἴκησιν ἄστρου[1]

The Platonic doctrine of the Immortality of the Soul is thus, we find, a doctrine of Metempsychosis, derived possibly from Oriental sources by Pythagoras, but at any rate reaching Plato through Pythagorean channels[2] The personal identity is unaffected by the successive incarnations, but the personal consciousness is liable to a periodic eclipse, at any rate to serious obscurations in the passage of

[8] Laws, p 897 A, where to Soul *before* it is linked to body, not only will, reflection, opinion, &c , are attributed, but also joy and sorrow, courage and fear, love and hate

[9] Tim 42 D, ἔσπειρε τοὺς μὲν εἰς Ἥλιον τοὺς δ' εἰς Σελήνην, τοὺς δ' εἰς τὰ ἄλλα ὅσα ὄργανα χρόνου

[1] A notion this, it may be observed, very different from that of emanation and absorption, with which some interpreters are inclined to identify it

[2] This he intimates plainly enough, when he makes Timaeus, a Pythagorean contemporary of Socrates, the mouthpiece of these doctrines A like intimation is conveyed in the Phaedo, by the introduction of the Pythagoreans Cebes and Simmias, of whom the former is mentioned in the Epistles as one of Plato's Italian intimates

the soul from one tabernacle to another. The Gods of the Mythus are twelve in number: but Plato in the Timaeus knows but of seven planets, the sun and moon included, for, as is well known, the earth was the centre of the planetary system in the eyes of most astronomers from Plato to Copernicus[3]. In explanation of the number twelve, a later Platonist[4] supposes the heaven divided by twelve concentric spheres, the outermost being that of the fixed stars, ἡ ἀπλανὴς σφαῖρα, next to that the sphere or orbit of Saturn (Cronos), then those of Jupiter, Mars, Venus, Mercury, the Sun and Moon, after these the sphere of Fire, of Air, of Water, and last of all the Earth, also ἀπλανής, though revolving, as Plato taught, upon her axis[5]. It is not impossible that he may have intended this twelve-fold distribution in the mythus before us, but as his purpose is not cosmical but moral, it was not worth his while to explain his meaning fully. It is however more than probable that by the οὐρανοῦ νῶτον (247 C), towards which at fixed periods the heavenly procession moves, he meant the outer surface of the sphere in which the fixed stars (the ἄστρα proper) are situated, and in the fields of space above he has placed the eternal Ideas on which the Gods and the more favoured of their mortal attendants feed their gaze. This part of the tale must be taken as purely figurative. The ideas were in Plato's view exempt from all conditions of time and space. They are the objects of pure intelligence, ψυχῆς κυβερνήτῃ μόνῳ θεαταὶ νῷ, "spiritual and spiritually discerned," and therefore stand in no relation to the fixed or any other stars. In truth, whatever may have been Plato's cosmical or astronomical theories, too much stress should not be laid upon the physical details, which belong, for the purposes of this mythus, entirely to the poetical investiture, the "machinery" of the tale. Nor are the discrepancies between this mythus and that in the Timaeus (quoted above) of any real importance. Whether, for instance, we regard the number of the twelve Gods as denoting the number of the spheres, or as introduced in mere accommodation to popular belief, is of little moment. Nor are the names of such of the twelve as Plato condescends to name,—Jupiter, Apollo, Mars, Juno, and Vesta,—to be pressed into accordance with any statements, Pythagorean or otherwise, which we may elsewhere

[3] The Pythagoreans made the earth a planet, as well as the sun, moon, &c., and conceived them all to revolve round a central fire, their Hestia.

[4] Iambl. ap. Stallb. Proll. ad Phaedr. p. lxx. ed. 2.

[5] Tim. 40 B, γῆν δὲ τροφὸν μὲν ἡμετέραν, εἱλλομένην δὲ περὶ τὸν διὰ παντὸς πόλον τεταμένον. Aristotle understood εἱλ. to mean revolving (κινουμένην). The later Platonists interpret σφιγγομένην, but this sense would have required the perfect participle. V. Arist. de Caelo, 2. 13, εἴλλεσθαι καὶ κινεῖσθαι. Aristoph. Nub. 761, μὴ νῦν περὶ σαυτὸν εἶλλε τὴν γνώμην ἀεί. Hestia, who in the Phaedric mythus μένει ἐν θεῶν οἴκῳ μόνη, will in this place represent the Earth.

meet with; for even in the Timaeus, a professedly physical work, Plato speaks lightly of the received nomenclature of Olympus[6] The really important feature in the mythus, and that for the sake of which its gorgeous machinery was constructed, is the doctrine of the divine original and subsequent fall of the human soul. The souls which follow in the train of their respective liege lords are called in one place δαίμονες They hold a subordinate rank in the heavenly hierarchy, being united to bodies of spiritual or ethereal substance, similar to those of the Gods themselves, but seemingly alloyed with baser matter[7]. The teams of the Gods obey the reins, and travel with equable and evenly poised motion (ἰσοῤῥόπως εὐήνια ὄντα πορεύεται, 247 B): but those of the attendant spirits are thrown out of balance by the greater weight of the steed which "partakes of baseness" (τῆς κακῆς μετέχει). Hence their ranks are disordered, their cars collide, and their plumage is ruffled and broken, insomuch that, a few favoured spirits excepted, they fall from sphere to sphere, lighting finally on the earth and there entering for the first time into tabernacles of human flesh. All souls, on their first descent from the empyrean, are incarnated as men[8], for all have had some glimpse of the eternal Ideas, and it is the prerogative of man to see the Idea as revealed in the objects of sense, the One in the Many—διὰ πολλῶν ἰέναι αἰσθήσεων εἰς ἓν λογισμῷ ξυναιρούμενον, 249 B, a privilege of which the irrational part of creation is *ex vi termini* incapable But the destinies of these fallen Souls vary, it seems, in a kind of compound proportion to the greatness and excellence of the heavenly Power in whose train they have followed, and to the clearer or more imperfect manifestations which have been afforded them of the supercelestial verities Those who have been enrolled under Jove (Zeus), and with him have gained the upper surface of the sphered heavens, after their fall—a fall occasioned in their case partly by some fatal mishap (συντυχίᾳ τινί), and not wholly by the pravity of steed or driver—enter the body of some man of the highest, that is of Jovial, temperament[9], and lead a life answerable to their glorious antecedents They addict themselves to the pursuit of

[6] Tim p 40 D Compare A Butler's Lectures, vol ii. p. 23, note 13

[7] Even Aristotle thought that the heavenly bodies were composed of a substance purer and more divine than any one of the four elements—earth, water, air, or fire This he denotes as the Fifth Substance or Essence, πέμπτη οὐσία, whence the Latin quinta essentia and our quintessence. It is not until their fall to our earth that the souls in this mythus are invested with an *earthy* body (σῶμα γήινον λαβοῦσαι). Yet from the first there is some mixture of evil in their composition, and in the Timaeus we are told that their union with the "spiritual body" they receive even in their original abode is dissoluble whereas the souls of the created Gods are ἄλυτα θεοῦ γε θέλοντος

[8] 248 C

[9] This follows from 252 E, οἱ μὲν οὖν Διὸς Δῖόν τινα εἶναι ζητοῦσι τὴν ψυχὴν τὸν ὑφ' αὐτῶν ἐρώμενον, where the comm refer to Phileb 30 D

Wisdom or of Beauty, or, finally, they indulge the passion for beautiful youths in a pure or philosophic spirit—παιδεραστοῦσι μετὰ φιλοσοφίας[1].

What then is this Platonic παιδεραστία, as set forth in the Phaedrus? It has been said already that it is a passion less free from alloy than that ἔρως with which Socrates was inspired by the young men of genius with whom he associated in the course of his missionary labours. In the first place the Platonic ἔρως is excited by the aspect of corporeal beauty[2]. All beauty of face or form[3] is according to Plato a copy or reflection of that perfect or ideal beauty which the Soul beheld in the heavenly places before her incarceration in the flesh. Beauty it is true is not the only 'Idea' thus incarnate. Wisdom, and we may suppose Virtue and Good too, have each their appropriate material antitypes, and if the eye could see them, as it beholds the beauty of outward form, they would stir the soul with "throes of direst love[4]." But as none of the bodily senses can vie in distinctness with that of sight, which brings the mind as it were face to face with its objects—and as of all the great archetypal forms Beauty is the only one which has access to the soul by this channel—we cannot wonder that warmer emotions are excited by it than by any other embodied Idea. It is the privilege of Beauty, says Plato, to be at once ἐκφανέστατον and ἐρασμιώτατον—most manifest and most lovable (250 D). The aspect of Beauty, however, works diversely on different natures. Those from whose souls, by lapse of time or contagion of the flesh, the memory of the glorious imagery they once beheld has faded, are stirred by no sacred awe at the aspect of beautiful forms, nor are they carried back in spirit[5] as into the presence of the primal Beauty: they are flushed with brute desire, and not ashamed or afraid to abandon themselves to pleasures from which Nature revolts. Whereas the true αὐτόπτης, he in whose soul the memory of the unveiled images—more august than those which the Eleusinian hierophant discloses to the trembling mystae—still lives fresh and undimmed, is smitten with a sacred horror akin to that which he felt when face to face with the divine archetype: he worships its image here below, and

[1] 219 A compared with 218 D.

[2] ὅταν θεοειδὲς πρόσωπον ἴδῃ κάλλος εὖ μεμιμημένον, ἤ τινα σώματος ἰδέαν, 251 A.

[3] He elsewhere adds 'of manners and of sciences,' Symp. 212 B.

[4] δεινοὺς γὰρ ἂν παρεῖχεν ἔρωτας, κ.τ.λ., 250 D.

[5] 250 E, οὐκ ὀξέως ἐνθένδε ἐκεῖσε φέρεται πρὸς αὐτὸ τὸ κάλλος . . . ὥστ' οὐ σέβεται προσορῶν, ἀλλ' ἡδονῇ παραδοὺς . . . καὶ ὕβρει προσομιλῶν οὐ δέδοικεν οὐδ' αἰσχύνεται παρὰ φύσιν ἡδονὴν διώκων.

but that he fears to be counted mad, would offer sacrifice to the idol of his heart.[6]

In this passage and in the sequel we have no difficulty in discerning the two Loves, the σκαιὸς and the δεξιὸς ἔρως, which, according to Plato, it is the chief merit of this Erotic Discourse to have set forth.[7] In both there is a sensuous element, which in lower natures gains the mastery and so gives character to the whole complex passion; whereas in those whose organization follows a higher type it is subdued or even absorbed by those emotions which are the natural allies of the reason. True Love is not therefore, according to Plato, a mere φιλία or friendly regard, warmed and heightened by congeniality of temper or pursuit; it is a passion which absorbs the whole complex nature of man, which carries him out of himself, causing him to spurn all restraints of convention or worldly expediency, to overleap every barrier, except those which his own reason and conscience erect, between his passion and its object. This, were that object other than is here supposed, would be a picture as philosophically true as it is vividly portrayed; in fact no philosopher has trodden this, the debatable ground of morality, with so firm a step before or since. No man can quarrel with Plato for refusing the name of ἔρως to any passion from which the physical element is excluded: the dark spot in his theory is the direction which that desire is supposed to take. But to have represented the other sex as the object of a refined and exalted passion is more than was to be expected from an Athenian of the fourth century before Christ. Even Plutarch, who elsewhere shows a juster feeling on these subjects, in his Eroticus speaks disdainfully of what he calls the Love of the Gynaeconitis.[8] This perversity of sentiment has been traced partly to the institution of the Gymnasium, and partly to the semi-Oriental depression to which the female sex, at least in Athens and the Ionian States, was condemned. Such women as Aristophanes depicts were certainly ill-fitted to inspire a lofty or virtuous affection; and passion being thus forbidden to flow in the channels Nature had marked out, it became of necessity erratic and perverse. This state of manners and sentiments caused to Plato the deepest solicitude; and in the Laws he speaks in terms of unequivocal reprobation of the passion alluded to, while he places

[6] πρῶτον μὲν ἔφριξε καί τι τῶν τότε ὑπῆλθεν αὐτὸν δειμάτων, εἶτα προσορῶν ὡς θεὸν σέβεται, κ τ λ 251 A

[7] 265 D, 266 A.

[8] Plut Erot 750 C, ἔρωτος ἀληθινοῦ οὐδὲν τῆς γυναικωνίτιδος μέτεστιν, οὐδ' ἐρᾶν ὑμᾶς ἔγωγέ φημι τοὺς γυναιξὶ προσπεπονθότας ἢ παρθένοις Ibid, ἔρως . . εὐφυοῦς καὶ ἁπαλῆς ψυχῆς ἁψάμενος εἰς ἀρετὴν διὰ φιλίας τελευτᾷ

restraints on the commerce of opposite sexes far more stringent than any legislator before his time had thought practicable or even desirable [9]. It is satisfactory to find that, before the close of its course, so great a mind had thus run itself clear of taint [1]. In the Republic,—the work of his mature, as the Laws was the offspring of his advanced age,—his views on these subjects are expressed with something of hesitation, and though it is clear in what direction his moral instincts pointed, in one place at least he makes concessions which we must lament to the popular sentiment of the day [2].

These remarks may serve to throw some light on the concluding portion of the Erotic Discourse [3], that portion of it which stands most in need of apology [4]. But in judging of this passage we must not leave out of account a consideration which Plato himself suggests to us in other parts of the Dialogue. We have already seen that this entire Discourse is intended as a pattern of philosophical Rhetoric. Now, one condition of a true Rhetoric is, that it shall adapt its arguments to the character of the hearer thus it shall know *οἷος ὑφ' οἵων λόγων πείθεται* (271 E). The hearer is in this case a man of passionate and excitable temperament, of tastes genial but imperfectly refined, and of faculties rather receptive than original For Phaedrus' sake, Socrates tells us, he has been compelled to use a diction more poetical than was meet (*ὀνόμασι ποιητικωτέροις τισὶν ἠναγκασμένος διὰ Φαῖδρον χρῆσθαι*), and for Phaedrus' sake, as we may well suppose, he has ventured into regions which might else have remained untrodden That this is no mere fancy, appears from Plato's language in another place (265 B)—a passage which sums up in brief nearly all that is worth saying on this subject After a short *résumé* of his theory of madness in its human or morbid, and in its divine aspect, he proceeds thus —"Of all these manifestations of madness, the Erotic we pronounced the best we then gave a figu-

[9] *τὸ τῶν ἀρρένων πάμπαν ἀφελοίμεθ' ἄν, τὸ δὲ γυναικῶν, κ.τ λ* Legg. viii 841 D

[1] By this I would not be understood to favour the idle calumnies which anti-Platonists like Athenaeus invented or propagated I think the tradition preserved by one of his biographers more probable than these *Πλάτων ὁ φιλόσοφος λέγεται μὴ γάμον τινὰ μηδὲ ὁμιλίαν σώματος καθάπαξ ἀνασχέσθαι* Hesych Miles Vit Plat init. The epigrams attributed to Plato, even if they are his, prove nothing, and some of them, among the rest that to Archeanassa, have been attributed with greater probability to other authors. Nor, had not his character been free from stain, would Aristotle have spoken of him as of *ἀνδρὸς ὃν οὐδ' αἰνεῖν τοῖσι κακοῖσι θέμις*.

[2] See Republ v p 468 B

[3] p 255 foll

[4] It seems impossible that Plato can seriously have entertained the paradox, that the *παιδῶν ἔρως* was a necessary step towards moral perfection All that can truly be gathered from his words is, that those who struggle victoriously with appetite, will come out from the conflict stronger and happier than they were before it commenced—that the trials of the soul are the occasions of its triumphs Compare A Butler's Lectures, II p 238

rative description, which I know not how to characterize, of the madness of the Lover, in which I doubt not we obtained some hold of the truth, though it is probable enough that in some directions we went astray[5] and so on the whole we concocted a Discourse not altogether unimpressive or unconvincing, and may flatter ourselves that we have gratified our Lord and Master Eros with a mythic hymn disfigured neither by want of skill nor want of piety[6]."

There remain two points which need further elucidation the "tripartition" of the Soul, and the doctrine of *ἀνάμνησις*. We have seen that the charioteer and his two steeds figure to us the three principles (*εἴδη*) which Plato in the Republic designates as *λόγος* or *τὸ λογιστικόν*, *θυμὸς* or *τὸ θυμοειδές*, and *ἐπιθυμία*. Of these the first and last are easily intelligible; but a few words on the second of the three may not be out of place. The author of the Magna Moralia attributed to Aristotle, presents us at the commencement of that treatise with a very concise sketch of the history of antecedent ethical speculation. Moral Philosophy, he tells us, originated in the Pythagorean schools: it was then taken up by Socrates, whose doctrines were modified and greatly improved by Plato. The Pythagorean theory, he says, was mixed with much alien matter. They conceived that the virtues were so many numbers. For instance, Justice was with them a square number (*ἀριθμὸς ἰσάκις ἴσος*). The doctrine of Socrates, though less fantastic, was not less arbitrary; for he insisted that all the virtues were but modifications of Science. For instance, Temperance (*σωφροσύνη*) was the knowledge of what was really pleasant or painful, Valour (*ἀνδρεία*) was the Science of what was really formidable or the contrary; Justice, of that which might or might not lawfully be done (*τῶν νομίμων τε καὶ μή*). These three examples are given us by Xenophon in the Memorabilia: but the critique which follows is Aristotle's. "In this way," he observes, "Socrates ignores and virtually annihilates sentiment and passion" (which are of course essential ingredients in human nature)[7]. This error, according to Aristotle, Plato saw and avoided, for he took pains to distinguish the rational from the irrational part of man's nature, and he assigned to each of these two principles their appropriate Virtues (*ἀπένειμεν ἑκάστῳ τὰς προσηκούσας ἀρετάς*). In the Allegory of the Phaedrus, the charioteer is of course the rational

[5] *τάχ' ἂν καὶ ἄλλοσε παραφερόμενοι*

[6] That of Lysias was neither *μέτριος* nor *εὔφημος*. It was coarse in sentiment and feeble in execution.

[7] This Socratic paradox was revived by the Stoics. Compare Galen Hipp. et Plat. T. v. p. 515, Kuhn. And ib. p. 595. Both these passages, as so much else in Galen, are highly interesting to the student of philosophical opinion.

(τὸ λόγον ἔχον), while the two steeds divide between them the irrational principle, under its twofold aspect of θυμὸς and ἐπιθυμία[8].

It has been usual to translate θυμὸς by the word 'iracundia,' and θυμοειδὲς by 'irascibile' or some equivalent Latin term. Hence Bacon, who apparently read his Plato in a Latin interpretation, censures him for using a term of too restricted meaning. Plato ought rather, he says, to have used a word equivalent to the Latin 'animositas[9].' Now it so happens that Plato's θυμοειδὲς is better translated by 'animositas' than by 'ira' or 'iracundia;' in fact, 'animositas' represents the meaning of the Greek better than any Latin word which we can imagine, and Bacon, who thought to censure Plato, has merely translated him. Anger, it is evident, is only one of many manifestations of the passionate or impulsive principle; and though in the Fourth Book of the Republic, p. 440 seq., where the theory is first propounded, anger or irascibility is the manifestation chiefly dwelt upon, it is evident from other passages in the same work that Plato intended by his θυμοειδὲς a much more comprehensive principle. Thus in B. VIII. p. 548 D we find φιλονεικία and φιλοτιμία, emulation and ambition expressly referred to this principle (ὑπὸ τοῦ θυμοειδοῦς κρατοῦντος φιλονεικίαι καὶ φιλοτιμίαι). An irascible man is not necessarily ambitious or a lover of distinction, though it may be true that a capacity of anger is an element in an ambitious man's constitution. But in p. 553 C, θαυμάζειν καὶ τιμᾶν[1] are mentioned among the functions of the very same principle. Now, if we turn to the Phaedrus, we find the nobler courser characterized as τιμῆς ἐραστὴς μετὰ σωφροσύνης τε καὶ αἰδοῦς, καὶ ἀληθινῆς δόξης ἑταῖρος: predicates evidently very inappropriate to the mere passion of anger[2], but agreeing perfectly with the attributes just cited from the

[8] This is one of the dichotomies which Plato so greatly affected. We have—

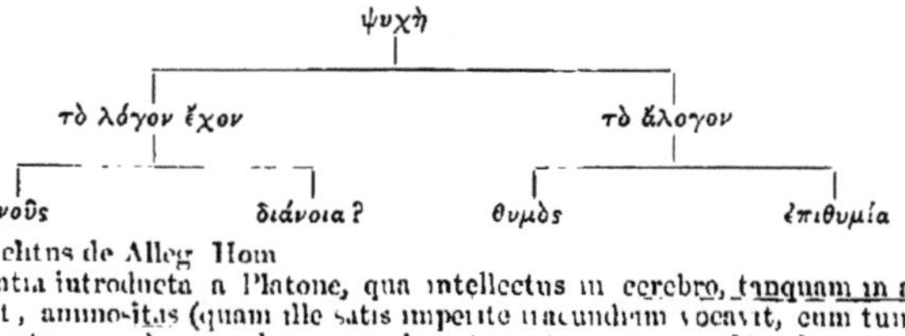

Comp. Heraclitus de Alleg. Hom.

[9] "Sententia introducta a Platone, qua intellectus in cerebro, tanquam in arce, collocatus est, animositas (quam ille satis imperite iracundiam vocavit, cum tumori et superbiae sit propior) in corde; concupiscentia autem et sensualitas in jecinore, neque prorsus contemnenda est neque cupide recipienda."—Bacon Aug. Sc. I. iv. c. 1, extr. Plato gives us the rationale of his own nomenclature in Repub. 580 E, τὸ δὲ τρίτον διὰ πολυειδίαν, κ.τ.λ.

[1] Compare Arist. Pol. VII. c. 7, ὁ θυμός ἐστιν ὁ ποιῶν τὸ φιλητικόν, αὕτη γάρ ἐστιν ἡ τῆς ψυχῆς δύναμις ᾗ φιλοῦμεν.

[2] In the Timaeus, a dialogue in which the psychology of man is treated in connexion with his physiology, Plato divides the body into three regions, corresponding

Republic[3] We shall therefore, I conceive, be justified in enlarging the term *θυμὸς* so as to include, not merely anger, but all the passions and sentiments which prompt to energetic action, and which are thus the natural counterpoise to the appetites, of which either sensual pleasure or mere bodily repletion (*πλησμονή*) is the object[4]. To descend to a more minute classification would lead us beyond the limits of the Platonic psychology, which, though sound as far as it goes, was undoubtedly imperfect, so far at least as its nature is to be made out from his written teaching. At the same time it is not difficult to divine the reasons which induced Plato to put anger as it were in the front rank of the impulses which ally themselves with the Reason in the inward struggles of the soul (*ὅπλα τίθεται μετὰ τοῦ λογιστικοῦ ἐν τῇ τῆς ψυχῆς στάσει*, Rep. iv 440 E). It is not too much to say, that without the capacity of being angry, moral disapprobation becomes impossible. The very terms by which we denote such disapprobation prove this. We speak of certain actions as vile, odious, abominable. But this is the language, not of pure intelligence, but of passion; it denotes that we have within us a principle which enables us to feel anger, indignation, hatred, at the spectacle of certain actions, or in the contemplation of certain states of mind in ourselves or in other men. The stronger our disapprobation, the more intense the language in which it is expressed, and the emotions of anger, hate, or scorn which prompt to the use of such language, are intense in the same proportion. But the actions

to the three main divisions of the soul. The *νοῦς*, or rational principle, he places in the head, or citadel (*ακρόπολις*), the approach to which is guarded by a narrow isthmus, the neck, which separates it from the thorax—and thus as it were ensures the safety of the governing powers above. In the thorax, a region parted in its turn from the lower region by the diaphragm, as by a wall, he plants that part of the soul which partakes of *ἀνδρεία* and *θυμός*, which here again he designates as *φιλόνεικον*—contentious or quarrelsome. The object of this arrangement, he tells us, is that these faculties, being within hearing of the reason, may help it in its warfare with the lower appetites, the *ἐπιθυμίαι*, which, as we should expect, are relegated to the inferior regions, the *φρένες* or diaphragm serving to divide the living dwelling-place of the soul, just as in a Greek house a cross-wall separated the *ἀνδρὼν* from the *γυναικωνῖτις*, the apartments of the male from those of the female inmates.—Tim. p. 70 A foll.

[3] There is therefore no ground for the suspicion expressed by Van Heusde, that "Plato cum Phaedrum scriberet nondum videtur notionem *θυμοῦ* satis sibi distincte proposuisse." Init. P. P. iii p. 26. See Repub. iv. 441, *καθάπερ ἐν τῇ πόλει ξυνεῖχεν αὐτὴν τρία γένη, χρηματιστικὸν ἐπικουρικὸν βουλευτικόν, οὕτω καὶ ἐν ψυχῇ τρίτον, τοῦτό ἐστι τὸ θυμοειδές, ἐπίκουρον ὂν τῷ λογιστικῷ φύσει, ἐὰν μὴ ὑπὸ κακῆς τροφῆς διαφθαρῇ*. Compare the *τροφῇ δοξαστῇ χρῶνται* of Phaedr. 248 B.

[4] In a MS of the late S. T. Coleridge (hitherto, so far as I know, unpublished), I remember, many years ago to have seen a distinction between the Appetites and what the writer proposed uncouthly, but expressively, to call the "Impetites." The details I am unable to recall, but the distinction seemed to me at the time to correspond pretty exactly to the Platonic distinction of *ἐπιθυμία* and *θυμός*, a correspondence of which Coleridge himself was apparently unconscious. The MS., I may a[illegible] ... [illegible]

or appetites which are the natural objects of such emotions, of this purified and well-directed anger, are mostly those which originate or reside in our lower or bestial nature these appetites are powerful incentives to action, whereas Reason, in and of itself, has no tendency to produce or restrain action, and would therefore be powerless in contending with the appetites, were it not allied with some more energetic principle. Its success in the conflict will depend, not on its own strength or clearness, but on the steadiness and intensity of the resistance which its ally opposes to the common enemy: in other words, our self-control will be proportionate to the anger we are capable of feeling towards all that is odious or evil. A well-directed irascibility is thus, we find, an indispensable element in the moral nature[5] We could not be moral, were we incapable of being made angry. To this extent it is true that anger is the natural ally of the reason Of course it does not follow that anger is the only or even the principal ingredient in the moral faculty. The power of hating certain qualities pre-supposes the power of loving or admiring their opposites[6] hence Plato is perfectly consistent with himself when he places wonder and reverence (τὸ τιμᾶν καὶ τὸ θαυμάζειν) in the same region of the soul with the malevolent emotions, and when he makes the θυμοειδὲς μέρος τῆς ψυχῆς, the impassioned or emotive principle, include both the one and the other And in the existing state of philosophical language, it does not seem that he could have selected a more expressive term than that which, as we have already observed, Bacon, with unconscious accuracy, represents by the Latin 'animositas'

In the struggle with the refractory horse, Plato represents the nobler one as helping the driver This however takes place only in the case of the well-trained philosophic nature, in which the sentiments are in harmony with the reason. The charioteer *reminds* his willing steed of that eternal beauty which they beheld together in the regions above the stars, being himself reminded of it by the spectacle of its incarnate antitype in the person of the beloved. (πάλιν εἶδεν αὐτὴν μετὰ σωφροσύνης ἐν ἁγνῷ βάθρῳ βεβῶσαν) This, if rationalized, might be understood to mean, that the intellect acts

[5] Compare the following passage in Sir J. Macintosh's Ethical Dissertation (Works, i p 321, Whewell), "When anger is duly moderated—when it is proportioned to the wrong—when it is detached from personal considerations—when dispositions and actions are its ultimate objects—it becomes a sense of justice, and is so purified as to be fitted to be a new element of conscience," with the context, and with Plato, Republ iv p 440 foll

[6] In the parable of the chariot, it is the business of the nobler steed to drag the soul upwards—not merely to contend with his baser yokefellow. He therefore represents the love of excellence (τὸ φιλόκαλον) as well as the principle which resists appetite

upon the sentiments through the medium of the imagination. It has however a more special meaning, which may be thus illustrated. The Platonic doctrine of Reminiscence or Suggestion (ἀνάμνησις)—Platonic in the strictest sense, for it was Plato's peculiar invention, and seems to have been dropped by his immediate successors—is briefly this. The mind is capable of apprehending certain ideas which experience alone is incapable of furnishing. Such, in particular, are the fundamental ideas of Geometry, which, though suggested to the mind by the senses, transcend in clearness and certainty the notions which reach us through the channels of sight or touch. Such, to borrow the instance given in the Phaedo, is the conception of equality, which, though originally no doubt *suggested* by the observation of apparent equality in the size of visible objects, would remain clear and certain, though it should be as demonstrable as it is probable that there are no two things of precisely equal dimensions in the universe. In modern phrase, there is in our perceptions of mathematical truth a rational as well as an empirical, an *à priori* as well as an *à posteriori*, element; or, to adopt a more antique phraseology, outward things partake of invisible realities, which are to be apprehended only by the eye of the mind—οὐσίας μετέχει ψυχῆς κυβερνήτῃ μόνῳ θεατῆς νῷ. In the Meno, Socrates is represented as giving an experimental proof of this doctrine, the experiment being tried upon a slave-boy whom Meno lends for the purpose, and in whose untutored mind the operator produces, to the entire satisfaction of his master, an ἀνάμνησις of a well-known proposition in Geometry [7]. Whatever we may think of the conclusiveness of this particular experiment, the general doctrine it was intended to illustrate is still maintained to be sound doctrine by many modern metaphysicians: in fact, had Plato stopped here, many would be of opinion that he had proved his point. But he did not stop at the fact, as at an ascertained ultimate fact of consciousness. He first extends the principle from the ideas of mathematical to those of moral or metaphysical relation, and then invents an hypothesis to account for the phenomenon in both cases. The great moral generalizations denoted by the words Good, Beautiful, and the like, he conceived, like the primary intuitions of Geometry, to contain an *à priori* element, for the existence of which experience is unable to account. These ideas, he argues, are not born with us—they are not "innate ideas," in the sense in which Locke and his followers use the phrase—a sense which Plato disavows as clearly as Locke himself. Not being born with us, whence do we obtain them? They are not to be found in the notions of the

[7] M[illegible] 82 [illegible] Ph[illegible] 72 [illegible] 67 And Post. i. 1

senses, for the senses tell us nothing about justice or goodness, but only about hot and cold, white and red, and the like. Neither can we obtain them by reflecting on the phenomena of sensation, for reflection can only arrange existing materials, it cannot enrich the mind with fresh matter. It remains then either that these ideas came to us at our birth—a supposition already rejected—or that, having been ours in a state of existence prior to birth, we have been reminded of them subsequently by experience. The antecedent existence of the human soul is thus, we see, an inference from a fact or supposed fact of consciousness, in other words, an hypothesis to account for such fact. The doctrine and the hypothesis are succinctly stated in a well-known passage of the Phaedo (72 E). "There is another theory of yours, Socrates," says Cebes in that dialogue, "which, if true, proves the antecedent existence of the Soul: a theory I have frequently heard you propose. It is to the effect, that what we call Learning is neither more nor less than an act of recollecting (ὅτι ἡμῖν ἡ μάθησις οὐκ ἄλλο τι ἢ ἀνάμνησις τυγχάνει οὖσα); if this, I say, be true, we must have learnt at some previous period the truths of which in this life we are from time to time reminded; but that would be impossible except on the supposition that our souls existed before they entered a human form: so that from this point of view also, the soul would appear to be immortal." On this hint Socrates speaks, and presents his hearers with an inductive proof of what he had shown experimentally in the Meno. It is remarkable that in both passages he rests the proof on the nature of mathematical conceptions, and asserts without proving, that his argument holds good of moral ideas also[8].

[8] οὐ γὰρ περὶ τοῦ ἴσου νῦν ὁ λόγος ἡμῖν μᾶλλόν τι ἢ καὶ περὶ αὐτοῦ τοῦ καλοῦ καὶ αὐτοῦ τοῦ ἀγαθοῦ καὶ δικαίου καὶ ὁσίου, καί, ὅπερ λέγω, περὶ ἁπάντων οἷς ἐπισφραγιζόμεθα τοῦτο ὃ ἔστι, καὶ ἐν ταῖς ἐρωτήσεσιν ἐρωτῶντες καὶ ἐν ταῖς ἀποκρίσεσιν ἀποκρινόμενοι, ὥστε ἀναγκαῖον ἡμῖν εἶναι τούτων ἁπάντων τὰς ἐπιστήμας πρὸ τοῦ γενέσθαι εἰληφέναι. Phaed p 75 D

APPENDIX II.

ON THE PHILOSOPHY OF ISOCRATES, AND HIS RELATION TO THE SOCRATIC SCHOOLS.

[Phaedrus, p. 278 E foll.]

THERE are few writers whose reputation has passed through so many vicissitudes as that of Isocrates. The ancient critics are divided in opinion as to his merits: Cicero, persuaded perhaps that it is his duty to err with Plato, is hyperbolical in his praises of an orator extolled in the Phaedrus, Dionysius of Halicarnassus, though in some points discriminating, is still on the whole highly favourable[1]; and the same may be said of Quintilian, and the grammarians and rhetoricians generally, whose esteem for Isocrates is significantly shown by the comparatively perfect state in which they have handed down his text. On the other hand, with the philosophers, from Aristotle downwards, he is by no means a favourite[2], and the last, though not the least of Greek critics, the author of the treatise *περὶ ὕψους*, speaks of him in terms bordering on contempt[3]. Descending to modern times, we find Isocrates in high favour among the literati of the Renaissance. The easiness of his Greek, the admiration of Cicero, the orthodoxy, apparent rather than real, of his ethical sentiments, combined to recommend him to the teachers of that day, and the same causes have helped in our own time to make him a favourite in quarters where Greek learning is still in a backward

[1] Dionysius extravagantly compares Isocrates to Polycletus and Phidias. His remark that Lysias *is* graceful, Isocrates *would be*, is much more happy: *πέφυκεν ἡ Λυσίου λέξις ἔχειν τὸ χαρίεν, ἡ δ' Ἰσοκράτους βούλεται.*

[2] The 30th Socratic Epistle, written apparently by a Platonist, is one proof of this.

[3] § 38. 2, *Ὁ γοῦν Ἰσοκράτης, οὐκ οἶδ' ὅπως, παιδὸς πρᾶγμα ἔπαθεν, διὰ τὴν τοῦ πάντα αὐξητικῶς ἐθέλειν λέγειν φιλοτιμίαν* κ.τ.λ.

state. But in proportion as Thucydides, Plato, Demosthenes, and the real representatives of Greek intellect come to be appreciated, we find that the reputation of Isocrates has invariably declined. Our own Dobree, who has done as much as any modern scholar towards the criticism and elucidation of his text, is at no pains to conceal his unfavourable opinion of the author whom he knows so well; and he concludes his ungrateful labours with the pathetic exclamation, "Tandem eluctatus sum taedium, quod summum fuit, relegendi et annotandi. Deo gratias!" If from England we turn to Germany, we find the most intelligent scholars of the same mind with Dobree. Niebuhr, as might have been expected, had no respect for Isocrates, either in his literary or his political character. "He is a thoroughly worthless and miserable author, and one of the most thoughtless and poorest minds. It is inconceivable to me how the ancients could so much esteem and admire him[4]." In another place he calls him a thoroughly bad citizen and an ineffable fool; strong language it must be confessed, but hardly more than the due of a publicist who traces all the misfortunes of his country to her naval supremacy[5], and who wrote a letter of congratulation to Philip after the battle of Chaeronea[6].

But with the literary or political merits of Isocrates we are not at present concerned. The passages in his writings to which attention will now be directed, relate rather to the literary history of his age and to his relations with other literary celebrities, especially Plato and other members of the Academy. At the same time they incidentally illustrate the personal character of the writer, and throw light on what we now call the "educational" notions of a period of high intellectual culture and refinement. They are also useful as showing the amount of egotism and self-praise which was tolerated by a Greek public, and put us in a better position for pronouncing on the curious question—Whether Plato's portraits of the earlier 'teachers of wisdom' are in these respects caricatures of their originals?

Plato and Isocrates were in the strictest sense contemporaries. Isocrates was but seven years older than Plato, and outlived him

[4] Lect. Anc. Hist. ii. p. 335.

[5] See the Oratio De Pace (B.C. 356) passim.

[6] Niebuhr apparently believes in the traditional story that the death of Isocrates was caused by the news of this disaster (Phil. Mus. i. 192). But the 2nd Epistle to Philip (Ep. iii.) bears every mark of genuineness, and so far from showing any trace of mortification or alarm, it ends with an expression of thankfulness that the writer had been spared to see the fulfilment of his political aspirations: ἃ νέος ὢν διενοούμην καὶ γράφειν ἐπεχείρουν ἔν τε τῷ πανηγυρικῷ λόγῳ καὶ ἐν τῷ πρὸς σὲ πεμφθέντι, ταῦτα νῦν τὰ μὲν ἤδη γιγνόμενα διὰ τῶν σῶν ἐφορῶ πράξεων, τὰ δ' ἐλπίζω γενήσεσθαι.

only about ten years. Unlike as they appear in character and genius, both were educators of youth, and in that capacity exerted a greater influence on their contemporaries than any other Athenians of their epoch[7]—that is to say, than any of the numerous teachers of Eloquence and Philosophy who flourished in the interval between the death of Socrates and the battle of Chaeronea. They professed, moreover, to belong to the same calling, for Isocrates insists strenuously on his right to be styled 'philosopher,' and speaks perpetually of ἡ ἐμὴ φιλοσοφία. This claim is to a certain extent admitted by Plato in the Phaedrus—ἔνεστι φιλοσοφία τις τῇ τοῦ ἀνδρὸς διανοίᾳ—possibly not without a reference to the reiterated assertions of Isocrates himself. Of the celebrities of the epoch, there was hardly one who had not at some period of his life studied under either Plato or Isocrates, and some are mentioned as having been pupils of both. Each seems to have taught on system, and their writings enable us to form a reasonably distinct idea of their respective methods of procedure.

At first sight it would appear that no two systems could be more directly opposed. The antithesis between Rhetoric and Dialectic, between the art which seeks only to persuade and that which professes to be satisfied with nothing short of conviction, represents pretty faithfully the relation between the methods of Isocrates and Plato. Yet their teaching may have had some elements in common. Isocrates, e.g., acknowledges the educational value of geometry and astronomy.[8] Those, he says, who apply themselves to the accurate study of these sciences, and are thus forced to fix their attention on obscure and difficult subjects without allowing their thoughts to wander, have their minds sharpened by these exercises and are enabled to learn and appreciate things of greater dignity and moment. By these more important things Isocrates means first the power of speaking and writing, and secondly the gift of political discernment and statesmanlike sagacity, as exemplified in his own political discourses. See, inter alia, Antid. § 196, 290, from a comparison of which passages we obtain a complete notion of what Isocrates means by "philosophy," a combination of the accomplishments of the ῥήτωρ and the πολιτικός. But in other respects Plato would have found little to object to in this view, for he too speaks of geometry and astronomy rather as parts of a proposed entire discipline than as sciences deserving to be cultivated for their own sake. I have no doubt that the passage quoted from the Antidosis refers specially to Plato and his followers,

[7] In Antid. 318, he says, that it had been objected to him that he had a larger number of disciples than all the philosophers put together.

[8] Antid. § 280–283 Bekk. Comp. Panath. § 26 sqq.

who in the vocabulary of Isocrates are denoted as οἱ δυναστεύοντες ἐν τοῖς ἐριστικοῖς λόγοις[9]. The instructions of these eristic dynasts, these Lords of Disputation, he proceeds to say, "are beneficial rather than injurious to their pupils, not to the extent they themselves pretend, but more than the public at large imagine," § 280. For the candour and tolerance implied in these expressions, Isocrates takes great credit to himself. These Eristics, he tells us, had dealt with him far less gently. They had blasphemed his favourite art (§ 276) as offensively as the lowest of the populace could do (βλασφημοῦσιν ὥσπερ οἱ φαυλότατοι τῶν ἀνδρῶν), not, he charitably adds, for want of knowing better, but in the hope, if not of drawing away his pupils, at any rate of exalting their own pursuits by comparison. He might, if so inclined, speak as bitterly of them as they had done of him—perhaps even more so, but this course he disdains. The men were harmless, though not so useful to the community as others whom he could name (ἧττον δ' ἑτέρων εὐεργετεῖν δυναμένους).

This passage indicates great soreness, and we naturally ask, Whence these tears? The answer is not far to seek. In a dialogue such as the Gorgias, written partly to show the shallowness of the culture imparted in the rhetorical schools, passages occur which could not fail to offend the susceptibility of so vain a man as Isocrates. It is indeed probable that the compliment passed upon him at the conclusion of the Phaedrus would be looked upon as but poor amends for the stinging sarcasms showered so profusely on his art and its professors in other parts of the dialogue. But the Gorgias contains no such propitiatory phrase; and though the master of Isocrates is treated respectfully by the philosophic satirist, the fool Polus and the libertine Callicles in effect represent between them the two elements, rhetorical and political, of which, as we have seen, the φιλοσοφία of Isocrates consists. Here, too, as in the Phaedrus, much contempt is poured upon the figures of rhetoric, those ἰδέαι λόγων, the use of which Isocrates inculcated on his pupils both by precept and example[1]. There are also passages in the Gorgias containing distinct

[9] In the Epistle to the young Alexander, he says, ἀκούω σε . . . τῶν φιλοσοφιῶν οὐκ ἀποδοκιμάζειν μὲν οὐδὲ τὴν περὶ τὰς ἔριδας . . . alluding to the lessons of his tutor Aristotle. Throughout, Isocrates is the only φιλόσοφος: the philosophers are mere ἐριστικοί, wranglers, word splitters, and so forth. The impudence of so nicknaming the Aristotelian philosophy is remarkable, but it does not diminish the interest of the notice.

[1] Thus, in Panath. 233 B, he boasts that his orations, πολλῶν μὲν ἐνθυμημάτων γέμειν, οὐκ ὀλίγων δ' ἀντιθέσεων καὶ παρισώσεων καὶ τῶν ἄλλων ἰδεῶν τῶν ἐν ταῖς ῥητορείαις διαλαμπουσῶν καὶ τοὺς ἀκούοντας ἐπισημαίνεσθαι καὶ θορυβεῖν ἀναγκαζουσῶν, "abound in the figures which light up a rhetorical composition, and extort the applause of an audience," where the word διαλαμπουσῶν reminds us of the so-styled λαμπάδες of Gorgias. So Antid. § 196, οἱ περὶ φιλοσοφίαν ὄντες τὰς ἰδέας ἁπάσας αἷς ὁ λόγος τυγχάνει χρώμενος διεξέρχονται τοῖς μαθηταῖς.

verbal parallelisms with corresponding passages in Isocrates. Who, for instance, can doubt that when Socrates speaks of rhetoric as *ἐπιτήδευμα ψυχῆς στοχαστικῆς καὶ ἀνδρείας* (Gorg 463), he is thinking of the boast of Isocrates, that to become an accomplished speaker is a matter requiring much study, *καὶ ψυχῆς ἀνδρικῆς καὶ δοξαστικῆς ἔργον εἶναι*[2]. Still less can we hesitate as to Isocrates' meaning, when he says in a very late oration[3], that of two bad things,—inflicting evil upon others and suffering it ourselves,—the infliction is much less bad than the endurance. For instance, if the choice were offered to the Athenians of unjustly tyrannizing over the Spartans, or submitting to their unjust domination, no sensible man would scruple to prefer the former alternative, though it is true that if you consult the self-styled philosophers, some few would maintain the opposite opinion, *ὀλίγοι δ' ἄν τινες τῶν προσποιουμένων εἶναι σοφῶν ἐρωτηθέντες οὐκ ἂν φήσαιεν*. The reference to the noble paradox of Socrates in the Gorgias, *ὅτι κρεῖττον ἀδικεῖσθαι ἢ ἀδικεῖν*, is not to be mistaken, nor in the 'pretenders to philosophy' can we fail to recognize the followers of Plato. On the other hand, when Callicles (Gorg. 484) is made to express a patronizing approval of philosophy as a pleasant and profitable employment for the youthful mind, but as deadly in its effects on the character if pushed too far, we are struck by the similarity of the sentiment to a passage in the well-known Antidosis of Isocrates, which, written late in the life of the orator, contains a statement and defence of the views which he had advocated during the whole of his professorial career. "I should recommend our younger men," he says, "to spend some time on these branches of education, but not to suffer their genius to waste and shrivel while they pore over unprofitable subtleties[4]."

In the Helenae Encomium, a scholastic exercise written apparently in rivalry of his master Gorgias, Isocrates begins his discourse with

[2] Contra Sophist 291 D. This was an early oration, Antid § 206, ὅτ' ἠρχόμην περὶ ταύτην εἶναι τὴν πραγματείαν, λόγον διέδωκα γράψας, κ τ λ

[3] Panath p 257, § 117. The Panath was written after the death of Plato, and when Isocrates was ninety-four years of age.

[4] § 287, Bekk. *διατρίψαι μὲν οὖν περὶ τὰς παιδείας ταύτας χρόνον τινὰ συμβουλεύσαιμ' ἂν τοῖς νεωτέροις, μὴ μέντοι περιιδεῖν τὴν φύσιν αὐτῶν κατασκελετευθεῖσαν ἐπὶ τούτοις.* § 288, *δεῖν δὲ τοὺς προύργου τι ποιεῖν βουλομένους καὶ τῶν λόγων τοὺς ματαίους καὶ τῶν πράξεων τὰς μηδὲν πρὸς τὸν βίον φερούσας ἀναιρεῖν ἐξ ἁπασῶν τῶν διατριβῶν.* It is remarkable that among the authors of *λόγοι μάταιοι* he mentions his own preceptor Gorgias, referring however to his metaphysical speculations, not to his rhetoric. So too in the Hel. Enc. 208 c, *Γοργίαν τὸν τολμήσαντα λέγειν ὡς οὐδὲν τῶν ὄντων ἐστίν.* It is highly probable that this passage is but a new version of remarks occurring in the earlier speech against the Sophists, which, as we have seen, Plato had probably read, and of which we have only a fragment remaining to us. Isocrates himself quotes his earlier speech in the Antidosis, and prides himself not a little on the consistency of his youthful and later opinions. Far from imitating the well known 'inconstantia' of Plato, it is evident that during a long life of teaching he had "learnt nothing and forgotten nothing."

a formal attack upon the leaders of the three principal Socratic sects. The attack is, so far as appears, entirely gratuitous, for it is not pretended that either Antisthenes, Plato, or Euclides, had breathed a word against the fame of Helen. Socrates, indeed, in the Phaedrus, alludes in complimentary language to the well-known poem in which Stesichorus had attempted to restore the tarnished reputation of this heroine, and Isocrates intimates very plainly that it would have been better for his followers had they devoted their powers to the discussion of equally edifying topics. There are some[5], he gravely complains, whose vanity is gratified if they can succeed even tolerably well in defending an absurd and paradoxical thesis; he is acquainted with persons who have grown grey (καταγεγηράκασιν) in arguing[6] that it is impossible to say that which is false, to contradict an adversary, or to hold two opposing arguments on the same theme; others who have spent a long life in defending the paradox, that Valour, and Wisdom, and Justice mean all the same thing, that we possess none of these virtues by nature, but that there is one science which includes all. Others, again, pass their time in eristic disputations which answer no end but that of giving trouble to their pupils. Trifling like this, he proceeds to say, has not even the merit of novelty, for it is well known that Protagoras and Gorgias, that Zeno and Melissus had in their day maintained still more startling paradoxes in books even more unreadable. It is clear from this passage that Isocrates is writing at a time when Socrates and the so-called Sophists had passed away, and when the ground was occupied by the now mature Socratic sects, and it is strange that the author of a Critical History of the Sophists should have maintained that the Helenae Encomium is an early work[7]. The passage shows considerable satirical ingenuity, and its writer probably prided himself on the happy expedient of interpolating Plato between two rivals, with one of whom the philosopher had been engaged in brisk controversy, while he looked upon the second as a well-meaning but somewhat narrow-minded brother in the faith[8].

[5] Hel. Enc. init., Εἰσί τινες οἳ μέγα φρονοῦσιν, ἢν ὑπόθεσιν παράδοξον ποιησάμενοι περὶ ταύτης ἀνεκτῶς εἰπεῖν δυνηθῶσιν.

[6] οἱ μὲν οὐ φάσκοντες οἷόν τ' εἶναι ψευδῆ λέγειν οὐδ' ἀντιλέγειν οὐδὲ δύο λόγω περὶ τῶν αὐτῶν πραγμάτων ἀντειπεῖν, οἱ δὲ διεξιόντες ὡς ἀνδρία καὶ σοφία καὶ δικαιοσύνη ταυτόν ἐστι, καὶ φύσει μὲν οὐδὲν αὐτῶν ἔχομεν, μία δ' ἐπιστήμη καθ' ἁπάντων ἐστίν· ἄλλοι δὲ περὶ τὰς ἔριδας διατρίβουσιν, κ.τ.λ.

[7] Geel, in an Epistle to Welcker, Rh. Mus. 1839. Antisthenes died at the age of sixty-seven, B.C. 367. The perfect καταγεγηράκασιν implies that both he and Plato were still alive; and we cannot therefore be far wrong if we fix B.C. 370 as the approximate date of the speech in question. At that date Plato would be fifty-nine, and Antisthenes about sixty-four.

[8] Euclides of Megara.

Equally well aimed is the bolt shot at Antisthenes, whose well-known dialectical paradoxes are refuted in more than one Platonic dialogue; and who, by the way, is said to have written a reply to one of the speeches of Isocrates[9].

Another reflection upon Plato seems to lurk in a passage of the Antidosis, § 303, where Isocrates complains that the epithet εὐφυής is much misapplied. People call those εὐφυεῖς, he says, who indulge in ribaldry, and have a talent for jesting and mimicry[1], whereas the word ought to be used to denote natural goodness of heart. This, it may be said, is perhaps intended rather for the comic poets, who did not spare Isocrates. But the poets of the middle comedy do not seem to have risen above mediocrity, and it is more likely that Isocrates had been vexed by hearing the epithet applied to Plato—the εὐφυής[2], or man of genius κατ' ἐξοχὴν of his day, one too, whose mimetic powers far transcend those of the poets referred to. In another passage he betrays vexation at the popularity of the Socratic dialogues, which he spitefully alludes to as τοὺς διαλόγους τοὺς ἐριστικοὺς καλουμένους, in which young men took far too much delight, but which their seniors could not endure· οἷς οἱ μὲν νεώτεροι μᾶλλον χαίρουσι τοῦ δέοντος, τῶν δὲ πρεσβυτέρων οὐδεὶς ἐστιν ὅστις ἂν ἀνεκτοὺς αὐτοὺς εἶναι φήσειεν. Panath. § 29, p. 238 B. This passage also points principally to Plato, whose dialogues far surpassed all others in popularity.

We have seen that Isocrates asserted his right to be called a philosopher, and that this claim was to a certain extent conceded by Plato, as it may have been by others. But this limited concession did not satisfy the vanity of Isocrates. His teaching was not only a philosophy, but *the* philosophy. All other professors, whether of rhetoric or dialectic, he qualifies with the dreaded name of σοφισταί. Not even Plato is excepted[3], when he is speaking by name of his two greatest works. If we ask what are the characteristics of the "philosopher" according to the Isocratic pattern, we shall find them the precise antithesis of those insisted on by the orthodox schools.

[9] Diog. Laert. in vita Antisthenis L. vi. 1. 15.

[1] Ammonius: εὐφυὴς λέγεται παρ' Ἀττικοῖς ὁ σκωπτικός.

[2] Plato is called εὔστοχος by Lucian in the Anthology.

[3] Philipp. § 12: ὁμοίως οἱ τοιοῦτοι τῶν λόγων ἄκυροι τυγχάνουσιν ὄντες τοῖς νόμοις καὶ ταῖς πολιτείαις ταῖς ὑπὸ τῶν σοφιστῶν γεγραμμέναις. The Philippus was written 346, Plato died circ. 348. The passage is remarkable as proving that the Laws were in general circulation within two years of Plato's death—a fact, it seems to me, quite decisive of the genuineness of that work. See the 30th Socratic Epistle, where the reference is recognized. If this is true, as with Spengel I believe it to be, it refutes the current tradition that the Laws was a posthumous work.

We know the pains taken by Plato in distinguishing between δόξαι and ἐπιστῆμαι, between the popular and the scientific way of handling a subject. This antithesis, which is admitted by all philosophic writers, however they may differ in its application, was by no means ignored by Isocrates. But he stands alone in claiming for the man of opinion, ὁ δοξαστικός, the title appropriated to the man of science. Those, he says, I call wise men, σοφοί, who are able to strike out the most probable opinions, and those I hold to be 'philosophers' whose studies enable them most readily to acquire this branch of wisdom[4]. He is aware that this opinion is paradoxical, and that he stands alone in maintaining it. In that wonderful effusion of senile self-complacency, the Panathenaicus[5], he boasts that his genius, though ill-fitted for the management of public affairs, and indeed for public speaking, enables him to arrive at the truth by the way of opinion far better than the pretenders to so-called science, δοξάσαι περὶ ἑκάστου τὴν ἀλήθειαν μᾶλλον δυναμένην τῶν εἰδέναι φασκόντων. And in a passage already quoted he extols rhetoric as the proper employment of a mind δοξαστικῆς καὶ ἀνδρείας, vigorous and fertile in opinion. Still more plainly antisocratic is a passage in the speech κατὰ τῶν σοφιστῶν, in which he says that he finds much more agreement among those who are content with δόξαι than among those who profess to be in possession of ἐπιστήμη[6]. In this description it does not appear that Plato is necessarily included, for the persons he alludes to are paid teachers, who have undersold Isocrates in the education market. He speaks of them as poor men (αὐτοὶ πολλῶν δεόμενοι), who took small fees from their pupils—three or four minae only for a complete course[7], a meanness of spirit, he thinks, much to be reprobated, and standing in disadvantageous contrast to his own more magnanimous practice[8]. Neither the poverty nor the fees are Platonic; but some of the minor Socratics are probably the offenders complained of[9].

[4] Antid. § 290, σοφοὺς νομίζω τοὺς δόξαις ἐπιτυγχάνειν ὡς ἐπὶ τὸ πολὺ τοῦ βελτίστου δυναμένους, φιλοσόφους δὲ τοὺς ἐν τούτοις διατρίβοντας, ἐξ ὧν τάχιστα λήψονται τὴν τοιαύτην φρόνησιν.

[5] p. 234 D sqq. [6] 292 C. [7] Ib. 291 D.

[8] Isocr. is said to have received 10 minae = 1000 drachms from each pupil. Plut. Vitae X Rhet. 838 A. His pupils were numerous. His course frequently lasted three or four years. Antid. § 93, Bekk. At the end of that time, when his pupils were about to depart (ἀποπλεῖν), they took leave often with tears. Ibid. 1000 drachms seems to have been the stated fee for a course. Demosth. adv. Lacrit. p. 938.

[9] The speech against the Sophists was written at the beginning, the Antidosis towards the end of the professorial life of Isocrates. In the former there is no passage which points to Plato, who had probably not yet come forward as the head of a school which was destined to throw all others into the shade. But the scientific aim of the teachers described, coupled with their moderate earnings, and contempt, genuine or affected, of 'filthy lucre' (ἀργυρίδιον καὶ χρυσίδιον τὸν

But it would be tedious to quote all the passages in which Isocrates gives expression to the jealous feelings which rankled in his mind. Those already referred to are sufficient to illustrate the opposition between his school and that of Plato, and to show that of the two rivals, if we may so call them, one at least was unfavourably disposed towards the other. It remains to ascertain, if possible, how far these feelings were reciprocated by Plato. And here it cannot but strike us as singular that the only passage in the Platonic dialogues in which Isocrates is named should be one in which he is favourably contrasted with a rival Logographus, in which his claim to be a philosopher is partially conceded, and he is pronounced to be capable of eminence in a still higher sphere of literature. This too at the end of a dialogue in which the Sicilian school, which Isocrates represented more truly than any other Attic writer, is assailed with mischievous raillery, insomuch that if no names of contemporaries had been mentioned, it would not have been unreasonable to suspect that he and not Lysias was the orator at whom Plato's censures were principally aimed[1]. For in the extant orations of Lysias we look in vain for any traces of the affectation which Plato ridicules; whereas the show-speeches of Isocrates are full of them. Of this difficulty the ancient critics do not seem to have been conscious. Cicero, who records in more than one place the feud between Isocrates and Aristotle, believes that Isocrates and Plato were the best of friends[2]. Nor was this, according to Cicero, a mere youthful friendship[3]. Such too seems to have been the traditional opinion of the schools. "The philosopher," says Laertius (iii. 9), "was a friend of Isocrates, and Praxiphanes has written a dialogue in which they are represented as conversing περὶ ποιητῶν in Plato's country-house, where Isocrates was a guest." This Praxiphanes was one of Aristotle's successors[4], and as a Peripatetic would not be prejudiced in favour of either of the illustrious disputants.

Nor is it easy to find any trace of a contrary opinion, if we except

πλοῦτον ἀποκαλοῦντες), are features which meet in the minor Socratics, and in them only.

[1] Compare in particular Phaedr. p. 267 A, τά τε αὖ σμικρὰ μεγάλα καὶ τὰ μεγάλα σμικρὰ φαίνεσθαι ποιοῦσι διὰ ῥώμην λόγου, καινά τ' ἀρχαίως καὶ τὰ ἐναντία καινῶς, κ.τ.λ., with Paneg. § 8, where Isocrates boasts: ὅτι οἱ λόγοι τοιαύτην ἔχουσι τὴν φύσιν, ὥσθ' οἷόν τ' εἶναι περὶ τῶν αὐτῶν πολλαχῶς ἐξηγήσασθαι, καὶ τά τε μεγάλα ταπεινὰ ποιῆσαι καὶ τοῖς μικροῖς μέγεθος περιθεῖναι, καὶ τὰ παλαιὰ καινῶς διελθεῖν καὶ περὶ τῶν νεωστὶ γεγενημένων ἀρχαίως εἰπεῖν. Plato jeeringly attributes this boast to Tisias and Gorgias. Isocrates adopts it as his own in perfect seriousness. The date of the Panegyricus is B.C. 380.

[2] "Exagitator omnium rhetorum hunc miratur unum. Me autem qui Isocratem non diligunt una cum Socrate et Platone errare patiantur." Brut. xiii. 42.

[3] "Ex eo seniore scribit Plato et scribit aequalis." Ibid.

[4] Anon. Vit. Aristotelis, in Appendix to Diogenes Laertius, ed. Didot, p. 13. Also quoted by Diog. Laert. and by Marcellinus in Vita Thucydidis.

a passage in that one of the Socratic Epistles, the XXXth[5], which alone has any pretension to authenticity. Had the tradition of a "simultas" between Plato and Isocrates reached the ears of Athenaeus, he would probably have made the most of it, for his learning was equalled by his virulence and love of defamation. We cannot therefore be surprised if some recent expositors of Plato have adhered to the old tradition, not reflecting that until recent times little or nothing had been done in the way of exhuming the allusions to contemporaries which lie beneath the surface of the Socratic Dialogues[6].

One of these personal allusions it is now time to discuss. In the Dialogue called Euthydemus occurs a passage in which Heindorf, Schleiermacher, Spengel, Dobree, and the Dutch scholars generally, see a distinct reference to Isocrates. The dialogue at the end of which this passage appears is a curious one. Socrates relates to his friend Criton a conversation between himself and a couple of foreigners, Dionysodorus and Euthydemus. These were sophists of the Eristic or Contentious sort, formidable in word-combat, and capable of refuting any proposition ὁμοίως ἐὰν ψευδὲς ἐάν τε ἀληθὲς ᾖ. The narrated dialogue consists of a series of quibbling arguments of the paltriest kind, and is apparently designed to bring into contempt a certain class or school of philosophic or pseudo-philosophic disputants. The motive of its publication by Plato it is not difficult to divine. We know from the passages already quoted from Isocrates that the epithet ἐριστικὸς was used by the rhetoricians as a convenient term of reproach to designate the stricter schools of philosophy, not only the minor Socratic sects and the obscurer pretenders to logical prowess—all in short who preferred the closed fist of logic to the open palm of rhetoric—but also Plato, Aristotle, and the professors of the Academy generally. Now Plato, in exalting Dialectic, which he represents as the prima philosophia, and its professors as alone philosophers, takes great pains to distinguish this queen of sciences from her spurious counterfeit, Eristic. This distinction is brought out with technical clearness in that masterly dialogue, the Philebus[7], and it affords the key to much of the subtle argumentation of the Sophistes and Politicus. But these are dialogues beyond the popular comprehension, and the Euthydemus seems to have been written to make the distinction palpable to ordinary minds. The rhetors had

[5] An Epistle purporting to be addressed to K. Philip, Ἰσοκράτης . . οὔτε Πλάτωνος ἐν τοῖς πρός σε πεμφθεῖσι λόγοις ἀπέσχηται.

[6] Is Dobree the first Commentator on Isocrates who suspected the anti-Platonic allusions?

[7] p. 17 A, οἷς διακεχώρισται τό τε διαλεκτικῶς πάλιν καὶ τὸ ἐριστικῶς ἡμᾶς ποιεῖσθαι πρὸς ἀλλήλους τοὺς λόγους.

vexed the Socratics by calling them Eristics See, says Plato, what an Eristic is, and how little he has in common with us or with our Master. Our contempt for verbal quibbles is as strong as yours, and far more intelligent; we know the false principles on which the Eristic art is founded, and are besides able to hold it up to ridicule with a force and humour of which you are incapable Of this design Plato gives us a plain intimation—first, in the model dialogue between Socrates and Clinias, p 278 E, which is meant by way of foil to the quibbling arguments of the two strangers; and secondly, in the concluding conversation between Socrates and Criton After he has finished his recital of the performance of the two sophists, Socrates ironically suggests that his friend would do well to join them, for among other recommendations they boasted, as other quacks since their day have done, that their course might be pursued without any interruption of ordinary business, ὅτι οὐδὲ τὸ χρηματίζεσθαί φασιν διακωλύειν οὐδὲν μὴ οὐ παραλαβεῖν ὁντινοῦν εὐπετῶς τὴν σφετέραν σοφίαν In declining this proposal, Criton takes occasion to offer to Socrates a respectful remonstrance. It seems ridiculous, he says, that *I* should admonish *you*, nevertheless I will tell you what somebody said of you in my hearing, a person who was actually present during the interview which you have just described The person, he goes on to say, was one who had no mean opinion of his own wisdom—one in fact of those who composed speeches for the law-courts with ability and success (ἀνὴρ οἰόμενος πάνυ εἶναι σοφός, τούτων τις τῶν περὶ τοὺς λόγους τοὺς εἰς τὰ δικαστήρια δεινῶν) After ironically expressing his surprise that Criton had not thought it worth his while to listen to wisdom such as this, this person had proceeded to express in no measured terms his contempt for philosophy, of which, as he professed to think, the two strangers were among the most eminent professors, and to intimate his surprise that a man like Socrates should have lent himself to so absurd an exhibition (πάνυ ἄν σε οἶμαι αἰσχυνθῆναι ὑπὲρ τοῦ σεαυτοῦ ἑταίρου οὕτως ἦν ἄτοπος ἐθέλων ἑαυτὸν παρέχειν ἀνθρώποις οἷς οὐδὲν μέλει ὅ τι ἂν λέγωσι, παντὸς δὲ ῥήματος ἀντέχονται) The fact was, the study and its professors were alike worthless and ridiculous Now, says Criton, though I entirely dissent from this estimate of philosophy, I do think the critic was right in censuring you for condescending to dispute in public with two such charlatans as those you have described

Now this passage, it may be said, though probably intended to account for the confusion in the mind of a superficial observer between the Dialecticians and Eristics, contains nothing which compels us to think of Isocrates in particular Why should not Lysias stand for the original of the picture, or why may not a class or school [illegible] With his usual address, Plato has contrived to put in a touch which enables us, as I think, to answer these inquiries. What did you think of the discussion? said Criton to the anonymous person of whom he speaks. Τί δὲ ἄλλο, ἦ δ' ὅς, ἢ οἷά περ ἂν ἀεί τις τῶν τοιούτων ἀκούσαι ληρούντων, καὶ περὶ οὐδενὸς ἀξίων ἀναξίαν σπουδὴν ποιουμένων. I am quoting, says Criton to Socrates, the very words this person used, οὑτωσὶ γάρ πως καὶ εἶπε τοῖς ὀνόμασι. This is an intimation that some one in particular is meant, and that the reader is expected to recognize the author by his style. The antithetic turn of the last clause, περὶ οὐδενὸς ἀξίων ἀναξίαν σπουδὴν ποιουμένων—a false antithesis by the way—the smoothness of the rhythm, and the frequent alliteration naturally suggest Isocrates. This impression is strengthened when Criton tells Socrates that his critic "was any thing but a speaker; in fact," says he, "I doubt whether he ever got up in court in his life, though they do say that he is thoroughly well acquainted with his profession, and that he writes capital speeches.[8]" It is added that "he is one of those whom Prodicus described as dwellers on the debateable land between the Philosophers and the Statesmen" (μεθόρια φιλοσόφου τε ἀνδρὸς καὶ πολιτικοῦ), a really happy description of Isocrates, but as little fitting Lysias as it would fit Isaeus or any other mere barrister or chamber-counsel of the day.[9] Socrates further observes that his censor is one of a set of men who deem themselves and are deemed by many others far the wisest of all. They flatter themselves that but for the philosophers their claim would be universally allowed, and that if they could destroy the reputation of their rivals, the palm would be unanimously awarded to their own profession. It is impossible to describe better the feeling which animates such speeches as the Panathenaicus and Antidosis, and when we are further told that these men μετρίως μὲν φιλοσοφίας ἔχειν μετρίως δὲ πολιτικῶν, we are inevitably reminded of the description of Isocrates in the Phaedrus as one in whose genius ἔνεστί τις φιλοσοφία. The finishing touch in the picture—ἐκτὸς δὲ ὄντες κινδύνων καὶ ἀγώνων καρποῦσθαι τὴν σοφίαν—agrees perfectly with the account of himself and his own way of life, which is given by Isocrates with no little self-gratulation in the Antidosis.[1] We may add that it is not appropriate to the metoec Lysias, whose abstinence from public affairs was owing not to choice but to necessity.

[8] Lysias did on one memorable occasion plead his own cause. The excellent speech κατὰ Ἐρατοσθένους was delivered by him during his brief tenure of the Athenian franchise. Whilst at Thurii he took an active and leading part in the local politics.

[9] Lysias was a clear-headed practical man, and seems to have made no pretension to philosophy. For this, among other things, he is rebuked in the Phaedrus.

[1] See especially §§ 158-9, Bekk. and § 162. With καρποῦσθαι τὴν σοφίαν compare the synonymous phrase ἀπολέλαυκα τοῦ πράγματος. Antid. § 208, Bekk.

In fact the combination of a smattering of philosophy, a measure of political knowledge, great talent as a writer of forensic speeches[2], and a boundless and intolerant vanity, is one which we find in the writings of Isocrates and in no others of that epoch[3]

The rebuke with which Socrates dismisses his anonymous critic is moderate and dignified. We ought not, he says, to be irritated by such pretensions to superiority, ill-founded as they are, for we have no right to quarrel with any man who can teach us any thing holding of wisdom—any one in short who works at his literary calling diligently, and expounds his views manfully, with vigour and perseverance (πάντ' ἄνδρα χρὴ ἀγαπᾶν ὅστις καὶ ὁτιοῦν λέγει ἐχόμενον φρονήσεως[4] πρᾶγμα, καὶ ἀνδρείως ἐπεξιὼν διαπονεῖται). The perseverance with which Isocrates inculcates—the ingenuity with which he amplifies—the very few ideas he possesses, is one of the most remarkable features in his writings.

On the whole, I think it will be agreed that there is a high degree of probability in the supposition that the passage commented on refers directly to Isocrates, and that if so, the tradition of his friendly relations with Plato is erroneous Plato could scarcely have failed to resent the querulous and contemptuous remarks upon himself and his school, with which, as we have seen, the speeches of Isocrates abound. But that his resentment amounted to enmity we have no reason to infer from this or any other passage, in fact, the remark of Socrates just quoted was apparently designed to calm the irritable feelings of Plato's admiring followers, who doubtless were exasperated by these attacks upon their master

If we now recur to the passage of the Phaedrus, we find a flattered likeness of the same original. In both we read of a successful speech-writer, in both of a speech-writer with some pretensions to philosophy. But in one of the two pictures shadows are put in which are wanting in the other, and the inference seems natural that Plato's feelings towards Isocrates had undergone a change in

[2] The forensic orations of Isocrates are his best They are free from the affectations of his show speeches, and are thought by Dion Hal. superior in some respects to the speeches of his rival Lysias

[3] At a later period of his life Isocrates expresses great soreness at the prevalent opinion of his arrogance and intolerance of other literary men He says he had been told that three or four Sophists of the rank and file (ἀγελαίων) had been discussing him in the Lyceum and that one of them (τὸν τολμηρότατον) had said, ὡς ἐγὼ πάντων καταφρονῶ τῶν τοιούτων, καὶ τάς τε φιλοσοφίας τῶν ἄλλων καὶ τὰς παιδείας ἁπάσας ἀναιρῶ, καὶ φημὶ πάντας ληρεῖν πλὴν τοὺς μετασχηκότας τῆς ἐμῆς διατριβῆς This he says surprised and distressed him, for he had always thought himself remarkable for modesty and humility, and a sworn foe to vanity and ostentation in other persons (ᾤμην ἐπιφανὴς εἶναι τοῖς ἀλαζονευομένοις πολεμῶν καὶ περὶ ἐμαυτοῦ μετρίως διειλεγμένος, μᾶλλον δὲ ταπεινῶς).

[4] Isocrates calls his own philoso[illegible] in Antid. § 290.

the interval between the composition of the two dialogues, whichever we assume to have been written first

But it is well known to persons conversant with recent Platonic literature that the passage of the Euthydemus is a main argument of those who support the old tradition that the Phaedrus was the first-written of the dialogues The date of the Euthydemus we have absolutely no means of determining, and if we set aside tradition, that of the Phaedrus may be said perhaps to be equally uncertain. Under such circumstances, we may venture, I think, to recognize in the portrait given in the Euthydemus the orator whose features are so faithfully portrayed, without thinking it necessary on that account to reject such internal indications of a later date as we may discover in the Phaedrus. I say nothing of the consideration, that the complimentary phrases put into the mouth of Socrates may have suggested to the readers of Plato a comparison between the prophecy and its fulfilment, neither favourable to the subject of the prediction, nor altogether undesigned by its author.

APPENDIX III.

THE EROTICUS OF CORNELIUS FRONTO.

THE following speech, though of little intrinsic value, is sufficiently curious to deserve a place in an edition of the Phaedrus. It was written as an imitation of the erotic discourse of Lysias, and, if it had no other use, might serve by way of foil to a composition, the literary merit of which is certainly underrated by Plato. But it is further entitled to notice on account of the circumstances under which it was written. Fronto, as is well known, was the tutor of the imperial philosopher, M. Aurelius, and seems to have written this speech for his pupil's delectation. The Latin letter which follows it was written by the young Caesar, who addresses his middle-aged friend in terms borrowed from the vocabulary of the lover. The 'erotic' language, which in this case it is fortunately impossible to misinterpret, illustrates what has been said above[1] respecting the use of such phraseology by Socrates and his followers, and enables us to avoid misunderstanding an expression in that one of the Platonic Epigrams which has perhaps the best claim to be accepted as genuine[2]. It is also worthy of note, that neither Fronto nor Aurelius seem to doubt that the speech in the Phaedrus was really written by Lysias. In the lists of this orator's works preserved by pseudo-Plutarch and other grammarians, we read of both ἐπιστολαὶ and ἐρωτικοί, and it is quite possible that specimens of either kind may have survived to Fronto's time. What may have been the precise difference between an "erotic speech" and an epistle it is hard to say. Fronto, though his speech is called ἐρωτικός, uses the verb ἐπιστέλλω at its commencement, and speaks of τὰ

[1] Appendix I. p. 152.

[2] That which ends with the line: ὦ ἐμὸν ἐκμήνας θυμὸν ἔρωτι Δίων. Diog. Laert. iii. c. 23.

πρότερον διὰ Λυσίου καὶ Πλάτωνος ἐπεσταλμένα Nor is there any thing in the form of these compositions to prevent us from calling them ἐπιστολαὶ if their authors had encouraged us to do so.

It is only necessary to add that the text as here given is taken, with a few variations, from the latest edition of the Letters of Fronto, published by Naber at Leipsic in 1867.

p. 234 van den Hout

('Ερωτικός)

Ὦ φίλε παῖ, τρίτον ἤδη σοι τοῦτο περὶ τῶν αὐτῶν ἐπιστέλλω, τὸ μὲν πρῶτον διὰ Λυσίου τοῦ Κεφάλου, δεύτερον δὲ διὰ Πλάτωνος τοῦ σοφοῦ, τὸ δὲ δὴ τρίτον διὰ τοῦδε τοῦ ξένου ἀνδρός, τὴν μὲν φωνὴν ὀλίγου δεῖν βαρβάρου, τὴν δὲ γνώμην, ὡς ἐγῷμαι, οὐ πάνυ ἀξυνέτου Γράφω δὲ νῦν οὐδέν τι τῶν[3] πρότερον γεγραμμένων ἐφαπτόμενος, μηδὲ ἀμελήσῃς τοῦ λόγου ὡς παλιλλογοῦντος. Εἰ δέ σοι δόξει τῶν πρότερον διὰ Λυσίου καὶ Πλάτωνος ἐπεσταλμένων πλείω τάδ' εἶναι, ἔστω σοι τεκμήριον, ὡς εὔλογα ἀξιῶ, ὅτι οὐκ ἀπορῶ λόγων Προσέχοις δ' ἂν ἤδη τὸν νοῦν, εἰ καινά τε ἅμα καὶ δίκαια λέγω

Ἔοικας, ὦ παῖ, πρὸ τοῦ λόγου πάντως βούλεσθαι μαθεῖν, τί δήποτέ γε μὴ ἐρῶν ἐγὼ μετὰ τοσαύτης σπουδῆς γλίχομαι τυχεῖν ὧνπερ οἱ ἐρῶντες. Τοῦτο δή σοι φράσω πρῶτον ὅπως ποτ' ἔχει Οὐ μὰ Δία πέφυκεν ὁρᾶν ὀξύτερον οὑτοσὶ ὁ πάνυ ἐραστὴς ἐμοῦ τοῦ μὴ ἐρῶντος, ἀλλ' ἔγωγε τοῦ σοῦ κάλλους αἰσθάνομαι οὐδενὸς ἧττον τῶν ἄλλων δυναίμην δ' ἂν εἰπεῖν ὅτι τούτου καὶ πολὺ ἀκριβέστερον Ὅπερ δὲ ἐπὶ τῶν πυρεττόντων καὶ τῶν εὖ μάλα ἐν παλαίστρᾳ γυμνασαμένων ὁρῶμεν, οὐκ ἐξ ὁμοίας αἰτίας ταὐτὸν συμβαίνειν διψῶσιν [μὲν] γὰρ ὁ μὲν ὑπὸ νόσου, ὁ δὲ ὑπὸ γυμνασιῶν· τοιάνδε τινὰ κἀμοί . . . . [4] λειτον τε ἅμα καὶ ὄλισθον. Ἀλλ' οὐκ ἔμοιγε ἐπ' ὀλέθρῳ πρόσει, οὐδὲ ἐπὶ βλάβῃ τινὶ ὁμιλήσεις, ἀλλ' ἐπὶ παντὶ ἀγαθῷ. Καὶ ὠφελοῦνται γὰρ καὶ διασώζονται οἱ καλοὶ ὑπὸ τῶν μὴ ἐρώντων μᾶλλον, ὥσπερ τὰ φυτὰ ὑπὸ τῶν ὑδάτων Οὐ γὰρ ἐρῶσιν οὔτε πηγαὶ οὔτε ποταμοὶ τῶν φυτῶν, ἀλλὰ παριόντες οὕτω δὴ καὶ παραῤῥέοντες, ἀνθεῖν αὐτὰ καὶ θάλλειν παρεσκεύασαν Χρήματα δὲ τὰ μὲν ὑπ' ἐμοῦ διδόμενα δικαίως ἂν καλοίης δῶρα, τὰ δ' ὑπ' ἐκείνου λύτρα. Μάντεων δὲ παῖδές φασιν καὶ τοῖς θεοῖς ἡδίους εἶναι τῶν θυσιῶν τὰς χαριστηρίους ἢ τὰς μειλιχίους ὧν τὰς μὲν οἱ εὐτυχοῦντες ἐπὶ φυλακῇ καὶ κτήσει τῶν ἀγαθῶν, τὰς δὲ οἱ κακῶς πράττοντες ἐπ' ἀποτροπῇ τῶν δεινῶν θύουσιν. Τάδε μὲν περὶ τῶν συμφερόντων καὶ τῶν σοί τε κἀκείνῳ ὠφελίμων εἰρήσθω.

[5] Εἰ δὲ [διὰ] τοῦτο δίκαιός ἐστιν τυχεῖν τῆς παρὰ σοῦ βοηθείας . . ερεισω συ τοῦτο . αὐτῷ πονερῷ δὲ τεκτηιω καὶ μηχανήσω τὰς θεττα

[3] ναν Naber, doubtless a misprint

[4] "Desiderantur paginae saltem duae" N

[5] "Sequuntur xiv versus evanidi, quos dabo fide Mai Plerique in iis absurda sunt" N

μεν . . ων . . ἐρᾷς . . δὲ πα εἶπε . . . τοτα κον . . (ἀ)ναίτιος . τινὸς διὰ τὴν αὐτῷ κατακο . . κο . . . πλὴν εἰ μή τι ὀφθεὶς ἠδίκηκας.

Μὴ ἀγνόει δὲ καὶ ἀδικηθεὶς αὐτὸς καὶ ὑβριζόμενος οὐ μετρίαν ἤδη ταύτην τὴν ὕβριν, τὸ ἅπαντας εἰδέναι τε καὶ φανερῶς οὕτως διαλέγεσθαι, ὅτι σου εἴη ὅδε ἐραστής φθάνεις δὲ καὶ πρίν τι τῶν τοιῶνδε πρᾶξαι, τοὔνομα τῆς πράξεως ὑπομένων Καλοῦσί γ' οὖν σε οἱ πλεῖστοι τῶν πολιτῶν τὸν τοῦδε ἐρώμενον ἐγὼ δέ σοι διαφυλάξω τοὔνομα καθαρὸν καὶ ἀνύβριστον Καλὸς γὰρ οὐχὶ ἐρώμενος τό γε κατ' ἐμὲ ὀνομασθήσει Εἰ δὲ τούτῳ ὡς δικαίῳ τινὶ χρήσεται, ὅτι μᾶλλον ἐπιθυμεῖ, ἴστω ὅτι οὐκ ἐπιθυμεῖ μᾶλλον, ἀλλ' ἰταμώτερον Τὰς δὲ μυίας καὶ τὰς ἐμπίδας μάλιστα ἀποσοβοῦμεν καὶ ἀπωθούμεθα, ὅτι ἀναιδέστατα καὶ ἰταμώτατα ἐπιπέτονται Τοῦτο μὲν οὖν καὶ τὰ θηρία ἐπίσταται φεύγειν μάλιστα πάντων τοὺς κυνηγέτας, καὶ τὰ πτηνὰ τοὺς θηρευτάς. Καὶ πάντα δὲ τὰ ζῷα τούτους μάλιστα ἐκτρέπεται τοὺς μάλιστα ἐνεδρεύοντας καὶ διώκοντας

Εἰ δέ τις οἴεται ἐνδοξότερον καὶ ἐντιμότερον εἶναι τὸ κάλλος διὰ τοὺς ἐραστάς, τοῦ παντὸς διαμαρτάνει Κινδυνεύετε μὲν γὰρ οἱ καλοὶ περὶ τοῦ κάλλους τῆς ἐς τοὺς ἀκούοντας πίστεως διὰ τοὺς ἐρῶντας [μετέχειν ?], δι' ἡμᾶς δὲ τοὺς ἄλλους βεβαιοτέραν τὴν δόξαν κέκτησθε. Εἰ γοῦν τις τῶν μηδέπω σε ἑωρακότων πυνθάνοιτο, ὁποῖός τις εἴης τὴν ὄψιν, ἐμοὶ μὲν ἂν πιστεῦσαι ἐπαινοῦντι, μαθὼν ὅτι οὐκ ἐρῶ· τῷ δ' ἀπιστῆσαι, ὡς οὐκ ἀληθῶς ἀλλ' ἐρωτικῶς ἐπαινοῦντι. Ὅσοις μὲν οὖν λώβη τις σώματος καὶ αἶσχος καὶ ἀμορφία πρόσεστιν, εὔξαιντ' ἂν εἰκότως ἐραστὰς αὐτοῖς γενέσθαι· οἱ γὰρ ἂν ὑπ' ἄλλων θεραπεύοιντο ἢ τῶν κατ' ἐρωτικὴν λύτταν καὶ ἀνάγκην προσιόντων Σὺ δὲ ἐν τῷ τοιῷδε κάλλει οὐκ ἔσθ' ὅτι καρπώσει πλέον ὑπ' ἔρωτος Οὐδὲν γὰρ ἧττον δέονταί σου οἱ μὴ ἐρῶντες Ἀχρεῖοι δὲ οἱ ἐρασταὶ τοῖς ὄντως καλοῖς οὐδὲν ἧττον ἢ τοῖς δικαίως ἐπαινουμένοις οἱ κόλακες. Ἀρετὴ δὲ καὶ δόξα καὶ τιμὴ καὶ κέρδος Κόσμος θαλάττῃ μὲν ναῦται καὶ κυβερνῆται καὶ τριήραρχοι καὶ ἔμποροι καὶ οἱ ἄλλως πλέοντες, οὐ μὰ Δία δελφῖνες, οἷς ἀδύνατον τὸ ζῆν ὅτι μὴ ἐν θαλάττῃ, καλοῖς δὲ ἡμεῖς οἱ τηνάλλως ἐπαινοῦντες καὶ ἀσπαζόμενοι, οὐχὶ ἐρασταί, οἷς ἀβίωτον ἂν εἴη στερομένοις τῶν παιδικῶν Εὕροις δ' ἂν σκοπῶν πλείστης ἀδοξίας αἰτίους[6] ὄντας τοὺς ἐραστάς ἀδοξίαν δὲ φεύγειν ἅπαντας μὲν χρὴ τοὺς εὐφρονοῦντας, μάλιστα δὲ τοὺς νέους, οἷς ἐπὶ μακρότερον ἐγκείσεται τὸ κακὸν ἐν ἀρχῇ μακροῦ βίου προσπεσόν.

Ὥσπερ οὖν ἱερῶν καὶ θυσίας, οὕτω καὶ τοῦ βίου τοὺς ἀρχομένους εὐλογίας μάλιστα πρ[έπει ἐπιμελεῖσθαι] . . . . . τοῖς τῶν . . . εἰς ἐσχάτην ἀδοξίαν α τούτους δὲ χρηστοὺς ἐραστὰς ἐξὸν εἰ . . πέντε καὶ . . . α ι εικ . . νον χρῆμα ἐρασταῖς . . του . . δὲ καὶ γὰρ οἱ ἐρῶντες διὰ τῶν τοιῶνδε φορημάτων οὐκ ἐκείνους τιμῶσιν, ἀλλ' αὐτοὶ ἀλαζονεύονταί τε καὶ ἐπιδείκνυνται, καὶ ὡς εἰπεῖν ἐξορχοῦνται τὸν ἔρωτα Συγγράφει δέ, ὥς φασιν, ὁ σὸς ἐραστὴς ἐρωτικά τινα περὶ σοῦ συγγράμματα, ὡς τούτῳ δὴ

[6] αἰτίους μέν. N

μάλιστά σε δελεάσων καὶ προσαξόμενος καὶ αἱρήσων τὰ δ' ἔστιν αἴσχη καὶ ὀνείδη καὶ βοή τις ἀκόλαστος ὑπ' οἴστρου προπεμπομένη, ὁποῖαι θηρίων ἢ βοσκημάτων ὑπ' ἔρωτος βρυχωμένων ἢ χρεμετιζόντων ἢ μυκωμένων ἢ ὠρυομένων Τούτοις ἔοικε τὰ τῶν ἐρώντων ᾄσματα Εἰ γοῦν ἐπιτρέψαις σαυτὸν τῷ ἐραστῇ χρῆσθαι ὅπου καὶ ὁπότε βούλοιτο, οὔτ' ἂν καιρὸν περιμείνας ἐπιτήδειον, οὔτε τόπον, οὔτε σχολήν, οὔτε ἐρημίαν, ἀλλὰ θηρίου δίκην ὑπὸ λύττης εὐθὺς ἔχοιτο ἂν καὶ βαίνειν προθυμοῖτο μηδὲν αἰδούμενος

Τοῦτο ἔτι προσθεὶς καταπαύσω τὸν λόγον, ὅτι πάντα θεῶν δῶρα καὶ ἔργα ὅσα ἐς ἀνθρώπων χρείαν τε καὶ τέρψιν καὶ ὠφέλειαν ἀφῖκται, τὰ μὲν αὐτῶν πάνυ καὶ πάντη θεῖα, γῆν φημι καὶ οὐρανὸν καὶ ἥλιον καὶ θάλατταν, ὑμνεῖν μὲν καὶ θαυμάζειν πεφύκαμεν, ἐρᾶν δ' οὔ, καλῶν δέ τινων φαυλοτέρων καὶ ἀτιμοτέρας μοίρας τετυχηκότων, τούτων ἤδη φθόνος καὶ ἔρως καὶ ζῆλος καὶ ἵμερος ἅπτεται Καὶ οἱ μέν τινες κέρδους ἐρῶσιν, οἱ δὲ ὄψων αὖ, οἱ δὲ οἴνου. Ἐν δὴ τῷ τοιῷδε ἀριθμῷ καὶ μερίδι καθίσταται τὸ κάλλος ὑπὸ τῶν ἐρώντων, ὅμοιον κέρδει καὶ ὄψῳ καὶ μέθῃ ὑπὸ δ' ἡμῶν τῶν θαυμαζόντων μέν, μὴ ἐρώντων δέ, ὅμοιον ἡλίῳ καὶ οὐρανῷ καὶ γῇ καὶ θαλάττῃ· τὰ γὰρ τοιαῦτα παντὸς ἔρωτος κρείττω καὶ ὑπέρτερα. Ἕν τί σοι φράσω πρὸς τούτοις, ὃ καὶ σὺ πρὸς τοὺς ἄλλους λέγων παῖδας, πιθανὸς εἶναι δόξεις Εἰκὸς δέ σε ἢ παρὰ μητρὸς ἢ τῶν ἀναθρεψαμένων μὴ ἀνήκοον εἶναι, ὅτι τῶν ἀνθῶν ἐστίν τι ὃ δὴ τοῦ ἡλίου ἐρᾷ καὶ πάσχει τὰ τῶν ἐρώντων, ἀνατέλλοντος ἐπαιρόμενον καὶ πορευομένου καταστρεφόμενον, δύνοντος δὲ περιτρεπόμενον ἀλλ' οὐδέν γε πλέον ἀπολαύει[7], οὐδὲ εὐμενεστέρου πειρᾶται διὰ τὸν ἔρωτα τοῦ ἡλίου Ἀτιμότατον γοῦν ἐστὶν φυτῶν καὶ ἀνθῶν οὔτε εἰς ἑορταζόντων θαλίας οὔτ' ἐς στεφάνους θεῶν ἢ ἀνθρώπων παραλαμβανόμενον Ἔοικας, ὦ παῖ, τὸ ἄνθος τοῦτο ἰδεῖν ἐθέλειν, ἀλλ' ἔγωγέ σοι ἐπιδείξω, εἰ εὐθὺς πρὸς τὸν Ἰλισὸν ἅμα ἄμφω βαδίσαιμεν.

Supersunt novem versus, quorum scriptura prorsus evanuit. Nihil apparet praeter correctoris subscriptionem

Feliciter

HAVE MI MAGISTER OPTUME

Age perge, quantum libet, comminare, et argumentorum globis comminare. numquam tu tamen erastem tuum, me dico, depuleris nec ego minus amare me Frontonem praedicabo, minusque amabo, quo tu tam variis tamque vehementibus sententiis adprobaris minus amantibus magis opitulandum ac largiendum esse Ego hercule te ita amore depereo neque deterrebor isto tuo dogmate ac si magis eris aliis non amantibus *facilis* et promptus, ego tamen *non minus te* [tuosque] amabo Ceterum quod ad sensuum densitatem, quod ad

[7] Naber gives ἀπόλλυσι, which has no meaning Cod. ΑΠΟΛΑΥCΕΙ, originally perhaps ΑΠΟΛΑΥCΕΙ. But the present is required by the context.

inventionis argutiarum[8], quod ad aemulationis tuae felicitatem adtinet, nolo quicquam dicere, [nisi] te multo placentis illos sibi et provocantis Atticos antevenisse.

Ac tamen nequeo quin dicam; amo enim, et hoc denique amantibus vere tribuendum esse censeo, quod victoriis τῶν ἐρωμένων magis gaude[rent. Vi]cimus igitur, [vici]mus inquam. Num . praestabilius . . . ubique eam sub . trapae . . . tram promsi . . . er quo . . adsis . . . disputari utra re magis caveret Quid de re ista [oro] . . mam tulerit an quod magister meus de Platone ?

Illud quidem non temere adiuraverio: siquis iste revera Phaeder fuit, si umquam is a Socrate afuit, non magis Socratem Phaedri desiderio quam me perisse [sines] . duo menses . arsisse . m . . amet, nisi confestim tuo amore corripitur Vale mihi maxima res sub caelo, gloria mea. Sufficit talem magistrum habuisse Domina mea mater te salutat

[8] Buttm argutiam

INDEX I.

T

Υ.

Φ

Χ

Ψ

INDEX II.

D.

E.

F.

G.

H.

I.

Q

R

V

W

X.

Z

THE END.

GILBERT AND RIVINGTON, PRINTERS, ST. JOHN'S SQUARE, LONDON.

A

CLASSIFIED CATALOGUE

OF

EDUCATIONAL WORKS

PUBLISHED BY

GEORGE BELL & SONS

LONDON: YORK STREET, COVENT GARDEN
NEW YORK: 66, FIFTH AVENUE; AND BOMBAY
CAMBRIDGE: DEIGHTON, BELL & CO

JULY, 1895

CONTENTS.

GREEK AND LATIN CLASSICS.

ANNOTATED AND CRITICAL EDITIONS.

AESCHYLUS Edited by F. A. PALEY, M.A., LL.D., late Classical Examiner to the University of London. *4th edition, revised.* 8vo, 8s. [*Bib. Class.*

— Edited by F. A. PALEY, M.A., LL.D. 6 vols. Fcap 8vo, 1s 6d. [*Camb. Texts with Notes.*

Agamemnon.	**Persae.**
Choephoroe.	**Prometheus Vinctus.**
Eumenides.	**Septem contra Thebas.**

ARISTOPHANIS Comoediae quae supersunt cum perditarum fragmentis tertiis curis, recognovit additis adnotatione critica, summariis, descriptione metrica, onomastico lexico HUBERTUS A. HOLDEN, LL.D. [late Fellow of Trinity College, Cambridge] Demy 8vo.

Vol. I., containing the Text expurgated, with Summaries and Critical Notes, 18s.

The Plays sold separately :

Acharnenses, 2s.	**Aves,** 2s.
Equites, 1s. 6d	**Lysistrata, et Thesmophoriazusae,** 4s.
Nubes, 2s.	**Ranae,** 2s.
Vespae, 2s	**Plutus,** 2s.
Pax, 2s	

Vol II Onomasticon Aristophaneum continens indicem geographicum et historicum 5s. 6d

— **The Peace.** A revised Text with English Notes and a Preface. By F. A. PALEY, M.A., LL.D. Post 8vo, 2s. 6d [*Pub Sch Ser.*

— **The Acharnians** A revised Text with English Notes and a Preface. By F. A. PALEY, M.A., LL.D. Post 8vo, 2s 6d. [*Pub Sch Ser.*

— **The Frogs** A revised Text with English Notes and a Preface By F. A. PALEY, M.A., LL.D Post 8vo, 2s. 6d. [*Pub Sch Ser.*

CAESAR De Bello Gallico. Edited by GEORGE LONG, M.A. *New edition.* Fcap 8vo, 4s.

Or in parts, Books I.-III, 1s 6d ; Books IV and V, 1s 6d, Books VI and VII, 1s 6d [*Gram Sch Class*

— **De Bello Gallico** Book I. Edited by GEORGE LONG, M.A. With Vocabulary by W. F. R. SHILLETO, M.A. 1s 6d. [*Lower Form Ser.*

— **De Bello Gallico** Book II Edited by GEORGE LONG, M.A. With Vocabulary by W. F. R. SHILLETO, M.A. Fcap 8vo, 1s. 6d [*Lower Form Ser.*

— **De Bello Gallico** Book III Edited by GEORGE LONG, M.A. With Vocabulary by W. F. R. SHILLETO, M.A. Fcap 8vo, 1s. 6d. [*Lower Form Ser.*

— **Seventh Campaign in Gaul** B.C. 52 De Bello Gallico, Lib VII Edited with Notes, Excursus, and Table of Idioms, by REV. W. COOKWORTHY COMPTON, M.A., Head Master of Dover College With Illustrations from Sketches by E. T. COMPTON, Maps and Plans. *2nd edition* Crown 8vo, 2s 6d net

"A really admirable class book"—*Spectator*

"One of the most original and interesting books which have been published in late years as aids to the study of classical literature. I think

CAESAR—*continued*
it gives the student a new idea of the way in which a classical book may be made a living reality."—*Rev. J. E. C. Welldon*, Harrow.

— **Easy Selections from the Helvetian War.** Edited by A. M. M. STEDMAN, M.A. With Introduction, Notes and Vocabulary. 18mo, 1*s.*, [*Primary Classics.*

CALPURNIUS SICULUS and M. AURELIUS OLYMPIUS NEMESIANUS. The Eclogues, with Introduction, Commentary, and Appendix. By C. H. KEENE, M.A. Crown 8vo, 6*s.*

CATULLUS, TIBULLUS, and PROPERTIUS. Selected Poems. Edited by the REV. A. H. WRATISLAW, late Head Master of Bury St. Edmunds School, and F. N. SUTTON, B.A. With Biographical Notices of the Poets. Fcap. 8vo, 2*s.* 6*d.* [*Gram. Sch. Class.*

CICERO'S Orations. Edited by G. LONG, M.A. 8vo. [*Bib. Class.*

Vol. I.—In Verrem. 8*s.*

Vol. II.—Pro P. Quintio—Pro Sex. Roscio—Pro Q. Roscio—Pro M. Tullio—Pro M. Fonteio—Pro A. Caecina—De Imperio Cn. Pompeii—Pro A. Cluentio—De Lege Agraria—Pro C. Rabirio. 8*s.*

Vols. III. and IV. *Out of print.*

— **De Senectute, De Amicitia, and Select Epistles.** Edited by GEORGE LONG, M.A. *New edition.* Fcap. 8vo, 3*s.* [*Gram. Sch. Class.*

— **De Amicitia.** Edited by GEORGE LONG, M.A. Fcap. 8vo, 1*s.* 6*d.* [*Camb. Texts with Notes.*

— **De Senectute.** Edited by GEORGE LONG, M.A. Fcap. 8vo, 1*s.* 6*d.* [*Camb. Texts with Notes.*

— **Epistolae Selectae.** Edited by GEORGE LONG, M.A. Fcap. 8vo, 1*s.* 6*d.* [*Camb. Texts with Notes.*

— **The Letters to Atticus.** Book I. With Notes, and an Essay on the Character of the Writer. By A. PRETOR, M.A., late of Trinity College, Fellow of St. Catherine's College, Cambridge. *3rd edition.* Post 8vo, 4*s.* 6*d.* [*Pub. Sch. Ser.*

CORNELIUS NEPOS. Edited by the late REV. J. F. MACMICHAEL, Head Master of the Grammar School, Ripon. Fcap. 8vo, 2*s.* [*Gram. Sch. Class.*

DEMOSTHENES. Edited by R. WHISTON, M.A., late Head Master of Rochester Grammar School. 2 vols. 8vo, 8*s.* each. [*Bib. Class.*

Vol. I.—Olynthiacs—Philippics—De Pace—Halonnesus—Chersonese—Letter of Philip—Duties of the State—Symmoriae—Rhodians—Megalopolitans—Treaty with Alexander—Crown.

Vol. II.—Embassy—Leptines—Meidias—Androtion—Aristocrates—Timocrates—Aristogeiton.

— **De Falsa Legatione.** By the late R. SHILLETO, M.A., Fellow of St. Peter's College, Cambridge. *8th edition.* Post 8vo, 6*s.* [*Pub. Sch. Ser.*

— **The Oration against the Law of Leptines.** With English Notes. By the late B. W. BEATSON, M.A., Fellow of Pembroke College. *3rd edition.* Post 8vo, 3*s.* 6*d.* [*Pub. Sch. Ser.*

EURIPIDES. By F. A. PALEY, M.A., LL.D. 3 vols. *2nd edition, revised.* 8vo, 8*s.* each. Vol. I. *Out of print.* [*Bib. Class.*

Vol. II.—Preface—Ion—Helena—Andromache—Electra—Bacchae—Hecuba. 2 Indexes.

Vol. III.—Preface—Hercules Furens—Phoenissae—Orestes—Iphigenia in Tauris—Iphigenia in Aulide—Cyclops. 2 Indexes.

EURIPIDES. Electra. Edited, with Introduction and Notes, by C. H. KEENE, M.A., Dublin, Ex-Scholar and Gold Medallist in Classics. Demy 8vo, 10*s.* 6*d.*

— Edited by F. A. PALEY, M.A., LL.D. 13 vols. Fcap. 8vo, 1*s.* 6*d.* each. [*Camb. Texts with Notes.*

Alcestis.	**Phoenissae.**
Medea.	**Troades.**
Hippolytus.	**Hercules Furens.**
Hecuba.	**Andromache.**
Bacchae.	**Iphigenia in Tauris.**
Ion (2*s.*).	**Supplices.**
Orestes.	

HERODOTUS. Edited by REV. J. W. BLAKESLEY, B.D. 2 vols. 8vo, 12*s.* [*Bib. Class.*

— **Easy Selections from the Persian Wars.** Edited by A. G. LIDDELL, M.A. With Introduction, Notes, and Vocabulary. 18mo, 1*s.* 6*d.* [*Primary Classics.*

HESIOD. Edited by F. A. PALEY, M.A., LL.D. *2nd edition, revised.* 8vo, 5*s.* [*Bib. Class.*

HOMER. Edited by F. A. PALEY, M.A., LL.D. 2 vols. *2nd edition, revised.* 14*s.* Vol. II. (Books XIII.-XXIV.) may be had separately. 6*s.* [*Bib. Class.*

— **Iliad.** Books I.-XII. Edited by F. A. PALEY, M.A., LL.D. Fcap. 8vo, 4*s.* 6*d.*

Also in 2 Parts. Books I.-VI. 2*s.* 6*d.* Books VII.-XII. 2*s.* 6*d.* [*Gram. Sch. Class.*

— **Iliad.** Book I. Edited by F. A. PALEY, M.A., LL.D. Fcap. 8vo, 1*s.* [*Camb. Text with Notes.*

HORACE. Edited by REV. A. J. MACLEANE, M.A. *4th edition*, revised by GEORGE LONG. 8vo, 8*s.* [*Bib. Class.*

— Edited by A. J. MACLEANE, M.A. With a short Life. Fcap. 8vo, 3*s.* 6*d.* Or, Part I., Odes, Carmen Seculare, and Epodes, 2*s.*; Part II., Satires, Epistles, and Art of Poetry, 2*s.* [*Gram. Sch. Class.*

— **Odes.** Book I. Edited by A. J. MACLEANE, M.A. With a Vocabulary by A. H. DENNIS, M.A. Fcap. 8vo, 1*s.* 6*d.* [*Lower Form Ser.*

JUVENAL: Sixteen Satires (expurgated). By HERMAN PRIOR, M.A., late Scholar of Trinity College, Oxford. Fcap. 8vo, 3*s.* 6*d.* [*Gram. Sch. Class.*

LIVY. The first five Books, with English Notes. By J. PRENDEVILLE. A new edition revised throughout, and the notes in great part re-written, by J. H. FREESE, M.A., late Fellow of St. John's College, Cambridge. Books I. II. III. IV. V. With Maps and Introductions. Fcap. 8vo, 1*s.* 6*d.* each.

— Book VI. Edited by E. S. WEYMOUTH, M.A., Lond., and G. F. HAMILTON, B.A. With Historical Introduction, Life of Livy, Notes, Examination Questions, Dictionary of Proper Names, and Map. Crown 8vo, 2*s.* 6*d.*

— Book XXI. By the REV. L. D. DOWDALL, M.A., late Scholar and University Student of Trinity College, Dublin, B.D., Ch. Ch. Oxon. Post 8vo, 2*s.* [*Pub. Sch. Ser.*

— Book XXII. Edited by the REV. L. D. DOWDALL, M.A., B.D. Post 8vo, 2*s.* [*Pub. Sch. Ser.*

LIVY Easy Selections from the Kings of Rome Edited by A. M. M. STEDMAN, M.A. With Introduction, Notes, and Vocabulary 18mo, 1s. 6d. [*Primary Class*

LUCAN The Pharsalia. By C. E. HASKINS, M.A., Fellow of St. John's College, Cambridge, with an Introduction by W. F. HEITLAND, M.A., Fellow and Tutor of St. John's College, Cambridge 8vo, 14s.

LUCRETIUS Titi Lucreti Cari De Rerum Natura Libri Sex. By the late H. A. J. MUNRO, M.A., Fellow of Trinity College, Cambridge *4th edition, finally revised.* 3 vols. Demy 8vo. Vols. I., II., Introduction, Text, and Notes, 18s. Vol. III., Translation, 6s.

MARTIAL. Select Epigrams. Edited by F. A. PALEY, M.A., LL.D., and the late W. H. STONE, Scholar of Trinity College, Cambridge. With a Life of the Poet Fcap 8vo, 4s. 6d. [*Gram. Sch. Class.*

OVID Fasti. Edited by F. A. PALEY, M.A., LL.D. *Second edition.* Fcap 8vo, 3s. 6d. [*Gram. Sch. Class.*

Or in 3 vols, 1s. 6d. each [*Grammar School Classics*], or 2s. each [*Camb. Texts with Notes*], Books I. and II., Books III. and IV., Books V. and VI.

— Selections from the Amores, Tristia, Heroides, and Metamorphoses. By A. J. MACLEANE, M.A. Fcap 8vo, 1s. 6d. [*Camb. Texts with Notes*

— Ars Amatoria et Amores. A School Edition. Carefully Revised and Edited, with some Literary Notes, by J. HERBERT WILLIAMS, M.A., late Demy of Magdalen College, Oxford Fcap 8vo, 3s. 6d.

— Heroides XIV. Edited, with Introductory Preface and English Notes, by ARTHUR PALMER, M.A., Professor of Latin at Trinity College, Dublin. Demy 8vo, 6s.

— Metamorphoses. Book XIII. A School Edition. With Introduction and Notes, by CHARLES HAINES KEENE, M.A., Dublin, Ex-Scholar and Gold Medallist in Classics *3rd edition* Fcap 8vo, 2s. 6d.

— Epistolarum ex Ponto Liber Primus With Introduction and Notes, by CHARLES HAINES KEENE, M.A. Crown 8vo, 3s.

PLATO The Apology of Socrates and Crito. With Notes, critical and exegetical, by WILHELM WAGNER, PH.D. *12th edition.* Post 8vo, 3s. 6d. A CHEAP EDITION Limp Cloth 2s. 6d. [*Pub. Sch. Ser.*

— Phaedo With Notes, critical and exegetical, and an Analysis, by WILHELM WAGNER, PH.D. *10th edition.* Post 8vo, 5s. 6d. [*Pub. Sch. Ser.*

— Protagoras. The Greek Text revised, with an Analysis and English Notes, by W. WAYTE, M.A., Classical Examiner at University College, London *7th edition* Post 8vo, 4s. 6d. [*Pub. Sch. Ser.*

— Euthyphro With Notes and Introduction by G. H. WELLS, M.A., Scholar of St. John's College, Oxford; Assistant Master at Merchant Taylors' School *3rd edition.* Post 8vo, 3s. [*Pub. Sch. Ser.*

— The Republic. Books I. and II. With Notes and Introduction by G. H. WELLS, M.A. *4th edition,* with the Introduction re-written. Post 8vo, 5s. [*Pub. Sch. Ser.*

— Euthydemus. With Notes and Introduction by G. H. WELLS, M.A. Post 8vo, 4s. [*Pub. Sch. Ser.*

— Phaedrus. By the late W. H. THOMPSON, D.D., Master of Trinity College, Cambridge 8vo, 5s. [*Bib. Class.*

— Gorgias. By the late W. H. THOMPSON, D.D., Master of Trinity College, Cambridge *New edition* 6s. [*Pub. Sch. Ser.*

PLAUTUS. Aulularia. With Notes, critical and exegetical, by W. WAGNER, PH.D. *5th edition.* Post 8vo, 4*s.* 6*d.* [*Pub. Sch. Ser.*

— **Trinummus.** With Notes, critical and exegetical, by WILHELM WAGNER, PH.D. *5th edition.* Post 8vo, 4*s.* 6*d.* [*Pub. Sch. Ser.*

— **Menaechmei.** With Notes, critical and exegetical, by WILHELM WAGNER, PH.D. *2nd edition.* Post 8vo, 4*s.* 6*d.* [*Pub. Sch. Ser.*

— **Mostellaria.** By E. A. SONNENSCHEIN, M.A., Professor of Classics at Mason College, Birmingham. Post 8vo, 5*s.* [*Pub. Sch. Ser.*

— **Captivi.** Abridged and Edited for the Use of Schools. With Introduction and Notes by J. H. FREESE, M.A., formerly Fellow of St. John's College, Cambridge. Fcap. 8vo, 1*s.* 6*d.*

PROPERTIUS. Sex. Aurelii Propertii Carmina. The Elegies of Propertius, with English Notes. By F. A. PALEY, M.A., LL.D. *2nd edition.* 8vo, 5*s.*

SALLUST: Catilina and Jugurtha. Edited, with Notes, by the late GEORGE LONG. *New edition, revised,* with the addition of the Chief Fragments of the Histories, by J. G. FRAZER, M.A., Fellow of Trinity College, Cambridge. Fcap. 8vo, 3*s.* 6*d.*, or separately, 2*s.* each. [*Gram. Sch. Class.*

SOPHOCLES. Edited by REV. F. H. BLAYDES, M.A. Vol. I. Oedipus Tyrannus—Oedipus Coloneus—Antigone. 8vo, 8*s.* [*Bib. Class.*

Vol. II. Philoctetes—Electra—Trachiniae—Ajax. By F. A. PALEY, M.A., LL.D. 8vo, 6*s.*, or the four Plays separately in limp cloth, 2*s.* 6*d.* each.

— **Trachiniae.** With Notes and Prolegomena. By ALFRED PRETOR, M.A., Fellow of St. Catherine's College, Cambridge. Post 8vo, 4*s.* 6*d.* [*Pub. Sch. Ser.*

— **The Oedipus Tyrannus of Sophocles.** By B. H. KENNEDY, D.D., Regius Professor of Greek and Hon. Fellow of St. John's College, Cambridge. With a Commentary containing a large number of Notes selected from the MS. of the late T. H. STEEL, M.A. Crown 8vo, 8*s.*

— — A SCHOOL EDITION. Post 8vo, 2*s.* 6*d.* [*Pub. Sch. Ser.*

— Edited by F. A. PALEY, M.A., LL.D. 5 vols. Fcap. 8vo, 1*s.* 6*d.* each. [*Camb. Texts with Notes.*

Oedipus Tyrannus.	**Electra.**
Oedipus Coloneus.	**Ajax.**
Antigone.	

TACITUS: Germania and Agricola. Edited by the late REV. P. FROST, late Fellow of St. John's College, Cambridge. Fcap. 8vo, 2*s.* 6*d.* [*Gram. Sch. Class.*

— **The Germania.** Edited, with Introduction and Notes, by R. F. DAVIS, M.A. Fcap. 8vo, 1*s.* 6*d.*

TERENCE. With Notes, critical and explanatory, by WILHELM WAGNER, PH.D. *3rd edition.* Post 8vo, 7*s.* 6*d.* [*Pub. Sch. Ser.*

— Edited by WILHELM WAGNER, PH.D. 4 vols. Fcap. 8vo, 1*s.* 6*d.* each. [*Camb. Texts with Notes.*

Andria.	**Hautontimorumenos.**
Adelphi.	**Phormio.**

THEOCRITUS. With short, critical and explanatory Latin Notes, by F. A. PALEY, M.A., LL.D. *2nd edition, revised.* Post 8vo, 4*s.* 6*d.* [*Pub. Sch. Ser.*

THUCYDIDES, Book VI. By T. W. DOUGAN, M.A., Fellow of St. John's College, Cambridge, Professor of Latin in Queen's College, Belfast. Edited with English notes. Post 8vo, 2*s.* [*Pub. Sch. Ser.*

— The History of the Peloponnesian War. With Notes and a careful Collation of the two Cambridge Manuscripts, and of the Aldine and Juntine Editions. By the late RICHARD SHILLETO, M.A., Fellow of St Peter's College, Cambridge. 8vo. Book I 6*s* 6*d*. Book II. 5*s*. 6*d*.

VIRGIL. By the late PROFESSOR CONINGTON, M.A. Revised by the late PROFESSOR NETTLESHIP, Corpus Professor of Latin at Oxford. 8vo. [*Bib. Class.*

Vol. I. The Bucolics and Georgics, with new Memoir and three Essays on Virgil's Commentators, Text, and Critics. *4th edition.* 10*s*. 6*d*.
Vol. II. The Aeneid, Books I.-VI. *4th edition.* 10*s*. 6*d*.
Vol. III. The Aeneid, Books VII.-XII. *3rd edition.* 10*s*. 6*d*.

— Abridged from PROFESSOR CONINGTON'S Edition, by the REV. J. G. SHEPPARD, D.C.L., H. NETTLESHIP, late Corpus Professor of Latin at the University of Oxford, and W. WAGNER, PH.D. 2 vols. Fcap. 8vo, 4*s*. 6*d*. each. [*Gram. Sch. Class.*

Vol. I. Bucolics, Georgics, and Aeneid, Books I.-IV.
Vol. II. Aeneid, Books V.-XII.
Also the Bucolics and Georgics, in one vol. 3*s*.

Or in 9 separate volumes (Grammar School Classics, with Notes at foot of page), price 1s. 6d. each.

Bucolics.	Aeneid, V. and VI.
Georgics, I. and II.	Aeneid, VII. and VIII.
Georgics, III. and IV.	Aeneid, IX. and X.
Aeneid, I. and II.	Aeneid, XI. and XII.
Aeneid, III. and IV.	

Or in 12 separate volumes (Cambridge Texts with Notes at end), price 1s. 6d. each.

Bucolics.	Aeneid, VII.
Georgics, I. and II.	Aeneid, VIII.
Georgics, III. and IV.	Aeneid, IX.
Aeneid, I. and II.	Aeneid, X.
Aeneid, III. and IV.	Aeneid, XI.
Aeneid, V. and VI. (price 2*s*.)	Aeneid, XII.

Aeneid, Book I. CONINGTON'S Edition abridged. With Vocabulary by W. F. R. SHILLETO, M.A. Fcap. 8vo, 1*s*. 6*d*. [*Lower Form Ser.*

XENOPHON. Anabasis. With Life, Itinerary, Index, and three Maps. Edited by the late J. F. MACMICHAEL. *Revised edition.* Fcap. 8vo, 3*s*. 6*d*. [*Gram. Sch. Class.*

Or in 4 separate volumes, price 1s. 6d. each.

Book I. (with Life, Introduction, Itinerary, and three Maps)—Books II. and III.—Books IV. and V.—Books VI. and VII.

— Anabasis. MACMICHAEL'S Edition, revised by J. E. MELHUISH, M.A., Assistant Master of St. Paul's School. In 6 volumes, fcap. 8vo. With Life, Itinerary, and Map to each volume, 1*s*. 6*d*. each. [*Camb. Texts with Notes.*

Book I.—Books II. and III.—Book IV.—Book V.—Book VI.—Book VII.

XENOPHON. Cyropaedia. Edited by G M GORHAM, M A, late Fellow of Trinity College, Cambridge *New edition* Fcap 8vo, 3*s* 6*d*
[*Gram Sch Class*

Also Books I. and II, 1*s* 6*d*, Books V and VI., 1*s* 6*d*

— Memorabilia Edited by PERCIVAL FROST, M A, late Fellow of St. John's College, Cambridge Fcap 8vo, 3*s* [*Gram. Sch Class.*

— Hellenica. Book I. Edited by L. D DOWDALL, M A, B.D Fcap. 8vo, 2*s* [*Camb Texts with Notes*

— Hellenica. Book II. By L. D. DOWDALL, M A, B D Fcap. 8vo, 2*s*. [*Camb. Texts with Notes*

TEXTS.

AESCHYLUS Ex novissima recensione F. A. PALEY, A M, LL.D Fcap. 8vo, 2*s*. [*Camb Texts*

CAESAR De Bello Gallico. Recognovit G. LONG, A M. Fcap 8vo, 1*s* 6*d*. [*Camb. Texts*

CATULLUS A New Text, with Critical Notes and an Introduction, by J P POSTGATE, M.A, LITT.D., Fellow of Trinity College, Cambridge, Professor of Comparative Philology at the University of London. Wide fcap. 8vo, 3*s*

CICERO De Senectute et de Amicitia, et Epistolae Selectae. Recensuit G LONG, A M Fcap 8vo, 1*s* 6*d* [*Camb. Texts.*

CICERONIS Orationes in Verrem. Ex recensione G. LONG, A.M. Fcap 8vo, 2*s*. 6*d* [*Camb. Texts.*

CORPUS POETARUM LATINORUM, a se aliisque denuo recognitorum et brevi lectionum varietate instructorum, edidit JOHANNES PERCIVAL POSTGATE. Tom. I —Ennius, Lucretius, Catullus, Horatius, Vergilius, Tibullus, Propertius, Ovidius. Large post 4to, 21*s*. net Also in 2 Parts, sewed, 9*s* each, net

*** To be completed in 4 parts, making 2 volumes

CORPUS POETARUM LATINORUM Edited by WALKER Containing —Catullus, Lucretius, Virgilius, Tibullus, Propertius, Ovidius, Horatius, Phaedrus, Lucanus, Persius, Juvenalis, Martialis, Sulpicia, Statius, Silius Italicus, Valerius Flaccus, Calpurnius Siculus, Ausonius, and Claudianus 1 vol 8vo, cloth, 18*s*

EURIPIDES Ex recensione F A PALEY, A M., LL D 3 vols Fcap 8vo, 2*s* each [*Camb. Texts*

Vol. I —Rhesus—Medea—Hippolytus—Alcestis—Heraclidae—Supplices—Troades

Vol II —Ion—Helena—Andromache—Electra—Bacchae—Hecuba

Vol III —Hercules Furens—Phoenissae—Orestes—Iphigenia in Tauris—Iphigenia in Aulide—Cyclops

HERODOTUS. Recensuit J G BLAKESLEY, S.T B. 2 vols Fcap 8vo, 2*s* 6*d* each [*Camb Texts*

HOMERI ILIAS I-XII Ex novissima recensione F. A PALEY, A M, LL D Fcap 8vo, 1*s* 6*d* [*Camb Texts*

HORATIUS. Ex recensione A. J. MACLEANE, A.M Fcap 8vo, 1*s*. 6*d* [*Camb. Texts*

JUVENAL ET PERSIUS Ex recensione A. J MACLEANE, A M. Fcap 8vo, 1*s* 6*d* [*Camb Texts.*

LUCRETIUS Recognovit H. A. J. MUNRO, A.M. Fcap. 8vo, 2s [*Camb Texts*.

PROPERTIUS. Sex Propertii Elegiarum Libri IV recensuit A. PALMER, collegii sacrosanctae et individuae Trinitatis juxta Dublinum Socius. Fcap 8vo 3s 6d

— Sexti Propertii Carmina Recognovit JOH. PERCIVAL POSTGATE, Large post 4to, boards, 3s 6d net

SALLUSTI CRISPI CATILINA ET JUGURTHA, Recognovit G LONG, A M Fcap 8vo, 1s 6d [*Camb. Texts*.

SOPHOCLES. Ex recensione F A PALEY, A M, LL.D. Fcap 8vo, 2s. 6d [*Camb Texts*.

TERENTI COMOEDIAE GUL WAGNER relegit et emendavit Fcap. 8vo, 2s. [*Camb Texts*.

THUCYDIDES Recensuit J G DONALDSON, S T.P 2 vols Fcap 8vo, 2s each. [*Camb. Texts*.

VERGILIUS Ex recensione J. CONINGTON, A M Fcap 8vo, 2s [*Camb Texts*

XENOPHONTIS EXPEDITIO CYRI Recensuit J F MACMICHAEL. A.B Fcap 8vo, 1s 6d. [*Camb. Texts*.

TRANSLATIONS.

AESCHYLUS, The Tragedies of. Translated into English verse by ANNA SWANWICK. *4th edition revised.* Small post 8vo, 5s

— The Tragedies of. Literally translated into Prose, by T. A. BUCKLEY, B.A. Small post 8vo, 3s 6d

— The Tragedies of Translated by WALTER HEADLAM, M A, Fellow of King's College, Cambridge [*Preparing*.

ANTONINUS (M Aurelius), The Thoughts of Translated by GEORGE LONG, M A *Revised edition* Small post 8vo, 3s 6d
Fine paper edition on handmade paper. Pott 8vo, 6s.

APOLLONIUS RHODIUS. The Argonautica Translated by E. P. COLERIDGE Small post 8vo, 5s

AMMIANUS MARCELLINUS. History of Rome during the Reigns of Constantius, Julian, Jovianus, Valentinian, and Valens Translated by PROF C. D YONGE, M A With a complete Index Small post 8vo, 7s 6d.

ARISTOPHANES, The Comedies of Literally translated by W. J. HICKIE *With Portrait* 2 vols Small post 8vo, 5s each.
Vol. I —Acharnians, Knights, Clouds, Wasps, Peace, and Birds.
Vol II —Lysistrata, Thesmophoriazusae, Frogs, Ecclesiazusae, and Plutus

— The Acharnians Translated by W H. COVINGTON, B A. With Memoir and Introduction. Crown 8vo, sewed, 1s

ARISTOTLE on the Athenian Constitution. Translated, with Notes and Introduction, by F G KENYON, M.A, Fellow of Magdalen College, Oxford. Pott 8vo, printed on handmade paper. *2nd edition* 4s 6d

— History of Animals. Translated by RICHARD CRESSWELL, M A Small post 8vo, 5s.

ARISTOTLE. Organon: or, Logical Treatises, and the Introduction of Porphyry. With Notes, Analysis, Introduction, and Index, by the REV. O. F. OWEN, M.A. 2 vols. Small post 8vo, 3*s.* 6*d.* each.

— **Rhetoric and Poetics.** Literally Translated, with Hobbes' Analysis, &c., by T. BUCKLEY, B.A. Small post 8vo, 5*s.*

— **Nicomachean Ethics.** Literally Translated, with Notes, an Analytical Introduction, &c., by the Venerable ARCHDEACON BROWNE, late Classical Professor of King's College. Small post 8vo, 5*s.*

— **Politics and Economics.** Translated, with Notes, Analyses, and Index, by E. WALFORD, M.A., and an Introductory Essay and a Life by DR. GILLIES. Small post 8vo, 5*s.*

— **Metaphysics.** Literally Translated, with Notes, Analysis, &c., by the REV. JOHN H. M'MAHON, M.A. Small post 8vo, 5*s.*

ARRIAN. Anabasis of Alexander, together with the Indica. Translated by F. J. CHINNOCK, M.A., LL.D. With Introduction, Notes, Maps, and Plans. Small post 8vo, 5*s.*

CAESAR. Commentaries on the Gallic and Civil Wars, with the Supplementary Books attributed to Hirtius, including the complete Alexandrian, African, and Spanish Wars. Translated by W. A. M'DEVITTE, B.A. Small post 8vo, 5*s.*

— **Gallic War.** Translated by W. A. M'DEVITTE, B.A. 2 vols., with Memoir and Map. Crown 8vo, sewed. Books I. to IV., Books V. to VII., 1*s.* each.

CALPURNIUS SICULUS, The Eclogues of. The Latin Text, with English Translation by F. J. L. SCOTT, M.A. Crown 8vo, 3*s.* 6*d.*

CATULLUS, TIBULLUS, and the Vigil of Venus. Prose Translation. Small post 8vo, 5*s.*

CICERO, The Orations of. Translated by PROF. C. D. YONGE, M.A. With Index. 4 vols. Small post 8vo, 5*s.* each.

— **On Oratory and Orators.** With Letters to Quintus and Brutus. Translated by the REV. J. S. WATSON, M.A. Small post 8vo, 5*s.*

— **On the Nature of the Gods.** Divination, Fate, Laws, a Republic, Consulship. Translated by PROF. C. D. YONGE, M.A., and FRANCIS BARHAM. Small post 8vo, 5*s.*

— **Academics,** De Finibus, and Tusculan Questions. By PROF. C. D. YONGE, M.A. Small post 8vo, 5*s.*

— **Offices;** or, Moral Duties. Cato Major, an Essay on Old Age; Laelius, an Essay on Friendship; Scipio's Dream; Paradoxes; Letter to Quintus on Magistrates. Translated by C. R. EDMONDS. *With Portrait*, 3*s.* 6*d.*

— **Old Age and Friendship.** Translated, with Memoir and Notes, by G. H. WELLS, M.A. Crown 8vo, sewed, 1*s.*

DEMOSTHENES, The Orations of. Translated, with Notes, Arguments, a Chronological Abstract, Appendices, and Index, by C. RANN KENNEDY. 5 vols. Small post 8vo.

Vol. I.—The Olynthiacs, Philippics. 3*s.* 6*d.*
Vol. II.—On the Crown and on the Embassy. 5*s.*
Vol. III.—Against Leptines, Midias, Androtion, and Aristocrates. 5*s.*
Vols. IV. and V.—Private and Miscellaneous Orations. 5*s.* each.

— **On the Crown.** Translated by C. RANN KENNEDY. Crown 8vo, sewed, 1*s.*

DIOGENES LAERTIUS. Translated by PROF. C. D. YONGE, M.A. Small post 8vo, 5*s.*

EPICTETUS, The Discourses of With the Encheiridion and Fragments Translated by GEORGE LONG, M A Small post 8vo, 5s
Fine Paper Edition, 2 vols. Pott 8vo, 10s 6d

EURIPIDES. A Prose Translation, from the Text of Paley. By E. P COLERIDGE, B.A 2 vols, 5s each
Vol I —Rhesus, Medea, Hippolytus, Alcestis, Heraclidæ, Supplices, Troades, Ion, Helena
Vol II —Andromache, Electra, Bacchae, Hecuba, Hercules Furens, Phoenissae, Orestes, Iphigenia in Tauris, Iphigenia in Aulis, Cyclops
*** The plays separately (except Rhesus, Helena, Electra, Iphigenia in Aulis, and Cyclops) Crown 8vo, sewed, 1s each

— Translated from the Text of Dindorf By T A BUCKLEY, B A. 2 vols small post 8vo, 5s each

GREEK ANTHOLOGY. Translated by GEORGE BURGES, M.A. Small post 8vo, 5s

HERODOTUS Translated by the REV HENRY CARY, M A. Small post 8vo, 3s 6d

— Analysis and Summary of. By J T. WHEELER. Small post 8vo, 5s

HESIOD, CALLIMACHUS, and THEOGNIS Translated by the REV J BANKS, M A. Small post 8vo, 5s

HOMER The Iliad. Translated by T. A BUCKLEY, B A Small post 8vo, 5s

— The Odyssey, Hymns, Epigrams, and Battle of the Frogs and Mice. Translated by T A BUCKLEY, B A Small post 8vo, 5s.

— The Iliad Books I -IV Translated into English Hexameter Verse, by HENRY SMITH WRIGHT, B A., late Scholar of Trinity College, Cambridge. Medium 8vo, 5s

HORACE Translated by Smart *Revised edition* By T. A. BUCKLEY, B A. Small post 8vo, 3s. 6d

— The Odes and Carmen Saeculare Translated into English Verse by the late JOHN CONINGTON, M A, Corpus Professor of Latin in the University of Oxford *11th edition.* Fcap 8vo 3s 6d

— The Satires and Epistles Translated into English Verse by PROF JOHN CONINGTON, M.A *8th edition.* Fcap. 8vo, 3s. 6d

— Odes and Epodes Translated by SIR STEPHEN E. DE VERE, BART *3rd edition, enlarged* Imperial 16mo 7s 6d net

ISOCRATES, The Orations of. Translated by J H FREESE, M A, late Fellow of St John's College, Cambridge, with Introductions and Notes Vol I Small post 8vo, 5s.

JUSTIN, CORNELIUS NEPOS, and EUTROPIUS. Translated by the REV J S WATSON, M A Small post 8vo, 5s

JUVENAL, PERSIUS, SULPICIA, and LUCILIUS. Translated by L. EVANS, M.A Small post 8vo, 5s

LIVY The History of Rome Translated by DR. SPILLAN, C EDMONDS, and others 4 vols small post 8vo, 5s each.

— Books I, II, III, IV A Revised Translation by J. H. FREESE, M.A, late Fellow of St John's College, Cambridge. With Memoir, and Maps. 4 vols, crown 8vo, sewed, 1s each.

— Book V and Book VI. A Revised Translation by E. S WEYMOUTH, M A., Lond With Memoir, and Maps Crown 8vo, sewed, 1s each.

— Book IX Translated by FRANCIS STORR, B A With Memoir Crown 8vo, sewed, 1s

LUCAN. The Pharsalia. Translated into Prose by H. T. RILEY Small post 8vo, 5s.

— The Pharsalia. Book I. Translated by FREDERICK CONWAY, M A With Memoir and Introduction Crown 8vo, sewed, 1s.

LUCIAN'S Dialogues of the Gods, of the Sea-Gods, and of the Dead. Translated by HOWARD WILLIAMS, M A Small post 8vo, 5s

LUCRETIUS Translated by the REV J. S WATSON, M A Small post 8vo, 5s

— Literally translated by the late H. A J MUNRO, M A *4th edition* Demy 8vo, 6s

MARTIAL'S Epigrams, complete. Literally translated into Prose, with the addition of Verse Translations selected from the Works of English Poets, and other sources Small post 8vo, 7s 6d

OVID, The Works of Translated. 3 vols Small post 8vo, 5s each

Vol. I —Fasti, Tristia, Pontic Epistles, Ibis, and Halieuticon

Vol II —Metamorphoses *With Frontispiece.*

Vol. III.—Heroides, Amours, Art of Love, Remedy of Love, and Minor Pieces *With Frontispiece.*

— Fasti. Translated by H T RILEY, B A 3 vols Crown 8vo, sewed, 1s each

— Tristia Translated by H T RILEY, B A Crown 8vo, sewed, 1s.

PINDAR Translated by DAWSON W TURNER Small post 8vo, 5s

PLATO Gorgias Translated by the late E M COPE, M A, Fellow of Trinity College. *2nd edition* 8vo, 7s

— Philebus Translated by F A PALEY, M A, LL D. Small 8vo, 4s.

— Theaetetus Translated by F A PALEY, M A, LL D Small 8vo, 4s

— The Works of Translated, with Introduction and Notes 6 vols. Small post 8vo, 5s each

Vol. I —The Apology of Socrates—Crito—Phaedo—Gorgias—Protagoras—Phaedrus—Theaetetus—Euthyphron—Lysis Translated by the REV H CARY

Vol II —The Republic—Timaeus—Critias Translated by HENRY DAVIS.

Vol. III —Meno—Euthydemus—The Sophist—Statesman—Cratylus—Parmenides—The Banquet Translated by G BURGES

Vol. IV —Philebus—Charmides—Laches—Menexenus—Hippias—Ion—The Two Alcibiades—Theages—Rivals—Hipparchus—Minos—Clitopho—Epistles. Translated by G BURGES

Vol. V.—The Laws. Translated by G BURGES

Vol. VI —The Doubtful Works Edited by G BURGES With General Index to the six volumes

— Apology, Crito, Phaedo, and Protagoras Translated by the REV. H. CARY. Small post 8vo, sewed, 1s, cloth, 1s 6d

— Dialogues. A Summary and Analysis of With Analytical Index, giving references to the Greek text of modern editions and to the above translations. By A DAY, LL.D. Small post 8vo, 5s

PLAUTUS, The Comedies of Translated by H. T RILEY, B A 2 vols. Small post 8vo, 5s each.

Vol I.—Trinummus—Miles Gloriosus—Bacchides—Stichus—Pseudolus—Menaechmei—Aulularia—Captivi—Asinaria—Curculio

Vol II —Amphitryon—Rudens—Mercator—Cistellaria—Truculentus—Persa—Casina—Poenulus—Epidicus—Mostellaria—Fragments

— Trinummus, Menaechmei, Aulularia, and Captivi Translated by H. T. RILEY, B A. Small post 8vo, sewed, 1s, cloth, 1s 6d.

PLINY. The Letters of Pliny the Younger Melmoth's Translation, revised, by the REV F. C T BOSANQUET, M.A Small post 8vo, 5*s*

PLUTARCH. Lives Translated by A STEWART, M A, late Fellow of Trinity College, Cambridge, and GEORGE LONG, M A 4 vols small post 8vo, 3*s.* 6*d* each.

— Morals Theosophical Essays Translated by C W KING, M A, late Fellow of Trinity College, Cambridge. Small post 8vo, 5*s.*

— Morals Ethical Essays. Translated by the REV. A. R. SHILLETO, M A. Small post 8vo, 5*s.*

PROPERTIUS. Translated by REV P. J F. GANTILLON, M A., and accompanied by Poetical Versions, from various sources Small post 8vo, 3*s* 6*d*

PRUDENTIUS, Translations from. A Selection from his Works, with a Translation into English Verse, and an Introduction and Notes, by FRANCIS ST. JOHN THACKERAY, M A, F S.A, Vicar of Mapledurham, formerly Fellow of Lincoln College, Oxford, and Assistant-Master at Eton. Wide post 8vo, 7*s* 6*d.*

QUINTILIAN Institutes of Oratory, or, Education of an Orator. Translated by the REV. J. S WATSON, M A. 2 vols small post 8vo, 5*s.* each

SALLUST, FLORUS, and **VELLEIUS PATERCULUS.** Translated by J S WATSON, M A Small post 8vo, 5*s*

SENECA: On Benefits Translated by A. STEWART, M A, late Fellow of Trinity College, Cambridge Small post 8vo, 3*s* 6*d.*

— **Minor Essays and On Clemency.** Translated by A. STEWART, M A Small post 8vo, 5*s.*

SOPHOCLES. Translated, with Memoir, Notes, etc, by E. P. COLERIDGE, B.A. Small post 8vo, 5*s*

Or the plays separately, crown 8vo, sewed, 1*s* each.

— **The Tragedies of** The Oxford Translation, with Notes, Arguments, and Introduction Small post 8vo, 5*s.*

— **The Dramas of** Rendered in English Verse, Dramatic and Lyric, by SIR GEORGE YOUNG, BART., M.A., formerly Fellow of Trinity College, Cambridge 8vo, 12*s* 6*d.*

— **The Œdipus Tyrannus** Translated into English Prose. By PROF. B. H KENNEDY. Crown 8vo, in paper wrapper, 1*s*

SUETONIUS Lives of the Twelve Caesars and Lives of the Grammarians. Thomson's revised Translation, by T FORESTER. Small post 8vo, 5*s*

TACITUS, The Works of Translated, with Notes and Index 2 vols. Small post 8vo, 5*s* each.

Vol I.—The Annals

Vol. II.—The History, Germania, Agricola, Oratory, and Index

TERENCE and **PHAEDRUS.** Translated by H. T. RILEY, B.A. Small post 8vo, 5*s*

THEOCRITUS, BION, MOSCHUS, and **TYRTAEUS.** Translated by the REV J BANKS, M A Small post 8vo, 5*s*

THEOCRITUS Translated into English Verse by C. S CALVERLEY, M.A, late Fellow of Christ's College, Cambridge. *New edition, revised.* Crown 8vo, 7*s.* 6*d.*

THUCYDIDES The Peloponnesian War Translated by the REV H. DALE. *With Portrait* 2 vols, 3s. 6d each

— **Analysis and Summary of.** By J. T WHEELER. Small post 8vo, 5s

VIRGIL. Translated by A. HAMILTON BRYCE, LL D. With Memoir and Introduction Small post 8vo, 3s 6d

Also in 6 vols, crown 8vo, sewed, 1s each

Georgics.	Æneid IV -VI
Bucolics	Æneid VII -IX.
Æneid I.-III.	Æneid X -XII

XENOPHON. The Works of. In 3 vols Small post 8vo, 5s each

Vol I —The Anabasis, and Memorabilia. Translated by the REV J S WATSON, M A With a Geographical Commentary, by W F AINSWORTH, F.S.A., F R.G.S, etc.

Vol. II —Cyropaedia and Hellenics. Translated by the REV. J S WATSON, M A, and the REV H DALE

Vol III.—The Minor Works Translated by the REV J S WATSON, M A

— **Anabasis.** Translated by the REV J. S. WATSON, M A With Memoir and Map. 3 vols.

— **Hellenics.** Books I and II. Translated by the REV. H. DALE, M A With Memoir

---

SABRINAE COROLLA In Hortulis Regiae Scholae Salopiensis contexuerunt tres viri floribus legendis *4th edition, revised and re-arranged* By the late BENJAMIN HALL KENNEDY, D D, Regius Professor of Greek at the University of Cambridge Large post 8vo, 10s 6d

SERTUM CARTHUSIANUM Floribus trium Seculorum Contextum Cura GULIELMI HAIG BROWN, Scholae Carthusianae Archididascali Demy 8vo, 5s

TRANSLATIONS into English and Latin. By C S CALVERLEY, M A, late Fellow of Christ's College, Cambridge *3rd edition* Crown 8vo, 7s 6d.

TRANSLATIONS from and into the Latin, Greek and English By R C JEBB, M A., Regius Professor of Greek in the University of Cambridge, H JACKSON, M A, LITT D, Fellows of Trinity College, Cambridge, and W E CURREY, M.A, formerly Fellow of Trinity College, Cambridge Crown 8vo *2nd edition, revised* 8s

GRAMMAR AND COMPOSITION

BADDELEY Auxilia Latina A Series of Progressive Latin Exercises By M J B BADDELEY, M A. Fcap 8vo Part I, Accidence *5th edition.* 2s. Part II *5th edition* 2s Key to Part II 2s 6d

BAIRD. Greek Verbs A Catalogue of Verbs, Irregular and Defective; their leading formations, tenses in use, and dialectic inflexions, with a copious Appendix, containing Paradigms for conjugation, Rules for formation of tenses, &c, &c By J S. BAIRD, T C D. *New edition, revised.* 2s 6d

— **Homeric Dialect** Its Leading Forms and Peculiarities By J. S BAIRD, T C D *New edition, revised* By the REV. W GUNION RUTHERFORD, M A, LL D, Head Master at Westminster School 1s.

BAKER Latin Prose for London Students. By ARTHUR BAKER, M A, Classical Master, Independent College, Taunton Fcap 8vo, 2*s*

BARRY. Notes on Greek Accents. By the RIGHT REV. A BARRY, D.D *New edition, re-written* 1*s*

CHURCH Latin Prose Lessons. By A J. CHURCH, M A, Professor of Latin at University College, London. *9th edition.* Fcap. 8vo, 2*s*. 6*d*

CLAPIN. Latin Primer. By the REV. A C CLAPIN, M A, Assistant Master at Sherborne School *4th edition* Fcap 8vo, 1*s*

COLLINS Latin Exercises and Grammar Papers By T COLLINS, M A, Head Master of the Latin School, Newport, Salop. *7th edition.* Fcap. 8vo, 2*s* 6*d*

— Unseen Papers in Latin Prose and Verse With Examination Questions. *7th edition* Fcap 8vo, 2*s* 6*d*

— Unseen Papers in Greek Prose and Verse With Examination Questions *4th edition* Fcap 8vo, 3*s*

— Easy Translations from Nepos, Caesar, Cicero, Livy, &c, for Retranslation into Latin. With Notes 2*s*

COMPTON Rudiments of Attic Construction and Idiom An Introduction to Greek Syntax for Beginners who have acquired some knowledge of Latin By the REV W COOKWORTHY COMPTON, M A, Head Master of Dover College Crown 8vo, 3*s*

FROST Eclogae Latinae, or, First Latin Reading Book. With Notes and Vocabulary by the late REV P. FROST, M A. Fcap 8vo, 1*s* 6*d*.

— Analecta Graeca Minora With Notes and Dictionary. *New edition* Fcap 8vo, 2*s*

— Materials for Latin Prose Composition By the late REV P FROST, M A *New edition* Fcap 8vo 2*s* Key. 4*s* net

— A Latin Verse Book *New edition.* Fcap 8vo, 2*s*. Key. 5*s* net

— Materials for Greek Prose Composition. *New edition.* Fcap 8vo, 2*s* 6*d* Key. 5*s*. net

— Greek Accidence. *New edition* 1*s*

— Latin Accidence. 1*s*

HARKNESS A Latin Grammar. By ALBERT HARKNESS Post 8vo, 6*s*.

KEY. A Latin Grammar By the late T. H. KEY, M A., F R S *6th thousand* Post 8vo, 8*s*

— A Short Latin Grammar for Schools *16th edition.* Post 8vo, 3*s* 6*d*

HOLDEN Foliorum Silvula Part I Passages for Translation into Latin Elegiac and Heroic Verse. By H. A. HOLDEN, LL D *11th edition* Post 8vo, 7*s*. 6*d*.

— Foliorum Silvula Part II. Select Passages for Translation into Latin Lyric and Comic Iambic Verse *3rd edition* Post 8vo, 5*s*.

— Foliorum Centuriae Select Passages for Translation into Latin and Greek Prose *10th edition* Post 8vo, 8*s*

JEBB, JACKSON, and CURREY. Extracts for Translation in Greek, Latin, and English By R C JEBB, LITT D, LL D, Regius Professor of Greek in the University of Cambridge; H JACKSON, LITT D, Fellow of Trinity College, Cambridge, and W. E. CURREY, M A., late Fellow of Trinity College, Cambridge. 4*s*. 6*d*.

Latin Syntax, Principles of. 1*s*.

Latin Versification 1*s*.

MASON. **Analytical Latin Exercises** By C. P. MASON, B.A. *4th edition.* Part I., 1s. 6d. Part II., 2s. 6d.

— **The Analysis of Sentences Applied to Latin.** Post 8vo, 1s. 6d.

NETTLESHIP. **Passages for Translation into Latin Prose.** Preceded by Essays on :—I. Political and Social Ideas. II. Range of Metaphorical Expression. III. Historical Development of Latin Prose Style in Antiquity. IV. Cautions as to Orthography. By H. NETTLESHIP, M.A., late Corpus Professor of Latin in the University of Oxford. Crown 8vo, 3s. A Key, 4s. 6d. net.

Notabilia Quaedam; or the Principal Tenses of most of the Irregular Greek Verbs, and Elementary Greek, Latin, and French Constructions. *New edition.* 1s.

PALEY. **Greek Particles** and their Combinations according to Attic Usage. A Short Treatise. By F. A. PALEY, M.A., LL.D. 2s. 6d.

PENROSE. **Latin Elegiac Verse,** Easy Exercises in. By the REV. J. PENROSE. *New edition.* 2s. (Key, 3s. 6d. net.)

PRESTON. **Greek Verse Composition.** By G. PRESTON, M.A. *5th edition.* Crown 8vo, 4s. 6d.

PRUEN. **Latin Examination Papers.** Comprising Lower, Middle, and Upper School Papers, and a number of the Woolwich and Sandhurst Standards. By G. G. PRUEN, M.A., Senior Classical Master in the Modern Department, Cheltenham College. Crown 8vo, 2s. 6d.

SEAGER. **Faciliora.** An Elementary Latin Book on a New Principle. By the REV. J. L. SEAGER, M.A. 2s. 6d.

STEDMAN (A. M. M.). **First Latin Lessons.** By A. M. M. STEDMAN, M.A., Wadham College, Oxford. *2nd edition, enlarged.* Crown 8vo, 2s.

— **Initia Latina.** Easy Lessons on Elementary Accidence. *2nd edition.* Fcap. 8vo, 1s.

— **First Latin Reader.** With Notes adapted to the Shorter Latin Primer and Vocabulary. Crown 8vo, 1s. 6d.

— **Easy Latin Passages** for Unseen Translation. *2nd and enlarged edition.* Fcap. 8vo, 1s. 6d.

— **Exempla Latina.** First Exercises in Latin Accidence. With Vocabulary. Crown 8vo, 1s. 6d.

— **The Latin Compound Sentence; Rules and Exercises.** Crown 8vo, 1s. 6d. With Vocabulary, 2s.

— **Easy Latin Exercises** on the Syntax of the Shorter and Revised Latin Primers. With Vocabulary. *3rd edition.* Crown 8vo, 2s. 6d.

— **Latin Examination Papers** in Miscellaneous Grammar and Idioms. *3rd edition.* 2s. 6d. Key (for Tutors only), 6s. net.

— **Notanda Quaedam.** Miscellaneous Latin Exercises. On Common Rules and Idioms. *2nd edition.* Fcap. 8vo 1s. 6d. With Vocabulary, 2s.

— **Latin Vocabularies** for Repetition. Arranged according to Subjects. *3rd edition.* Fcap. 8vo, 1s. 6d.

— **First Greek Lessons.** [*In preparation.*

— **Easy Greek Passages** for Unseen Translation. Fcap. 8vo, 1s. 6d.

— **Easy Greek Exercises** on Elementary Syntax. [*In preparation.*

— **Greek Vocabularies** for Repetition. Fcap. 8vo, 1s. 6d.

— **Greek Testament Selections** for the Use of Schools. *2nd edition.* With Introduction, Notes, and Vocabulary. Fcap. 8vo, 2s. 6d.

— **Greek Examination Papers** in Miscellaneous Grammar and Idioms. *2nd edition.* 2s. 6d. Key (for Tutors only), 6s. net.

THACKERAY. Anthologia Graeca A Selection of Greek Poetry, with Notes By F. ST. JOHN THACKERAY. *5th edition.* 16mo, 4*s*. 6*d*

— Anthologia Latina A Selection of Latin Poetry, from Naevius to Boethius, with Notes By REV F. ST. JOHN THACKERAY. *6th edition.* 16mo, 4*s* 6*d*.

— Hints and Cautions on Attic Greek Prose Composition. Crown 8vo, 3*s* 6*d*

— Exercises on the Irregular and Defective Greek Verbs 1*s* 6*d*

WELLS Tales for Latin Prose Composition. With Notes and Vocabulary. By G. H. WELLS, M.A, Assistant Master at Merchant Taylor's School. Fcap. 8vo, 2*s*

HISTORY, GEOGRAPHY, AND REFERENCE BOOKS, ETC.

TEUFFEL'S History of Roman Literature. *5th edition,* revised by DR SCHWABE, translated by PROFESSOR G C W WARR, M A, King's College, London Medium 8vo 2 vols 30*s* Vol I. (The Republican Period), 15*s* Vol II (The Imperial Period), 15*s*.

KEIGHTLEY'S Mythology of Ancient Greece and Italy. *4th edition,* revised by the late LEONHARD SCHMITZ, PH D, LL D, Classical Examiner to the University of London With 12 Plates Small post 8vo, 5*s*.

DONALDSON'S Theatre of the Greeks. *10th edition* Small post 8vo, 5*s*.

DICTIONARY OF LATIN AND GREEK QUOTATIONS; including Proverbs, Maxims, Mottoes, Law Terms and Phrases With all the Quantities marked, and English Translations With Index Verborum. Small post 8vo, 5*s*

A GUIDE TO THE CHOICE OF CLASSICAL BOOKS By J B. MAYOR, M A, Professor of Moral Philosophy at King's College, late Fellow and Tutor of St John's College, Cambridge. *3rd edition,* with Supplementary List. Crown 8vo, 4*s*. 6*d* Supplement separate, 1*s* 6*d*.

PAUSANIAS' Description of Greece. Newly translated, with Notes and Index, by A. R. SHILLETO, M A. 2 vols Small post 8vo, 5*s*. each.

STRABO'S Geography. Translated by W FALCONER, M.A, and H C. HAMILTON 3 vols Small post 8vo, 5*s* each

AN ATLAS OF CLASSICAL GEOGRAPHY By W. HUGHES and G LONG, M A Containing Ten selected Maps Imp 8vo, 3*s*

AN ATLAS OF CLASSICAL GEOGRAPHY Twenty-four Maps by W HUGHES and GEORGE LONG, M A With coloured outlines. Imperial 8vo, 6*s*

ATLAS OF CLASSICAL GEOGRAPHY. 22 large Coloured Maps. With a complete Index. Imp. 8vo, chiefly engraved by the Messrs Walker. 7*s*. 6*d*.

MATHEMATICS.

ARITHMETIC AND ALGEBRA.

BARRACLOUGH (T.). The Eclipse Mental Arithmetic. By TITUS BARRACLOUGH, Board School, Halifax. Standards I., II., and III., sewed, *6d.*; Standards II., III., and IV., sewed, *6d.* net; Book III., Part A, sewed, *4d.*; Book III., Part B, cloth, *1s. 6d.*

BEARD (W. S.). Graduated Exercises in Addition (Simple and Compound). For Candidates for Commercial Certificates and Civil Service appointments. By W. S. BEARD, F.R.G.S., Head Master of the Modern School, Fareham. *3rd edition.* Fcap. 4to, *1s.*

— *See* **PENDLEBURY.**

ELSEE (C.). Arithmetic. By the REV. C. ELSEE, M.A., late Fellow of St. John's College, Cambridge, Senior Mathematical Master at Rugby School. *14th edition.* Fcap. 8vo, *3s. 6d.*
[*Camb. School and College Texts.*

— **Algebra.** By the REV. C. ELSEE, M.A. *8th edition.* Fcap. 8vo, *4s.*
[*Camb. S. and C. Texts.*

FILIPOWSKI (H. E.). Anti-Logarithms, A Table of. By H. E. FILIPOWSKI. *3rd edition.* 8vo, *15s.*

GOUDIE (W. P.). *See* **Watson.**

HATHORNTHWAITE (J. T.). Elementary Algebra for Indian Schools. By J. T. HATHORNTHWAITE, M.A., Principal and Professor of Mathematics at Elphinstone College, Bombay. Crown 8vo, *2s.*

HUNTER (J.). Supplementary Arithmetic, with Answers. By REV. J. HUNTER, M.A. Fcap. 8vo, *3s.*

MACMICHAEL (W. F.) and PROWDE SMITH (R.). Algebra. A Progressive Course of Examples. By the REV. W. F. MACMICHAEL, and R. PROWDE SMITH, M.A. *4th edition.* Fcap. 8vo, *3s. 6d.* With answers, *4s. 6d.* [*Camb. S. and C. Texts.*

MATHEWS (G. B.). Theory of Numbers. An account of the Theories of Congruencies and of Arithmetical Forms. By G. B. MATHEWS, M.A., Professor of Mathematics in the University College of North Wales. Part I. Demy 8vo, *12s.*

MOORE (B. T). Elementary Treatise on Mensuration. By B. T. MOORE, M.A., Fellow of Pembroke College, Cambridge.
[*New edition preparing.*

PENDLEBURY (C.). Arithmetic. With Examination Papers and 8,000 Examples. By CHARLES PENDLEBURY, M.A., F.R.A.S., Senior Mathematical Master of St. Paul's, Author of "Lenses and Systems of Lenses, treated after the manner of Gauss." *7th edition.* Crown 8vo. Complete, with or without Answers, *4s. 6d.* In Two Parts, with or without Answers, *2s. 6d.* each.
Key to Part II. *7s. 6d.* net. [*Camb. Math. Ser.*

— **Examples in Arithmetic.** Extracted from Pendlebury's Arithmetic. With or without Answers. *5th edition.* Crown 8vo, *3s.*, or in Two Parts, *1s. 6d.* and *2s.* [*Camb. Math. Ser.*

— **Examination Papers in Arithmetic.** Consisting of 140 papers, each containing 7 questions; and a collection of 357 more difficult problems. *2nd edition.* Crown 8vo, *2s. 6d.* Key, for Tutors only, *5s.* net.

PENDLEBURY (C.) and TAIT (T. S.). Arithmetic for Indian Schools. By C. PENDLEBURY, M.A. and T. S. TAIT, M.A., B.SC., Principal of Baroda College. Crown 8vo, 3*s.* [*Camb. Math. Ser.*

PENDLEBURY (C.) and BEARD (W. S.). Arithmetic for the Standards. By C. PENDLEBURY, M.A., F.R.A.S., and W. S. BEARD, F.R.G.S. Standards I., II., III., sewed, 2*d.* each, cloth, 3*d.* each; IV., V., VI., sewed, 3*d.* each, cloth, 4*d.* each; VII., sewed, 6*d.*, cloth, 8*d.* Answers to I. and II., 4*d.*, III.-VII., 4*d.* each.

— **Elementary Arithmetic.** *3rd edition.* Crown 8vo, 1*s.* 6*d.*

POPE (L. J.) Lessons in Elementary Algebra. By L. J. POPE, B.A. (Lond.), Assistant Master at the Oratory School, Birmingham. First Series, up to and including Simple Equations and Problems. Crown 8vo, 1*s.* 6*d.*

PROWDE SMITH (R.) *See* Macmichael.

SHAW (S. J. D.) Arithmetic Papers. Set in the Cambridge Higher Local Examination, from June, 1869, to June, 1887, inclusive, reprinted by permission of the Syndicate. By S. J. D. SHAW, Mathematical Lecturer of Newnham College. Crown 8vo, 2*s.* 6*d.*; Key, 4*s.* 6*d.* net.

TAIT (T. S.) *See* Pendlebury.

WATSON (J.) and GOUDIE (W. P.) Arithmetic. A Progressive Course of Examples. With Answers. By J. WATSON, M.A., Corpus Christi College, Cambridge, formerly Senior Mathematical Master of the Ordnance School, Carshalton. *7th edition, revised and enlarged.* By W. P. GOUDIE, B.A. Lond. Fcap. 8vo, 2*s.* 6*d.* [*Camb. S. and C. Texts.*

WHITWORTH (W. A.). Algebra. Choice and Chance. An Elementary Treatise on Permutations, Combinations, and Probability, with 640 Exercises and Answers. By W. A. WHITWORTH, M.A., Fellow of St. John's College, Cambridge. *4th edition, revised and enlarged.* Crown 8vo, 6*s.* [*Camb. Math. Ser.*

WRIGLEY (A.) Arithmetic. By A. WRIGLEY, M.A., St. John's College. Fcap. 8vo, 3*s.* 6*d.* [*Camb. S. and C. Texts.*

BOOK-KEEPING.

CRELLIN (P.). A New Manual of Book-keeping, combining the Theory and Practice, with Specimens of a set of Books. By PHILLIP CRELLIN, Chartered Accountant. Crown 8vo, 3*s.* 6*d.*

— **Book-keeping for Teachers and Pupils.** Crown 8vo, 1*s.* 6*d.* Key, 2*s.* net.

FOSTER (B. W.) Double Entry Elucidated. By B. W. FOSTER. *14th edition.* Fcap. 4to, 3*s.* 6*d.*

MEDHURST (J. T.). Examination Papers in Book-keeping. Compiled by JOHN T. MEDHURST, A.K.C., F.S.S., Fellow of the Society of Accountants and Auditors, and Lecturer at the City of London College. *3rd edition.* Crown 8vo, 3*s.*

THOMSON (A. W.) A Text-Book of the Principles and Practice of Book-keeping. By PROFESSOR A. W. THOMSON, B.SC., Royal Agricultural College, Cirencester. *2nd edition, revised.* Crown 8vo, 5*s.*

GEOMETRY AND EUCLID.

BESANT (W. H.). Conic Sections treated Geometrically. By W. H. BESANT, SC D., F R.S., Fellow of St. John's College, Cambridge. *9th edition.* Crown 8vo, 4s. 6d. net Key, 5s net. [*Camb Math. Ser.*

BRASSE (J) The Enunciations and Figures of Euclid, prepared for Students in Geometry By the REV J BRASSE, D D. *New edition.* Fcap. 8vo, 1s Without the Figures, 6d

DEIGHTON (H) Euclid Books I-VI, and part of Book XI., newly translated from the Greek Text, with Supplementary Propositions, Chapters on Modern Geometry, and numerous Exercises By HORACE DEIGHTON, M A, Head Master of Harrison College, Barbados *3rd edition* 4s 6d, or Books I-IV, 3s Books V-XI, 2s 6d Key, 5s net [*Camb Math Ser.*

Also issued in parts:—Book I, 1s; Books I and II, 1s 6d; Books I-III, 2s. 6d, Books III and IV, 1s 6d

DIXON (E T.). The Foundations of Geometry. By EDWARD T. DIXON, late Royal Artillery Demy 8vo, 6s

MASON (C. P.). Euclid. The First Two Books Explained to Beginners. By C P MASON, B A *2nd edition* Fcap 8vo, 2s. 6d

McDOWELL (J) Exercises on Euclid and in Modern Geometry, containing Applications of the Principles and Processes of Modern Pure Geometry. By the late J MCDOWELL, M.A, F.R A S., Pembroke College, Cambridge, and Trinity College, Dublin. *4th edition.* 6s. [*Camb Math. Ser.*

TAYLOR (C) An Introduction to the Ancient and Modern Geometry of Conics, with Historical Notes and Prolegomena 15s.

— The Elementary Geometry of Conics By C. TAYLOR, D D, Master of St John's College. *7th edition, revised* With a Chapter on the Line Infinity, and a new treatment of the Hyperbola Crown 8vo, 4s. 6d [*Camb. Math Ser.*

WEBB (R). The Definitions of Euclid With Explanations and Exercises, and an Appendix of Exercises on the First Book by R. WEBB, M A Crown 8vo, 1s 6d.

WILLIS (H G) Geometrical Conic Sections An Elementary Treatise By H G WILLIS, M A, Clare College, Cambridge, Assistant Master of Manchester Grammar School. Crown 8vo, 5s. [*Camb Math. Ser.*

ANALYTICAL GEOMETRY, ETC

ALDIS (W S). Solid Geometry, An Elementary Treatise on By W. S ALDIS, M A, late Professor of Mathematics in the University College, Auckland, New Zealand *4th edition, revised* Crown 8vo, 6s [*Camb Math Ser.*

BESANT (W. H). Notes on Roulettes and Glissettes. By W. H BESANT, SC D., F R.S *2nd edition, enlarged.* Crown 8vo, 5s [*Camb Math Ser.*

CAYLEY (A.). **Elliptic Functions, An Elementary Treatise on.** By ARTHUR CAYLEY, Sadlerian Professor of Pure Mathematics in the University of Cambridge. *2nd edition.* Demy 8vo. 15s.

TURNBULL (W. P.) **Analytical Plane Geometry, An Introduction to.** By W. P. TURNBULL, M.A., sometime Fellow of Trinity College. 8vo, 12s.

VYVYAN (T. G.) **Analytical Geometry for Schools.** By REV. T. VYVYAN, M.A., Fellow of Gonville and Caius College, and Mathematical Master of Charterhouse. *6th edition.* 8vo, 4s. 6d. [*Camb. S. and C. Texts.*

— **Analytical Geometry for Beginners.** Part I. The Straight Line and Circle. Crown 8vo, 2s. 6d. [*Camb. Math. Ser.*

WHITWORTH (W. A.) **Trilinear Co-ordinates,** and other methods of Modern Analytical Geometry of Two Dimensions. By W. A. WHITWORTH, M.A., late Professor of Mathematics in Queen's College, Liverpool, and Scholar of St. John's College, Cambridge. 8vo, 16s.

TRIGONOMETRY

DYER (J. M.) and WHITCOMBE (R. H.). **Elementary Trigonometry.** By J. M. DYER, M.A. (Senior Mathematical Scholar at Oxford), and REV. R. H. WHITCOMBE, Assistant Masters at Eton College. *2nd edition.* Crown 8vo, 4s. 6d. [*Camb. Math. Ser.*

PENDLEBURY (C.) **Elementary Trigonometry.** By CHARLES PENDLEBURY, M.A., F.R.A.S., Senior Mathematical Master at St. Paul's School. Crown 8vo, 4s. 6d. [*Camb. Math. Ser.*

VYVYAN (T. G.) **Introduction to Plane Trigonometry.** By the REV. T. G. VYVYAN, M.A., formerly Fellow of Gonville and Caius College, Senior Mathematical Master of Charterhouse. *3rd edition, revised and augmented.* Crown 8vo, 3s. 6d. [*Camb. Math. Ser.*

WARD (G. H.) **Examination Papers in Trigonometry.** By G. H. WARD, M.A., Assistant Master at St. Paul's School. Crown 8vo, 2s. 6d. Key, 5s. net.

MECHANICS AND NATURAL PHILOSOPHY.

ALDIS (W. S.). **Geometrical Optics, An Elementary Treatise on.** By W. S. ALDIS, M.A. *4th edition.* Crown 8vo, 4s. [*Camb. Math. Ser.*

— **An Introductory Treatise on Rigid Dynamics.** Crown 8vo, 4s. [*Camb. Math. Ser.*

— **Fresnel's Theory** of Double Refraction, A Chapter on. *2nd edition, revised.* 8vo, 2s.

BASSET (A. B.) **A Treatise on Hydrodynamics,** with numerous Examples. By A. B. BASSET, M.A., F.R.S., Trinity College, Cambridge. Demy 8vo. Vol. I., price 10s. 6d.; Vol. II., 12s. 6d.

— **An Elementary Treatise on Hydrodynamics and Sound.** Demy 8vo, 7s. 6d.

— **A Treatise on Physical Optics.** Demy 8vo, 16s.

BESANT (W. H.) **Elementary Hydrostatics.** By W. H. BESANT, SC.D., F.R.S. *16th edition.* Crown 8vo, 4s. 6d. Solutions, 5s. net. [*Camb. Math. Ser.*

— **Hydromechanics, A Treatise on.** Part I. Hydrostatics. *5th edition, revised, and enlarged.* Crown 8vo, 5s. [*Camb. Math. Ser.*

BESANT (W. H.). A Treatise on Dynamics. *2nd edition.* Crown 8vo, 10*s*. 6*d* [*Camb Math Ser*

CHALLIS (PROF). Pure and Applied Calculation. By the late REV J CHALLIS, M A, F.R S, &c. Demy 8vo, 15*s*.

— **Physics,** The Mathematical Principle of Demy 8vo, 5*s*.

— **Lectures on Practical Astronomy** Demy 8vo, 10*s*.

EVANS (J. H) and MAIN (P. T) Newton's Principia, The First Three Sections of, with an Appendix; and the Ninth and Eleventh Sections. By J H EVANS, M.A, St. John's College. The *5th edition*, edited by P. T MAIN, M A, Lecturer and Fellow of St. John's College Fcap 8vo, 4*s*. [*Camb S and C. Texts.*

GALLATLY (W) Elementary Physics, Examples and Examination Papers in. Statics, Dynamics, Hydrostatics, Heat, Light, Chemistry, Electricity, London Matriculation, Cambridge B A, Edinburgh, Glasgow, South Kensington, Cambridge Junior and Senior Papers, and Answers By W GALLATLY, M A, Pembroke College, Cambridge, Assistant Examiner, London University Crown 8vo, 4*s* [*Camb Math. Ser*

GARNETT (W). Elementary Dynamics for the use of Colleges and Schools By WILLIAM GARNETT, M A, D C L, Fellow of St John's College, late Principal of the Durham College of Science, Newcastle-upon-Tyne *5th edition, revised.* Crown 8vo, 6*s* [*Camb. Math Ser*

— **Heat,** An Elementary Treatise on *6th edition, revised* Crown 8vo, 4*s* 6*d* [*Camb Math Ser.*

GOODWIN (H.). Statics By H. GOODWIN, D D, late Bishop of Carlisle. *2nd edition.* Fcap 8vo, 3*s* [*Camb. S. and C Texts.*

HOROBIN (J C) Elementary Mechanics. Stage I. II. and III, 1*s*. 6*d*. each By J. C. HOROBIN, M A, Principal of Homerton New College, Cambridge.

— **Theoretical Mechanics.** Division I Crown 8vo, 2*s* 6*d*.

*** This book covers the ground of the Elementary Stage of Division I of Subject VI of the "Science Directory," and is intended for the examination of the Science and Art Department

JESSOP (C M) The Elements of Applied Mathematics Including Kinetics, Statics and Hydrostatics By C M. JESSOP, M A, late Fellow of Clare College, Cambridge, Lecturer in Mathematics in the Durham College of Science, Newcastle-on-Tyne. Crown 8vo, 6*s*. [*Camb. Math. Ser*

MAIN (P. T) Plane Astronomy, An Introduction to By P T MAIN, M A, Lecturer and Fellow of St. John's College. *6th edition, revised* Fcap 8vo, 4*s* [*Camb S and C. Texts.*

PARKINSON (R M). Structural Mechanics By R. M PARKINSON, ASSOC M I C E. Crown 8vo, 4*s* 6*d*

PENDLEBURY (C). Lenses and Systems of Lenses, Treated after the Manner of Gauss. By CHARLES PENDLEBURY, M A, F R A S., Senior Mathematical Master of St Paul's School, late Scholar of St. John's College, Cambridge Demy 8vo, 5*s*

STEELE (R E) Natural Science Examination Papers. By R. E STEELE, M.A, F C S, Chief Natural Science Master, Bradford Grammar School. Crown 8vo Part I, Inorganic Chemistry, 2*s*. 6*d*. Part II, Physics (Sound, Light, Heat, Magnetism, Electricity), 2*s*. 6*d* [*School Exam. Series.*

WALTON (W.). **Theoretical Mechanics, Problems in** By W WALTON, M.A, Fellow and Assistant Tutor of Trinity Hall, Mathematical Lecturer at Magdalene College *3rd edition, revised* Demy 8vo, 16*s*
— **Elementary Mechanics, Problems in.** *2nd edition* Crown 8vo, 6*s*.
[*Camb. Math. Ser.*

DAVIS (J. F) **Army Mathematical Papers** Being Ten Years' Woolwich and Sandhurst Preliminary Papers Edited, with Answers, by J F. DAVIS, D LIT., M.A. Lond Crown 8vo, 2*s*. 6*d*

DYER (J M) and PROWDE SMITH (R). **Mathematical Examples** A Collection of Examples in Arithmetic, Algebra, Trigonometry, Mensuration, Theory of Equations, Analytical Geometry, Statics, Dynamics, with Answers, &c For Army and Indian Civil Service Candidates By J M DYER, M A., Assistant Master, Eton College (Senior Mathematical Scholar at Oxford), and R. PROWDE SMITH, M A. Crown 8vo, 6*s*. [*Camb Math Ser*

GOODWIN (H) **Problems and Examples,** adapted to "Goodwin's Elementary Course of Mathematics." By T. G. VYVYAN, M.A. *3rd edition.* 8vo, 5*s*., Solutions, *3rd edition*, 8vo, 9*s*.

SMALLEY (G. R) **A Compendium of Facts and Formulae in Pure Mathematics and Natural Philosophy.** By G R SMALLEY, F R A S *New edition, revised and enlarged* By J MCDOWELL, M A, F R.A S Fcap 8vo, 2*s*

WRIGLEY (A). **Collection of Examples and Problems in Arithmetic,** Algebra, Geometry, Logarithms, Trigonometry, Conic Sections, Mechanics, &c, with Answers and Occasional Hints. By the REV A WRIGLEY. *10th edition, 20th thousand* Demy 8vo, 3*s*. 6*d*

A Key By J C PLATTS, M A and the REV A WRIGLEY. *2nd edition.* Demy 8vo, 5*s*. net.

MODERN LANGUAGES.

ENGLISH.

ADAMS (E) **The Elements of the English Language** By ERNEST ADAMS, PH D. *26th edition.* Revised by J. F DAVIS, D LIT., M A, (LOND) Post 8vo, 4*s* 6*d*

— **The Rudiments of English Grammar and Analysis** By ERNEST ADAMS, PH D *19th thousand* Fcap 8vo, 1*s*.

ALFORD (DEAN). **The Queen's English** A Manual of Idiom and Usage. By the late HENRY ALFORD, D D, Dean of Canterbury. *6th edition.* Small post 8vo Sewed, 1*s*, cloth, 1*s* 6*d*

ASCHAM'S Scholemaster Edited by PROFESSOR J E B MAYOR. Small post 8vo, sewed, 1*s*

BELL'S ENGLISH CLASSICS A New Series, Edited for use in Schools, with Introduction and Notes Crown 8vo

BACON'S Essays Modernized Edited by F J ROWE, M A, Professor of English Literature at Presidency College, Calcutta

BROWNING'S Strafford Edited by E H HICKEY With Introduction by S R GARDINER, LL D 2*s*. 6*d*

BELL'S ENGLISH CLASSICS—*continued*

BURKE'S Letters on a Regicide Peace. I and II Edited by H. G. KEENE, M.A., C.I.E. 3*s*., sewed, 2*s*

BYRON'S Childe Harold Edited by H. G. KEENE, M.A., C.I.E., Author of "A Manual of French Literature," etc 3*s*. 6*d*. Also Cantos I and II separately, sewed, 1*s*. 9*d*

— Siege of Corinth Edited by P. HORDERN, late Director of Public Instruction in Burma 1*s*. 6*d*., sewed 1*s*

CHAUCER, SELECTIONS FROM Edited by J. B. BILDERBECK, B.A., Professor of English Literature, Presidency College, Madras [*Preparing*

DE QUINCEY'S Revolt of the Tartars and The English Mail-Coach Edited by CECIL M. BARROW, M.A., Principal of Victoria College, Palghât, and MARK HUNTER, B.A., Principal of Coimbatore College 3*s*. sewed, 1*s*

DE QUINCEY'S Opium Eater Edited by MARK HUNTER, B.A. [*In the press*

GOLDSMITH'S Good-Natured Man and She Stoops to Conquer. Edited by K. DEIGHTON Each, 2*s*. cloth, 1*s*. 6*d*. sewed The two plays together, sewed, 2*s*. 6*d*

IRVING'S Sketch Book Edited by R. G. OXENHAM, M.A.

JOHNSON'S Life of Addison Edited by F. RYLAND, Author of "The Students' Handbook of Psychology," etc 2*s*. 6*d*

— Life of Swift Edited by F. RYLAND, M.A. 2*s*

— Life of Pope Edited by F. RYLAND, M.A. 2*s*. 6*d*

— Life of Milton Edited by F. RYLAND, M.A. 2*s*. 6*d*

— Life of Dryden Edited by F. RYLAND, M.A. 2*s*. 6*d*

LAMB'S Essays Selected and Edited by K. DEIGHTON 3*s*., sewed, 2*s*

LONGFELLOW'S Evangeline Edited by M. T. QUINN, M.A. [*In the press*

MACAULAY'S Lays of Ancient Rome. Edited by P. HORDERN 2*s*. 6*d*., sewed, 1*s*. 9*d*

— Essay on Clive Edited by CECIL BARROW, M.A. 2*s*., sewed, 1*s*. 6*d*

MASSINGER'S A New Way to Pay Old Debts Edited by K. DEIGHTON 3*s*.; sewed, 2*s*

MILTON'S Paradise Lost Books III and IV Edited by R. G. OXENHAM, M.A., Principal of Elphinstone College, Bombay 2*s*., sewed, 1*s*. 6*d*., or separately, sewed, 10*d*. each

— Paradise Regained Edited by K. DEIGHTON 2*s*. 6*d*., sewed, 1*s*. 9*d*

POPE, SELECTIONS FROM Containing Essay on Criticism, Rape of the Lock, Temple of Fame, Windsor Forest Edited by K. DEIGHTON 2*s*. 6*d*.; sewed, 1*s*. 9*d*

SHAKESPEARE'S Julius Caesar Edited by T. DUFF BARNETT, B.A. (Lond.) 2*s*

— Merchant of Venice Edited by T. DUFF BARNETT, B.A. (Lond.) 2*s*.

— Tempest Edited by T. DUFF BARNETT, B.A. (Lond.) 2*s*

Others to follow

BELL'S READING BOOKS. Post 8vo, cloth, illustrated.

Infants

Infant's Primer. 3*d*.
Tot and the Cat 6*d*.
The Old Boathouse. 6*d*
The Cat and the Hen. 6*d*.

Standard I.

School Primer. 6*d*
The Two Parrots 6*d*.
The Three Monkeys. 6*d*
The New-born Lamb. 6*d*.
The Blind Boy. 6*d*

Standard II.

The Lost Pigs 6*d*
Story of a Cat. 6*d*.
Queen Bee and Busy Bee. 6*d*
Gulls' Crag. 6*d*

Standard III.

Great Deeds in English History. 1*s*.
Adventures of a Donkey. 1*s*.
Grimm's Tales. 1*s*.
Great Englishmen. 1*s*.
Andersen's Tales. 1*s*.
Life of Columbus. 1*s*.

Standard IV

Uncle Tom's Cabin. 1*s*
Great Englishwomen 1*s*.
Great Scotsmen 1*s*.
Edgeworth's Tales 1*s*.
Gatty's Parables from Nature. 1*s*.
Scott's Talisman 1*s*

BELL'S READING BOOKS—*continued*

Standard V.

Dickens' Oliver Twist. 1*s*.
Dickens' Little Nell 1*s*
Masterman Ready. 1*s*
Marryat's Poor Jack. 1*s*.
Arabian Nights 1*s*
Gulliver's Travels. 1*s*
Lyrical Poetry for Boys and Girls. 1*s*
Vicar of Wakefield. 1*s*

Standards VI and VII.

Lamb's Tales from Shakespeare 1*s*
Robinson Crusoe. 1*s*.
Tales of the Coast. 1*s*
Settlers in Canada 1*s*
Southey's Life of Nelson 1*s*.
Sir Roger de Coverley. 1*s*.

BELL'S GEOGRAPHICAL READERS. By M. J. BARRINGTON-WARD, M.A. (Worcester College, Oxford)

The Child's Geography Illustrated Stiff paper cover, 6*d*.
The Map and the Compass (Standard I) Illustrated. Cloth, 8*d*
The Round World. (Standard II) Illustrated Cloth, 10*d*
About England (Standard III) With Illustrations and Coloured Map Cloth, 1*s* 4*d*

BELL'S ANIMAL LIFE READERS A Series of Reading Books for the Standards, designed to inculcate the humane treatment of animals. Edited by EDITH CARRINGTON and ERNEST BELL. Illustrated by HARRISON WEIR and others [*In preparation.*

EDWARDS (F.) Examples for Analysis in Verse and Prose Selected and arranged by F. EDWARDS. *New edition* Fcap 8vo, cloth, 1*s*

GOLDSMITH. The Deserted Village. Edited, with Notes and Life, by C. P. MASON, B.A, F.C.P *4th edition* Crown 8vo, 1*s*.

HANDBOOKS OF ENGLISH LITERATURE. Edited by J W HALES, M A, formerly Clark Lecturer in English Literature at Trinity College, Cambridge, Professor of English Literature at King's College, London Crown 8vo, 3*s* 6*d* each

The Age of Pope By JOHN DENNIS.
The Age of Dryden. By R. GARNETT, LL D., C B.

In preparation.

The Age of Chaucer By PROFESSOR HALES.
The Age of Shakespeare By PROFESSOR HALES.
The Age of Milton By J. BASS MULLINGER, M A.
The Age of Wordsworth By PROFESSOR C. H. HERFORD, LITT D

HAZLITT (W.) Lectures on the Literature of the Age of Elizabeth. Small post 8vo, sewed, 1*s*
— Lectures on the English Poets. Small post 8vo, sewed, 1*s*.
— Lectures on the English Comic Writers. Small post 8vo, sewed, 1*s*

LAMB (C) Specimens of English Dramatic Poets of the Time of Elizabeth With Notes. Small post 8vo, 3*s* 6*d*.

MASON (C. P) Grammars by C. P MASON, B A, F.C P, Fellow of University College, London
— First Notions of Grammar for Young Learners Fcap. 8vo 95*th thousand* Cloth, 1*s*
— First Steps in English Grammar, for Junior Classes. Demy 18mo. 59*th thousand*. 1*s*.

MASON (C. P.). **Outlines of English Grammar, for the Use of Junior Classes.** *17th edition* *97th thousand* Crown 8vo, 2*s*.

— **English Grammar,** including the principles of Grammatical Analysis. *36th edition, revised* *153rd thousand.* Crown 8vo, green cloth, 3*s* 6*d*

— **A Shorter English Grammar,** with copious and carefully graduated Exercises, based upon the author's English Grammar. *9th edition.* *49th thousand* Crown 8vo, brown cloth, 3*s* 6*d*

— **Practice and Help in the Analysis of Sentences** Price 2*s* Cloth

— **English Grammar Practice,** consisting of the Exercises of the Shorter English Grammar published in a separate form *3rd edition* Crown 8vo, 1*s*

— **Remarks on the Subjunctive and the so-called Potential Mood** 6*d*, sewn

— **Blank Sheets** Ruled and headed for Analysis 1*s* per dozen.

MILTON: Paradise Lost Books I, II, and III Edited, with Notes on the Analysis and Parsing, and Explanatory Remarks, by C P MASON, B A, F C P Crown 8vo.

Book I. With Life. *5th edition* 1*s*.
Book II With Life *3rd edition* 1*s*
Book III With Life *2nd edition.* 1*s*

— **Paradise Lost** Books V.-VIII With Notes for the Use of Schools. By C. M LUMBY 2*s*. 6*d*

PRICE (A C) **Elements of Comparative Grammar and Philology** For Use in Schools By A C PRICE, M A, Assistant Master at Leeds Grammar School Crown 8vo, 2*s*. 6*d*.

SHAKESPEARE. Notes on Shakespeare's Plays. With Introduction, Summary, Notes (Etymological and Explanatory), Prosody, Grammatical Peculiarities, etc By T DUFF BARNETT, B.A Lond, late Second Master in the Brighton Grammar School Specially adapted for the Local and Preliminary Examinations Crown 8vo, 1*s* each

Midsummer Night's Dream —Julius Cæsar.—The Tempest —Macbeth —Henry V.—Hamlet —Merchant of Venice.—King Richard II —King John —King Richard III —King Lear.—Coriolanus.—Twelfth Night —As You Like it —Much Ado About Nothing.

"The Notes are comprehensive and concise"—*Educational Times.*
"Comprehensive, practical, and reliable"—*Schoolmaster*

— **Hints for Shakespeare-Study.** Exemplified in an Analytical Study of Julius Cæsar. By MARY GRAFTON MOBERLY *2nd edition* Crown 8vo, sewed, 1*s*

— **Coleridge's Lectures and Notes on Shakespeare and other English Poets** Edited by T ASHE, B A. Small post 8vo, 3*s* 6*d*.

— **Shakespeare's Dramatic Art.** The History and Character of Shakespeare's Plays By DR. HERMANN ULRICI. Translated by L DORA SCHMITZ. 2 vols small post 8vo, 3*s*. 6*d* each.

— **William Shakespeare.** A Literary Biography By KARL ELZE, PH.D, LL.D. Translated by L DORA SCHMITZ. Small post 8vo, 5*s*

— **Hazlitt's Lectures on the Characters of Shakespeare's Plays.** Small post 8vo, 1*s*.

See **BELL'S ENGLISH CLASSICS.**

SKEAT (W. W.). **Questions for Examinations in English Literature.** With a Preface containing brief hints on the study of English. Arranged by the REV. W. W. SKEAT, LITT.D., Elrington and Bosworth Professor of Anglo-Saxon in the University of Cambridge. *3rd edition.* Crown 8vo, 2*s.* 6*d.*

SMITH (C. J.) **Synonyms and Antonyms of the English Language.** Collected and Contrasted by the VEN. C. J. SMITH, M.A. *2nd edition, revised.* Small post 8vo, 5*s.*

— **Synonyms Discriminated.** A Dictionary of Synonymous Words in the English Language. Illustrated with Quotations from Standard Writers. By the late VEN. C. J. SMITH, M.A. With the Author's latest Corrections and Additions, edited by the REV. H. PERCY SMITH, M.A., of Balliol College, Oxford, Vicar of Great Barton, Suffolk. *4th edition.* Demy 8vo, 14*s.*

TEN BRINK'S History of English Literature. Vol. I. Early English Literature (to Wiclif). Translated into English by HORACE M. KENNEDY, Professor of German Literature in the Brooklyn Collegiate Institute. Small post 8vo, 3*s.* 6*d.*

— Vol. II. (Wiclif, Chaucer, Earliest Drama, Renaissance). Translated by W. CLARKE ROBINSON, PH.D. Small post 8vo, 3*s.* 6*d.*

— **Lectures on Shakespeare.** Translated by JULIA FRANKLIN. Small post 8vo, 3*s.* 6*d.*

THOMSON: Spring. Edited by C. P. MASON, B.A., F.C.P. With Life. *2nd edition.* Crown 8vo, 1*s.*

— **Winter.** Edited by C. P. MASON, B.A., F.C.P. With Life. Crown 8vo, 1*s.*

WEBSTER'S INTERNATIONAL DICTIONARY of the English Language. Including Scientific, Technical, and Biblical Words and Terms, with their Significations, Pronunciations, Alternative Spellings, Derivations, Synonyms, and numerous illustrative Quotations, with various valuable literary Appendices, with 83 extra pages of Illustrations grouped and classified, rendering the work a COMPLETE LITERARY AND SCIENTIFIC REFERENCE-BOOK. *New edition* (1890). Thoroughly revised and enlarged under the supervision of NOAH PORTER, D.D., LL.D. 1 vol. (2,118 pages, 3,500 woodcuts), 4to, cloth, 31*s.* 6*d.*; half calf, £2 2*s.*; half russia, £2 5*s.*; calf, £2 8*s.*; or in 2 vols. cloth, £1 14*s.*

Prospectuses, with specimen pages, sent post free on application.

WEBSTER'S BRIEF INTERNATIONAL DICTIONARY. A Pronouncing Dictionary of the English Language, abridged from Webster's International Dictionary. With a Treatise on Pronunciation, List of Prefixes and Suffixes, Rules for Spelling, a Pronouncing Vocabulary of Proper Names in History, Geography, and Mythology, and Tables of English and Indian Money, Weights, and Measures. With 564 pages and 800 Illustrations. Demy 8vo, 3*s.*

WRIGHT (T.). **Dictionary of Obsolete and Provincial English.** Containing Words from the English Writers previous to the 19th century, which are no longer in use, or are not used in the same sense, and Words which are now used only in the Provincial Dialects. Compiled by THOMAS WRIGHT, M.A., F.S.A., etc. 2 vols. 5*s.* each.

FRENCH CLASS BOOKS.

BOWER (A. M.). The Public Examination French Reader With a Vocabulary to every extract, suitable for all Students who are preparing for a French Examination. By A. M. BOWER, F.R.G.S., late Master in University College School, etc. Cloth, 3*s* 6*d*.

BARBIER (PAUL) A Graduated French Examination Course By PAUL BARBIER, Lecturer in the South Wales University College, etc. Crown 8vo, 3*s*

BARRERE (A.) Junior Graduated French Course. Affording Materials for Translation, Grammar, and Conversation. By A. BARRÈRE, Professor R.M.A., Woolwich 1*s* 6*d*.

— **Elements of French Grammar and First Steps in Idioms.** With numerous Exercises and a Vocabulary. Being an Introduction to the Précis of Comparative French Grammar. Crown 8vo, 2*s*

— **Precis of Comparative French Grammar and Idioms and Guide to Examinations** *4th edition* 3*s* 6*d*

— **Récits Militaires** From Valmy (1792) to the Siege of Paris (1870). With English Notes and Biographical Notices *2nd edition* Crown 8vo, 3*s*

CLAPIN (A. C.). French Grammar for Public Schools By the REV. A. C. CLAPIN, M.A., St John's College, Cambridge, and Bachelier-ès-lettres of the University of France. Fcap. 8vo. *14th edition* 2*s* 6*d*
Key to the Exercises. 3*s*. 6*d* net

— **French Primer** Elementary French Grammar and Exercises for Junior Forms in Public and Preparatory Schools Fcap 8vo *10th edition* 1*s*

— **Primer of French Philology.** With Exercises for Public Schools *7th edition* Fcap 8vo, 1*s*.

— **English Passages for Translation into French** Crown 8vo, 2*s* 6*d*.
Key (for Tutors only), 4*s* net

DAVIS (J. F.) Army Examination Papers in French. Questions set at the Preliminary Examinations for Sandhurst and Woolwich, from Nov., 1876, to June, 1890, with Vocabulary. By J. F. DAVIS, D.LIT., M.A., Lond. Crown 8vo, 2*s* 6*d*

DAVIS (J. F.) and THOMAS (F.). An Elementary French Reader. Compiled, with a Vocabulary, by J. F. DAVIS, M.A., D.LIT., and FERDINAND THOMAS, Assistant Examiners in the University of London. Crown 8vo, 2*s*

DELILLE'S GRADUATED FRENCH COURSE.

- **The Beginner's own French Book** 2*s* Key, 2*s*
- **Easy French Poetry for Beginners** 2*s*.
- **French Grammar** 3*s*. Key, 3*s*
- **Repertoire des Prosateurs** 3*s* 6*d*
- **Modèles de Poesie.** 3*s* 6*d*
- **Manuel Etymologique** 2*s* 6*d*
- **Synoptical Table of French Verbs** 6*d*

ESCLANGON (A.) The French Verb Newly Treated · an Easy, Uniform, and Synthetic Method of its Conjugation By A. ESCLANGON, Examiner in the University of London. Small 4to, 5*s*.

GASC (F. E. A.). First French Book, being a New, Practical, and Easy Method of Learning the Elements of the French Language *Reset and thoroughly revised* *116th thousand* Crown 8vo, 1*s*

— **Second French Book;** being a Grammar and Exercise Book, on a new and practical plan, and intended as a sequel to the "First French Book." *52nd thousand.* Fcap 8vo, 1*s* 6*d*

GASC (F. E. A.). Key to First and Second French Books. *6th edition*, Fcap. 8vo, 3*s*. 6*d*. net.

— **French Fables**, for Beginners, in Prose, with an Index of all the Words at the end of the work. *17th thousand*. 12mo, 1*s*. 6*d*.

— **Select Fables of La Fontaine.** *19th thousand*. Fcap. 8vo, 1*s*. 6*d*.

— **Histoires Amusantes et Instructives**; or, Selections of Complete Stories from the best French modern authors, who have written for the young. With English notes. *17th thousand*. Fcap. 8vo, 2*s*.

— **Practical Guide to Modern French Conversation**, containing:— I. The most current and useful Phrases in Everyday Talk. II. Everybody's necessary Questions and Answers in Travel-Talk. *19th edition*. Fcap. 8vo, 1*s*. 6*d*.

— **French Poetry for the Young.** With Notes, and preceded by a few plain Rules of French Prosody. *5th edition, revised*. Fcap. 8vo, 1*s*. 6*d*.

— **French Prose Composition**, Materials for. With copious footnotes, and hints for idiomatic renderings. *21st thousand*. Fcap. 8vo, 3*s*.

Key. *2nd edition*. 6*s*. net.

— **Prosateurs Contemporains**; or, Selections in Prose chiefly from contemporary French literature. With notes. *11th edition*. 12mo, 3*s*. 6*d*.

— **Le Petit Compagnon**; a French Talk-Book for Little Children. *14th edition*. 16mo, 1*s*. 6*d*.

— **French and English Dictionary**, with upwards of Fifteen Thousand new words, senses, &c., hitherto unpublished. *5th edition, with numerous additions and corrections*. In one vol. 8vo, cloth, 10*s*. 6*d*. **In use at Harrow, Rugby, Shrewsbury, &c.**

— **Pocket Dictionary** of the French and English Languages; for the everyday purposes of Travellers and Students. Containing more than Five Thousand modern and current words, senses, and idiomatic phrases and renderings, not found in any other dictionary of the two languages. *New edition*. *53rd thousand*. 16mo, cloth, 2*s*. 6*d*.

GOSSET (A.). Manual of French Prosody for the use of English Students. By ARTHUR GOSSET, M.A., Fellow of New College, Oxford. Crown 8vo, 3*s*.

"This is the very book we have been looking for. We hailed the title with delight, and were not disappointed by the perusal. The reader who has mastered the contents will know, what not one in a thousand of Englishmen who read French knows, the rules of French poetry."—*Journal of Education*.

LE NOUVEAU TRESOR; designed to facilitate the Translation of English into French at Sight. By M. E. S. *18th edition*. Fcap. 8vo, 1*s*. 6*d*.

STEDMAN (A. M. M.). French Examination Papers in Miscellaneous Grammar and Idioms. Compiled by A. M. M. STEDMAN, M.A. *5th edition*. Crown 8vo, 2*s*. 6*d*.

A Key. By G. A. SCHRUMPF. For Tutors only. 6*s*. net.

— **Easy French Passages for Unseen Translation.** Fcap. 8vo, 1*s*. 6*d*.

— **Easy French Exercises on Elementary Syntax.** Crown 8vo, 2*s*. 6*d*.

— **First French Lessons.** Crown 8vo, 1*s*.

— **French Vocabularies for Repetition.** Fcap. 8vo, 1*s*.

— **Steps to French.** 12mo, 8*d*.

FRENCH ANNOTATED EDITIONS.

BALZAC Ursule Mirouet. By HONORÉ DE BALZAC Edited, with Introduction and Notes, by JAMES BOIELLE, B.-ès-L., Senior French Master, Dulwich College. 3*s*.

CLARÉTIE Pierrille. By JULES CLARÉTIE With 27 Illustrations Edited, with Introduction and Notes, by JAMES BOIELLE, B.-ès-L. 2*s* 6*d*

DAUDET. La Belle Nivernaise. Histoire d'un vieux bateau et de son equipage. By ALPHONSE DAUDET Edited, with Introduction and Notes, by JAMES BOIELLE, B.-ès-L With Six Illustrations. 2*s*.

FÉNELON. Aventures de Télémaque. Edited by C J DELILLE. *4th edition* Fcap 8vo, 2*s* 6*d*.

GOMBERT'S FRENCH DRAMA. Re-edited, with Notes, by F E A GASC Sewed, 6*d*. each.

MOLIÈRE.

Le Misanthrope.	Les Fourberies de Scapin
L'Avare	Les Précieuses Ridicules
Le Bourgeois Gentilhomme	L'Ecole des Femmes
Le Tartuffe	L'Ecole des Maris.
Le Malade Imaginaire	Le Médecin Malgre Lui.
Les Femmes Savantes.	

RACINE.

La Thébaïde, ou Les Frères Ennemis.	Britannicus.
Andromaque	Phedre.
Les Plaideurs.	Esther
Iphigénie.	Athalie

CORNEILLE

Le Cid.	Cinna
Horace.	Polyeucte

VOLTAIRE.—Zaire.

GREVILLE. Le Moulin Frappier. By HENRY GREVILLE Edited, with Introduction and Notes, by JAMES BOIELLE, B.-ès-L. 3*s*.

HUGO Bug Jargal. Edited, with Introduction and Notes, by JAMES BOIELLE, B.-ès-L 3*s*.

LA FONTAINE. Select Fables. Edited by F E A GASC *19th thousand* Fcap. 8vo, 1*s*. 6*d*

LAMARTINE Le Tailleur de Pierres de Saint-Point Edited with Notes by JAMES BOIELLE, B.-ès-L *6th thousand.* Fcap 8vo, 1*s* 6*d*

SAINTINE Picciola. Edited by DR DUBUC *16th thousand* Fcap 8vo, 1*s* 6*d*.

VOLTAIRE Charles XII. Edited by L. DIREY *7th edition.* Fcap 8vo, 1*s* 6*d*.

GERMAN CLASS BOOKS.

BUCHHEIM (DR. C A) German Prose Composition. Consisting of Selections from Modern English Writers With grammatical notes, idiomatic renderings, and general introduction By C. A BUCHHEIM, PH D, Professor of the German Language and Literature in King's College, and

Examiner in German to the London University. *14th edition, enlarged and revised.* With a list of subjects for original composition Fcap 8vo, 4s 6d. A KEY to the 1st and 2nd parts. *3rd edition* 3s net To the 3rd and 4th parts 4s net.

BUCHHEIM (DR C A.) **First Book of German Prose.** Being Parts I. and II of the above With Vocabulary by H. R. Fcap 8vo, 1s. 6d

CLAPIN (A C.). **A German Grammar for Public Schools** By the REV A. C CLAPIN, and F HOLL-MULLER, Assistant Master at the Bruton Grammar School *6th edition.* Fcap. 8vo, 2s 6d

— **A German Primer** With Exercises *2nd edition* Fcap 8vo, 1s

German. The Candidate's Vade Mecum Five Hundred Easy Sentences and Idioms. By an Army Tutor. Cloth, 1s. For Army Prelim. Exam

LANGE (F) **A Complete German Course for Use in Public Schools.** By F LANGE, PH D , Professor R M A Woolwich, Examiner in German to the College of Preceptors, London ; Examiner in German at the Victoria University, Manchester Crown 8vo

Concise German Grammar With special reference to Phonology, Comparative Philology, English and German Equivalents and Idioms. Comprising Materials for Translation, Grammar, and Conversation. Elementary, 2s.; Intermediate, 2s ; Advanced, 3s 6d

Progressive German Examination Course Comprising the Elements of German Grammar, an Historic Sketch of the Teutonic Languages, English and German Equivalents, Materials for Translation, Dictation, Extempore Conversation, and Complete Vocabularies I. Elementary Course, 2s. II. Intermediate Course, 2s. III Advanced Course. *Second revised edition* 1s 6d.

Elementary German Reader. A Graduated Collection of Readings in Prose and Poetry. With English Notes and a Vocabulary *4th edition* 1s 6d.

Advanced German Reader A Graduated Collection of Readings in Prose and Poetry. With English Notes by F. LANGE, PH D., and J F. DAVIS, D LIT *2nd edition* 3s

MORICH (R J.) **German Examination Papers in Miscellaneous Grammar and Idioms.** By R J. MORICH, Manchester Grammar School. *2nd edition* Crown 8vo, 2s 6d. A Key, for Tutors only 5s net

STOCK (DR.) **Wortfolge, or Rules and Exercises on the order of Words in German Sentences.** With a Vocabulary. By the late FREDERICK STOCK, D LIT , M A Fcap 8vo, 1s 6d.

KLUGE'S Etymological Dictionary of the German Language. Translated by J. F. DAVIS, D LIT. (Lond.). Crown 4to, 18s.

GERMAN ANNOTATED EDITIONS.

AUERBACH (B) **Auf Wache.** Novelle von BERTHOLD AUERBACH. **Der Gefrorene Kuss.** Novelle von OTTO ROQUETTE Edited by A A. MACDONELL, M.A., PH D. *2nd edition* Crown 8vo, 2s

BENEDIX (J R) **Doktor Wespe.** Lustspiel in fünf Aufzugen von JULIUS RODERICH BENEDIX. Edited by PROFESSOR F. LANGE, PH D, Crown 8vo, 2s. 6d.

EBERS (G.) Eine Frage. Idyll von GEORG EBERS. Edited by F. STORR, B.A., Chief Master of Modern Subjects in Merchant Taylors' School. Crown 8vo, 2s.

FREYTAG (G.). Die Journalisten. Lustspiel von GUSTAV FREYTAG. Edited by PROFESSOR F. LANGE, PH.D. *4th revised edition.* Crown 8vo, 2s. 6d.

— SOLL UND HABEN. Roman von GUSTAV FREYTAG. Edited by W. HANBY CRUMP, M.A. Crown 8vo, 2s. 6d.

GERMAN BALLADS from Uhland, Goethe, and Schiller. With Introductions, Copious and Biographical Notices. Edited by C. L. BIELEFELD. *4th edition.* Fcap. 8vo, 1s. 6d.

GERMAN EPIC TALES IN PROSE. I. Die Nibelungen, von A. F. C. VILMAR. II. Walther und Hildegund, von ALBERT RICHTER. Edited by KARL NEUHAUS, PH.D., the International College, Isleworth. Crown 8vo, 2s. 6d.

GOETHE. Hermann und Dorothea. With Introduction, Notes, and Arguments. By E. BELL, M.A., and E. WOLFEL. *2nd edition.* Fcap. 8vo, 1s. 6d.

GOETHE. FAUST. Part I. German Text with Hayward's Prose Translation and Notes. Revised, With Introduction by C. A. BUCHHEIM, PH.D., Professor of German Language and Literature at King's College, London. Small post 8vo, 5s.

GUTZKOW (K.). Zopf und Schwert. Lustspiel von KARL GUTZKOW. Edited by PROFESSOR F. LANGE, PH.D. Crown 8vo, 2s. 6d.

HEY'S FABELN FUR KINDER. Illustrated by O. SPECKTER. Edited, with an Introduction, Grammatical Summary, Words, and a complete Vocabulary, by PROFESSOR F. LANGE, PH.D. Crown 8vo, 1s. 6d.

— The same. With a Phonetic Introduction, and Phonetic Transcription of the Text. By PROFESSOR F. LANGE, PH.D. Crown 8vo, 2s.

HEYSE (P.). Hans Lange. Schauspiel von PAUL HEYSE. Edited by A. A. MACDONELL, M.A., PH.D., Taylorian Teacher, Oxford University. Crown 8vo, 2s.

HOFFMANN (E. T. A.). Meister Martin, der Kufner. Erzahlung von E. T. A. HOFFMANN. Edited by F. LANGE, PH.D. *2nd edition.* Crown 8vo, 1s. 6d.

MOSER (G. VON). Der Bibliothekar. Lustspiel von G. VON MOSER. Edited by F. LANGE, PH.D. *4th edition.* Crown 8vo, 2s.

ROQUETTE (O.). *See* Auerbach.

SCHEFFEL (V. VON). Ekkehard. Erzahlung des zehnten Jahrhunderts, von VICTOR VON SCHEFFEL. Abridged edition, with Introduction and Notes by HERMAN HAGER, PH.D., Lecturer in the German Language and Literature in The Owens College, Victoria University, Manchester. Crown 8vo, 3s.

SCHILLER'S Wallenstein. Complete Text, comprising the Weimar Prologue, Lager, Piccolomini, and Wallenstein's Tod. Edited by DR. BUCHHEIM, Professor of German in King's College, London. *6th edition.* Fcap. 8vo, 5s. Or the Lager and Piccolomini, 2s. 6d. Wallenstein's Tod, 2s. 6d.

— Maid of Orleans. With English Notes by DR. WILHELM WAGNER. *3rd edition.* Fcap. 8vo, 1s. 6d.

— Maria Stuart. Edited by V. KASTNER, B.-ès-L., Lecturer on French Language and Literature at Victoria University, Manchester. *3rd edition.* Fcap. 8vo, 1s. 6d.

ITALIAN

CLAPIN (A. C.) Italian Primer. With Exercises. By the REV. A. C. CLAPIN, M.A., B.-ès-L. *3rd edition.* Fcap. 8vo, 1s.

DANTE. The Inferno. A Literal Prose Translation, with the Text of the Original collated with the best editions, printed on the same page, and Explanatory Notes. By JOHN A. CARLYLE, M.D. With Portrait. *2nd edition.* Small post 8vo, 5s.

— **The Purgatorio.** A Literal Prose Translation, with the Text of Bianchi printed on the same page, and Explanatory Notes. By W. S. DUGDALE. Small post 8vo, 5s.

BELL'S MODERN TRANSLATIONS

A Series of Translations from Modern Languages, with Memoirs, Introductions, etc. Crown 8vo, 1s each.

GOETHE. Egmont. Translated by ANNA SWANWICK.

— **Iphigenia in Tauris.** Translated by ANNA SWANWICK.

HAUFF. The Caravan. Translated by S. MENDEL.

— **The Inn in the Spessart.** Translated by S. MENDEL.

LESSING. Laokoon. Translated by E. C. BEASLEY.

— **Nathan the Wise.** Translated by R. DILLON BOYLAN.

— **Minna von Barnhelm.** Translated by ERNEST BELL, M.A.

MOLIÈRE. The Misanthrope. Translated by C. HERON WALL.

— **The Doctor in Spite of Himself.** (Le Médecin malgré lui.) Translated by C. HERON WALL.

— **Tartuffe, or, The Impostor.** Translated by C. HERON WALL.

— **The Miser.** (L'Avare.) Translated by C. HERON WALL.

— **The Shopkeeper turned Gentleman.** (Le Bourgeois Gentilhomme.) Translated by C. HERON WALL.

RACINE. Athalie. Translated by R. BRUCE BOSWELL, M.A.

— **Esther.** Translated by R. BRUCE BOSWELL, M.A.

SCHILLER. William Tell. Translated by SIR THEODORE MARTIN, K.C.B., LL.D. *New edition, entirely revised.*

— **The Maid of Orleans.** Translated by ANNA SWANWICK.

— **Mary Stuart.** Translated by J. MELLISH.

— **Wallenstein's Camp and the Piccolomini.** Translated by J. CHURCHILL and S. T. COLERIDGE.

— **The Death of Wallenstein.** Translated by S. T. COLERIDGE.

*** For other Translations of Modern Languages, *see* the Catalogue of Bohn's Libraries, which will be forwarded on application.

SCIENCE, TECHNOLOGY, AND ART.

CHEMISTRY

COOKE (S.) First Principles of Chemistry. An Introduction to Modern Chemistry for Schools and Colleges. By SAMUEL COOKE, M.A., B.E., Assoc. Mem. Inst. C.E., Principal of the College of Science, Poona. *6th edition, revised.* Crown 8vo, 2s. 6d.

— **The Student's Practical Chemistry.** Test Tables for Qualitative Analysis. *3rd edition, revised and enlarged.* Demy 8vo, 1s.

STOCKHARDT (J A) Experimental Chemistry Founded on the work of J. A. STOCKHARDT A Handbook for the Study of Science by Simple Experiments. By C W HEATON, F I C, F C S, Lecturer in Chemistry in the Medical School of Charing Cross Hospital, Examiner in Chemistry to the Royal College of Physicians, etc. *Revised edition* 5s.

WILLIAMS (W M) The Framework of Chemistry Part I Typical Facts and Elementary Theory By W M WILLIAMS, M A., St John's College, Oxford, Science Master, King Henry VIII.'s School, Coventry. Crown 8vo, paper boards, 9d net.

BOTANY.

EGERTON-WARBURTON (G) Names and Synonyms of British Plants By the REV G EGERTON-WARBURTON Fcap 8vo, 3s 6d. (*Uniform with Hayward's Botanist's Pocket Book*)

HAYWARD (W R.). The Botanist's Pocket Book Containing in a tabulated form, the chief characteristics of British Plants, with the botanical names, soil, or situation, colour, growth, and time of flowering of every plant, arranged under its own order, with a copious Index. By W R HAYWARD *6th edition, revised* Fcap. 8vo, cloth limp, 4s 6d

MASSEE (G.). British Fungus-Flora A Classified Text-Book of Mycology. By GEORGE MASSEE, Author of "The Plant World" With numerous Illustrations. 4 vols post 8vo, 7s 6d each.

SOWERBY'S English Botany Containing a Description and Life-size Drawing of every British Plant. Edited and brought up to the present standard of scientific knowledge, by T BOSWELL (late SYME), LL.D, F L.S, etc. *3rd edition, entirely revised* With Descriptions of all the Species by the Editor, assisted by N E. BROWN 12 vols, with 1,937 *coloured plates*, £24 3s in cloth, £26 11s in half-morocco, and £30 9s. in whole morocco Also in 89 parts, 5s., except Part 89, containing an Index to the whole work, 7s 6d

*** A Supplement, to be completed in 8 or 9 parts, is now publishing Parts I, II, and III ready, 5s. each, or bound together, making Vol XIII of the complete work, 17s

TURNBULL (R) Index of British Plants, according to the London Catalogue (Eighth Edition), including the Synonyms used by the principal authors, an Alphabetical List of English Names, etc. By ROBERT TURNBULL. Paper cover, 2s. 6d., cloth, 3s.

GEOLOGY.

JUKES-BROWNE (A. J.). Student's Handbook of Physical Geology. By A J JUKES-BROWNE, B A, F G S., of the Geological Survey of England and Wales With numerous Diagrams and Illustrations. *2nd edition, much enlarged*, 7s 6d

-- **Student's Handbook of Historical Geology.** With numerous Diagrams and Illustrations 6s

"An admirably planned and well executed 'Handbook of Historical Geology'"—*Journal of Education*

— **The Building of the British Isles** A Study in Geographical Evolution. With Maps *2nd edition revised.* 7s 6d

MEDICINE.

CARRINGTON (R. E.), and LANE (W. A.). A Manual of Dissections of the Human Body. By the late R. E. CARRINGTON, M.D. (Lond.), F.R.C.P., Senior Assistant Physician, Guy's Hospital. *2nd edition.* Revised and enlarged by W. ARBUTHNOT LANE, M.S., F.R.C.S., Assistant Surgeon to Guy's Hospital, etc. Crown 8vo, 9*s.*

"As solid a piece of work as ever was put into a book; accurate from beginning to end, and unique of its kind."—*British Medical Journal.*

HILTON'S Rest and Pain. Lectures on the Influence of Mechanical and Physiological Rest in the Treatment of Accidents and Surgical Diseases, and the Diagnostic Value of Pain. By the late JOHN HILTON, F.R.S., F.R.C.S., etc. Edited by W. H. A. JACOBSON, M.A., M.CH. (Oxon.), F.R.C.S. *5th edition.* 9*s.*

HOBLYN'S Dictionary of Terms used in Medicine and the Collateral Sciences. *12th edition.* Revised and enlarged by J. A. P. PRICE, B.A., M.D. (Oxon.). 10*s.* 6*d.*

LANE (W. A.). Manual of Operative Surgery. For Practitioners and Students. By W. ARBUTHNOT LANE, M.B., M.S., F.R.C.S., Assistant Surgeon to Guy's Hospital. Crown 8vo, 8*s.* 6*d.*

SHARP (W.) Therapeutics founded on Antipraxy. By WILLIAM SHARP, M.D., F.R.S. Demy 8vo, 6*s.*

BELL'S AGRICULTURAL SERIES.

In crown 8vo, Illustrated, 160 pages, cloth, 2s. 6d. each.

CHEAL (J.). Fruit Culture. A Treatise on Planting, Growing, Storage of Hardy Fruits for Market and Private Growers. By J. CHEAL, F.R.H.S., Member of Fruit Committee, Royal Hort. Society, etc.

FREAM (DR.). Soils and their Properties. By DR. WILLIAM FREAM, B.SC. (Lond.), F.L.S., F.G.S., F.S.S., Associate of the Surveyor's Institution, Consulting Botanist to the British Dairy Farmers' Association and the Royal Counties Agricultural Society; Prof. of Nat. Hist. in Downton College, and formerly in the Royal Agric. Coll., Cirencester.

GRIFFITHS (DR.). Manures and their Uses. By DR. A. B. GRIFFITHS, F.R.S.E., F.C.S., late Principal of the School of Science, Lincoln; Membre de la Société Chimique de Paris; Author of "A Treatise on Manures," etc., etc. *In use at Downton College.*

— The Diseases of Crops and their Remedies.

MALDEN (W. J.). Tillage and Implements. By W. J. MALDEN, Prof. of Agriculture in the College, Downton.

SHELDON (PROF.). The Farm and the Dairy. By PROFESSOR J. P. SHELDON, formerly of the Royal Agricultural College, and of the Downton College of Agriculture, late Special Commissioner of the Canadian Government. *In use at Downton College.*

Specially adapted for Agricultural Classes. Crown 8vo. Illustrated. 1*s.* each.

Practical Dairy Farming. By PROFESSOR SHELDON. Reprinted from the author's larger work entitled "The Farm and the Dairy."

Practical Fruit Growing. By J. CHEAL, F.R.H.S. Reprinted from the author's larger work, entitled "Fruit Culture."

TECHNOLOGICAL HANDBOOKS.

Edited by Sir H Trueman Wood

Specially adapted for candidates in the examinations of the City Guilds Institute Illustrated and uniformly printed in small post 8vo.

BEAUMONT (R) Woollen and Worsted Cloth Manufacture By ROBERTS BEAUMONT, Professor of Textile Industry, Yorkshire College, Leeds; Examiner in Cloth Weaving to the City and Guilds of London Institute *2nd edition.* 7s 6d

BENEDIKT (R), and KNECHT (E) Coal-tar Colours, The Chemistry of. With special reference to their application to Dyeing, etc. By DR. R BENEDIKT, Professor of Chemistry in the University of Vienna. Translated by E KNECHT, PH D of the Technical College, Bradford. *2nd and enlarged edition,* 6s 6d

CROOKES (W) Dyeing and Tissue-Printing By WILLIAM CROOKES, F R S., V P C S 5s.

GADD (W. L) Soap Mauufacture. By W. LAWRENCE GADD, F I C, F C S., Registered Lecturer on Soap-Making and the Technology of Oils and Fats, also on Bleaching, Dyeing, and Calico Printing, to the City and Guilds of London Institute 5s

HELLYER (S S) Plumbing: Its Principles and Practice. By S. STEVENS HELLYER. With numerous Illustrations 5s

HORNBY (J) Gas Manufacture. By J HORNBY, F I C, Lecturer under the City and Guilds of London Institute. [*In the press*

HURST (G.H) Silk-Dyeing and Finishing. By G H HURST F C.S, Lecturer at the Manchester Technical School, Silver Medallist, City and Guilds of London Institute With Illustrations and numerous Coloured Patterns. 7s. 6d

JACOBI (C T) Printing A Practical Treatise By C T JACOBI, Manager of the Chiswick Press, Examiner in Typography to the City and Guilds of London Institute With numerous Illustrrations 5s.

MARSDEN (R) Cotton Spinning Its Development, Principles, and Practice, with Appendix on Steam Boilers and Engines By R MARSDEN, Editor of the "Textile Manufacturer" *4th edition* 6s 6d

— Cotton Weaving With numerous Illustrations [*In the press*

POWELL (H), CHANCE (H), and HARRIS (H G) Glass Manufacture Introductory Essay, by H POWELL, B A (Whitefriars Glass Works), Sheet Glass, by HENRY CHANCE, M A. (Chance Bros., Birmingham) Plate Glass, by H G HARRIS, Assoc Memb Inst C E 3s 6d

ZAEHNSDORF (J W) Bookbinding By J W. ZAEHNSDORF, Examiner in Bookbinding to the City and Guilds of London Institute With 8 Coloured Plates and numerous Diagrams *2nd edition, revised and enlarged.* 5s

*** *Complete List of Technical Books on Application.*

MUSIC.

BANISTER (H C) A Text Book of Music By H C BANISTER, Professor of Harmony and Composition at the R A of Music, at the Guildhall School of Music, and at the Royal Normal Coll and Acad of Music for the Blind *15th edition.* Fcap. 8vo. 5s

This Manual contains chapters on Notation, Harmony, and Counterpoint,

BANISTER (H. C.)—*continued.*
Modulation, Rhythm, Canon, Fugue, Voices, and Instruments, together with exercises on Harmony, an Appendix of Examination Pape s, and a copious Index and Glossary of Musical Terms.
— Lectures on Musical Analysis. Embracing Sonata Form, Fugue, etc, Illustrated by the Works of the Classical Masters *2nd edition, revised* Crown 8vo, *7s. 6d.*
— Musical Art and Study Papers for Musicians Fcap 8vo, *2s.*
CHATER (THOMAS) Scientific Voice, Artistic Singing, and Effective Speaking A Treatise on the Organs of the Voice, their Natural Functions, Scientific Development, Proper Training, and Artistic Use By THOMAS CHATER With Diagrams. Wide fcap *2s 6d*
HUNT (H. G BONAVIA) A Concise History of Music, from the Commencement of the Christian era to the present time. For the use of Students By REV. H G. BONAVIA HUNT, Mus. Doc Dublin; Warden of Trinity College, London; and Lecturer on Musical History in the same College. *13th edition, revised to date* (1895) Fcap. 8vo, *3s 6d.*

ART.

BARTER (S.) Manual Instruction—Woodwork. By S. BARTER Organizer and Instructor for the London School Board, and to the Joint Committee on Manual Training of the School Board for London, the City and Guilds of London Institute, and the Worshipful Company of Drapers. With over 300 Illustrations Fcap 4to, cloth *7s 6d.*
BELL (SIR CHARLES) The Anatomy and Philosophy of Expression, as connected with the Fine Arts By SIR CHARLES BELL, K H. *7th edition, revised. 5s.*
BRYAN'S Biographical and Critical Dictionary of Painters and Engravers. With a List of Ciphers, Monograms, and Marks A new Edition, thoroughly Revised and Enlarged By R E GRAVES and WALTER ARMSTRONG 2 volumes. Imp 8vo, buckram, *3l 3s*
CHEVREUL on Colour Containing the Principles of Harmony and Contrast of Colours, and their Application to the Arts. *3rd edition,* with Introduction Index and several Plates *5s* —With an additional series of 16 Plates in Colours, *7s 6d*
DELAMOTTE (P H) The Art of Sketching from Nature By P. H DELAMOTTE, Professor of Drawing at King's College, London. Illustrated by Twenty-four Woodcuts and Twenty Coloured Plates, arranged progressively, from Water-colour Drawings by PROUT, E W COOKE, R A, GIRTIN, VARLEY, DE WINT, and the Author *New edition* Imp 4to, *21s*
FLAXMAN'S CLASSICAL COMPOSITIONS, reprinted in a cheap form for the use of Art Students. Oblong paper covers, *2s. 6d* each.
Homer 2 vols —Æschylus —Hesiod —Dante.
— Lectures on Sculpture, as delivered before the President and Members of the Royal Academy With Portrait and 53 plates *6s*
HARRIS (R) Note-book of Geometrical Drawing. By R. HARRIS, Art Master at St Paul's School *New edition, enlarged* Crown 8vo.
HEATON (MRS). A Concise History of Painting. By the late MRS. CHARLES HEATON. *New edition.* Revised by COSMO MONKHOUSE. *5s.*

LELAND (C G) Drawing and Designing In a series of Lessons for School use and Self Instruction By CHARLES G LELAND, M A, F R L S Paper cover, 1s, or in cloth, 1s. 6d

— **Leather Work:** Stamped, Moulded, and Cut, Cuir-Bouille, Sewn, etc. With numerous Illustrations Fcap. 4to, 5s

— **Manual of Wood Carving** By CHARLES G LELAND, M A, F R I S. Revised by J J HOLTZAPFFEL, A M INST C E. With numerous Illustrations. Fcap 4to, 5s

— **Metal Work.** With numerous Illustrations. Fcap 4to, 5s

LEONARDO DA VINCI'S Treatise on Painting Translated from the Italian by J F RIGAUD, R A With a Life of Leonardo and an Account of his Works, by J W BROWN. With numerous Plates 5s

MOODY (F W.) Lectures and Lessons on Art. By the late F. W. MOODY, Instructor in Decorative Art at South Kensington Museum With Diagrams to illustrate Composition and other matters *A new and cheaper edition* Demy 8vo, sewed, 4s 6d

STRANGE (E F) Alphabets a Handbook of Lettering, compiled for the use of Artists, Designers, Handicraftsmen, and Students With complete Historical and Practical Descriptions. By EDWARD F. STRANGE. With more than 200 Illustrations Imperial 16mo, 8s 6d net.

WHITE (GLEESON) Practical Designing A Handbook on the Preparation of Working Drawings, showing the Technical Methods employed in preparing them for the Manufacturer and the Limits imposed on the Design by the Mechanism of Reproduction and the Materials employed. Edited by GLEESON WHITE Freely Illustrated. *2nd edition* Crown 8vo, 6s net.

Contents —Bookbinding, by H ORRINSMITH—Carpets, by ALEXANDER MILLAR—Drawing for Reproduction, by the Editor—Pottery, by W. P. RIX—Metal Work, by R LL RATHBONE—Stained Glass, by SELWYN IMAGE—Tiles, by OWEN CARTER—Woven Fabrics, Printed Fabrics, and Floorcloths, by ARTHUR SILVER—Wall Papers, by G C HAITÉ

MENTAL, MORAL, AND SOCIAL SCIENCES.

PSYCHOLOGY AND ETHICS

ANTONINUS (M Aurelius) The Thoughts of. Translated literally, with Notes, Biographical Sketch, Introductory Essay on the Philosophy, and Index, by GEORGE LONG, M A *Revised edition* Small post 8vo, 3s 6d, *or new edition on Handmade paper, buckram,* 6s

BACON'S Novum Organum and Advancement of Learning. Edited, with Notes, by J DEVEY, M A. Small post 8vo, 5s

EPICTETUS The Discourses of With the Encheiridion and Fragments Translated with Notes, a Life of Epictetus, a View of his Philosophy, and Index, by GEORGE LONG, M A Small post 8vo, 5s, *or new edition on Handmade paper*, 2 vols, *buckram*, 10s 6d

KANT'S Critique of Pure Reason Translated by J M D MEIKLEJOHN, Professor of Education at St Andrew's University Small post 8vo, 5s

— **Prolegomena and Metaphysical Foundations of Science.** With Life. Translated by E BELFORT BAX Small post 8vo, 5s.

LOCKE'S Philosophical Works. Edited by J A. ST. JOHN. 2 vols. Small post 8vo, 3s 6d. each

RYLAND (F.) **The Student's Manual of Psychology and Ethics,** designed chiefly for the London B A and B Sc By F RYLAND, M A, late Scholar of St John's College, Cambridge. Cloth, red edges. *5th edition, revised and enlarged.* With lists of books for Students, and Examination Papers set at London University Crown 8vo, 3s 6d.

— **Ethics** An Introductory Manual for the use of University Students. With an Appendix containing List of Books recommended, and Examination Questions Crown 8vo, 3s 6d.

— **Logic** An Introductory Manual. Crown 8vo [*In the press*

SCHOPENHAUER on the Fourfold Root of the Principle of Sufficient Reason, and On the Will in Nature. Translated by MADAME HILLEBRAND Small post 8vo, 5s

— **Essays** Selected and Translated With a Biographical Introduction and Sketch of his Philosophy, by E BELFORT BAX. Small post 8vo, 5s

SMITH (Adam) Theory of Moral Sentiments. With Memoir of the Author by DUGALD STEWART Small post 8vo, 3s 6d

SPINOZA'S Chief Works. Translated with Introduction, by R. H. M. ELWES 2 vols Small post 8vo, 5s. each

Vol I.—Tractatus Theologico-Politicus—Political Treatise.

II —Improvement of the Understanding—Ethics—Letters

HISTORY OF PHILOSOPHY.

BAX (E B) Handbook of the History of Philosophy. By E BELFORT BAX *2nd edition, revised.* Small post 8vo, 5s

DRAPER (J W) A History of the Intellectual Development of Europe. By JOHN WILLIAM DRAPER, M D, LL D With Index 2 vols. Small post 8vo, 5s each

FALCKENBERG (R) History of Modern Philosophy By RICHARD FALCKENBERG, Professor of Philosophy in the University of Erlangen. Translated by Professor A C ARMSTRONG Demy 8vo, 16s

HEGEL'S Lectures on the Philosophy of History Translated by J. SIBREE, M.A Small post 8vo, 5s.

LAW AND POLITICAL ECONOMY.

KENT'S Commentary on International Law. Edited by J T ABDY, LL D, Judge of County Courts and Law Professor at Gresham College, late Regius Professor of Laws in the University of Cambridge *2nd edition, revised and brought down to a recent date* Crown 8vo, 10s. 6d.

LAWRENCE (T. J) Essays on some Disputed Questions in Modern International Law By T J LAWRENCE, M A, LL M *2nd edition, revised and enlarged* Crown 8vo, 6s

— **Handbook of Public International Law.** *2nd edition.* Fcap 8vo, 3s

MONTESQUIEU'S Spirit of Laws. A New Edition, revised and corrected, with D'Alembert's Analysis, Additional Notes, and a Memoir, by J V. PRITCHARD, A M. 2 vols Small post 8vo, 3s 6d each

PROTHERO (M) Political Economy By MICHAEL PROTHERO, M A. Crown 8vo, 4s 6d

RICARDO on the Principles of Political Economy and Taxation. Edited by E C. K GONNER, M.A., Lecturer in University College, Liverpool Small post 8vo, 5s

SMITH (Adam) The Wealth of Nations An Inquiry into the Nature and Causes of Reprinted from the Sixth Edition, with an Introduction by ERNEST BELFORT BAX 2 vols. Small post 8vo, 3s. 6d each

HISTORY.

BOWES (A.). A Practical Synopsis of English History, or, A General Summary of Dates and Events By ARTHUR BOWES *10th edition* Revised and brought down to the present time Demy 8vo, 1s

COXE (W.) History of the House of Austria, 1218-1792 By ARCHDN. COXE, M.A., F.R S Together with a Continuation from the Accession of Francis I. to the Revolution of 1848 4 vols Small post 8vo 3s 6d. each

DENTON (W.) England in the Fifteenth Century. By the late REV. W DENTON, M A, Worcester College, Oxford. Demy 8vo, 12s.

DYER (Dr T H). History of Modern Europe, from the Taking of Constantinople to the Establishment of the German Empire, A D 1453-1871. By DR T. H DYER *A new edition.* In 5 vols. £2 12s 6d.

GIBBON'S Decline and Fall of the Roman Empire. Complete and Unabridged, with Variorum Notes Edited by an English Churchman. With 2 Maps 7 vols Small post 8vo, 3s 6d each

GREGOROVIUS' History of the City of Rome in the Middle Ages. Translated by ANNIE HAMILTON Vols I, II, and III Crown 8vo, 6s each net

GUIZOT'S History of the English Revolution of 1640. Translated by WILLIAM HAZLITT. Small post 8vo, 3s. 6d

— History of Civilization, from the Fall of the Roman Empire to the French Revolution Translated by WILLIAM HAZLITT. 3 vols Small post 8vo, 3s 6d each.

HENDERSON (E F) Select Historical Documents of the Middle Ages Including the most famous Charters relating to England, the Empire, the Church, etc, from the sixth to the fourteenth centuries. Translated and edited, with Introductions, by ERNEST F. HENDERSON, A B, A M, PH D Small post 8vo, 5s.

— A History of Germany in the Middle Ages Post 8vo, 7s 6d net

HOOPER (George) The Campaign of Sedan. The Downfall of the Second Empire, August-September, 1870. By GEORGE HOOPER. With General Map and Six Plans of Battle Demy 8vo, 14s

— Waterloo. The Downfall of the First Napoleon a History of the Campaign of 1815 With Maps and Plans Small post 8vo, 3s. 6d

LAMARTINE'S History of the Girondists Translated by H. T. RYDE. 3 vols Small post 8vo, 3s 6d each.

— History of the Restoration of Monarchy in France (a Sequel to his History of the Girondists) 4 vols Small post 8vo, 3s 6d each

— History of the French Revolution of 1848 Small post 8vo, 3s 6d

LAPPENBERG'S History of England under the Anglo Saxon Kings. Translated by the late B. THORPE, F S A. *New edition,* revised by E C OTTE. 2 vols. Small post 8vo, 3s 6d each

LONG (G) The Decline of the Roman Republic From the Destruction of Carthage to the Death of Cæsar. By the late GEORGE LONG, M A Demy 8vo In 5 vols. 5s each

MACHIAVELLI'S History of Florence, and of the Affairs of Italy from the Earliest Times to the Death of Lorenzo the Magnificent together with the Prince, Savonarola, various Historical Tracts, and a Memoir of Machiavelli Small post 8vo, 3s 6d.

MARTINEAU (H) History of England from 1800-15 By HARRIET MARTINEAU. Small post 8vo, 3s. 6d.

MARTINEAU (H.). History of the Thirty Years' Peace, 1815-46. 4 vols. Small post 8vo, 3*s.* 6*d.* each.

MAURICE (C. E.). The Revolutionary Movement of 1848-9 in Italy, Austria, Hungary, and Germany. With some Examination of the previous Thirty-three Years. By C. EDMUND MAURICE. With an engraved Frontispiece and other Illustrations. Demy 8vo, 16*s.*

MENZEL'S History of Germany, from the Earliest Period to 1842. 3 vols. Small post 8vo, 3*s.* 6*d.* each.

MICHELET'S History of the French Revolution from its earliest indications to the flight of the King in 1791. Small post 8vo, 3*s.* 6*d.*

MIGNET'S History of the French Revolution, from 1789 to 1814. Small post 8vo, 3*s.* 6*d.*

PARNELL (A.). The War of the Succession in Spain during the Reign of Queen Anne, 1702-1711. Based on Original Manuscripts and Contemporary Records. By COL. THE HON. ARTHUR PARNELL, R.E. Demy 8vo, 14*s.* With Map, etc.

RANKE (L.). History of the Latin and Teutonic Nations, 1494-1514. Translated by P. A. ASHWORTH. Small post 8vo, 3*s.* 6*d.*

— **History of the Popes,** their Church and State, and especially of their conflicts with Protestantism in the 16th and 17th centuries. Translated by E. FOSTER. 3 vols. Small post 8vo, 3*s.* 6*d.* each.

— **History of Servia and the Servian Revolution.** Translated by MRS. KERR. Small post 8vo, 3*s.* 6*d.*

SIX OLD ENGLISH CHRONICLES: viz., Asser's Life of Alfred and the Chronicles of Ethelwerd, Gildas, Nennius, Geoffrey of Monmouth, and Richard of Cirencester. Edited, with Notes and Index, by J. A. GILES, D.C.L. Small post 8vo, 5*s.*

STRICKLAND (Agnes). The Lives of the Queens of England; from the Norman Conquest to the Reign of Queen Anne. By AGNES STRICKLAND. 6 vols. 5*s.* each.

— **The Lives of the Queens of England.** Abridged edition for the use of Schools and Families. Post 8vo, 6*s.* 6*d.*

THIERRY'S History of the Conquest of England by the Normans; its Causes, and its Consequences in England, Scotland, Ireland, and the Continent. Translated from the 7th Paris edition by WILLIAM HAZLITT. 2 vols. Small post 8vo, 3*s.* 6*d.* each.

WRIGHT (H. F.). The Intermediate History of England, with Notes, Supplements, Glossary, and a Mnemonic System. For Army and Civil Service Candidates. By H. F. WRIGHT, M.A., LL.M. Crown 8vo, 6*s.*

For other Works of value to Students of History, see Catalogue of Bohn's Libraries, sent post-free on application.

DIVINITY, ETC.

ALFORD (DEAN). Greek Testament. With a Critically revised Text, a digest of Various Readings, Marginal References to verbal and idiomatic usage, Prolegomena, and a Critical and Exegetical Commentary. For the use of theological students and ministers. By the late HENRY ALFORD, D.D., Dean of Canterbury. 4 vols. 8vo. £5 2*s.* Sold separately.

— **The New Testament for English Readers.** Containing the Authorized Version, with additional Corrections of Readings and Renderings, Marginal References, and a Critical and Explanatory Commentary. In 2 vols. £2 14*s.* 6*d.* Also sold in 4 parts separately.

AUGUSTINE de Civitate Dei. Books XI. and XII. By the REV. HENRY D. GEE, B.D., F.S.A. I. Text only. 2*s.* II. Introduction and Translation. 3*s.*

BARRETT (A. C.). Companion to the Greek Testament. By the late A. C. BARRETT, M.A., Caius College, Cambridge. 5*th edition.* Fcap. 8vo, 5*s.*

BARRY (BP.). Notes on the Catechism. For the use of Schools. By the RT. REV. BISHOP BARRY, D.D. 10*th edition.* Fcap. 2*s.*

BLEEK. Introduction to the Old Testament. By FRIEDRICH BLEEK. Edited by JOHANN BLEEK and ADOLF KAMPHAUSEN. Translated from the second edition of the German by G. H. VENABLES under the supervision of the REV. E. VENABLES, Residentiary Canon, of Lincoln. 2*nd edition*, with Corrections. With Index. 2 vols. small post 8vo, 5*s.* each.

BUTLER (BP.). Analogy of Religion. With Analytical Introduction and copious Index, by the late RT. REV. DR. STEERE. Fcap. 3*s.* 6*d.*

EUSEBIUS. Ecclesiastical History of Eusebius Pamphilus, Bishop of Cæsarea. Translated from the Greek by REV. C. F. CRUSE, M.A. With Notes, a Life of Eusebius, and Chronological Table. Sm. post 8vo, 5*s.*

GREGORY (DR.). Letters on the Evidences, Doctrines, and Duties of the Christian Religion. By DR. OLINTHUS GREGORY, F.R.A.S. Small post 8vo, 3*s.* 6*d.*

HUMPHRY (W. G.). Book of Common Prayer. An Historical and Explanatory Treatise on the. By W. G. HUMPHRY, B.D., late Fellow of Trinity College, Cambridge, Prebendary of St. Paul's, and Vicar of St. Martin's-in-the-Fields, Westminster. 6*th edition.* Fcap. 8vo, 2*s.* 6*d.*

Cheap Edition, for Sunday School Teachers. 1*s.*

JOSEPHUS (FLAVIUS). The Works of. WHISTON'S Translation. Revised by REV. A. R. SHILLETO, M.A. With Topographical and Geographical Notes by COLONEL SIR C. W. WILSON, K.C.B. 5 vols. 3*s.* 6*d.* each.

LUMBY (DR.). The History of the Creeds. I. Ante-Nicene. II. Nicene and Constantinopolitan. III. The Apostolic Creed. IV. The Quicunque, commonly called the Creed of St. Athanasius. By J. RAWSON LUMBY, D.D., Norrisian Professor of Divinity, Fellow of St. Catherine's College, and late Fellow of Magdalene College, Cambridge. 3*rd edition, revised.* Crown 8vo, 7*s.* 6*d.*

— **Compendium of English Church History, from 1688-1830.** With a Preface by J. RAWSON LUMBY, D.D. Crown 8vo, 6*s.*

MACMICHAEL (J. F.). The New Testament in Greek. With English Notes and Preface, Synopsis, and Chronological Tables. By the late REV. J. F. MACMICHAEL. Fcap. 8vo (730 pp.), 4*s.* 6*d.*

Also the **Four Gospels**, and the **Acts of the Apostles**, separately. In paper wrappers, 6*d.* each.

MILLER (E.). Guide to the Textual Criticism of the New Testament. By REV. E. MILLER, M.A., Oxon, Rector of Bucknell, Bicester. Crown 8vo, 4*s.*

NEANDER (DR. A.). History of the Christian Religion and Church. Translated by J. TORREY. 10 vols. small post 8vo, 3*s.* 6*d.* each.

— **Life of Jesus Christ.** Translated by J. MCCLINTOCK and C. BLUMENTHAL. Small post 8vo, 3*s.* 6*d.*

— **History of the Planting and Training of the Christian Church by the Apostles.** Translated by J. E. RYLAND. 2 vols. 3*s.* 6*d.* each.

— **Lectures on the History of Christian Dogmas.** Edited by DR. JACOBI. Translated by J. E. RYLAND. 2 vols. small post 8vo, 3*s.* 6*d.* each.

NEANDER (DR. A.) Memorials of Christian Life in the Early and Middle Ages Translated by J. E. RYLAND. Small post 8vo, 3s 6d

PEARSON (BP.). On the Creed. Carefully printed from an Early Edition. Edited by E. WALFORD, M.A. Post 8vo, 5s.

PEROWNE (BP.) The Book of Psalms A New Translation, with Introductions and Notes, Critical and Explanatory By the RIGHT REV. J. J. STEWART PEROWNE, D.D. Bishop of Worcester 8vo Vol. I. *8th edition, revised* 18s. Vol. II *7th edition, revised* 16s

— The Book of Psalms Abridged Edition for Schools. Crown 8vo *7th edition* 10s 6d

SADLER (M. F.) The Church Teacher's Manual of Christian Instruction Being the Church Catechism, Expanded and Explained in Question and Answer For the use of the Clergyman, Parent, and Teacher By the REV. M. F. SADLER, Prebendary of Wells, and Rector of Honiton. *43rd thousand* 2s 6d

*** A Complete List of Prebendary Sadler's Works will be sent on application

SCRIVENER (DR.). A Plain Introduction to the Criticism of the New Testament With Forty-four Facsimiles from Ancient Manuscripts For the use of Biblical Students By the late F. H. SCRIVENER, M.A., D.C.L., LL.D., Prebendary of Exeter *4th edition*, thoroughly revised, by the REV. E. MILLER, formerly Fellow and Tutor of New College, Oxford. 2 vols demy 8vo, 32s.

— Novum Testamentum Græce, Textus Stephanici, 1550 Accedunt variae lectiones editionum Bezae, Elzevirii, Lachmanni, Tischendorfii, Tregellesii, curante F. H. A. SCRIVENER, A.M., D.C.L., LL.D. *Revised edition* 4s 6d

— Novum Testamentum Græce [Editio Major] textus Stephanici, A.D. 1556. Cum variis lectionibus editionum Bezae, Elzevirii, Lachmanni, Tischendorfii, Tregellesii, Westcott Hortii, versionis Anglicanæ emendatorum curante F. H. A. SCRIVENER, A.M., D.C.L., LL.D., accedunt parallela s. scripturæ loca Small post 8vo. *2nd edition* 7s 6d

An Edition on writing-paper, with margin for notes 4to, half bound, 12s.

WHEATLEY. A Rational Illustration of the Book of Common Prayer Being the Substance of everything Liturgical in Bishop Sparrow, Mr. L'Estrange, Dr. Comber, Dr Nicholls, and all former Ritualist Commentators upon the same subject Small post 8vo, 3s 6d

WHITAKER (C.). Rufinus and His Times With the Text of his Commentary on the Apostles' Creed and a Translation To which is added a Condensed History of the Creeds and Councils By the REV. CHARLES WHITAKER, B.A., Vicar of Natland, Kendal Demy 8vo, 5s.

Or in separate Parts —1. Latin Text, with Various Readings, 2s 6d. 2 Summary of the History of the Creeds, 1s 6d 3. Charts of the Heresies of the Times preceding Rufinus, and the First Four General Councils, 6d each.

— St. Augustine De Fide et Symbolo—Sermo ad Catechumenos St. Leo ad Flavianum Epistola—Latin Text, with Literal Translation, Notes, and History of Creeds and Councils 5s Also separately, Literal Translation. 2s

— Student's Help to the Prayer-Book 3s.

SUMMARY OF SERIES.

BIBLIOTHECA CLASSICA.
PUBLIC SCHOOL SERIES
CAMBRIDGE GREEK AND LATIN TEXTS.
CAMBRIDGE TEXTS WITH NOTES
GRAMMAR SCHOOL CLASSICS.
PRIMARY CLASSICS.
BELL'S CLASSICAL TRANSLATIONS.
CAMBRIDGE MATHEMATICAL SERIES.
CAMBRIDGE SCHOOL AND COLLEGE TEXT BOOKS.
FOREIGN CLASSICS
MODERN FRENCH AUTHORS
MODERN GERMAN AUTHORS.
GOMBERT'S FRENCH DRAMA.
BELL'S MODERN TRANSLATIONS.
BELL'S ENGLISH CLASSICS
HANDBOOKS OF ENGLISH LITERATURE.
TECHNOLOGICAL HANDBOOKS.
BELL'S AGRICULTURAL SERIES
BELL'S READING BOOKS AND GEOGRAPHICAL READERS.

BIBLIOTHECA CLASSICA.

AESCHYLUS By DR PALEY 8s
CICERO By G LONG Vols I and II 8s each.
DEMOSTHENES By R WHISTON 2 Vols 8s each
EURIPIDES By DR PALEY Vols II and III 8s. each.
HERODOTUS. By DR BLAKESLEY 2 Vols 12s.
HESIOD By DR. PALEY. 5s
HOMER By DR PALEY 2 Vols 14s
HORACE. By A J. MACLEANE 8s
PLATO Phaedrus By DR THOMPSON 5s
SOPHOCLES Vol I By F H BLAYDES 5s
— Vol II. By DR PALEY 6s
VIRGIL. By CONINGTON AND NETTLESHIP 3 Vols 10s 6d each

PUBLIC SCHOOL SERIES.

ARISTOPHANES Peace By DR PALEY 2s 6d.
— Acharnians By DR PALEY 2s 6d.
— Frogs By DR PALEY 2s 6d
CICERO Letters to Atticus Book I By A PRETOR 4s 6d.
DEMOSTHENES De Falsa Legatione By R SHILLETO 6s
— Adv Leptinem By B W BEATSON 3s 6d
LIVY. Books XXI and XXII By L D DOWDALL 2s each
PLATO Apology of Socrates and Crito By DR. W. WAGNER. 3s 6d. and 2s 6d.
— Phaedo. By DR W. WAGNER 5s 6d
— Protagoras By W WAYTE 4s 6d
— Gorgias By DR THOMPSON 6s
— Euthyphro By G. H WELLS 3s
— Euthydemus By G H WELLS 4s
— Republic By G H WELLS 5s.
PLAUTUS Aulularia By DR W WAGNER. 4s. 6d.
— Trinummus By DR W WAGNER 4s 6d
— Menaechmei By DR W WAGNER 4s 6d
— Mostellaria. By E. A SONNENSCHEIN 5s.

PUBLIC SCHOOL SERIES—*continued.*

SOPHOCLES. Trachiniae. By A. PRETOR. 4*s.* 6*d.*
— Oedipus Tyrannus. By B. H. KENNEDY. 2*s.* 6*d.*
TERENCE. By DR. W. WAGNER. 7*s.* 6*d.*
THEOCRITUS. By DR. PALEY. 4*s.* 6*d.*
THUCYDIDES. Book VI. By T. W. DOUGAN. 2*s.*

CAMBRIDGE GREEK AND LATIN TEXTS.

AESCHYLUS. By DR. PALEY. 2*s.*
CAESAR. By G. LONG. 1*s.* 6*d.*
CICERO. De Senectute, de Amicitia, et Epistolae Selectae. By G. LONG. 1*s.* 6*d.*
— Orationes in Verrem. By G. LONG. 2*s.* 6*d.*
EURIPIDES. By DR. PALEY. 3 Vols. 2*s.* each.
HERODOTUS. By DR. BLAKESLEY. 2 Vols. 2*s.* 6*d.* each.
HOMER'S Iliad. By DR. PALEY. 1*s.* 6*d.*
HORACE. By A. J. MACLEANE. 1*s.* 6*d.*
JUVENAL AND PERSIUS. By A. J. MACLEANE. 1*s.* 6*d.*
LUCRETIUS. By H. A. J. MUNRO. 2*s.*
SOPHOCLES. By DR. PALEY. 2*s.* 6*d.*
TERENCE. By DR. W. WAGNER. 2*s.*
THUCYDIDES. By DR. DONALDSON. 2 Vols. 2*s.* each.
VIRGIL. By PROF. CONINGTON. 2*s.*
XENOPHON. By J. F. MACMICHAEL. 1*s.* 6*d.*
NOVUM TESTAMENTUM GRAECE. By DR. SCRIVENER. 4*s.* 6*d.*

CAMBRIDGE TEXTS WITH NOTES.

AESCHYLUS. By DR. PALEY. 6 Vols. 1*s.* 6*d.* each.
EURIPIDES. By DR. PALEY. 13 Vols. (Ion, 2*s.*) 1*s.* 6*d.* each.
HOMER'S Iliad. By DR. PALEY. 1*s.*
SOPHOCLES. By DR. PALEY. 5 Vols. 1*s.* 6*d.* each.
XENOPHON. Hellenica. By REV. L. D. DOWDALL. Books I. and II. 2*s.* each.
— Anabasis. By J. F. MACMICHAEL. 6 Vols. 1*s.* 6*d.* each.
CICERO. De Senectute, de Amicitia, et Epistolae Selectae. By G. LONG. 3 Vols. 1*s.* 6*d.* each.
OVID. Selections. By A. J. MACLEANE. 1*s.* 6*d.*
— Fasti. By DR. PALEY. 3 Vols. 2*s.* each.
TERENCE. By DR. W. WAGNER. 4 Vols. 1*s.* 6*d.* each.
VIRGIL. By PROF. CONINGTON. 12 Vols. 1*s.* 6*d.* each.

GRAMMAR SCHOOL CLASSICS.

CAESAR, De Bello Gallico. By G. LONG. 4*s.*, or in 3 parts, 1*s.* 6*d.* each.
CATULLUS, TIBULLUS, and PROPERTIUS. By A. H. WRATISLAW, and F. N. SUTTON. 2*s.* 6*d.*
CORNELIUS NEPOS. By J. F. MACMICHAEL. 2*s.*
CICERO. De Senectute, De Amicitia, and Select Epistles. By G. LONG. 3*s.*
HOMER. Iliad. By DR. PALEY. Books I.-XII. 4*s.* 6*d.*, or in 2 Parts, 2*s.* 6*d.* each.
HORACE. By A. J. MACLEANE. 3*s.* 6*d.*, or in 2 Parts, 2*s.* each.
JUVENAL. By HERMAN PRIOR. 3*s.* 6*d.*
MARTIAL. By DR. PALEY and W. H. STONE. 4*s.* 6*d.*
OVID. Fasti. By DR. PALEY. 3*s.* 6*d.*, or in 3 Parts, 1*s.* 6*d.* each.
SALLUST. Catilina and Jugurtha. By G. LONG and J. G. FRAZER. 3*s.* 6*d.*, or in 2 Parts, 2*s.* each.
TACITUS. Germania and Agricola. By P. FROST. 2*s.* 6*d.*
VIRGIL. CONINGTON'S edition abridged. 2 Vols. 4*s.* 6*d.* each, or in 9 Parts, 1*s.* 6*d.* each.
— Bucolics and Georgics. CONINGTON'S edition abridged. 3*s.*
XENOPHON. By J. F. MACMICHAEL. 3*s.* 6*d.*, or in 4 Parts, 1*s.* 6*d.* each.
— Cyropaedia. By G. M. GORHAM. 3*s.* 6*d.*, or in 2 Parts, 1*s.* 6*d.* each.
— Memorabilia. By PERCIVAL FROST. 3*s.*

PRIMARY CLASSICS.

EASY SELECTIONS FROM CAESAR. By A. M. M. STEDMAN. 1*s.*
EASY SELECTIONS FROM LIVY. By A. M. M. STEDMAN. 1*s.* 6*d.*
EASY SELECTIONS FROM HERODOTUS. By A. G. LIDDELL. 1*s.* 6*d.*

BELL'S CLASSICAL TRANSLATIONS.

AESCHYLUS. By WALTER HEADLAM. 6 Vols. [*In the press.*
ARISTOPHANES. Acharnians. By W. H. COVINGTON. 1*s.*
CAESAR'S Gallic War. By W. A. MCDEVITTE. 2 Vols. 1*s.* each.
CICERO. Friendship and Old Age. By G. H. WELLS. 1*s.*
DEMOSTHENES. On the Crown. By C. RANN KENNEDY. 1*s.*
EURIPIDES. 14 Vols. By E. P. COLERIDGE. 1*s.* each.
LIVY. Books I.-IV. By J. H. FREESE. 1*s.* each.
— Book V. By E. S. WEYMOUTH. 1*s.*
— Book IX. By F. STORR. 1*s.*
LUCAN: The Pharsalia. Book I. By F. CONWAY. 1*s.*
OVID. Fasti. 3 Vols. By H. T. RILEY. 1*s.* each.
— Tristia. By H. T. RILEY. 1*s.*
SOPHOCLES. 7 Vols. By E. P. COLERIDGE. 1*s.* each.
VIRGIL. 6 Vols. By A. HAMILTON BRYCE. 1*s.* each.
XENOPHON. Anabasis. 3 Vols. By J. S. WATSON. 1*s.* each.
— Hellenics. Books I. and II. By H. DALE. 1*s.*

CAMBRIDGE MATHEMATICAL SERIES.

ARITHMETIC. By C. PENDLEBURY. 4*s.* 6*d.*, or in 2 Parts, 2*s.* 6*d.* each. Key to Part II. 7*s.* 6*d.* net.
EXAMPLES IN ARITHMETIC. By C. PENDLEBURY. 3*s.*, or in 2 Parts, 1*s.* 6*d.* and 2*s.*
ARITHMETIC FOR INDIAN SCHOOLS. By PENDLEBURY and TAIT. 3*s.*
ELEMENTARY ALGEBRA. By J. T. HATHORNTHWAITE. 2*s.*
CHOICE AND CHANCE. By W. A. WHITWORTH. 6*s.*
EUCLID. By H. DEIGHTON. 4*s.* 6*d.*, or Books I.-IV., 3*s.*; Books V.-XI., 2*s.* 6*d.*; or Book I., 1*s.*; Books I. and II., 1*s.* 6*d.*; Books I.-III., 2*s.* 6*d.*; Books III. and IV., 1*s.* 6*d.* KEY. 5*s.* net.
EXERCISES ON EUCLID, &c. By J. MCDOWELL. 6*s.*
ELEMENTARY MENSURATION. By B. T. MOORE.
ELEMENTARY TRIGONOMETRY. By C. PENDLEBURY. 4*s.* 6*d.*
ELEMENTARY TRIGONOMETRY. By DYER and WHITCOMBE. 4*s.* 6*d.*
PLANE TRIGONOMETRY. By T. G. VYVYAN. 3*s.* 6*d.*
ANALYTICAL GEOMETRY FOR BEGINNERS. Part I. By T. G. VYVYAN. 2*s.* 6*d.*
ELEMENTARY GEOMETRY OF CONICS. By DR. TAYLOR. 4*s.* 6*d.*
GEOMETRICAL CONIC SECTIONS. By DR. W. H. BESANT. 4*s.* 6*d.* Key, 5*s.* net.
GEOMETRICAL CONIC SECTIONS. By H. G. WILLIS. 5*s.*
SOLID GEOMETRY. By W. S. ALDIS. 6*s.*
GEOMETRICAL OPTICS. By W. S. ALDIS. 4*s.*
ROULETTES AND GLISSETTES. By DR. W. H. BESANT. 5*s.*
ELEMENTARY HYDROSTATICS. By DR. W. H. BESANT. 4*s.* 6*d.* Solutions. 5*s.* net
HYDROMECHANICS. Part I. Hydrostatics. By DR. W. H. BESANT. 5*s.*
DYNAMICS. By DR. W. H. BESANT. 10*s.* 6*d.*
RIGID DYNAMICS. By W. S. ALDIS. 4*s.*
ELEMENTARY DYNAMICS. By DR. W. GARNETT. 6*s.*
ELEMENTARY TREATISE ON HEAT. By DR. W. GARNETT. 4*s.* 6*d.*
ELEMENTS OF APPLIED MATHEMATICS. By C. M. JESSOP. 6*s.*
PROBLEMS IN ELEMENTARY MECHANICS. By W. WALTON. 6*s.*
EXAMPLES IN ELEMENTARY PHYSICS. By W. GALLATLY. 4*s.*
MATHEMATICAL EXAMPLES. By DYER and PROWDE SMITH. 6*s.*

CAMBRIDGE SCHOOL AND COLLEGE TEXT BOOKS.

ARITHMETIC. By C. ELSEE. 3*s.* 6*d.* By A. WRIGLEY. 3*s.* 6*d.*
EXAMPLES IN ARITHMETIC. By WATSON and GOUDIE. 2*s.* 6*d.*
ALGEBRA. By C. ELSEE. 4*s.*
EXAMPLES IN ALGEBRA. By MACMICHAEL and PROWDE SMITH. 3*s.* 6*d.* and 4*s.* 6*d.*
PLANE ASTRONOMY. By P. T. MAIN. 4*s.*
STATICS. By BISHOP GOODWIN. 3*s.*
NEWTON'S *Principia.* By EVANS and MAIN. 4*s.*

CAMBRIDGE SCHOOL TEXTS—*continued.*

ANALYTICAL GEOMETRY. By T. G. VYVYAN. 4*s.* 6*d.*
COMPANION TO THE GREEK TESTAMENT. By A. C. BARRETT. 5*s.*
TREATISE ON THE BOOK OF COMMON PRAYER. By W. G. HUMPHRY. 2*s.* 6*d.*
TEXT BOOK OF MUSIC. By H. C. BANISTER. 5*s.*
CONCISE HISTORY OF MUSIC. By DR. H. G. BONAVIA HUNT. 3*s.* 6*d*

FOREIGN CLASSICS.

FÉNELON'S Télémaque. By C. J. DELILLE. 2*s.* 6*d.*
LA FONTAINE'S Select Fables. By F. E. A. GASC. 1*s.* 6*d.*
LAMARTINE'S Le Tailleur de Pierres de Saint-Point. By J. BOÏELLE. 1*s.* 6*d.*
SAINTINE'S Picciola. By DR. DUBUC. 1*s.* 6*d.*
VOLTAIRE'S Charles XII. By L. DIREY. 1*s.* 6*d.*
GERMAN BALLADS. By C. L. BIELEFELD. 1*s.* 6*d.*
GOETHE'S Hermann und Dorothea. By E. BELL and E. WÖLFEL. 1*s.* 6*d.*
SCHILLER'S Wallenstein. By DR. BUCHHEIM. 5*s.*, or in 2 Parts, 2*s.* 6*d.* each.
— Maid of Orleans. By DR. W. WAGNER. 1*s.* 6*d.*
— Maria Stuart. By V. KASTNER. 1*s.* 6*d.*

MODERN FRENCH AUTHORS.

BALZAC'S Ursule Mirouët. By J. BOÏELLE. 3*s.*
CLARÉTIE'S Pierrille. By J. BOÏELLE. 2*s.* 6*d.*
DAUDET'S La Belle Nivernaise. By J. BOÏELLE. 2*s.*
GREVILLE'S Le Moulin Frappier. By J. BOÏELLE. 3*s.*
HUGO'S Bug Jargal. By J. BOÏELLE. 3*s.*

MODERN GERMAN AUTHORS.

HEY'S Fabeln für Kinder. By PROF. LANGE. 1*s.* 6*d.*
— — with Phonetic Transcription of Text, &c. 2*s.*
FREYTAG'S Soll und Haben. By W. H. CRUMP. 2*s.* 6*d.*
BENEDIX'S Doktor Wespe. By PROF. LANGE. 2*s.* 6*d.*
HOFFMANN'S Meister Martin. By PROF. LANGE. 1*s.* 6*d.*
HEYSE'S Hans Lange. By A. A. MACDONELL. 2*s.*
AUERBACH'S Auf Wache, and Roquette's Der Gefrorene Kuss. By A. A. MACDONELL. 2*s.*
MOSER'S Der Bibliothekar. By PROF. LANGE. 2*s.*
EBERS' Eine Frage. By F. STORR. 2*s.*
FREYTAG'S Die Journalisten. By PROF. LANGE. 2*s.* 6*d.*
GUTZKOW'S Zopf und Schwert. By PROF. LANGE. 2*s.* 6*d.*
GERMAN EPIC TALES. By DR. KARL NEUHAUS. 2*s.* 6*d.*
SCHEFFEL'S Ekkehard. By DR. H. HAGER. 3*s.*

The following Series are given in full in the body of the Catalogue.

GOMBERT'S French Drama. *See page* 31.
BELL'S Modern Translations. *See page* 34.
BELL'S English Classics. *See pp.* 24, 25.
HANDBOOKS OF ENGLISH LITERATURE. *See page* 26.
TECHNOLOGICAL HANDBOOKS. *See page* 37.
BELL'S Agricultural Series. *See page* 36.
BELL'S Reading Books and Geographical Readers. *See pp.* 25, 26.

CHISWICK PRESS:—C. WHITTINGHAM AND CO., TOOKS COURT, CHANCERY LANE.

Lightning Source UK Ltd.
Milton Keynes UK
UKHW022310080223
416651UK00001B/231

9 781015 870635